GWT in Action

GWT in Action

EASY AJAX WITH THE GOOGLE WEB TOOLKIT

ROBERT HANSON
ADAM TACY

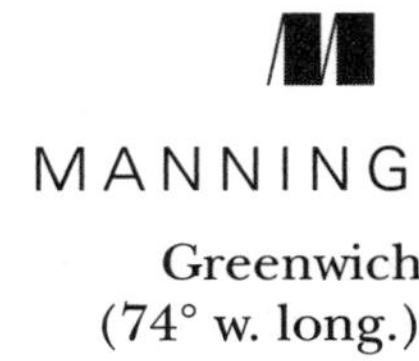

MANNING
Greenwich
(74° w. long.)

For online information and ordering of this and other Manning books, please visit www.manning.com. The publisher offers discounts on this book when ordered in quantity. For more information, please contact:

Special Sales Department
Manning Publications Co.
Sound View Court 3B fax: (609) 877-8256
Greenwich, CT 06830 email: orders@manning.com

Manning Publications Co.
Sound View Court 3B
Greenwich, CT 06830

Copyeditor: Tiffany Taylor
Typesetters: Gordan Salinovic
Cover designer: Leslie Haimes

ISBN 1-933988-23-1
Printed in the United States of America
1 2 3 4 5 6 7 8 9 10 – MAL – 13 12 11 10 09 08 07

To my son, David

Thank you for letting me shorten playtime so many times,
so that Daddy could work on his book.

—RH

To my parents

Everything I have achieved is because of something you did for me.
Thank you.

—AT

brief contents

contents

PART 2 BUILDING USER INTERFACES 107

preface

In the middle of 2005, we noticed that something was different. The Web had reinvented itself, and terms like *Ajax* and *Web 2.0* were being created to help define the new technologies and ideas. JavaScript tools like Scriptaculous, Prototype, and DWR were entering the scene, making it much easier to use JavaScript for interactive interfaces and making Ajax easier to employ. At the same time, Ajax applications, such as Flickr and Google Mail, were beginning to revolutionize the way users expected to use the Web.

We experimented with the new JavaScript libraries, but developing applications seemed more difficult than it needed to be. We also had difficulty seeing how to effectively manage a project using JavaScript—we were used to the ease of development that comes with typed languages, testing, and powerful IDEs with debugging capabilities. Sure, you can manage a successful JavaScript project, but the need to develop and maintain several different versions of code for differing browsers is a headache. Also, in our experience, it isn't easy to find enough JavaScript developers who are aware of the necessary browser issues and nuances and who are also at a sufficient comfort level with production quality development processes to deliver a large project (compared to the number of Java programmers).

In May 2006, a news item from the JavaOne conference announced the Google Web Toolkit. It was described as a toolkit that let you write client-side code in Java and compile it to JavaScript. It was like Christmas, and we hurried to download and exploit these new toys.

We were early adopters, quickly joining in with the rest of the GWT community in test-driving this new tool. Each day, developers posted to the developers' list the source code of widgets they had created. Everyone was trying to show what they could do and share their code with others. This led Robert to start the GWT Widget Library project on SourceForge. Before long, we were working together on the code for Adam's `EditableLabel` for the GWT Widget Library. We worked well together, and we shared a huge enthusiasm for this new technology. When Manning asked if we would write a book, we jumped at the chance to share everything we had learned to date.

To paraphrase the first few paragraphs of this book, instead of taking tools to the Ajax space, Google has taken Ajax to the tools. We can now use fully fledged IDEs, and GWT manages all the messing around associated with browser differences. Just as important is the fact that by using Java and all the normal Java tools (IDEs, Ant, Maven, and so on), GWT fits into our development processes as a hand does into a glove, plus it supports internationalization and unit testing right out of the box.

Let's be clear: GWT won't solve every problem you have when it comes to creating Ajax applications, and some elements could be improved (now that it's open source, it can only get better). But GWT takes a massive step toward maturing the process of creating and maintaining Ajax applications. We finish the book with the following statement, which sums up our view of GWT: "…we don't even want to think about the amount of effort that would be required to program, let alone debug, any issues or perform maintenance across six different browsers for an application such as the Dashboard (developed in this book) directly in JavaScript."

GWT has proven to be a viable alternative to pure JavaScript development. Each major release of GWT brings new features; and month after month new applications are being released by eager developers. We hope that through this book, we can share our enthusiasm for GWT and make it easier for you to get the most out of this technology.

acknowledgments

Although there are only two names on the cover, writing and producing this book has been a tremendous undertaking by a large cast. We couldn't have written this book without them.

We would like to begin our thanks with Michael Stephens from Manning for getting this project started. We want to thank him for his honesty about how much work this book would really be, and for his guidance and encouragement along the way to get us through it. We couldn't have done this book without you.

We wish to thank Manning's publisher, Marjan Bace, for green-lighting the project and heading up a great team at Manning. Our thanks also go out to the entire Manning team for helping us turn our rough ideas into a finished work that goes far beyond what we could have accomplished on our own. This includes the fantastic work done by Olivia DiFeterici, Gabriel Dobrescu, Christina Downs, Leslie Haimes, Cynthia Kane, Dottie Marsico, Mary Piergies, Gordan Salinovic, Maureen Spencer, Tiffany Taylor, Karen Tegtmeyer, Ron Tomich, and Megan Yockey. Thanks to all of you for being part of the team.

We also want to thank Phil Hanna, our technical editor. Phil is an accomplished author with several books under his belt, so we were elated when he joined the team.

We need to thank each and every reviewer for their comments. All of them spent their free time to help us with our project, and for that we are grateful. Special thanks to Julian Seidenberg, Mike Buksas, Denis Kurilenko, Bernard Farrell, Deepak Vohra, Carlo Bottiglieri, Scott Stirling, Goldy Luka, Jeff Cunningham,

Eric Raymond, Andrew Grothe, Noel Rappin, Christopher Haupt, Benjamin Gorlick, Aleksey Nudelman, and Ernest Friedman-Hill.

Last, and perhaps the most important contributor to this book, is everyone from the GWT community. This book was in no small part guided by your questions and discussions on the GWT developers' forum. This includes not only GWT users, but also the entire GWT team at Google. Thank you all.

about this book

The Google Web Toolkit (GWT) slashes through the issues that surround multi-browser Ajax development. It moves the development lifecycle into the type-safe language of Java while retaining the capability to access JavaScript and third-party libraries. GWT offers the opportunity to develop your Ajax application once for use in multiple browsers and configurations.

GWT in Action aims to give you a solid foundation for developing GWT applications. It puts all the tools and development tasks into the context of typical application development, ensuring that you can understand and avoid the problems faced in GWT development. Throughout the book, the development of a Dashboard application, together with various component applications for the Dashboard, provides the mechanism we use to explain GWT concepts.

We start by providing a solid background on the basics, looking at the tools that are used and where they're used in a typical development lifecycle. Then, we consider widgets, panels, and events, discussing those provided by GWT and how to create your own (leaning heavily on our experience from developing components for the GWT Widget Library).

Additionally, we tackle some of GWT's more advanced aspects that are not currently documented in other publications, such as the following:

- Writing code that handles internalization and browser differences:
  Why send IE and Firefox markup for Flash movies when you can send just the appropriate one? And, how can you change the way applications work based on locale as well as changing whole components of your application?
- Driving alternatives in application functionality through GWT properties:
  The Dashboard example comes in two flavors: Internet and intranet versions. Which one is shown to the user is driven by user-defined properties that you'll define and manage.
- Harnessing the powerful GWT generator concept:
  You'll learn to introspect classes and tags in comments at compile time to produce new Java classes.
- Describing the development of composite objects:
  You'll see how to build the `EditableLabel` we built for the GWT Widget Library. You'll also construct new composite widgets using other composite widgets—for example, building a complex color picker widget from a number of GWT slider widgets. Finally, you'll learn how to apply CSS consistently to components.
- Integrating with JavaScript through the JavaScript Native Interface (JSNI):
  We'll discuss interapplication communication via JavaScript. You'll build wrappers to simple and complex third-party JavaScript libraries (such as the Google Ajax Search component found in the GWT Widget Library).

Any substantial application requires server-side components, and many books can tell you about all the server-side development techniques (Java, PHP, and so on) for which GWT is highly flexible and which it can plug into. Our approach in *GWT in Action* is to concentrate several chapters on ensuring you get a thorough understanding of GWT's client-server communication techniques; for example:

- JSON processing using proxy servers (the Yahoo Search component)
- GWT-RPC: the technique, the problem, and the solutions (see the Server Status component)
- XML processing (used in the menu for the complete Dashboard application)
- Form handling, including uploading files
- Using traditional Ajax communication

The key point is to get a good understanding of each approach in GWT so you see the flexibility and can choose your server side appropriately (or, if your server side is a given, so you thoroughly understand the technique you'll be using).

By the end of the book, you'll understand how the Dashboard application (http://dashboard.manning-sandbox.com) referred to throughout is architected, how it's constructed, and how it works.

Who should read this book?

The book is aimed at anyone with an interest in GWT. We appreciate that the readership will come from varied backgrounds—JavaScript programmers looking to see what the fuss is all about, Java programmers learning that they can now program Ajax applications simply, server-side developers interested in understanding GWT-RPC, web designers looking to understand what this useful maturing of development means to them, and many others.

Readers looking for a gentle introduction to GWT concepts and components will appreciate the easy way in which these topics are introduced. The book has been particularly designed to reduce the large number of gotchas that are found when you first look at GWT. More advanced readers will find that the book contains many aspects you have perhaps thought of but not yet figured out how to implement—and, we hope, a few you haven't thought of!

You should be familiar with the concept of Java classes and packages, although we feel this is something you can pick up as you read the book, follow the code samples, and use an IDE. A lot of GWT (and Java) issues revolve around classpaths and GWT's package structure, so we recommend a thorough reading of chapter 9 if you're getting stuck.

Roadmap

Chapter 1 introduces GWT and examines where it sits in relation to complementary and competing technologies. It also shows how easy it is to get a first GWT application up and running.

Chapter 2 provides a detailed understanding of the steps required to build the default GWT application using the GWT command-line tools, indicating what each tool is, why it's used, and when you should use it. This chapter also discusses alternative approaches to creating your application, including by hand and by using an IDE wizard.

Chapter 3 is the first step you'll take away from the default GWT application and toward the initial version of the Dashboard. We'll explain what default files you need to change/replace and why.

Chapter 4 starts our discussion of standard GWT components. It looks at widgets, but not in a textbook style. Using component applications from the running Dashboard application, you'll get insight into the use of key widgets from GWT. The second part of the chapter looks at building your own widgets, including the GWT Widget Libraries `PNGImage` widget and two widgets that extend the standard `MenuItem` widget.

Chapter 5 covers panels, looking at how they're used in the Dashboard and how to extend and create your own panels—including the `DashboardPanel` used for the Dashboard application components.

Chapter 6 introduces event handling as performed by GWT and explains how to harness it for your own components. You'll see how to handle new events for widgets as well as plumb together the event handling for double-clicks and so on.

Chapter 7 finishes the four key aspects of GWT application components by thoroughly discussing the development of composite widgets. We lean on the `EditableLabel`, which has been around for nearly a year and is included in the GWT Widget Library. You'll also build some slider composite widgets, culminating in a sliding color-picker widget.

Chapter 8 is where you'll learn how to harness any JavaScript library you may have and want to interact with. The GWT Widget Library includes a GWT widget that wraps the Google Ajax Search functionality; you'll learn how we built that component as well as how to wrap the Google Video Search component.

Chapter 9 wraps up the direct user interface components included in the book. You'll learn the details of using the GWT module's XML configuration file to, among other things, inject resources, alter the project layout, invoke class replacement and generation, and include server components. You'll also see how to include third-party GWT libraries, as well as how to create you own libraries of GWT code.

Chapter 10 takes you into the world of GWT-RPC, where you'll learn how to pass Java objects between the web browser and your Java servlets.

Chapter 11 expands on the previous chapter by showing you common usage patterns and custom serialization for GWT-RPC. This include polling techniques, including how to emulate server-push.

Chapter 12 looks at GWT's support for classic Ajax and HTML forms. These tools offer flexibility, allowing your GWT application to connect to any server-side application. This chapter provides real-world examples for loading external configuration data and using GWT to upload files to the server.

Chapter 13 finishes our discussion of client-server communication with GWT's support of the JavaScript Object Notation (JSON) message format. We'll explain what JSON is and provide an example of using it to communicate with the Yahoo Search API.

Chapter 14 looks at GWT's powerful generators. You'll learn how to build generators that introspect code at compile time to generate new subclasses with additional functionality. You'll also see how these generators can promote comments written in code to be displayed in dialogs to the user at runtime.

Chapter 15 rounds off the advanced techniques by thoroughly covering properties, including internationalization both in the normal sense of changing text for labels and menus, and so on, and also in terms of changing whole components of your application based on the defined locale. You'll also use properties to drive the selection of the view that is presented to the user.

Chapter 16 shows you how to test your GWT code with JUnit and how to deploy your finished application to the server. You'll learn how to organize your deployed code to reduce clutter on the server.

Chapter 17 completes the book by investigating the underlying mechanisms of GWT, for those interested in delving a little deeper. You'll see how bootstrapping works (including the changes introduced by GWT 1.4), what your compiled code should look like, and what the various output files produced by the compiler are related to.

Code conventions and downloads

This book contains copious amounts of code and examples. The whole substantial GWT application, called the Dashboard, is referred to throughout the book and is available from www.manning.com/hanson or www.manning.com/GWTinAction.

The additional libraries that are used by the application code and that you need to download separately are as follows:

- JSON classes used in the server-side code, from http://JSON.org.
- File upload server-side processing from Apache Commons (commons-fileupload.jar, commons-io.jar, commons-codec.jar). Apache Commons is at http://jakarta.apache.org/commons/.
- The Apache Commons commons-httpclient component, which the proxy server implementation used in one component relies on.
- GWT Widget Library (http://gwt-widget.sourceforge.net/).

Source code in listings or in text is in a `fixed-width font` to separate it from ordinary text. Additionally, Java method names, component parameters, object properties, and HTML and XML elements and attributes in text are also presented using `fixed-width font`. Java method names generally don't include the signature (the list of parameter types).

Java, HTML, and XML can all be verbose. In many cases, the original source code (available online) has been reformatted, adding line breaks and reworking indentation, to accommodate the available page space in the book. In rare cases, even this wasn't enough, and listings include line-continuation markers. Additionally, comments in the source code have been removed from the listings.

Code annotations accompany many of the source code listings, highlighting important concepts. In some cases, numbered bullets link to explanations that follow the listing.

GWT was originally a closed-source development program, but it's now open-source. You can download the binary packages for your platform (Windows, Linux, Mac OX) from here: http://code.google.com/webtoolkit/versions.html. If you're interested in contributing to the platform or living on the bleeding edge of development, then you can grab the source code from the SVN archive here: http://code.google.com/webtoolkit/makinggwtbetter.html.

Author Online

The purchase of *GWT in Action* includes free access to a private web forum run by Manning Publications, where you can make comments about the book, ask technical questions, and receive help from the authors and from other users. To access the forum and subscribe to it, point your web browser to www.manning.com/GWTinAction or www.manning.com/hanson. This page provides information on how to get on the forum once you are registered, what kind of help is available, and the rules of conduct on the forum.

Manning's commitment to our readers is to provide a venue where a meaningful dialogue between individual readers and between readers and the authors can take place. It's not a commitment to any specific amount of participation on the part of the authors, whose contribution to the forum remains voluntary (and unpaid). We suggest you try asking the authors some challenging questions lest their interest stray! The Author Online forum and the archives of previous discussions will be accessible from the publisher's web site as long as the book is in print.

About the authors

ROBERT HANSON is a senior Internet engineer specializing in Java application development and maintenance. Robert is the creator of the popular open source *GWT Widget Library* found at http://gwt-widget.sourceforge.net and also maintains a blog at http://roberthanson.blogspot.com where he talks about GWT and other topics relating to the industry. You can contact him at iamroberthanson@gmail.com.

ADAM TACY works as a project manager at WM-data in the Nordics, specializing in delivery of new/leading-edge projects while enjoying the associated risks and need to establish repeatable processes. He was a (grateful) early adopter of GWT and has contributed to the GWT Widget Library. In his spare time, you can find him falling through ice, mishandling kite-surf equipment, and enjoying all things Norwegian, Swedish, and Finnish while missing good old British bacon and beer. You can contact him at adam.tacy@gmail.com.

about the title

By combining introductions, overviews, and how-to examples, the *In Action* books are designed to help learning *and* remembering. According to research in cognitive science, the things people remember are things they discover during self-motivated exploration.

Although no one at Manning is a cognitive scientist, we are convinced that for learning to become permanent it must pass through stages of exploration, play, and, interestingly, re-telling of what is being learned. People understand and remember new things, which is to say they master them, only after actively exploring them. Humans learn *in action.* An essential part of an *In Action* guide is that it is example-driven. It encourages the reader to try things out, to play with new code, and explore new ideas.

There is another, more mundane, reason for the title of this book: our readers are busy. They use books to do a job or solve a problem. They need books that allow them to jump in and jump out easily and learn just what they want just when they want it. They need books that aid them *in action.* The books in this series are designed for such readers.

about the cover illustration

The figure on the cover of *GWT in Action* is a "Janissary in Ceremonial Dress." Janissaries were an elite corps of soldiers in the service of the Ottoman Empire, loyal only to the Sultan. The illustration is taken from a collection of costumes of the Ottoman Empire published on January 1, 1802, by William Miller of Old Bond Street, London. The title page is missing from the collection and we have been unable to track it down to date. The book's table of contents identifies the figures in both English and French, and each illustration bears the names of two artists who worked on it, both of whom would no doubt be surprised to find their art gracing the front cover of a computer programming book... two hundred years later.

The collection was purchased by a Manning editor at an antiquarian flea market in the "Garage" on West 26th Street in Manhattan. The seller was an American based in Ankara, Turkey, and the transaction took place just as he was packing up his stand for the day. The Manning editor did not have on his person the substantial amount of cash that was required for the purchase and a credit card and check were both politely turned down. With the seller flying back to Ankara that evening the situation was getting hopeless. What was the solution? It turned out to be nothing more than an old-fashioned verbal agreement sealed with a handshake. The seller simply proposed that the money be transferred to him by wire and the editor walked out with the bank information on a piece of paper and the portfolio of images under his arm. Needless to say, we transferred the funds the next day, and we remain grateful and impressed by this unknown person's trust in one of us. It recalls something that might have happened a long time ago.

The pictures from the Ottoman collection, like the other illustrations that appear on our covers, bring to life the richness and variety of dress customs of two centuries ago. They recall the sense of isolation and distance of that period—and of every other historic period except our own hyperkinetic present.

Dress codes have changed since then and the diversity by region, so rich at the time, has faded away. It is now often hard to tell the inhabitant of one continent from another. Perhaps, trying to view it optimistically, we have traded a cultural and visual diversity for a more varied personal life. Or a more varied and interesting intellectual and technical life.

We at Manning celebrate the inventiveness, the initiative, and, yes, the fun of the computer business with book covers based on the rich diversity of regional life of two centuries ago, brought back to life by the pictures from this collection.

Part 1

Getting started

Part 1 introduces you to the Google Web Toolkit by providing an overview of what the toolkit includes and how it compares to similar technologies. Following the introduction, this part of the book provides instruction for getting your first GWT application up and running, using the GWT command-line tools to generate skeleton code. Finally, we'll take a detailed look at the skeleton code and, more important, explain how to extend it.

1 Introducing GWT

This chapter covers

- High-level overview of GWT's toolset
- Comparison of GWT to similar technologies
- An example of a GWT application

In May 2006, Google released the Google Web Toolkit (GWT), a set of development tools, programming utilities, and widgets that let you create rich Internet applications differently than you may have done before. The difference between GWT and all those other frameworks is that with GWT you write your browser-side code in Java instead of JavaScript. For those of us who rely on Java as a trusted tool, this is a monumental difference over traditional JavaScript coding. It means that besides gaining all the advantages of Java as a programming language, you also get immediate access to a gazillion Java development tools that are already available. Instead of trying to build a new tool to support the development of rich Internet applications in JavaScript, Google has altered the paradigm, allowing these applications to be written in Java, making use of tools that already exist.

The need to write code in Java instead of JavaScript is rooted in the ever-increasing size and complexity of rich Internet applications. Large applications are difficult to manage, and Java was designed to make large application development manageable. While bringing all of Java's benefits to rich Internet applications, GWT still allows you to interact with existing JavaScript code. When you embrace GWT, it doesn't mean that you need to throw away all your old JavaScript code: GWT makes every attempt to be flexible with regard to integration, allowing it to integrate not only with existing JavaScript code, but also with your existing server-side services.

At the core of GWT is a Java-to-JavaScript compiler that produces code capable of running on Internet Explorer, Firefox, Mozilla, Safari, and Opera. The compiler converts the Java syntax to JavaScript, utilizing JavaScript versions of commonly used Java classes like `Vector`, `HashMap`, and `Date`. The compiler can then weave in JavaScript that you've referenced in your code, allowing you to utilize popular libraries like `Scriptaculous`, `JSCalendar`, and `TinyMCE`.

Beyond the compiler, GWT also includes a large library of widgets and panels, making it effortless to build a web application that looks more like a desktop application. The widget library includes the usual suspects like text boxes, drop-down menus, and other form fields. In addition, it includes complex widgets including a menu bar, tree control, dialog box, tab panel, stack panel, and others.

When it comes to communication with the server, GWT has a tool for every job. First, it includes several wrappers of varying complexity and capability around the JavaScript `XMLHttpRequest` object, an object often associated with Asynchronous JavaScript + XML (Ajax) development. Another tool provided by GWT is a set of classes for supporting the JavaScript Object Notation (JSON) message format. JSON is a popular message format known for its simplicity and widespread availability. GWT also provides some of its own special sauce in the form of a tool that lets you send Java objects between the browser and server without the need to translate them into an intermediate message format.

These tools for communication allow you to access server-side services written in any language, and make it possible to integrate with frameworks such as JavaServer Faces (JSF), Spring, Struts, and Enterprise JavaBeans (EJBs). This flexibility means GWT doesn't make more work for you; instead, it allows you to continue to use the same server-side tools you're using today.

But being able to write rich Internet applications in Java isn't enough to make them easier to write. Toward this end, GWT provides support for the JUnit testing framework and a special hosted-mode browser that lets you develop and debug in Java without ever needing to deploy your code to a server. This is a real time-saver!

As you can see, GWT is a rich topic, and we still haven't mentioned half of what there is to cover. In this chapter, we begin the exploration of GWT gently, spending some time enumerating each of GWT's major features that will be covered throughout the book. Along the way, we provide short code snippets to help you better understand how you'll use the feature in practice.

After exploring the main features of GWT, we'll compare GWT to some of the other toolkits. Our selection of frameworks for the comparisons is based on questions we've seen posed by non-GWT developers. Our hope is that by making these comparisons, we can better explain what GWT is and what it isn't. Again, we provide code snippets for the purpose of comparison, but not quite a working application.

At the end of chapter 1, we wrap up the tour by providing you with a complete, working example application. This example will start you in the process of developing rich Internet applications with GWT. Let's get down to business and find out what GWT is all about, beginning with an overview of the primary features that make this toolkit so useful to web application developers.

1.1 A walk through GWT

GWT provides a rich set of tools focused on solving the problem of moving the desktop application into the browser, including a rich set of widgets and many other tools. The GWT toolbox provides an XML parser, several tools for communicating with the server, internationalization and configuration tools, and a browser-history management system. Figure 1.1 provides a visual map of the central aspects of GWT, each of which will be described in this section. In the figure, you can see that the tools can be divided into those that are tied to the compiler, and the Java libraries that make up the GWT API.

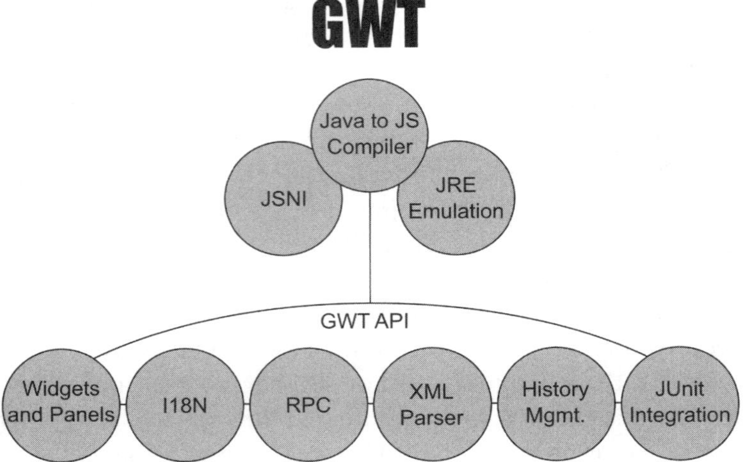

Figure 1.1 GWT provides a comprehensive set of tools to meet the challenge of developing modern rich Internet applications. From UI components to configuration tools to server communication techniques, GWT's tools help web apps look, act, and feel more like full-featured desktop apps.

We'll cover each of these tools in turn beginning with the compiler, the most important piece of the puzzle, along with the accompanying Java emulation library. We'll move on to provide information about the rich widget library and show you how GWT lets you interface your new GWT code with your existing JavaScript libraries. We'll then hop over and examine GWT's support for internationalization and see what Remote Procedure Call (RPC) services GWT has to offer for communicating with server-side services. Finally, we'll wrap up the examination by looking at the XML parser API, browser-history management API, and close with a strong dose of JUnit integration. By the end of this section, you should have a good idea of what GWT is capable of, and we hope you'll be as excited as we are about this new technology.

Our tour of the features in GWT will mimic the ordering you see in figure 1.1 from top to bottom and left to right. We'll begin with the keystone of the diagram, the Java-to-JavaScript compiler.

1.1.1 Explaining GWT's Java-to-JavaScript compiler

The most obvious place to start looking at what GWT provides is the one tool that defines it: the compiler. The GWT compiler's responsibility is to convert your Java code into JavaScript code, in much the same way the Java compiler compiles your Java code into bytecode. You compile your project by running the Java program `com.google.gwt.dev.GWTCompiler`, passing it the location of your module definition file along with some other parameters. A *module* is a set of related Java classes and files accompanied by a single configuration file. The module definition typically includes an entry point, which is a class that executes when the application starts.

The compiler starts with the entry-point class, following dependencies required to compile the Java code. The GWT compiler works differently than the standard Java compiler because it doesn't compile everything in the module; it includes only what is being used. This is useful in that it lets you develop a large library of supporting components and tools, and the compiler includes only those classes and methods used by the entry-point class.

The compiler has three style modes that determine what the resulting JavaScript looks like. The default style is `obfuscate`, which makes the JavaScript look like alphabet soup. Everything is compressed and nearly impossible to decipher. This isn't done to prevent it from being read, although that could be seen as a benefit for preventing code theft; instead, it helps keep the resulting JavaScript file as small as possible. This is a real concern as your application gets larger.

This snippet of JavaScript code is the output of the GWT compiler using the obfuscated compiling mode. You can see that it's as compressed as it can be, with no hint as to what the method is used for:

```
function b(){return this.c + '@' + this.d();}
```

The next style is `pretty`, which generates readable JavaScript. This compiled code snippet is derived from the same original Java source code as the obfuscated sample. You can now see that the code is a `toString()` method, a common method for Java classes, but you still can't tell what class this code is for:

```
function _toString(){
  return this._typeName + '@' + this._hashCode();
}
```

The last style is `detailed`, which produces JavaScript code that looks like the `pretty` style with the addition of the full class name as part of the JavaScript method name. This makes it easy to trace the JavaScript code back to the originating Java code. In this code sample, compiled in `detailed` mode, you can easily see that this is the `toString()` method for `java.lang.Object`, the root of all Java classes.

```
function java_lang_Object_toString__(){
  return this.java_lang_Object_typeName + '@' + this.hashCode__();
}
```

The `pretty` and `detailed` styles are typically used only during development so that JavaScript errors in your browser are easier to track back to the source Java code. For production, using `obfuscated` is favorable because it keeps the JavaScript file size down and can help to hide trade secrets.

Another important aspect of the compiler is that it compiles from Java source code, not compiled Java binaries. This means the source for all the Java classes you're using must be available. This plays a role when you want to distribute GWT code for reuse. When you build distributable Java Archive (JAR) files, you must include both the Java source and compiled Java class files. The GWT compiler also requires that the source code be compliant with the Java 1.4 syntax. This is expected to change eventually, but for now you can't use generics, enums, and other Java 1.5 features in your application. Note that this restriction applies only to code that will be compiled to JavaScript; it doesn't limit what Java version you can use to write server components that will communicate with the browser.

One last feature to note is that when your code is compiled to JavaScript, it results in a different JavaScript file for each browser type and target locale. The supported browsers include Internet Explorer, Firefox, Mozilla, Opera, and Safari. Typically, this means your application will be compiled to a minimum of four or five separate JavaScript files. Each of these files is meant to run on a specific browser type, version, and locale. A bootstrap script, initially loaded by the browser, automatically pulls the correct file when the application is loaded. The benefit of this process is that the code loaded by the browser doesn't contain code it can't use. Typically, this doesn't result in huge bandwidth savings; but in some cases, especially when you're providing the interface in multiple locale settings, the size can be reduced significantly.

Following our diagram in figure 1.1, we'll next look at a core feature of the GWT compiler: its ability to let Java code interact with native JavaScript code via the JavaScript Native Interface.

1.1.2 Using JSNI to execute JavaScript from Java

Although GWT code is written in Java instead of JavaScript, sometimes you need to write code that can make direct JavaScript calls. There are several reasons why you might need to do this. You may need to make a call to the browser's API for which no GWT equivalent exists. Another perhaps more common reason is if you want to use some super-fantastic JavaScript library.

The JavaScript Native Interface (JSNI) lets you execute JavaScript from Java as well as execute Java from JavaScript. This is made possible by the GWT compiler, which can merge native JavaScript code with the JavaScript code generated from

Java. We'll get into the finer points of doing this in chapter 8, but here are some examples to give you an idea how this works.

This first example is basic but reveals how the mechanism works:

```
public native int addTwoNumbers (int x, int y)
/*-{
  var result = x + y;
  return result;
}-*/;
```

In Java, you can declare a method as *native*, alerting the compiler that the implementation of the method will be written in some other language. Per the Java language specification, when you declare a method as being native, you aren't allowed to specify a code block for the method. If you haven't seen this before, this mechanism was built into Java to let Java code call methods in compiled libraries written in languages like C and C++.

When you inspect this method, you see that what appears to be a block of code is all contained in a multiline Java comment. Inside this comment is the native JavaScript code that will be executed when the method is called. This satisfies the Java syntax requirement of not allowing a code block for native methods, but provides the JavaScript that the GWT compiler can use to allow execution of this code.

This example passes a Java `List` object to the method and uses JavaScript to add two items to it:

```
public native void fillData (List data)
/*-{
    data.@java.util.List::add(Ljava/lang/Object;)('item1');
    data.@java.util.List::add(Ljava/lang/Object;)('item2');
}-*/;
```

Because you're calling the `add()` method on a Java object, you need to use a special syntax to provide details on the object and method we're referencing. Here you let the GWT compiler know that the variable data is an instance of `java.util.List` and that the `add()` method takes a single `java.lang.Object` argument. This mechanism is fairly easy to use once you understand the special syntax, and it lets you include any needed JavaScript code in the same source file as your Java code. Chapter 8 gets into the details of the syntax.

Moving on to the next component of GWT from figure 1.1, and keeping in line with the relationship between Java and JavaScript in GWT, we need to visit the JRE Emulation Library, a mapping of Java Runtime Environment (JRE) classes to their JavaScript equivalents.

1.1.3 Accessing the JRE emulation library

We mentioned earlier that the GWT compiler needs access to the Java source code for any class you're using in your code. This requirement doesn't stop with the use of just external libraries; it includes the JRE as well. To provide developers with the ability to use some of the JRE classes, GWT provides the JRE Emulation Library. This library contains the most commonly used parts of the full JRE, which you can use in your projects and compile to JavaScript.

Tables 1.1 and 1.2 enumerate the available classes of the JRE that may be utilized in your GWT applications from the `java.lang` package and the `java.util` package, respectively. If you look through the lists carefully, you'll likely see that several classes you might consider important are missing. For example, the `java.util.Date` class is available, but not `java.util.Calendar` or any date-formatting tools.

Table 1.1 Classes from `java.lang.*` that are available in GWT

Classes		
`Boolean`	`Byte`	`Character`
`Class`	`Double`	`Float`
`Integer`	`Long`	`Math`
`Number`	`Object`	`Short`
`String`	`StringBuffer`	`System`
Exceptions/Errors		
`AssertionError`	`ArrayStoreException`	`ClassCastException`
`Exception`	`Error`	`IllegalArgument-Exception`
`IllegalStateException`	`IndexOutOfBounds-Exception`	`NegativeArraySize-Exception`
`NullPointerException`	`NumberFormatException`	`RuntimeException`
`StringIndexOutOfBounds-Exception`	`Throwable`	`UnsupportedOperation-Exception`
Interfaces		
`CharSequence`	`Cloneable`	`Comparable`

Table 1.2 Classes from `java.util.*` that are available in GWT

Classes		
AbstractCollection	AbstractList	AbstractMap
AbstractSet	ArrayList	Arrays
Collections	Date	HashMap
LinkedHashMap[a]	ListIterator[a]	HashSet
SortedMap[a]	Stack	TreeMap[a]
Vector		
Exceptions/Errors		
EmptyStackException	NoSuchElementException	TooManyListenersException
Interfaces		
Collection	Comparator	EventListener
Iterator	List	Map
RandomAccess	Set	

a. Targeted for inclusion in the 1.4 release of GWT

When you start using these classes, you'll notice some additional differences. Some of the functionality differs from the JRE versions in subtle ways. As of this writing, the following restrictions apply:

- `Double` and `Float` should not be used as `HashMap` keys for performance reasons.
- For `String.replaceAll`, `String.replaceFirst`, and `String.split`, the regular expressions vary from the standard Java implementation.
- `StringBuffer(int)` behaves the same as `StringBuffer()`.
- `System.out` and `System.err` are available but have no functionality in web mode.
- The stack-trace-related methods in `Throwable` aren't functional due to the lack of stack-trace support.
- The implementation of the `Vector` class doesn't include any of the capacity and growth-management functionality of the normal Java implementation, nor is there any checking of index validity.

In general, this isn't as limiting as we have made it sound. In many cases, you can get around the problem by using other Java classes, writing your own code to perform a specific function, or making direct use of the JavaScript API. As GWT gains momentum, it's likely a lot of these holes will be filled by either the GWT library itself or open source libraries.

Now we want to switch gears. As you saw in figure 1.1, the components of GWT are roughly divided into those relating to the compiler and those relating to the GWT API. In the next section, we'll begin our tour of the GWT API by looking at the GWT widget and panel library, the visual components that are used to build your user interface.

1.1.4 Understanding GWT's widget and panel library

GWT ships with a large set of widgets and panels. The distinction between widgets and panels is that a *widget* is some sort of control used by a user, and a *panel* is a container into which controls can be placed. For example, a button or text box is a widget, and a table that displays the button and text box left-to-right on the page is a panel. But panels in GWT aren't just for layout; some panels offer interactivity. Generally speaking, GWT uses three types of components: widgets, panels for layout, and interactive panels. Figure 1.2 shows a small sample of some of the available widgets and panels.

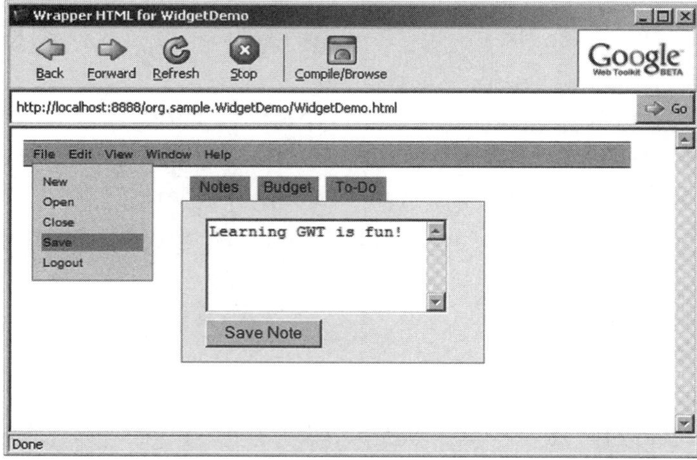

Figure 1.2 GWT ships with a set of widgets and panels that allow you to quickly create a rich Internet application without needing to worry about the HTML and JavaScript details.

The MenuBar, a widget, is shown across the top of the page. The TabPanel, an interactive panel, appears in the middle of the page, acting as a container for a TextArea and Button widget. The MenuBar and TabPanel are then contained in an AbsolutePanel that allows for exact positioning of the components it contains.

If you're familiar with Java's Swing library, then you may be familiar with using layout managers to organize the components inside of a panel; but this is difficult to map to HTML elements, so GWT takes a different approach. Instead of layout managers, GWT provides a set of panels that display their children in a specific manner. For example, the HorizontalPanel displays its child widgets from left to right, FlowPanel displays its children using normal HTML flow rules, and the AbsolutePanel provides exact positioning of the components it contains.

The widgets provided by GWT generally map back to a specific HTML equivalent. This includes form fields like Button, TextBox, TextArea, Checkbox, RadioButton, and FormPanel. In addition, there are several variations of the HTML table element, including the base class HTMLTable and two specialized subclasses, Grid and FlexTable.

GWT also comes with several rich components that are familiar in desktop applications but not so much in web applications. The TabPanel lets you place different widgets on different tabs, and the widgets displayed depend on the currently selected tab, like the tabbed browsing in Firefox and Internet Explorer 7. The MenuBar provides an easy way to create a multilevel menu for your application. Then there are PopupPanel, StackPanel, and others.

Although GWT includes more than 30 widgets and panels, it's likely that they won't meet all your needs. To fill this void, open source projects make specialized widget, tools, and panels available to use in your own projects. The list of widgets includes calendars, sortable tables, calculators, drawing panels, tooltip panels, and others. There are also a number of widgets available that wrap existing JavaScript libraries, like the Google Maps API, Google Search API, and Scriptaculous effects. In addition to HTML-based widgets, widgets are available for Scalar Vector Graphics (SVG), a markup language for creating extremely rich vector-based graphics. We'll discuss how to use third-party libraries in your projects, as well as a few of our favorite libraries, in chapter 9.

When you build your own widgets by extending those that come with GWT, it's often required that you access the browser's underlying JavaScript objects. It would be great it we could forget about the underlying JavaScript, but that isn't always possible. Fortunately, GWT provides facilities for interfacing Java with the underlying JavaScript.

Next, we'll look at a different part of the GWT API. GWT provides a set of tools for internationalization and configuration, allowing you to present your newly developed user interface in several languages.

1.1.5 Examining GWT's internationalization and configuration tools

GWT provides several techniques that can aid you with internationalization and configuration issues. This may seem like an odd pair, but they're similar in that you want the ability to store text strings or numeric values in a properties file and to access them from your application. GWT provides two primary mechanisms that should handle most needs: static inclusion at compile time, and dynamic inclusion at runtime. The static method is accomplished by implementing the `Constants` or `Messages` interface, whereas the dynamic method uses the GWT `Dictionary` class.

You include settings statically at compile time by implementing an interface, either `Constants` or `Messages`, and by creating a single method for each property you want to use. For example, perhaps you want to use a properties file to store a welcome message along with the image path of your application's logo. You provide a method for each in your interface:

```
public interface MySettings extends Constants
{
  String welcomeMessage();
  String logoImage();
}
```

Once you have your interface, you can use GWT to dynamically create an instance of this interface, and it automatically attaches the properties file settings to it. You can also set up several properties to be used for different locales—for example, if you wanted the text to change based on the language of the reader.

The `Messages` interface differs from `Constants` in that you may specify arguments to the methods, which are then used to fill placeholders in the property text. For example, you may want to alter the previous interface to allow the person's name to be included in the greeting message. Your properties file might look like the following:

```
welcomeMessage = Welcome to my book {0} {1}
logoImage = /images/logo.jpg
```

The placeholder `{0}` is used to mark the place where the first variable should be inserted into the message and `{1}` for the second. The interface you use for `Constants` needs to be modified to use the `Messages` interface instead, and you add two arguments to your method:

```
public interface MySettings extends Messages
{
  String welcomeMessage(String fname, String lname);
  String logoImage();
}
```

One of the benefits of using these two interfaces is that the messages from your properties file are statically included in your compiled JavaScript. This means the performance of using a value from a properties file is about the same as using a hard-coded string in the application. The compiler also includes only properties that are referenced. This makes it possible to use only a few properties from a large properties file without having all the properties embedded in your JavaScript code.

If you're only using this mechanism for specifying settings that you don't want to hard-code into your application, then you'll likely have a single properties file; but if you want to provide for localization, you'll have one properties file for each supported language. When you compile your code with multiple properties files, the GWT compiler creates a different set of JavaScript files for each locale supplied. If you're supporting a lot of locales, this results in a lot of files; but the benefit is that each JavaScript file has only a single set of properties embedded in it, making the file size smaller.

On the flip side of the coin, there are occasions where the property values are generated dynamically—for example, the details of a specific user. In this case, you need a dynamic runtime mechanism to look up property information. For this purpose, GWT provides a `Dictionary` class, which doesn't use properties files. Instead, you can use the `Dictionary` object to grab settings that have been embedded in the HTML as JavaScript objects:

```
var MySettings = {
  welcomeMessage: "Welcome to my book",
  logoImage: "/images/logo.jpg"
};
```

In the GWT application, you load the JavaScript object into a `Dictionary` instance by using the static method `Dictionary.getDictionary()`, passing the JavaScript variable name as an argument. You can then use the methods of the returned `Dictionary` object to get the individual settings. This mechanism is ideal when you want to pass data to your GWT application:

```
Dictionary settings = Dictionary.getDictionary("MySettings");
String logo = settings.get("logoImage");
```

The configuration mechanisms provided by GWT, covered in detail in chapter 15, handle most of your configuration and internationalization issues and allow for both dynamic and static properties.

So far, we've looked at the compiler and its supporting tools for compiling your code, we've introduced you to widgets and panels for building the user interface, and we've examined internationalization tools so that you can make the UI available in a dozen different languages. Now we'll take it one step further and look at the tools that GWT provides for communicating with the server and making your applications truly interactive.

1.1.6 Calling remote procedures with GWT

Most nontrivial GWT applications need the ability to communicate information between the browser client and the server. For instance, perhaps the application needs to fetch data to display to the user, or to log the user into the application, or to load an external data file. Fortunately, today's browsers include a special JavaScript object called `XMLHttpRequest` that allows communication between the browser and server without forcing a page refresh like traditional HTML forms do. This special JavaScript object is the basis for making browser-based Remote Procedure Calls (RPCs).

GWT provides two tools that sit on top of the `XMLHttpRequest` object. The first is the `RequestBuilder` class, which is essentially a wrapper around this object, although it's a bit more Java-like in its usage. The second tool, GWT-RPC, is more elaborate and lets you send and receive real Java objects between the client and server. We'll begin with the `RequestBuilder` class and give you a feel for what RPC looks like in GWT.

Making RPC requests with RequestBuilder

The `RequestBuilder` class lets you create a request to be submitted to the server, gives you the ability to fire off the request, and provides access to the results sent back from the server. The short code example in listing 1.1 gives a feel for how it works.

Listing 1.1 An example of an RPC call using `RequestBuilder`

```
String url = "/service/search";
RequestBuilder rb = new RequestBuilder(RequestBuilder.GET, url);      ❶

try {
  Request request = rb.sendRequest("term=GWT+in+Action",      ❷
    new RequestCallback() {                                   ❸
      public void onResponseReceived (Request req, Response res) {
```

```
          // process here
        }

        public void onError (Request req, Throwable exception) {
          // handle error here
        }
    });
  }
  catch (RequestException e) {
    // handle exception here
  }
```

If you aren't used to using anonymous classes, then this example may look a little foreign, so we'll explain it a little. You begin by creating a new instance of the `RequestBuilder` ❶ by specifying the HTTP method and target URL to use. Then, you can use various methods of the `RequestBuilder` instance to set a timeout, add HTTP headers to the request, and even set the username and password for hitting URLs that require authentication. All these options will be covered in detail in chapter 12.

Next, you fire off a request to the server by calling `sendRequest()` ❷ on the `RequestBuilder` instance. This method returns a handle to the request, which is of type `Request`. For long-running requests, you can use the returned `Request` to check on the status of a request or even cancel it. The `sendRequest()` method takes two arguments: a `String` that is sent to the server with the request, and a `RequestCallback` instance to handle the response and any error that might occur. Listing 1.1 uses an anonymous class ❸ that implements the `RequestCallback`, essentially an inline class, for this second parameter to keep the example short; but if the response handler will contain more than a few lines of code, it's preferable to create a separate class.

You use a handler class to handle the response because RPC calls from the browser occur *asynchronously*. The term *asynchronous* in this context means that the `sendRequest()` method returns immediately, without waiting for the server to respond, putting the server request and the execution of the JavaScript code out of sync. When the server does eventually respond, the handler is triggered, just like an event handler. There is a good reason for the call to happen asynchronously. For the browser to handle the call synchronously, it would need to stop handling events, and it would appear frozen from the user's perspective. This definitely wouldn't be desirable.

Another notable attribute is that the response to a call made with `RequestBuilder` is text. This text can be an XML file, HTML code, simple plain text, or JSON code.

JSON is a simple message format for sending structured data, and it's specifically geared for use in the browser. In chapter 13, we'll take a long look at how to use JSON on both the client and server, but for now a brief example will suffice:

```
JSONObject obj = new JSONObject();
obj.put("title", new JSONString("GWT in Action"));
obj.put("author", new JSONString("Hanson and Tacy"));
obj.put("pages", new JSONNumber(600));
String serializedObj = obj.toString();
```

This code sample creates a `JSONObject` and populates it with several properties, just like you would with a Java `HashMap`. Calling the `toString()` method returns the serialized form of the object as a text string. The next step, not shown, would be to use the `RequestBuilder` class to send this serialized data to the server for processing.

The JSON implementation that comes with GWT is limited to use in the browser only, so you need to find your own JSON implementation for use on the server. Fortunately it's fairly easy to find a JSON implementation by visiting http://json.org, the home of the JSON format. When you look for an implementation, you'll notice that you aren't limited to just Java; there are JSON libraries for dozens of languages. This makes JSON a truly universal format, allowing you to pair your GWT application with an application written in any language on the server.

For those of us running only Java on the server, using JSON can feel awkward. On the browser client, you need to copy the data from your Java object into a JSON object; then, on the server, copy the JSON object back into a Java object. When you're using Java on the server, it makes more sense to deal with Java objects directly without the JSON middle-man, and that is where GWT-RPC fits in.

Communicating with GWT-RPC

The GWT-RPC mechanism lets you send Java objects between the client and server with only a little additional work on both the client and server sides. We'll get into the finer points of using GWT-RPC, and show you some common usage patterns, in chapters 10 and 11, but for now we'll stick to the basics.

You first define a service interface that will be implemented by the server. For example, if you're creating a password service, it might look something like the following:

```
public interface PasswordService extends RemoteService {
  Boolean changePassword (String user,
     String oldPass, String newPass);
}
```

Nothing too complex here. The interface defines one method for changing the user's password. The only requirement is that the interface must extend the `RemoteService` interface supplied by GWT. Next comes the implementation of the server. Again, this is about as easy as it gets:

```
public class PasswordServiceImpl
  extends RemoteServiceServlet
  implements PasswordService {

  public Boolean changePassword (String user,
       String old, String new) {
    // add code here
  }
}
```

The implementation implements the interface you defined for your service and extends the `RemoteServiceServlet`. The `RemoteServiceServlet` is where all the magic happens. This servlet receives the data from the server, which we already mentioned must be text due to the way the underlying `XMLHttpRequest` object works, and deserializes the text data into Java objects. The Java objects are then passed to the implemented `changePassword()` method for processing. On the return trip, the `RemoteServiceServlet` serializes the return value into text, which can then be sent back to the browser.

So far, so good. You created a service interface and coded the implementation on the server in a specific way. Coding the client-side call is just as easy:

```
service.changePassword("jdoe", "abc123", "m@tr1x",
  new AsyncCallback()
  {
    public void onSuccess (Object result) {
      Window.alert("password changed");
    }

    public void onFailure (Throwable ex) {
        Window.alert("uh oh!");
    }
  });
```

Here you call the `changePassword()` method, and in the call you include an additional `AsyncCallback` handler. This is just like the `RequestCallback` you used with the `RequestBuilder`; it handles the result that is passed back from the server.

To be honest, we aren't giving you the whole story; for example, you may have noticed that we never showed you the code to create the `service` object on the client-side. We did this because we want to provide the flavor of what GWT-RPC provides without getting into all the details. We found that GWT-RPC is easy to use once you go through a few iterations of using it and when you understand its limitations. We'll provide those details in chapters 10 and 11 so that you can take full advantage of GWT-RPC.

Following our diagram from figure 1.1, we move on to a topic that is somewhat related to RPC. Earlier in the section, we mentioned that `RequestBuilder` receives a text response from the server, and we included XML in the list of formats the text may be in. It would be difficult to use XML data without an XML parser, so it's a good thing GWT has that, too.

1.1.7 Investigating GWT's XML parser

In the last five or so years, XML has become a part of our daily lives as developers. The configuration of your Java server uses an XML format, the RSS feeds you consume and supply are XML, and often so are the protocols you use to communicate with remote services, as in the case of SOAP and XML-RPC. To make it as simple as possible to deal with these data formats on the client browser, GWT provides a Document Object Model (DOM) based XML parser. DOM-based XML parsers consume the XML and create an object tree. You can then use the DOM API to traverse the tree and read its contents.

GWT takes advantage of the fact that modern browsers have the ability to parse XML and create a DOM tree. Because the parsing is done by the browser and not by GWT, you get the performance benefit of native code execution. This code sample shows you how the `XMLParser` is used to create a `Document` object, through which the entire DOM tree can be traversed:

```
Document doc = XMLParser.parse(responseText);
Element root = doc.getDocumentElement();

NodeList children = root.getChildNodes();
for (int i = 0; i < children.getLength(); i++) {
  doSomethingWithNode(children.item(i));
}
```

From the `Document` object, you can grab the root element, and in an XML document there can be only one. From the root element, you can iterate through the children, and their children, and so on. The GWT DOM implementation is based on the standard provided by the World Wide Web Consortium (W3C), the same people who standardized HTML. In chapter 12, we'll use RequestBuilder with GWT's XML parser to load a set of bookmarks from an XML file sitting on the server and present them as a menu list.

Next, we'll continue with our exploration of the various GWT APIs and show how GWT can manage your browser history.

1.1.8 Managing the browser history

One of the valid complaints about rich Internet applications is that they break the browser's Back button. What we mean is that if you replace a piece of content on the web page dynamically with JavaScript, the browser doesn't count that as a page change. Often, the user sees the content of the page change, so they assume they can click the Back button in the browser to get back to the previous content; but their assumption is false. This behavior is due to the fact that changing the content of a page programmatically is fairly new to many users, and they don't understand it. To provide a solid user experience, we need to write the application so that the back button behaves in a manner that the user expects.

The popular solution to this problem tends to be a little complicated to implement and use. It requires adding a hidden frame to your page and doing some amount of scripting to get it to work. In the case of GWT, all the hard work has been done for you. To access it, you need to write an event handler that implements the HistoryListener interface and register it with the History object. Here you register an instance of a user defined class MyHistoryListener:

```
History.addHistoryListener(new MyHistoryListener());
```

With the listener registered, you can emulate a page change by creating a new history token. A *token* is a keyword that defines the content change. For example, you might create a token overview for the page with information about your company and a token reports for a different page showing reporting information. Note that when we say *page*, we don't mean that the browser is loading a different URL. This is GWT, after all, so a *page* can be content loaded by selecting a tab on a TabPanel or selecting an option from a MenuBar:

```
History.newItem("overview");
History.newItem("reports");
```

Creating a new token does two things. First, it invisibly loads a hidden frame on the web page with a new page. Because the hidden frame is loaded with a different page, the browser counts this as a new page view and adds it to the browser history. Second, it calls the onHistoryChanged() method of the HistoryListener to indicate a content change:

```
public class MyHistoryListener implements HistoryListener {
  public void onHistoryChanged (String historyToken) {
    if (historyToken.equals("overview")) {
      // display overview panel
    }
    else if (historyToken.equals("reports")) {
      // display reports panel
    }
  }
}
```

We hope you can see how this works. Because the hidden frame has changed, clicking the Back button in the browser changes it back. This in turn triggers another call to the HistoryListener with the previous token. And don't forget the browser's Forward button—now that you've gone back into the history, the Forward button will move you forward again. This behavior is exactly what the user expects. We'll discuss the history mechanism a little more in chapter 4.

Now, we'll move on to the last major API feature: the testing framework. Being able to test JavaScript code properly has proven to be a fairly difficult task due to the lack of good testing tools, and often it's done poorly. GWT again makes your life easy by allowing you to test your GWT code with the Java developers' favorite testing framework, JUnit.

1.1.9 Introducing GWT's JUnit integration

It has always been a best practice to write automated tests for code, and various frameworks have been made available over the years to make the process easier. JUnit is the most popular tool of this variety used by Java developers, and it's integrated with many IDEs. Instead of creating a new framework for GWT from scratch, GWT provides support for JUnit so that you don't need to learn yet another testing framework.

To create a new test case, you create a class that extends GWTTestCase, which in turn extends JUnit's own TestCase class. You then need to implement just one required method, getModuleName(), followed by any number of specific tests. GWT uses the module name to locate the project configuration file. We'll delve into the details in chapter 16, but for now let's look at a short example:

```
public class MathTest extends GWTTestCase
{
  public String getModuleName ()
  {
    return "org.mycompany.MyApplication";
  }
```

```
    public void testAbsoluteValue ()
    {
      int absVal = Math.abs(-5);
      assertEquals(5, absVal);
    }

}
```

Here we included only one test, which verifies that the absolute value of –5 is 5. This is obviously true, but if it were false, the `assertEquals()` method would trigger an exception that would be reported by the JUnit test runner.

In addition to the usual JUnit-style testing, `GWTTestCase` also lets you test RPC calls to the server. GWT starts up its own version of Tomcat; executes your compiled GWT code; and tests that when your client-side code calls the server-side application, it gets the expected results. In short, it does things you couldn't do otherwise without having someone sit in front of a browser to test your application. No offense to real user testing, but if you have a large suite of tests that you want to run over and over, it isn't realistic to always do this manually.

With the end of this section on JUnit, we also finish our look at GWT's major features. Next, we'll show you how GWT compares to other technologies.

1.2 GWT vs. other solutions

GWT isn't the first tool to try to make it easy to build rich Internet applications; and as web technologies constantly evolve, it undoubtedly won't be the last. In this section, we'll look at several other technologies that are often lumped into the same category as GWT and explain where the differences lie.

In each of the following sections, we'll provide a code example for creating a text box and a button. You'll fill the text box with the word *clicked* when the button is clicked with the mouse. Finally, we'll compare the code example provided to the GWT reference implementation and discuss the important differences. Figure 1.3 shows the GWT reference implementation in a web browser when the application starts and after the action button has been clicked.

Figure 1.3 The GWT reference implementation of a text box and a button before and after the action button is clicked

To begin, we need to examine the GWT reference implementation, shown in listing 1.2.

Listing 1.2 An implementation of a simple `Button` event in GWT

```
final TextBox text = new TextBox();
text.setText("text box");

final Button button = new Button();
button.setText("Click Me");

button.addClickListener(new ClickListener()
{
    public void onClick (Widget sender)
    {
        text.setText("clicked");
    }
});

Panel main = new FlowPanel();
RootPanel.get().add(main);

main.add(text);
main.add(button);
```

❶ Create text box
❷ Create button
❸ Attach event handler
❹ Attach main panel
❺ Attach widgets to panel

This is the first example of GWT code that we've looked at, so it deserves a thorough explanation:

❶ Create a new text box, which, displayed in the browser, looks like a normal text box that you might find in a form on the Web.

❷ Create a button and set the text to display on the button. Note that at this point, neither the text box nor button has been attached to the web page.

❸ Add an event handler to the button by adding a click listener object, which is called when a user clicks the button. Notice that the object you add as a listener is an anonymous class. If you haven't seen this type of Java construct before, it may seem a little unnatural at first, but all you're doing is creating an new object that implements the interface `ClickListener`.

❹ Add a panel to your window, and then ❺ add the text box and button to the panel.

When you run this GWT code, it renders an HTML page with a text box and button; when the button is clicked, the code changes the text in the text box. In the following sections, we'll port this simple code to a few other frameworks and discuss how they differ from GWT. Note that we're making every attempt to be unbiased as we describe the competing frameworks. We believe that each tool is different from the next, and each has its own strengths and weaknesses.

With that in mind, let's begin our tour with Swing, followed by Echo2, JavaServer Faces, and Ruby on Rails.

1.2.1 GWT vs. Swing

Swing is the standard toolkit for building GUI applications in Java. This may seem like a strange choice of tools to compare GWT to, because Swing isn't typically associated with web applications. We're comparing Swing to GWT because the two frameworks are similar in the way you write code for them. Listing 1.3 shows the Swing version of the application.

Listing 1.3 An implementation of a simple `Button` event in Swing

```
final JTextField text = new JTextField();      // Create text box
text.setText("text box");

final JButton button = new JButton();          // Create button
button.setText("Click Me");

button.addActionListener(new ActionListener()  // Attach event handler
{
    public void actionPerformed (ActionEvent e)
    {
        text.setText("clicked");
    }
});

final JFrame rootPanel = new JFrame();
Panel main = new Panel();                      // Attach main panel
rootPanel.getContentPane().add(main);

main.add(text);                                // Attach widgets to panel
main.add(button);

rootPanel.setVisible(true);
rootPanel.pack();
```

This Swing code should look vaguely similar to the GWT reference example; in fact, it's nearly identical. There are a few name changes; for instance, GWT's `ClickListener` interface is called `ActionListener` in Swing.

For Swing developers, there are a few important differences between GWT and Swing. First, the components that ship with GWT don't follow the Model View Controller (MVC) pattern: No model object can be shared by multiple components to keep them in sync. Second, GWT doesn't use layout managers to control the layout. Instead, you use panels that have built-in layout styles. For example, the GWT `HorizontalPanel` arranges its child components left-to-right across the page, whereas the `DockPanel` lets you add widgets to the panel in a similar fashion to the Swing's `BorderLayout`.

These differences are fairly easy to work with, and GWT is a friendly environment for Swing developers. Next, we'll look at Echo2, which lets you write applications in a similar manner to GWT but takes a different approach.

1.2.2 GWT vs. Echo2

Echo2 is another popular web toolkit in the same problem space as GWT, and it's similar to GWT in how it's used to create the UI. You use the API to create instances of components and then add them to the display. Listing 1.4 shows the Echo2 version of the GWT reference example; the two versions look nearly identical.

Listing 1.4 An implementation of a simple `Button` event in Echo2

```
final TextField text = new TextField();        | Create text
text.setText("text box");                      | box

final Button button = new Button();            | Create
button.setText("Click Me");                    | button

button.addActionListener(new ActionListener()
{
    public void actionPerformed (ActionEvent evt)      Attach event
    {                                                  handler
        text.setText("clicked");
    }
});

Window window = new Window();
window.setContent(new ContentPane());
Row main = new Row();                          | Attach
window.getContent().add(main);                 | main panel

main.add(text);            | Attach widgets
main.add(button);          | to panel
```

Although both frameworks use similar APIs, they work in an entirely different fashion. Applications written for Echo2 run on the server, not the client. With GWT, you compile your Java source to JavaScript and run it on the browser. With Echo2, you compile your Java source to Java class files and run them on the server. This also means that when a client-side event is triggered, it may need to be handled on the server.

The consequence is that an interface built with Echo2 needs to hit the server more often, but it doesn't have to deal with an RPC API because the RPC happens all by itself. It also means that Echo2 doesn't need to send all the JavaScript to the browser at once; it sends only what it needs to given the current state of the application. Finally, you're tied to using a Java application server because this is required to host an Echo2 application.

Next up is another Java-based framework called JavaServer Faces.

1.2.3 GWT vs. JavaServer Faces

JavaServer Faces (JSF) is a web framework for Java-based web applications. It uses managed Java beans on the server, which represent the model, plus a set of tag libraries that can be used with a JSP page to reference the properties of the model. In a standard JSF implementation, all the processing is done on the server, and the web page reloads for each transaction. The fact that the page needs to reload for each transaction doesn't make JSF a viable rich client for built-in components, but with additional effort it's possible. For the sake of comparison, we'll provide a standard non-Ajax JSF application that can perform the same action as our reference GWT application.

The first step in creating a JSF application is to create a class to represent the model, as shown in listing 1.5. Our example's model is simple; it contains only one property, named `text`. In standard Java bean fashion, you make the property private to the class and provide accessors for getting and setting the value. To this you also need to add a method named `changeText()`, which is triggered when the command button is clicked.

Listing 1.5 A JSF-managed bean that represents a simple model with a single property `text` and a single command

```
package org.gwtbook;

public class SampleBean
{
    private String text = "text box";

    public String getText ()
```

```
    {
        return text;
    }

    public void setText (String text)
    {
        this.text = text;
    }

    public void changeText ()
    {
        this.text = "clicked";
    }
}
```

The next step is to register this class as a managed bean in the JSF configuration file (see listing 1.6). Provide the name `sampleBean` for the managed bean; this name will be used to reference it in the JSP code to follow.

Listing 1.6 A snippet of the JSF configuration file that defines a managed bean

```
<managed-bean>
  <managed-bean-name>sampleBean</managed-bean-name>
  <managed-bean-class>org.gwtbook.SampleBean</managed-bean-class>
  <managed-bean-scope>request</managed-bean-scope>
</managed-bean>
```

The JSP page, shown in listing 1.7, looks similar to a standard JSP page. It uses two JSF tag libraries to specify the view and controls you're using. For the value in the `inputText` tag, you reference the `text` property of your managed bean using the JSF expression language. In the `actionButton` tag you see it again, but this time it references the `changeText()` method.

Listing 1.7 The HTML code and tags used to render a button and link it to your managed bean

```
<%@taglib uri="http://java.sun.com/jsf/core" prefix="f"%>
<%@taglib uri="http://java.sun.com/jsf/html" prefix="h"%>
<f:view>
<html>
<head>
  <title>JSF Example</title>
</head>
<body>
```

```
    <h:form>
      <h:inputText value="#{sampleBean.text}"/>
      <h:commandButton
            value="Click Me"
            action="#{sampleBean.changeText}"/>
    </h:form>

  </body>
  </html>
  </f:view>
```

JSF is different from GWT in that JSF provides little in the way of support for rich client-side functionality. It's possible to build reusable client-side components by doing some of the work in JavaScript, but custom components have little reuse value. Because JSF integrates with the client side, it's in competition with GWT, but there is some potential for integrating the two.

Next, we'll compare GWT to Ruby on Rails, a popular non-Java framework for writing web applications.

1.2.4 GWT vs. Ruby on Rails

The title of this section is a little misleading because GWT and Ruby on Rails don't compete, although they overlap in some respects. Ruby on Rails is a rapid development framework that uses the Ruby language. It provides the server side of the equation and is specifically designed to handle a lot of the back-end work automatically for you. On the client side, Ruby on Rails provides some support for Ajax, allowing you to use the Java equivalent of a tag library in your HTML code. The end result is that Ruby on Rails can send data to the server triggered by a user action and display a response in the page. However, it isn't designed for complex interactions between the client and server.

GWT is client-centric, and most of what GWT does is on the client side of the picture. It lets you develop and display widgets using Java and write Java handlers to trap user-triggered actions. GWT can communicate with the server as needed, which may be driven by user interaction or perhaps a timed event. GWT then lets you compile all the Java code to JavaScript so that the program can be run in the browser. On the server, GWT only provides a mechanism for serializing and deserializing Java objects so they can be received from the browser and sent back; it doesn't get involved in other aspects of the server.

Instead of competition between GWT and Ruby on Rails, we find an opportunity for integration. This is in part driven by the fact that GWT provides several nonproprietary schemes for passing data between client and server. We're finding that many developers who are starting to use GWT are using non-Java technologies on the server and are looking at GWT to provide only client-side functionality.

1.3 Building your first GWT application

Like most developers, the first thing we want to do when we try a new technology is to build something with it. We could write pages and pages explaining how to use GWT, and we will, but that can't replace having a running example in front of you. Toward that end, this section will be drastically light on details, and we'll focus only on getting your first GWT application up and running.

In this section, we'll assume that you've downloaded and uncompressed the appropriate GWT distribution for your platform and verified that you have a version of Java installed on your workstation that can be used with GWT. If you haven't, you can download GWT from http://code.google.com/webtoolkit/ and Java from http://java.sun.com. Let's get to it and build something.

1.3.1 Building and running an example application

GWT ships with an `applicationCreator` tool that creates a directory structure and populates it with sample code. This tool is your friend; you'll likely use it to create the skeleton for every GWT application you write. We'll cover it in much greater detail in the next chapter.

To run the tool, open a command prompt or shell, and navigate to the directory where you unpacked GWT. As arguments to the command, specify an output directory named Sample and specify the Java class that you want the tool to create:

```
applicationCreator -out Sample org.sample.client.App
```

The output of this command looks like this on Windows and is similar on all other platforms:

```
Created directory Sample\src
Created directory Sample\src\org\sample
Created directory Sample\src\org\sample\client
Created directory Sample\src\org\sample\public
Created file Sample\src\org\sample\App.gwt.xml
Created file Sample\src\org\sample\public\App.html
Created file Sample\src\org\sample\client\App.java
Created file Sample\App-shell.cmd
Created file Sample\App-compile.cmd
```

That's it. You've written your first fully functional GWT application.

Granted, you haven't seen it run, but rest assured that this little application will compile to JavaScript and execute. Before you run it, we suggest that you explore each of the generated files:

- *App.gwt.xml*—The configuration file for the module. It's used to define the entry-point class, dependencies, and compiler directives. The entry-point class is the class that is executed when the module loads into your browser.
- *App.html*—The HTML page that loads and executes the application. We don't want to get into the specifics about how the HTML loads the module, but it may be worth looking at. This file is well commented.
- *App.java*—A sample entry-point class generated by the `applicationCreator` tool. This is where you put the Java code that you want to be compiled to JavaScript.
- *App-shell.cmd*—A simple shell script that executes the *hosted-browser* that ships with GWT. The hosted-browser works like your web browser, but it's specifically tailored for GWT development. Executing this launches the application.
- *App-compile.cmd*—Another simple shell script that executes the Java to JavaScript compiler. Just like the App-shell script, this script references the module configuration file, which provides the details about what needs to be compiled. Running this creates a directory called www and generates the JavaScript there.

The next step is to run the application; if you haven't guessed already by looking at the generated source code, it's a "Hello World" application. You have two options for doing this: You may either run the App-shell script to launch the hosted-browser, or run the App-compile script and then open the App.html file in the www directory in your browser. We recommend that you do both. It's worth experimenting a little to see how each of these approaches works, because you'll use both frequently when you develop your own applications.

Figure 1.4 shows the application running in Firefox. It's a basic application that presents a button that toggles the visibility of the "Hello World!" message. From browsing through the project files, you may have noticed that the text at the top of the page is in the HTML page, and only the button and the "Hello World!" label are referenced in the Java file. This is a good example of how GWT can mix HTML content with application logic, allowing you to leverage the skills of a designer without needing to teach them GWT.

Figure 1.4 Sample generated "Hello World" application running in JavaScript. This is what you should see on your screen; if you don't, you may want to go back and make sure you followed along exactly.

That is a wonderful example, but if you're like us, you've lost count of how many "Hello World" examples you've seen. Let's have some fun and alter the code to do something a little more exciting.

1.3.2 Building Tic-Tac-Toe with GWT

First things first: If you have a favorite IDE or text editor, now is the time to start it up. In this section, you'll use the files created with the `applicationCreator` in the previous section to do something fun. If you want to use your IDE for this project, you need to add the gwt-user.jar file that came with the GWT distribution to your classpath. It doesn't matter what IDE or text editor you use at this point, but it's worth noting that GWT provides additional support for Eclipse users, as you'll see in chapter 2. You should also set the project to use Java 1.4 compatibility. As of this writing, GWT doesn't yet support the new Java 5 syntax constructs for client-side code, so for now you need to limit yourself to Java 1.4. The client-side code is considered to be any Java code that will be compiled into JavaScript and run in the browser.

Next, we need to decide what to build. This early in the book, we don't want to overwhelm you with advanced GWT concepts like internationalization or remote procedure calls, so we'll stick to something simple: a simple rendition of Tic-Tac-Toe.

Designing theTic-Tac-Toe game

You'll build a Tic-Tac-Toe game by starting with the `Grid` widget from the GWT library. The `Grid` control renders an HTML table with a specific number of columns and rows. In this example, you'll use this to build the regulation 3x3 Tic-Tac-Toe grid, but you may alter the code to use a more challenging 4x4 or even 5x5 grid.

In each of the cells of the `Grid` control, you'll put a blank `Button` control. The end result looks something like figure 1.5. Unless you're using a visual designer to build your GWT application, it's usually a good idea to sketch out your application before you build it, like we did with this diagram.

The logic of the application is simple. When the first player clicks a button, you change the text of the button to display an X. When the next player clicks a different button, you change the text of the button to display O. You toggle back and forth between X and O as the game progresses.

You also need to perform a check before changing the text of a button. If the button clicked by the player already contains a marker, then you display an alert message that tells the player they must select a different square.

All the changes you'll make are in the App.java file created by the `applicationCreator` tool; if you want to follow along, open that file now. Let's write the code to make this work.

Writing the Tic-Tac-Toe game

To build the Tic-Tac-Toe game, you need to import the needed Java classes for the project. In the App.java file, replace the generated `import` lines with the following `import` lines for this project:

```
import com.google.gwt.core.client.EntryPoint;
import com.google.gwt.user.client.Window;
import com.google.gwt.user.client.ui.*;
```

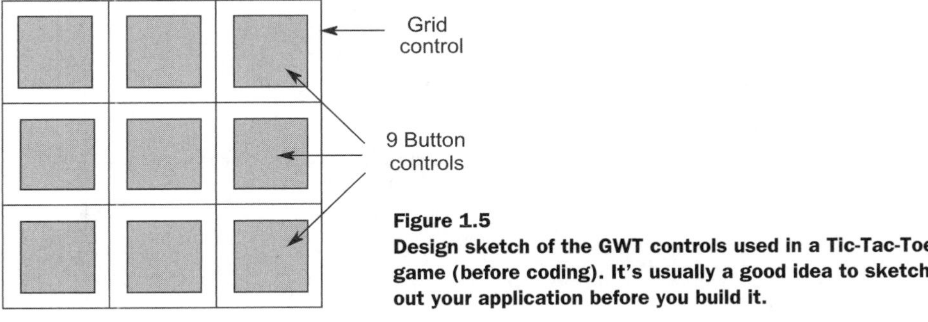

Figure 1.5
Design sketch of the GWT controls used in a Tic-Tac-Toe game (before coding). It's usually a good idea to sketch out your application before you build it.

The EntryPoint interface is required to be implemented by the main class of the module. The EntryPoint interface requires the implementation of the method onModuleLoad(). This method has the same purpose as the main() method in a regular Java application or the service() method in a Java servlet. This is the method that starts the application.

The Window class is roughly equivalent to the window JavaScript object. It provides access to the browser window to do things, such as to determine the browser's height and width or to display an alert message to the user.

The third import imports the entire GWT UI package. This includes dozens of widgets, listeners, and panels that you'll see more of as you progress through the chapters. For now, we won't get into any of the details of what classes this includes; we'll focus on the project at hand.

Listing 1.8 shows the code for the class, which replaces the existing generated code in the App.java file.

Listing 1.8 A simple Tic-Tac-Toe implementation in GWT

```
public class App implements EntryPoint {

  private boolean playerToggle = true;                      ❶
  private ClickListener listener = new TicTacClick();

  public void onModuleLoad() {
    Grid grid = new Grid(3, 3);       ❷

    for (int col = 0; col < 3; col++) {
      for (int row = 0; row < 3; row++) {
        Button button = new Button();          ❸
        button.setPixelSize(30, 30);

        button.addClickListener(listener);     ❹

        grid.setWidget(col, row, button);      ❺
      }
    }

    RootPanel.get().add(grid);       ❻
  }

  private class TicTacClick implements ClickListener {
    public void onClick(Widget sender) {
      // todo                                                  ❼
    }
  }
}
```

You begin by defining a boolean value ❶ to keep track of whose turn it is so you know if you should display an X or O, and you create an listener instance that will be used to handle click events. We'll provide more information about this listener shortly. Next, you create a 3x3 `Grid` control ❷. At this point, the control isn't displayed on the page, but it's constructed in memory. As you loop through the 3x3 `Grid`, you create the `Button` control ❸ that appears in that square. You also set the width and height to 30 pixels. Alternatively, you could use CSS in the HTML page to specify the height and width, but for now this will suffice.

After you create the `Button` control, you register the listener ❹ that you created earlier to receive click events for the `Button`. The listener is an instance of the private class `TicTacClick`, which handles the click event; but for now we haven't provided any code for it. Once the `Button` has been created, you need to add it to the `Grid` ❺. Here you use the `col` and `row` loop variables to place it in the right cell.

Once the `Buttons` are added to the `Grid`, you need to add the `Grid` to the page ❻. The `RootPanel` class represents the top-level panel on the HTML page, and here you add the `Grid` to your `RootPanel`. By calling `RootPanel.get()`, you add the `Grid` to the bottom of the page. Alternatively, you can pass a `String` argument to the `get()` method to specify the HTML element ID where the control should be added. This lets you add controls not only to the end of the page, but also inside any HTML element that has an ID attribute.

❼ This code handles the `Button` clicks and make the Xs and Os appear. We didn't want to put all the code into a single listing, so we'll look at this next. Replace segment ❼ with the code from listing 1.9.

Listing 1.9 A click listener class for the Tic-Tac-Toe implementation

```
private class TicTacClick implements ClickListener {

  public void onClick(Widget sender) {        ❶
    Button button = (Button) sender;

    if (button.getText().equals("")) {        ❷

      if (playerToggle) {
        button.setText("X");
      }                                       ❸
      else {
        button.setText("O");
      }
      playerToggle = !playerToggle;
    }
```

```
      else {
        Window.alert("That square is already taken ");     ❹
      }
    }
  }
```

The TicTacClick class implements ClickListener ❶, which requires that you implement the method onClick(). This method is called whenever a click event is triggered, and, as a parameter to this method, you receive a reference to the object that was clicked. In this case, you know it's a Button control that was clicked, so you can cast it as such.

You need to test if this specific Button has been clicked before ❷, and, if it has, you need to alert the player that they must select a different square. The getText() property of the Button returns the text displayed in this control.

Remember the boolean toggle property you created in your class? You created it to toggle between player turns. If the value is true, you display an X ❸, and, if it's false, you display an O. You then toggle the playerToggle value so that it switches the displayed value the next time a Button is clicked.

If the Button is already displaying text, you drop down to this else condition. Here you use the Window object ❹, which is the equivalent of the JavaScript window object, to display a message to the user indicating that they need to select a different square.

If you typed everything in exactly the same as we did, your Tic-Tac-Toe game should look like figure 1.6, which shows the game in the hosted-mode browser.

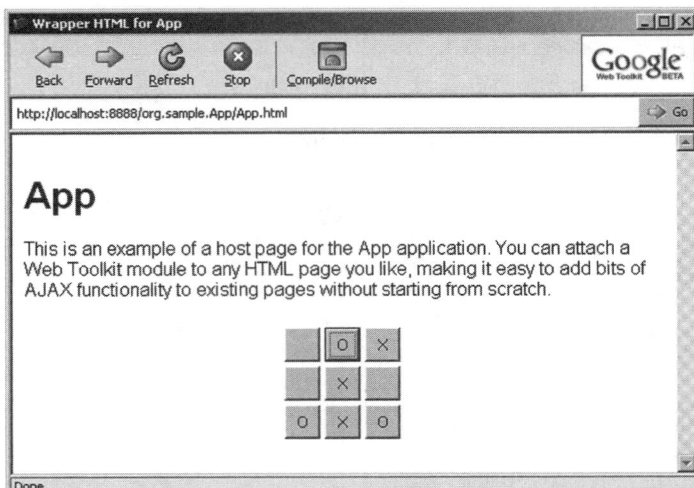

Figure 1.6 Tic-Tac-Toe GWT application running in the hosted-mode browser. This is how your screen should appear if you're following along with the code.

This application is a trivial example, but we hope it has given you a small taste of what GWT is capable of. Throughout this book, we'll provide increasingly complex examples as we examine the full breadth of GWT's capabilities.

We need to wrap things up and start getting into the fine details. Let's summarize what you've seen thus far and prepare for the rest of the GWT adventure.

1.4 Summary

GWT adds a new tool to the web developer's tool belt, helping to solve some of the hardships involved with developing complex rich Internet applications. GWT changes the way you write rich clients by allowing you to write web applications the same way you write desktop applications with Swing. With GWT, you write code in Java, using a plethora of fancy Java tools like Eclipse and JUnit, without the need to learn the intricacies of JavaScript. GWT provides an abstraction on top of the HTML DOM, allowing you to use a single Java API without having to worry about differences in implementations across browsers. When you're done with your Java application, you can then compile your code to JavaScript, which is suitable for running on today's popular browsers.

Tools like Echo2 attempt to do this as well, but they require a Java application server to serve the application. GWT lets you instead create an application that compiles completely to JavaScript and can be served by any web server. This allows GWT to be easily integrated with existing applications no matter what type of server you're running.

An important part of what GWT has to offer is its toolset for making RPCs. It provides a simple RPC mechanism for passing Java objects between the client and server. It does so by serializing and deserializing the objects on both client and server, allowing you to pass custom beans without having to worry about serialization details. GWT also allows communication to non-Java applications via the standard JSON. JSON libraries are available for most languages, making integration a relatively simple task.

GWT as a whole lets you develop web applications at a higher level of abstraction and leverages the tools already available for the Java language. It provides an easier way to build rich Internet applications. In the chapters that follow, we'll get into the details of doing this. We'll show you how to set up your development environment, build an application with existing widgets, create new widgets, communicate with the server, and much more. First, let's start by expanding the default application we began in chapter 1 and then applying that to a running Dashboard example we'll return to throughout the book.

2 Creating the default application

This chapter covers

- Starting a new GWT project
- Preparing for internationalization
- Creating JUnit tests
- Importing the application into your IDE

Chapter 1 got you up and running with your first GWT application; it was a quick and dirty approach, but it worked, and you quickly had a fully functioning Tic-Tac-Toe application. Now it's time to start shoring up your approach and take the first few steps toward building a full-scale application. Over the next two chapters, you'll create the first version of the Dashboard application, which is an example you'll keep expanding and adding to as you progress through this book.

You should read this chapter and the next together, because they're both needed to create the first version of the Dashboard. We split the discussion into two chapters so that in this chapter, we can explain the tasks that are necessary for every GWT application—these initial steps result in the production of an application that we call the *GWT default application*. Then, in chapter 3, we go through the steps needed to specialize the default application in order to produce your own application (in this case, the GWT Dashboard). If you're using a wizard provided by an IDE, then it may perform the steps necessary to generate the default application for you.

To help us explain how the contents of the two chapters go together, we first present a typical development lifecycle, which a real-world programmer might apply when developing GWT applications. With one possible specific high-level web development process in mind, chapter 2 looks again at the tools you used in chapter 1; but this time we'll consider them in detail. You'll actively use those tools shown first in chapter 1, which we'll refer to as the *creation tools*, to create the default directory structure and files used as the basis for the example Dashboard application. This step is performed for all GWT applications you build, and the output is the GWT default application that you first saw in figure 1.4 in section 1.3.1.

Let's take the first step toward building the Dashboard's directory and code structure by examining how you build the GWT default application.

2.1 The GWT application development lifecycle

You can create GWT applications three ways. The first way is to use the set of creation tools provided in the GWT download. These tools let you quickly create a directory and file structure suitable for your GWT application, which is also in line with the structure the GWT compiler expects. You saw these tools in use when you created the Tic-Tac-Toe application in chapter 1. If you use these creation tools, then the result is, by default, independent of any IDE that you may be using. By providing the extra `-eclipse` flag to the creation tools, you direct them to generate an additional set of files that enable the whole structure to be easily imported into the Eclipse IDE. (Eclipse isn't the only IDE you can use; GWT just makes it easy to integrate with Eclipse without using an IDE-specific wizard—it's also possible to import Eclipse projects into some of the other more common IDEs.)

As GWT matures, more third-party tools are appearing on the market that hide the need to use the GWT creation tools. In some cases, these third-party tools come in the form of wizards that IDEs support; in other cases, new IDEs are being built or tweaked specifically to support GWT application development. If you're using one of these tools, then generally the tool provides specific use instructions; but often, running an IDE-specific wizard results in a default application similar to that produced by the GWT creation tools.

If you don't want to use the GWT-provided tools or a tool provided by your IDE, then it's possible to create the directory structure and basic files yourself. You may want to do this, for example, if you're working in an environment where system restrictions prevent you from using the standard structure. Taking this approach means you will more than likely have to deal in more detail with the application's Module XML file (see chapter 9) in order to tell the compiler all the paths to the necessary files.

Figure 2.1 summarizes the three methods of creating GWT applications.

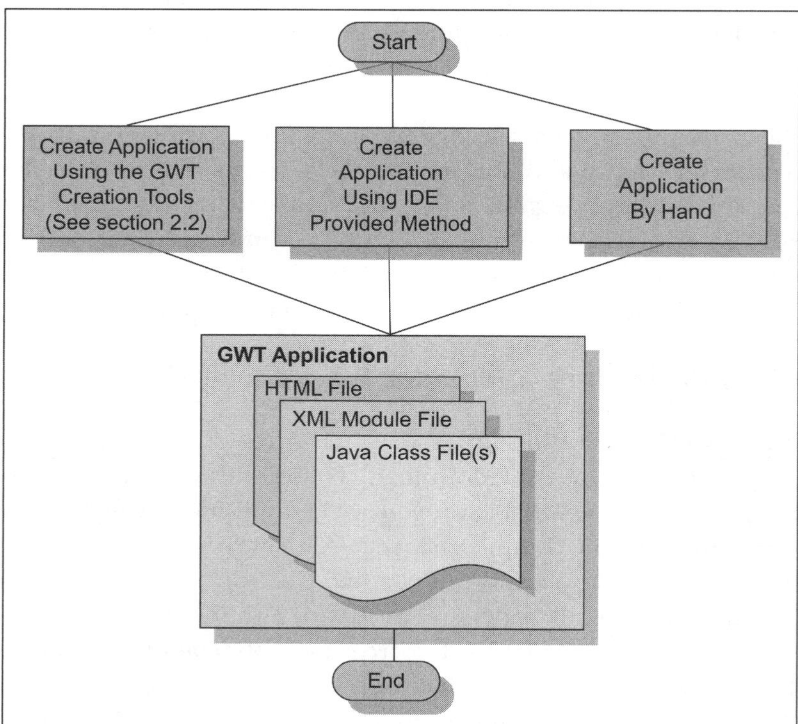

Figure 2.1 The three ways to create a GWT application: using the GWT tools, using a plug-in for an IDE, and creating the structure and files by hand. This chapter uses the GWT creation tools.

All three approaches lead to the production of the same set of basic files that represent the GWT default application—which is good, because all those files are necessary for your application to work. For simplicity at this stage in GWT's maturity, this book will follow the first approach—using the set of creation tools provided by the GWT distribution.

Looking at the other two approaches identified in figure 2.1, probably the most error-prone way to create a GWT application's structure and files is to do so by hand. We advise against this approach, although it can be useful if your environment forces you to use a different directory structure than the default. We won't discuss this "by hand" approach in this book; it isn't difficult, but it requires a lot of attention to detail to make sure all the necessary files are in the correct places, the hosted mode and compile tools have the correct classpaths set, and so on. We'd risk spending more of our time explaining that than getting going with development!

Even though we're using Eclipse in this book, GWT isn't tied to Eclipse; the files produced can be imported into any IDE, or your application can be created using the command-line tools. Eclipse, like any IDE, has pluses and minuses; but it's free and, probably more important, widely used. This book won't get into the pros and cons of any particular IDE. GWT provides great support at the creation-tool level for Eclipse, so we'll continue with that. Don't worry if you aren't using Eclipse as your IDE, in section 2.2.6, we'll look briefly at how you can import the files into other IDEs.

The GWT creation tools we discuss in this chapter—together with the GWT hosted-browser, GWT compiler, and your choice of web server and browsers—provide complete development and test environments. Figure 2.2 shows a simplified view of the lifecycle stages in which the creation tools and other tools just mentioned are typically used. (If you followed one of the other approaches indicated in figure 2.1, you would do so in figure 2.2's Stage 1.)

Table 2.1 details each stage of this typical web-application development lifecycle.

The remainder of this chapter and all of chapter 3 are given over to showing this theory in practice by stepping through each of the lifecycle stages in turn to produce the first basic version of the Dashboard application. You'll perform all the steps in Stage 1, using the GWT creation tools to create the directory and default code and load the application into the Eclipse IDE. (If you want to use your IDE's plug-in to create the structure for you, then you can try running it according to its manual now and pick us up again in chapter 3, where we should have similar structures.)

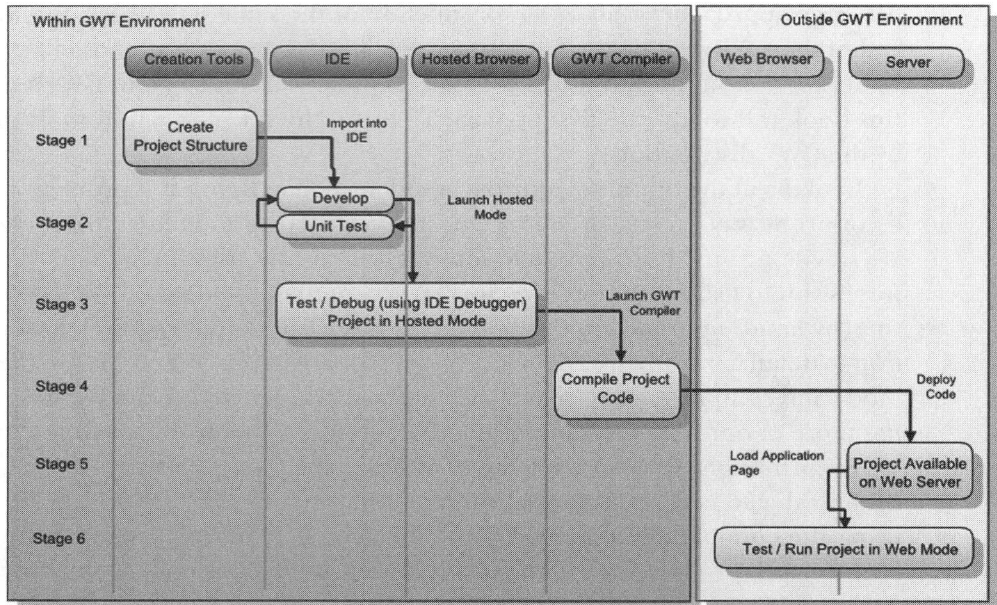

Figure 2.2 Generic lifecycle of GWT application development, showing along the top which tools are used and down the side the stage in which they're used. Some of the stages (for example, Stage 2) can be repeated many times before moving to the next stage. This is a waterfall approach; you may also follow a more rapid application development process by cycling between Stages 2, 3, 4, 5, and 6 as necessary.

Table 2.1 Stages involved in the typical development of a GWT application (the stages are shown in figure 2.2)

Stage	Description
1	The directory and code structure for the project is established. This can be performed using one of the three approaches suggested in figure 2.1—using the GWT creation tools, using an IDE-specific wizard, or by hand. If you use the GWT creation tools, they create a default application (you saw this in chapter 1). Often, if you used the GWT creation tools or the by-hand method, the next step you want to take is to import the basic outline of your project into an IDE. If you're using the GWT creation tools and the Eclipse IDE, then by adding the `-eclipse` flag to the command-line tools, you create all the additional files required to easily import your directory and code structure into Eclipse as an Eclipse project.
2	Once the directory and code structure is created, application development can proceed. Typically, you replace the default files created for you by the GWT creation tools or your IDE's wizard and add other files that you require for your application: additional Java classes, Cascading Style Sheets (CSS), images, and so on.

Table 2.1 Stages involved in the typical development of a GWT application (the stages are shown in figure 2.2) *(continued)*

Stage	Description
3	The development period typically contains several cycles that move between writing your application and testing in hosted mode, using the hosted-browser (Stage 3). You can launch hosted mode either directly from a shell window or from within your IDE. It acts as a managed environment, executing your code as pure Java code and deploying any server-side Java code you've developed into its own internal web server. Errors and exceptions that are raised in hosted mode, as well as any output from the GWT logging you may have included in your code, are safely captured by this managed environment. Compare this to web mode, where your application becomes JavaScript code and is executed directly by a web browser—it has no guaranteed safe management of exceptions and errors. Another benefit of hosted mode comes from the ability to link it to your IDE's debugger for both client and server-side Java code debugging.
4	When you're happy with the developed code in hosted mode, it's time to compile your Java code into JavaScript for use in web mode (Stage 4). You start compilation by invoking the GWT compiler: The resulting files are then ready to be viewed in a web browser. If you have only client-side code at this point, you can open the application directly from the filesystem; but if you have server-side code, you need to deploy the code to a web server. The compilation process produces a number of files that are required; chapter 17 discusses this process.
5	A compiled application is typically deployed to your standard test environment's web server so you can check the deployment process as well as ensure that the code executes correctly. Deploying is largely dependent on your web server; but if you have no server-side code, you can check web mode directly from your filesystem by double-clicking your application's HTML file from the compiled directory.
6	To finish development, check your functionality in a number of browsers in web mode before the final production release. It's nice to trust GWT and Google when they say that you can write once and run in many browsers, but maybe you're like us and don't take everything at face value!

When producing a GWT application, you always start by creating the GWT default application in order to ensure that the file and directory structure is complete and correct. After producing the GWT default application, you need to take the resulting files and turn them into your own application. You'll do this work in chapter 3, where we first look at what is produced as the default application and then discuss the changes you need to make to produce the first version of the Dashboard. But as we mentioned, your first task is to go through all the Stage 1 steps to create the default directory and code structure.

2.2 Stage 1: Creating a GWT application

Looking into the GWT distribution you downloaded in chapter 1, you should see four command-line applications, all ending with the word *Creator*. Table 2.2 summarizes the functionality of these tools. They help you create the directory and file structure of a GWT application, and they also create a set of default files that go together to make the default application. In this stage, we'll look at each of these creation tools in turn, see how they can be invoked, and discuss the outputs they produce. The result is the GWT default application, which can support internationalization as well as some basic unit tests.

DEFINITION The GWT default application is the application created by the `applicationCreator` tool. It's useful because you can quickly check that the creation tools have executed correctly by running it. Creating your own application means changing the files provided in the default application—something we cover in chapter 3.

Table 2.2 GWT provides a number of creation tools that you can use to quickly develop the default GWT application. These tools are used at various stages in the typical development lifecycle.

Stage	Tool name	Overview
1A	`projectCreator`	GWT provides tight integration with the Eclipse IDE, and if you're going to use this IDE, you need to execute this tool first. If you aren't using Eclipse, you can safely ignore this stage. This tool establishes the necessary files required to enable the directory and file structure to be easily loaded into the Eclipse IDE as an Eclipse project. This essentially means at this stage creating the necessary .project and .classpath files.
1B	`applicationCreator`	This tool performs the following three functions: ▪ Creates the Java package structure in a directory that holds your GWT application. ▪ Creates default HTML and Java files together with a basic module XML file that is used to tie the GWT application together. These created files are the default application that you saw in chapter 1. For most applications, you overwrite all these files in Stage 2 of the lifecycle. ▪ Creates the command-line scripts that can be used to launch the GWT application in hosted mode and to compile it for web mode.

Table 2.2 GWT provides a number of creation tools that you can use to quickly develop the default GWT application. These tools are used at various stages in the typical development lifecycle. *(continued)*

Stage	Tool name	Overview
1C	`i18nCreator`	I18n is an abbreviation for internationalization (i + 18 missing letters + n). This tool performs the following two functions: ▪ Creates a simple properties file containing the key/value pairs that act as constants or messages in an application that uses the GWT i18n capabilities ▪ Creates a new command-line tool specifically for the GWT application being created, which you'll need to use in Stage 1D
1D	*`Appl`*`-i18n`	This command-line application is created by the `i18nCreator` tool in Stage 1C. Its purpose is to take the properties file containing constants or messages and produce a corresponding Java interface file. The resulting interface file is used in your GWT application code when you need to access i18n constants and/or messages from the properties files. In the compilation process, GWT binds together the interface file with the properties file so that the functionality works seamlessly. Don't worry; we explain this in detail in chapter 15.
1E	`junitCreator`	If you're going to perform unit testing of your GWT application using the JUnit tool, then the `junitCreator` tool creates a suitable directory and file structure. Your unit tests are written into the file created by this tool.
1F	Import to IDE	The final optional step in Stage 1 is importing the directory and code structure created by the creation tools into an IDE. If you performed Stage 1A and ensured that the `-eclipse` flag was used in the other tools, then your GWT application can easily be imported into the Eclipse IDE. If you aren't using Eclipse, then it's still possible to import the directory structure and files into other IDEs.

Although table 2.2 gives a good overview of each of the tools, it doesn't explain which tools are optional and in what order they should be used. When we, the authors, develop GWT applications, we follow the flow given in figure 2.3. This figure helps you understand when and where to use each of the tools in Stage 1 of the development lifecycle.

If you've created GWT applications before, you may wonder where the commands for compiling and executing a project in hosted mode are in figure 2.3. They aren't provided as standard command-line tools because they require some knowledge of your project name and the necessary classpaths. Don't worry, though: GWT doesn't require you to have all this knowledge about classpaths. The

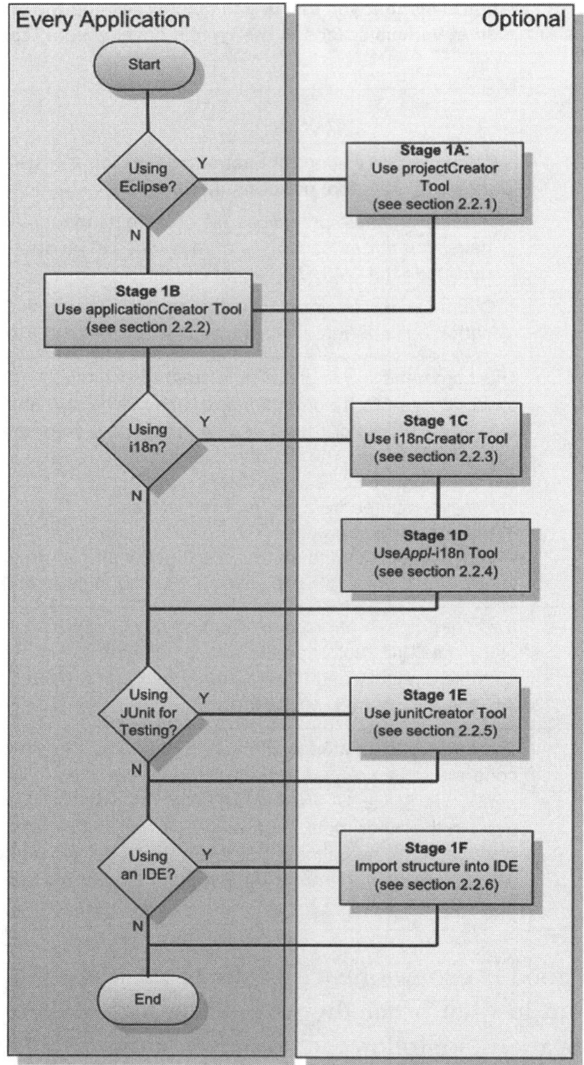

Figure 2.3
How the various GWT creation tools are used together in the development of the structure and files for the GWT default application (the application you have at the end of this chapter)

`applicationCreator` tool creates the necessary commands for compiling and hosted mode.

If you use the creation tools to create an application, then the simplest application that can be created by following the path through figure 2.3 uses only the `applicationCreator` tool. This results in just the plain box-standard GWT default application files being produced. Following all the steps in figure 2.3 results in the generation of the GWT default application again, but this time it includes the files necessary to support internationalization and unit testing. If you're using Eclipse as the IDE, then you need to add the `-eclipse` flag when you execute these other creation commands to ensure that the required launch files for Eclipse are produced or appropriately updated. Don't forget that if you're using Eclipse, the first tool you need to execute is the `projectCreator` tool so that a number of Eclipse project-specific files are created.

Because the `projectCreator` tool is executed first when you use Eclipse, that's where you start the process of creating the GWT default application (which will, in chapter 3, turn into the Dashboard application). In the rest of this section, you'll follow all the steps in table 2.2 to create a GWT default application that supports internationalization and unit testing. We assume that you're using Eclipse as your IDE; however, if you aren't using Eclipse or an IDE that can import an Eclipse project, you can skip to Stage 1B (section 2.2.2) to create the GWT application.

2.2.1 Creating the project

Using the Eclipse editor as your IDE, you can quickly create the necessary Eclipse project structure and files by using the `projectCreator` command-line tool. Doing this and using the `-eclipse` flag in the other creation tools makes it easy to import your project directly into Eclipse, because it produces certain project files that Eclipse uses to describe classpaths and applications.

If you're using Eclipse, then you should execute the `projectCreator` command as the first step in the development process. Run the following command now to create the DashboardPrj Eclipse project in the DashboardDir directory:

```
projectCreator -eclipse DashboardPrj -out DashboardDir
```

The `projectCreator` command gives the following response if it executes successfully, having produced a source directory (src) and Eclipse-specific .project and .classpath files in the newly created DashboardDir directory:

```
Created directory DashboardDir\src
Created directory DashboardDir\test
Created file DashboardDir\.project
Created file DashboardDir\.classpath
```

The .project and .classpath files will be manipulated by some of the tools you apply in later steps of Stage 1, so if you don't create these files first, those tools will fail. If you don't get this output, then the tool will try to tell you what went wrong—most likely, issues with file permissions on directories at this stage.

NOTE If you forget to run `projectCreator` before `applicationCreator`, then it isn't the end of the world. You can run it afterward; just remember to use the `-ignore` parameter.

The full format for the `projectCreator` command is

```
projectCreator [-ant AntFile]
               [-eclipse ProjName]
               [-out DirName]
               [-overwrite]
               [-ignore]
```

The various flags used in the command are as follows:

- `-ant AntFile`—Requests the tool to produce an Ant build file to compile the source code of the project. The suffix .ant.xml is added to the value provided as the parameter. (Optional.)
- `-eclipse ProjName`—The Eclipse project name.
- `-out DirName`—The directory into which to write output files. (Defaults to current.)
- `-overwrite`—Overwrites any existing files in the output directory. (Optional.)
- `-ignore`—Ignores any existing files in the output directory; doesn't overwrite. (Optional.)

`-ant AntFile` refers to an argument that creates an Ant file. Including such a flag in the arguments to the `projectCreator` tool directs the tool to produce a valid Ant file with actions for compiling, packaging, and cleaning your GWT application (Ant is a popular tool used to ease the process of building and deploying applications). By default, the extension `ant.xml` is appended to the name you provide with the `ant` flag. You use the `ant` flag only if you intend to use the Ant tool to build/deploy your projects. If you're considering using Ant, then listing 2.1 shows the default contents of Dashboard.ant.xml that will be produced if you use the `-ant Dashboard` flag in the creation step.

Listing 2.1 Ant control file output produced when you use the `-ant` flag in the `projectCreator` tool

```
<?xml version="1.0" encoding="utf-8" ?>
<project name="Dashboard" default="compile" basedir=".">
  <description>
    Dashboard build file.  This is used to package up your project
    as a jar, if you want to distribute it. This isn't needed
    for normal operation.
  </description>

  <!-- set classpath -->
  <path id="project.class.path">
    <pathelement path="${java.class.path}/"/>
    <pathelement path=
  "C:/GWT/trunk/build/dist/Windows/gwt-windows-0.0.0/gwt-user.jar"/>
    <!-- Additional dependencies (such as junit) go here -->
  </path>
  <target name="compile" description="Compile src to bin">
    <mkdir dir="bin"/>
    <javac srcdir="src:test" destdir="bin" includes="**" debug="on"
         debuglevel="lines,vars,source" source="1.4">
      <classpath refid="project.class.path"/>
    </javac>
  </target>
  <target name="package" depends="compile" description=
      "Package up the project as a jar">
    <jar destfile="Dashboard.jar">
      <fileset dir="bin">
        <include name="**/*.class"/>
      </fileset>
      <!-- Get everything; source, modules, html files -->
      <fileset dir="src">
        <include name="**"/>
      </fileset>
      <fileset dir="test">
        <include name="**"/>
      </fileset>
    </jar>
  </target>
  <target name="clean">
    <!-- Delete the bin directory tree -->
    <delete file="Dashboard.jar"/>
    <delete>
      <fileset dir="bin" includes="**/*.class"/>
    </delete>
  </target>
  <target name="all" depends="package"/>
</project>
```

Compile target

Package target

Clean target

"All" target

At this point, you've created the basic directory structure and files required for an Eclipse project; this makes it easy to import your project into the Eclipse IDE (or another IDE that can import Eclipse projects). In a little while, we'll show you how to load this project into the Eclipse editor. But first, we should note that you've created only the structure for an Eclipse project and not any GWT-specific files. Creating those GWT default application files is the next step as you rejoin the mainstream development path.

2.2.2 Creating an application

In this step, you'll create the directory structure and files that make up the GWT default application (which in the example will be transformed into the Dashboard application, so you'll set up the files using that name). The structure and files produced in this step are independent from any IDE you may be using. If you're using the Eclipse IDE, then you just created an Eclipse project, and this step will add the GWT default application's files to that project.

The `applicationCreator` tool creates a GWT application that conforms to the GWT expected directory structure (more on this in chapter 9) and also generates the hosted-mode and web-mode scripts. You use this tool to create a new GWT application (don't forget that if you're using the Eclipse IDE, you should run the `projectCreator` tool first, as discussed in section 2.2.1).

To create the GWT default application, you need to execute one of the two command lines shown in table 2.3. There is a non-Eclipse version to use if you aren't using Eclipse as your IDE and an Eclipse version to use if you are (the difference being the inclusion of the `-eclipse DashboardPrj` flag in the Eclipse version—don't worry, we'll explain the syntax and flags shortly).

Table 2.3 Two different versions of the `applicationCreator` tool in action, using the specific code to create the Dashboard application. If you're using the Eclipse version, you should have executed the `projectCreator` tool first.

Version	Command line
Non-Eclipse	`applicationCreator -out DashboardDir org.gwtbook.client.Dashboard`
Eclipse	`applicationCreator -eclipse DashboardPrj -out DashboardDir org.gwtbook.client.Dashboard`

Running either of the command-line versions listed in table 2.3 produces the following output:

```
Created directory DashboardDir\src\org\gwtbook
Created directory DashboardDir\src\org\gwtbook\client
Created directory DashboardDir\src\org\gwtbook\public
Created file DashboardDir\src\org\gwtbook\Dashboard.gwt.xml
Created file DashboardDir\src\org\gwtbook\public\Dashboard.html
Created file DashboardDir\src\org\gwtbook\client\Dashboard.java
Created file DashboardDir\Dashboard-shell.cmd
Created file DashboardDir\Dashboard-compile.cmd
```

The `applicationCreator` tool creates the expected Java package structure under the src directory; the module XML file Dashboard.gwt.xml, which we discuss in detail in chapter 9; the hosted-mode and web-mode command-line tools; and the default application's HTML and Java files.

If you use the Eclipse version, then the project name you used to create the project is added as an extra parameter with the `-eclipse` flag. This tells the command to create an Eclipse launch configuration specifically for this project, and results in the following additional output:

```
Created file DashboardDir\Dashboard.launch
```

If you examine the directory structure of the Dashboard application now, you'll see the structure shown in figure 2.4.

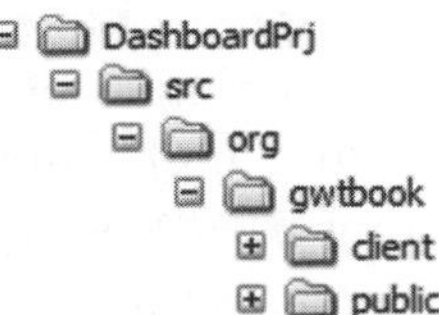

Figure 2.4 Examining the directory structure created by the GWT `applicationCreator` tool—in this case, for the Dashboard application. You can see the `org.gwtbook.client` package structure under the src directory, which is where your Java code will go. The application's basic HTML file is stored under the public directory.

NOTE If you can't use the default directory and file layout for your application (perhaps you have coding standards that are in conflict, or your system setup prevents using it), then you can create the directory structure by hand. But you need to ensure that the command tools' paths are set up correctly and that the GWT compiler can find the source code and public folders, by setting the `source` and `public` attributes in the module XML file (see chapter 9).

As you saw in figure 2.3 (which showed how the GWT creation tools are used together to develop the directory and file structure of a GWT application), the `applicationCreator` tool is all you need to create the structure of the basic GWT default application. To double-check that the `applicationCreator` tool has executed successfully, you can run the default application by executing the `Dashboard-shell` command. Doing so rewards you with the application shown in figure 2.5.

Figure 2.5
The default application created by the GWT creation tools. The files that produce this application are created by executing the `applicationCreator` tool and are usually replaced by your own files when you develop an application (we get to this in chapter 3). The default application is a useful tool to show that the creation tools have worked and that the basic dependencies are correct.

But where did this application come from? If you look in the src/org/gwtbook/client directory of DashboardDir, you'll find the Dashboard.java file, which created the application shown in figure 2.5. The contents of this file are repeated in listing 2.2. (Note that for brevity, we don't show the `import` statements and comment lines that are produced—typically, we won't show these in our code listings unless explicitly necessary.)

Listing 2.2 First view of the GWT code that adds a label and a button to the screen

```
public void onModuleLoad() {
   final Button button = new Button("Click me");
   final Label label = new Label();

   button.addClickListener(new ClickListener() {
      public void onClick(Widget sender) {
         if (label.getText().equals(""))
            label.setText("Hello World!");
         else
            label.setText("");
      }
   });

   RootPanel.get("slot1").add(button);
   RootPanel.get("slot2").add(label);
}
```

Annotations: Create GWT Button (on `final Button button = new Button("Click me");`); Create GWT Label (on `final Label label = new Label();`); Add ClickListener to Button (on `button.addClickListener(...)`); Add Button to web page (on `RootPanel.get("slot1").add(button);`); Add Label to web page (on `RootPanel.get("slot2").add(label);`)

This code, together with the Dasboard.html file in the src/org/gwtbook/public directory, generates the output shown in figure 2.5. We won't go through what these files contain at the moment; we just wanted to let you see that this default application isn't created magically by GWT. To get the look and feel of the Dashboard application (or any other application), you need to replace these files with your functionality—but we leave that until Stage 2 of the development process, in chapter 3.

If you look at the command in full, you see that to create a GWT application, you call `applicationCreator` from the command line using the following template:

```
applicationCreator       [-out DirName]
                         [-eclipse ProjName]
                         [-overwrite]
                         [-ignore]
                         className
```

The options that are available for this command are as follows:

- `-out`—The directory into which to write output files. (Defaults to current.)
- `-eclipse`—Name of the Eclipse project previously used in the `projectCreator` tool execution. (Optional.)
- `-overwrite`—Overwrites any existing files. (Optional.)
- `-ignore`—Ignores any existing files; doesn't overwrite. (Optional.)

The command provides some flexibility over the output, allowing you to change the default directory (if you don't provide one, then the command writes all its output to the current directory). You can also tell the tool to overwrite any existing files or ignore them using the `-overwrite` and `-ignore` flags, respectively. If the application is being created with a view toward importing it into Eclipse, then you should add the `-eclipse` flag as well as the project name you used in section 2.2.1.

NOTE GWT requires the package name for your application's main code to have the subpackage `client` at the end. Not including it will cause the GWT compiler to raise an error.

The final input to the `applicationCreator` command is the class name. It needs to be a fully qualified class name constructed in the particular style shown in figure 2.6. It follows the Sun standard for fully qualified class names in Java but specifically requires that the last nested package name be called `client`. This restriction isn't required by Java, but it's enforced by GWT.

It's useful to follow this GWT-specific format, because in chapter 9, we'll talk about the Java package structure for an application. Later still, we'll introduce server code under the `org.gwtbook.server` package and code for automatically generating new code under the `org.gwtbook.rebind` package.

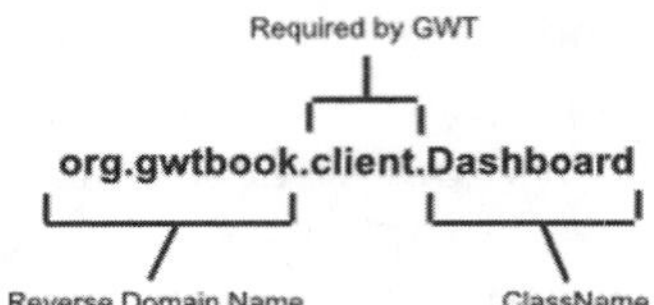

Figure 2.6 Breakdown of a GWT fully qualified Java class name for your application. This is standard Java syntax, but GWT requires that your user interface code always be under a subpackage called `client`. (We cover other special subpackage names such as `server` and `rebind` at various points later in this book.)

Up to this point, you've created your project and basic application. If you wanted to, you could already run the `Dashboard-shell` command script to execute the application, as you saw in figure 2.5. For certain applications—those that have no internationalization and/or those for which you have no desire to perform unit testing with JUnit—this is all you need to do. However, in this example you'll add internationalization to the Dashboard; therefore, you'll go through the next two optional stages, 1C and 1D.

2.2.3 Setting up internationalization

Internationalization allows you to display different interfaces depending on the locale from which the application is being viewed (for example, the Dashboard will have different languages in the menus). We discuss internationalization (also known as i18n) in detail in chapter 15; but because this is the next step in Stage 1, you'll set up your application structure now so that i18n is supported. The `i18nCreator` tool lets you set up this structure. It's useful to note that you don't need to set up your i18n approach at this point; you can defer it until later in the development lifecycle if you wish. However, because you know you're going to use it, you'll set it up now.

The rationale behind GWT internationalization is to allow your application to replace specific constants and messages on the UI with a locale-specific version. For example, the Dashboard application will use both English and Swedish a little later. The generation of this functionality is a two-step process; the first step, which uses the `i18nCreator` tool, creates a sample properties file and a new script. The second step involves entering some constants or messages into the properties file and then executing the script generated by this tool. The output from the second stage is a Java interface file that is used in your application. Trust us: It's a lot easier in practice than it may sound!

NOTE Internationalization (i18n) is easy to set up and use in GWT. You just create some properties files and a simple Java interface; at compile time, GWT creates all the necessary Java plumbing code for you.

To add i18n to your existing structure, you need to select the appropriate command line to execute from table 2.4—either the Eclipse or non-Eclipse version—and execute it now.

Table 2.4 The different versions of the `i18nCreator` tool used to create the framework for the Dashboard internationalization

Version	Command line
Non-Eclipse	`i18nCreator -out DashboardDir org.gwtbook.client.DashboardConstants`
Eclipse	`i18nCreator -eclipse DashboardPrj -out DashboardDir org.gwtbook.client.DashboardConstants`

Successful output of executing either of the `i18nCreator` commands is as follows:

```
Created file
  DashboardDir\src\org\gwtbook\client\DashboardConstants.properties
Created file DashboardDir\DashboardConstants-i18n.cmd
```

The tool has created a sample properties file called DashboardConstants.properties that sits where the main code is, and a new command-line tool called `DashboardConstants-i18n` where the rest of the creator commands are. You'll use this new `DashboardConstants-i18n` command-line tool in Stage 1D.

If you use the Eclipse version, then the command also asks the tool to output the necessary Eclipse launch configurations for the second script:

```
Created file DashboardDir\DashboardConstants-i18n.launch
```

You've seen the internationalization tool in action, and you've created a simple structure into which to place the internationalization aspects of the Dashboard application (in this case, you created the structure necessary for constants—in chapter 15, we'll also look at internationalizing messages). Let's take a moment to look at the command line for this tool in detail and see what other arguments you can pass to the tool to alter its behavior. The tool is called using the following template:

```
i18nCreator [-eclipse ProjName]
            [-out DirName]
            [-createMessages]
            [-overwrite]
            [-ignore]
            interfaceName
```

The options that are available to the command are as follows:

- `-eclipse`—Name of the eclipse project. (Optional.)
- `-out`—The directory into which to write output files. (Defaults to current.)
- `-createMessages`—By default, the tool produces an interface that extends the GWT `Constants` interface; if you wish it to extend the GWT `Messages` interface instead, add this flag.
- `-overwrite`—Overwrites any existing files. (Optional.)
- `-ignore`—Ignores any existing files; doesn't overwrite. (Optional.)

By default, the tool produces output files that support the GWT i18n approach for constants, but adding the flag `-createMessages` alters the output to suit the GWT i18n approach for messages instead (we'll explain the differences between constants and messages in chapter 15). You can also direct the tool to overwrite or ignore any existing files in the directory indicated by the value passed to the `-out` flag.

This concludes the first part of setting up internationalization. You've laid the foundation for the i18n of your application; the next stage is to get your i18n approach ready for use in your code—that is, to create the specific locale properties files that contain the locale-specific constants or messages. Remember that for the Dashboard example, you'll be changing the text in the menu system based on the locale. In the next section, we'll focus on creating the properties files that contain the menu text.

2.2.4 Implementing internationalization

In the previous stage, the `i18nCreator` tool created a dummy properties file as well as a new `DashboardConstants-i18n` command-line application; but you can't yet use these files in your application, because they contain no data. In Stage 1D, you create the link between the properties file and your application code. To create that link, you must create key/value pairs for constants in the properties file and then execute the `DashboardConstants-i18n` command-line application. This tool takes that properties file and produces a Java interface class that contains a method for each key. It's these methods in the Java interface that you use in your application.

This step of Stage 1 may be performed more than once, possibly during the later stages of development. Each time new constants and/or messages are added to your properties file, this stage should be executed to ensure that the Java interface file is up to date. If you executed the `DashboardConstants-i18n` command line now, you'd get a simple interface file reflecting the default properties file.

When you update your i18n properties file in chapter 3, you'll run the `Dash-boardConstants-18n` command line again to make sure you take advantage of and gain access to the new constants.

That concludes the creation of internationalization. In the final step of using the creation tools (from figure 2.3), you'll set the foundations for unit testing. Although this step is optional, we feel that unit testing is an important part of development. It isn't necessary to perform this step at this stage; you can jump to section 2.2.6 if you wish to start getting your framework into an IDE or to chapter 3 if you want to start building the Dashboard functionality without an IDE.

2.2.5 Creating unit test cases

JUnit is a powerful approach to testing, and it's beneficial that GWT includes a simple way of integrating unit tests into your development approach. Undoubtedly, JUnit deserves—and has—a wealth of books written about it, and we won't attempt to cover using JUnit here. If you're interested in knowing more about JUnit, we recommend *JUnit in Action* by Vincent Massol and Ted Husted. (In chapter 16, we look at GWT testing in more detail.)

NOTE GWT makes writing and creating JUnit tests for your code a painless (maybe enjoyable is going too far) process.

Before you can begin creating a JUnit test-case structure, you need to have the JUnit JAR file somewhere on your development system that you can refer to (you can download it from http://www.junit.org). To add JUnit tests to the Dashboard example, execute one of the two versions listed in table 2.5 (for simplicity, we're assuming that the JUnit JAR is stored in the root of the C:\ directory; if you have it somewhere else, then you should replace the argument to the first parameter with your location).

Table 2.5 The different versions of the `junitCreator` tool used to create the framework for the Dashboard JUnit testing.

Version	Command Line
Non-Eclipse	`junitCreator -junit c:\junit.jar -module org.gwtbook.Dashboard -out DashboardDir org.gwtbook.client.test.DashboardTest`
Eclipse	`junitCreator -junit c:\junit.jar -eclipse DashboardPrj -module org.gwtbook.Dashboard -out DashboardDir org.gwtbook.client.test.DashboardTest`

Running either command creates a suitable directory and file structure ready to accept the unit-test code for any unit testing you may wish to perform on the Dashboard example (the Eclipse version provides more files for easy integration with Eclipse). You ask for the test class to be called `DashboardTest` and to be in the package `org.gwtbook.client.test`. The script creates a new directory called test under DashboardDir and stores your generated test-class files under that. Because you're creating the tests in the same package as the code, there is no need for the `junitCreator` command to alter the Dashboard module.

Successful output of both versions of the `junitCreator` command is as follows:

```
Created directory DashboaradDir\test\org\gwtbook\client\test
Created file DashboardDir\test\org\gwtbook\client\test\DashboardTest.java
Created file DashboardDir\DashboardTest-hosted.cmd
Created file DashboardDir\DashboardTest-web.cmd
```

If you're using the Eclipse version, then the following two lines are appended to the output, indicating the creation of the associated hosted-mode and web-mode launch scripts for Eclipse:

```
Created file DashboardDir\DashboardTest-hosted.launch
Created file DashboardDir\DashboardTest-web.launch
```

The `junitCreator` tool creates the necessary classes with stubs in them; places the necessary links in the GWT application module; and, if you're using Eclipse, creates the appropriate launch configurations. The full template for the command is

```
junitCreator      -junit PathToJUnitJarFile
                  [-eclipse ProjName]
                  [-module ModName]
                  [-out DirName]
                  [-ignore]
                  [-overwrite]
                  className
```

The options that are available to the command are as follows:

- `-junit`—Path to the JUnit libraries.
- `-eclipse`—Name of the Eclipse project. (Optional.)
- `-module`—The GWT module of the application you wish to test.
- `-out`—The directory into which to write output files. (Defaults to current.)
- `-overwrite`—Overwrites any existing files. (Optional.)
- `-ignore`—Ignores any existing files; doesn't overwrite. (Optional.)

The flags -eclipse, -out, -overwrite, and -ignore are the same as those discussed for the previous two tools. The -junit flag is required, and its value must point to the installation of the JUnit classes in your system. The -module flag must indicate the GWT module you want to test.

Running the junitCreator tool won't, unfortunately, create unit tests for you; it does, however, manipulate the necessary files and create a sensible directory structure, shown in figure 2.7. In addition, it creates a simple Java class file in which you can place your unit tests.

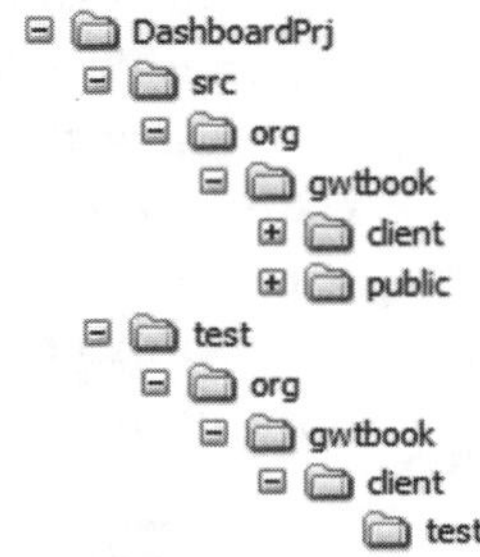

Figure 2.7 The directory structure that exists after you execute the GWT junitCreator tool. Notice that the structure for the application you saw in figure 2.4 is still intact. The new structure for testing sits under the test directory.

We'll look at using JUnit testing in more detail when we get to chapter 16.

Let's take a second to recap where you are with respect to creating the GWT default application. You've created the directory and code structure for the GWT default application, and you've added support for internationalization. If you took the last step, you've also incorporated unit testing. These steps are common to all GWT applications you'll build; only by altering and adding to the default application code do you begin to create your own application.

Before you start building the Dashboard application in the next chapter, let's look at the final Stage 1 application development task: importing your project into an IDE. We recommend this optional step because it makes code development/debugging much easier and quicker.

2.2.6 Importing into your IDE

We're convinced that a great benefit of GWT is the ability to use a familiar development environment in the development of your web applications (the GWT team members often say on the forums that they chose Java not because they're Java addicts but because at this moment in time it has great tool support).

Right now, GWT integrates easily into Eclipse, and other IDEs are rapidly delivering easier integration approaches. There are even approaches to build GUI development tools for GWT in a similar manner to Matisse (the NetBeans IDE GUI builder).

In this section, we'll demonstrate the use of Eclipse as an IDE and also the generic steps you can take to use another IDE if you created your application following the instructions given in the early part of this chapter.

Importing into Eclipse

Importing a project into Eclipse after you create it using the project and application creator tools is simple and quick. In the Eclipse Package Explorer window, right-click, and select the Import option. Figure 2.8 shows this step, together with the next step of choosing the Existing Projects into Workspace option under the General folder.

Click the Next button, and then click the Browse button next to the Select Root Directory option. Navigate the filesystem to find DashboardDir, and select it; see figure 2.9. Click OK.

At this point, you can decide where you want Eclipse to store the project file—in the Import Projects dialog box, if you select the Copy Projects into Workspace

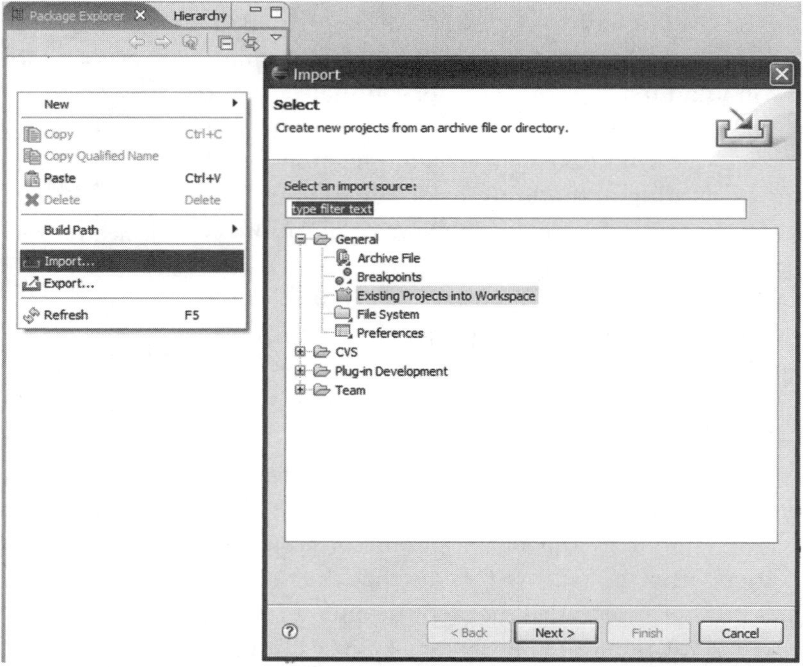

Figure 2.8 To import the newly created Dashboard project into the Eclipse IDE for development of the application, right-click the Eclipse Package Explorer window and select Import.

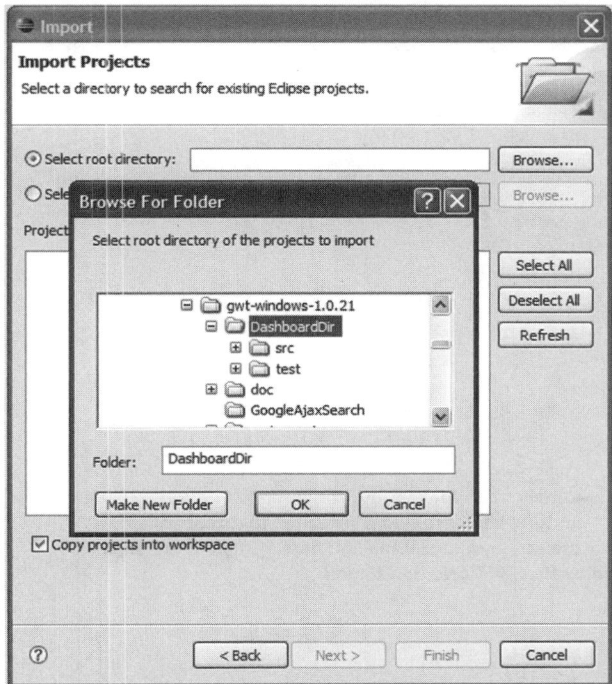

Figure 2.9 The second stage of importing the Dashboard project into Eclipse: finding the project that you're importing in your directory structure.

check box, Eclipse copies all the project files into its workspace directory. If you don't select this option, Eclipse leaves the files where they are. It's important to remember which way you choose, because that dictates where you'll need to pick up the GWT-generated files from later for web deployment (GWT will place them relative to the source files).

Regardless of which choice you make about where to store the project files, now you should click the Finish button to import the project. A short while later, you'll see a view similar to that shown in figure 2.10. The project is now loaded into Eclipse.

Eclipse isn't the only IDE you can use to develop GWT projects, although it's the easiest to integrate straight out of the box using the tools provided in GWT. In case you choose not to use the `-eclipse` flag with the creation tools, or if you wish to import your files into a different IDE, we'll look at the steps to do that next.

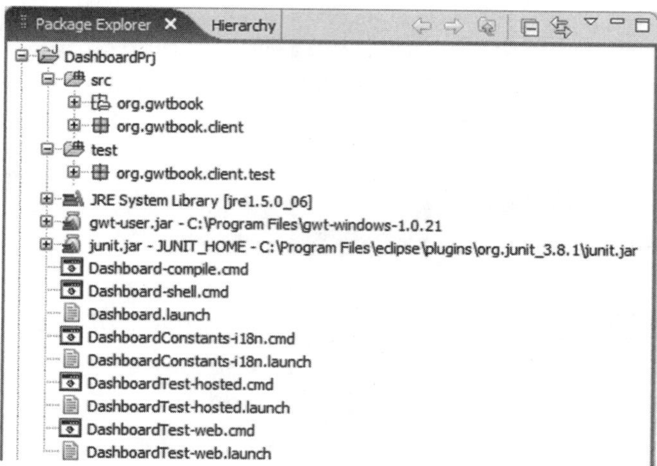

Figure 2.10 The GWT Dashboard application loaded into the Eclipse Package Explorer window, showing the directory structure, the Java and HTML files together with the associated module XML file, and the range of command-line applications and Eclipse launch configurations generated by the GWT creation tools.

Using other IDEs

With GWT, you aren't restricted to using the Eclipse IDE. If you wish, you can use a text editor and command-line execution of tools. If you do use an IDE, then you can import the structure you've just created.

You've already seen how the `applicationCreator` tool creates the correct file structure for a GWT application, so you're up and running from that point. Follow these steps if you're using an IDE for which there is no existing GWT support:

1. Create the application using `applicationCreator` (and both `i18nCreator` and `junitCreator` if you want that functionality).
2. Import the code into your IDE, preserving the file structure just produced.
3. Add the gwt-user.jar file to your IDE's classpath and any path required for auto-completion to operate correctly.
4. Hook up your IDE to execute the `application-shell` and `application-compile` scripts.
5. For debugging, hook your IDE debugger up to port 9000, which is the port on which hosted mode allows debugging connections.

Using Ant scripts will significantly increase the ease of development and testing, and you can find some references to scripts that others have built on the GWT forum.

IDEs such as NetBeans can import Eclipse projects, so this may be a smoother way to ensure that all the configuration needed for your application is imported.

The alternative is to use an IDE that has a GWT wizard built for it, such as IntelliJ, which creates the necessary files and configuration for instant use in that IDE. Finally, some extensions to Eclipse exist, such as Googlipse and GWTDesigner; they allow you to develop GWT applications graphically and thus create the necessary configurations for you at project creation time.

One way or another, you've arrived at the point where your project structure is in place and you have the ability to start building your new GWT application, either in a text editor or in an IDE. You've executed the default application to make sure everything has been created correctly, and now you're ready to change that default to your own application.

2.3 Summary

This chapter has covered the first step in developing a GWT application created using the default GWT creation tools. You now have the directory and file structure for the default GWT application, which forms the basis for the Dashboard example you'll build on throughout the rest of the book.

You may think we've used a lot of pages for what is effectively the GWT "Hello World" example, but the GWT structure isn't as simple as typing four lines of code and saying, "there you are." However, you've done the hard part; continuing to develop your application from this point is much more like writing a few lines of code and executing it. Although it may have seemed like a long path to get to this point, you've seen that with a bit of practice and knowing what you're doing, completing Stage 1 takes only a few minutes.

The key benefit of using the GWT creation tools is that they generate the directory structure and file contents in such a way that they correctly tie together. You can easily check that the structure is correct by executing the default application. This puts you in a safe position to begin replacing the default files with the files needed for your own application, and that means heading on to chapter 3.

3 Advancing to your own application

This chapter covers

- GWT module definition
- Hosted-mode browsers
- Compiling a GWT application
- Running a GWT application

Generating the GWT default application is great, and if you follow the steps in the previous chapter time and time again, you'll consistently get the default application. We doubt, though, that this is all you'll use GWT for; it would be a pretty dull technology if that were all it did!

Stage 1 of the lifecycle is generally performed for all GWT applications. It isn't wasted work, because it provides a solid foundation of files and directories that enables you to confidently build your own applications. However, going through the remaining stages in the lifecycle is the key. In this chapter, we'll cover the remaining stages in the lifecycle in the context of the specific example we introduced in chapter 2: a Dashboard application.

3.1 Describing the application example

Throughout the rest of this book, we'll go through the remaining steps of the lifecycle that are necessary to transform the default application into the application you want to build. In this case, that happens to be the Dashboard application shown in figure 3.1.

The key functionality of the Dashboard application, where a number of component applications will sit, can be summed up as follows:

- Providing a simple windowing system that lets you drag and minimize component applications.
- Implementing drop functionality for windows. If you drop one on the trash icon, it's removed from the display.
- Supporting a menu system that displays option menu bars for in-focus windows (it's the responsibility of the windowed application to place and remove its option menu).
- Letting you extend the menu system with a bookmark listing that loads bookmarks from an XML file.
- Using GWT generators to automatically generate an About menu item whose display contains information gleaned from introspecting the component application's Java class.
- Supporting internationalization by using constants for the menu bar and messages for the initial name of the Dashboard.

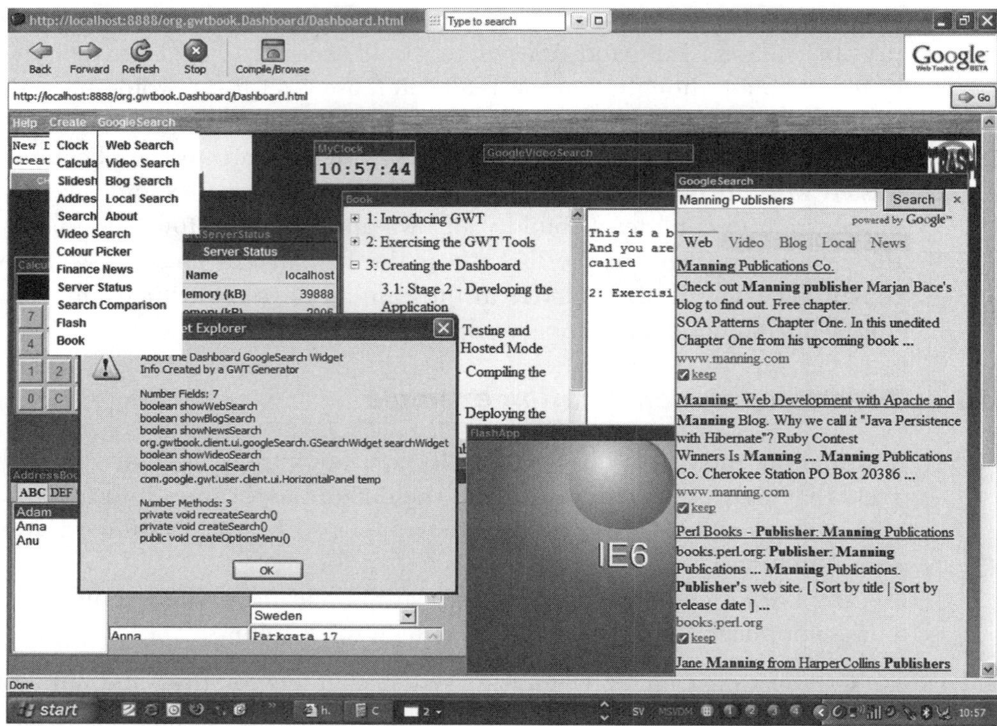

Figure 3.1 ***GWT in Action*** **Dashboard running in hosted mode, showing a number of component applications; an About Box automatically created by GWT generators that have introspected the application's class; and a couple of open menu bars, one showing options for the component application in focus and the other listing the component applications that can be executed. Although this may look intimidating, it shows what you can do with GWT. Throughout this book and the code, you'll see how this is achieved.**

Component application is the name we give to the individual applications you can create in the Dashboard—for example, the Calculator, Google Search, and Server Status components. We won't show how to build these applications in detail in this book; rather, we'll point out parts of them to demonstrate key GWT concepts. (You can download the source code for the complete Dashboard application and a large number of component applications from http://www.manning.com/hanson.)

This application is too ambitious to build in one short chapter. To show how the remaining lifecycle stages are used, we'll take the default application from chapter 2 and build a basic version of the Dashboard, shown in figure 3.2.

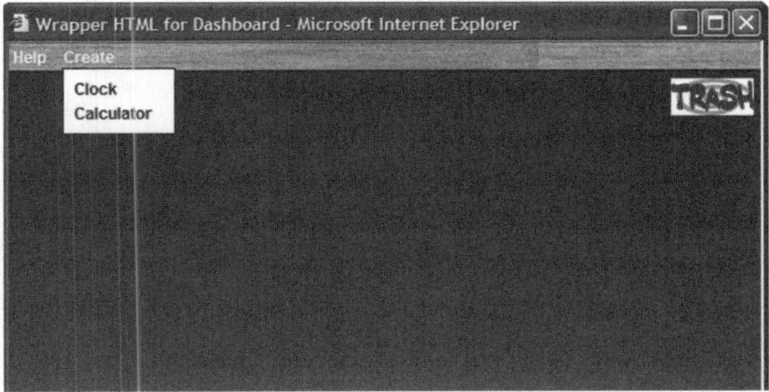

Figure 3.2 The Dashboard application you'll build in this chapter by taking the default application created at the end of chapter 2 and altering the files. Comparing this figure to the full Dashboard application shown in figure 3.1, you can see that it's much simpler, but that's what we want for now.

Stage 1 of the lifecycle got you to the start of this chapter and is generally performed for all GWT applications. As we promised, the rest of chapter 3 steps through the remaining stages in the web application development lifecycle. If you're following along as you build the Dashboard application, then there will be some hands-on work for you in this chapter as you alter the default files created for the default application, starting with Stage 2 where you build the application.

3.2 Stage 2: Developing your application

Stage 1 laid the solid foundations for the GWT application. In Stage 2, you'll move on to alter the files provided by the default application to build your own GWT application (this stage is required for all GWT applications built using the GWT creation tools and most of those built using IDE specific plug-ins).

When you build small applications, it's possible—although not always advisable, because surprisingly often, prototypes try to head toward production systems—to get away with sitting down, writing some code, and hoping it meets the need. As you step up to building larger and larger applications, you must take a more structured approach in order to keep track of where you are, enable multiple developers to work on the code, and make an application that is maintainable in the future.

The approach we've typically taken to building the applications, and that we've done in the background for the Dashboard, is shown in figure 3.3. We start, not surprisingly, by defining the functionality we wish to implement; then, we design

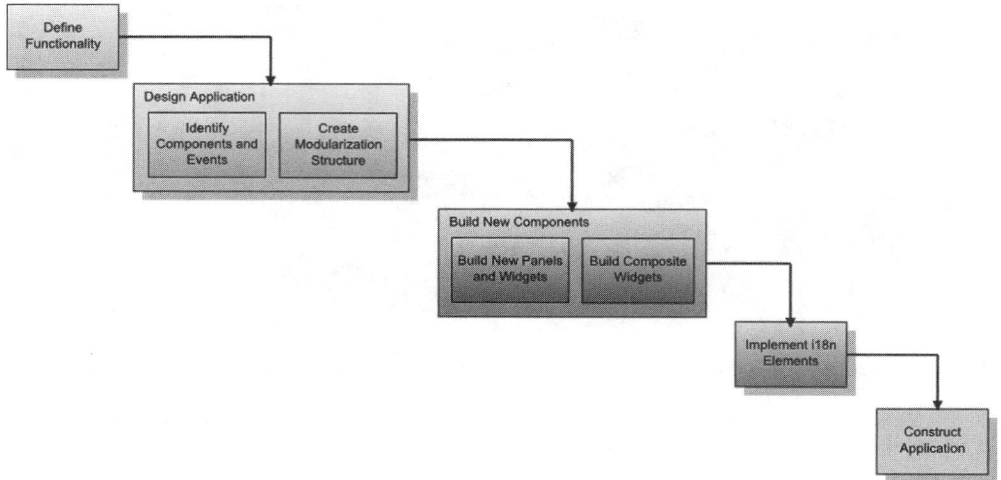

Figure 3.3 Typical steps in Stage 2 (developing the application) from the application development lifecycle process introduced in chapter 2 for developing a new GWT application (but not showing the testing tasks that would normally be present)

the application to meet that functionality by identifying components and events we'll use as well as how we'll use GWT's modularization capabilities. We create the design of the application and end up with a construction step that involves building the various components that make up the application.

Each of the five steps takes you nearer the end goal of a completed application. For the Dashboard, you can define the functionality as a simple menu system that implements internationalization text for the English and Swedish languages, with an icon for the trash can. Why did we pick Swedish? Well, one of the authors lives in Sweden, and it also gives you a good opportunity to use extended characters such as ä, ö, and å in the internationalization files. You have no new widgets or panels to build, and the modularization is negligible (we discuss modularization in much more detail in chapter 9). The next step in Stage 2 is to address internationalization.

3.2.1 Implementing internationalization

When you executed the i18n tools in chapter 2, it created a default properties file (DashboardConstants.properties) and a `DashboardConstants-i18n` command-line tool. You may have executed this new command-line tool at that point, and it produced a simple DashboardConstants.java file, which was fairly empty because you hadn't yet defined any constants in the DashboardConstants.properties file.

Now we'll go through the process of adding internationalization aspects for the Dashboard, which in this case means creating the text that will appear in the menu for both the English and Swedish locales. Examples appear in figures 3.4 and 3.5.

Figure 3.4 The Dashboard when the locale is left as the default locale. The menu bar is written in English.

We mentioned in chapter 2 that the second part of the internationalization step was the only part of Stage 1 that might be used again in later stages to ensure that the DashboardConstants.java file matched the available keys. This is now demonstrated: Following the update to the properties files that you're about to perform, you'll need to execute the `DashboardConstants-i18n` creator tool again. First you'll update the key/value pairs that you require for the Dashboard example by replacing the DashboardConstants.properties file with the constants for the default locale (the locale used if the requested one isn't available). To do so, replace the contents of DashboardConstants.properties with those shown in listing 3.1.

Figure 3.5 The Dashboard when the locale is set to Swedish. The menu bar is now written in Swedish. (The locale was changed by adding the parameter `?locale=sv` to the end of the URL.)

Listing 3.1 Key/value pairs for menu constants in the default locale

```
AboutMenuItemName: About
CalculatorMenuItemName: Calculator
ClockMenuItemName: Clock
CreateMenuName: Create
HelpMenuName: Help
```

Now, when you use the key `HelpMenuName` in the Java code, you get the constant value `Help`.

The format of these properties files follows the traditional Java properties file format (with the slight exception that the file should be encoded as UTF-8 format and can therefore include Unicode characters directly). In the example, you use a colon as the separator between keys and values, but it's equally valid to use an equals sign (=) or whitespace character (a space or tab, but not a newline marker, because that indicates the start of a new key and implies that the last key had an empty string as its value). There is no need to do this in the value because all characters up to the line feed are treated as part of the value.

That set of key/pairs is great for the default locale, but you also want to deal with the Swedish locale. To do so, you need to add a new properties file that contains the same keys as in listing 3.1 but with the values in Swedish. You have to do this for all the specific locales you want to make available in the application. (As you'll see later in the book, these properties files exist in a hierarchy. If entries are missing, the value from a file higher in the hierarchy is used instead—if no such value exists, then the GWT compiler raises an error.) These new files must be named according to a well-defined naming convention (discussed in more detail in chapter 15) to ensure that GWT can deal with them.

For now, you need to create a properties file for the Swedish locale. To do so, create a new file called DashboardConstants_sv.properties in the same location as the default properties file, and fill it with the contents shown in listing 3.2. (Don't worry if your keyboard doesn't have these characters. You can always use the electronic copies of the files available at http://www.manning.com/hanson.)

Listing 3.2 Key/value pairs used for menu constants in the Swedish locale

```
AboutMenuItemName: Om
CalculatorMenuItemName: Kalkylator
ClockMenuItemName: Klocka
CreateMenuName: Nya
HelpMenuName: Hjälp
```

NOTE You should set the encoding of your properties files to UTF-8 using your editor; otherwise, GWT won't be able to cope with any special characters—in the case of Swedish, this means the Ä, Ö, and Å characters, but other languages have their own specifics, too!

To set the encoding of your properties files to UTF-8 in Eclipse, select the file in the Package Explorer, right-click it, and select Properties. In the dialog box that opens, select Other for the file encoding; and in the drop-down box, choose the UTF-8 option (if just encoding the language file still does not work, try encoding the whole project). For other IDEs, see the appropriate IDE manual.

You now create a simple interface file that allows you to refer to constants in the code. You create this file, or update it if you've previously done this task, by executing the `DashboardConstants-i18n` tool. This tool takes the default properties file and creates items in the interface file for each key (note that if the locale-specific files have more keys than the default file, they will be ignored; if the locale-specific files have keys missing, then the default values are used).

Because you've changed the default properties file, execute the `Dashboard-Constants-i18n` command now to refresh the interface file. Doing so creates (or replaces, if it already exists) the DashboardConstants.java file in the client directory. This new file contains the code shown in listing 3.3, including one method declaration for each of the keys in the properties file.

Listing 3.3 Java interface file created by running the `Dashboard-Constants-i18n` application

```
package org.gwtbook.client;

import com.google.gwt.i18n.client.Constants;

public interface DashboardConstants extends Constants {
  String AboutMenuItemName();
  String CalculatorMenuItemName();
  String ClockMenuItemName();
  String CreateMenuName();
  String HelpMenuName();
}
```

That is all you need to implement the back-end aspects of internationalization—relatively easy, at least compared to doing this yourself in JavaScript! To use the locales in code, you amend the module XML file as shown in listing 3.9 and then you use the `GWT.create()` method shown later in listing 3.7 to get the correct set of constants for the locale the application is told it's in. You can change locales in one of two ways. The simplest is to add the following text to the URL used to view the application: `?locale=sv`. The other is to set it in the module XML file, as discussed in section 3.2.2. (Chapter 15 discusses how to use the dynamic string i18n approach GWT provides when you're dealing with legacy code.)

At first glance, the interface and properties files seem to sit in useless isolation—and that is true, except when you execute or compile the code. When that occurs, the GWT system steps in, binding together the properties files and this interface to produce new Java classes that the code uses (this is performed by GWT generators, and there is more on this topic in chapter 14). To use these constants, you need to use a GWT concept called *deferred binding* in the upgraded Dashboard.java file.

DEFINITION *Deferred binding* allows you to write code that is syntactically correct at development time, but with the exact semantics/functionality deferred until runtime. (Technically this occurs at compile-time, because that is where GWT resolves these deferred choices; but conceptually they're resolved at runtime.)

3.2.2 Constructing the application

In this section, you'll examine and alter the contents of the default files; in particular, you'll alter the HTML page (Dashboard.html) and the Java file (Dashboard.java) as well as add a style sheet (Dashboard.css). When you're developing applications using the creation tools, you'll typically need to alter the following files:

- *HTML file*—This is the HTML document into which the GWT application will be loaded. The default file is simple and is unlikely to meet your needs for a real application, so you'll almost by default end up replacing it.

  What it's replaced with depends on how you'll be using your GWT application. If your application will be placed into a brand-new page, you have a lot of flexibility; but sometimes your application will be going into an existing web page, in which case you should use an HTML file representative of that page.
- *Module XML file*—This file indicates a number of aspects of the current GWT application (module) to the GWT compiler. Normally, each application has one module XML file (in the example, it's Dashboard.gwt.xml), unless you start making your applications modular. In that case, there will be a number of XML module files (we cover this in chapter 8 when we discuss how the Dashboard application will be built).
- *Java code files*—This set of Java classes and interfaces goes together to make up the application. The default application always provides one file, in this case the Dashboard.java file, which provides the basic interface between the application and the GWT loading mechanism. For the Dashboard example, you've also implemented internationalization, so you have a DashboardConstants.java file too. In practice, you'll end up replacing these files to reflect the needs of your application as well as adding other Java files to represent other aspects of the application. For example, as you progress through this book, you'll build new widgets and panels as well as applications that sit in the Dashboard.

Although it's physically possible to place the details of all these Dashboard components in one massive Dashboard.java file, doing so is considered bad programming practice and is a support nightmare! In practice, each of these components consists of one or more Java class files, which all need to be created from scratch.

For each of the default GWT application files you'll replace, we'll look at what the original file contains and how it works, and then show the replacement file. In a GWT application, the HTML file acts as the container into which the application is delivered; it makes sense that this is the first file we'll examine and change.

Constructing the HTML file

There is nothing unusual in the default Dashboard.html file created by the tools. It's simple HTML consisting of a standard head and body block, with a title and some style information. When viewed in a web browser, it produces output similar to that shown in figure 3.6, with a header, some text, and an HTML table that contains two cells named `slot1` and `slot2`. (We used Firefox's Web Developer extension to allow you to easily see the DOM elements and their names on the web page.)

The important parts of the HTML file, in a GWT application sense, are the table cells `slot1` and `slot2`. When the default application loads, this is where the `Button` and the `Label` you saw in chapter 1 are placed.

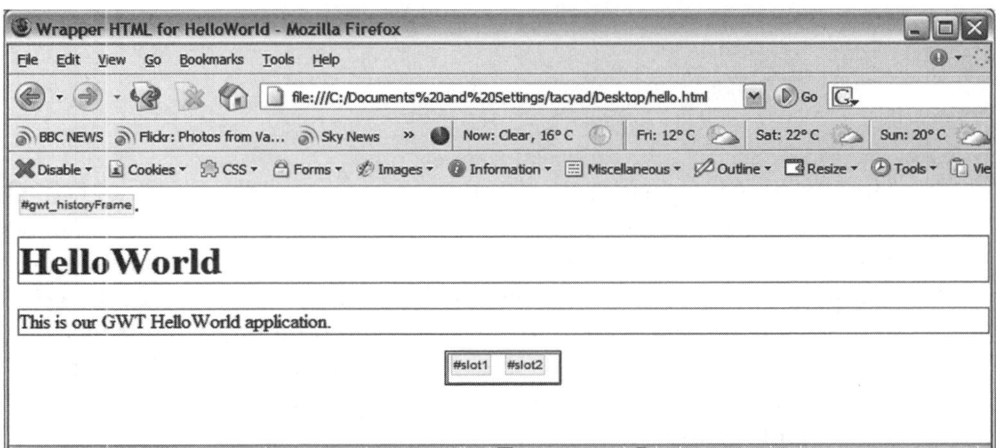

Figure 3.6 The HelloWorld HTML file displayed in Firefox using the Web Developer extension tool to highlight the DOM elements. You can see the GWT History frame, the title, some text, and the two slots where the default application will place its widgets.

The HTML that renders figure 3.6 is shown in listing 3.4.

Listing 3.4 Dashboard.html file provided for the default GWT application

```
<html>
   <head>
      <title>Wrapper HTML for Dashboard</title>
      <meta name='gwt:module' content='org.gwtbook.Dashboard'>     ❶ Identify application
   </head>
   <body>
      <script language="javascript"
              src="gwt.js"></script>                        ❷ Load GWT framework
      <iframe id="__gwt_historyFrame"
              style="width:0;height:0;border:0">            ❸ Support GWT history
      </iframe>
      <h1>Dashboard</h1>
      <p>
         This is an example of a host page for the Dashboard
         application. You can attach a Web Toolkit module to
         any HTML page you like, making it easy to add bits
         of AJAX functionality to existing pages
         without starting from scratch.
      </p>
      <table align=center>
         <tr>
            <td id="slot1"></td><td id="slot2"></td>     ❹ Create application holding positions
         </tr>
      </table>
   </body>
</html>
```

The GWT-specific parts of the HTML come at points ❶, ❷, ❸, and ❹. ❶ and ❷ are mandatory, and your application can't work without them being present. ❸ is required only if you're going to use GWT history functions. It's normally required, but not mandatory, to have some form of named element(s) in the HTML file ❹ in order for your application to know where to position itself once loaded. What is important for this example is that there are named DOM elements that can be found in the web page, not the fact that they're called `slot1` and `slot2` or that they're table cells.

Let's examine the default HTML file in a little more detail. A meta-tag is introduced in the head section ❶ for each GWT application to be included in the web page. In the case of the default example, there is only one application, so only one `gwt:module` meta-tag is required. You set the `content` attribute of the meta-tag to be the class name of the application, `org.mycompany.Dashboard`, which informs the GWT loading mechanism where to look to initialize the application (we cover the GWT loading mechanism in chapter 17—the process just described covers GWT up to version 1.3, from version 1.4 this gets slightly simpler where only one JavaScript file directly related to your application is loaded, see chapter 17 for details).

In addition to the meta-tags for the module, the GWT loading mechanism recognizes three other meta-tags; these are shown in table 3.1 (with definitions taken directly from the GWT code).

Table 3.1 Meta-tags that can be entered into an application's HTML file. Each meta-tag controls an aspect of the GWT application.

Meta-tag	Description
`gwt:module`	Indicates that a module definition is coming. The value of the `content` attribute is the class you define that implements the `EntryPoint` interface. **Example** `<meta name="gwt:module" content="qualified_class_name">`
`gwt:property`	Defines a deferred binding client property. It can cover many aspects—for example, the locale of the application (which drives the loading of other locale-specific constant files, if you defined them). **Example** `<meta name="gwt:property" content="_name_=_value_">`
`gwt:onPropertyErrorFn`	Specifies the name of a function to call if a client property is set to an invalid value (meaning that no matching compilation is found). **Example** `<meta name="gwt:onPropertyErrorFn" content="_fnName_">`
`gwt-onLoadErrorFn`	Specifies the name of a function to call if an exception happens during bootstrapping or if a module throws an exception out of `onModuleLoad()`; the function should take a `message` parameter. **Example** `<meta name="gwt:onLoadErrorFn" content="_fnName_">`

At ❷ in listing 3.4, you include the main GWT JavaScript file, gwt.js, which is provided in the GWT distribution. The purpose of this file is to initiate and manage the application loading mechanism, which is discussed in chapter 17, as well as to perform some other administrative tasks. Google indicates that this tag could be placed in the header block, but there is a gain in startup speed if it's included in the body—we'll trust them on that point.

The default application's HTML includes an iframe ❸; it's optional, but the creation tools include it by default. It's used by the GWT history functions, and you should remove it only if you know for sure you won't be using these functions. It's particularly useful, because poor design and development of Ajax solutions run the risk of breaking the user's expected behavior of how browser history works (it's no longer necessary to refresh the browser page every time a screen update is required). GWT solves this problem by using an iframe in which history can be stored and retrieved.

The final element of the HTML that we'll discuss is at ❹ in listing 3.4, where you can find the named DOM elements in which you'll place the application components. In the default application, there are two table cells called `slot1` and `slot2` into which the Java code places the button and the text displayed when the button is clicked.

It's worth noting here that you don't need to place GWT components in a table; any named DOM container will do (such as a span or a div). Also, it isn't always necessary to have a separate element for each GWT component that you place in the web page. The Google example could easily be implemented using a GWT panel in which the button and message were placed. The panel itself would then be placed as one element on the screen; but now we're straying into composite widgets and layout design territory, which is a subject for chapter 7. When you develop the Dashboard, you'll see that you need no named DOM element.

In the case of the Dashboard application, replace the contents of the Dashboard.html file with the code shown in listing 3.5.

Listing 3.5 Dashboard.html file used for the first version of the Dashboard example application

```
<html>
   <head>
      <title>Wrapper HTML for Dashboard</title>
      <meta name='gwt:module' content='org.gwtbook.Dashboard'>    ❶ Identify application
   </head>
   <body>
      <script language="javascript" src="gwt.js">    ❷ Load GWT framework
      </script>
      <iframe id="__gwt_historyFrame"    ❷ Support GWT history
```

```
            style="width:0;height:0;border:0">
      </iframe>
   </body>
</html>
```

In this new file, you can see that the two mandatory elements are still there (❶ and ❷), and you also keep the history capability ❸, because that will be used by the Dashboard components later. The big difference in this HTML is that you deliberately don't include any named DOM elements, such as `slot1` or `slot2`, from the default application. The main benefit of named DOM elements is to allow the GWT applications to seamlessly fit into existing web pages at specific locations; the Dashboard application takes over the whole real estate of the web page, so named slots are relatively meaningless.

The new Dashboard.HTML file is nothing out of the ordinary. If you have a GWT application, to go into any existing web page, you just identify a named DOM container for it and include the relevant meta-tag and gwt.js script. But how does the GWT application bind itself to that named container (or display in the browser, in the case of the Dashboard) and provide the necessary functionality? That comes in the Java code.

Altering the application files

Along with the HTML file, altering the application's Java file (Dashboard.java in this case) is a key step in the process of moving away from the default application. The code that is provided by default in the Dashboard.java file is shown in listing 3.6.

Listing 3.6 Default application's Dashboard.java Java code

```
package org.gwtbook.client;

import com.google.gwt.core.client.EntryPoint;
import com.google.gwt.user.client.ui.Button;
import com.google.gwt.user.client.ui.ClickListener;
import com.google.gwt.user.client.ui.Label;
import com.google.gwt.user.client.ui.RootPanel;
import com.google.gwt.user.client.ui.Widget

public class Dashboard implements EntryPoint {          ❶ Implement EntryPoint

   public void onModuleLoad() {                         ❷ Define initial functionality
      final Button button = new Button("Click me");     ❸ Create button
      final Label label = new Label("");                ❹ Create label
```

```
        button.addClickListener(new ClickListener() {
           public void onClick(Widget sender) {
              if (label.getText().equals(""))
                 label.setText("Hello World");
              else
                 label.setText("");
           }
        });
        RootPanel.get("slot1").add(button);
        RootPanel.get("slot2").add(label);
     }
  }
```

❺ **Add ClickListener to button**

❻ **Add button and label to web page**

This is simple Java code, which breaks down as follows. The Java class name must be the same as the filename, and in this case it's called `Dashboard` ❶. For GWT applications, there must be one class in your application known as the *entry point class*, which provides an `onModuleLoad()` method (the GWT loading mechanism calls this method to start your application). This class is identified to GWT by implementing the `EntryPoint` interface, as this class does.

Because this class implements the `EntryPoint` interface, it must provide the `onModuleLoad()` method ❷. For the default application, this method creates the necessary GWT widgets (a button and a label) and adds a click listener to the button. This click listener contains an `onClick()` method, which is called when the button is clicked.

In segment ❸ of the code, you create a GWT widget—in this case, a `Button` widget. In the Java code, this is treated like any other object: It's created, and you can perform a number of actions on it through the `Button` class's member functions. When executing in hosted or web mode, this object becomes a direct representation of a DOM button and is so displayed in the web page. We'll look at all the widgets GWT provides in more detail in the next chapter.

At ❹, you create a GWT Java `Label` object, which in Java code acts as a simple object but in hosted or web mode becomes a direct representation of a DOM `div` element whose inner text can be altered.

Most functionality on the UI aspects of a GWT application are driven by events—a user clicks something, or something is dragged or changed in some way. GWT manages these events through listeners added to GWT widget objects. At ❺, you add a click listener to the `Button` widget. When the button is clicked, the `onClick()` method is called to update the text value of the `Label` (causing it either to be blank or to say Hello World). Event handling is covered in more detail in chapter 6.

Now that you know how the default application Java code works, let's introduce the Java code for the application (you should replace the existing Dashboard.java contents in your project with that shown in listing 3.7).

Listing 3.7 Dashboard.java Java code for the first version of the Dashboard application

```
package org.gwtbook.client;

import com.google.gwt.core.client.EntryPoint;
import com.google.gwt.core.client.GWT;
import com.google.gwt.user.client.Command;
import com.google.gwt.user.client.Window;
import com.google.gwt.user.client.ui.MenuBar;
import com.google.gwt.user.client.ui.RootPanel;

public class Dashboard implements EntryPoint{                  ❶ Implement EntryPoint
   public void onModuleLoad(){                                 ❷ Define initial functionality
      MenuBar menu = new MenuBar();
      MenuBar menuCreate = new MenuBar(true);                  ❸ Create menu bars
      MenuBar menuHelp = new MenuBar(true);
      MenuBar login = new MenuBar(true);
      Image trash = new Image("trash.png");
      DashboardConstants constants =                           ❹ Access internationalization constants
         (DashboardConstants) GWT.create(DashboardConstants.class);

      menuHelp.addItem(constants.AboutMenuItemName(),          ❺ Define menu items
                       new DummyCommand());
      menuCreate.addItem(constants.ClockMenuItemName(),
                       new DummyCommand());
      menuCreate.addItem(constants.CalculatorMenuItemName(),
                         new DummyCommand());
      menu.addItem(constants.HelpMenuName(), menuHelp);        ❻ Build menu system
      menu.addItem(constants.CreateMenuName(), menuCreate);
      RootPanel.get().add(menu);                               ❼ Add components to web page
      RootPanel.get().add(trash);
      menuCreate.addStyleName("submenu");
      menuHelp.addStyleName("submenu");                        ❽ Apply styling to components
      trash.setStyleName("trash");
   }

   public class DummyCommand implements Command{               ❾ Define dummy command
      public void execute() {
         Window.alert("Menu Item Clicked");
      }
   }
}
```

As we walk through this code, you'll see a number of similarities to and differences from the default application. The class is still the `EntryPoint` to the application and is still called `Dashboard` ❶. Because this is the `EntryPoint` class, it must implement the `onModuleLoad()` method ❷.

In the default application, you created `Button` and `Label` widgets. For the first version of the Dashboard, you create `MenuBar` widgets instead ❸. As we mentioned previously, we'll talk more about widgets in chapter 4.

When you created the Dashboard directory and code structure using the tools, we said you'd implement internationalization, and you created a `DashboardConstants` interface file using the tools. We also said that you access these constants through a GWT concept called *deferred binding*.

At ❹ you request the correct binding between the interface file and locale-specific properties files (you'll create these shortly) to ensure that the correct locale constants are available. `GWT.create()` is a special method that works differently in hosted and web mode, but all you need to worry about here is that the method selects the correct set of locale-specific constants or messages. (We'll cover internationalization in much more detail in chapter 15).

❺ is similar to where you added a `ClickListener` to the `Button` in the default application, except here you add `MenuItems` to `MenuBars` and indicate that when these `MenuItems` are clicked, the code should perform the `execute()` method of the new `DummyCommand` object you create for each `MenuItem`. You set the text to be shown for each `MenuItem` to be the value returned from constant object created at ❻. This is how you show different constant values (effectively language, in this case) for different locales.

To finish the menu system, you add two different `MenuBars` to the root `MenuBar` displayed at the top of the screen. In the default application, you used this `RootPanel.get()` method with specific named elements on the HTML page as a parameter to insert the widgets at specific locations. In the Dashboard, you don't define any named elements in the HTML file; instead, you let the `RootPanel` place the widgets in-line from the top of the page ❼. On the screen, you put the menu first and then the image for the trash icon. This approach works well for the Dashboard—different approaches work better for different applications.

If you're checking back in the book to see what this looks like, you may wonder how the trash icon appears directly under the menu bar and on the right side of the page—because this isn't how placing elements in-line works. The answer is the use of Cascading Style Sheets (CSS).

The final step of the application setup adds names from a CSS to the objects you've created ❽. You explicitly set the style for the submenus and the trash icon.

In a corresponding CSS definition, you enter the stylistic aspects for the components. The styling for the trash icon includes the statement `float: right`, which is how the icon is made to float to the right side of the page.

When you created the `MenuItems`, you told them that if they're clicked, they should call the `execute()` method of an object of type `DummyCommand`; then, the text *Menu Item Clicked* appears on the screen. ❾ provides a simple implementation of the `Command` interface, which creates a JavaScript alert box on the screen with the text *Menu Item Clicked* in it.

DON'T FORGET

First—Currently, the Java you use in your client-side code must comply to Java 1.4 standards: no generics, and so on. Your IDE is probably set to the Java 5.0 standard by default, so even though your IDE says you have valid code, it may fail in the GWT compiler. (If you're new to Java, don't worry; Java 5.0 is the next version after 1.4—GWT isn't that far behind!) The easiest thing to do for simple projects is set your IDE to use the 1.4 standard. In Eclipse, right-click the project in the Package Explorer, and select the Properties option; then, under the Java Compiler tree, set the compliance to Java 1.4 mode. If you're using server-side code, there is no such restriction on the Java used for it.

Second—Any Java packages that you include in client-side code must have the source code visible to the GWT compiler and must follow the same restrictions as code you write (that is, they must be compliant with Java 1.4).

Third—Your client-side Java code becomes compiled as JavaScript—don't expect your Java code to do anything JavaScript can't do. In particular, this means you can't access the user's filesystem (except through the standard file-upload browser functionality, which we'll look at in chapter 12); and, from client-side code, you can't directly access a database on your server (to do this, you need to get your client-side code to talk to server-side code, which we thoroughly go through in chapters 10–13).

All GWT applications are glued together with one or more corresponding module XML files. Simple applications have only one of these files. When you build the full Dashboard application later, you'll see that there is a module XML file for the Dashboard application as well as one each for most of the component applications.

Examining the module XML file

Under the src/org/gwtbook folder, you find the Dashboard.gwt.xml module file. This file is always named *YourApplicationName*.gwt.xml and is used by GWT to control the compilation (the generation of what GWT calls *permutations*) of your application as well as GWT module inheritance. GWT creates a new JavaScript file for each permutation of various options, such as browser types and included locales (in chapter 15, we'll look at exactly what you can do in this area). The file can contain many elements, all of which are described in glorious detail in chapter 9; but right now it describes the view of the default application (see listing 3.8). You need to replace this content with that shown in listing 3.9.

Listing 3.8 Default application's Dashboard.gwt.xml file

```
<module>
   <inherits
       name="com.google.gwt.user.User" />
   <entry-point
       class="org.gwtbook.client.Dashboard" />
</module>
```

Listing 3.9 New XML module file to represent the Dashboard application

```
<module>
   <inherits
       name='com.google.gwt.user.User'/>            ❶ Inherit standard GWT functionality
   <inherits
       name="com.google.gwt.i18n.I18N" />           ❷ Inherit GWT internationalization
   <extend-property
       name="locale"
       values="sv" />                               ❸ Swedish locale
   <entry-point
       class='org.gwtbook.client.Dashboard'/>       ❹ Entry point
   <stylesheet
       src="Dashboard.css" />                       ❺ Style sheet
</module>
```

This module file is slightly more than that provided with the default application; let's look at what it contains. At ❶ you indicate that this application inherits the functionality in the `User` GWT module—almost all applications include this entry.

Next ❷, you say that you also inherit the functionality in the `I18N` GWT module—unfortunately, i18n functionality isn't part of the default include mentioned in ❶, and you need to specifically inherit this module if you have i18n aspects in the code.

❸ indicates to the application that it needs to manage the Swedish locale in addition to the default one. If you don't include this entry, then even if you have code for the Swedish locale, it will never be accessible (additional locales require additional entries in this file).

When looking at the Java code, we talked about the need for a class to implement the `EntryPoint` interface and act as the starting point of the application. At ❹ in the module XML file, you tell the compiler which class implements this `EntryPoint` interface.

Finally, at ❺ you inject the style sheet as discussed in the last chapter.

With the completion of this module XML file, the first version of the Dashboard application is functionally complete, but it's still missing the styling needed to make it look like figure 3.2.

REMEMBER A GWT module XML file and the Java classpath are only loosely related. The XML file points out GWT dependencies; the classpath points out Java dependencies. If a particular module is mentioned in a module XML file but its source code isn't on the Java classpath, then compilation will fail.

3.2.3 *Applying styling*

The most obvious instance of styling applied to the application (obvious if you're running the code rather than looking at the black-and-white picture in the book!) is the fading blue background given to the Dashboard. Without the styling, the Dashboard would appear as shown in figure 3.7.

Setting a background image on a web page is an easy task to accomplish when you're using normal HTML and a CSS; you just set an entry for the `body` element in the style sheet. For example:

```
body {
   margin: 0;
   padding: 0;
   background: #111fff;
   background-image:url("DashboardBackground.jpg");
}
```

You then link the style sheet into the HTML.

Figure 3.7
This is what the Dashboard application looks like if you forget to apply any styling—not quite the same view as in figure 3.2.

How do you do this in GWT? After compilation, GWT is simple HTML and JavaScript, so the same CSS approach works perfectly well. You should create a Dashboard.css file and store it in the src/org/gwtbook/public directory. In that file, enter the code shown in listing 3.10.

Listing 3.10 Part of the CSS for the first version of the Dashboard application

```
body {                                          ❶ Style body
   margin: 0;
   padding: 0;
   background: #111fff;
   background-image:url("DashboardBackground.jpg");
}

.trash {                                        ❷ Style trash icon
   float: right;
   margin: 5px;
}

.gwt-MenuBar {                                  ❸ Style menu bar
   background: #66a;
   background-image:url("BrushedSteelGrayBackground.jpg");
   border-bottom: 2px solid #000;
   cursor: pointer;
}
```

This style sheet mentions a couple of graphics files, which you use to give the look—you can either grab them from the electronic part of this book or supply your own. Either way, they need to be stored in the same directory as the style sheet.

The style sheet shows three different ways of styling GWT components. You can style standard HTML elements using the normal way of defining styling for that element. In listing 3.10, ❶ shows the styling for the `body` element, which among other things sets the background image of the body element to DashboardBackground.gif. When the application loads, it expects to find that image file in the src/org/gwtbook/public folder in hosted mode (it's possible to change this default location, as we'll discuss in chapter 9) or the public path in web mode.

It's possible to set the style name of GWT components using the `setStyleName()` method, as you saw at ❽ of the Java code in listing 3.7. There you set the style name (you're setting the CSS class name for the DOM element) of the trash object as follows:

```
trash.setStyleName("trash");
```

At ❷ in this style sheet is the corresponding CSS used to style that element. Note that in the CSS, you need to start the name with a period (.), which isn't present in the name used in your Java code—if you don't do so, then the styling isn't applied (that has caught us a few times!). You can give an element multiple CSS class names by using the `addStyleName()` method (the `setStyleName()` method removes all previous CSS class names associated with the element first and then applies the provided CSS class name—so, if you call `setStyleName()` with the empty string, "", you clear all associated CSS class names).

Finally, all GWT widgets come with a set of default style names already applied, and you can use those in the style sheet without having to name them in the code. To get the names of the styles set as default, you need to go to the GWT web site and navigate through the class hierarchy to the UI object you're interested in.

You style the root `MenuBar` a lovely shade of brushed steel in the Dashboard application. To do this, navigate to the `MenuBar` object on the GWT web site to see the standard GWT style names for a `MenuBar` (at the time of writing, that web site is at http://code.google.com/webtoolkit/documentation/com.google.gwt.user.client.ui.MenuBar.html; see figure 3.8).

Class MenuBar

```
public class MenuBar
extends Widget
implements PopupListener
```

A standard menu bar widget. A menu bar can contain any number of menu items, each of w
cascaded menu bar.

CSS Style Rules

```
*

    *
    .gwt-MenuBar { the menu bar itself }
    .gwt-MenuBar .gwt-MenuItem { menu items }
    .gwt-MenuBar .gwt-MenuItem-selected { selected menu items }
```

Figure 3.8 Identifying the default style names for standard GWT widgets from the GWT web site. In this case, you're looking at the `MenuBar` definition from the GWT web page, and you can see the CSS Style Rules section.

Under the CSS Style Rules section, you can see three entries for the `MenuItem`, which match those given at ❸ in listing 3.10.

To complete the linkage between application and style sheet, we need to decide where to place the link to the style sheet. You have two choices. First, you can edit the Dashboard.html file and add the following in the HTML's `HEAD` section (just as you normally would in an HTML file to which you were linking a style sheet):

```
<link rel=stylesheet href="Dashboard.css">
```

Second, you can create an entry in the module XML file to inject the CSS resource into the application. The benefit of this approach is that you can keep style-specific information logically with the application; if you embed the application in another HTML file, you don't need to alter that HTML file. To use the injection method, place the following into the module XML file:

```
<stylesheet src="Dashboard.css"/>
```

If you add that line to the Dashboard.gwt.xml file you altered earlier, then you're ready to get on with testing and debugging the application in hosted mode.

3.3 Stage 3: Testing and debugging in hosted mode

Hosted mode is a managed environment provided as part of the GWT distribution. You saw in the process diagram in chapter 2 that hosted mode is the environment where you perform the majority of system testing and debugging.

In the Windows operating system, hosted mode uses the version of Internet Explorer that is installed on your machine as the display technology; the other GWT distribution includes a prebuilt Mozilla instance (unfortunately, you can't change these defaults). When running your code in hosted mode, your Java code isn't compiled into JavaScript; rather it's interpreted. This allows you the distinct advantage of being able to link the execution of the application in hosted mode to the debugging capabilities of your IDE.

In this section, we'll look at the process of running the example in hosted mode both from the command line and from within the Eclipse IDE's program-launch capability. We'll also discuss how you can debug your application at runtime in the Eclipse IDE (this process is similar for other IDEs). Let's prepare for hosted mode.

3.3.1 Preparing for hosted mode

In hosted mode, the application is executed through a managed environment that is provided by the GWT distribution. The client-side code executes in a managed web browser, where the Java code is effectively interpreted and any errors or issues are captured and reported in a controller window. Hosted mode also includes an embedded version of the Tomcat servlet engine into which any server-side Java code is deployed automatically.

When you executed the application creation tool in chapter 2, it created a script for you called `Dashboard-shell`, in the DashboardDir directory. This script launches hosted mode. If you haven't used the creation tools or are just interested in the contents of the default script, it appears in listing 3.11 (for the Windows environment—the Mac and Linux versions are similar).

Listing 3.11 Default contents of the `Dashboard-shell` command-line script

```
@java -cp "%~dp0\src;%~dp0\bin;gwt-user.jar;gwt-dev-windows.jar"
      com.google.gwt.dev.GWTShell -out "%~dp0\www" %*
      org.gwtbook.Dashboard/Dashboard.html
```

The hosted-mode script can take a number of arguments. The default set is shown in listing 3.11, and the following sections describe all the possible arguments and what they mean.

-noserver

This argument prevents the embedded Tomcat server from starting up. It's useful to do this if you've deployed your server-side code to your own servlet engine. By default, this value is false, meaning that the Tomcat server embedded within the hosted mode software is used.

-whitelist "list"

By default, hosted mode prevents the user/code from navigating to URLs outside of the applications scope—the whitelist is empty (the whitelist is a list that contains URLs the hosted mode is allowed to navigate to—the opposite, a list where the hosted mode is not allowed to navigate to is called the blacklist, and you'll see that in a short while). If you wish to allow the user/code to do so, then the URLs that will be navigated must be added to a whitelist using a regular expression approach.

For example, if you want the application to navigate to the Swedish Google search site, and you don't add the URL to the whitelist, then you'll see the error message shown in figure 3.9.

To add http://www.google.se to the whitelist, you add the following entry to the `Dashboard-shell` command script:

```
-whitelist " ^http[:][/][/]www[.]google[.]se"
```

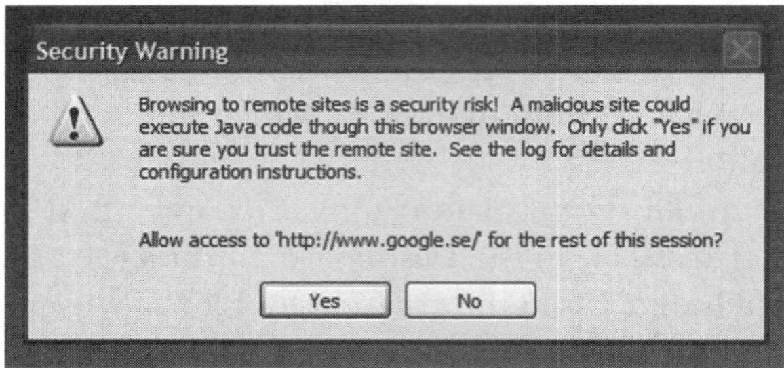

Figure 3.9 The security warning that GWT hosted mode raises if the user or code tries to navigate to a URL that isn't specifically included on the whitelist

Now, when you or the code attempts to navigate to this Google site, no security warning is presented, but the browser navigates to the requested location.

-blacklist "list"

Similar to the whitelist approach, hosted mode can explicitly bar URLs if they're placed on the blacklist; by default, the blacklist is empty. To add http://www.google.se to the blacklist, add the following entry to the `Dashboard-shell` command script:

```
-blacklist " ^http[:][/][/]www[.]google[.]se"
```

Now, when you or the code attempts to navigate to this Google site, no security warning is presented to the user, but the browser doesn't navigate to the requested location. If you look at the hosted mode console after you try to navigate to a location on the blacklist, you see the output in figure 3.10.

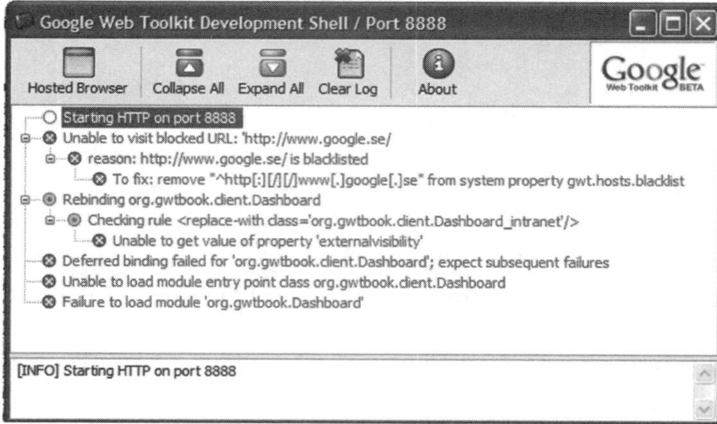

Figure 3.10 The output on the hosted-mode console if you try to navigate to a URL that is specifically included on the blacklist

-logLevel level

Running GWT hosted mode with default settings means that the logging level is set to `INFO`. You can alter this level by providing the `-logLevel` argument to the hosted-mode browser. Seven levels of logging are available:

- `ERROR`
- `WARN`
- `INFO`
- `TRACE`
- `DEBUG`
- `SPAM`
- `ALL`

The levels reside in a hierarchy the same as that in Log4J (see section 3.7.1). This means that if you set/leave the logging level at `INFO`, then all `INFO`, `WARN`, and `ERROR` messages are displayed; if it's set to `DEBUG`, then all `DEBUG`, `TRACE`, `INFO`, `WARN`, and `ERROR` messages are shown. This logging can be extensive; figure 3.11 shows logging set to `ALL` for the Dashboard application.

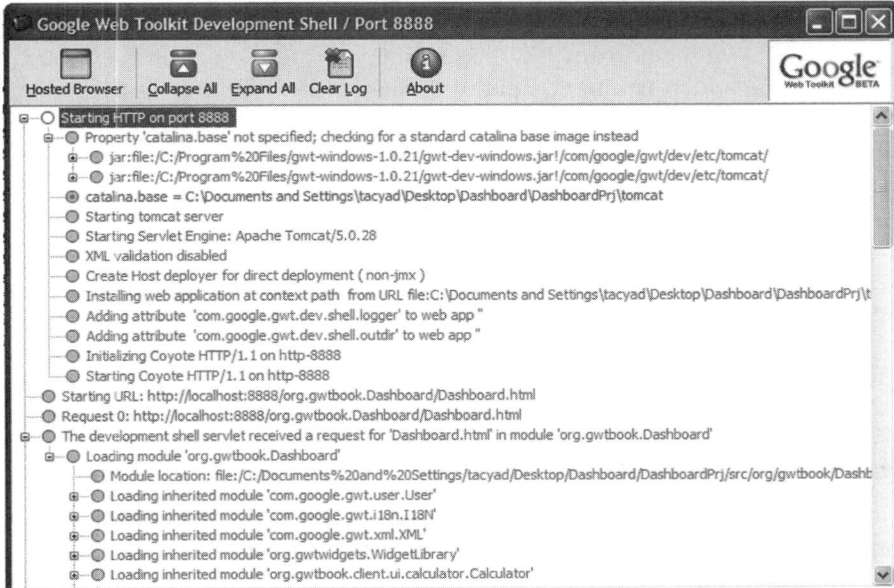

Figure 3.11 The detailed output that results when the full Dashboard project starts and the logging level is set to `ALL`

Setting the log level to `ALL` produces an extremely detailed log of exactly what the system is producing—it isn't likely that you'll use this level all the time, if at all. However, section 3.7.1 discusses how you hook into this logging mechanism for your code.

-gen "location"

This argument indicates the directory into which files produced by any GWT generators in your project are placed (so they can be reviewed at a later date if required). We cover GWT generators in detail in chapter 14.

-out "location"

Including the `-out` argument indicates to hosted mode that the files produced for the application should be stored in a particular directory (rather than the default location, which is the current user directory).

-style value

This argument alters the way in which the code is created. There are three options: `OBFUSCATED`, `PRETTY`, and `DETAILED`; each one alters the readability of any produced JavaScript code. Obfuscated code has a small size footprint but is effectively not readable, whereas detailed output contains as much information as the compiler can stuff in.

DON'T FORGET If you include any Java libraries in your development, then they need to be added to the classpath defined on the first line of the hosted-mode execution script. Otherwise, they won't be available to your code (this includes any libraries you're using for the client and server sides).

When this script is executed, hosted mode for the application is invoked, as you'll see in the next section.

TIP Although the arguments are normally added to the application's shell command script, if you're using an IDE such as Eclipse, then you need to add them to the launch configuration. In Eclipse, you do so by right-clicking the project, selecting Run As > Run, and then adding the arguments to the Arguments tab (see figure 3.13).

3.3.2 Running the Dashboard in hosted mode

Firing up the application in hosted mode from the command line is as simple as typing the following command in the root directory of the application (in this case, DashboardDir):

```
Dashboard-shell
```

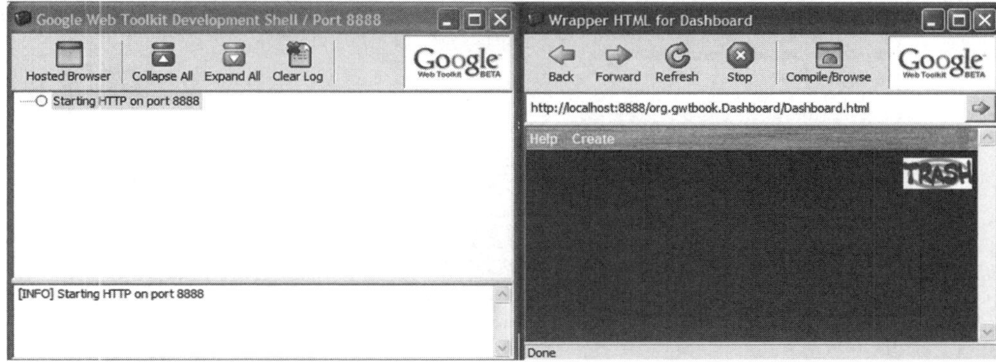

Figure 3.12 Dashboard application running in hosted mode. The left window is the hosted console, and the right is the hosted browser with the Dashboard application running.

After a short delay, two new windows open. The first is the hosted development controller, where you can examine any error messages, and so on; the second is the application. In the case of the Dashboard, you should see something resembling figure 3.12.

If you're using the Eclipse editor, then it's possible to launch the program from within Eclipse. To do so, run the project as a Java application. Right-click the project, and select Run As and then Java Application. The `projectCreator` tool created all the details Eclipse needs to know to run the program. To see this information in more detail, either look at the Dashboard.launch file or right-click and select Run; the dialog box in figure 3.13 opens. Clicking Run launches hosted mode from Eclipse, and you should see the same view as in figure 3.12 after a short startup delay.

There isn't a lot of testing you can do for the Dashboard, because at this time it doesn't do much. You can try the menus to confirm that you get back the message *Menu Item Clicked*, or change the locale to see the difference. Changing the locale is as simple as adding the text `?locale=sv` to the end of the URL and clicking Refresh. If you do this, assuming you made all the changes along with us, you should see the Swedish version of the page shown earlier in figure 3.5.

The other task you can perform in Stage 3 of the development is debugging the application. You'll do this through Eclipse in the next section.

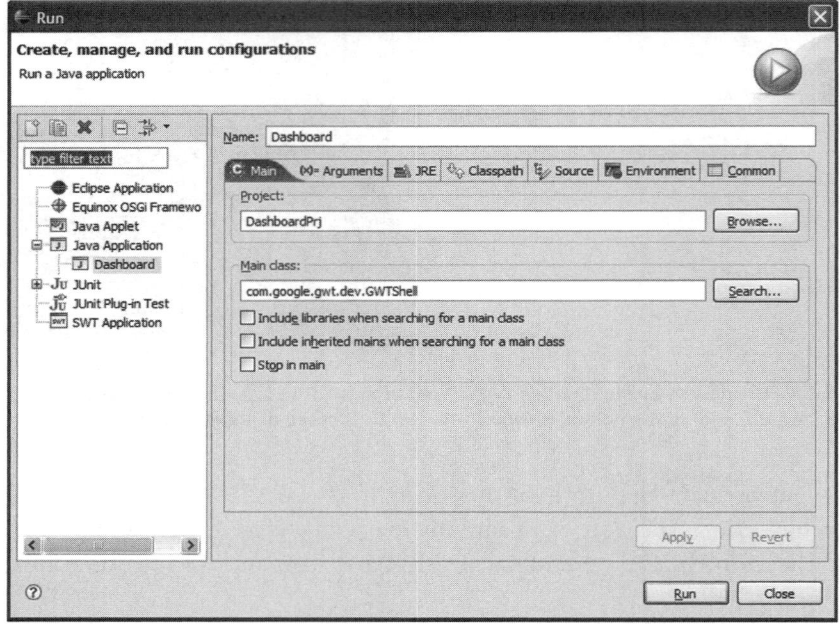

Figure 3.13 Running hosted mode from Eclipse by clicking the Run As option. This dialog box shows that the Java class to be executed is `com.google.gwt.dev.GWTShell`, which is part of the GWT system. Here, you can add to the classpath any libraries you're using (in the case, you aren't using any at this stage).

3.3.3 *Debugging the Dashboard in hosted mode through Eclipse*

Debugging in Eclipse works the same way as debugging any Java application (and this applies to both client and server [RPC] side code, although you haven't got any server-side code yet). Follow these steps to debug an application:

1. Set the breakpoints in the code where you wish the debugger to step in. Figure 3.14 shows a breakpoint set at the point where you display an alert to the screen when a user selects a menu option. This is indicated by the little blue ball in the left sidebar.
2. Execute the application in debug mode. In Eclipse, you do this in the same manner you did when launching hosted mode, except you select Debug As rather than Run As: Right-click the project in Package Explorer, select Debug As, and then select Java Application.

```
public class DummyCommand implements Command{
        /**
         * We are required to implement the execute() method.
         */
    public void execute() {
            Window.alert("Menu Item Clicked");
    }
}
```

Figure 3.14 Setting a breakpoint in the Eclipse IDE at the start of the `changeLabel()` method. To do so, click in the gray bar next to the `Window.alert()` command. Eclipse shows a little blue circle indicating that a breakpoint has been set.

3 When you execute the application in debug mode, the hosted browser is launched, and everything works as normal until you click the button. When you do, normal execution is suspended and the Eclipse debugger traps the execution point and presents the screen shown in figure 3.15.

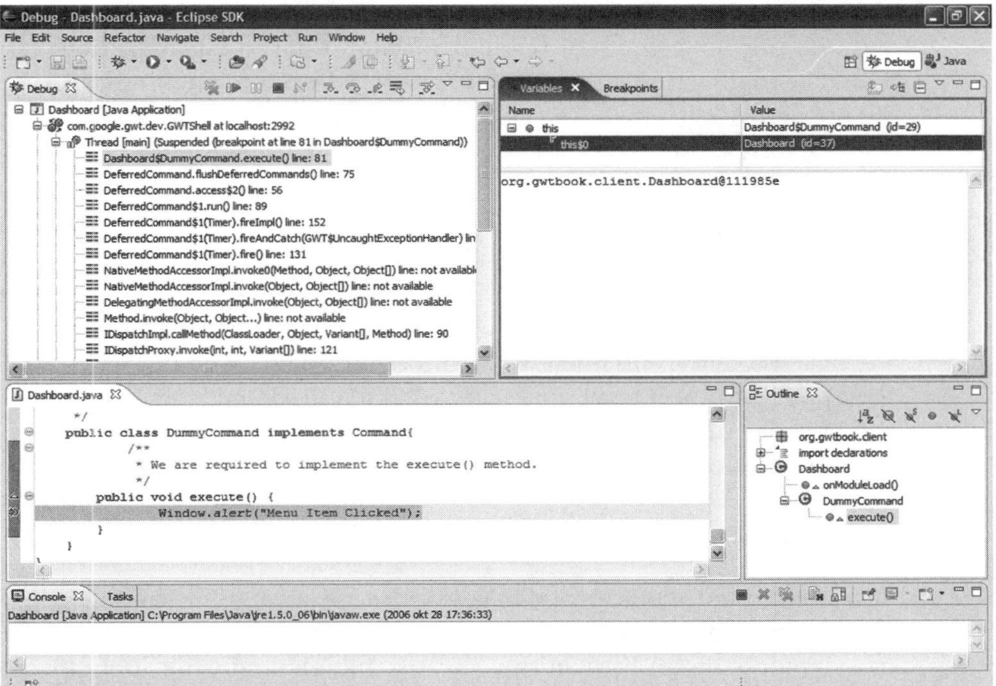

Figure 3.15 The view shown in the Eclipse debugger when the code reaches the breakpoint you previously set in figure 3.11.

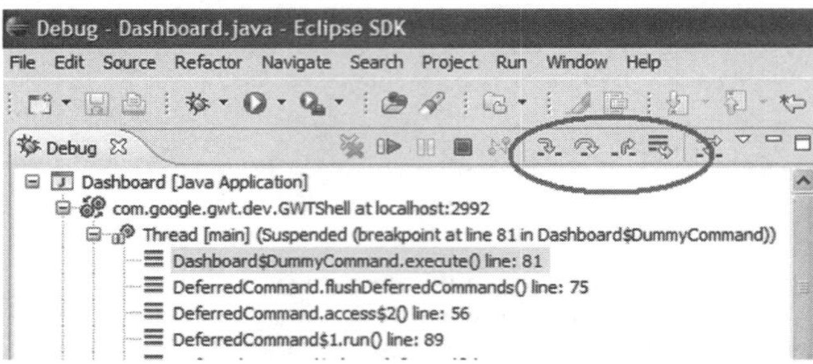

Figure 3.16 You can use the buttons on the debugger's toolbar to navigate throughout the code in debug mode. From left to right, the buttons are circled: Step Into, Step Over, Step Out, and Drop to Frame.

4 You can now step through and into the code using the navigation buttons at the top of the Debug window (see figure 3.16).

The debugger is immensely helpful when it comes to understanding the null pointer errors that seem to inevitably appear when you're building complicated applications (so far, you may have experienced them when you forgot to create objects (widgets and panels) before trying to use them—school child errors, yes; but with the debugger, they're quickly found. You can't imagine how difficult this would be to do by looking at the JavaScript code, not to mention ensuring it's consistent across all browser versions you would have to maintain in a non-GWT approach. It's also useful when you're using the more advanced techniques of remote procedure calling (RPC), where Java code is deployed onto a server. When you execute such applications through hosted mode, you can hook your debugger up to both client- and server-side code.

You're almost at the end of the development lifecycle for the first version of the Dashboard example. You created the project structure, replaced or amended the necessary files, and filled them with appropriate content. Then, you launched the application in hosted mode and tried a little debugging as well as setting up the basis for unit testing. Now, it's time to take the final step toward a complete GWT application and exercise it in web mode, where it runs for real.

3.4 Stage 4: Compiling the code

Whereas hosted mode provides you with a protected environment in which to perform system testing because the Java code is interpreted and can be debugged, in web mode the application runs for real. In web mode, the application has been compiled into the web technologies we discussed in chapter 1. No longer is the application Java code; you now have a number of JavaScript files (*permutations*, as they're called in GWT) for each browser and locale combination.

As you create more complex applications, including and managing different GWT properties, then the number of permutations will increase—the full Dashboard, for example, will come with an intranet and Internet version selected by setting an `externalvisibility` property. This means the permutation matrix space will cover browsers, locales, and external visibilities—luckily, GWT takes care of all that for you, as well as selecting the correct permutation to show the user.

The first step in executing the application in web mode is to compile the Java code. In chapter 17, we take a more detailed look at the functionality and outputs from the compilation process, but let's take a moment now to discuss how you invoke the compiler and see what the resulting files are.

3.4.1 Compiling the code/preparing for web mode

In web mode, an application is executed through a normal web browser; therefore, the GWT application needs to be compiled from Java to JavaScript before this happens. You perform compilation by executing the compilation script, which has also thoughtfully been created by the application-creator command. It's in the DashboardDir directory and is called `Dashboard-compile`. The contents of this default command look like:

```
@java -cp "%~dp0\src;%~dp0\bin;gwt-user.jar;gwt-dev-windows.jar"
      com.google.gwt.dev.GWTCompiler -out "%~dp0\www" %*
      org.gwtbook.Dashboard
```

DON'T FORGET Again, if you're including any Java libraries in your development, they must be added to the classpath defined on the first line of the compiler script. Otherwise, they won't be available to the compiler, and you'll get compilation errors.

The following sections describes the possible arguments to the compiler and what they mean:

-logLevel level

As with hosted mode, you can set the logging level used during the compilation process by providing the `-logLevel` argument to the compiler. The same seven levels of logging are available (`ERROR`, `WARN`, `INFO`, `TRACE`, `DEBUG`, `SPAM`, and `ALL`). The levels reside in the same hierarchy as for hosted mode.

-treeLogger

Passing the compiler the `-treeLogger` flag directs the compiler to produce its output in a standard GWT `TreeLogger` format in a new window (see figure 3.17).

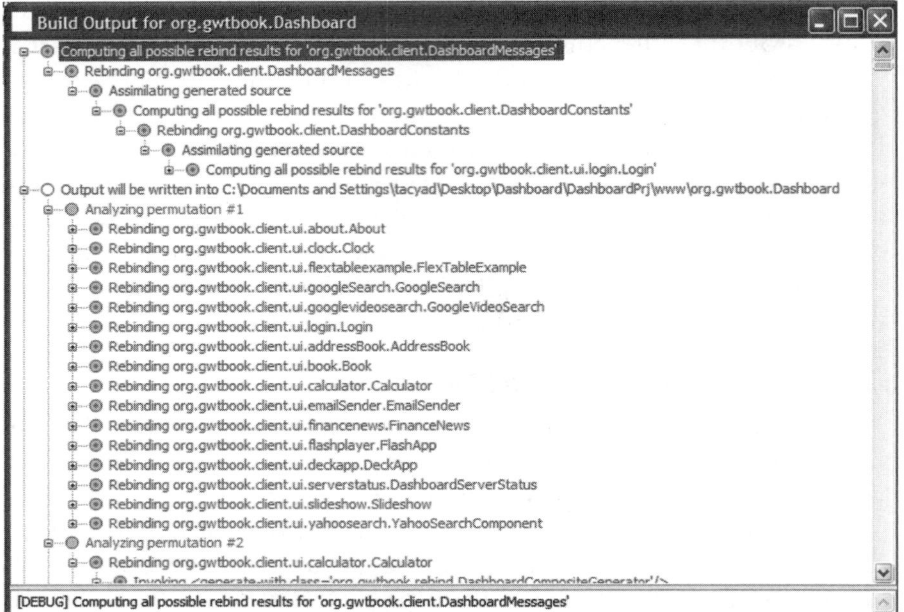

Figure 3.17 Setting the `treeLogger` flag for the GWT compiler causes it to produce its output in a new window in a tree style. You can then easily navigate and check the output of the compilation process.

-gen "location"

This argument indicates the directory into which files produced by any GWT generators that are in your project are placed (so they can be reviewed at a later date if required). We cover GWT generators in detail in chapter 14.

-out "location"

Including the `-out` argument indicates to the compiler that the output files produced for the application should be stored in a particular directory (rather than the default location, which is the current user directory).

-style value

This argument alters the way in which the code is created. There are three options: `OBFUSCATED`, `PRETTY`, and `DETAILED`; each one alters the readability of any produced JavaScript code. Obfuscated code has a small size footprint but is effectively not readable, whereas detailed output contains as much information as the compiler can stuff in.

For production-ready code, you'll probably prefer the small footprint size created by setting the style to OBFUSCATED. But in development, you may like to use PRETTY or DETAILED if you wish to look at the produced JavaScript code.

When the compiler is invoked, it takes the Java classes and translates them into a number of JavaScript files. Each JavaScript file (a permutation, in GWT parlance) represents a version of the application for each property value the application is concerned with. Normally, those properties are restricted to browser types and any internationalization that may be going on. In the case of the full Dashboard, you get 18 different permutations—one for each of the browsers, locales, and external visibility options. Let's look at the files that are produced.

NOTE The default values for heap size of the Java Virtual Machine (JVM) used for compilation aren't optimal, and you should consider changing them. In the authors' development environment, we add the arguments -Xms256m and -Xmx512m just before the -cp argument in the compiler scripts. This has the benefit of substantially speeding up compilation (on our machines, from around 15 minutes to just over 40 seconds!) and avoiding the potential for heap-size errors generated by the compilation process.

3.4.2 Viewing the compilation results

You perform compilation by executing the following command:

```
Dashboard-compile
```

When compilation has finished, your application is compiled into an org.mycompany.Dashboard directory under the DashboardDir/www/ directory (which is created if it doesn't already exist). Figure 3.18 shows a typical subset of the files produced for the Dashboard application.

We discuss these files in more detail in later chapters; for now, we can say that the XML files correspond directly to the HTML files with the same name—they list the decisions made by the GWT compiler when generating the permutations of code. For example, the XML file named 127D3E5E8741F096957AE332A38198D0.xml contains the rebind decisions shown here that indicate the 127D3E5E8741-F096957AE332A38198D0.nocache.html file is specifically the version for the Opera browser when the application is using the Swedish locale:

```
<rebind-decision
   in="org.gwtbook.client.DashboardConstants"
   out="org.gwtbook.client.DashboardConstants_sv"/>
<rebind-decision
   in="com.gootgle.gwt.user.client.impl.DOMImpl"
   out="com.google.gwt.user.client.impl.DOMImplOpera"/>
```

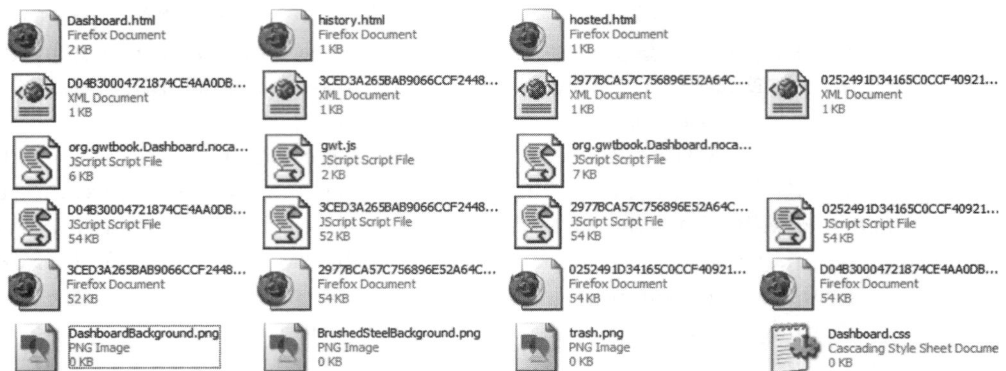

Figure 3.18 The output of compiling the Dashboard GWT application for web mode. You can see three HTML files that form the framework for the application. A number of XML files detail the choices made by the compiler for several permutations, followed by a similar number of HTML and JavaScript files (whose names match the previous HTML files). The remaining files are the image and style-sheet resources.

(The file names are based on MD5 hashing, so it's unlikely that you'll have exactly the same filenames. The conceptual link between the XML and HTML files will still exist and be valid.)

We cover the process of compilation in chapter 17. For now, you have a compiled application, and it's time to deploy that code.

3.5 Stage 5: Deploying the code

Once the application has been compiled, you can take the next step to execute it in web mode, by deploying it to your favorite web server. We cover deployment in detail in chapter 16 because the more complicated your application becomes, the more complicated deployment can be. For now, you can perform a simple deployment because you have no server-side code.

NOTE When you have server-side code (in Java), then you need to ensure that you create a web.xml file that details the services you're deploying to the servlet engine (in hosted mode, this is all automatically done for you). Even if you include your service endpoints (see chapters 10–14) in the GWT module XML file (see chapter 9), you still need to create a web.xml file for them to be visible to your web-mode deployment.

3.5.1 Deploying to a web server

We developed the examples for this book with the Apache web server as the target, and in that case deploying this example was as simple as copying across the files in the compilation directory to the web server's root directory (or, if you prefer, a specific folder under the root directory). If you want to save space on the deployment, then you don't need all the XML files we previously discussed, because they're only used by the compiler to keep track of where it is.

If you don't have a web server, we recommend that you get one. Apache is free, runs on most systems, and is simple to use in a basic way (if you only ever use client-side code, then you can use the basic Apache HTTP server from http://httpd.apache.org/; but if you use GWT RPC server-side code or other Java-based server code, then Apache Tomcat is a better idea (http://tomcat.apache.org/). On those occasions where your application uses only client-side code, you can "deploy" to the filesystem.

3.5.2 Deploying to a filesystem

If you don't have a web server, or you want to make a quick check of functionality in browsers, then you can still "deploy" this version of the Dashboard, because most operating systems allow you to double-click the Dashboard.html file in the compilation folder. The limitations of this approach are that you can't execute any server-related code—for example, if you try this for the full Dashboard example in the downloadable code, you'll receive an error notification because the code can't call the server to retrieve the XML file necessary for the Bookmark menu.

This limitation isn't significant—especially if you want to check some functionality quickly. If you want to always deploy to a server, it's worth taking the extra effort and using Maven or Ant to build automatic packaging and deployment tasks that greatly reduce your effort of deploying to a server.

This is a basic deployment. In chapter 16, we'll go into detail on the subject of deployment. After the application has been deployed, it's time to run it.

3.6 Stage 6: Running in web mode

Running the application in web mode is a case of navigating to the correct URL on your web server. The final result of the Dashboard application that you're been building in this chapter can be seen in figure 3.19 (running on the Opera browser).

If you have errors at this phase, they're probably related to the deployment you just performed. You'll normally take a good look at the deployment to identify where it has gone wrong.

To round off the discussion of the application, we'll discuss adding logging capability to check on the progress of the application as it executes.

Figure 3.19 The Dashboard application in web mode in the Opera browser. Any of the supported browsers can be used for web mode; we chose Opera because we normally use Firefox and wanted to see the application in another browser.

3.7 Implementing application logging

Logging information is useful both for tracing errors and for understanding service workloads. Modern logging frameworks make for a flexible, and often light, approach to capturing in-process information for applications. However, logging for a web application is an interesting topic; for a start, what do you log—and more important, where do you store logs?

With a non-Ajax approach, such as Struts used in a pure way, every action on the screen results in server calls and a redrawing of the web page, which means you can log every action the user makes—but you're hoping to get many thousands of visitors per hour, and logging all of their activities could generate substantial logs that are unwieldy.

Ajax complicates the last approach slightly, because a lot more functionality occurs on the user's machine, meaning there is potentially not as much client-server communication. However, a web application doesn't get access to the user's filesystem for security reasons, so you can't store log files there. How is this logging issue solved in GWT?

3.7.1 Logging information on the client-side

If you're a JavaScript developer coming to GWT, used to the extensive logging needed in that language to understand errors, then chances are you'll look for, and perhaps become frustrated with, the client-side logging capabilities offered by GWT. But—and this is a key point—you should move your mindset toward using the much more powerful Java debuggers available to you now instead of relying on output messages and log statements.

Typically, you should rely heavily on the GWT compiler; but in rare cases, issues occur in the JavaScript code. To debug these, your best chance is to ensure that the code is compiled in detailed or pretty mode (by supplying the -style DETAILED or PRETTY flag to the compiler) and then adding debug statements to the human-readable JavaScript code (you'll rarely need to do this).

If you're a Java developer and used to frameworks such as Log4J, then you too may be slightly disappointed. GWT has limited capability for client-side logging: the only built-in client-side logging capability for web mode is the `Window.alert()` method, which isn't that user friendly; in hosted mode, this is only slightly improved by the addition of a log method in the GWT class.

However, as we discussed earlier, if you're logging for information purposes, there is limited benefit in client-side logging for an Ajax application (inability to access those logs). If you're logging for the purpose of debugging, then the `GWT.log()` method can help identify where issues may be occurring, but the real power comes from the debugging capability of your IDE.

Other frameworks/toolsets provide more comprehensive JavaScript logging on the client side, but this is because they're unable to be debugged like GWT is in Java. One that we've used, for example, is provided by the Yahoo UI Widgets. Figure 3.20 shows the logger from this toolkit.

Many times, you may wish to use logging in other frameworks/toolkits because it's useful to debug errors, identify uninstantiated objects, and confirm that you're

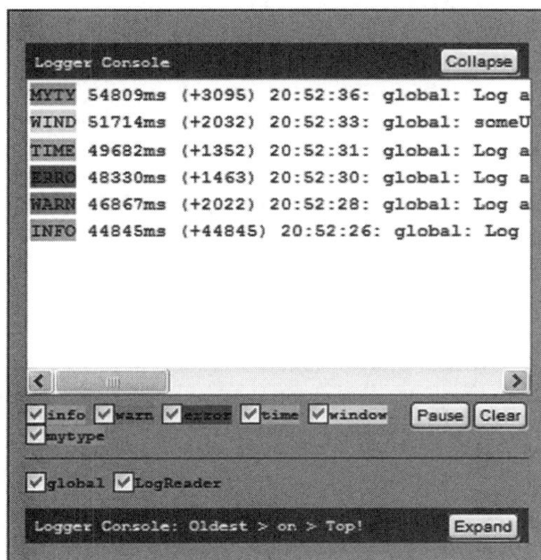

Figure 3.20
Client-side logging capabilities provided by the Yahoo UI widget framework. GWT doesn't provide such extensive client-side logging capabilities, but that is related to the philosophy of being able to use Java IDE and debuggers rather than trying to fix issues by reading logs from running programs.

calling valid methods. Remember that when you're writing GWT programs, you're writing your code in Java, and you can use the power of your IDE's debugger to capture all these issues.

Sometimes, you may wish to get notification that your code is following particular paths while you're developing code, and you may not want to always invoke the IDE's debugger (or you may even be developing without an IDE). In this case, GWT provides a basic logging capability (but it's only valid in hosted mode). You can use the `GWT.log()` method to output messages to the hosted mode console.

In your code, place the logging messages where you wish, and GWT duly prints them to the hosted browser window as required. For example, if you add logging to the Dashboard example's `onModuleLoad()` method, then when you execute the Dashboard in hosted mode, you see the view shown in figure 3.21.

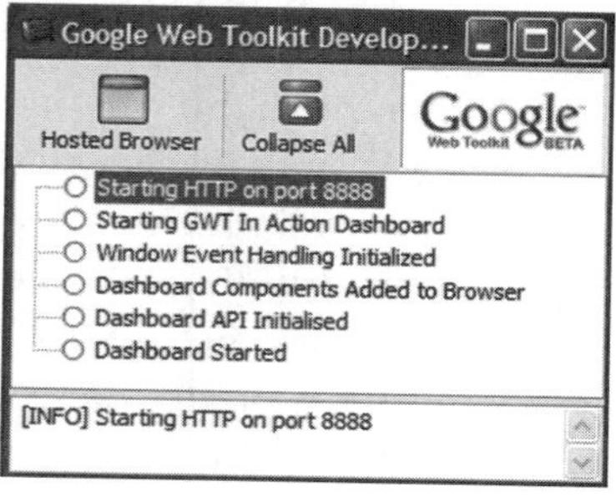

Figure 3.21 Using GWT's basic log capability, `GWT.log()`, to display log messages in the hosted browser window when the Dashboard application executes

You can add this logging capability to the `onModuleLoad()` method using the code shown in listing 3.12.

Listing 3.12 Updating the Dashboard's `onModuleLoad()` method to log basic runtime information

```
public void onModuleLoad(){
   GWT.log("Starting GWT In Action Dashboard",null);

   // Create Dashboard Name EditableLabel
   // Create Menu System
   // Create Trash Icon
   // Set up window event handling

   GWT.log("Window Event Handling Initialized",null);

   // Add components to the browser

   GWT.log("Dashboard Components Added to Browser",null);

   //Start API listening

   GWT.log("Dashboard API Initialised",null);
   GWT.log("Dashboard Started",null);
}
```

Using the `GWT.log()` method means deciding which of the two arguments to pass in (you can pass only one argument; the other must be null). The first argument is plain text and is the approach you use in the Dashboard. The second argument is an object that is an instance of the `Throwable` object—a GWT exception.

Finally, if you want to implement a logging system on the client side for web mode, you can wrap an existing JavaScript logging framework—for example, Log4-JavaScript (http://log4javascript.sourceforge.net/) with some JavaScript Native Interface (JSNI) and then access it through that (we talk about wrapping JavaScript libraries more in chapter 8). However, if you've followed a development lifecycle that only uses web mode as the last stage, then there is limited benefit from client-side logging a GWT application. You can use a basic approach to client-side logging in web mode and put your messages on the screen using the JavaScript alert functionality, but again, this is useful only if you have an error that appears in your compiled code and not Java code—which should be rare.

Of much more use and interest is logging on the server side.

3.7.2 Logging information on the server-side

Logging on the server side is much more open than on the client side, and you're free to choose the most familiar/useful framework. If your server-side code is Java, then a good recommendation is to base your logging on an approach such as Log4J from the Apache Foundation. Because there are no restrictions on the Java used on server-side code, this recommendation fits well for RPC- and J2EE-based approaches.

If you're using other languages, then you can find implementations of Log4J for them, too, such as Log4PHP (http://logging.apache.org/log4php/) or Log4Perl (http://log4perl.sourceforge.net/). The scope of these logging packages is worth chapters of their own, but we focus on GWT rather than logging in this book. For more information about this type of logging, we recommend starting with the Log4J documentation (http://logging.apache.org/log4j/docs/manual.html).

You've seen that it's possible to perform logging on both the client and server side, but that in a web application, true logging is best performed on the server side. Logging on the client side to debug code isn't necessary with GWT because you should develop in Java in an IDE that reduces errors on the client side to functional misunderstandings.

That's it for logging, and for now, it's time to take a well-deserved break and grab some coffee; you've reached the end of building your first application. After your coffee, we'll look at the basics of GWT while building up to the more complicated version of the Dashboard.

3.8 Summary

Congratulations—that's it. You've taken the first run through the whole development lifecycle of a real GWT application, and you've run the first version of the *GWT in Action* Dashboard application! Over the coming chapters, we'll expand on all the concepts we've talked about in the last two chapters and examine how the full Dashboard example was built. Figure 3.22 shows a schematic of the Dashboard, identifying the components you'll build over the next four chapters, including `ToggleMenuItem`, `EditableLabel`, `DashboardComposite`, and `DashboardPanel` (in which `DashboardComposites` sit).

If you haven't seen GWT before, then these last two chapters have taken you through the development lifecycle to the point that you're in possession of a working GWT application that includes some aspects of styling and internationalization. We'll build on the foundations laid down in this chapter throughout this book as you continue to construct the Dashboard application.

You should take away two key points from chapters 2 and 3. First, GWT is flexible in terms of how you create and build an application. We feel that at the moment, the smoothest way to develop a GWT application is to use the GWT command-line creation tools with the `-eclipse` parameter and then import the application into Eclipse for development. As time progresses, the plug-ins for the other IDEs will improve, and they should become the preferred way of creating GWT applications; but we aren't there yet.

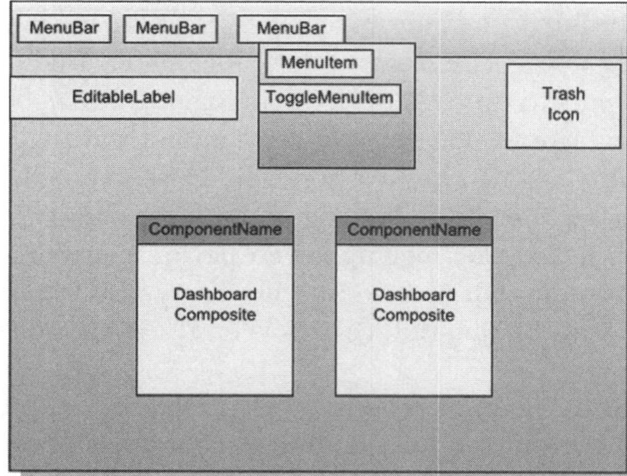

Figure 3.22
The design of the Dashboard application and the various components that are used. We'll discuss most of these components over the next few chapters.

Second, the GWT creation tools always create the default application, and if you don't at a minimum change the application's Java file, then you'll get the default application displayed in hosted and/or web mode. Just adding your own Java files achieves nothing, unless you alter the main Java file for the application.

Creating applications is a straightforward process as long as you remember several key points:

- Java code used on the client side must comply with the requirements of Java 1.4 (not the later versions).
- Any libraries that you wish to include on the client side must also comply with the GWT Java requirements, and you must have the source code available because that is what the GWT compiler uses to create the JavaScript.
- If you use any Java libraries, then they need to be added to the hosted and web modes' classpaths in the respective command-line scripts.

We've reached the conclusion of part 1 of the trail. If you look back over your shoulder, in the distance you see the land of Ajax, with all its cross-browser scripting problems and issues over maintaining several versions of JavaScript for the same applications. In front of you lies the world of GWT, where all those issues are significantly reduced.

There is still a tricky trail to follow to complete the Dashboard, but you've taken the first steps by defining the basic structure. In the next part of this book, you'll learn the basics of GWT: the core user interface components. We'll look at widgets, panels, events, composite widgets, and JSNI components as we ready you for building the UI parts of the full Dashboard.

Part 2

Building user interfaces

Part 1 introduced you to the fundamentals of building and compiling your GWT application. This part of the book explores the user-interface components that you'll use to create your GWT applications. We'll begin with an introduction to GWT's widgets and panels and then discuss event-handling and creating composite widgets. Next, we'll explain how to use the JavaScript Native Interface to interact with JavaScript code external to the GWT application. This part of the book concludes by showing you how to wrap your GWT module as a reusable library for other GWT applications.

4 Working with widgets

This chapter covers

- How widgets work
- Using GWT's widgets
- Interacting with widgets
- Creating new widgets

Now that you've wet your toes by building the first version of the Dashboard application, you'll take the next few steps toward building the full version, which uses many different types of widgets and panels as well as handling different types of events. To get there, we first need to tell you exactly what these components are!

This chapter deals specifically with *widgets*, which are the visible components of a GWT application that a user sees on the browser page: for example buttons, labels, images, and the menu system. Imagine buying a new plasma television and then finding out that the manufacturer hasn't provided any control buttons or a remote. This is what your application would be like without widgets: useless.

DEFINITION *Widgets* are the visible components of a GWT application that a user can see on the browser page.

Over this and the next five chapters, we'll cover some of the basics of GWT to get you into a position to fully understand how the Dashboard is constructed. Along the way, you'll build a few of the necessary components for the Dashboard. These chapters cover the concepts shown in table 4.1.

Table 4.1 The five chapters involved in covering the GWT basics of widgets, panels, events, composite widgets, and using the JavaScript Native Interface (JSNI)

Chapter	Component covered	Details
4	Widgets	Widgets are the visible components of a GWT application that the user sees on the screen: buttons, labels, menu bars, and so on. You'll build two widgets used in the Dashboard: `PNGImage` and `ToggleMenuItem`.
5	Panels	Panels help you structure the view on the screen; they can be used to position (with panels such as `VerticalPanel`) and manage the visibility of widgets (with panels such as `DeckPanel`). You'll construct the `DashboardContainer` panel, which holds all the Dashboard component applications you'll build later in the book.
6	Events	Functionality in GWT is driven by events: for example, when a user clicks a button, when a form submission returns, or when the user drops a component they have been dragging. You'll extend the `DashboardContainer` from chapter 5 to handle double-click and focus events.

Table 4.1 The five chapters involved in covering the GWT basics of widgets, panels, events, composite widgets, and using the JavaScript Native Interface (JSNI) ***(continued)***

Chapter	Component covered	Details
7	Composite widgets	Combining all the power of the last three chapters, we finally come to composite widgets. These are widgets made up of other widgets, usually placed in one or more different panels; they're the most powerful form of component you can create. You'll build the `EditableLabel` composite and the `Dashboard-Composite` object, which are used in the Dashboard.
8	JavaScript Native Interface (JSNI)	JSNI affords you access to native JavaScript. You can think of it in a similar manner to using assembly language code in a C program. Chapter 8 discusses the appropriate places to use JSNI and how you can wrap existing third-party JavaScript libraries for use in the GWT programs.

As we've said, this chapter covers widgets, and we'll start by looking at what widgets are. Next, we'll take a quick look at the widgets that come standard with GWT, including how to use them in the components of the Dashboard.

In the second part of this chapter, you'll learn how to create your own widgets, just in case those provided as standard aren't enough or don't meet your needs. In that discussion, you'll build a `PNGImage` widget to allow you to use PNG images in the Dashboard (within GWT 1.3, the `Image` widget doesn't properly support transparency of PNG images in all browsers, so you have to build your own widget to do this). You'll also extend the `MenuItem` widget so that it meets the Dashboard application's needs. If you're ready, then we'll jump in and define what a widget is.

4.1 What is a widget?

Widgets are one of four fundamental building blocks of GWT applications—the others being panels, events, server communication (including remote procedure calling [RPC], Form submission, JavaScript Object Notation [JSON], and XML handling, as well as the traditional Asynchronous JavaScript and XML [Ajax] `XMLHttpRequest`). When a user fires up your GWT application, they're looking at a set of widgets that have been positioned by panels and that react to events. Widgets, just like the buttons on the plasma television remote control we mentioned earlier, are the components the user interacts with. Luckily, GWT provides many different widgets for free, and these include the usual suspects: buttons (such as the one shown in figure 4.1), text boxes, and menus.

Click me

Figure 4.1 Button widget shown as rendered HTML in the Firefox browser

Most applications are built using multiple widgets, which you put in panels to provide some structure—this is obvious if you look at the Dashboard's Calculator component application (see figure 4.2).

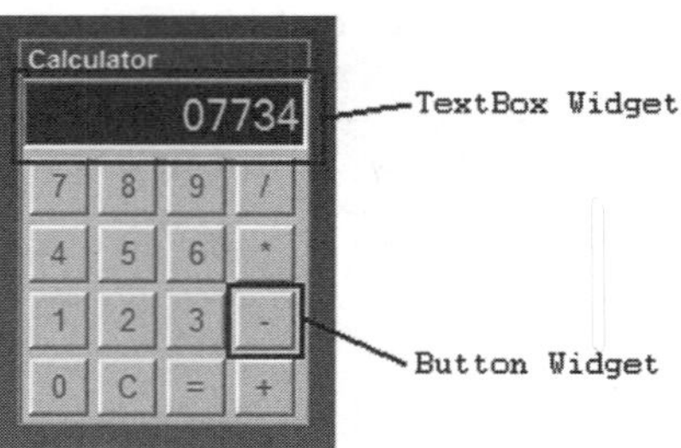

Figure 4.2 Calculator application from the Dashboard, showing how a number of widgets can be put together to create a complete application

Widgets, as well as panels, which we'll look at in the next chapter, have a dual existence in GWT: You can think of them as both Java objects and DOM elements. The Java object view is the one you use in day-to-day programming to create applications. The DOM view is the view that the Java objects from your program have when you think of them in the context of what is displayed in the web browser. You'll look at both of these views in the next two sections, starting with the Java object view of widgets.

4.1.1 Using widgets as Java objects

The purpose of GWT is to develop rich Internet applications once, in Java, and then have the GWT compiler generate the HTML and JavaScript necessary for the application to work in a variety of different browsers. To achieve this, you must have a way of representing various browser objects, which GWT calls *widgets,* in the Java programs.

This approach takes advantage of the object-oriented programming world's ability to model objects and concepts as programming objects. For example, in a GWT program, you can happily use a Java object called `Button`. This `Button` object models various properties that you expect a button to have, such as being able to set the visible text and click the button. You can model all the components you wish to see in a browser—the widgets—as Java objects with methods and properties.

During your everyday programming use of GWT, you'll consider all widgets in their natural Java object form. The button we mentioned in this section's introduction is created by calling the constructor of the GWT Java `Button` class as follows:

```
Button theButton = new Button("Click Me");
```

This code creates a new GWT button Java object on which you can then execute various class methods. The tasks shown in table 4.2 are typical operations you can perform on a GWT `Button` widget.

Table 4.2 Functionality that results from applying some Java `Button` class methods to the Java `Button` object

Code	Description
`theButton.setStyleName("buttonStyle");`	Sets the Cascading Style Sheet (CSS) class name for the button. A corresponding entry should be found in the CSS style sheet attached to the web document, although its name must be prefixed with a period: for example, `.buttonStyle{…}`.

`theButton.addClickListener(`
`new ClickListener(){`
`   public void onClick(Widget sender){`
`   }`
`});`
	Adds a `ClickListener` (an event listener that specifically listens for mouse click events) to the button. When the button is clicked, the code in the `onClick()` method defined in the `ClickListener` is executed.

`theButton.setText("Go on, click me");`	Changes the text shown on the button from the original Click Me to "Go on, click me".
`theButton.setVisible(false);`	Hides the button on the web browser so that it's no longer visible.

The Java view of widgets is straightforward to anyone familiar with writing Java programs or using similar high-level object based language; you create objects from classes and call methods that those classes have. What the Java view doesn't give you is an understanding of how these widgets are displayed on a web page. That is provided by the widget's alternative DOM representation.

4.1.2 Considering widgets as DOM elements

The Java representation of the widget you've just seen works great in the Java code and allows you to build GWT applications as you want, using any number of widgets and using their associated methods to build the functionality. However, you can't display these Java objects in a web browser, so you don't yet have an Ajax application. This is where the alternative DOM representation of widgets comes in.

The Document Object Model (DOM) is the browser's view of the web page you see. You can access and alter the DOM using a variety of languages, and the effects of most manipulations are immediately visible on the current browser page. Manipulations can include adding or removing elements, hiding or making elements visible, or changing their location. In the case of GWT, this manipulation is eventually performed through JavaScript in the compiled code; but in your program, you use Java. Next, we'll look at how to bridge that gap.

All GWT widgets have an alternative DOM representation that is built in parallel with the Java object. The Java constructor is generally responsible for creating this DOM representation; if you look at the detail of the constructor for the `Button` class, you see the following definition:

```
public Button() {
   super(DOM.createButton());
   adjustType(getElement());
   setStyleName("gwt-Button");
}
```

The call to `DOM.createButton()` creates the DOM element `<button>` through the GWT DOM classes. Also, in the constructor of the parent, the `setElement()` method is called to set the widget's Java class DOM representation to this new `<button>` element. Using this value set by the `setElement()` method, you get access to the DOM representation from the Java view (to do so, you use the `getElement()` method). If you were to look at the DOM representation of a GWT Java button, you would see that it looks like this:

```
<button class="gwt-Button"
        eventbits="7041"
        onchange="null"
        onload="null"
        onerror="null">
      Click me
</button>
```

This is the standard DOM representation of a `<button>` object with a couple of additional GWT-specific attributes. These additional attributes (`eventbits`, `onload`, and so on) are set by the object's Java constructor when this DOM representation is created. Don't be confused by the name of the first attribute, `class`; this refers to the CSS styling that can be applied to a widget, rather than the Java class name of the widget.

The next attribute, `eventBits`, is one that occurs in many widgets. It indicates to GWT what type of events are listened to (*sunk*) by that particular widget; we'll go into this in more detail in chapter 6, but it will keep popping up in examples until we get there. A widget sinks browser events that it's interested in handling.

One golden rule that applies to this DOM representation is that you shouldn't rely on the fact that a particular widget is implemented as a particular DOM element, because nothing stops future implementations of widgets from being represented using different DOM elements than previous versions. By focusing your programming efforts on the Java code view using the methods provided by each GWT widget class to perform functionality, you protect yourself against possible future changes at the DOM level. As a rule, you should need to access the DOM in your applications only on rare occasions, if ever.

Now that you know what a widget is and how it's represented both in Java and the DOM, we'll take a quick tour of the widgets that are available as part of the GWT distribution.

4.2 The standard GWT widgets

The standard GWT distribution comes with a wide range of widgets for use in applications. These widgets cover the types of areas you would expect: buttons, text boxes, so on. However, some widgets you may expect are missing—for example, progress bars and sliders, although you'll build one of them in chapter 7.

In the set of widgets, the designers of GWT have implemented a strong hierarchy of Java classes in order to provide an element of consistency across widgets where that consistency naturally exists. Take the `TextBox`, `TextArea`, and `PasswordTextBox` widgets; it isn't unreasonable to expect them to share certain properties. GWT recognizes this fact and captures the common properties in a `TextBoxBase` class, which these three widgets inherit. To get a snapshot of this hierarchy, cast your eye over figure 4.3.

You can see in this hierarchy that all widgets ultimately inherit from the `UIObject` class, which contains a number of essential housekeeping and property aspects. In the `UIObject` class, you'll find the `setElement()` method, which we discussed previously regarding its use to set the physical link between a widget's Java object and DOM views. Subclasses of `UIObject` must call this method as the *first* thing they do before any other methods are called, to ensure that the link to a `Browser` element is established.

NOTE All GWT widgets inherit from the `UIObject` class. This class provides a common set of methods and attributes for all widgets, including setting size, visibility, and style names, as well as providing the link between the Java and DOM representations.

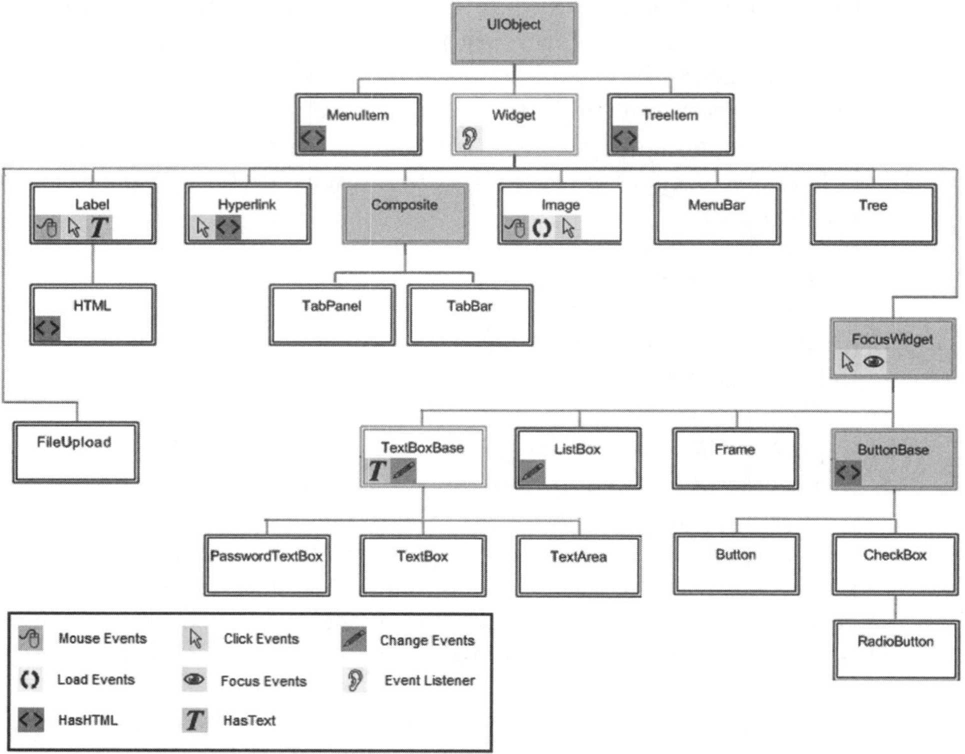

Figure 4.3 GWT widget class hierarchy, showing the widgets from GWT 1.3 (more widgets are added continuously in new releases, but looking at GWT 1.3 widgets shows the hierarchy in a nice, succinct manner), also indicating the types of event listeners that can be registered against each widget and whether they have text and/or HTML associated with them

We won't go through all the methods in the `UIObject` class, but we'll highlight the typical functionality you can expect all widgets to inherit. The `UIObject` class provides access to a wide range of DOM functionality without your having to access the DOM directly. For example you can set the height of a GWT `UIObject` using the `setHeight()` method, which in turn uses the `setStyleAttribute()` method from the DOM class:

```
public void setHeight(String height) {
   DOM.setStyleAttribute(element, "height", height);
}
```

The other methods written in this style include the ability to set the width, title (what is displayed when a mouse hovers over an element), and both width and height at the same time through the `setSize()` method. All these methods take `Strings` as parameters, such as `setSize("100px","200px")`. Meanwhile, the `set-PixelSize()` method allows integers, such as `setPixelSize(100,200)`. Although these methods for setting style attributes are available, we recommend that styling generally be performed using CSS. This is because it allows a nice separation between functional code and how the application looks (and it also lets you hand off to the design department to style the application they way they do best).

After `UIObject`, all widgets (except `TreeItem` and `MenuItem`) must inherit from the `Widget` class; it provides widgets with their widget-ness, including the methods that are called when a widget is attached or detached from a panel. This class also contains the default implementation of the `onBrowserEvent()` method, which lets a widget manage any events it has sunk (you'll see this in action in chapter 6).

In the next section, we'll look briefly at some of the widgets you get for free with the GWT distribution as well as how you'll use them in the Dashboard application. We won't aim to talk about all the widgets, because the set is growing with each new GWT release; those we'll cover are shown in figure 4.4.

As we discuss the widgets in this chapter, we'll include simple code showing their use and point out where in the Dashboard application you use them. This code may look a little alien in some places; don't worry, we haven't introduced most of the concepts used in the code yet, because they come in the next few chapters, but in most cases you should be able to see what is happening.

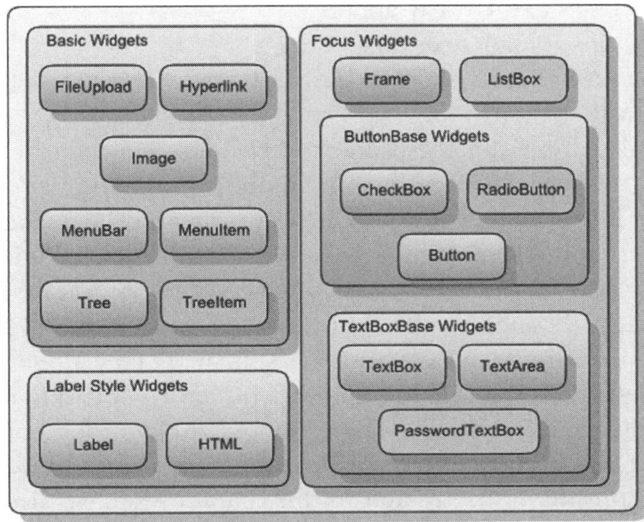

Figure 4.4 Summary of widgets included in GWT, indicating how they will be grouped and discussed in this chapter

There are a couple of principles to bear in mind as you read the next few sections. First, this isn't intended to be a complete walkthrough of the GWT API for widgets; to do that would border on the excessively boring. Instead, we'll try to show some of the key methods and pitfalls, as well as where you use the methods in the Dashboard application, so you can look in the code. In general, where a `getter` method is used, such as `getText()`, the GWT API provides the appropriate `setter` method too (`setText()`). Finally, we often don't include names or number of parameters for a method, unless it's really necessary; this allows us to write a book focused on what can be done without getting bogged down in details. The online GWT API reference (`http://code.google.com/webtoolkit/documentation/gwt.html`) is an invaluable source of help for the details, as is the use of a good IDE.

We'll break the discussion of widgets into the following five main categories of widgets shown in figure 4.4: basic, label style, focus, ButtonBase, and TextBox-Base. Let's start by looking at basic widgets.

4.2.1 Interacting with the basic widgets

We define the basic widgets as those that inherit directly from the `Widget` class. There are five of these widgets which we'll briefly consider next in the context of the Dashboard application you're building. Sometimes we'll also show a code sample in isolation to emphasize a particular point or property.

Uploading files with the FileUpload widget

The `FileUpload` widget acts as a GWT wrapper to the standard browser file-upload text box—the one you use to let the user upload a file from their machine to your server. (See figure 4.5.)

Figure 4.5 The `FileUpload` widget

Remember that this is only the client-side component—clicking the Browse button allows the user to select a file on their computer through the standard File Search dialog box, but it doesn't let you save a file to your server. That takes a little more work. This widget should be embedded in a form that has its encoding set to multipart. When ready, you submit the form to your server to process the uploading of the file selected (an example of this functionality is provided in the `FileUploadServlet` class in the server package of the Dashboard). This widget doesn't provide any server-side code to handle file upload; you have to provide that, but you're free to do so in your favorite server-side language. We'll look at such a `FileUpload` widget in more detail when we discuss server-side components in chapter 12; we'll also consider it briefly later in this chapter when we discuss how to build widgets.

NOTE Because your GWT application becomes JavaScript code, access to files falls under the same restrictions as JavaScript. This means no direct saving of files to a user's machines; and the only way to access files on a user's machine is to use the `FileUpload` widget.

The `FileUpload` widget is one of the most inconsistently implemented widgets across browsers; different browsers allow differing security restrictions and abilities to style it. Most browsers, for example, won't let you set the default value of the text box because that would allow a web application to go fishing for files. As with all widgets, remember that if you can't do something with the widget in HTML and JavaScript, then you can't do it in GWT. GWT only provides a `getFilename()` method that retrieves the filename selected by a user. Don't confuse this method with the `getName()` and `setName()` methods, which are used to set the DOM name of the `FileUpload` widget.

But enough of file uploading until chapter 12. We'll now continue looking at some of the other basic widgets that GWT provides.

Navigating your application with hyperlinks

The `Hyperlink` widget acts as an internal hyperlink in your GWT application. To the user, it looks exactly like a normal hyperlink on the web page; when they click it, they expect navigation to occur in the application. This action is usually coded as manipulating the GWT `History` object to change the application state—you can see how this works in the Dashboard's `Slideshow` application (`org.gwtbook.client.ui.slideshow.Slideshow`). The application has two hyperlinks at the bottom, as shown in figure 4.6, which enable the user to move the slideshow to the start or the end.

Figure 4.6 Two `Hyperlink` widgets (Start and End) in action at the bottom of the Slideshow Dashboard application

Any component that uses a `Hyperlink` widget should also extend the `HistoryListener` interface and implement the `onHistoryChange()` method to catch and manage clicks the hyperlinks. As you can see, the Dashboard's `Slideshow` component implements two hyperlinks, which can be found in the code as follows:

```
Hyperlink startLink = new Hyperlink("Start","0");        ❶
Hyperlink endLink = new Hyperlink("End",""+(maxNumberImages-1));    ❷
```

Each `Hyperlink` widget constructor comprises two elements: the text to be displayed on the screen and a history token (which can be any arbitrary string). In the Slideshow's case, all the history tokens represent numbers of a picture, starting at 0 for the first and ending at the maximum number of images in the slideshow minus one. It's easy to have a hyperlink that points to the start and end of the slideshow by using the appropriate values in the `Hyperlink` constructor—"0" for the start (as shown in ❶) and the string representation of the largest image number (as shown in ❷).

When you're using GWT `History`, remember to include the following line in the body of your HTML page:

```
<iframe id="__gwt_historyFrame"
        style="width:0;height:0;border:0">
</iframe>
```

Failure to include the history frame will result in errors, because it's used in GWT's approach to storing and retrieving history tokens. This error in hosted web mode is visible by errors in the hosted web mode console, as shown in figure 4.7 (however, you'll get no similar warning in web mode).

Starting HTTP on port 8888
Rebinding org.gwtbook.client.ui.slideshow.Slideshow
Unable to initialize the history subsystem; did you include the history frame in your host page? Try <iframe id='__gwt_historyFrame' style='width:0;height:0;border:0'></iframe>

Figure 4.7 Error raised when you try to use the GWT `History` subsystem in hosted mode without its being properly initialized

(The rebinding message in figure 4.7 is a result of GWT manipulation you'll perform later in the book using GWT generators to take the basic component application and automatically generate new code to show an About menu item.)

Using methods in the `Hyperlink` class, it's easy to get the history token associated with a particular link (`getTargetHistoryToken()`) or update the token if you wish (`setTargetHistoryToken()`). Similarly, you can set the hyperlink's text or get it through the `setText()` and `getText()` methods respectively (or the HTML using `setHTML()` and `getHTML()` if you've created the hyperlink so the text is treated as HTML, using the `Hyperlink(String, boolean, String)` constructor instead of the more simple `Hyperlink(String, String)` version), which treats the hyperlink as simple text.

Treating hyperlink text as HTML means that any mark-up code—such as text in bold, underlines, and images—is displayed. If you want a normal hyperlink to, say, another HTML page, then use the `HTML` widget, which we'll look at later, rather than a `Hyperlink` widget that has its text set to some HTML.

Hyperlinks are one way to navigate through an application; another is to use a menu system.

Navigating your application using menus

The menu system provided by GWT is based on the MenuBar and MenuItem widgets. MenuItems are added to MenuBars, and MenuBars are added to other MenuBars, to create your application's menu system. Figure 4.8 shows the Dashboard menu system, where Clock, Calculator, and Slideshow MenuItems are added to a Create MenuBar; this Create MenuBar and a Help MenuBar are then added to another MenuBar, which is displayed on the browser page.

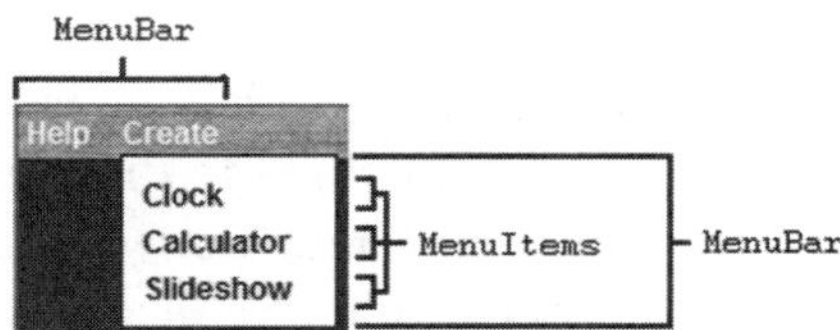

Figure 4.8 MenuBar and MenuItem widgets used in the Dashboard application. In this example, three MenuItems are placed in one MenuBar, which is then added to an overall MenuBar.

In the Dashboard class (org.gwtbook.client.Dashboard), you define one global MenuBar using the following code:

```
MenuBar menu = new MenuBar();
```

This simple line creates a horizontal menu bar. (It could just as easily be created using the alternative constructor, which takes a boolean parameter whose value is set to false: for example, new MenuBar(false). If the parameter is set to true, a vertical MenuBar is created.) At present, the Dashboard will have two standard menu bars; you'll create two additional ones later in this book, and further down the Dashboard code you can find two methods used to build the create and help menu bars. The method buildHelpMenu(), shown in listing 4.1, builds the initial Create menu bar using vertical menu bars.

Listing 4.1 Building the Dashboard's Create menu bar and menu items, and the nested Locale menu bar

```
protected MenuBar buildHelpMenu(){
   MenuBar menuHelp = new MenuBar(true);                    ❶ Create vertical
   MenuBar menuLocale = new MenuBar(true);                     MenuBars


   menuLocale.addItem(constants.EnglishLocale(),
                      new ChangeLocaleToEnglishCommand());   ❷ Add MenuItem
   menuLocale.addItem(constants.SwedishLocale(),                to MenuBar
                      new ChangeLocaleToSwedishCommand());
   menuHelp.addItem(constants.LocaleMenuItemName(), menuLocale);   Add MenuBar
   return menuHelp;                                                to MenuBar
}
```

You create vertical menu bars by passing the Boolean value `true` as a parameter in the constructor (see ❶). In a `MenuBar`, one or more `MenuItems` or other `MenuBars` go together to give the visual structure shown in figure 4.8. It's possible to create `MenuItems` inline in the code, which is what you do at ❷ where the first parameter to the `addItem()` method is a new `MenuItem`. Each `MenuItem` is bound to a segment of code, the second parameter to the `addItem()` method, which is executed when that menu item is clicked.

You use the *command pattern* to describe the command that will be executed when a menu item is clicked. In practice, this means you create a new instance of either the GWT `Command` class or a subclass, which contains an `execute()` method where the code is stored. For the Dashboard, we decided to define a number of `Command` subclasses as inner classes to the Dashboard, because this best met our needs. An example of one of these classes is shown in listing 4.2 (this command is attached to the `MenuItems` defined in ❷ of listing 4.1).

Listing 4.2 A subclass of the `Command` class to change the application locale to English

```
class ChangeLocaleToEnglishCommand implements Command{
  public void execute(){
    Window.removeWindowCloseListener(dashboardWindowCloseListener);
    changeLocale("");
  }
}
```

Using the command pattern allows the GWT application to turn a request for future functionality into an object that can be passed around the code; the defined functionality can then be invoked later. In the case of the menu items, GWT provides the plumbing so that when a menu item is clicked, the associated command's `execute()` method is invoked. In this example, when the user clicks a menu item whose command is set to an instance of the `ChangeLocaleToEnglishCommand` class, then this `execute()` method is invoked, and a `WindowCloseListener` is removed from the application before the `changeLocale()` method is called. (Otherwise, you invoke both of the window-closing events you'll set up in chapter 6—in the case of the Dashboard, these event handlers display two alert boxes, which you don't want to happen if you're just changing the locale.)

You can interrogate a `MenuItem` to find out what its parent menu is through its `getParentMenu()` method, as well as find out whether it opens a submenu through its `getSubMenu()` method. Similarly, you can set the submenu of a `MenuItem` through the `setSubMenu()` method, but not its parent menu. In some applications, you may need to change the command associated with a particular `MenuItem` (`setCommand()`) or find out what that command is (`getCommand()`).

The final implementation aspect of a `MenuItem` we want to discuss relates to the text shown as the item itself. This text can be treated either as pure text or as HTML, depending on whether a Boolean parameter is provided in the constructor of the `MenuItem`. As with any widget that can allow HTML to be set, you should always take care that you don't expose the application to script-based security issues. Creating a menu item using `new MenuItem(String, true, Command)` treats the `String` as HTML; using the `MenuItem(String, false, Command)` or `MenuItem(String, Command)` constructor treats it as pure text.

A `MenuBar` widget lets you define whether its child menus open automatically or wait for the user to click them to open. The `setAutoOpen()` method achieves this. In the Dashboard, you do this in the `onModuleLoad()` method, where you create the whole menu system using the code shown in listing 4.3.

Listing 4.3 Creating the Dashboard's menu system

```
MenuBar menuCreate = buildCreateMenu();                          Build
MenuBar menuHelp = buildHelpMenu();                              submenus
menu.addItem(constants.HelpMenuName(),menuHelp);                 Add submenus
menu.addItem(constants.CreateMenuName(),menuCreate);             to MenuBar
menu.setAutoOpen(true);    <------  Set submenus to auto-open
```

At the top of the screen is the Dashboard's menu system, shown in figure 4.9, which is involved in the code a number of times. The Help and Create menu bars are created as simple implementations for an Internet view (in the `Dashboard` class) and then overridden to provide a more functional intranet version (in the `Dashboard_intranet` class). The version used, intranet or Internet, is chosen by using GWT user-defined properties and setting the user-defined `externalvisibility` property in the Dashboard.html file (we describe all this in chapter 15).

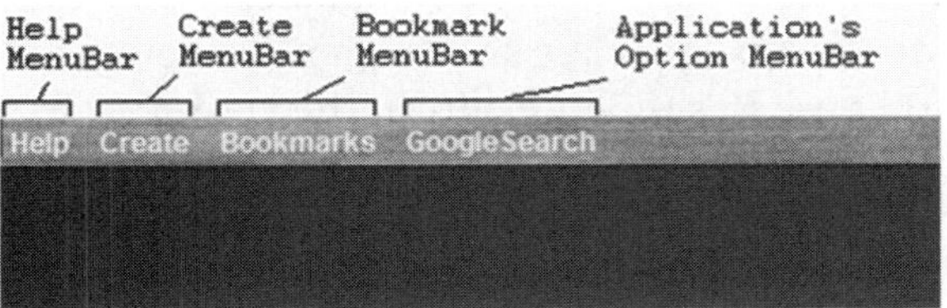

Figure 4.9 The Dashboard menu system, showing the four possible menu bars. The Help and Create menu bars are always present, the Bookmarks menu is loaded as XML from the server, and the option menu bar is shown when a component application gains focus.

The text for these two menu bars is created using GWT internationalization constants set up for a default (English) locale and an alternative Swedish locale. This internationalization approach, which we looked at briefly in chapter 3, is expanded on in chapter 15.

You also use the two new `MenuItem` widgets you'll create later in this chapter in the Dashboard's menu system. When running in intranet mode, the Help menu bar lets the user turn on/off the confirmation requested when they delete a component application; they do this through a `TwoComponentMenuItem`. In both modes, the user can change the locale through two `TwoComponentMenuItems`: one for each locale supported by the application. You can see the intranet view of the Help menu in figure 4.10, where both new widgets are in use.

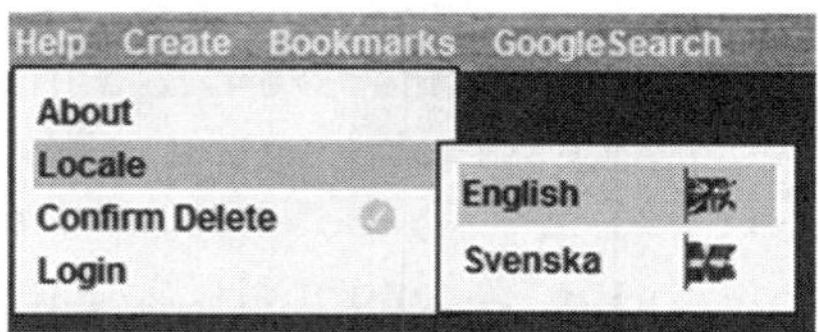

Figure 4.10 Examining the Dashboard's menu system and showing off the two new `MenuItem` widgets built in this chapter. The English and Swedish locale `MenuItems` are instances of the `TwoComponentMenuItem`, and the Confirm Delete `MenuItem` is an instance of the `ToggleMenuItem` (it's shown in the ON state).

You also manipulate the menu bar in two further ways. First, you create a bookmark menu bar whose contents are loaded from an external XML file using the GWT implementation of the `XMLHttpRequest` object; this is covered in chapter 12. Second, each component application can register an option menu, which is shown in the main menu when the application gains focus (you use a GWT generator, discussed in chapter 14, to automatically generate an `About` item in the option menu for each application; it lists all the methods and fields included in the application). Figure 4.10 shows the option menu for the Google Search component application. These component applications also have some generic functional requirements placed on them.

The final point to note about the `MenuBar` is that it implements the `PopupListener` interface, which allows functionality to be fired when the `MenuBar` is closed. If you wish to use different functionality than the standard when the `MenuBar` closes, then you can override the existing class and implement your own `onPopupClosed()` method. (You don't use this functionality in the Dashboard.)

Managing the view of data using trees

We've nearly completed our look at most of the basic widgets in GWT. Two are left, the first of which is the `Tree` widget. This widget provides applications with a standard hierarchical tree comprising `TreeItem` widgets. (See figure 4.11.)

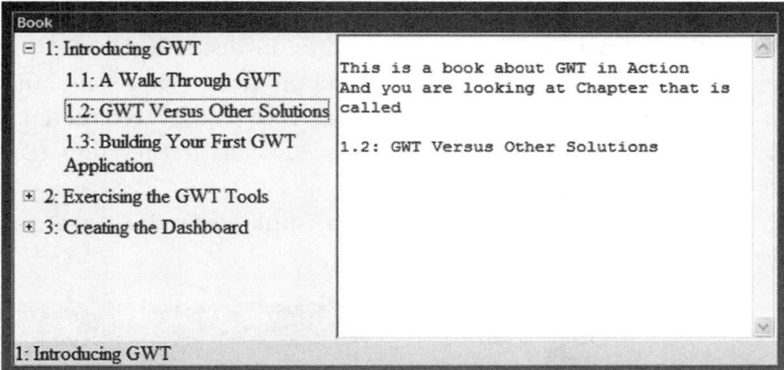

Figure 4.11 The Dashboard's Book application, showing the `Tree` widget on the left. In chapter 6, you'll see how events are used when `TreeItems` are selected or expanded.

A `Tree` is built similarly to the way you built a menu earlier. In that case, you added a number of `MenuItems` to a `MenuBar`; here, you'll add `TreeItems` to a `Tree`. The constructors for a `TreeItem` are flexible and allow you to create an empty `TreeItem` or `TreeItems` from `Strings` or other widgets (which could mean a standard widget or a composite widget). In listing 4.4, which comes from the Dashboard's Book application (`org.gwtbook.client.ui.book.Book`), you build a simple tree to represent the top-level structure of the book.

Listing 4.4 Creating the Dashboard's Book tree system

```
private Tree buildTOC(){
   TreeItem chapter1 = new TreeItem("1: Introducing GWT");
   chapter1.addItem("1.1: A Walk Through GWT");
   chapter1.addItem("1.2: GWT Versus Other Solutions");
   :
   TreeItem chapter2 = new TreeItem("2: Exercising the GWT Tools");
   chapter2.addItem("2.1: Setting up Dashboard Version 1");
   :
   TreeItem chapter3 = new TreeItem("3: Creating the Dashboard");
   chapter3.addItem("3.1: Stage 2 - Developing the Application");
   :
   Tree t = new Tree();
   t.addItem(chapter1); t.addItem(chapter2); t.addItem(chapter3);
   return t;
}
```

Build chapter 1 tree

Build chapter 2 tree

Build chapter 3 tree

Build table of contents tree

Unlike in the menu system, you don't add commands to MenuItems to implement functionality when they're clicked or expanded; instead, you implement a TreeListener. Doing so requires you to implement two methods: an onTreeItemSelected() method, which is fired when a MenuItem is selected; and the onTreeItemStateChanged() method, which is invoked if the state (opened or closed) of a TreeItem changes.

For the Dashboard Book application, you implement the TreeListener as shown in listing 4.5.

Listing 4.5 Adding event handling to the Dashboard's Book tree to change the display text

```
Tree theTree = buildTOC();
theTree.addTreeListener(new TreeListener(){
   public void onTreeItemSelected(TreeItem item) {       ❶ Fired when TreeItem selected
      changeText(item.getText());                       ❷ Get text from selected item
   }

   public void onTreeItemStateChanged(TreeItem item) {   ❸ Fired when TreeItem state changes
      if (item.getState()){                             ❹ Get state of changed item
         currChapter.setText(item.getText());           ❺ Retrieve text
      } else {
         currChapter.setText("----------");
      }
   }
});
```

This listener calls the Dashboard application's changeText() method ❷ to fill in the text box at right in the Book application with text when a TreeItem is selected ❶. When the state of a TreeItem changes, then the onTreeItemStateChanged() method ❸ is called. This method retrieves the state of the MenuItem that was changed ❹ and, if this item is now open, places the text of the time at the bottom of the widget by retrieving it using the getText() method ❺. Otherwise, it places dashes as the text.

A TreeItem comes with a host of helper methods that you can invoke to learn more about or change existing properties of the item. You can find out the child at a particular index (getChild(int index)), count the number of children (getChildCount()), or get the index of a particular child (getChildIndex(TreeItem)). Additionally, you can get the Tree a particular TreeItem is in (getTree()), find out if an item's children are currently displayed (getState()), determine its parent item (`getParentItem()`), and find out whether it's currently selected (`isSelected()`).

A `TreeItem` may have a widget associated with it, though if it does, it can't directly have text associated (unless it's set up as a composite widget). Often, you may associate a `CheckBox`, for example, with `TreeItems`. You associate a widget with a `TreeItem` either through the `setWidget()` method or by using the `TreeItem(Widget)` constructor.

Finally, the various states of the `TreeItem`, whether an item is closed or open, are shown as images. By default, these images are in the public folder of your application and are called tree_closed.gif, tree_open.gif, and tree_white.gif. You can replace these images with your own versions if you wish—just keep the names the same. If you'd like to store the images in a different directory, indicate the location using the `setImageBase()` method.

Viewing images

If you wish to display an image in a GWT application, you can use the `Image` basic widget. This widget allows images to be loaded and displayed, as you can see in figure 4.12.

An interesting aspect of the `Image` widget is the ability to add a `LoadListener` to it so that a particular action can be performed when the image has completed loading (`onLoad()`), or another action can be performed if there is an error loading the image (`onError()`).

TIP The `LoadListener` will work only if the `Image` is added to the browser page, usually via a panel, which is itself added to the browser. Just creating the Java object and adding a `LoadListener` isn't enough to catch the events, due to the way in which the GWT event-handling system works (see chapter 6).

Figure 4.12
The `Image` widget in the Dashboard's Slideshow application

Listing 4.6 shows the code from the Dashboard's Slideshow component (`org.gwt.client.ui.slideshow.Slideshow`), which can be used to preload images into an application.

Listing 4.6 Preloading Slideshow images with a `LoadListener`

```
Image[] testLoading = new Image[maxNumberImages];
preloadImages.setVisible(false);
for(int loop=0;loop<maxNumberImages;loop++){
   testLoading[loop] = new Image(theImages[loop][1]);
   testLoading[loop].addLoadListener(new LoadListener(){
      public void onError(Widget sender) {
         Window.alert("Expected Error - onError() Method works.");
      }
      public void onLoad(Widget sender) {
         Window.setTitle("Loaded Image: "+imageName);
      }
   });
   preloadImages.add(testLoading[loop]);
}
```

❶ Hide panel
❷ Add Load-Listener
❸ Define onError code
❹ Define onLoad code

The `preloadImages` object is a `HorizontalPanel`, which you add to the application specifically for the future use of preloading images. Due to the way the GWT event mechanism works, you need to have the images loading into a component that is added to the browser page (if they aren't, then there is no hook into the event mechanism, and the `LoadListener` is ignored). However, there is no requirement for the component to be visible, so in ❶ you set it to be invisible to avoid an unsightly mess!

You add a new `LoadListener` at ❷ and define the `onError()` method to just put a JavaScript alert on the screen if there is an error ❸; or, if the image loads, you change the title bar of the browser window to show the image name using the `Window.setTitle()` method ❹.

Once you have an `Image` object, it's possible to use the `prefetch()`or `setUrl()` method to load a new image rather than creating new objects as you did in the example. Either way is valid, and you'll choose which way to set it up in your own applications.

You should also be aware that when you use a transparent PNG image over another image in Internet Explorer 5.5 and 6, ugly backgrounds start to get applied. You'll build a new widget later in this chapter that overcomes these problems.

An exciting addition that came with GWT 1.4 is the ability to bundle together and clip images. The original `Image` class gained a new method that allows you to

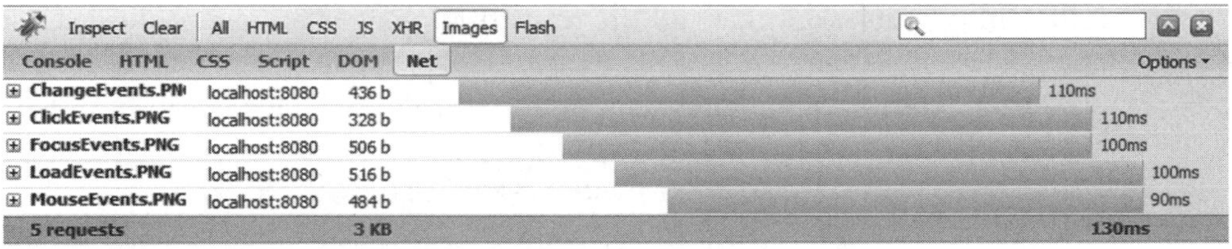

Figure 4.13 The Dashboard's Server Status application showing GWT `Label` widgets in action

display only a portion of the image. For example, to display only the top left 50x50 pixel square of an image, you can use the constructor `new Image("image.png", 0, 0, 50, 50)`.

The ultimate purpose of clipping an image is optimizing the load time of your GWT application. Loading one image containing a number of images you'll use is more efficient than loading each of the images individually. Let's look at an HTML page that loads the five images displayed in the Events Widget Browser Dashboard application. When you have a simple page that loads all five images separately, the Firebug extension to Firefox reports the timelines shown in figure 4.13.

The five images take around 130ms to download. The images are coming from a web server local to the machine; but look at the results shown in figure 4.14, where we manually created an image that contains all the five images in one.

You're down to 50ms to load the images. Extend this to a larger application that is loading images across a real network, and you can begin to see that there are distinct advantages to bundling images together. There's a disadvantage as well, though: Do you want to manually manipulate all the images you have into one? Luckily, GWT provides the `ImageBundle` class that gets around this problem. You provide your images as you want and create an interface that extends `ImageBundle` that references your images, and GWT does the work of putting them together for you. Let's look at that in more detail.

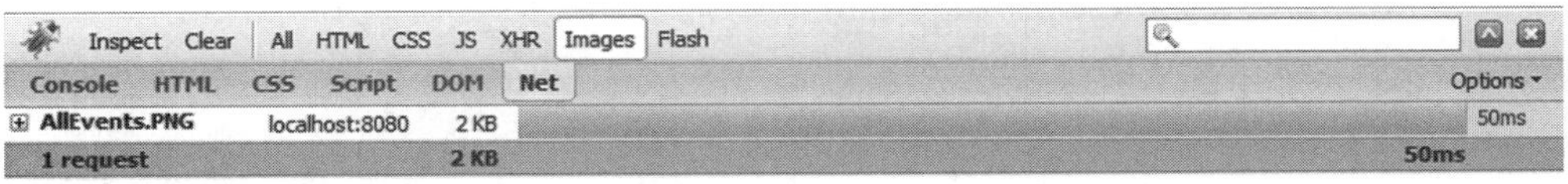

Figure 4.14 All five images displayed in one

In the Public folder of the Dashboard application, create a ToolbarImages folder into which you place all the individual images for the toolbar. Then, in the `org.gwtbook.client.ui.EventsWidgetBrowser` package, create a new interface class that extends `ImageBundle`; a sample of that interface is shown in listing 4.7.

Listing 4.7 Creating an `ImageBundle`

```
public interface ToolBarImageBundle extends ImageBundle{      ❶ Point to resource
   /**
   * @gwt.resource org/gwtbook/public/ToolbarImages/ChangeEvents.png
   */
   AbstractImagePrototype ChangeEvents();      ❷ Create method

   /**
   * @gwt.resource org/gwtbook/public/ToolbarImages/ClickEvents.png
   */
   AbstractImagePrototype ClickEvents();
}
```

The interface defines a method ❷ for each image that will be bundled together, and the GWT-generated implementations of these methods are used to extract the clipped images. By default, GWT takes the images from within the package in which the bundle interface is defined (this is different from other images/resources) and looks for an image named after the method name. To play nicer with the application structure, you can direct GWT to take the resource from a location of your choosing. This is achieved by using annotations in the comments; for example, ❶ tells the compiler to get the image returned by the `ChangeEvents()` method from the ToolbarImages directory.

Using the bundled image is simple. Listing 4.8 shows the case of creating an instance of your image bundle, via the deferred binding approach. With access to the image bundle, you call the appropriate methods for the image we wish to use, and that method returns an `AbstractImagePrototype`. To get the `Image` you're after, you call the `createImage()` method on the `AbstractImagePrototype`. Now, you have a standard `Image` that can be added to your application.

Listing 4.8 Creating an `ImageBundle`

```
ToolBarImageBundle toolBarImages =                          Create image bundle object
      (ToolBarImageBundle)GWT.create(ToolBarImageBundle.class);
AbstractImagePrototype changeEventImagePrototype =
      toolBarImages.ChangeEvents();   <-- Create Image Prototype
Image changeEventImage = changeEventImagePrototype.createImage()   Create image
```

But images aren't the only thing you can display on the application. You also have a range of ways to display text.

4.2.2 Displaying text on the application

The `Image` widget we looked at just now is useful for displaying pictures and images on the web browser. However, many applications need to show text either as passive information or more actively or funkily. As we dig down into the hierarchy of widgets, two widgets allow you to present text on the screen: `Label` and `HTML`.

Showing text as a label

A `Label` widget contains arbitrary text, which is displayed exactly as written. This means the `Label` created by the code `new Label("Hi <B>there</B>")` appears on the browser page exactly as "Hi <b>there</b>"—the word *there* isn't interpreted as HTML and isn't shown in bold text.

It's possible to control the horizontal alignment of labels, although by default the size of a `Label` widget is the size of the text it encloses. Right-aligning, using the following command

```
theLabel.setHorizontalAlignment(HorizontalAlignmentConstant.ALIGN_RIGHT)
```

has little visible affect unless you use a style sheet (or, less preferably, the `theLabel.setWidth()` method) to set the width of the label to be longer than the text. The alignment you see in the Dashboard's Server Status application (`org.gwtbook.client.ui.serverstatus.ServerStatus`), shown in figure 4.15, is achieved by aligning `Labels` in a `Grid` panel (see chapter 5). A `Label` may also word-wrap if the `setWordWrap()` method is called; this method takes a Boolean variable that is set to `true` if the `Label` should word-wrap and `false` otherwise.

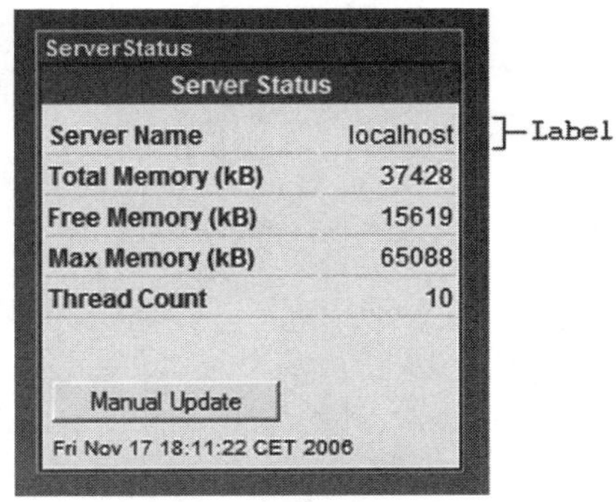

Figure 4.15 The Dashboard's Server Status application showing GWT `Label` widgets in action

GWT allows you to add `ClickListener` and `MouseListener` to a standard `Label` widget, offering the possibility of capturing the user trying to interact with the `Label`. By default, no action occurs; you have to add click or mouse listeners. In the `EditableLabel` widget you'll build in chapter 7 (`org.gwtbook.client.ui.EditableLabel`), when a user clicks the label, you present a text box instead of the label; they can use it to change the text of the label. You add the click listener as shown in listing 4.9.

Listing 4.9 Adding a `ClickListener` to the GWT `EditableLabel` widget

```
text = new Label(labelText);
text.setStyleName("editableLabel-label");
text.addClickListener(new ClickListener()
{
   public void onClick (Widget sender){
      changeTextLabel();
   }
});
```

The `ClickListener` acts similarly to the `Command` you used in the `MenuItem` widget. It registers an `onClick()` method that GWT executes when the user of the application clicks the label.

Once you have a label, you can change the text programmatically using the `setText()` method (as well as get the current text using the `getText()` method). See listing 4.10.

Listing 4.10 Changing the label text in the Clock application through the `setText()` method

```
Date d = new Date();
if (! local) {
   d = new Date(d.getTime() - (d.getTimezoneOffset() * 60 * 1000));
}
clockLabel.setText(d.getHours() +                 <-- Set label to
           ":" + twoDigit(d.getMinutes()) +           new time
           ":" + twoDigit(d.getSeconds()));
```

You can also use a slightly more active text-presenting widget if you wish: the `HTML` widget.

Making text active using the HTML widget

If you want to provide more funkiness with the presentation of text, then the `HTML` widget may be the component you're looking for. It acts the same as a `Label` widget, but—this is important—it interprets any text as arbitrary HTML. Whereas in the label the text "Hi <B>there</B>" is written as is, if you write the code `new HTML("Hi <B>there</B>")`, the text is displayed as "Hi **there**".

The HTML widget is also useful if you wish to provide a true hyperlink. When we looked at the Hyperlink widget, you learned that you can present what looks like a hyperlink to the user, but when clicked, it only changes the historical aspect of the application. If you use an HTML widget instead, then you can provide proper links, as you'll do later in the About application to link to the book's web pages:

```
new HTML("<a href='http://www.manning.com/hanson'>Manning</a>");
```

You must be careful with this widget because allowing arbitrary HTML can expose security issues to your application if maliciously constructed HTML is used. Also consider whether the HTML Panel we'll discuss in chapter 5 is more appropriate for your needs.

Labels and HTML are a useful way of presenting information to a user, but there is another half of interacting with the user: capturing their input.

4.2.3 Grabbing the user's interaction using focus widgets

You can grab user input using one of a number of widgets in GWT, all of which fall under the FocusWidget hierarchy shown earlier in figure 4.3. These widgets inherit from the FocusWidget class; but before we look at them in detail, you should understand that FocusWidget isn't a widget in the normal sense—you can't create an instance of it and display it on the browser. Yes, it extends the Widget class, but its only purpose is to provide a class that handles focus, click, and keyboard events that can be extended to provide the necessary common functionality across its children. So, it's defined as an *abstract* class.

Although it's abstract, FocusWidget provides the common functionality for all focus widgets; this includes setting the widgets position in the browser's tab index through the setTabIndex() method. A widget's tab index indicates the ordering in which it will highlight when the user uses the Tab key to move through webpage elements. Setting tab indexes is particularly useful to the user if widgets are used in a form; correspondingly, the standard form components are subclasses of FocusWidget.

You can also use the setAccessKey(char key) method to assign a special key combination that, when pressed, gives the widget focus—or you can do this programmatically through the setFocus() method. In the EditableLabel widget you'll build in chapter 7, you change a Label widget into TextArea for editing.

Once the widget swapping has taken place, to make sure the `TextArea` immediately has focus, you call the `setFocus()` method on it (see listing 4.11).

Listing 4.11 Setting the `TextArea` widget to have the focus in the `EditableLabel` widget

```
changeTextArea.setText(originalText);      <-- Set text from FocusWidget
changeTextArea.setVisible(true);           <-- Set visibility inherited from UIObject
changeTextArea.setEnabled(true);           <-- Set FocusWidget as enabled
changeTextArea.setFocus(true);             <-- Set focus inherited from FocusWidget
```

In GWT, two widgets extend `FocusWidget` directly to produce new widgets: `Frame` and `ListBox`. We'll look at them next, as well as two additional abstract subclasses of focus widgets (`TextBoxBase` and `ButtonBase`), which in turn have more widgets as their children.

Framing an area of interest

In the Dashboard, we wanted to introduce flexibility into the About component application (`org.gwtbook.client.ui.about.About`). Rather than hard-code the about message, we decided that it should be loaded from a separate HTML file. To support that functionality, you use the `Frame` widget, into which you can easily load a new HTML page. You do this either through the constructor, such as `new Frame("resource-to-load")`, or through the widget's `frame.setURL("resource-to-load")` method.

Figure 4.16 shows the basic About component application in the Dashboard, where the contents are loaded from another HTML file (About.html, if you've downloaded the example code). Because the widget represents an `IFRAME` DOM element, this content can easily be created from a static HTML file, JSP, servlet, PHP script, .NET application, and so on.

A subclass of the `Frame` widget is the `NamedFrame` widget, which lets you associate a name. These `NamedFrames` are typically used as targets for the `FormPanel`—and you'll see this in action in chapter 12, when we deal with forms.

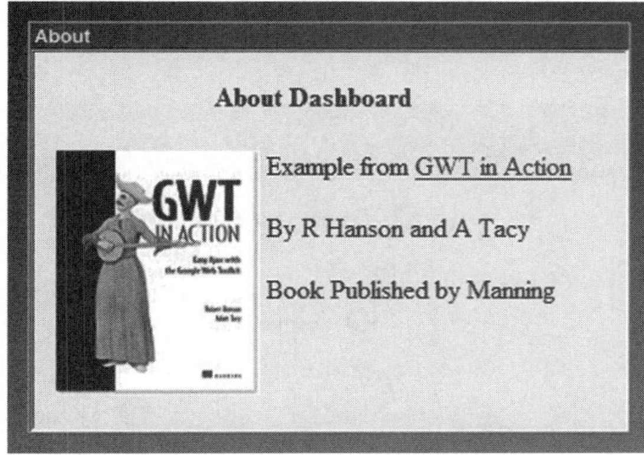

Figure 4.16
Using the `Frame` widget in the Dashboard About dialog. The contents of this display are loaded from another HTML file into a frame.

Listing options

The `ListBox` widget is used extensively in the Dashboard's Address Book application (`org.gwtbook.client.ui.addressbook.AddressBook`), as shown in figure 4.17. It presents a list of choices to the user, either as a drop-down or as a standard list box. In the Address Book application, you use the list-box form for selecting names and in drop-down form for selecting countries.

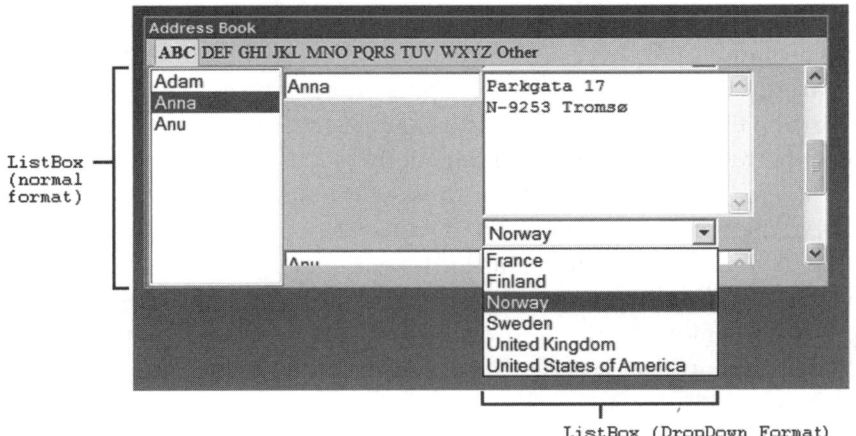

Figure 4.17 The Dashboard Address Book application uses both forms of the `ListBox` widget. Names are stored in a normal format list box, and countries are selected from a list box in its drop-down style.

To create a normal format list box, you use the standard constructor `new ListBox()`, as shown in listing 4.12.

Listing 4.12 Creating a standard `ListBox` and adding a `ChangeListener` to the Address Book application

```
addressLinks = new ListBox();                          ❶ Create standard ListBox

addressLinks.setVisibleItemCount(10);                  ❷ Set number of visible items

super.add(addressLinks);
addressLinks.addChangeListener(new ChangeListener(){   ❸ Add ChangeListener

   public void onChange(Widget sender) {
      int val = addressLinks.getSelectedIndex();       ❹ Get selected index

      String text = addressLinks.getItemText(val);     ❺ Get selected text

      showAddress(text);
   }
});
```

After creating the `ListBox` object ❶, you set the maximum number of visible items that will be shown ❷ through the `setVisibleItemCount(number)` method; this is effectively the height of the list box. For the Address Book, you display 10 items as standard; if there are more, then the widget acquires a scroll bar.

Having a list box provides a way of presenting choices to the user. To understand which item the user selects, you add a `ChangeListener` to the `ListBox` ❸. When the selected value in the list box is changed, the `onChange()` method is called. You use this change listener to show the address of the new person by first finding out the index of the option the user selected (using the `getSelectedIndex()` method, ❹) and then passing that index value as the parameter to the `getItemText()` method to get the text representation of the selected option ❺. This returned text is then used as a parameter in the Address Book's `showAddress()` method.

The alternative view of `ListBox` as a drop-down box of options is created by setting the visible item count to 1. For variety in the Address Book, you subclass the `ListBox` widget to provide a country choice drop-down widget, as shown in listing 4.13.

Listing 4.13 Creating a drop-down list box for the Dashboard's Address Book application

```
private class CountryChoiceBox extends ListBox{
   public CountryChoiceBox(){
      super();                          <-- Call parent constructor
      this.setVisibleItemCount(1);      <-- Set widget to be drop-down
      this.addItem("France");
      this.addItem("Finland");
      this.addItem("Norway");
      this.addItem("Sweden");
      this.addItem("United Kingdom");
      this.addItem("United States of America");   Add options
   }
}
```

You select an option programmatically using the `setSelectedIndex(value)` method. This method works best, and makes more sense, when the list box is in its drop-down view; you use it in the Dashboard to ensure that the correct country option is shown for each address.

One thing you don't do in any of the Dashboard component applications is allow the list box to have multiple selections. To do so is just a case of using the `setMultipleSelect()` method. If you do that, then you need to be a little more intelligent when getting the selected item, because the `getSelectedItem()` method returns only the first selected item. To get all the selected items, you need to iterate over all the items, calling the `isItemSelected()` method for each item to determine whether it's selected.

Clicking your way through an application

Using a list box gives the user a wide range of choices. If you wish to be more careful about the range of choices offered to the user, then you should consider using one of the widgets that extends the `ButtonBase` widgets.

These widgets include `Button` along with `RadioButton` and `CheckBox`. `ButtonBase` provides the standard methods common to its three children—for example, setting and getting the text associated with them through the `setText()` and `getText()` methods or the similar methods for the HTML (`setHTML()` and `getHTML()`).

Let's look at these three children and how you use them in the Dashboard.

Pushing the button

The `Button` widget is one you've already seen in this chapter. It's a push button in the style normally found on web pages. It's created by calling the constructor as follows:

```
new Button("7");
```

You can see the Dashboard's calculator buttons all lined up in figure 4.18. You add them to a `Grid` panel and also apply some CSS styling to change the normal gray button/black text to a light blue button/green text—although that may not be visible in the book!

Figure 4.18 A range of `Button` widgets set out to form the keypad of the Calculator Dashboard application

Normally, you register a `ClickListener` with the `Button` in order to perform some functionality when the button is clicked. For the keys that represent the operation buttons (plus and so on) in the Dashboard's Calculator application (`org.gwtbook.client.ui.calculator.Calculator`), you add click listeners to the button:

```
Button w = new Button("+");
w.addClickListener(new ClickListener(){
   public void onClick(Widget sender) {
      performCalculation(op);
   }
});
```

When you press keyboard buttons while focused in the Dashboard Calculator application, you wish to perform the same functionality as if you clicked the buttons. You achieve this by programmatically executing the clicking of a button by calling the `button.click()` method.

Buttons are one subclass of the `ButtonBase` widget, but there are two more. Next, we'll look at the `CheckBox`.

Checking the box

The `CheckBox` widget implements the standard browser check box functionality (see figure 4.19). In normal pre-Ajax applications, this widget was usually found in a `Form`, and the values were submitted to the server when the form is submitted. In the Ajax world, this isn't a constraint anymore; yes, it's still found in forms, but it can also function as a standalone component. If you're using it standalone, you can add a `ClickListener` to it, so that some segment of code can be executed when the element is checked or unchecked. You'll do this in chapter 5 for the Dashboard application.

Figure 4.19 `CheckBox` components in action

Making the choice

The final widget we'll look at that's included with the GWT distribution as a subclass of `ButtonBase` is the `RadioButton` widget, which provides the implementation of a set of mutually exclusive selections. As with the `CheckBox`, it's common to see this either in a form or standing alone. Unlike `CheckBox`, you need a way to indicate which RadioButtons are included in a particular group. You do this in the constructor, which has three forms, all of which require the definition of a group name. Listing 4.14 shows the construction of two groups of radio buttons.

Listing 4.14 Creating two groups of a radio buttons

```
RadioButton rb1  =  new  RadioButton("Grp1")
RadioButton rb2 = new RadioButton("Grp1",  "Second Choice");
RadioButton rb3 = new RadioButton("Grp1",  "<B>Third</B> Choice",true);
RadioButton rb10 = new RadioButton("Grp2","Other");
RadioButton rb11 = new RadioButton("Grp2",  "Other 2");

rb1.addClickListener(new ClickListener(){
   public void onClick(Widget sender) {
      performAction1(op);
   }
});
rb2.addClickListener(new ClickListener(){
   public void onClick(Widget sender) {
      performAction2(op);
   }
});
```

Create Grpl Radio-Buttons

Create Grp2 RadioButtons

Add ClickListeners per RadioButton

If management of choices isn't the purpose of your application and you need a freer way to let users express themselves, then the next set of widgets in the TextBoxBase family are probably the ones you're after.

4.2.4 Getting user input through text input

Extending the FocusWidget is the TextBoxBase widget, which again isn't a widget but an abstract class providing standard functionality for the PasswordTextBox, TextArea, and TextBox widgets. The TextBoxBase class provides the type of functionality you would expect for an editable text element on screen: for example, canceling keypresses, setting and getting the visible text, setting the cursor position, and trapping a keypress and replacing it in the text box with a different character.

TextBoxBase provides a number of methods that you'd reasonably expect a widget that extends it to implement. You can get all the text in the widget with the getText() method or just get the text the user selected using the getSelectedText() method. In addition, you can get the length of the selected text using getSelectionLength() and the cursor position with getCursorPos()). It's also possible to set all these properties using the opposite methods, such as setText() and setCursorPos(), or to select all the text using the selectAll() method.

Let's look the three child widgets of TextBoxBase and how you use them in the Dashboard.

Securing password entry

The PasswordTextBox widget represents the standard browser text box that masks its input when the user types in values. It's commonly used to allow application users to enter passwords. The Dashboard includes a simple security application called the Login component (org.gwtbook.client.ui.login.Login), which uses the Password TextBox as shown in figure 4.20.

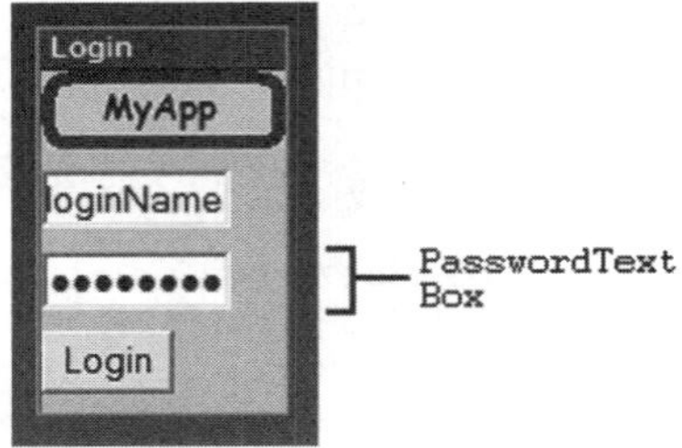

Figure 4.20 PasswordTextBox in the Dashboard Login application hides the characters being typed for the password.

This widget is easily created using the PasswordTextBox() constructor, but it includes no other methods except those inherited from the TextBoxBase widget.

Entering multiple lines of text

The TextArea widget allows application users to enter text that has multiple lines. In the Dashboard, you use this widget in the EditableLabel composite widget (see chapter 7) as shown in action in figure 4.21.

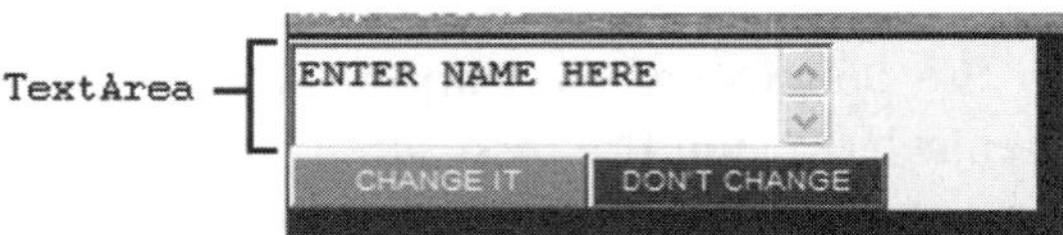

Figure 4.21 Using the TextArea in the EditableLabel composite widget built for the Dashboard (we'll look at this in more detail in chapter 7)

Creating a TextArea is a simple case of using the TextArea() constructor. From there, you can set the width and height of the TextArea either through CSS or by using the provided setCharacterWidth() and setVisibleLines() methods.

Sometimes you don't need multiple lines of text, and in that case the TextBox widget is more appropriate.

Entering a single line of text

If you don't need multiple lines of text that can be edited, then TextBox is probably a more appropriate widget. In the Dashboard, you use text boxes in a number of places, including in the Calculator Dashboard application; a user can enter numbers directly in the screen area as well as by clicking buttons (see figure 4.22).

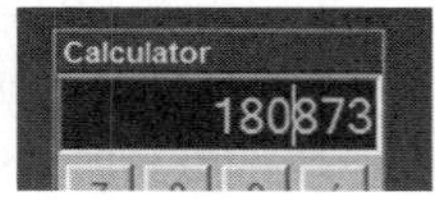

Figure 4.22 The TextBox widget in the Dashboard Calculator application

One aspect of TextBoxBase widgets we haven't discussed is the ability to trap keypresses and either change or cancel them through using a KeyboardListener. In the Calculator, you don't want users to have the ability to enter anything except numerical characters in the text box. You achieve this using the code given in listing 4.15.

Listing 4.15 Cancelling keypresses in the Calculator display through a KeyboardListener

```
theDisplay.addKeyboardListener(new KeyboardListenerAdapter(){
   public void onKeyPress(Widget sender,
                          char keyCode,
                          int modifiers) {
      if (!Character.isDigit(keyCode)){
         ((TextBox)sender).cancelKey();
      }
   }
});
```

Add KeyboardListenerAdapter

Check which key was pressed

Cancel invalid keypresses

First, you associate a KeyboardListenerAdapter with the text box (theDisplay) and then override its onKeyPress() method. In that method, you check to see if the keyCode is a digit by using the Java Character.isDigit() method. If it isn't a digit, then you cancel the keypress—which means it doesn't reach the widget and therefore is never displayed on the browser. The syntax to do this may be a little strange; you have to cast the sender object into a TextBox object before you can call the cancelKey() method, because the listener method only deals with pure Widget class objects.

Just as you can alter some of the stylistic aspects of the TextArea via either the preferred approach of CSS or programmatically, you can do the same with TextBox. Programmatically, you use the setMaxLength() and setVisibleLength() methods. The first method defined the maximum number of characters that can be typed into the text box; the second the maximum number of characters that are visible at any one time.

We hope this discussion has shown that many widgets are available for you to use in your applications and indicated where you'll use them in future development in this book. However, sometimes this set of simple widgets isn't enough or doesn't fulfill the needs of your application. In these cases, you can either create your own widget or extend an existing one.

4.3 Creating new widgets

Although GWT provides an extensive set of widgets, it can be the case that you don't have the functionality you need for your application. This may be because the provided widgets aren't quite right, or a basic widget is missing. There are three ways to create new widgets, as shown in figure 4.23.

In this section, we'll look at the first two approaches: creating new widgets directly from the DOM and by extending an existing widget. Remember that when we say a *basic widget*, we're referring to a widget that represents some basic functionality a browser can provide—anything more complicated involves the third approach: creating composite widgets. We'll discuss composites in detail in chapter 7; they're used if you need to create a widget that is made up of two or more existing widgets.

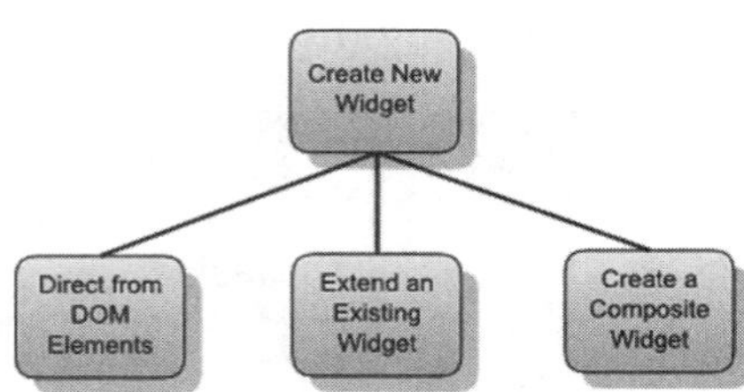

Figure 4.23 The three options available for creating a new widget in GWT. In this section, we'll look at following two methods: directly from the DOM and extending an existing widget (chapter 7 covers composite widgets in detail).

For the first approach, we struggled to find an example to include in this book, because the current GWT distribution has been comprehensive enough for our purposes. Earlier distributions were missing a `FileUpload` widget, so we built one; we'll look at how we did that in this section. When it comes to extending existing widgets, you'll build three new widgets for the Dashboard. The first is the `PNGImage` widget, which extends the standard `Image` widget to cope with some IE 5.5 and 6 problems with displaying PNG image transparency (you'll use this for the trash-can icon to allow PNG images to be used there).

The second new widget extends the `MenuItem` widget to create the Dashboard's `ToggleMenuItem` widget. GWT provides a `MenuItem` widget that is used in menus, but it consists just of text. The `ToggleMenuItem` will consist of text and one of two images indicating the toggled state of the menu item (imagine that these images consist of a check or a blank image indicating that the functionality represented by the menu item is on or off).

Let's assume that you need to create a new widget. First, you'll see how you do that through manipulation of the DOM.

4.3.1 Creating new widgets by manipulating the DOM

The first approach we'll discuss when you need to create a new widget is how to do so by manipulating the DOM directly (this is generally the way the standard GWT widgets are constructed). You won't have to do this often, because most widgets are already built; and you should do this only on those occasions when a basic browser widget is missing.

When writing this book, we couldn't think of a widget that needed to be built this way, but we recalled that when we started using GWT, a basic widget was missing: `FileUpload`. There is now a standard GWT version, so we'll look at how you built that.

Developing the FileUpload widget

You want the version of the `FileUpload` widget to look like exactly like the standard browser file-upload box shown in figure 4.24.

Browse...

Figure 4.24 Standard browser file-upload GWT widget (this is how you want the widget to appear)

The first step when creating a new widget is to decide which DOM element the widget will implement. In this case, it's a simple choice: Because you want a `FileUpload` widget, you need to use a DOM `<input>` element whose `type` attribute is set to `file` (this is the only way in a browser to create the widget shown in figure 4.24).

Next, you decide where the new widget will sit in the hierarchy that already exists. The approach sometimes involves a little trial and error because the hierarchy is large. Taking a common-sense approach, you want the widget to be notified of focus events and clicks, so you choose for it to sit under the `FocusWidget` class.

The widget is rather like a text box, and a user may expect it to behave in such a way, so `TextBoxBase` is also a good candidate; but there are a number of issues with this. It isn't possible to set the text of the underlying input DOM element due to valid security restrictions implemented by most browsers. Plus, the notion of text alignment isn't valid for this type of widget. Choose for this widget to extend `FocusWidget` as well as implement the `HasText` interface (which indicates that there is text you can set and get in this widget).

The widget consists of the code shown in listing 4.16.

Listing 4.16 The `FileUpload` widget

```
package org.gwtbook.client;
import com.google.gwt.user.client.DOM;
import com.google.gwt.user.client.ui.FocusWidget;
import com.google.gwt.user.client.ui.HasText;

public class FileUpload extends FocusWidget implements HasText{    <-- 1 Extend FocusWidget

   public FileUpload(String name){                                   <-- 2 Implement constructor
      super(DOM.createElement("input"));
      DOM.setAttribute(getElement(), "type", "file");
      DOM.setAttribute(getElement(), "name", name);
   }
```

```
    public String getText(){
        return DOM.getAttribute(getElement(), "value");
    }

    public void setText(String text){
        throw new RuntimeException("Not possible to set Text");
    }
}
```

Implement get and set methods ❸

At ❶, you state the name of the new widget and say that it will extend the FocusWidget class as just discussed. You'll inherit a number of methods from there. You also say that this widget will implement the HasText interface, which means you have to provide setText() and getText() methods.

Next ❷, you define the constructor of this widget. Here you introduce the direct DOM manipulation we've discussed in this section so far. Initially, you need to create the DOM input element, using the following code:

```
DOM.createElement("input")
```

This creates the <input> element, which you then use in the FocusWidget's constructor, which is accessed through the call to super() to establish the widget. This also sets the element field of the widget to be this new <input> element.

To complete the widget, you use more DOM manipulation approaches to set the type of the element (file) and its name:

```
DOM.setAttribute(getElement(), "type", "file");
DOM.setAttribute(getElement(), "name", name);
```

The getElement() method retrieves the widget's underlying element that was set in the call to the FocusWidget's constructor. You use this returned element in the two setAttribute() calls to set both the type and name attributes.

After the constructor has completed the element, you have the following DOM element held as the Java object:

```
<INPUT type="file" name="name" __eventBits="7040"/>
```

The eventBits has been set, although you haven't asked for it. These values appeared because you're extending the FocusWidget that has these values set.

Because you've implemented the HasText interface, you need to provide the two methods that this interface requires. First is the getText() method. For the FileUpload widget, it makes sense that the value returned is the value of the filename selected by the user. To get this value, you must perform some more DOM manipulation; this time, you use the getAttribute() method, as follows, to retrieve the value of the file input box ❸:

```
return DOM.getAttribute(getElement(), "value");
```

Another consequence of implementing the `HasText` interface is that you must provide the `setText()` method ❸. The majority of browsers place security restrictions on setting the text of a browser file-upload input, so you raise an exception if this method is called:

```
throw new RuntimeException("Not possible to set Text");
```

You can now use the new widget like any other widget by creating a new instance of it in the Java code, such as this:

```
FileUpload myUpload = new FileUpload();
```

As it turns out, this version isn't too far off the version that now ships with GWT, although that one is a little fancier and more flexible. The steps required to create a new widget by manipulating the DOM are summarized in table 4.3.

Table 4.3 Steps to create a new widget through DOM manipulation

Step	Action	Description
1	Identify the DOM	Identify which DOM element(s) the widget will wrap.
2	Locate the widget on the hierarchy	Locate where on the hierarchy this new widget should sit. Should it be directly under the `Widget` class, or can it take advantage of inheriting from a widget further down the hierarchy?
3	Identify interfaces to implement	Identify what interfaces (in addition to those it inherits) the widget should implement. We'll cover event interfaces in chapter 6.
4	Implement the constructor	Create the constructor using the appropriate DOM methods to create the element and add necessary attributes to the DOM element. If the widget is to sink events that aren't included in the hierarchy, then use the `sinkEvents()` method to indicate this. Don't forget to override the `onBrowserEvent()` method in the next step.
5	Implement the required methods	You now need to implement three types of methods: ▪ Those methods required by the interfaces, which you said in step 2 the widget will implement. ▪ Override the `onBrowserEvent()` method if you sink additional events not performed by other widgets above you in the hierarchy. ▪ Those methods you wish to create.

That is all there is to it to building a simple new widget from scratch. As we've said, though, it isn't easy to see where this situation will arise, given the increasing completeness of the provided GWT widgets. Most of the time, new widgets come from extending existing ones or creating composite widgets (as you'll see in chapter 7). The next section looks at how you extend existing widgets; you'll build three concrete examples for use in the Dashboard later on.

4.3.2 Creating new widgets by extending existing widgets

Instead of creating a widget directly from scratch, there are occasions where you can create a new widget by extending an existing one that almost has the functionality you need. In this section, you'll see three examples. The first extends the `Image` widget to allow it to cope with displaying transparency in the IE 5.5 and IE 6 browsers, which you need for the trash-can icon in the Dashboard example. Second, you'll build a widget that extends the standard `MenuItem` widget by letting you display another widget after the menu text; you'll then extend that widget to create a third one that allows you to toggle the widget shown after the text between two different widgets when the menu item is clicked.

The new widgets will follow the development steps shown in table 4.4. These are comfortingly similar to the steps involved in developing a widget from scratch—except you no longer need to identify DOM elements and where in the hierarchy the widget will sit, because these are given by the widget you choose to extend.

Table 4.4 Extending an existing widget to create a new one

Step	Action	Description
1	Identify the widget's functionality	Define exactly what you wish the new widget to do.
2	Identify the widget to extend	Identify which widget provides the closest match to the functionality you require. Sometimes you'll find a widget that provides not enough functionality in one area but too much in another. This is easy to fix, because you can override methods to provide both more and less functionality (sometimes this over-functionality is in the event-handling area, in which case you can use `unsinkEvents()` and/or alter the `onBrowserEvent()` method).
3	Identify interfaces to implement	Do you need to implement any new interfaces for this new widget? We'll cover event interfaces in chapter 6.

Table 4.4 Extending an existing widget to create a new one *(continued)*

Step	Action	Description
4	Implement the constructor	Create the constructor using the appropriate calls to `super()` to invoke the parent widget's constructor, and implement any additional code required for this new widget. If the widget is to sink events that aren't included in the parent, then use the `sinkEvents()` method to indicate this. Similarly, if you wish your new widget to not manage events that the parent widget does, then use the `unsinkEvents()` method (and don't forget to override the `onBrowserEvent()` method in the next step).
5	Implement the required methods	You now need to implement three types of methods: ■ Those methods required by the interfaces, which you said in step 2 the widget will implement. Or, override those methods required by the parent's interface that you wish to implement differently. ■ Override the `onBrowserEvent()` method if you sink additional events not managed by the parent, or if you unsink events that are managed by the parent. ■ Those methods you wish to create.

Let's create the first of three new widgets you'll be using in the Dashboard: the `PNGImage` widget.

Developing the Dashboard's PNGImage widget

The Dashboard application displays a trash-can image that sits at upper right on screen. In chapter 3, you implemented this as a simple `Image` widget. However, the `Image` widget that comes with GWT isn't that successful in displaying a transparent PNG image over another when you're using IE 5.5 or 6. This is what you could end up doing in the Dashboard, where the trash icon sits on top of a background image. Also, when you build the slider widget in chapter 7, you'll be sliding a thumbnail image over a background scale image; if you use the standard `Image` widget, and the programmer provides two PNG images, then it will look messy.

The problem is that the transparent PNG images acquires a halo effect in IE 5.5 (see figure 4.25) and a horrible background in IE 6 (see figure 4.26).

The third-party GWT Widget Library includes a `PNGImage` widget that overcomes this problem. In this section, we'll walk through the steps we took to develop this widget (to avoid importing the GWT Widget Library into the project yet, you'll create the `PNGImage` widget under the `org.gwtbook.client.ui` package).

Figure 4.25 PNG image transparency problem in IE 5.5: a white halo around the star using the GWT `Image` widget

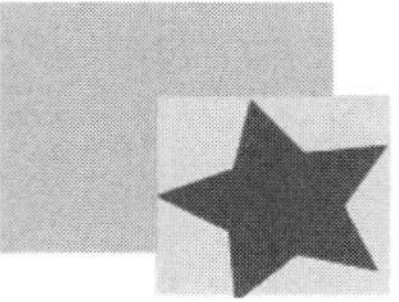

Figure 4.26 PNG image transparency problem in IE 6: a gray background around the star using the GWT `Image` widget

Rather than try to create a completely new widget, we decided that `PNGImage` should behave as much as possible like the standard GWT `Image` widget, and therefore inheritance from the standard `Image` widget was the way forward. The widget is made from three classes: a main widget class and two implementation classes (one for IE and one for other browsers). The full code for the implementation class of the `PNGImage` is shown in listing 4.17.

Listing 4.17 The main GWT `PNGImage` class

```
package org.gwtbook.client.ui;

import org.gwtbook.client.ui.impl.PNGImageImpl;
import com.google.gwt.core.client.GWT;
import com.google.gwt.user.client.Event;
import com.google.gwt.user.client.ui.Image;

public class PNGImage extends Image                          ❶ Extend Image class
{
   private PNGImageImpl impl;

   public PNGImage (String url, int width, int height){
      impl = (PNGImageImpl) GWT.create(PNGImageImpl.class);  ❷ Defer binding of implementation class

      setElement(impl.createElement(url, width, height));    ❸ Set widget's DOM element
      sinkEvents(Event.ONCLICK | Event.MOUSEEVENTS |         ❹ Sink events
                 Event.ONLOAD | Event.ONERROR);
   }

   public String getUrl (){                                  ❺ Provide getURL method
      return impl.getUrl(this);
   }

   public void setUrl (String url){                          ❻ Disable setURL method
      throw new RuntimeException("Not allowed for a PNG image");
   }
}
```

Having identified the functionality required for the PNGImage to be exactly the same as the Image widget, except to be able to handle PNG transparency, you indicate that the definition of the PNGImage class extends the Image widget ❶. There are no new interfaces that you wish PNGImage to implement, because you want PNGImage to behave the same as Image.

At ❷ you use code similar to that which we looked at when we discussed internationalization. Although in this case, instead of deferring picking the right Java class until you know the locale, you defer the binding until you know the browser in which the code is being executed (this is known technically as *deferred binding*, which we'll cover in chapter 15—it's used here because you need to implement different code depending on whether the browser is IE 5.5/6 or not). If the browser isn't IE 5.5/6, then the deferred binding picks a class called PNGImageImpl; if not, then it picks a class called PNGImageImplIE6.

At ❸, you create the DOM object that represents the PNG image. You do so by calling the create method on whichever version of the PNGImageImpl class has been selected by the compiler under the deferred binding rules. In the case where the browser isn't IE 5.5/6, the create method contains the following code to create a standard <image> DOM element and set some attributes:

```
Element result = DOM.createImg();
DOM.setAttribute(result, "src", url);
DOM.setIntAttribute(result, "width", width);
DOM.setIntAttribute(result, "height", height);
return result;
```

If the browser is IE 5.5/6, then the create method in the PNGImageImplIE6 class is used. First, it determines whether the image is a PNG image (by crudely looking at the extension). If the file isn't a PNG image, then the normal constructor is used to create an <img> element. Otherwise, you need to apply a specific IE AlphaImageLoader filter to the image. You do this by creating a <div> element and then setting the innerHTML of that DIV to include the PNGImage plus a specific IE AlphaImageLoader filter, as follows:

```
Element div = DOM.createDiv();
DOM.setInnerHTML(div, "<span style=\"display:inline-block;width:" +
                    width + "px;height:" + height + "px;"+
 filter:progid:DXImageTransform.Microsoft.AlphaImageLoader(src='" +
                    url + "', sizingMethod='scale')\"></span>");
```

In all cases, a DOM element is returned to the constructor in the PNGImage class. This element is then set as the element of the PNGImage widget. You can find the full code for the implementation classes in the electronic downloads for the book (http://www.manning.com/hanson).

The events that this widget must sink are the same as for the `Image` widget, so normally you wouldn't need to include a new `sinkEvents()` call. However, in this case you don't call the `Image` constructor using (`super()`), so you must explicitly identify the events you'll sink ❹. You don't need to override the `onBrowserEvent()` method because that is directly inherited from the parent `Image` widget.

To finalize the widget, you ensure that the methods from the `Image` class you inherit are handled appropriately. The `getURL()` method ❺ of the `Image` class is no longer valid in this implementation, so you override it and make it call the browser-specific implementation you're using to return the correct value.

Finally, for PNG images, it isn't possible to set the URL, because it's for an `Image` widget. This is a case where the parent widget provides more functionality than you can support in the extended widget. You solved this problem by raising a `RuntimeException` if someone wishes to try to call this method ❻.

The corrected `PNGImage` now displays correctly in IE 5.5/6, as shown in figure 4.27. The halo effect from IE 5.5 and background from IE 6 are gone, and `PNGImage` displays a PNG image correctly in all browsers.

You create the new `PNGImage` object using the standard Java call to its constructor:

```
PNGImage myImage = new PNGImage("star.png",100,100);
```

Now that you have the `PNGImage` class, you can represent the trash icon in the Dashboard application and use safely when building the sliders—both of which we cover later in this book. Next we'll look at developing another widget that you need for the Dashboard—the `ToggleMenuItem` widget.

Figure 4.27 Corrected IE PNG handling with no halo or background using the new `PNGImage` widget, which extends the GWT Image widget

4.4 Developing the Dashboard's ToggleMenuItem widget

As we explained earlier, GWT provides a useful widget called the `MenuItem`. One or more of these menu items are placed in a menu bar to create the GWT menu system. Useful as it is, it isn't immediately obvious how to use `MenuItem` to display menu items that has two components—for example, the menu item and a shortcut key, or a menu item followed by an image.

In this section, you'll first build a `TwoComponentMenuItem` widget that allows you to place some text followed by another widget (which could be a `Label` representing a shortcut key combination, or an `Image`). The content of a `MenuItem` is generally text, although you have the option of that text being interpreted as HTML; this is the hook you'll use to build this new widget. In the Dashboard, you'll use this widget to indicate the locales, as shown in figure 4.28.

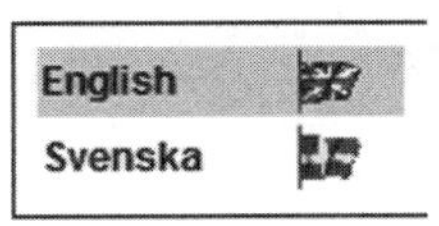

Figure 4.28 Example of the `TwoComponentMenuItem` in the Dashboard. It displays an animated GIF of a country flag related to the selectable locale.

Once you have a widget that allows you to place two components in a menu item, you can extend that to get to the widget you need for the Dashboard, which shows one of two images after the text depending on an internal state. When the widget is clicked, the state and image change, as shown in figure 4.29. This widget is called the `ToggleMenuItem`.

For the Dashboard, you use this widget to indicate to the user whether they will be asked to confirm that a component should be deleted. On the left side of figure 4.29, you indicate that the user will be asked for confirmation; if the user clicks the menu item, then the right side of figure 4.29 is visible. Let's build the `TwoComponentMenuItem` first and then look at the `ToggleMenuItem`.

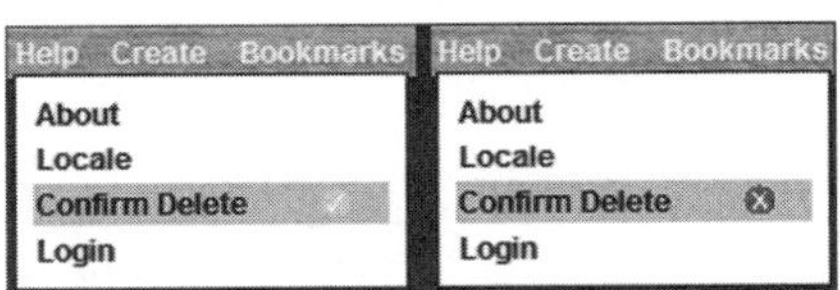

Figure 4.29 Various states of the `ToggleMenuItem` in the Dashboard example's Help manu bar. (You show the Confirm Delete functionality as either enabled or disabled.)

4.4.1 Building the TwoComponentMenuItem

The `TwoComponentMenuItem` provides a widget that displays the text in a normal `MenuItem` followed by a second widget, as shown in figure 4.30. This second widget could be text showing which shortcut key combination can be used—for example, Ctrl + O to fire the command behind the menu, or perhaps an image.

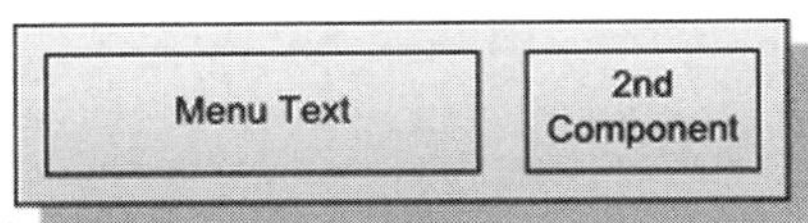

Figure 4.30 Schematic of the `TwoComponentMenuItem`

You implement `TwoComponentMenuItem` as shown in listing 4.18.

Listing 4.18 The `TwoComponentMenuItem` class

```
package org.gwtbook.client;

import com.google.gwt.user.client.Command;
import com.google.gwt.user.client.ui.HTML;
import com.google.gwt.user.client.ui.HorizontalPanel;
import com.google.gwt.user.client.ui.Label;
import com.google.gwt.user.client.ui.MenuItem;
import com.google.gwt.user.client.ui.Widget;

public class TwoComponentMenuItem extends MenuItem{        ❶ Extend MenuItem widget

   protected HorizontalPanel theMenuItem = new HorizontalPanel();   ❷ Create HorizontalPanel to hold two components

   public TwoComponentMenuItem(String theText,
                               Widget secondComponent,
                               Command theCommand){
      super(theText,true,theCommand);                       ❸ Call parent's constructor
      theMenuItem.add(new Label(theText+" "));              ❹ Set components of new widget
      theMenuItem.add(secondComponent);
      this.setSecondComponent(secondComponent);             ❺ Set rightmost component as widget
   }

   public void setSecondComponent(Widget newComponent){    ❻ Define SetSecondComponent method
      theMenuItem.remove(1);
      theMenuItem.add(newComponent);
      SimplePanel dummyContainer = new SimplePanel();
      dummyContainer.add(theMenuItem);
      String test = DOM.getInnerHTML(dummyContainer.getElement());
      this.setHTML(test);
   }

   public void setFirstComponent(String newComponent){     ❼ SetFirstComponent method
      theMenuItem.remove(0);
      theMenuItem.insert(new Label(newComponent),0);
      SimplePanel dummyContainer = new SimplePanel();
      dummyContainer.add(theMenuItem);
      String test = DOM.getInnerHTML(dummyContainer.getElement());
      this.setHTML(test);
   }

   public void setText(String theText){                    ❽ Standard setText method
      setFirstElement(theText);
   }
}
```

The `TwoComponentMenuItem` extends the `MenuItem` class ❶, so everything there is available to you in the class and you can use this class everywhere you would use a

MenuItem. To provide the ability to handle two components, you create a HorizontalPanel ❷ that will hold the two components: The first element is a Label that contains the text, and the second is whatever widget is passed in to the class.

In the widget's constructor, you first call the MenuItem constructor ❸ to make sure you're creating a valid MenuItem, but you let it know that you'll be treating the text component as a piece of HTML text. Next, you create a Label ❹ using the text passed in for the menu and add it to the HorizontalPanel as well as adding the second component directly to the same HorizontalPanel. Then, you call the setSecondComponent() method ❺—you have to add the second component prior to calling the method to set it; or the method would break because it first removes the second component (as you'll see next).

To create the view of the two components on screen, you perform some GWT and DOM magic ❻. First, you remove any existing second component from the HorizontalPanel, and then you add the new second component. So far, this is simple GWT. Next, you want to get access to the HTML of the HorizontalPanel; you do so by juggling with the DOM. You put the HorizontalPanel into a SimplePanel and then retrieve the inner HTML of the SimplePanel. A similar process is shown to set the first element in ❼, but note that the code now removes the first component (index 0), which makes the second component become the first. The implication is that when you add a new first component, you must insert it before the existing first component and so use the insert() method as opposed to the add() method.

Finalizing the component is a case of overriding the setText() method, because you need to put any text in the HorizontalPanel instead of straight into the widget. To change the text, you set a new first element as shown in the override method ❽.

As with the PNGImage and FileUpload, you create the new widget using its constructor:

```
TwoComponentMenuItem myMenuItem =
     new TwoComponentMenuItem("MenuItem",
                              new Image("myMenuImage.jpg"),
                              new Command(){
                                 public void execute(){
                                    Window.alert("Menu Clicked");
                                 }
                              });
```

With the TwoComponentMenuItem in place, you can look at specializing it by extending the class to create the Dashboard's ToggleMenuItem widget.

4.4.2 Building the ToggleMenuItem

With the `TwoComponentMenuItem` widget built, you can extend it to provide the `ToggleMenuItem` as shown in listing 4.19. This widget shows one of two different images depending upon an internal status. For the Dashboard, you wish to show a check image if a certain piece of functionality is enabled and a cross image if it isn't (although you could easily show a check and no image as the disabled view in other scenarios).

Listing 4.19 The `ToggleMenuItem` class

```
package org.gwtbook.client;

import com.google.gwt.user.client.Command;
import com.google.gwt.user.client.ui.Image;

public class ToggleMenuItem extends TwoComponentMenuItem{      ❶ Extend TwoComponent MenuItem

   public class ToggleMenuItemStates{                           ❷ Define widget states
      static public final boolean ON = true;
      static public final boolean OFF = false;
   }

   Widget[] states;                    ❸ Define array to store toggle widgets
   boolean state = true;               ❹ Define Boolean to store current state

   public ToggleMenuItem(String theText,
                         Widget onState,
                         Widget offState,
                         Command command){
      super(theText, onState, command);    ❺ Call parent's constructor
      states = new Widget[2];              ❻ Set up state variables
      states[0] = onState;
      states[1] = offState;
   }

   public void toggle(){                   ❼ Provide method to toggle widget
      setSecondComponent(states[state?1:0]);
      state = !state;
   }

   public boolean getState(){              ❽ Get widget's current state
      return state;
   }
}
```

For the ToggleMenuItem, you're extending the TwoComponentMenuItem; you say so in the definition of the class ❶. Through the inheritance hierarchy, this widget inherits MenuItem and can be used anywhere a MenuItem could.

The second component of this widget is one of two different widgets (in the Dashboard you use Images), which you hold in the array of Widgets you create at ❸. To determine which widget you'll show by default, you set the state value of this ToggleMenuItem widget to be true ❹.

Creating the widget is performed by the constructor, which first calls the parent constructor to ensure that this ToggleMenuItem will act in a similar manner to a TwoComponentMenuItem ❺ and sets the second component as the image representing the first state. It then creates an array and stores the two Widgets passed in as parameters as the alternative two states' widgets ❻.

We've talked a little about states in this widget, and at ❷ you define an inner class that contains the available states (ON and OFF). Toggling the state of the menu item is performed through the toggle() method ❼, which it's expected will be called by the user's code. This method sets the second component of the ToggleMenuItem widget to be the widget representing the state you're currently not in, and then it changes the internal representation of the state. You return the current state of the widget by calling the getState() method defined at ❽.

You could continue the hierarchy of MenuItems, building many different types if you wished (to build the menu items you're familiar with from desktop applications), but we'll leave it with these two. With this class developed, you now have the set of basic widgets that you need to develop the Dashboard example; but we still need to look at panels and events.

4.5 Summary

That concludes the first part of the journey through the GWT basics, covering widgets. You've seen that GWT provides quite a few standard widgets; but where the functionality you need isn't present, then it's relatively simple to create your own widgets. You can do this either by starting from scratch or by extending an existing widget (if you need more complicated functionality, which is better implemented as two or more simple widgets put together, then you should consider composite widgets, which are discussed in chapter 7).

The fact that widgets have two alternative views, the Java object and the DOM representation, can be a little strange at first. However, 99 percent of the time you only have to consider the Java object view. One of the few times you need to think of the widget in its DOM view is if you're creating new widgets. It can be dangerous to rely on the DOM view of the widget, because there is no guarantee that future versions of GWT will use the same DOM construct for a particular widget.

In the second half of the chapter, you constructed three widgets that will be used in the running Dashboard application—the `PNGImage` together with the `TwoComponentMenuItem` and `ToggleMenuItem`—and we discussed how they're created. To keep going with the Dashboard, we next need to look at how you visually arrange widgets in the application. You'll do that in chapter 5 by using panels.

5 Working with panels

This chapter covers

- How panels work
- Using GWT's panels
- Composite panels
- Creating new panels

If widgets can be said to provide user interface functionality, then panels provide the application's layout and visual organization. Think again of the new Plasma television from chapter 4—thankfully, the manufacturer provides a remote control with lots of buttons (widgets) on it; but what if the labels didn't match the buttons, and the buttons were all over the place? Then it wouldn't be a useful remote control! Panels allow you to control the visual structure (ensure the right labels are with the right buttons, and they're all in the right place) of your GWT applications.

DEFINITION *Panels* provide the means to visually organize and lay out a GWT application.

Panels let you visually organize and lay out a GWT application. In this chapter, we'll define what panels are; then, we'll take a tour of the panels provided in the standard GWT distribution and how you'll use them in the Dashboard. As we move into the second part of this chapter, you'll begin building your own panels. Like widgets, there probably won't be many times when you'll need to build a panel from scratch, because a range of panels are prebuilt; but we'll look at the steps involved in doing so. We'll also look at creating new panels by extending existing panels, which is a much more common situation. We'll end the chapter by building the first version of the `DashboardPanel`, into which all the component Dashboard applications (such as the Calculator, Server Status, and Clock) you build as part of the larger Dashboard example will sit.

Let's get straight to business by defining GWT panels.

5.1 What is a panel?

Panels are the building blocks of a GWT application's structural, and sometimes functional, makeup. They allow you to position widgets where you need them to make the application's functionality make sense—putting labels next to the right buttons, making sure particular components are hidden until needed, and so on.

This notion starts with the `RootPanel`, which is a direct interface into the browser's current web page. You saw this in action in chapter 3, where we discussed how the GWT default application inserted a `Button` and a `Label` into two named table cells on the screen and how you'll insert Dashboard components into the Dashboard example. `RootPanel` is a special case because it captures the browser page directly; all other panels have no knowledge of the browser until they're added through methods in the `RootPanel` class. Outside of the `RootPanel`, panels exist to be the containers into which widgets (and often other panels) are placed, sometimes recursively, to give the necessary structure to your application.

GWT provides a number of different panels, ranging from a simple `FlowPanel`, where components are laid out flowing from top left to bottom right, to more complicated panels, such as `DeckPanel`, where child widgets are held like a deck of cards with only one widget visible at a time. There is a panel for almost every need you can think of. Where panels aren't yet available in the core toolkit, you'll probably find one in a third-party library or later versions of GWT. (For example, GWT 1.0 had no `FormPanel`, so the GWT Widget Library provided one; then, in GWT 1.3 a native implementation was provided. In this chapter, we look mainly at the panels from GWT 1.3, but GWT 1.4 adds various new panels such as three types of `SplitPanels`, and so on—it's a constantly growing set.)

Panels, like the widgets we looked at in the last chapter, have a dual existence in GWT—they can be thought of as Java objects and DOM elements.

5.1.1 Using panels as Java Objects

Just as with the widgets in chapter 4, your everyday programming view of panels will be their Java object view. For example, when you create a `FlowPanel` (a panel that lets any widgets added to it flow within the constraints of the panel size), you use the following Java code:

```
FlowPanel theFlowPanel = new FlowPanel();
```

This code creates a new `FlowPanel` Java object, which you can then execute a number of class methods on. Some of these methods are listed in table 5.1.

Table 5.1 Applying some of the Java `Panel` class methods to the Java `FlowPanel` object

Code	Description
`theFlowPanel.setStyleName("buttonStyle");`	Sets the Cascading Style Sheet (CSS) style name for the `FlowPanel`. A corresponding entry should be found in the CSS style sheet attached to the web document.
`theFlowPanel.add(new Label("Test"));`	Adds a new `Label` widget to the `FlowPanel`.
`theFlowPanel.iterator();`	Retrieves a Java iterator object to allow you to iterate over all the widgets that have been added to the `FlowPanel`.

All panels are created this way—even the more complicated VerticalPanel, which places widgets on top of each other in a column. This is created in Java code as simply as this:

```
VerticalPanel theVerticalPanel = new VerticalPanel();
```

The Java object view of panels lets you treat the panel as a pure Java object. Although methods such as add() allow you a peek of how the panel behaves and may appear on the browser, they don't let you fully understand how they behave. For that, we need to consider the panel in its alternative view, as a DOM element.

5.1.2 Considering panels as DOM elements

The DOM element view of panels is displayed in the web browser. When a panel is created using the Java constructor, that constructor is responsible for creating the necessary DOM element for the panel. For example, the FlowPanel we looked at in the previous section has a Java constructor defined as follows:

```
public FlowPanel() {
   setElement(DOM.createDiv());
}
```

Therefore, when you create a FlowPanel Java object, you're also creating a DOM div element. If you were to look directly at the DOM element of this FlowPanel, you would see the following:

```
<div>
</div>
```

Not the most exciting of panels, but it works as described. If you add two other FlowPanels to it, they're added directly inside the first panel, but there are no instructions about how to position the new panels (next to or on top of)—they flow according to the browser's rule, as follows:

```
<div>
   <div></div>
   <div></div>
</div>
```

The second and third lines are the two new FlowPanels added to the original FlowPanel.

Unlike widgets, where functionality of the component is determined by the type of widget—a Button is a button, an Image an image—panels are harder to understand because they're more abstract in concept. If you just looked at the DOM element from the FlowPanel, it would be hard to tell what type of panel it was. The defining property of a panel is how it deals with other user interface components that are added to it. You can see this easier if we look at the `VerticalPanel`. It has this DOM element representation:

```
<table cellSpacing="0" cellPadding="0">
   <tbody>
   </tbody>
</table>
```

If you add the same two `FlowPanels` you added to the `FlowPanel` just now to this `VerticalPanel`, then the DOM element becomes the following:

```
<table cellSpacing="0" cellPadding="0">
   <tbody>
      <tr>
         <td style="VERTICAL-ALIGN: top" align="left">   <-- 1 Top half of VerticalPanel
            <div></div>   <-- First FlowPanel
         </td>
      </tr>
      <tr>
         <td style="VERTICAL-ALIGN: top" align="left">   Bottom half of Vertical Panel
            <div></div>   <-- Second FlowPanel
         </td>
      </tr>
   </tbody>
</table>
```

When you add a new widget to the `VerticalPanel`, its `add()` method creates a new `tr` DOM element into which it places the new widget. Then, this new DOM element is added at the end of the existing table. You can see this in the previous code snippet, where the two `FlowPanels` are captured in separate cells in the table structure, and each cell is held on a separate row.

Each panel defines its own `add()` and `insert()` methods, among others, and these give the panel its layout properties. Each panel can have widgets or other panels added to it; you can do this recursively to build the structure you need for your application, such that a panel may contain other panels that contain widgets.

Notice at ❶ that the vertical alignment of the `VerticalPanel` cell that holds the first `FlowPanel` is set to align the component vertically. To change this, use the `setVerticalAlignment()` method of the `VerticalPanel`. (There is also a `setHorizontalAlignment()` method). A number of panels control formatting in a similar manner.

At the heart of the GWT system is the `RootPanel`—the panel that links the application to the browser window. It provides references to particular DOM elements on the page, rather than strictly being a panel itself. There are two ways to use the object. The first is to pass a DOM name that you know exists, such as `RootPanel.get("MyDomArea")`, in which case a DOM element reference to

`MyDomArea` is returned. The second approach is to call `RootPanel.get()`—the lack of parameters means the result will be a reference to the page's `Body` element.

As we mentioned previously for widgets, you shouldn't rely on the fact that a particular DOM element is used to implement any particular panel, because it isn't guaranteed that it will remain that way in future GWT releases. The only exception is that three panels are set up specifically to be HTML tables and used that way; we'll come to those when we discuss the classes of panels in the next section.

5.2 The standard GWT panels

The standard GWT distribution comes with a wide range of panels that cover many different circumstances. To make sense of the panels, it's useful to split them up into five families, which correspond to the breakdown shown in the class hierarchy in figure 5.1:

- *Simple panels*—These panels are based on a `div` element and may contain only one widget. (This is a semantic distinction rather than a practical one, because this one widget may be a panel containing other widgets/panels, or a composite widget.)
- *Complex panels*—Complex panels allow any number of widgets and are usually based on a `div` or `table` element. However, when you use these widgets, you shouldn't rely on knowing their internal structure because that could change in the future.
- *HTML table panels*—These types of panels are based on HTML tables and should be expected to behave in that manner.
- *Composite panels*—Composite panels are a combination of other panels put together to provide some new functionality.
- *Split panels*—New in GWT 1.4 is the SplitPanel family, which provides a sliding bar between two widgets that allows them to be resized (but we won't discuss it in this book).

You can see in this hierarchy that all panels in GWT subclass the `Panel` abstract class. This `Panel` class subclasses the `Widget` class (and hence `UIObject`), so in a sense a panel is a widget. You can make panels sink events and override the `onBrowserEvent()` method, as you'll see you can for widgets in the next chapter (Complex panels are the exception because they're composite widgets rather than panels, but they behave in a similar manner to panels; we've shown this linkage as a dotted line in the hierarchy. We'll cover composite widgets in detail in chapter 7.)

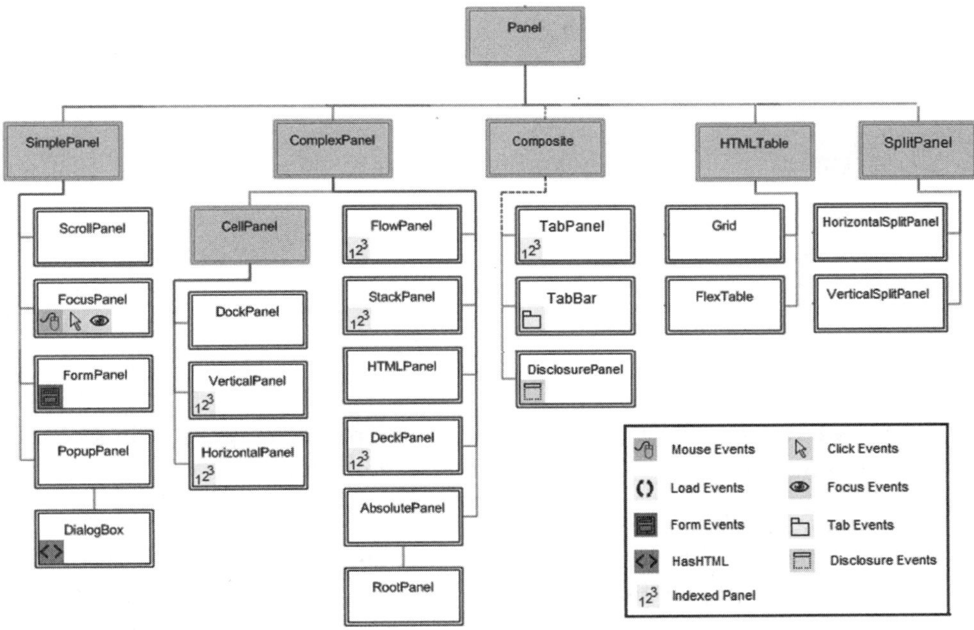

Figure 5.1 Class hierarchy of panels provided with the GWT 1.3 framework, showing the different types of panels available

The defining difference between panels and widgets comes in the panel's implementation of the `HasWidgets` interface. This interface requires panels to provide the ability to add and remove widgets from the component that implements it. It's therefore possible to add widgets and panels to a panel, but you can't add panels or widgets to a widget (because it doesn't implement the `HasWidgets` interface). Additionally, when a panel is added to the browser, the panel's `onAttach()` method is called; it iterates over all the widgets the panel contains, calling their `onAttach()` methods (when you add a widget to the browser on its own, the same mechanism occurs because you're adding the widget to the `RootPanel`; it's just less obvious).

In the next section, we'll take a quick tour through the panels that come as standard with GWT which we use in the Dashboard application. The starting point for exploring the panels will be the `SimplePanel` family.

5.2.1 Interacting with simple panels

The `SimplePanel` family provides panels that restrict the number of widgets that can be added to one. If we strip it down to its bare bones, the `SimplePanel` class extends the abstract `Panel` class and has a single variable for holding details of its one widget.

Figure 5.1 shows the following five `SimplePanel` panels:

- `PopupPanel`
- `DialogBox`
- `FormPanel`
- `FocusPanel`
- `ScrollPanel`

Let's look at each of them, discussing any peculiarities or points of interest and where you'll use them in the Dashboard application.

Popping up displays

A `PopupPanel` "pops" up over other widgets on your page—you could use it, for example, to implement tooltip functionality (which is what you'll do in the Dashboard's Server Status component application, shown in figure 5.2).

Google is particularly proud of this component because it even pops up over list boxes, which normally is a problem for this type of functionality.
The panel can be set to auto-hide if the user clicks outside it. And be aware that it previews browser events—if a widget you're developing doesn't get the events you expect, make sure no unexpectedly open `PopupPanels` are grabbing and deleting

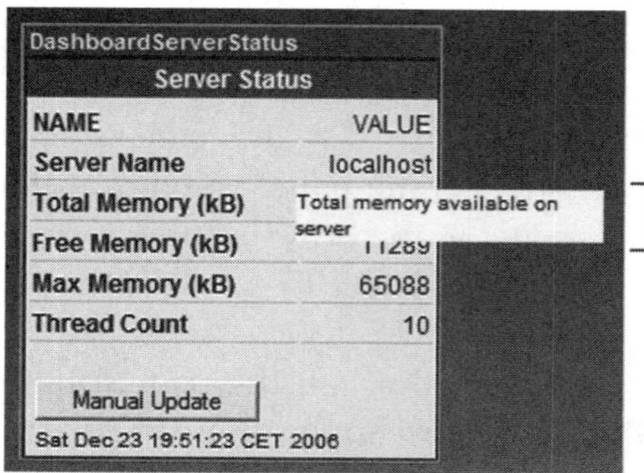

Figure 5.2
Displaying a Dashboard tooltip by clicking a Server Status attribute name (you create the tooltip by subclassing the `PopupPanel`)

that event! This caused a problem with the `ToolTip` class, but we'll discuss that in more detail in chapter 6.

A subclass of `PopupPanel` is the `DialogBox` panel, which the Dashboard component applications use heavily.

Communicating in a dialog

The `DialogBox` panel is a particular instance of a `PopupPanel` that can contain a single widget and a caption at the top—which can be seen in figure 5.3.

The user can drag the panel around by clicking the caption and dragging the mouse, although the panel doesn't naturally contain a close button.

When you look at figure 5.3, you may question whether this is a simple panel, because there appears to be more than one widget in the dialog box: your widget and a `Label` widget for the caption. Although `DialogBox` seems to have many widgets associated with it, it doesn't (really). We get into an argument of semantics that many politicians would be proud of—because a panel is a widget, if you add any type of panel to a simple panel, you're adding only one widget (the panel you add may be complicated, with many widgets added to it, but you're still adding only one "widget" to the dialog box).

To create a `DialogBox`, you use one of the two constructors that GWT provides. The first takes no parameters, and the second takes a boolean parameter to specify the auto-hide capability (`true` to hide the dialog if a user clicks somewhere else, `false` otherwise).

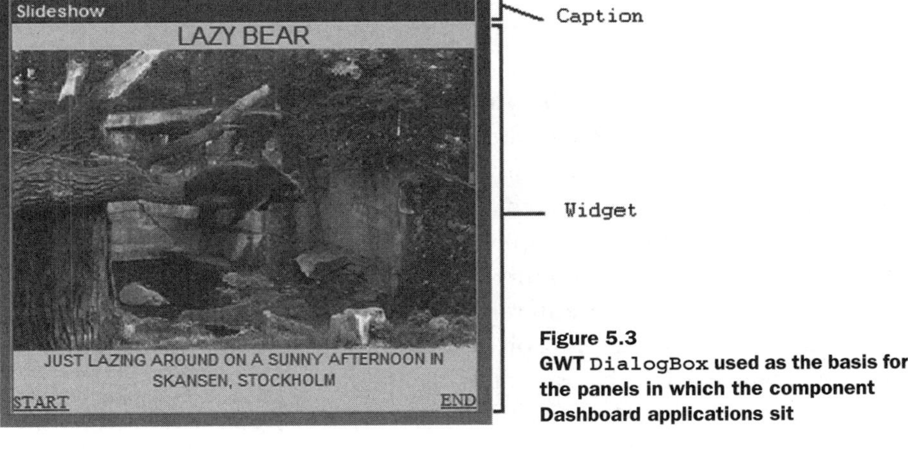

Figure 5.3
GWT `DialogBox` used as the basis for the panels in which the component Dashboard applications sit

Once a DialogBox is created, you need to set the two component parts: the caption and the widget. You set the former using the setText() or setHTML() method and the latter using the setWidget() method. Generally, you create a DialogBox as shown in listing 5.1.

Listing 5.1 Creating a dialog using the DialogBox class

```
final DialogBox theDialog = new DialogBox(true);      <-- Create DialogBox object
theDialog.setText("A Dialog");                         <-- Set caption text
VerticalPanel thePanel = new VerticalPanel();
Label theMessage = new Label("Some Dialog Text");
Button okButton = new Button("OK");
okButton.addClickListener(new ClickListener() {           Create dialog's widget
   public void onClick(Widget sender) {
      theDialog.hide();
   }
});
thePanel.add(theMessage);
thePanel.add(okButton);
theDialog.setWidget(thePanel);    <-- Set dialog's widget
```

You'll create a subclass of DialogBox later in this chapter for use in the Dashboard example. Let's look at another panel you use in the Dashboard, although as part of an application.

Forming an opinion

The FormPanel was introduced into GWT in version 1.1 to allow the management of forms and is probably the most functionally active panel in the set. You can set all sorts of attributes, such as the form's encoding, the method of sending to the server (post or get) and the action (what happens when the form is submitted). In chapter 13, we'll show a complete example of this panel together with how it's submitted to the server and how you handle the events related to submission and return of results. For now, the form shown in figure 5.4 is what we're talking about—and we hope it seems familiar to you as an outline of a standard HTML form.

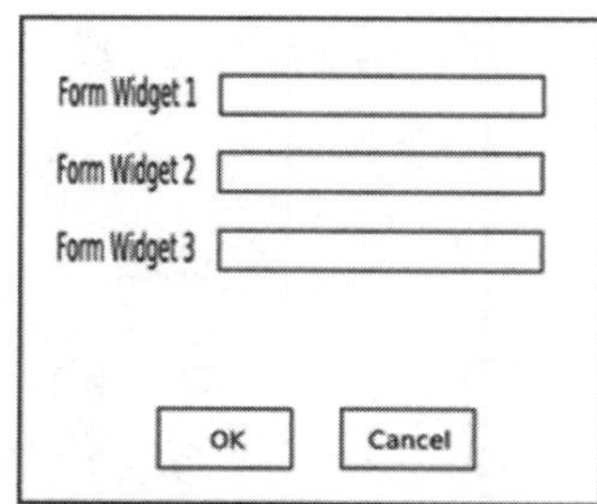

Figure 5.4 Example of the FormPanel. It's a simple panel, but it performs the same trick you saw with DialogBox: The form components—text boxes, labels, radio buttons, and so on—must be added to a particular panel, and then that panel is added to the FormPanel.

Submission of a form occurs programmatically by calling the FormPanel's submit() method as the result of some other user interaction—usually, by adding a ClickListener to a submit Button added to the form. We'll look more at ClickListeners in the next chapter, on events; but one panel manages many different types of events: the FocusPanel.

Focusing user actions

A FocusPanel acts similarly to the FocusWidget you saw in the previous chapter. It lets its contents become focusable and adds the ability to capture mouse and keyboard events that occur anywhere on the panel. You'll use a FocusPanel in the Calculator component application to let you capture keypresses on the keyboard, as you can see in figure 5.5.

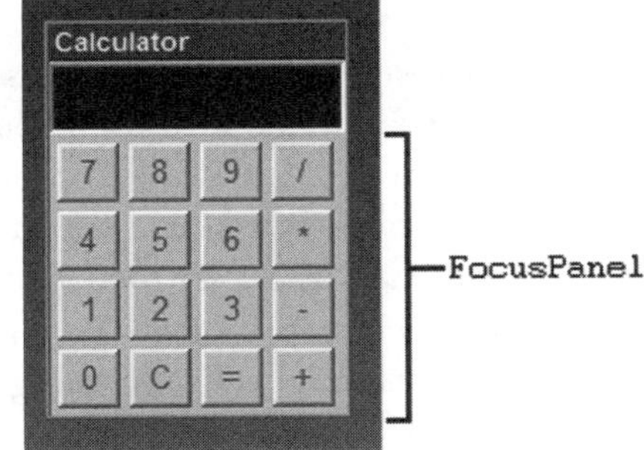

Figure 5.5 The Calculator Dashboard application you'll build in this book places its keypad inside a FocusPanel, which enables you to capture physical computer keypresses and pretend the user has mouse-clicked one of the calculator's buttons.

Unlike the FocusWidget, which you can't create instances of, you can create instances of FocusPanel. In order for it to have any functionality, you need to place content in it (you could use it on its own, giving it dimensions through CSS or the setWidth()/Height() methods, but we're not sure what purpose an empty focus area has).

In the Dashboard's Calculator application, you'll place the calculator keys inside a FocusPanel so that you can capture physical keyboard presses (see listing 5.2).

Listing 5.2 Using a FocusPanel in the Calculator by adding buttons and a KeyboardListener

```
FocusPanel theKeypad = new FocusPanel();
:
theKeyPad.add(theKeys);                                          ❶ Add widget to FocusPanel
theKeyPad.addKeyboardListener(new KeyboardListenerAdapter(){     ❷ Add KeyListener to FocusPanel
   public void onKeyPress(Widget sender,
                          char keyCode,
                         int modifiers) {                        Implement key event-handling
      //code that handles keypress goes here.
   }
});
theKeyPad.setTabIndex(0);                                        ❸ Set widget's tab index
theKeyPad.setAccessKey('+');                                     ❹ Set browser access key
```

By adding the calculator's grid of buttons, `theKeys`, to the `theKeyPad FocusPanel` ❶, you can add `ClickListeners`, `FocusListeners`, `MouseListeners`, and `KeyboardListeners`. We chose to add a `KeyboardListener` ❷ to process any keyboard keypresses. This way, the user can use the physical keyboard to enter numbers and operations in the calculator as if they were clicking the buttons directly.

The `FocusPanel`, like the `FocusWidget`, lets you set its position in the browser's tab index through the `setTabIndex()` method ❸. If the tab index is shared between multiple `FocusWidgets` or `FocusPanels`, then the ordering given by the browser when the user presses the Tab key is arbitrary; however, if the `FocusPanel` is in sequence with the `FocusWidget`, then that ordering is upheld.

Finally, you set up a special access key ❹ for the focus area such that if the user presses the browser's modifier key and the special key, then the widget automatically receives focus. In Firefox and Internet Explorer, the special modifier key is Alt; in Opera, it's the Shift-Esc key combination. Or, you can set the focus programmatically by using the `setFocus()` method with a boolean variable as the parameter.

In addition to focusing on a panel, the user may wish to scroll up and down (or even across) a panel.

Scrolling through information

A `ScrollPanel` allows a user to scroll around a widget that is larger than the dimensions of the `ScrollPanel`. By default, the panel always shows both scroll bars, although it's possible to set it such that they're shown only when necessary. This is the panel we have the most problems with, because unless you set dimensions for it (either—preferably—through CSS, or programmatically using the `setWidth()/setHeight()` methods), it expands to the size of the widget you place in it—and therefore you get no scrolling capability. You must set the `ScrollPanel` dimensions to less than the widget it contains to enact the scrolling.

You can set a widget to always be visible in the scroll panel. You'll use that functionality in the Dashboard's Address Book application to quickly show the relevant address details when a name is selected from the list of names (see figure 5.6).

The Address Book uses the code shown in listing 5.3 to create and use a `ScrollPanel`.

Listing 5.3 Using a ScrollPanel in the Dashboard's Address Book

```
visibleAddresses = new ScrollPanel();                              <-- Create ScrollPanel
visibleAddresses.setStyleName("addressBook-visibleAddress");      <-- Set ScrollPanel's CSS style name
visibleAddresses.add(theAddresses);                               <-- Add panel to ScrollPanel
visibleAddresses.addScrollListener(new ScrollListener(){          <-- Add ScrollListener
   public void onScroll(Widget widget,
                        int scrollLeft,
                        int scrollTop) {
      int widgetCount = theAddresses.getWidgetCount();            <-- Scroll event-handling
      int panelHeight = theAddresses.getOffsetHeight();
      int widgetHeight = panelHeight/widgetCount;
      int widgetNumber = scrollTop/widgetHeight;
      addressLinks.setSelectedIndex(widgetNumber);
   }
});
```

If the panel/widget added to the `ScrollPanel` has dimensions less than the `ScrollPanel`, then by default, no scroll bars are displayed. Scroll bars are added automatically once the dimensions of the component added to the `ScrollPanel` grow out of the `ScrollPanel`'s dimensions. To have scroll bars always present, you use the `setAlwaysShowScrollBars()` method on the panel.

You can programmatically set the position of the scroll bars for the panel using two methods the panel provides. To set vertical position, use the `setScrollPosition()` method; to set the horizontal scroll-bar position, use the `setHorizontalPosition()` method. Alternatively, you can set the position of the bars relative to a widget that you want visible using the `ensureVisible()` method. This last method is used in the `AddressBook` to show the address selected by the user (see listing 5.4).

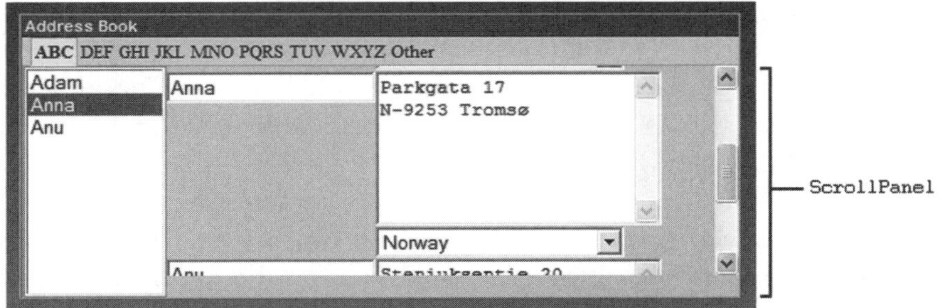

Figure 5.6 The Dashboard's Address Book application uses a `ScrollPanel` when displaying a list of addresses.

Listing 5.4 Setting the scroll-bar position relative to an element

```
private void showAddress(String index){
   AddressDetails address = (AddressDetails) addresses.get(index);
   visibleAddresses.ensureVisible(address);
}
```

In the `showAddress()` method, you get the `AddressDetails` object that should now be seen and then use the `ensureVisible()` method to make it visible.

These simple panels were restricted to adding only one widget. Although that's mainly a semantic restriction, if you wish to use a panel that explicitly allows the addition of multiple widgets, you need to consider either a `ComplexPanel` or `HTMLTable` family panel. In the next section, we'll look at the `ComplexPanel` family and, after that, `HTMLTable`.

5.2.2 *Considering more complex panels*

The `ComplexPanel` family of panels lets you add one or more widgets, which makes them more advanced compared to the `SimplePanel` family we just looked at (which allows only one widget per panel).

Presentational aspects of complex panels are delegated to the subclasses, which must decide what DOM elements they use to provide their visual behavior. Some of the subclasses use `div` elements (for example, the `DeckPanel`) and others use `table` elements (for example, the `HorizontalPanel` and `VerticalPanel`). This difference is driven by the ease with which visual behavior can be implemented. In the case of the `DeckPanel`, only one widget is visible at any given time; it's easier to place each widget in separate `div` elements and then manipulate the `visibility` style property of the individual `div`s. Horizontal and vertical panels are easier to construct as tables in HTML—but we should be clear here that you shouldn't rely on the fact that they're implemented as tables, because that could change in future releases (if you need to rely on a table structure, then you should use the `HTMLTable` family of panels we'll discuss later).

A complex panel lets you retrieve an iterator to access its child widgets (to get the iterator, you call the `iterator()` method on the panel). To get a list of a panel's child widgets instead of an iterator, you use the `getChildren()` method, which returns a `WidgetCollection` object.

You add widgets using the `add()` method. An `insert()` method is provided that lets you insert new widgets before a particular index in the widget collection.

GWT provides nine complex panels:

- `AbsolutePanel`
- `RootPanel`
- `HTMLPanel`
- `FlowPanel`
- `DeckPanel`
- `StackPanel`
- `DockPanel`
- `HorizontalPanel`
- `VerticalPanel`

Let's look at the salient points of each of them in turn.

Positioning components absolutely

In an absolute panel, you can position widgets wherever you wish. You add widgets by specifying the particular x and y coordinates at which they should appear in the panel. This is achieved using the constructor's `add(Widget, x, y)` method; or, if the widget is already added, then you can change its position with the `setPosition(Widget,x,y)` method.

Widgets can overlap if they're so arranged, but you can't directly alter the z-index of an absolute panel with the standard implementation. If you're interested in finding the position of a widget in an absolute panel, you can use the `getWidgetTop()` and `getWidgetLeft()` methods, which retrieve values of the top and left of the widget relative to the panel it's in.

Note that an absolute panel won't resize itself to make room for widgets you add; all the other panels generally do. If you add an extra widget to a horizontal panel, it will grow to the right to make room—but not so for the absolute panel. If you add a widget in a position that is outside the existing visible area for an absolute panel, then the panel will happily place it there. Should you then wish for it to be displayed, you must either move the widget or explicitly resize the panel.

This panel is also the parent of `RootPanel`, which we'll look at next.

Interfacing with the browser through the RootPanel

A special case of `AbsolutePanel` is `RootPanel`, which gives your application direct access to the browser page. `RootPanel` is mainly used to add your application's components to the view the user gets, as you saw back in section 3.1.2.

`RootPanel` provides functionality to get specific named DOM elements from the DOM representation of the current browser page using the `get(elementName)` method, or a reference to the DOM `body` using the `get()` method. You've seen both these techniques used: the first in the default application to place the button

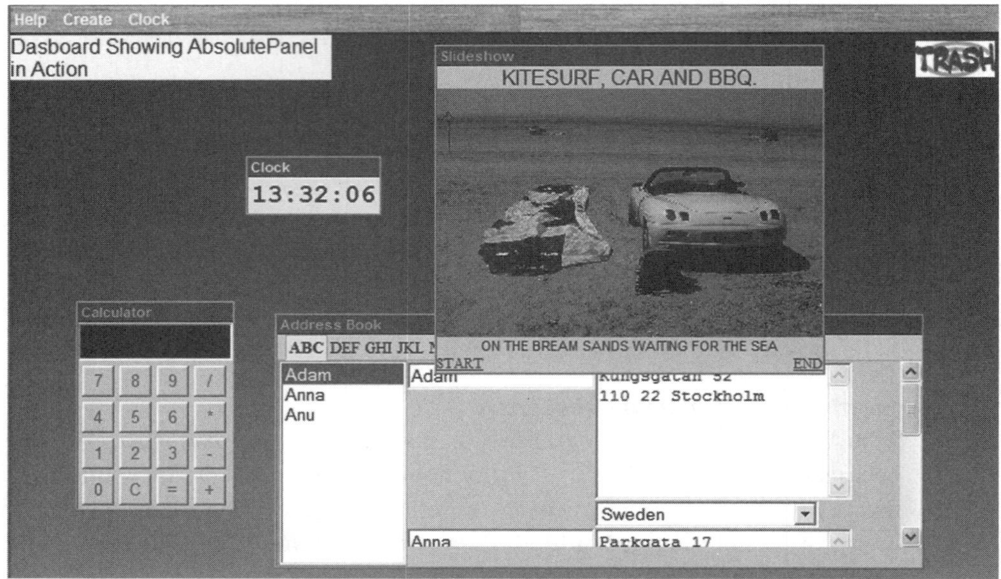

Figure 5.7 The Dashboard showing how to use the `RootPanel` for positioning Dashboard applications where you want (`RootPanel` is really an implementation of an `AbsolutePanel`)

and label in desired locations on the screen, and the second in the Dashboard where you place widgets as they come. Figure 5.7 shows what happens when you add a number of widgets to the browser using the second approach.

Slightly more controlled, but still flexible, is the `HTMLPanel`.

Adding new HTML areas

The `HTMLPanel` lets you include standard HTML code in it. You use the constructor to add an HTML string to the panel, and you add widgets to named elements in that HTML. This is performed in a similar manner to how widgets are added to the `RootPanel`, but using the `add(Widget,String)` method.

You don't use this panel in the Dashboard—we couldn't manage to use every single GWT component in our example application!

`RootPanel` and `AbsolutePanel` are extremely relaxed about laying out components, giving you total control over positioning. Now we'll move on to panels that are more controlling. Let's ease ourselves in by first looking at the `FlowPanel`.

Flowing components

A `FlowPanel` lets the widgets that are added to it flow in a left to right, top to bottom manner, as if you were adding widgets directly to the browser page. This is the same manner they would appear if they were added to the browser screen. Figure 5.8 shows this flow in action as you have added four widgets to the panel in sequential order.

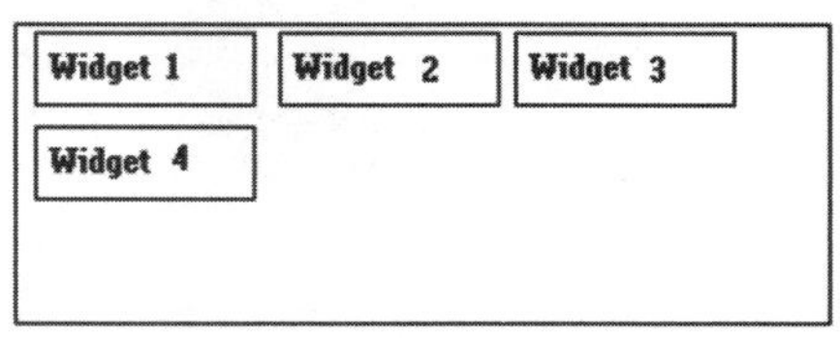

Figure 5.8 Result of adding four widgets to a `FlowPanel`—the widgets were added in sequential number order and flowed left to right, top to bottom.

The panel also implements the `IndexedPanel` interface, which enforces an explicit ordering on its children. This means you can get a widget with a particular number using the `getWidget(int)` method and always be guaranteed that it will be the same widget. You can also get the index of a widget through the `getWidgetIndex(Widget)` method and a count of the widgets in a panel with the `getWidgetCount()` method. Finally, you can remove a widget using the `remove(int widgetIndex)` method as well as the standard panel `remove(Widget)` method.

In terms of layout, `FlowPanel` allows the most flexibility for styling through CSS after the `AbsolutePanel`. You'll make use of this in the `EditableLabel` component you'll build in chapter 7, where you'll place a text area and two buttons in a `FlowPanel`; by varying the width of the container, you can move the buttons from the right of the text to under it (you can also achieve the same effect using CSS commands). See figure 5.9.

Figure 5.9 Using the `FlowPanel` in the `EditableLabel` component of the Dashboard. In this example, three components (a text area and two buttons) flow from left to right and top to bottom into the shape of the outer container.

If you want to let the application have even more control over positioning, perhaps not showing parts of the application, then the `DeckPanel` is a great choice.

Decking out an application

You can add numerous widgets to a `DeckPanel`, but only one widget is visible at any given time. The panel acts like a pack of cards. In the GWT implementation, this panel is used by the `TabPanel` implementation, where clicking a tab makes the widget for that tab visible, as you'll see later. You'll also use it in the Dashboard for the Security application, the three decks of which are shown in figure 5.10. Only one of these decks is visible at a time, and you default to deck 1 to allow the

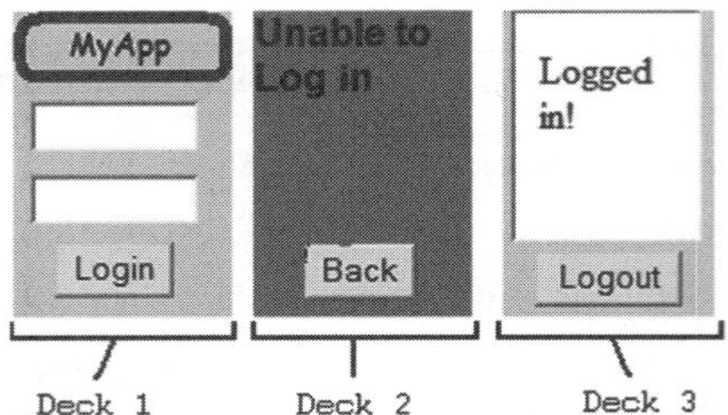

Figure 5.10
The three decks of the Dashboard's login functionality, showing the default view, a failed login, and a successful login. Only one of these decks is visible at a time.

user to log in—if they're unsuccessful, then they're shown deck 2; if they succeed, then they're shown deck 3.

To create the `Login` widget, you use the code shown in listing 5.5 in the constructor of the composite widget.

Listing 5.5 Creating the `DeckPanel` for the Dashboard's login application

```
application = new DeckPanel();                       <- Create DeckPanel
application.add(createLoginPanel());                 
application.add(createLoggedInPanel());              Add new widget/panels as decks
application.add(createErrorPanel());                 
application.setStyleName("login-visiblePanel");
application.showWidget(LOGIN_PANEL);                 <- Show first deck
```

This panel also implements the `IndexedPanel` interface, which means that when widgets are added, they're ordered and can be indexed—this ordering gives you confidence that the correct deck is displayed in the Security application. On top of this, you can set the current visible widget through the `showWidget(int)` method as well as get the current visible widget through the `getVisibleWidget()` method.

If you want a panel that acts in a similar way to `DeckPanel` but lets you choose which panel is visible, then you should use the `StackPanel`.

Stacking components together

`StackPanel` and `DeckPanel` share similar functionality, in that they both show only one widget at a time; but in a `StackPanel`, a header for each widget is visible and can be selected to show the widget.

Figure 5.11 shows the Dashboard's Search Comparison application. There are two panels (two different versions of the Google search widget we'll cover later in the book), but only panel 2, the video search, is currently visible. Clicking header 1 for the blog search displays that panel, as shown on the right in the figure.

To create the `StackPanel` in figure 5.11, you use the code shown in listing 5.6.

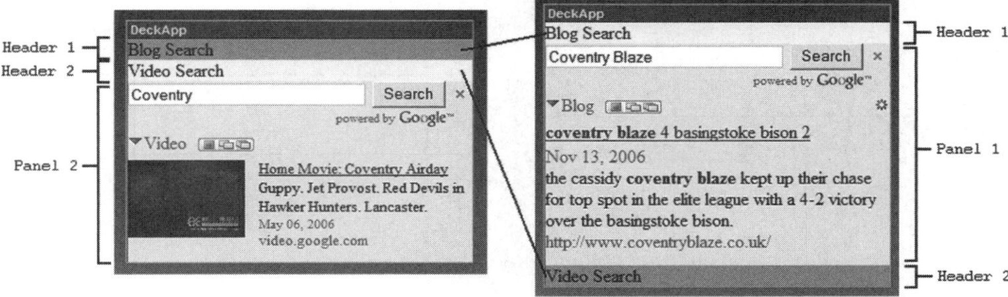

Figure 5.11 `StackPanel` **is similar to** `DeckPanel` **but lets you select a label to show each panel (only one of which is visible at a time, depending on whether you click Blog Search or Video Search).**

Listing 5.6 Creating the `DeckPanel` for the Dashboard's Search Comparison application

```
StackPanel theStack = new StackPanel();                            ❶ Create StackPanel
theStack.add(createGoogleBlogSearch(),"Blog Search");              ❷ Add panel
theStack.add(createGoogleVideoSearch(),"Video Search");              to stack
```

The stack is created using the constructor shown in ❶. You then add new widgets to the stack panel using the `add()` method ❷, which should be given a widget and some header text as parameters. The header text can also be HTML text if a third parameter, a boolean, is given and set to `true`. This third way lets you add images to the header text. You can also change the text associated with a widget through the `setStackText()` method for a particular widget index—which means you need to find the index of the widget you wish to set the text for. If it's the currently selected widget, you can use the `getSelectedIndex()` method.

To programmatically show a new stack, you use the `showStack()` method.

Docking components

The `DockPanel` is reminiscent of the Swing `BorderLayout`. It lets you add multiple widgets to the North, West, East, and South; but only one widget can be added to the Center space, which can take up any remaining space on the widget. The layout of the `DockPanel` is shown in figure 5.12.

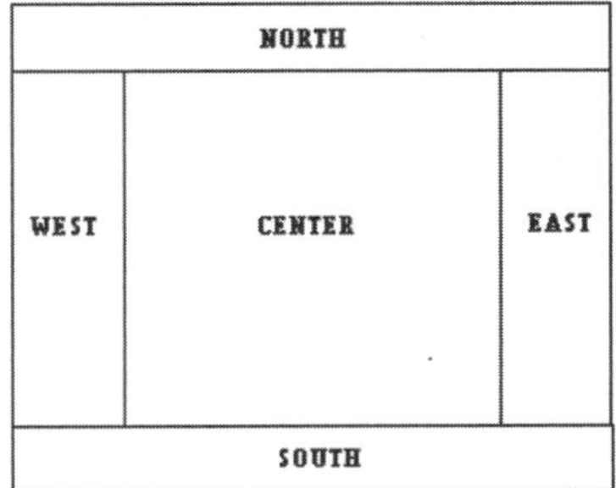

Figure 5.12 Schematic of the `DockPanel` showing the five areas where widgets can be placed

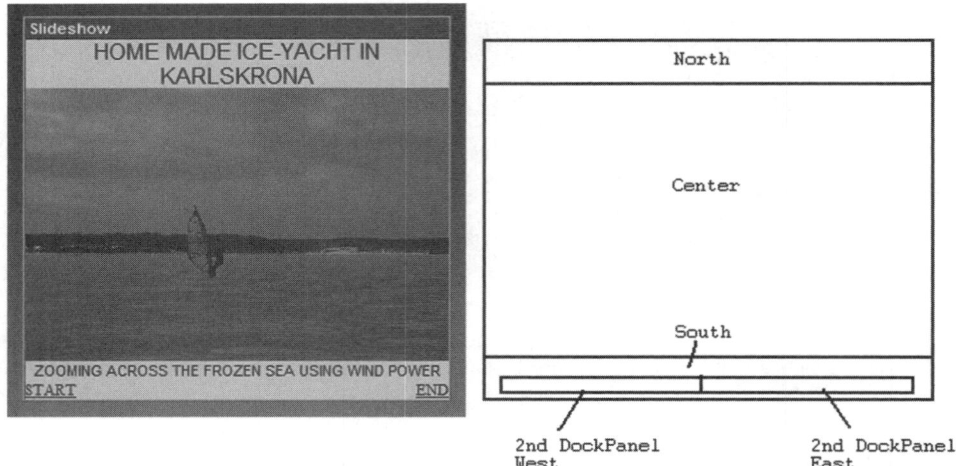

Figure 5.13 Use of the `DockPanel` in the Slideshow application. The outer dock panel doesn't use the East and West areas, whereas the dock panel in the South area of the first uses only the East and West areas to position the Start and End hyperlinks.

If no widget is added to a particular area, then that area's space is "lost". You'll use of this property in the Dashboard's Slideshow application, where you use two `DockPanels`, one inside the other (see figure 5.13).

When you add widgets, you must explicitly set where the widget will reside in the `DockPanel` using static constants from that class, such as `DockPanel.NORTH`. Only one widget can sit in the `DockPanel.CENTER` location; trying to place more than one widget there raises an exception, although it's possible to add more than one widget to the other areas, as you can see in listing 5.7.

Listing 5.7 Creating the `DockPanel` for the Dashboard's Slideshow application

```
DockPanel thePanel = new DockPanel();                  <-- Create DockPanel
thePanel.add(theTitle,DockPanel.NORTH);                <-- Add widget to North
thePanel.add(theImage,DockPanel.CENTER);
thePanel.add(theName,DockPanel.SOUTH);                 | Add multiple
thePanel.add(navPanel,DockPanel.SOUTH);                | widgets to South
thePanel.add(preloadImages, DockPanel.SOUTH);
```

`DockPanel` extends the `CellPanel`, as do the horizontal and vertical panels we'll look at next. This `CellPanel` allows widgets contained in cells of an HTML table; you can set horizontal and vertical layouts using constants from the HasVerticalAlignment and HasHorizontalAlignment classes, but using CSS styling is preferred.

If you want to guarantee that widgets are always kept in a horizontal line, you should use the HorizontalPanel.

Laying out horizontally

A HorizontalPanel adds widgets in a horizontal line from left to right. There isn't much more to say about this panel than that; it's good at doing its one job. You used this panel when you created the TwoComponentMenuItem widget in chapter 4; it's shown in figure 5.14.

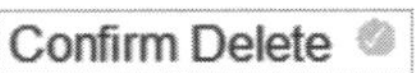

Figure 5.14 HorizontalPanel used in the TwoComponentMenuItem widget built in chapter 4 to position both components horizontally across the page

For this component, you create a HorizontalPanel that contains two widgets. Listing 5.8 shows where you use the horizontal panel.

Listing 5.8 Creating the HorizontalPanel for the Dashboard's menu

```
private HorizontalPanel theMenuItem = new HorizontalPanel();   <-- Create HorizontalPanel
theMenuItem.remove(1);   <-- Remove existing widget
theMenuItem.add(newComponent);   <-- Add component to HorizontalPanel
SimplePanel dummyContainer = new SimplePanel();
dummyContainer.add(theMenuItem);
String test = DOM.getInnerHTML(dummyContainer.getElement());
this.setHTML(test);
```

With the horizontal panel in place, listing 5.8 shows how the second component is changed. You first remove the image—it's at index 1, because the widget collection is zero indexed—and then add the new image using the standard add() method. The remaining part of this code extracts the HTML relating to the panel so it can be added to the menu item; we covered that functionality in section 4.4.1.

If you want the widgets to go down instead of across, then you need the VerticalPanel.

Laying out vertically

Diametrically opposite the HorizontalPanel is the VerticalPanel, which does an excellent job of keeping widgets stacked on top of each other. You'll use it, for example, in the Dashboard Security application to keep the components lined up, as shown in figure 5.15.

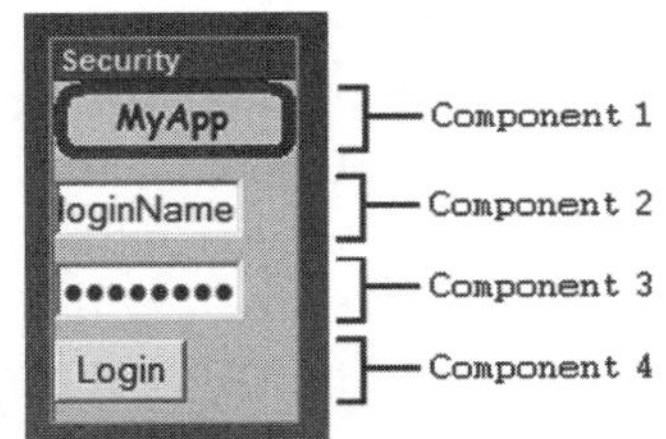

Figure 5.15 Using the VerticalPanel to position all the components used in the first deck of the Dashboard's login application

It's created using the code shown in listing 5.9.

Listing 5.9 Creating the `VerticalPanel` for the Dashboard's login component application

```
loginPanel = new VerticalPanel();
loginPanel.add(appImage);
loginPanel.add(userName);
loginPanel.add(password);
loginPanel.add(loginButton);
```

Whether the complex panel uses a `div` or `table` DOM elements is transparent to you. It's nice to be aware of the underlying implementation, but you shouldn't rely on it, because among other things, it may change in the future. If you need to manage a panel as a table—for example, to insert widgets in the fourth column and third row—then you need to consider the final family of panels: `HTMLTable`.

5.2.3 Considering HTML table-based panels

Three GWT-provided panels act explicitly as if they have a table structure: `HTMLTable`, `FlexTable`, and `Grid`. You can insert GWT widgets at determined column/row locations and manipulate the style name of specific cells.

The first panel is a basic HTML table that is then specialized by the second two panels. The key difference between the second two panels is that `Grid` is of a fixed size and needs to be explicitly resized if columns/rows outside the initially set size are to be accessed. The `FlexTable` panel, on the other hand, creates new grid cells as and when needed.

Implementing an HTMLTable

The `HTMLTable` panel provides all the basics for building HTML tables in GWT, although you can't create an instance of it—you must use one of its children. It can create an empty table; add or remove cells, rows, and columns; and check whether particular rows, columns, or cells exist. It also lets you set or remove widgets for particular cells as well as set things such as cell padding and spacing.

You can add a `TableListener` to a child of `HTMLTable` panel, which is fired when cells in the table are clicked. For example, the code shown in listing 5.10 uses the grid panel and can be used to provide functionality that sorts a table based on a column when the header of that column is clicked.

Listing 5.10 Adding a `TableListener` to reorder data by clicking elements in the header row

```
final int HEADERROW = 0;
Grid myTable = new Grid();                                   Create HTMLTable
myTable.addTableListener(new TableListener(){                AddTableListener
   public void onCellClicked(SourcesTableEvents sender,
                             int row,
                             int cell){                      onCellClicked method
      if (row==HEADERROW){                                   Check if clicked row was header
         orderTableOn(cell);                                 Order table (application method)
      }
   }
});
```

Individual cells can be assigned their own CSS class name and have certain stylistic attributes altered programmatically. You do this using the `CellFormatter` object from the `HTMLTable` class, which is subclassed by `Grid` and `FlexTable`. Table 5.2 shows how to set the format of a cell and a whole row for a `Grid`.

Table 5.2 Ways to format in a `Grid`

Task	Code
Formatting a cell	`Grid g;` `g.getCellFormatter().setStyleName(0,0,"header");`
Formatting a row	`Grid g;` `g.getRowFormatter().setStyleName(0,"header");`

The key aspect of `HTMLTable` is that it provides the basis for the next two panels.

Flexing a table layout

A `FlexTable` is essentially a table where rows and columns are created implicitly to match the size needed when the program adds widgets. For example, if the `FlexTable` is initially dimensioned as a 4x4 grid, and the program adds a widget to column 10, row 15, then the `FlexTable` automatically grows to be a 10x15 grid.

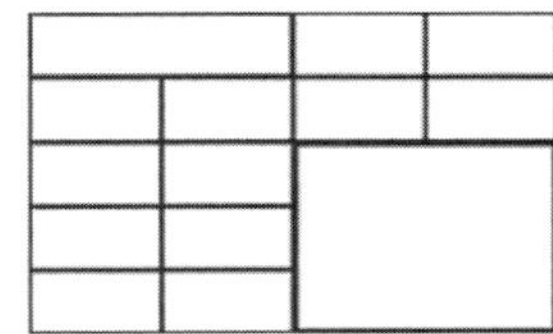

Figure 5.16 Example of a `FlexTable` with some row and column spanning

Additionally, rows and columns can span a number of other columns or rows, which isn't possible using a `Grid`; see figure 5.16.

FlexTable provides an additional class to allow rows and columns to span a number of cells: FlexCellFormatter. You can set row and column spanning as simply as in listing 5.11.

Listing 5.11 Using a FlexCellFormatter on a FlexTable

```
flextable = new FlexTable();
   FlexCellFormatter formatter =
      flextable.getFlexCellFormatter();
   formatter.setColSpan(0, 0, 2);                ❶ Set cell (0,0) to span two columns
   formatter.setRowSpan(0,0,2);                  ❷ Set cell (0,0) to span two rows
   for(int loop1=0;loop1<6;loop1++){
      for(int loop2=0;loop2<5;loop2++){
         flextable.setText(loop1,loop2,"("+loop1+","+loop2+")");   ❸ Fill cells (0,0) to (5,4) with text
   }

   }
   formatter.addStyleName (1,1,"flexTable");     ❹ Set style for cell (l,l)
```

In this example, you span cell (0,0) across the first two rows and columns ❶ ❷. Then ❸ you try to fill the cells. But notice in figure 5.17 that this spanning affects the positioning of the neighboring cells—row 0 appears one column longer, and row 1 appears two columns longer. This should be expected; it's caused by the spanning, but it may cause you to think your application is wrong if you forget this!

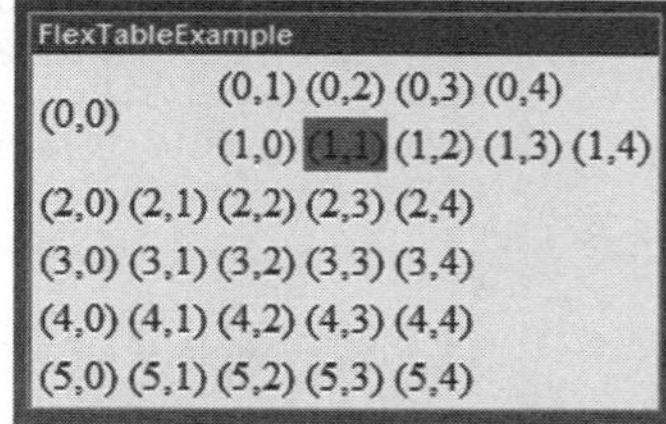

Figure 5.17 Result of trying to span the first two cells in rows 1 and 2, columns 1 and 2

At ❹, you apply styling directly to the cell at column 1, row 1, which you can see in figure 5.17. The Server Status component also uses a table formatter to give its table's header cells a different style than the rest of the table cells.

You need to be acutely aware of how the formatter works; otherwise, you'll get results that you may not expect.

WARNING One thing to be aware of regarding tables in GWT is that there is currently a performance hit if tables become exceptionally large. An approach to minimize this issue is to implement data pagination: If the table can show 10 items, and you have 100 pieces of data in your database, then fetch only the relevant 10 you need at a time.

If you don't need the flexibility of a flex table, then you use Grid.

Gridding components together

A grid provides the same container style as `FlexTable` but is less flexible in terms of positioning widgets. If a grid is created with dimensions 4x4, and then you need to add a widget at column 10, row 15, you must explicitly resize the grid to 10x15 before you can add the widget. Unlike in a flex table, you can't span rows or columns in a grid. You use `Grid` in the Dashboard's Calculator to lay out the buttons, as shown in figure 5.18.

Figure 5.18 Buttons laid out using the `Grid` panel to provide a uniform keypad for the Calculator Dashboard application

The final family we need to look at is the composite panel family.

WARNING Grid becomes unhappy if you try and place a widget in a cell that doesn't exist. However, the error from GWT in Hosted Mode won't tell you this; it complains about other things.

5.2.4 Considering composite panels

The final family of panels is the composite panel family. There are two panels in this family, although you'll normally use only `TabPanel` (it uses the `TabBar`).

Creating a TabBar

The `TabBar` composite panel wraps a `HorizontalPanel` to provide functionality for tabs. It sinks `onClick` events and allows applications to register `TabListeners` against it to be notified when tabs are selected.

Creating a TabPanel

A `TabPanel` is a combination of two other panels. It uses a `DeckPanel` to contain the visible contents of the tab displays so that only one deck is visible at a time. It adds a `TabBar` to contain the tabs that can be clicked and registers a `TabListener` in order to be notified when elements in the `TabBar` are clicked, which then shows the correct deck in the `DeckPanel`. You can see this arrangement in figure 5.19.

Disclosing panels

GWT 1.4 introduced a new composite panel, called DisclosurePanel—effectively a panel with a title, where the panel is hidden until the title is clicked upon. The panel is hidden again when the title is again clicked upon.

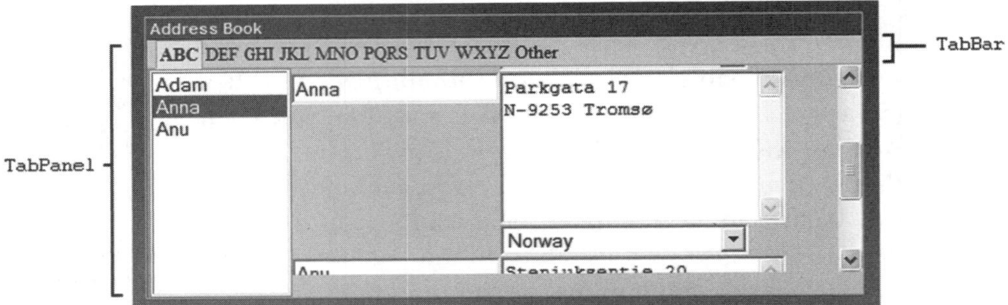

Figure 5.19 How a `TabPanel` is constructed

5.2.5 *Splitting panels*

Also new in GWT 1.4 were a family of splitter panels (an abstract base class and two concrete classes: HorizontalSplitPanel and VerticalSplitPanel). Both concrete implementations allow widgets to be placed either side of a split bar, which can be slid in one plane, e.g. left to right for the HorizontalSplitPanel. Sliding the bar alters the visible width of each side and thus hides and shows the contained widgets.

That's all the panels that are provided free with the GWT distribution you use in the Dashboard. Because it's an extensive list, it isn't likely that you'll need to create your own panels. However, we should never say never; in the next two sections, we'll take a closer look at the process used to create a new panel.

5.3 *Creating new panels*

In this section, you'll begin to construct a new panel that allows only `Button` widgets to be added. Initially, we'll examine how it can be constructed from scratch by manipulating DOM elements; then, we'll explain how to build the same panel by extending an existing panel.

Once we've shown the basics of extending a panel, we'll turn our attention to extending the `DialogBox` to provide the first version of the panel you'll use for all the Dashboard component applications (you'll extend this panel in the next chapter to handle more events and the "drop" part of drag and drop).

BE AWARE It's often tempting to implement a component by extending a panel rather than creating a composite widget (see chapter 7). If you extend a panel, then you're conceptually saying to people that they can expect to add widgets to and remove them from the panel. Make sure that's what you want to say; if not, consider the composite widget approach.

5.3.1 Creating a new panel from scratch

If you want to create a panel from scratch, then you need to think what DOM element is best suited to representing the panel. In this section, you'll build a panel that holds only clickable widgets but isn't concerned with any structural aspects, so it seems reasonable that a div is suitable.

Listing 5.12 shows the code for the panel, including the add(), remove(), and iterator() methods that make the panel functionally useful.

Listing 5.12 Creating a ButtonPanel from scratch

```
public class ButtonPanel extends Panel{          ❶ Extend panel

   private WidgetCollection children = new WidgetCollection(this);   ❷ Create empty widget collection

   public Iterator iterator() {      ❸ iterator() method
      return children.iterator();
   }

   public boolean remove(Widget w) {      ❹ remove() method
      if (!children.contains(w))
         return false;
      disown(w);
      children.remove(w);
      return true;
   }

   public void add(Widget w){      ❺ add() method
      if (w.getParent() == this)
         return;
      if (!(w instanceof Button))      ❻ Check that widget is a Button
         throw new RuntimeException("Widget must be a Button");
      adopt(w, getElement());
      children.insert(w, children.size());
   }

   public ButtonPanel(){      ❼ Construct new panel
      setElement(DOM.createDiv());
   }
}
```

The new panel must declare that it will be a new subclass of the abstract Panel class, which implements the HasWidgets interface ❶. By doing this, you need to provide an implementation of the remove() and iterator() methods, as well as the add() method.

Because you aren't implementing a simple type of panel, you must allow for one or more widgets to be added to this panel. You need a way to manage and keep track of them, and this is possible using the `WidgetCollection` object ❷.

It's a requirement of the `HasWidgets` interface that the panel must provide a method that returns an `iterator` ❸. In the panel's case, this `iterator` is created by returning the `iterator` provided by the `WidgetCollection` object (this is the same way all the panels, except those in the `SimplePanel` family, perform this task). If the `iterator()` method doesn't return a valid `iterator` object, then the panel will fail to attach completely to the browser. (The failure is that, when attaching the panel to the browser, an attempt is made to access all of the panel's children through the `iterator`; if that is null, then a null pointer exception is raised.)

The `remove()` method ❹ is relatively simple, but it needs to make sure you remove the requested widget from both the DOM and Java views of the panel. You remove the widget from the DOM by invoking the superclass's `disown()` method. *Disowning* a widget is the process implemented in the `Panel` class that ensures both that the widget is removed from the panel and that the panel is removed from being the parent of the widget. The widget is removed from the GWT Java code representation by using the `remove()` method on the `WidgetCollection`.

The process to add a widget generally depends on the panel's behavior. For example, a `VerticalPanel` always adds new widgets to the bottom of its panel; a `HorizontalPanel` always adds them to the rightmost side. For this panel, you're lazy and allow the DOM to decide where to place the new widget you add ❺.

The first check in the `add()` method is to ensure that the widget you're adding doesn't already have you as its parent (in which case it's already added). Next, you check that the widget is a `Button` by seeing whether the widget is an instance of the `Button` class using the code `if (!(w instanceof Button))` ❻. If both these checks are passed, then you `adopt()` the widget and add it to the GWT Java representation in the `WidgetCollection`.

Adopting a widget is the mechanism to ensure that a widget belongs to one and only one parent (panel)—it ensures that the widget is attached at both the DOM and GWT levels. Initially, the widget is removed from any parents it already has; then, it's appended as a child into a panel's DOM element; and finally the parent of the widget is set as this panel. This `adopt()` method must be called once in the process of adding a widget to a panel. The `adopt()` method is defined in the `Panel` class as follows:

```
protected void adopt(Widget w, Element container) {
   w.removeFromParent();
   if (container != null)
```

```
        DOM.appendChild(container, w.getElement());
    w.setParent(this);
}
```

The underlying HTML element for this panel is the nice and safe `div` element, so the constructor for the `ButtonPanel` sets the panels DOM element as a newly created `div` DOM element ❼.

The `Panel` class is responsible for managing its process of attaching and detaching from the browser's DOM and ensuring that all of its child widgets' `onAttach()` or `onDetach()` methods are called.

At this point, you have created the first panel. The steps to implement a completely new panel are summarized in table 5.3.

Table 5.3 Summary of the steps required to create a new low-level panel

Step	Name	Description
1	Extend	Create a new class that extends the `Panel` class; or, if the widgets must be ordered in a particular manner, extends the `IndexedPanel` class.
2	Implement iterator	Implement the `iterator()` method to return a valid `iterator` over the panel's widgets.
3	Implement key methods	Implement the following methods: ■ `remove()`—Removes a specified widget. This method must also call the `disown()` method for the widget being removed. ■ `add()`—Adds a widget to the panel. Often, in more complicated panels, this method calls an `insert()` method to add the widget at a particular position in the panel. If not, then this method must call the `adopt()` method. ■ `insert()`—Optionally provided in complex panels to insert a widget into a particular position. Where it's provided, it's mainly called by the `add()` method. If this method is provided, then it must call the `adopt()` method to ensure that the widget is properly adopted by the panel.
4	Implement useful methods	With the basics in place, you can now add additional methods that you feel are useful to the functionality of your newly created panel.

Creating a panel from scratch is the most basic approach. Next, we'll look at creating a panel from one of the existing panels. There is a diversity of existing panels, and after reading the next section, you may agree that creating panels from scratch is a last resort.

5.3.2 Creating a new panel by extending an existing panel

You saw earlier in this chapter that GWT is distributed with a large range of differing panel layouts. This range means that before creating a new panel from scratch, you should look to see whether extending an existing panel is the best approach.

To do so, the first step is to decide which family this new panel will be a member of—will it be a simple, a complex, or an `HTMLTable` panel? This decision will affect the functionality that the user expects from the panel. If it's a simple panel, then you won't be able to put more than one widget in it; if it's an `HTMLTable` panel, then you should be able to expect to apply `CellFormatter` objects to positions in the panel.

Once the family is selected, you need to choose the most appropriate panel to extend and then do so, being careful to ensure that you override any methods as necessary. Let's revisit the `ButtonPanel` you just created and see if you can reimplement it by extending an existing panel.

Re-creating the ButtonPanel

The definition of the `ButtonPanel`, a panel where a number of `Buttons` can be added, implies that you need the ability to add more than one widget; so, you shouldn't use the `SimplePanel` family. You don't particularly care about the order of the buttons, apart from them being displayed in a left-right manner as they're added; and you aren't interested in displaying them conceptually as a table. This means the best-fit family is `ComplexPanel`.

In this family, `FlowPanel` and `HorizontalPanel` fit the best. Because you haven't defined that the buttons must always be in a horizontal line, you'll extend `FlowPanel`. The new panel class becomes simple and is defined in listing 5.13.

Listing 5.13 Creating the `ButtonPanel` by extending the existing `FlowPanel` public class

```
ButtonPanel2 extends FlowPanel{                    ❶ Extend FlowPanel
   public void add(Widget w){                      ❷ add() method
      if (w.getParent() == this)
         return;
      if (!(w instanceof Button))                  ❸ Is widget a button?
         throw new RuntimeException("Widget must be a Button");
      super.add(w);                                ❹ Add widget through parent's add() method
   }
}
```

In this approach, you inherit all the functionality needed from `FlowPanel` ❶ but override the `add()` method ❷ in order to retain the restriction that widgets being added are `Buttons` ❸. Notice that you don't need to define how the widgets are added because you rely on the `add()` method in the `FlowPanel` class by calling `super.add(w)` at the end of the method definition ❹.

You can see that listing 5.13 is much simpler than the class you created in listing 5.12, and that the only reason for having to extend `FlowPanel` was to add the check that widgets are clickable. The general steps for creating a new panel by extending an existing one are shown in table 5.4.

Table 5.4 Summary of the steps required to extend an existing panel

Step	Name	Description
1	Identify class to extend	Determine which `Panel` class is the most suitable for you to extend for your situation.
2	Implement key methods	Implement (override) the following methods as required: ■ `remove()`—Removes a specified widget. This method must also call the `disown()` method for the widget being removed. ■ `add()`—Adds a widget to the panel. Often, in more complicated panels, this method calls an `insert()` method to add the widget at a particular position in the panel. If not, then this method must call the `adopt()` method. ■ `insert()`—Optionally provided in complex panels to insert a widget into a particular position. Where it's provided, it's mainly called by the `add()` method. If this method is provided, then it must call the `adopt()` method to ensure that the widget is properly adopted by the panel.

We've looked at panels in detail and have shown how to create your own panels if you wish. With this experience in your hands, you can take the next step in the development of the Dashboard by creating the panel in which all the component Dashboard applications will sit.

5.4 Creating the Dashboard panel

We've arrived at the section where you'll take your knowledge of existing panels and how new ones are built and apply it to the Dashboard application. If you recall, the Dashboard lets users open a number of applications, such as a Clock or a Slideshow. These applications should open in their own window in the Dashboard, and the user should be able to drag them around. The target is to display the component applications in a panel that looks like figure 5.20.

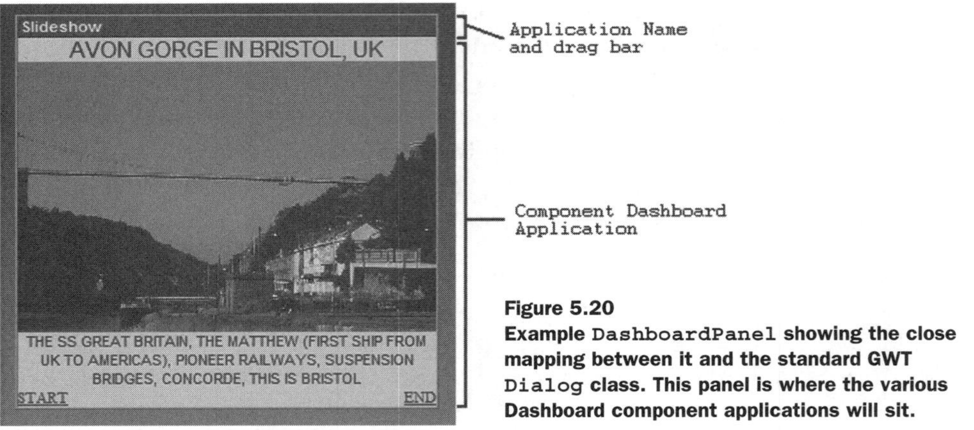

Figure 5.20 Example `DashboardPanel` showing the close mapping between it and the standard GWT `Dialog` class. This panel is where the various Dashboard component applications will sit.

Just by looking at figure 5.20, it's obvious that the `DialogBox` panel is the closest match, and you could leave it just like that—this panel has a caption area where you can store the title and an area for the widget where the application can go. However, you need the panel to perform a couple of other tasks.

The panels must have unique IDs in case you need to refer to them individually in the future, and you need to keep track of which panel is currently active. You also need to prevent anyone from creating a panel that doesn't have an associated application as well as prevent the previewing of events that comes standard in the `DialogBox` class (if you don't do this last step, then all the panels will try to preview events, preventing you from clicking menu bars, and so on). Listing 5.14 shows the code for the first version of this new panel (you'll build up this panel in the next chapter, so it's called `DashboardPanelFirst` here; but we refer to it in both chapters as `DashboardPanel` unless we need to distinguish between the versions. In the downloadable code you will see only the final version of the DashboardPanel).

Listing 5.14 Extending `DialogBox` to provide the first version of the `DashboardPanel` class

```
public class DashboardPanelFirst extends DialogBox{           // 1 Extend DialogBox
   protected int id;                                          // 2 Initialize variables
   protected static int lastId = 0;
   protected static DashboardPanelFirst current = null;
   protected DashboardComposite parkComponent;

   public boolean onEventPreview(Event event){ return true; } // 3 Cancel DialogBox event preview
   public static DashboardPanelFirst getCurrent(){ return current; }
   public int getId(){ return id; }
```

```
    protected native boolean getConfirmDelete()/*-{          <-- 4 Confirm delete
       return $wnd.confirmDelete;
    }-*/;

    protected void removeFromDashboard(){          <-- 5 Remove DashboardPanel
       if (getConfirmDelete()){
          if(Window.confirm("Are you sure you want to delete this?"))
             hide();
             parkComponent.removeMenu();
       } else {
          hide();
          parkComponent.removeMenu();
       }
    }
                                                   6 Add application to DashboardPanel
    protected void addDashboardComponent(DashboardComposite comp,          <--
                                         boolean showAtStart) {
       parkComponent = comp;
       this.setText(comp.getName());
       this.setWidget(comp);
       if(showAtStart){
          this.show();
       }
    }
                                                   7 Constructor
    public DashboardPanelFirst(DashboardComposite component){          <--
       super();
       this.id = ++lastId;
       addDashboardComponent(component, true);
    }
                                                   8 Disallow constructor with no arguments
    public DashboardPanelFirst(){          <--
       throw new RuntimeException("Cannot create new Dashboard
           Application without an associated DashboardComposite");
    }
 }
```

You formally indicate ❶ that this class will extend the standard `DialogBox` panel and will, therefore, behave in a similar manner.

A variable called `id` is created ❷; it will contain the ID of this panel. Each `DashboardPanel` will have its own unique ID, and you use the static variable `lastId` to hold the value of the last ID you set for a newly created `DashboardPanel`. The static modifier means that this variable is accessible to all objects in the Java Virtual Machine.

Similarly, the `static current` variable holds a reference to which `DashboardPanel` is the one that is currently focused. The last class variable you define, `parkComponent`, will eventually hold the Dashboard application; you'll use this more in the next chapter when we discuss how the panel handles events.

As we mentioned in the introductory text, you need to prevent this version of the `DialogBox` from previewing events, and you do this at ❸ by overriding the `onEventPreview()` method to return the value `true`.

When someone tries to close this panel, you wish to check with the overall Dashboard application whether you should ask the user for confirmation. You do this by checking the value of the `confirmDelete` JavaScript variable held in the Dashboard HTML file. To do that, you use JavaScript Native Interface (JSNI), which you can see at ❹; we'll go into detail on this in chapter 8. This method is used at ❺, where the `DashboardPanel` is removed from the Dashboard by confirming with the user if you need to; you also remove any menu item the application may have added to the Dashboard's menu.

❻ adds a component Dashboard application to the panel. You set the caption of the panel to be the name of the component as well as using the panel's parent `setWidget()` method in order to add the application widget to the panel.

When you create the panel, you should use this constructor ❼; then, you call the parent's constructor to ensure you have a valid `DialogBox`, and you set the `id` of this panel to be one greater than the previous value of the static `lastId` variable (which is also then updated). Next, you call the `addDashboardComponent()` method to tie the application provided as an argument into this panel. Trying to use the default constructor ❽, you raise a `RuntimeException` to prevent instances of the panel from being created that don't have an application component initially.

You need to develop this panel further to give you the full functionality you need, but to do that means you need to understand GWT event handling (which is the topic of the next chapter). You want the panel to handle focus events. *Gaining focus* means the application registers an option menu in the Dashboard menu system. If a component application loses focus, then its option menu is removed from the Dashboard's menu, to be replaced by the option menu of the new application that has gained focus.

The developer of an application is responsible for providing the option menu they want, but you'll make sure all applications have at least an About menu item in an option menu, which, when selected, displays internal information about the component application (see figure 5.21).
You'll do that by automatically taking the provided class and creating a new one at runtime using GWT generators. But you must wait until chapter 14 to see how this is done.

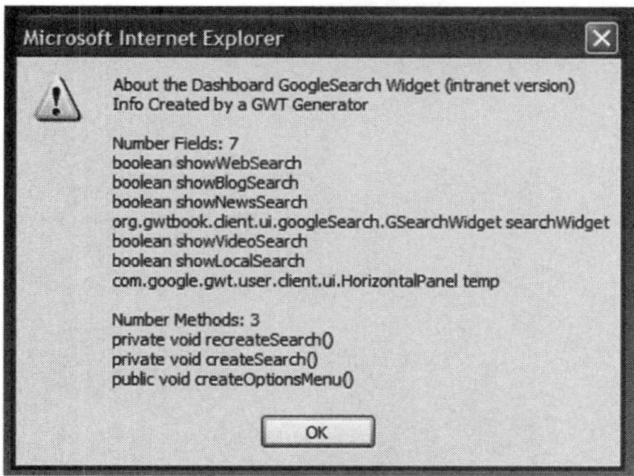

Figure 5.21
An example of the About menu automatically created by using GWT generators and introspecting an existing GWT Java class

5.5 Summary

This concludes the second part of our journey through the GWT basics, which has looked at panels. We hope you're convinced that GWT provides a large number of panels as standard, and this list is growing with each release. Where the functionality you need isn't present, it's relatively simple to create your own panel. You can do this either by starting from scratch or, more preferably, by extending an existing panel.

Panels are similar to widgets in that they have two alternative views: the Java object and the DOM view. As with widgets, you'll spend 99 percent of the time considering the Java object view and only get interested in the DOM view if you're creating new panels. It can also be as dangerous with panels as it is with widgets to start relying on the DOM view of the widget, because there is no guarantee that future versions of GWT will use the same DOM construct for a particular panel. However, three panels are specifically tied to DOM representation, which you can rely on: the `HTMLTable`, `FlexTable`, and `Grid` panels.

In the second half of this chapter, you constructed a `ButtonPanel` from scratch as well as by extending an existing panel. The knowledge you gained allowed you to build the first version of the `DashboardPanel`, which will be heavily used in the Dashboard example. To complete this panel, you need to handle double-clicks on the title and implement some drag-and-drop functionality; this requires you to have a good understanding of how GWT handles events, which is the topic of the next chapter.

6 Handling events

This chapter covers

- GWT event model
- Listening and previewing events
- Event types
- Implementing drag and drop

Finishing off the trilogy of GWT basics, and coming just before we pull everything together in the chapter on developing composite widgets, we'll now cover how events are handled in GWT. Remember the plasma television remote control with buttons that are labeled nicely and set out in a sensible way? When you push the buttons, you want something to happen—you want the remote control to handle the button-click event and change the channel or alter the volume. It's exactly the same in GWT applications; widgets are laid out in panels, and when the user interacts with them, you want things to happen—you must handle events.

Event-handling has popped up a few times already: In chapter 2, we discussed the default application that uses a click listener on a button to show text; you created the `PNGImage` widget in chapter 4 that sank events in the constructor; and we explored some of the other widgets in chapter 4.

This chapter explains the event-handling concept in GWT, including how it manages and differs from the standard browser way of handling events. You'll also take the dashboard panel (`DashboardPanelFirst`) that you built in chapter 5 and extend it so that it can handle mouse double-clicks and drag-and-drop capability (a mouse double-click toggles the minimized/full view of the component). Let's start looking at how GWT deals with events.

6.1 Exploring events

Event handling in web applications ties visual elements the user sees to the functionality of the application. This could be through clicking a button, dragging a component, changing a value, or a number of other events. GWT supports all the events that a browser can manage, as shown in table 6.1.

Table 6.1 Browser events that a GWT application can handle, together with internal GWT values that may be assigned to them

Event	Description
`BUTTON_LEFT`	The left mouse button was clicked.
`BUTTON_MIDDLE`	The middle mouse button was clicked.
`BUTTON_RIGHT`	The right mouse button was clicked.
`ONBLUR`	An element lost keyboard focus.
`ONCHANGE`	The value of an input element has changed.
`ONCLICK`	A user clicked an element.

Table 6.1 Browser events that a GWT application can handle, together with internal GWT values that may be assigned to them *(continued)*

Event	Description
ONDBLCLICK	A user double-clicked an element.
ONERROR	A JavaScript error occurred (this error event is most often found when the loading of an image fails).
ONFOCUS	The opposite of the ONBLUR event: An element received keyboard focus.
ONKEYDOWN	A user pressed a key.
ONKEYPRESS	A character was generated from a keypress (either directly or through autorepeat).
ONKEYUP	A user released a key.
ONLOAD	An element (normally an IMG) finished loading.
ONLOSECAPTURE	An element that had mouse capture lost it.
ONMOUSEDOWN	The user clicked a mouse button over an element.
ONMOUSEMOVE	The mouse moved within an element's area.
ONMOUSEOUT	The mouse moved out of an element's area.
ONMOUSEOVER	The mouse moved into an element's area.
ONMOUSEUP	The user released a mouse button over an element.
ONSCROLL	A scrollable element's scroll offset changed.
FOCUSEVENTS	This is a bitmask covering both the focus and blur events. ONFOCUS | ONBLUR
KEYEVENTS	This is a bitmask covering the down, up, and press keyboard events. ONKEYDOWN | ONKEYPRESS | ONKEYUP
MOUSEEVENTS	This is a bitmask covering the down, up, move, over, and out mouse events. Note that this doesn't include the click or double-click events. ONMOUSEDOWN | ONMOUSEUP | ONMOUSEMOVE | ONMOUSEOVER | ONMOUSEOUT

GWT also manages a range of other events that are more application specific in the same manner as browser events. These events include:

- *Form submission events*—Used to handle submission of a form and when a form submission is completed
- *Pop-up closure*—Raised when a pop-up (such as a menu bar) closes
- *Table-cell clicks*—Can manage user clicks in the cells of a GWT table
- *Tab events*—Used to manage events such as the user clicking a tab
- *Tree events*—Fired when items in the tree are selected or the state of them is changed (the item is opened or closed)
- *Window resize*—Fired whenever the browser window is resized
- *Window close*—Fired just before the browser window is closed

Supporting event handling in a multitude of browsers can be a tricky business, with not all browsers following the same standard way of handling events. In the next couple of sections, we'll look at how the browsers differ, which is important in order for you to understand why GWT introduces its own model to solve these differences.

6.1.1 Identifying event model browser differences

The largest difference between handling events in browsers is whether events are *captured* or *bubbled* through elements. Imagine the situation where you have a couple of nested elements (Elements 1 and 2) in an overall web document. Further imagine that on each element and the document, you've placed an object that listens for a mouse click. When you click Element 1, different browsers take different approaches to handle that click.

In Internet Explorer (IE), the model that is invoked is called *event bubbling*. Element 1 is the first to receive notification of the click, followed by Element 2, and then eventually the Document—you can see this case in figure 6.1.

Other browsers generally use an approach called *event capturing*. The Document is the first component to receive notification when Element 1 is clicked, followed by Element 2 and then finally Element 1 itself (see figure 6.2).

If you rely on the browser to handle events, then you can potentially get inconsistencies across implementations. In the worse case, Element 2 may depend on the event handler for Element 1 setting some values before it can execute properly. With an event-bubbling strategy, that dependency is fine; but for an event-capture model, it breaks because the event handler for Element 2 runs before Element 1.

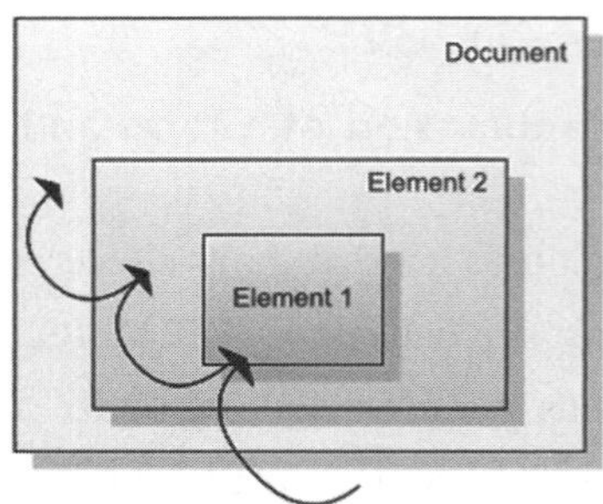

Figure 6.1 Summary of the process of event bubbling (the IE model)

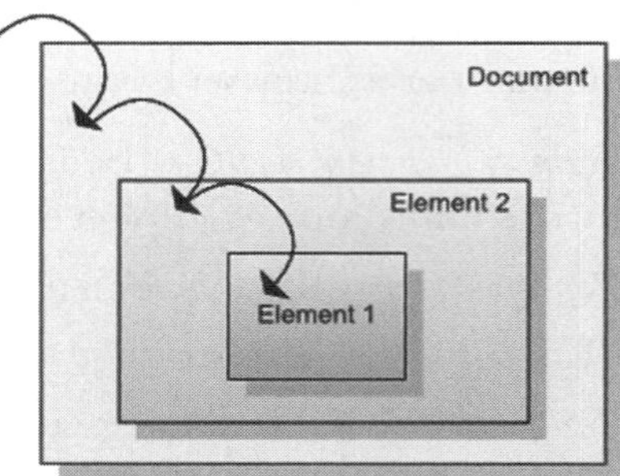

Figure 6.2 Summary of the process of event capture (the Netscape model)

All browsers that GWT supports, except IE, support the unified World Wide Web Consortium (W3C) DOM event-handling standard. This requires browsers to implement both bubbling and capturing, and events are registered using an `addEventListener()` method, which has a boolean parameter to say whether the listener is to be fired on capture or bubble. By using the flexibility of the browsers that support the W3C model, GWT can make all browsers implement the event-bubbling approach. GWT then places its own `Listener` model on top of this to provide a well-controlled event-handling mechanism.

6.1.2 Understanding the GWT event model

One of the first things a GWT application does when it loads is to register a single global event handler at the browser's document level. It performs this through the `init()` method of the DOM class, which has two implementations: one for IE and one for all the other browsers GWT supports. For IE, this is performed in the `DOMImplIE6` class:

```
$doc.body.onclick       = $doc.body.onmousedown  =
$doc.body.onmouseup     = $doc.body.onmousemove  =
$doc.body.onkeydown     = $doc.body.onkeypress   =
$doc.body.onkeyup       = $doc.body.onfocus      =
$doc.body.onblur        = $doc.body.ondblclick   =
$wnd.__dispatchEvent;
```

Don't worry too much about the notation here; we're using JavaScript Native Interface code (JSNI), which is explained in more detail in chapter 8. If you are interested now, then `$doc` is GWT's way of referencing the JavaScript document object and `$wnd` the JavaScript window object.

For all browser events in the document, the `dispatchEvent()` method at the browser level should be called. Because this is IE, the effect is that any event that happens on the browser page is handled at the document level first. For all other browsers, similar functionality is performed using the W3C-defined `addEventListener()` method and setting the last parameter to be `true`, which indicates that the event should be performed in the capture phase (the Document element gets to handle the event first). The code can be found in the `DOMImplStandard` class:

```
$wnd.addEventListener('click',
                      $wnd.__dispatchCapturedMouseEvent,
                      true);
$wnd.addEventListener('dblclick',
                      $wnd.__dispatchCapturedMouseEvent,
                       true);
:
$wnd.addEventListener('keypress',
                       $wnd.__dispatchCapturedEvent,
                       true);
```

Here you're calling slightly different JavaScript methods (`__dispatchCapturedMouseEvent()` and `__dispatchCapturedEvent()`) than in the IE version, but the functionality is broadly similar. All of these methods are written in JSNI language, which we'll cover in chapter 8.

By default, any new widget or panel does not listen for any events, and everything is handled at the document level. To get a widget/panel to listen to events, you need to understand the lifecycle of event handling, which we'll discus next. This lifecycle is summarized in figure 6.3.

Creating a widget/panel

When you create a widget, you need to tell it to sink the appropriate events, using the `sinkEvents()` method. This results in the widget being set up to listen for particular events—all widgets implement the `EventListener` interface by default.

If you sink events, then you also need to provide a way of handling those sunk events; you do so by overriding the `onBrowserEvent()` method (defined in the `com.google.gwt.user.client.ui.Widget` class).

One word of caution: If you're trying to sink new events in an existing widget, you need to create a subclass of the existing widget and then add the appropriate `sinkEvent()` and `onBrowserEvent()` code—you must also remember to call the parent's existing method, through `super.onBrowserEvent()`, to ensure your subclass acts the same as the parent (we'll discuss this more in the next few sections).

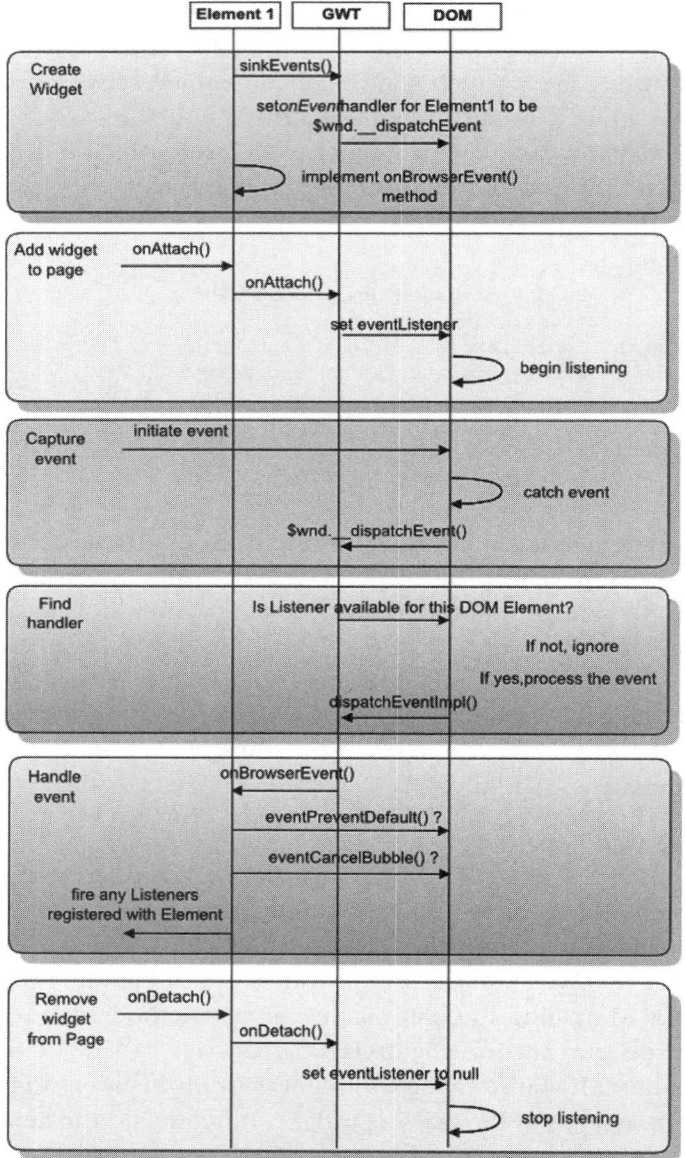

Figure 6.3 Lifecycle of event handling for a widget/panel (the element) in GWT

Once the code is in place and you've created an instance of the object, then you need to add it to the page before it starts managing events.

Adding a widget to a page

A widget/panel won't start listening for events until it's added into the DOM structure of the page. This point can sometimes catch you out, particularly if you forget about the dual Java object/DOM existence of widgets and panels.

GWT takes care of the mechanism for you; all you need to do is add the widget/panel directly to the browser page using `RootPanel.get().add(widget/panel)` or add it to another panel, which is then itself added to other panels and then to the browser page. When a component is added to the browser page its `onAttach()` method is called, if the object is a panel it then calls all of its children's `onAttach()` methods. A widget's `onAttach()` method, which is eventually called, registers itself as an event listener within the DOM hierarchy, and the widget is now listening and ready to capture events.

Capturing an event

Capturing events takes place as you have registered in the browser's event-handling mechanism—in IE it occurs at the element clicked upon and in other browsers directly at the document level.

Once the event is captured, the JavaScript method `$wnd__dispatchEvent()` is called. This method was created in the DOM implementation's `init()` method. It performs the next task of finding an appropriate handler for the event just captured.

Finding a handler

When an event is captured, the GWT application checks if the element the event has occurred on has a listener attached to it. If so, then it calls the `dispatchEvent()` method in the DOM class, passing in the event, the element, and a reference to the element's listener `EventListener`. (In versions previous to GWT 1.4, the process began walking up the DOM hierarchy until it found a listener registered that can handle the event received. Upon finding one, it calls back into the GWT code for the dispatched event to be handled, but from GWT 1.4 this walking the DOM is no longer performed.)

Handling an event

Handling the event is achieved by calling the `onBrowserEvent()` method of the `EventListener` instance passed to the dispatch method in the DOM class. As we just mentioned, this is a reference to the widget, so the `onBrowserEvent()` code you implemented in the first step is now invoked.

You can perform some options at this point in the event lifecycle. You can request that the event bubbling be cancelled using the `DOM.eventCancelBubble()` method; this prevents any other widgets in the bubble hierarchy from seeing the event. You can also request that the default browser action for an event be prevented, using the `DOM.eventPreventDefault()` method (although this doesn't stop context menus in browsers).

Finally, you can feed the event further back into the code by making use of the `Listener` pattern set up for event management. We'll cover this in more detail shortly.

Removing a widget from a page

The widget stops listening only when it's removed from the browser page. It's removed directly or because the panel it sits in has been removed. The process is the opposite of that you saw when you added a widget to the browser; it's performed through the `onDetach()` method, which ultimately sets the event listener for the widget to null.

In the next couple of sections, we'll consider some of these steps in detail to more fully explain the concepts.

6.2 Listening to events

As you've just seen, event handling in GWT is initially set up at the document level. If a widget wishes to handle events itself, then it needs to register that fact by sinking the event, which can be done either explicitly or implicitly through inheritance. Let's look at the explicit approach. (The implicit approach occurs when you inherit from a class that already explicitly sinks events. You'll see that later when you build the drag-and-drop capability for the `DashboardPanel`.)

6.2.1 Sinking events

The first way a widget can register interest in events is to use the `sinkEvents()` method. Using this method, you can tell the GWT application and browser what types of events the widget is interested in. A widget can sink all browser events shown in table 6.1; when it does so, it registers the `$wnd.__dispatchEvent()` method for events the widget should sink. It also updates the DOM element representation of the widget to show which events it's interested in. In the Dashboard, you want the `DashboardPanel` to handle the double-click event—the result of which you can see in figure 6.4, where if the user double-clicks the container, you wish it to shrink to

Figure 6.4 The effect of introducing double-clicking event handling in the `DashboardPanel`. The image on the left shows the Slideshow application in full-mode. On the right, double-clicking the application shrinks it to the title-bar.

display only the title. Double-clicking again restores the panel (to achieve this, you remove the visible widget and replace it with an image of size 1 pixel by 1 pixel).

Back in chapter 5, we introduced the first version of the `DashboardPanel`, the constructor for which is shown in listings 6.1. Then, in listing 6.2, we introduce the second version of `DashboardPanel`, which shows how to start sinking the new event.

Listing 6.1 Previous `DashboardPanelFirst` constructor code

```
public DashboardPanelFirst(DashboardComposite component){
   super();
   addDashboardComponent(component, true);

}
```

Listing 6.2 `DashboardPanelSecond` constructor code, including the `sinkEvent()` method for double-clicks

```
public DashboardPanelSecond(DashboardComposite component){
   super();
   this.id = ++lastId;
   this.sinkEvents(Event.ONDBLCLICK);      <-- (1) Sink double-click event
}
```

Listing 6.1 shows the original dashboard's panel constructor (DashboardPanelFirst) created at the end of chapter 5. The updated code in listing 6.2 includes an extra line ❶ that registers this widget as sinking the double-click event. Remember that back in section 4.2, we looked at the DOM view of the Button widget and saw that it looked like this:

```
<button class="gwt-Button"
   eventBits="7041"
   onChange="null"
   onLoad="null"
   onError="null">
      Click me
</button>
```

At the time, we said not to worry about what the eventBits attribute was; but now we can reveal that this attribute is altered when you call the sinkEvent() method using the values shown in Event handling in web applications ties visual elements the user sees to the functionality of the application. This could be through clicking a button, dragging a component, changing a value, or a number of other events. GWT supports all the events that a browser can manage, as you saw in table 6.1.

If you compare the DOM representation of the dashboard panels from before (listing 6.3) and after (listing 6.4) you run the sinkEvents() method, you can see that you've acquired an extra attribute eventBits. (We got these views by running the Dashboard application in Eclipse in debug mode and placing a break point just before the onSink() method. We were then able to inspect variables; we looked at the this element when in the DashboardPanel code, and Eclipse showed us these representations.)

Listing 6.3 DashboardPanel's DOM view before calling the onSink() event

```
<DIV class=gwt-DialogBox
     style="POSITION: absolute">
  <TABLE cellSpacing=0 cellPadding=0>
    <TBODY>
      <TR>
        <TD align=left>
            </TD>
         </TR>
      <TR></TR>
    </TBODY>
  </TABLE>
</DIV>
```

Listing 6.4 DashboardPanel's DOM view after calling the onSink() event

```
<DIV class=gwt-DialogBox
     style="POSITION: absolute"
     __eventBits="2">                         <-- Sink the double-click event
  <TABLE cellSpacing=0 cellPadding=0>
    <TBODY>
       <TR>
         <TD align=left>
            </TD>
         </TR>
       <TR></TR>
    </TBODY>
  </TABLE>
</DIV>
```

The value of the eventBits field is set to 2—which is exactly what you'd expect if you look at the bitwise value of double-click in the GWT code. You don't need to limit yourself to adding events one at a time by logically OR-ing events together; for example, to sink the onLoad and onChange events at the same time, you write sinkEvents(Event.ONLOAD | Event.ONCHANGE).

You set bits in the eventBits field so that GWT can keep a record of what events a particular widget is handling; the field doesn't play a part in event handling. You'll see in a short while that when an event occurs on a widget that is sinking those events, then that widget's onBrowserEvent() method is called; if you want to handle the event, you need to override the widget's default onBrowserEvent() method.

6.2.2 Managing sunk events with the onBrowserEvent() method

Once you've indicated that a widget should sink particular events, you must set up the application to handle those events. You do that in the widget's code by overriding the onBrowserEvent() method. The default implementation of this method is defined in the Widget class as an empty method, consistent with the GWT model of not handling events unless explicitly directed to.

For the DashboardPanel, which extends DialogBox, you must handle all the DialogBox sunk events plus the onDblClick event you registered in the last section. You can easily handle all the DialogBox sunk events by calling the parent's onBrowserEvent() method. The onBrowserEvent() method can be written as in listing 6.5.

Listing 6.5 Implementing the `DashboardPanel` `onBrowserEvent()` method to handle double-click events

```
public void onBrowserEvent(Event event) {
    super.onBrowserEvent(event);                    ❶ Call parent event handler
    int type = DOM.eventGetType(event);             ❷ Decipher current event
    switch (type) {
        case Event.ONDBLCLICK: {                    ❸ Recognize double-click event
            toggleShow();
            break;
        }
    }
}
```

The first line of listing 6.5 tells you that you wish the `DashboardPanel` panel to handle events the same way as the parent panel (`DialogBox`). This is done by calling the parent's `onBrowserEvent()` ❶. You now handle the event by first deciphering the event type ❷ by calling the `eventGetType()` method in the GWT DOM class, which returns an integer value representing the event.

The `Event` object is a strange beast; it provides an opaque interface into the JavaScript event you're dealing with. You shouldn't create these events as normal Java objects; they appear as necessary, controlled by GWT (opaque JavaScript objects are explained in more depth in the JSNI chapter, chapter 8).

If the event you're dealing with is determined to be a double-click ❸, then you execute the `toggleShow()` method, which is defined in listing 6.6.

Listing 6.6 Toggling the visibility of the application

```
public void toggleShow(){
    if(visible){                                    Already hidden?
        int width = this.getOffsetWidth();
        Image empty = new Image("hidden.png");
        empty.setWidth(width+"px");                 Hide application
        empty.setHeight("1px");
        this.setWidget(empty);
    } else {
        this.setWidget(parkComponent);              Show application
    }
    visible = !visible;                             Toggle visibility flag
}
```

This method toggles the visibility of the application part of the `DashboardPanel` by showing either the application or a small image; providing the functionality you wanted in figure 6.4. When you shrink the panel, you programmatically alter the widget's width and height styling.

You can also unsink events from widgets using the `unsinkEvents()` method, which alters the `eventBits` attribute of the widget and removes the event listener for that type of event.

A number of helper methods go with the `Event` object to allow you to get particular attributes of the event. These are as follows:

- `eventGetAltKey()`—Returns `true` if the Alt key was pressed when the event occurred.
- `eventGetButton()`—Indicates which mouse button was clicked during the event. It returns a bit field made up from `Event.BUTTON_LEFT`, `Event.BUTTON_MIDDLE`, and `Event.BUTTON_RIGHT`.
- `eventGetClientX()`—Gets the mouse x-position within the browser window's client area.
- `eventGetClientY()`—Similar to the previous method, but returns the mouse y-position in the browser window's client area.
- `eventGetCtrlKey()`—Returns `true` if the Ctrl key was pressed when the event occurred.
- `eventGetFromElement()`—Valid only for the `ONMOUSEOVER` event. Returns the element from which the mouse was moved.
- `eventGetKeyCode()`—If the event was `ONKEYPRESS`, returns the Unicode value of the character. Otherwise, for the `ONKEYDOWN` and `ONKEYUP` events, returns the code associated with the key.
- `eventGetRepeat()`—Returns `true` if the key event was generated by an autorepeat.
- `eventGetScreenX()`—Determines the mouse x-position on the user's display; note the difference from to `eventGetClientX`.
- `eventGetScreenY()`—Similar to the previous method, but returns the mouse y-position in the user's display.
- `eventGetShiftKey()`—Returns `true` if the Shift key was pressed when the event occurred.
- `eventGetTarget()`—Returns the element that was the target of this particular event.

- `eventGetToElement()`—Valid only for the `ONMOUSEOVER` event and returns the element to which the mouse was moved.
- `eventGetType()`—Returns the event type.
- `eventGetTypeString()`—Returns the event type as a `String`.

Helper methods are particularly useful if you want to capture events such as right mouse clicks, which aren't directly available in GWT. If you're trying to capture right mouse clicks, you sink the `Event.ONMOUSEDOWN` event in the widget to capture the mouse-down event. Then, in the overridden `onBrowserEvent()` method, you check whether the event is a mouse down, and then check the button that was clicked. The result, in the Dashboard's Address Book application, is shown in figure 6.5.

Listing 6.7 shows how this functionality is implemented in the Address Book.

Listing 6.7 Capturing right mouse clicks

```
public void onBrowserEvent(Event event) {
   int type = DOM.eventGetType(event);
   switch (type) {
      case Event.ONMOUSEDOWN: {                          ❶
         switch (DOM.eventGetButton(event)) {            ❷
            case Event.BUTTON_RIGHT:
               Window.alert("Pressed the Right Button"); ❸
               break;
         }
         break;
      }
   }
}
```

❶ Is event a mouse down?
❷ Which button was clicked?
❸ Alert user that right button was clicked

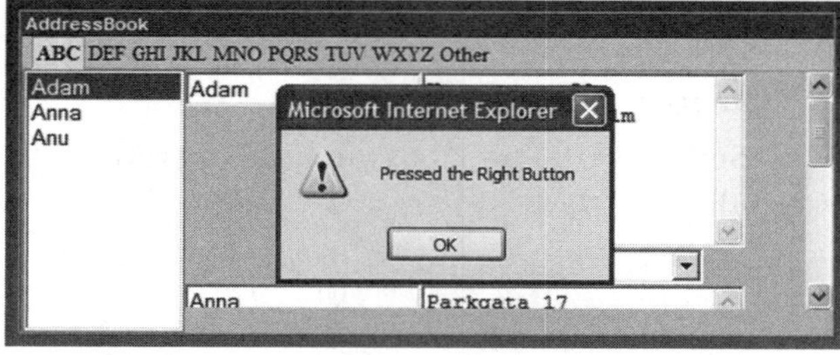

Figure 6.5 Capturing right mouse button clicks in the Dashboard's Address Book application

First, you check for the onMouseDown event ❶. Having confirmed that this is the event you're dealing with, you use the eventGetButton() helper method ❷ to determine whether this is a right click. If it's a right click, then you bring up an alert box ❸.

The final piece in the event-handling jigsaw is understanding how events that are sunk actually get handled by the onBrowserEvent() method you've just seen.

6.2.3 Linking sunk events to the onBrowserEvent() method

If you have a widget that sinks events, and you've defined an onBrowserEvent() method, how do the two get linked together? The answer comes in a mixture of Java and JSNI code (don't worry, GWT does this all for you).

Remember that the onSink() method registers the fact that the element should call the $wnd.__dispatchEvent method. This method is defined in the DOM implementation classes, such as the DOMmplIE6 class's init() methods. Listing 6.8 shows the part of the init() method that is responsible for setting up event handling.

Listing 6.8 Definition of the GWT dispatchEvent() method

```
$wnd.__dispatchEvent = function() {
    if ($wnd.event.returnValue == null) {
        $wnd.event.returnValue = true;
    if (!@com.google.gwt.user.client.DOM::previewEvent(
                Lcom/google/gwt/user/client/Event;)($wnd.event))
        return;
    }
    if (this.__listener)
        @com.google.gwt.user.client.DOM::dispatchEvent(
                Lcom/google/gwt/user/client/Event;
                Lcom/google/gwt/user/client/Element;
                Lcom/google/gwt/user/client/EventListener;)
                ($wnd.event, this, this.__listener);
};
```

❶ Check if should preview event
❷ Check if has Listener
❸ Call dispatchEvent() method

The first segment of the code ❶ checks to see if the element the event was captured on has been set up to preview events. If so, then it calls the previewEvent() method, and no further event-processing takes place. For IE6, the event previewing is as simple as shown in ❶, but for the other browsers you need a little more processing to prevent the event propagating (remember, they all use the DOM standard model). In the DOMImplStandard class is this additional code:

```
evt.stopPropagation();
evt.preventDefault();
```

Once you've determined there is no event previewing, at ❷ you check to see whether a listener is associated with the element the event occurred on. If so, you then make a JSNI call from JavaScript back into the Java program. We'll cover the JSNI in much more detail in chapter 8; for now, we can say that this code calls the `dispatchEvent()` method in the DOM class, which takes three arguments: the event, the element, and the listener ❸.

In the DOM class, this method eventually calls the `listener.onBrowserEvent()` method.

As well as handling events, it's possible to register a widget as previewing events.

6.2.4 Previewing events

By implementing the `EventPreview` interface, a widget can register itself as being able to preview events that are occurring on the browser document. When a component that implements `EventPreview` is active on the document, then all events are routed to it.

The events should be handled by the `onEventPreview()` method, which normally returns `false` if it decides to do something with the event and `true` otherwise. This has an important implication if you're inheriting from classes that have event preview. If that class returns `false` for an event you wish to handle, then you won't see that event occurring. You have this situation in the `DashboardPanel`.

`DashboardPanel` extends `DialogBox`, which in turn extends the `PopupPanel` class, and it's here that you find the `onEventPreview()` method that `DashboardPanel` will inherit. This inherited method is shown in listing 6.9.

Listing 6.9 `onEventPreview()` method for the `PopupPanel`

```
public boolean onEventPreview(Event event) {
   int type = DOM.eventGetType(event);
   switch (type) {
      case Event.ONKEYDOWN: {
         return onKeyDownPreview((char) DOM.eventGetKeyCode(event),
         KeyboardListenerCollection.getKeyboardModifiers(event));
      }
      case Event.ONKEYUP: {
         return onKeyUpPreview((char) DOM.eventGetKeyCode(event),
         KeyboardListenerCollection.getKeyboardModifiers(event));
      }
      case Event.ONKEYPRESS: {
         return onKeyPressPreview((char) DOM.eventGetKeyCode(event),
```

❶ Determine event type
❷ Manage key-down event
❸ Preview key value

```
            KeyboardListenerCollection.getKeyboardModifiers(event));
         }
         case Event.ONMOUSEDOWN:
         case Event.ONMOUSEUP:
         case Event.ONMOUSEMOVE:
         case Event.ONCLICK:
         case Event.ONDBLCLICK: {                        ❹ Preview double-click
            if (DOM.getCaptureElement() == null) {
               Element target = DOM.eventGetTarget(event);
               if (!DOM.isOrHasChild(getElement(), target)) {
                  if (autoHide && (type == Event.ONCLICK)) {
                     hide(true);
                     return true;
                  }
                  return false;
               }
            }
            break;
         }
      }
      return true;
   }
```

As with the `onBrowserEvent()` method, when you preview events, you must first decipher the type of event you're previewing ❶ by calling the `eventGetType()` method. If the event you're previewing is key down ❷, which is either when it's pressed or when it's on its key-repeat cycle, then you call a helper method to work out what to do with this key. The `eventGetKeyCode()` method is one of a number of methods that allow you to get details about the event you're looking at; in this case, it returns the ASCII value of the key being pressed ❸.

The `DialogBox` also previews the double-click event ❹. You may question why this method handles the double-click event. Remember that this is event previewing, not event handling, and this is one of five mouse events handled by the code that follows, which closes the pop-up if a mouse event happens outside it.

You don't want any of this previewing functionality in the `DashboardPanel`. If you leave it there, then each new component application opened will grab all the events, and you'll be at the mercy of other classes as to whether you receive them. To get us to the situation you want for `DashboardPanel`, you must override the `onEventPreview()` method with this simple one:

```
public boolean onEventPreview(Event event){
   return true;
}
```

We should summarize the current position of the `DashboardPanel`, which can now handle double-click events; it's shown as `DashboardPanelSecond` in listing 6.10.

Listing 6.10 Adding code to the `DashboardPanel` to handle double click events that are sunk.

```
public class DashboardPanelSecond extends DashboardPanelFirst
{
   public boolean onEventPreview(Event event){ return true; }      <- Suppress event preview
   public void toggleShow(){                       <- Toggle view of Dashboard Panel
      if(visible){
         int width = this.getOffsetWidth();
         Image empty = new Image("hidden.png");
         empty.setWidth(width+"px");
         this.setWidget(empty);
      } else {
         this.setWidget(parkComponent);
      }
      visible = !visible;
   }

   public void onBrowserEvent(Event event) {        <- Handle double-click
      super.onBrowserEvent(event);
      int type = DOM.eventGetType(event);
      switch (type) {
         case Event.ONDBLCLICK: {
            toggleShow();
            break;
         }
      }
   }

   public DashboardPanelSecond(DashboardComposite component){
      super(component);
      this.sinkEvents(Event.ONDBLCLICK);            <- Sink double-click
   }

   public DashboardPanelSecond(){
      super();
   }
}
```

This works because the `Widget` class extends the `EventListener` interface, and GWT knows how to plug it all together. Another way to explicitly handle events is to make the classes extend higher-level listener interfaces.

6.2.5 Handling events by extending the listener classes

Event handling can also be performed by creating new classes that extend the higher-level event listeners. As we've talked about before, the standard `Widget` class extends the `EventListener` class, but you can also extend the higher-level listeners, such as `MouseListener`. This is done, for example, by the `DialogBox`, which you're extending already for the `DashboardPanel`. Listing 6.11 shows how this is set up.

Listing 6.11 Filtered view of the `DialogBox` class that shows how mouse events are handled

```
public class DialogBox
       extends PopupPanel
       implements HasHTML, MouseListener {          <-- 1 Implement MouseListener

   private HTML caption = new HTML();

   public DialogBox() {
      // Some other bits of code                     Add listener to
      caption.addMouseListener(this);           <--  component
   }

   public void onMouseMove(Widget sender, int x, int y){}
     public void onMouseUp(Widget sender, int x, int y){}
     public void onMouseEnter(Widget sender){}          Interface's
     public void onMouseLeave(Widget sender){}          required methods
}
```

The class definition ❶ says it will implement the `MouseListener` interface. This means you should find implementations of all the expected methods, such as `onMouseDown()`, `onMouseMove()`, and so on. The last step in the constructor of the `DialogBox` adds this class (or object, as it will be at the time) as the `MouseListener` on the `caption` object of the `DialogBox`.

This isn't as strange as it may seem. The `caption` object is defined as an HTML widget; and if you looked in the class definition of the HTML object, you would see that it implements the `SourcesMouseEvents` interface that, as you've seen in this chapter, allows you to register and un-register `MouseListeners`.

By registering the complete `DialogBox` as the `MouseListener` for the caption component of the `DialogBox`, you encapsulate the whole functionality in one class. It just so happens in this case that the functionality is dragging; this arrangement provides you with a panel that can be dragged by clicking only the caption.

These `Listener` objects can also be used externally to register particular listeners against widgets that allow you to move (or change) events further into the application's code.

6.2.6 Moving events further into your GWT code

Once the widgets have captured events, you'll often feed that information back into the code, just as the center gets the ball back to the quarterback, or the rugby ball needs to be recycled from a ruck. The following code gives an example of what we mean:

```
Button theButton = new Button("Click Me");
theButton.addClickListener(new ClickListener(){
   public void onClick(Widget sender){
      Window.alert("Button was Clicked");
   }
});
```

This code registers a `ClickListener` with a `Button` so that when the button is clicked, the text "Button was Clicked" appears in a JavaScript alert box. Notice that you haven't had to sink events or override the `onBrowserEvent()` to do this. The `Button` object implements the `SourcesClickEvents` interface.

Let's see how it does this by looking at the button. It's complicated to show this example using the exact GWT `Button` because the aspects we want to demonstrate are distributed through its widget hierarchy, so we'll flatten that hierarchy and look at the `Button` shown in listing 6.12.

Listing 6.12 Sample `Button` class that ties together all aspects of GWT event handling

```
public class Button
       extends Widget
       implements SourcesClickEvents{        <-- (1) Implement SourcesClickEvents interface

   private ClickListenerCollection clickListeners;   <-- (2) Create collection of ClickListeners

   public Button(){
      setElement(DOM.createButton());
      this.sinkEvents(Event.ONCLICK);        <-- (3) Sink click event
   }

   public onBrowserEvent(Event evt){         <-- (4) Override onBrowserEvent()
      switch(DOM.getEventType(evt)){
         case Event.ONCLICK:
            if(clickListeners != null)
```

```
                clickListeners.fireClick(this);        ◁┐ Fire
            break;                                    ❺ ClickListeners
        }
    }
    public void addClickListener(ClickListener listener){    ◁┐ Add
        if (clickListener == null){                         ❻ ClickListener
            clickListener = new ClickListenerCollection();
        }
        clickListener.add(listener);
    }

    public void removeClickListener(ClickListener listener){   ◁┐
        if (clickListener != null){                     Remove  │
            clickListener.remove(listener);        ClickListener ❼
        }
    }
}
```

You tell the world that you'll be implementing the `SourcesClickEvents` interface ❶. This means you must provide the `addClickListener()` method to register `ClickListeners` with this Button, and a `removeClickListener()` method to remove any `ClickListener` previously added if you wished to do so. (In the real GWT `Button` class, this interface is implemented along with a couple of others in the `FocusWidget` class, which is then subclassed as the `ButtonBase` class; then, that is subclassed as the real `Button` class—and that's why we flattened it out a bit for this discussion!)

To support this notion of listeners, you create a `ClickListenerCollection` object ❷, which you'll use to store the `ClickListeners` that will be registered against the component. The `ClickListenerCollection` also provides simple methods such as `fireClick()`, which fires the `onClick` events to all `ClickListeners` it holds.

Managing the interface to the user's event is the code you've seen a number of times now: the sinking of events ❸ and the `onBrowser()` event method ❹. What is new here is that on receiving an `onClick` event on the `Button`, you pull out the `ClickListenerCollection` object and execute the `fireClick()` method on it ❺. This has the effect of firing an `onClick` event to all the `ClickListeners` registered with the `Button`.

These `ClickListeners` are registered with the `Button` through the `addClickListener()` method ❻, which adds any new `ClickListener` objects to the `ClickListenerCollection` (and creates it if it doesn't already exist).

You created `ClickListeners` in other components of the code, usually close to where the `Button` was created, in a style similar to the following:

```
Button theButton = new Button();
theButton.addClickListener(new ClickListener(){
   public void onClick(Widget sender){
      //Do something when the button is clicked.
   }
});
```

This little piece of code creates a new `Button` and then adds a `ClickListener` to it (as a Java anonymous type). When the button is clicked, the code in listing 6.12's `onBrowserEvent()` executes this `ClickListener`'s `onClick()` method, and thus the event happening at the `Button` class is moved to the area of code just defined. It's feasible that other `EventListeners` are registered with this piece of code and that the `onClick()` method might in turn fire them off, too.

As well as being able to add `ClickListeners` to the `Button`, you wish to have the ability to remove `ClickListeners`, which is what the code does at this point ❼. If you want to remove listeners, then you shouldn't add them as anonymous classes; define them first as their own objects, and then add them. (Otherwise, you have no handle to the object to remove!)

By making the object implement one of the many `SourcesEvents` interfaces, you indicate that it will allow the adding and removing of particular `EventListeners` and that somewhere in the code, you'll be firing the necessary events.

This approach allows you to start moving events around in the code, and not necessarily just those events that the browser raises. You can also use this methodology to change the type of events handled internally in the GWT code. For example, if the widget detects a mouse click internally, it could present that externally as another type of event.

Why would you do this? To make the event more meaningful to the user. For example, the `HTMLTable` panel detects mouse clicks in cells of the table, but it presents `CellClicked` events telling you which row and column were clicked rather than just the fact a mouse click event occurred.

You can also make actions that happen in the application be treated as events. You'll use this approach in the `EditableLabel` widget described in chapter 7, where you allow the user to change a label by editing it. When the user has finished editing and accepted the change, you fire a change event to any `ChangeListeners` that are registered with the widget (we'll also look at this functionality in section 6.3.1).

Let's turn back to the Dashboard example. You wish to do a couple of things whenever the panel gets focus, such as adding an option menu to the Dashboard menu for the component application. To achieve this, you need to make a couple of changes to the `DashboardPanel` class to let you add and remove `FocusListeners`. The intention is that each `DashboardPanel` will contain one small application object, which will extend a class called `DashboardComposite`. You'll define that class in the next chapter; for now, you should know that this class extends `FocusListener`. The third version of the `DashboardPanel` panel is defined in listing 6.13 (note that this inheritance is purely representative—in the downloadable code, at http://www.manning.com/hanson, only the final version of the `DashboardPanel` class is provided).

Listing 6.13 Third version of the `DashboardPanel`, showing how the code handles focus events

```
public class DashboardPanelThird
       extends DashboardPanelSecond
       implements SourcesFocusEvents            ❶ Implement SourcesFocusEvents interface
{
   FocusListenerCollection listeners =          ◁ Create ListenerCollection object
       new FocusListenerCollection();

   public void addFocusListener(FocusListener listener){     ◁ Add FocusListener
      listeners.add(listener);
   }

   public void removeFocusListener(FocusListener listener){  ◁ Remove FocusListener
      listeners.remove(listener);
   }

   private addDashboardComponent(DashboardComposite component,
                                 boolean showAtStart){
      super(component, showAtStart);
      this.addFocusListener(component);         ◁ Add component as listener
   }
}
```

One key thing to note is that you add a `DashboardComposite` as the `FocusListener`, which means the panel must implement the `SourcesFocusEvents` interface ❶. This drives the need to include a `FocusListenerCollection` and the `addFocusListener()` and `removeFocusListener()` methods.

All this talk so far has been about how easy it is to handle events raised in the browser. But there is a small problem: The browser often has its own default event handling.

6.2.7 Preventing default browser event handling

Sometimes you want to prevent the standard event handling that a browser provides. The most obvious instance is the context menus that a browser displays when a user right clicks; but that unfortunately isn't always handled by events, so it's a little complicated to manage. Another default event that you may wish to prevent the browser from handling is dragging images.

In the browser window, it's possible to drag an image from the browser page into the address bar and for that image to then be displayed. For the trash icon in the Dashboard, you create a specific `TrashIcon` class, and in it you specifically prevent this functionality. To do so, you override the `onBrowserEvent()` method in the `TrashIcon` class, as shown in listing 6.14.

Listing 6.14 Overriding the `onBrowserEvent()` method

```
public void onBrowserEvent(Event event){
   DOM.eventPreventDefault(event);
   super.onBrowserEvent(event);
}
```

In the second line, you call the `eventPreventDefault()` method to stop the browser from taking its default action. You can try it for yourself in the running application; it isn't possible to drag the trash icon image onto the address bar.

GWT includes many different types of events and handling classes, and it's worthwhile to look at some of them now. We'll refer back to the Dashboard and its component applications for examples of their use.

6.3 Handling standard browser events

We've covered quite a bit in the first part of this chapter, and you've seen all the components that go together to handle events in GWT. At the start of the chapter, we indicated in table 6.1 that GWT manages a wide range of events. Over the next few sections, we'll look at all these events and how you've used them in the Dashboard and its component application.

The pattern you use for handling events generally summarizes the sets of classes discussed so far in this chapter. Any component you wish to be able to add appropriate `Listeners` to or remove them from will implement the appropriate `SourcesEvent` interface, requiring you to implement methods that allow you to add and remove `Listeners` to/from a related `Collections` object. When you wish to fire events, you use the methods in the appropriate `Collections` object. In general, you'll add listeners as anonymous classes; for example:

```
object.addListener(new Listener(){
   public void listenerMethod1(){
      // Appropriate code to handle event goes here.
   }
});
```

Sometimes you'll use an associated `Adapter` class instead of the `Listener` to avoid having to leave a large number of the required methods of a listener defined as blank methods, which makes the code look messy. The `Adapter` class already provides implementations for all the `Listener`'s methods, so when you create a new subclass of the `Adapter`, we only override those methods you're interested in. Table 6.2 summarizes all of these types together for the `Keyboard` events, and it's possible to do this for all the event types in GWT.

Table 6.2 Summary of components involved in `Keyboard` events

<table>
<tr><th colspan="3"><code>SourcesEvent</code> interface: <code>SourcesKeyboardEvents</code></th></tr>
<tr><td>Methods</td><td colspan="2"><code>addKeyboardListener(KeyboardListener c)</code>
<code>removeKeyboardListener(KeyboardListener c)</code></td></tr>
<tr><th colspan="3">Related collections object</th></tr>
<tr><td>Name</td><td colspan="2"><code>KeyboardListenerCollection</code></td></tr>
<tr><td rowspan="2">Methods</td><td><code>fireKeyboardEvent(Widget w)</code></td><td>Fires the keyboard event on all registered <code>KeyboardListeners</code> in the <code>KeyboardListenerCollection</code>. If the event isn't a keyboard event, then no action is taken.</td></tr>
<tr><td><code>fireKeyDown(Widget w, char keyCode, int modifiers)</code></td><td>Fires the <code>keyDown</code> event to all registered <code>KeyboardListeners</code> in the <code>KeyboardListenerCollection</code>.
The <code>keyCode</code> is the Java representation of the key pressed.
The <code>modifiers</code> argument relates to the modifier key that was pressed when the event occurred. It can be one of the following values:
<code>KeyboardListener.MODIFIER_SHIFT</code>
<code>KeyboardListener.MODIFIER_CTRL</code>
<code>KeyboardListener.MODIFIER_ALT</code></td></tr>
</table>

Table 6.2 Summary of components involved in `Keyboard` events *(continued)*

Methods *(continued)*	`fireKeyPress(Widget w,`
	`char keyCode,`
	`int modifiers)`
		Fires the `keyPress` event to all registered `KeyboardListeners` in the `KeyboardListenerCollection`.

	`fireKeyUp(Widget w,`
	`char keyCode,`
	`int modifiers)`
		Fires the `keyUp` event to all registered `KeyboardListeners` in the `KeyboardListenerCollection`.

	`getKeyboardModifiers(` `Event e)`	
Listener interface: `KeyboardListener`		

Methods	`onKeyDown(Widget w`
	`char keyCode,`
	`int modifiers)`
		Fired whenever the widget gains focus.

	`onKeyPress(Widget w`
	`char keyCode,`
	`int modifiers)`
		Fired when a widget loses focus.

	`onKeyUp(Widget w`
	`char keyCode,`
	`int modifiers))`	

Related adapter class		
Name	`KeyboardListenerAdapter`	

As we have previously done for widgets and panels, we'll now walk through all the different types of events that can happen and look briefly at where you use them in the Dashboard or its component applications, pointing out any useful tidbits of information as we go.

6.3.1 *Reacting to change*

`ChangeListeners` are useful if you wish to be notified when a component has changed. You use this fact in the Dashboard's Address Book application. When the user selects a new name—for example, changing the selection from Adam to Anu, as shown in figure 6.6—you need to change the displayed address.

In listing 6.15, you create a new `ListBox` widget and then add a `ChangeListener` to it so you're informed whenever the user changes the selected items in the list.

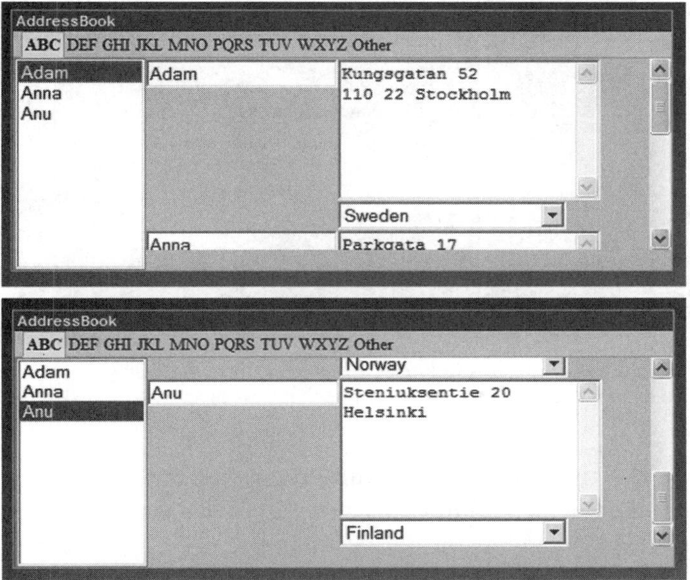

Figure 6.6 Selecting a name in the list box at left in the Dashboard's Address Book application automatically selects the appropriate address on the scroll panel on the right via functionality stored in a `ChangeListener` registered against the list box.

Listing 6.15 Adding a `ChangeListener` to the Address Book's Names list box

```
addressLinks = new ListBox();                       <-- Create ListBox
addressLinks.setVisibleItemCount(10);
super.add(addressLinks);
addressLinks.addChangeListener(new ChangeListener(){   <-- Add ChangeListener
   public void onChange(Widget sender) {               <-- onChange() method
      int val = addressLinks.getSelectedIndex();
      String text = addressLinks.getItemText(val);
      showAddress(text);
   }
});
```

The `onChange()` method is called whenever the user changes the selected items in the list. In this case, you implement it so that it gets the text of the newly selected name and then calls a helper method to display the correct name on the panel.

Most of the other listeners we'll look at are mainly useful when you're dealing with low-level widgets such as buttons, text boxes, and so on. `ChangeListener` is useful wherever you may want to indicate to other registered listeners that the

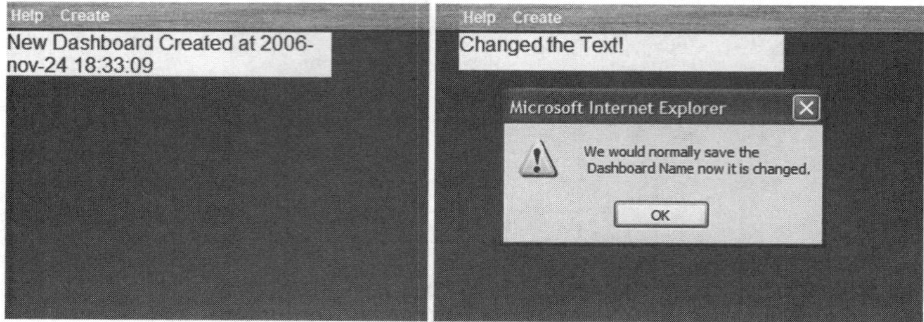

Figure 6.7 A `ChangeListener` is registered against the `EditableLabel` widget, which is fired when the user changes the `EditableLabel` text. Normally the change would be saved in a database, but here you raise an alert box.

state has changed. You use this ability in the `EditableLabel` composite widget, which you'll build in chapter 7, to indicate when the user has changed text. In the example code, you display an alert message (see figure 6.7); but in a real application, you might use this change listener to fire off functionality to save the new value to a database.

The `EditableLabel` is made up of a `TextArea`, a `TextBox`, some `Buttons`, and a `Label` widget; the `TextArea/TextBox` is visible if the user is editing the label, and the user must click an OK button for the change to take place. Using a change listener on the underlying text box isn't suitable, because the user may cancel their change. Instead, you make the `EditableLabel` widget implement the `SourcesChangeEvents` interface. This means that in the Dashboard class, you can create a new instance, as shown in listing 6.16.

Listing 6.16 Creating an `EditableLabel` and adding a `ChangeListener`

```
dashboardName = new EditableLabel(                              Create
   messages.DashboardDefaultNameMessage(message),               EditableLabel
   constants.NameChangeOK(),
   constants.NameChangeCANCEL());                               Add
   dashboardName.setWordWrap(true);                             ChangeListener
   dashboardName.addChangeListener(new ChangeListener(){
      public void onChange(Widget sender) {
         Window.alert("We would normally save the \n Dashboard
                      Name now it is changed.");                onChange()
      }                                                         method
   }
});
```

Within the editable label code, when the label is changed, you fire the onChange event, as shown in listing 6.17, on the set of ChangeListeners registered in the ChangeListenerCollection called changeListeners.

Listing 6.17 Firing the onChange event from the EditableLabel

```
private void setTextLabel (){
   if(text.getWordWrap()){
      text.setText(changeTextArea.getText());
   } else {
      text.setText(changeText.getText());
   }
   restoreVisibility();
   if (changeListeners!=null)changeListeners.fireChange(this);
}
```

Firing a ChangeListener

Change events are abstract notions, which can be used to your advantage as we just discussed. Most events in GWT are much more concrete, such as handling mouse clicks.

6.3.2 Clicking around

The most common place to find ClickListeners is registered against Buttons, but they can also be registered against the other widgets in the Focus-Widget hierarchy (Image, Label, Hyperlink, PasswordTextBox, TextArea, TextBox, ListBox, Button, CheckBox, and RadioButton) and the FocusPanel.

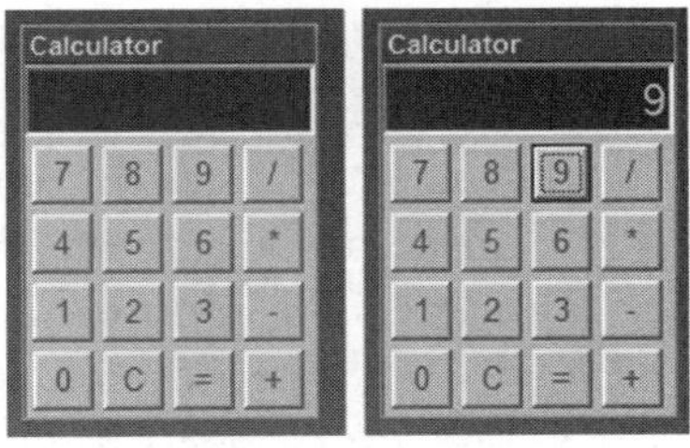

Figure 6.8 Clicking the 9 button on the Dashboard's Calculator application enters a number into the display via a ClickListener registered on the button.

In the Dashboard, as with most user interface–style applications, you use them extensively; but the largest number is used in the Dashboard's Calculator application. Figure 6.8 shows the visible affects of a ClickListener registered against the number 9 button: Clicking it places the number 9 into the calculator's display.

The code in listing 6.18 ties the button to displaying the text.

Listing 6.18 Adding a ClickListener to the number 9 button in the Dashboard's Calculator

```
private void addNumberButtonPressAction(Button button,
                                        final char numberChar){
   button.unsinkEvents(Event.KEYEVENTS);                   // Unsink keyboard events on button
   button.addClickListener(new ClickListener(){             // Add ClickListener
      public void onClick(final Widget sender) {           // onClick() Method
         sender.setStyleName("calculator-Button-selected");
         displayNumber(numberChar);                         // Display digit
            Timer t = new Timer(){
               public void run() {
                  sender.setStyleName("calculator-Button");
               }
            };
         t.schedule(CHANGE_STYLE_DELAY);
      }
});
```

The ClickListener is added to the button, and you implement the necessary onClick() method to call the helper method displayNumber(), which puts the correct number on the calculator's display.

6.3.3 Gaining/Losing focus

You saw earlier in this chapter how you made the DashboardPanel manage FocusEvents, so in this section we won't go over this type of event handling again in detail. Figure 6.9 shows the effect of the FocusListener that the code in listing 6.13 applies to the DashboardPanel: Once the component application gains focus, a new option menu appears. When this component loses focus (because the user selects another dashboard component application), the menu disappears and is replaced by the other application's menu.

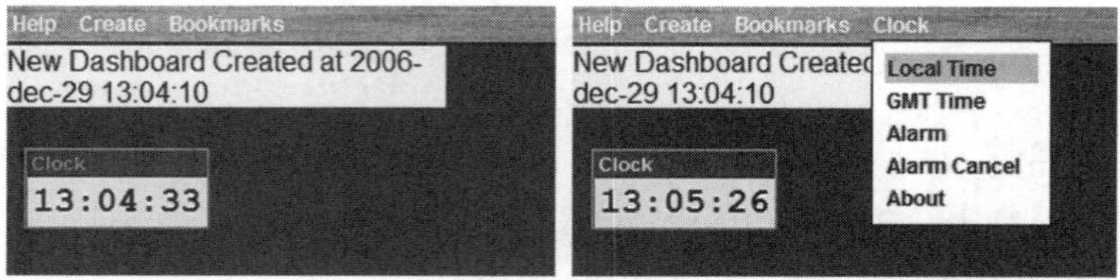

Figure 6.9 Methods in the Dashboard container's FocusListener are fired when the user focuses on the Dashboard's Clock application to display an option menu in the menu system.

6.3.4 Capturing keyboard inputs

The Dashboard's Calculator application makes the heaviest use of keyboard events in our Dashboard. Both the onscreen keypad (which is a `FocusPanel`) and the display (a `TextBox`) handle keyboard events, in accordance with the classes and methods shown in table 6.2.

If you look at the keyboard event listener added to the display object, shown in listing 6.19, you can see that it uses the `KeyboardListenerAdapter` class; you don't have to provide implementations for all three `KeyboardListener` methods.

Listing 6.19 Adding a `KeyboardListenerAdapter` to the Calculator display

```
theDisplay.addKeyboardListener(new KeyboardListenerAdapter(){
   public void onKeyPress(Widget sender,
                          char keyCode,
                          int modifiers) {
      if (!Character.isDigit(keyCode)){
         ((TextBox)sender).cancelKey();
      }
   }
});
```

Within the implementation, you make sure the keypress is a digit. Otherwise, you ignore the functionality (you can easily expand this to manage operators if you want).

6.3.5 Loading images

In chapter 4, you saw how to use the load-event listener when dealing with the Dashboard's Slideshow application, where you tried to load seven images and only six were available. The missing image caused the alert shown in figure 6.10 to be displayed to the user through the `onError()` method.

The two things to remember are that `LoadListeners` only apply to images at present, unless you want to implement your own widget and have that handle load listeners; and if the image isn't attached to the browser, then `LoadListener` methods aren't fired. This second point is due to the way GWT manages events,

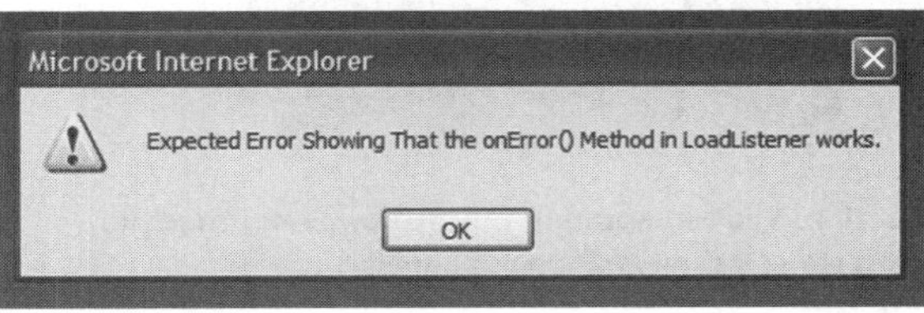

Figure 6.10 Showing an error when an image in the Slideshow component application can't be found

as you saw earlier in figure 6.3. To prevent messy displays, it's always possible to set the visibility of the image to false, using `image.setVisibility(false)`, prior to loading and subsequently display when the load is successful.

6.3.6 *Managing mouse inputs*

Later in this chapter, you'll see how to implement drag-and-drop functionality for the `DashboardPanel`, which enables you to move your component applications around in a similar manner to that shown in figure 6.11. This requires you to use some of the classes and methods associated with the mouse event handling capabilities of GWT.

In the drag-and-drop capability, you need to capture `onMouseDown` events to start the dragging, `onMouseMove` events to drag a component, and `onMouseUp` events to stop the dragging and drop the component. We'll look at the code for this in more detail later in this chapter.

6.3.7 *Scrolling*

When a component that implements the `SourcesScrollEvents` interface is scrolled, it can inform any `ScrollListeners` registered with it about that scrolling. Normally, only the `ScrollPanel` listens for and manages this event; you use it

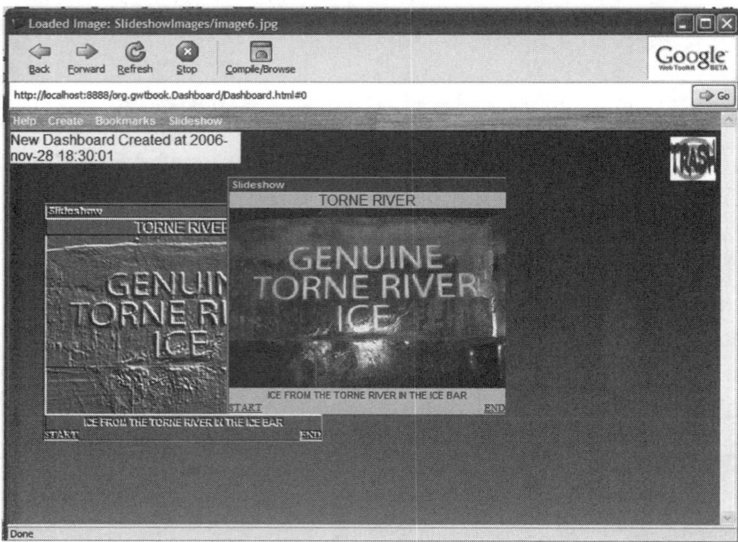

Figure 6.11 The MouseListener in action. You're capturing `MouseDown`, `MouseMove`, and `MouseUp` events in the Dashboard panel's drag-and-drop capability.

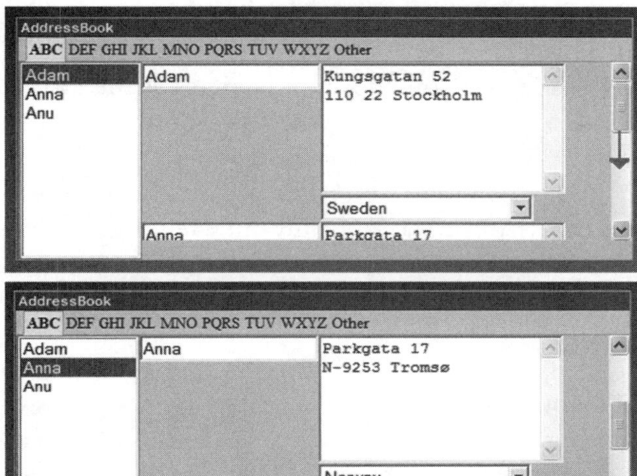

Figure 6.12 Scrolling through addresses not only changes the displayed address but also changes the list box on the left via functionality registered in a `ScrollListener`.

in the Dashboard's Address Book application so that when a user scrolls down the list of addresses, the selected index in the `ListBox` is also updated. If you look at figure 6.12, you see the effect of the user dragging the scroll bar downward. The top image shows the address for Adam; as the scroll bar goes down, the address for Anna is shown, while at the same time the selected index changes to show the updated name.

Adding a `ScrollListener` is no harder than adding the listener to the `ScrollPanel`, which you see happening in listing 6.20.

Listing 6.20 Adding a `ScrollListener` to the Address Book's `ScrollPanel`

```
visibleAddresses.addScrollListener(new ScrollListener(){      // Add ScrollListener to ScrollPanel
   public void onScroll(Widget widget,                        // Required onScroll() method
                        int scrollLeft,
                        int scrollTop) {
      int widgetCount = theAddresses.getWidgetCount();
      int panelHeight = theAddresses.getOffsetHeight();
      int widgetHeight = panelHeight/widgetCount;
      int widgetNumber = scrollTop/widgetHeight;
      addressLinks.setSelectedIndex(widgetNumber);
   }
});
```

For this application, this works well when you scrolling downward but isn't perfect when you scroll upward. This is because it changes the selected name as soon as any part of the address is visible. Scrolling down, it changes as the top of the new address appears; but scrolling up, it changes when the bottom appears, which doesn't look great—but we'll leave that to you to fix if you want.

In the standard GWT implementation, you can't add a `ScrollListener` to the browser window, but you can (from GWT 1.4) find out the scroll position of the window by using the `Window.getScrollLeft()` and `Window.getScrollTop()` methods. There are also some other events you can handle at the window level.

6.3.8 Window resize events

Two events can be managed through the GWT `Window` class: resizing and closing windows. If you register a `WindowResizeListener` with the browser, using the code shown in listing 6.21, then every time the browser window is resized you get an alert box telling you the new size, as you can see in figure 6.13.

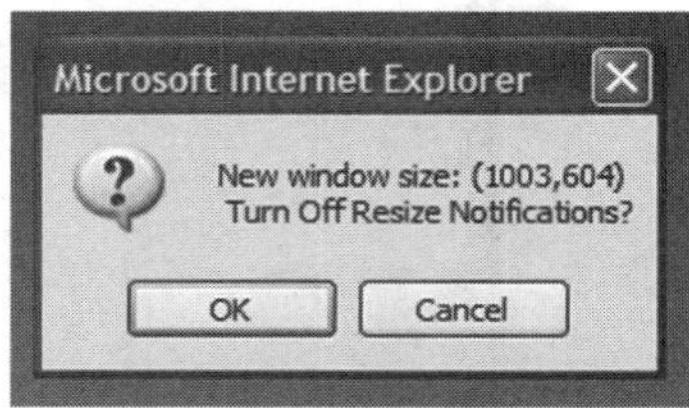

Figure 6.13 The result of resizing the browser window with a `WindowResizeListener` set up to display the new size

A `WindowResizeListener` is added to the browser using the GWT Window class, as shown in listing 6.21.

Listing 6.21 Adding a `WindowResizeListener` to the Dashboard

```
Window.addWindowResizeListener(new WindowResizeListener(){     Add Window-
   public void onWindowResized(int x, int y){                  ResizeListener
      if(informResize){
         if(Window.confirm("New window size: ("+x+","+y+") "
                        +"\n Turn Off Resize Notifications?")){
            Window.removeWindowResizeListener(this);   Remove
         }                                             WindowResizeListener
      }
      informResize = !informResize;     (1) Preventing double
   }                                        event handling
});
```

This event gets fired twice within GWT due to the event-handling mechanism—so don't be surprised to see this message twice if you write the code. To overcome this in the Dashboard, you include an additional variable and check it before displaying the confirmation box. The final part of the code inverts that variable so you don't see the message the second time.

BE AWARE The `WindowResize` event is fired twice in GWT (even with GWT 1.4's new approach to handling events). A simple boolean variable that can be checked and inverted gets around this problem—you use this in the Dashboard's resize listener.

Getting a message indicating the resize can be useful, but it can also be a little annoying, so you include the ability ❶ to remove the `WindowResizeListener` when the user clicks OK in the confirm box (which is launched by the `onWidowResizing()` method).

As well as the browser window being resized, it can be closed. To manage that, you use a `WindowCloseListener`.

6.3.9 Window close events

The other event you can manage through the `Window` class is the user trying to close the window or navigate to another page. In the Dashboard's `onModuleLoad()` method, you implement a simple `WindowCloseListener`, which presents the user with the confirmation box shown in figure 6.14.

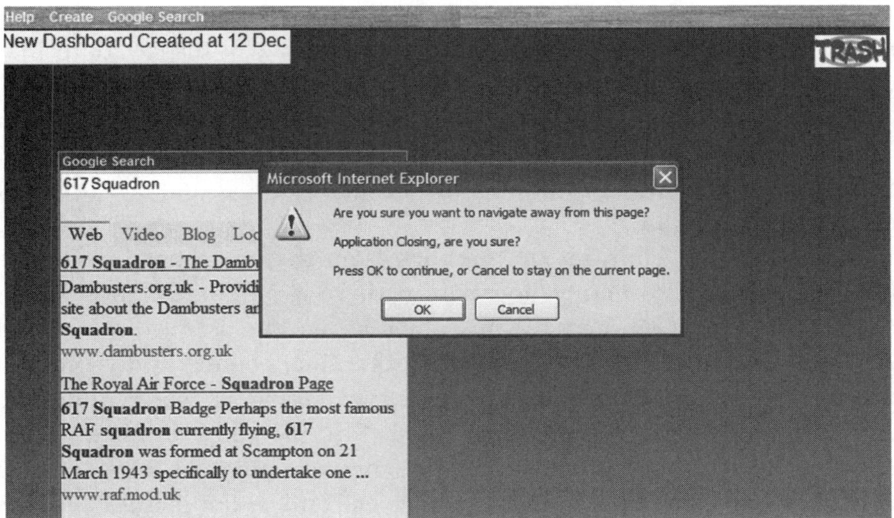

Figure 6.14 The Dashboard application, displaying a confirmation message after you try to navigate away from it

You do this by using the code shown in listing 6.22.

Listing 6.22 Listening to Window closure events from the Dashboard code

```
Window.addWindowCloseListener(new WindowCloseListener(){
   public String onWindowClosing() {              <-- Runs when window is closing
      return "Application Closing, are you sure?";
   }
   public void onWindowClosed() {                   <-- Runs when window is closed
      Window.alert("Here is where we would save state
                   to the server");
   }
});
```

You add a new `WindowCloseListener` as an anonymous type, and this must define two methods: `onWindowClosing()` and `onWindowClosed()`. The first method is called by your application when someone tries to navigate away from it. In figure 6.14, we tried to navigate away from the Dashboard to www.manning.com, and the application caught this and displayed the confirmation message.

The `onWindowClosing()` method can return a Java `String`. If you choose to return the null object, then no confirmation message is displayed. By making the `onWindowClosing()` method return a `String`, that gets displayed in the default confirmation message. You can see this in figure 6.14, where the text "Application Closing, are you sure?" has been inserted into the confirmation message. (JavaScript places our message between the two lines of text it always presents, as you can see in figure 6.14.)

Once the user confirms the message from the `onWindowClosing()` method, they're navigated to the new location. If there is no confirmation message (the `onWindowClosing()` returns the null object), then the user is directly navigated.

The `WindowCloseListener` gives you one final chance to do something after the closing event is handled—through the `onWindowClosed()` method. Many applications want to do something just before the windows close: for example, cleaning up state, potentially saving the current state, and more. GWT uses this mechanism to clean up all the event listeners, and so on, that it has added to the page before the navigation continues.

The `onWindowClosed()` method is the last piece of code executed by the application before either the window closes or the user is navigated to their new location. Execution of this method is shown in figure 6.15. In the Dashboard you just display a JavaScript alert message to show the functionality has happened.

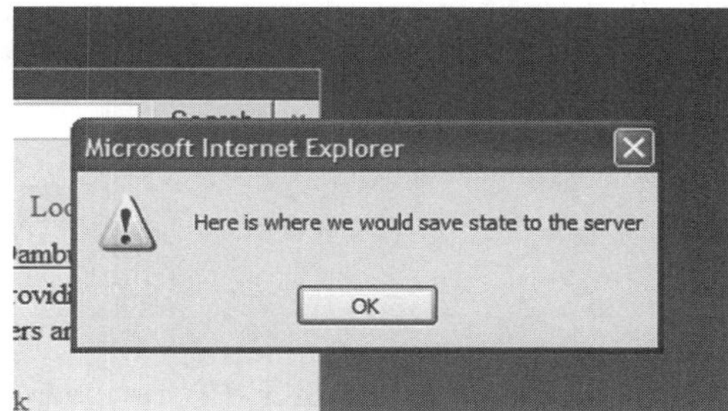

Figure 6.15
The Dashboard application executing the `onWindowClosed()` method, which would normally be used to save the application's state but in this case displays an alert message

You should be careful to understand what happens in this final `onWindowClosed()` method. The code you write in the method is guaranteed to be executed to completion; for example, if you write some code that loops through the numbers 0 to 400,000 before allowing the browser to close, then this will be done.

However, you need to be careful when it comes to asynchronous processing, such as an Ajax call in this final code. For example, you may want to try to save some state information for the application to the server if the user navigates away. You could write a well-formed request as shown in listing 6.23.

Listing 6.23 Failing AJAX Handling in an `onWindowClosed()` method

```
WindowCloseListener dashboardWindowCloseListener =
      new WindowCloseListener(){
   public void onWindowClosed() {
      String stateString = "Some state information";
      RequestBuilder rb = new RequestBuilder(RequestBuilder.POST,
                                      GWT.getModuleBaseURL()+
                                      "saveState");
      try {
         rb.sendRequest(stateString, new RequestCallback(){      ❶ Send Ajax request
            public void onError(Request request,
                                Throwable exception) {          Handle communication errors
               Window.alert("Unable to save");
            }

            public void onResponseReceived(Request request,
                                      Response response){      Handle response from server
               if(response.getStatusCode()!=200){
                  Window.alert("Unable to save state");
               } else {
                  Window.alert("Saved");
               }
            }
         });
      } catch (RequestException e) {
```

```
            GWT.log("Could not send search request", e);
         }
      }

      public String onWindowClosing() {
         return null;
      }
   };
```

We'll cover these types of requests in detail in chapter 12. In essence, what you're trying to do is make a request to the server to save the "Some state information" `String` and then report to the user if there has been an error in handling this request.

Because this code is placed in the close-listener method, then it's reasonable to expect that the request is constructed ❶. Can it be guaranteed that the request is sent? That's a good question. It relies on the underlying JavaScript and browser being able to create the `XMLHttpRequest` object and fire it before the browser unloads the application, and that appears to depend on a wide range of factors (the browser, whether proxy connections are involved, is it a navigation to another page or the window closing, and so on).

Is this approach to saving state reliable? It depends on your view of the data being saved and what experience you wish to provide for your user. Your application may have two types of information: data that is important to the user (text they're typing in, for example); and other information, such as which widget was last shown on a `StackPanel`.

The former data is important to keep safe and should be saved continuously while the application is executing. That way, if the browser is closed in error by the user or operating system, then only the data since the last update is lost. You may decide that it would be nice, but not critical, to save the UI information so that when the user runs the application, they get the same view again. If this second kind of data is lost, it may not be a problem; and because you want the last view status before navigating away, you may pick this Ajax attempt (however, never underestimate the need for a good user experience).

One thing you definitely can't rely on is being able to handle any response from the server in this situation. If your browser has managed to get the request off, then your application continues executing the rest of the close listener code. Because the `XMLHttpRequest` is asynchronous, and your close listener code is executing locally, there is a significant chance that your code will complete and the browser will load the new page before your response gets back. At that point, there is no longer any code in the browser that can handle it.

Our advice is to understand the importance of the data and to understand whether you're in a controlled environment that will offer a repeatable experience. If your application is for the Internet rather than a corporate intranet, then you have no control over how the network/systems are set up, and you should avoid trying to save data at the last minute.

Of course, making sure the user confirms that they've saved the data before the application closes is by far the most reliable approach, and you can do that using the `onWindowClosing()` method and popping up an appropriate message such as "Application closing—have you saved your data? (Click Cancel if you need to save the data.)"

Not just the standard browser events are handled by GWT in the way we have discussed in this chapter. Other types of events are handled in a similar manner, with equivalent classes.

6.4 Handling other event types

GWT handles five more types of events with the same type of listener pattern as the standard browser events:

- Form
- Popup
- Table
- Tree
- Tab

For each of these types, we'll look at how you use and manage them in the Dashboard application or its components. Again, this section isn't meant to provide a definitive reference to events; we'll provide pointers on key aspects and some identification as to where in the code you can see how you use them.

6.4.1 Handling forms

We'll cover forms in some detail in chapter 12, so we'll point you in the direction of that chapter if you want to learn more.

6.4.2 Reacting to closing pop-ups

You can register an event handler for when pop-ups are closed. The Dashboard's `Tooltip` (see figure 6.16), which is a subclass of the `PopupPanel`, sets up a timer that autocloses the pop-up after a delay. If you close the tooltip in another way,

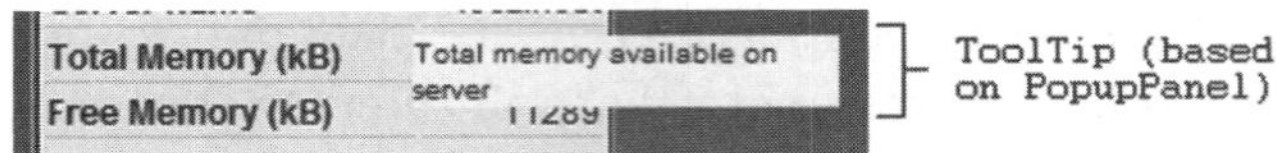

Figure 6.16 The `PopupPanel`-based `ToolTip` on the Server Status component application. This tooltip disappears after a predetermined time (or if another tooltip is opened).

such as by clicking another part of the application, then you need to cancel that timed hide event to avoid having surplus timers running (we're not exactly sure of the impact of this, but we doubt it's good, so it's best to avoid if you can!).

You only attach tooltips to the Server Status component application (in case you thought they were going to be everywhere—of course, you can always expand the Dashboard to use them where you wish).

By registering a `PopupListener`, which cancels the timer when the pop-up is closed, you avoid that issue—see the `onPopupClosed()` method in listing 6.24.

Listing 6.24 The `ToolTip onPopupClosed()` implementation

```
this.addPopupListener(new PopupListener(){
   public void onPopupClosed(PopupPanel sender,
                              boolean autoClosed) {
      removeDelay.cancel();
   }
});
```

The `removeDelay` object is an instance of a GWT timer that is ordinarily invoked after a scheduled delay to close the pop-up. Here you cancel that timer schedule as soon as the pop-up is closed.

6.4.3 *Tab events*

GWT allows you to manage events that occur when the user clicks the tabs in a tab panel. You can implement handlers for two types of events: `onBefore` and `onSelected`. The first of these events is fired after a user clicks a tab but before the associated tab panel is displayed. You use this in the Dashboard's Address Book component (see figure 6.17) to prevent a user from going to a tab where no addresses are available.

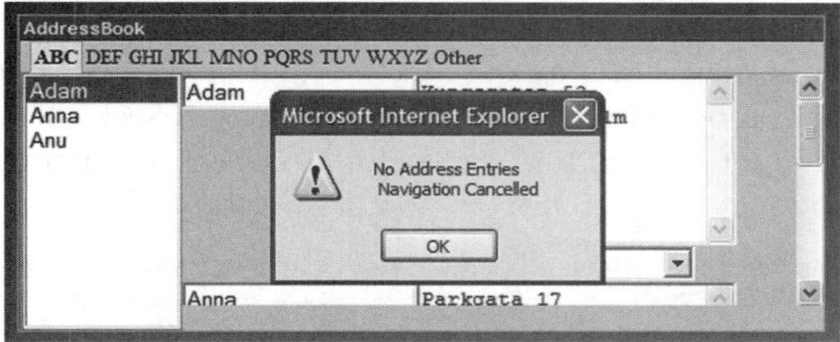

Figure 6.17 Using the `onBefore` event handler for tabs to prevent the user from going to Address Book tabs that contain no addresses

The code to achieve this affect is shown in listing 6.25.

Listing 6.25 Adding a `TabListener` to the Address Book

```
addresses.addTabListener(new TabListener(){                    <-- Add TabListener
   public boolean onBeforeTabSelected(SourcesTabEvents sender,
                                          int tabIndex) {      <-- Do something before going to selected tab
      VerticalPanel vp = getAddressPanel(tabIndex);
      int val = vp.getWidgetCount();
      if (val == 0){
         Window.alert("No Address Entries\n Navigation Cancelled");
         return false;       <-- Disallow selected tab
      }
      return true;      <-- Allow navigation to selected tab
   }

   public void onTabSelected(SourcesTabEvents sender,          <-- Do something when going to selected tab
                             int tabIndex) {
   }
});
```

When using the `onBeforeTabSelect()` method, you need to return a boolean value. This value determines whether GWT allows the selected tab to be shown. A `false` value prevents the selection of the tab, whereas a `true` value lets the tab be selected.

The `onTabSelected()` method allows you to implement functionality for the new tab, which might include operations to initialize the panel. In the Dashboard case, you don't implement anything.

6.4.4 *Tabling events*

The most classic use of table events we can think of is to develop a table of data in which clicking headings reorders the data. In the Dashboard's Server Status component application, you set up a `TableListener` for all cells of the table, as shown in listing 6.26.

Listing 6.26 Adding a `TableListener` to perform tasks on the Server Status data

```
serverStats.addTableListener(new TableListener(){
   public void onCellClicked(SourcesTableEvents sender,
                             int row, int cell) {
      if (row == HEADER_ROW){
         if (cell == STATNAME_COL)
            Window.alert("Would re-order based on statistic
                          name here");
         else
            Window.alert("Would re-order based on statistic
                          values here");
      } else {
         Widget clickedOn = serverStats.getWidget(row, cell);
         int toolY = clickedOn.getAbsoluteTop();
         int toolX = clickedOn.getAbsoluteLeft() +
                     clickedOn.getOffsetWidth();
         switch(row){
            case SERVERNAME_ROW: new ToolTip(
                "The name of the server being monitored",
                toolX, toolY);
            break;
         :
         }
      }
   }
});
```

❶ Select Status Name column
❷ Identify widget clicked, if not in header
❸ Calculate position for tooltip
Create tooltip

Clicks on the table are handled by the `onCellClicked()` method. If the user clicks in the header row, then you can invoke functionality to reorder the data ❶—although for the sake of brevity in the examples, we don't. Clicking elsewhere in the table means you wish to show a tooltip explaining what the data means. The problem is that you can't tell x and y positions for the mouse click within a `TableListener`. To overcome that restriction, you identify the widget that was clicked (which is possible because each cell contains a widget ❷) and then calculate the position where the tooltip should be shown to be the upper-right position of that widget ❸.

6.4.5 Tree events

In the Dashboard's Book component application, we'll look into how tree events can be managed, through the `TreeListener`. Figure 6.18 shows tree events being managed in the Book application. In the top image, no tree items have been selected; in the bottom image, we have opened (changed the state) of item 3 and selected the tree item related to chapter 3.1 of the book.

By changing the state of a tree item, you fire the `onTreeItemStateChanges()` method, which in the Dashboard's `Book` object sets the label at the bottom of the component to read the same as the menu item (see ❶ in listing 6.27).

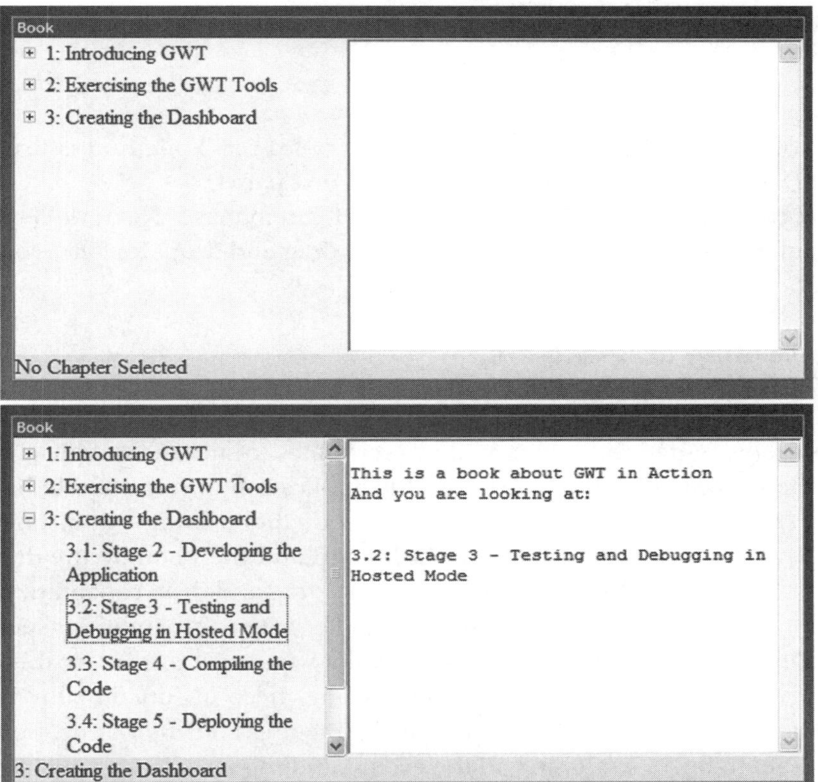

Figure 6.18 Tree events being fired on the `Book` widget

Listing 6.27 Implementing the `TreeListener` on the Dashboard's Book component application

```
theTree.addTreeListener(new TreeListener(){
   public void onTreeItemStateChanged(TreeItem item) {      ❶
      if(item.getState()){
         currChapter.setText(item.getText());
      } else {
         currChapter.setText("------");
      }
   }

   public void onTreeItemSelected(TreeItem item) {      ❷
      changeText(item.getText());
   }
});
```

When you select an item, then the `onTreeItemSelect()` method is fired, which for the Dashboard ❷ sets the text shown in a text panel.

That concludes our look at the events GWT can manage. Next, we'll use all the information you've seen by implementing drag-and-drop for the component applications used in the Dashboard.

6.5 Implementing drag-and-drop

So far, you've been building the `DashboardPanel` panel based on the `DialogBox`, and you've extended that functionality a few times to sink the double-click event, to handle toggling of the view, to show the application or just the title bar, and to handle `FocusEvents`. The one piece of functionality missing—until now—is the ability to drag the panel around the Dashboard and then handle the dropping it on the trash icon. GWT currently has no native drag-and-drop capability, but some libraries are beginning to add windowing-like system capabilities (such as the GWT Window Manager: http://www.gwtwindowmanager.org/). In this section, though, we'll examine how to add this missing piece of functionality by implementing your own code. We'll look first at dragging and then at dropping. This way, you get to begin exercising all the event-handling knowledge you have gained from this chapter.

6.5.1 Implementing the drag part

Think of the act of dragging a component: You press the mouse button down on the panel and keep it down while dragging the panel. The dragging should stop when you release the mouse button. In these terms, you can envisage that you need to use the onMouseDown, onMouseMove, and onMouseUp events. Do you need to sink these events? To answer that question, we need to look at the components of DialogBox to see if the events are already sunk.

The definition of DialogBox implements the MouseListener interface:

```
public class DialogBox
       extends PopupPanel
       implements HasHTML, MouseListener
```

The MouseListener requires the implementation of the following methods:

- onMouseDown(Widget sender, int x, int y)
- onMouseEnter(Widget sender)
- onMouseLeave(Widget sender)
- onMouseMove(Widget sender, int x, int y)
- onMouseUp(Widget sender, int x, int y)

The DialogBox class already implements its own drag functionality. In this section, you'll extend this functionality to meet your needs. The DialogBox implements dragging in the following three phases: starting to drag, dragging, and stopping the drag.

Starting to drag

Dragging starts when the user creates an onMouseDown event over the panel and is implemented by the code in listing 6.28.

Listing 6.28 Event-handling code for the onMouseDown event in the DialogBox component

```
public void onMouseDown(Widget sender, int x, int y) {     ❶ Set dragging
   dragging = true;                                           flag to true
   DOM.setCapture(caption.getElement());            ❷ Capture DOM element
   dragStartX = x;        ❸ Log initial
   dragStartY = y;          coordinates
}
```

You set an internal variable called dragging to true so you know the drag state of the panel ❶. Then, by calling the DOM method setCapture() ❷, you ensure that DialogBox's caption receives all mouse events directly (this is cancelled when you call the releaseCapture() method later in the code, as you'll see).

To understand where the user has dragged to, and hence where you need to reposition the dialog box from, you store the screen coordinates of the mouse cursor when the `onMouseDown` event was received (provided as parameters to the `onMouseDown()` method, which is called by the `MouseListener`) ❸.

Now that you've captured the `onMouseDown` event and set up some preliminary variables, the next stage is when the user drags the component.

Dragging

When the user drags the component, you need to determine where the mouse cursor is now on the screen. You know the mouse has moved because it raises an `onMouseMove` event. The handler for such an event is shown in listing 6.29.

Listing 6.29 Event-handling code for the `onMouseMove` event in the `DialogBox` component

```
public void onMouseMove(Widget sender, int x, int y) {
   if (dragging) {
      int absX = x + getAbsoluteLeft();
      int absY = y + getAbsoluteTop();
      setPopupPosition(absX - dragStartX, absY - dragStartY);
   }
}
```

❶ Check for dragging
❷ Find new coordinates
❸ Move panel across page

If you're handling an `onMouseMove` event, then you first check to see whether the panel has been set to be in a dragging state by a previous `onMouseDown` event. If it hasn't, then you ignore the rest of the code ❶.

Assuming the widget is in a dragging state, you identify the x and y positions to which you need to move the widget. You do this by taking the new coordinates of the mouse cursor (from the event) and then adding those to the leftmost and topmost point of the panel in the browser's coordinate system ❷.

Finally ❸, you call the `setPopupPosition()` method of the `PopupPanel` (which is the parent of `DialogBox`) to move the panel to the correct position. Notice that you subtract the initial x and y values stored in the previous section, hence why we had to store them originally.

The panel continues being dragged while the `onMouseDown` event is called. When the user releases the mouse button, then an `onMouseUp` event is called.

Stopping the drag

Dragging stops when an `onMouseUp` event is captured. The code in listing 6.30 shows what the `DialogBox` does to handle an `onMouseUp` event.

Listing 6.30 Event-handling code for the `onMouseUp` event in the `DialogBox` component

```
public void onMouseUp(Widget sender, int x, int y) {
   dragging = false;
   DOM.releaseCapture(caption.getElement());
}
```

Set dragging flag to false

Release DOM element

You set the drag state of the panel to false and then call the DOM method `releaseCapture()` to stop the element from receiving all mouse-related events.

This functionality works fine for the `DialogBox` (and it's a good template for any type of dragging capability that you need for your own application). For the Dashboard, you'll go slightly further and extend this basic ability.

DashboardPanel onMouseDown

At the start of dragging, you'll change the style of the panel (in the Dashboard, you'll change the text color of the caption), and you'll also fire an `onFocus` event against any of the `FocusListeners` registered with this panel. The code for the `DashboardPanel` is shown in listing 6.31.

Listing 6.31 Event-handling code for the `onMouseDown` event in the `DashboardPanel` component

```
public void onMouseDown(Widget sender, int x, int y)
{
   super.onMouseDown(sender, x, y);
   if (DashboardPanel.current != null) {
      DashboardPanel.current.listeners.
         fireLostFocus(DashboardPanel.current);
      DashboardPanel.current.
         removeStyleName("selectedDashboardComponent");
   }
   DashboardPanel.current = this;
   addStyleName("selectedDashboardComponent");
   DashboardPanel.current.listeners.fireFocus(this);
}
```

1. Handle as normal
2. Check if we have focus
3. Lose focus on old panel
4. Set this as current panel
5. Set CSS style to show we have focus
6. Fire our focus listener

The `DashboardPanel` panel still wants to act as much as possible like the `DialogBox` from which it inherits, so you execute the `DialogBox`'s `onMouseDown()` method first ❶ before trying any of your own functionality. With the `DialogBox`'s standard functionality executed, the next check you perform is to see if the static variable `DashboardPanel.current` is set to null ❷. If it is, that means no `DashboardPanel` currently has focus, so you can jump to step ❹.

If the `current` variable is set, then currently another `DashboardPanel` has focus; you need to remove the focus from it (step ❸). You do that by firing its `onLostFocus` event through its `FocusListeners` object. This invokes the `onLostFocus()` method for the component Dashboard application, which requests that application to remove any option menu it has placed in the Dashboard's menu bar. Once the `onLostFocus` event is fired, you remove the styling name that gave it the styling of a focused panel.

In ❹ you set this panel as the current `DashboardPanel` object, which has the focus in the Dashboard, and then change the style of the panel to be that of a panel with focus ❺.

Finally ❻, you fire the `onFocus` event for the new current `DashboardPanel`, which results in the new component application registering any option menu it has in the Dashboard's menu.

Catching the mouse-down is the initialization part of dragging. Next, you need to handle when the user starts moving the mouse while keeping the mouse button down.

DashboardPanel onMouseMove

There is no need to override the `DialogBox`'s `onMouseMove()` method because it does exactly what you require: It moves the panel as you move the mouse. Dragging stops when the user releases the mouse button, and the code gets an `onMouseUp` event.

DashboardPanel onMouseUp

The final action to handle while dragging is to process the mouse-up action. You need to release the capture of the element and then, crucially, detect where the component has been dropped. If it's dropped on top of the trash icon, then the `DashboardPanel` being dragged should be removed from the Dashboard. The `onMouseUp()` code is shown in listing 6.32.

Listing 6.32 Event-handling code for the `onMouseUp` event in the `DashboardPanel` component

```
public void onMouseUp(Widget sender, int x, int y)
{
   super.onMouseUp(sender, x, y);
   if (detectCollision(this, trash)) {
      removeFromDashboard();
   }
}
```

You first call the standard onMouseUp() functionality of the DialogBox and then perform a collision-detection check, which is at the heart of the drop capability.

6.5.2 Implementing the drop part

Dragging is only one part of the drag and drop functionality you require for the DashboardPanel. The final part of the previous section showed you how to deal with letting go of the mouse button, which is technically the drop part; but you need to implement functionality to see if the user has dropped the component on another particular area.

The detection algorithm is based on checking whether two components overlap. If they do, then you can say that one component has been dropped on the other. You can easily check by looking at the boundaries of the objects; for example, if the right part of one object is less than the left part of another, then they aren't overlapping.

Listing 6.33 Event-handling code for the onMouseUp event in the DashboardPanel component

```
boolean detectCollision(Widget w1, Widget w2)
{
    int left1, left2, right1, right2;
    int top1, top2, bottom1, bottom2;
    left1 = w1.getAbsoluteLeft();
    left2 = w2.getAbsoluteLeft();
    right1 = w1.getAbsoluteLeft() + w1.getOffsetWidth();
    right2 = w2.getAbsoluteLeft() + w2.getOffsetWidth();
    top1 = w1.getAbsoluteTop();
    top2 = w2.getAbsoluteTop();
    bottom1 = w1.getAbsoluteTop() + w1.getOffsetHeight();
    bottom2 = w2.getAbsoluteTop() + w2.getOffsetHeight();
    if (bottom1 < top2) return false;
    if (top1 > bottom2) return false;
    if (right1 < left2) return false;
    if (left1 > right2) return false;
    return true;
}
```

Calculate boundaries ❶

Determine collisions

The code in listing 6.33 shows how to check for collisions. We'll explain how in more detail now. ❶ is dedicated to calculating the numerical outer boundaries of the two components, because you wish to see if they've collided according to the following cases.

Case 1: Widget 1 above widget 2

Collision case 1 checks whether the situation shown in figure 6.19 is true, where the y index of the bottom of widget 1 is less than the y index of the top of widget 2. If this is so, then the widgets haven't collided.

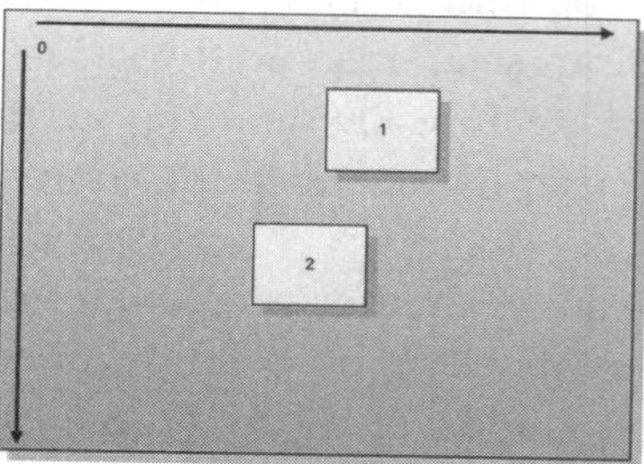

Figure 6.19
Checking for vertical collision. The test fails because the y-index of the bottom of 1 has a lower y index than the top of 2.

Case 2: Widget 1 below widget 2

Similarly, if the y index of the top of widget 1 is greater than the y index of the bottom of widget 2, then they can't have collided (see figure 6.20).

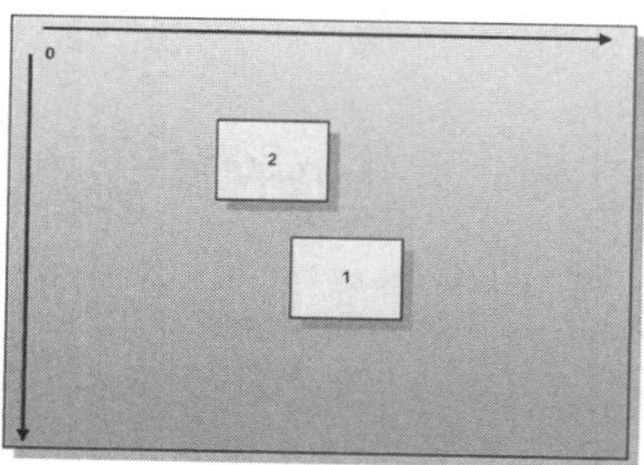

Figure 6.20
Checking for vertical collision. The test fails because the y-index of the top of 1 is greater than the y-index of the bottom of 2.

Case 3: Widget 1 to the left of widget 2

Collision case 3 determines whether a horizontal collision has occurred by checking whether the x index of the right side of widget 1 is less than the x index of the left side of widget 2. If it's less, then the components haven't collided (see figure 6.21).

Figure 6.21
Checking for horizontal collision. The test fails because the x-index of the right side of 1 is less than the x-index of the left of 2.

Case 4: Widget 1 to the right of widget 2

Finally, collision case 4 checks whether the x index of the left side of widget 1 is greater than the x index of the right side of widget 2, as shown in figure 6.22. If it is, then the widgets haven't collided.

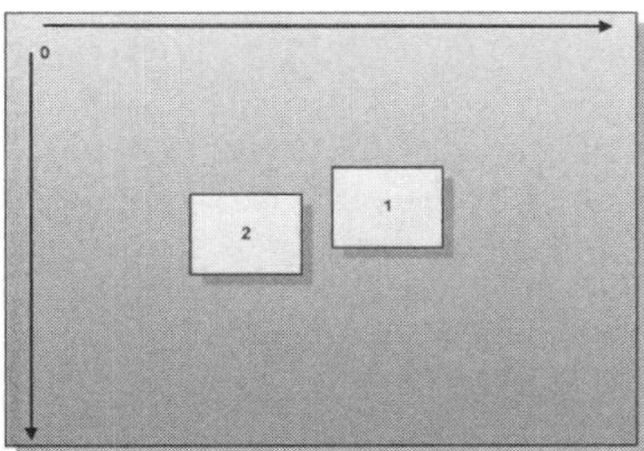

Figure 6.22
Checking for horizontal collision. The test fails because the x-index of the left part of 1 is greater than the x-index of the right part of 2.

With the complete code for drag-and-drop in place, you can finish the `DashboardPanel` class, which is shown in listing 6.34. (Note that the downloadable code doesn't have this inheritance from `DashboardFirst` through to this example; it has only the one class called `DashboardPanel`, which contains all the necessary functionality.)

Listing 6.34 Final version of the `DashboardPanel`

```
public class DashboardPanel
      extends DashboardPanelThird
{
   public void onMouseDown(Widget sender, int x, int y){      ◁ Calculate Boundaries
      super.onMouseDown(sender, x, y);
      if (DashboardPanel.current != null) {
         DashboardPanel.current.listeners.
            fireLostFocus(DashboardPanel.current);
         DashboardPanel.current.
            removeStyleName("selectedDashboardComponent");
      }
      DashboardPanel.current = this;
      addStyleName("selectedDashboardComponent");
      DashboardPanel.current.listeners.fireFocus(this);
   }

   public void onMouseUp(Widget sender, int x, int y){      ◁ Determine Collisions
      super.onMouseUp(sender, x, y);
      if (detectCollision(this, trash)) {
         removeFromDashboard();
      }
   }
```

```
    boolean detectCollision(Widget w1, Widget w2)
    {
        int left1, left2;
        int right1, right2;
        int top1, top2;
        int bottom1, bottom2;
        left1 = w1.getAbsoluteLeft();
        left2 = w2.getAbsoluteLeft();
        right1 = w1.getAbsoluteLeft() + w1.getOffsetWidth();
        right2 = w2.getAbsoluteLeft() + w2.getOffsetWidth();
        top1 = w1.getAbsoluteTop();
        top2 = w2.getAbsoluteTop();
        bottom1 = w1.getAbsoluteTop() + w1.getOffsetHeight();
        bottom2 = w2.getAbsoluteTop() + w2.getOffsetHeight();
        if (bottom1 < top2) return false;
        if (top1 > bottom2) return false;
        if (right1 < left2) return false;
        if (left1 > right2) return false;
        return true;

}
```

This final listing completes our journey exploring events and developing the `DashboardPanel`, which you'll continuously use throughout the elements of the Dashboard example. We've briefly mentioned the `DashboardComposite` in this chapter; in chapter 7, we'll tie widgets, panels, and events together to produce composite widgets.

6.6 Summary

We've reached the end of our journey through the basics of GWT, where we have covered widgets, panels, and events. We think you'll agree that GWT provides a wide range of these components, and if you think in a purely Java way, they are relatively easy to build and plug together.

The event handling in GWT requires you to think much less about how it might be happening in the browser and more about how it works in the Java code. This is a good thing, because it means you aren't constantly worrying about how it's working in the browser, not least because of the browser differences!

In general, you need to tell widgets to sink events and then handle those sunk events in an `onBrowserEvent()` method. You can pass events around the code by using the `EventListener` and `SourcesEvent` interface frameworks, which also keeps you away from browser differences in event handling.

Unlike widgets and panels, you can't build new low-level browser events, but it's possible to create higher-level events—for example, the way GWT provides `CellClick` events for the `HTMLTable`. Although we didn't look at building events in this chapter, you can follow the pattern provided many times already in GWT. Also, in the next chapter, you'll see how to trap mouse-up events and export them as change events in the slider.

Next, you'll pull together all your knowledge of widgets, panels, and events to produce composite widgets.

7 Creating composite widgets

This chapter covers

- Building composite widgets
- Layout selection
- GWT interfaces
- Styling widgets

Composite widgets are powerful elements of GWT. They're widgets that you create yourself using existing widgets, composites, and panels; they're almost mini-GWT applications. A typical composite includes a number of different widgets and panels and ties all that functionality together using events, which is why we had to leave the definition of composite widgets until this point.

In this chapter, we'll look at building two composite widgets that will be used in the Dashboard application. The first composite widget is one you can also find a version of in the GWT Widget Library—the `EditableLabel`. On screen, it resembles normal text until you click it, at which time it switches to a text box in which you can update the text—when you click the OK or Cancel button, it returns to being a simple piece of text.

After building the `EditableLabel` composite, we'll look at a much more complicated composite, but show how easy it is to start pulling it together. We'll show the outline of a slider class, which is a composite made from two images, and then explain how by putting together a few of these sliders, you can produce a rich color-picker widget.

The third composite you'll build in this chapter is the `DashboardComposite` class. This isn't a composite in the sense of the `EditableLabel`; rather, it's an extension of the GWT `Composite` class specifically for use in the Dashboard example. It provides the normal `Composite` functionality, plus it provides the capability of adding an option menu to the Dashboard's main menu as well as handling focus events for the Dashboard applications.

Let's start by expanding on the brief definition of what a composite widget is.

7.1 What is a composite widget?

Although GWT provides a large number of widgets, and you saw in chapter 4 how you can create your own widgets, there will be occasions where you want to manage a collection of these widgets, laid out in a particular way, as a single "widget" itself. This is where composite widgets come in.

DEFINITION A *composite widget* is a collection of widgets (standard GWT widgets, user-defined widgets, or other composite widgets), laid out in a particular manner and providing some specific functionality, which you wish to manage as a single entity.

To some extent, composite widgets are mini-GWT applications. You build them from a set of widgets, lay them out using panels, and handle the events using the standard event-handling process—all of which we've described in the last three chapters. In this chapter, you'll build the `EditableLabel` composite widget, which includes a `Label`, `TextBox`, `TextArea` and two `Button` widgets; some of these are shown in action in figure 7.1.

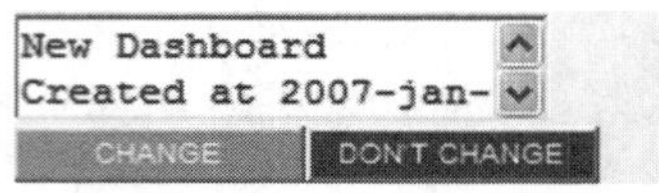

Figure 7.1 The `EditableLabel` composite widget in action in the Dashboard

By building the `EditableLabel` as a composite widget, you can treat it like any other widget in the code by creating instances of it using

```
EditableLabel newLabel = new EditableLabel();
```

You can also add it to the browser page, or any other panel, with code similar to this:

```
RootPanel.get().add(newLabel);
```

Defining a composite widget is easy as long as you remember two things: first, the composite widget class must extend the GWT `Composite` class; and second, you must call the `initWidget()` method, passing in the main container of the composite widget as a parameter before the end of the constructor. Failure to call the `initWidget()` method will result in exceptions being thrown in your code and the program ceasing to work.

You generally define composite widgets to sit within an overall panel and add the widgets you need (in their own panels if necessary) to that overall panel. You pass this overall panel as a parameter to the `initWidget()` method.

Because composite widgets are like mini-applications, it's useful to have a process in mind for how to develop them (which can also be applied to applications).

7.2 Composite widget development steps

Building composites is like building miniature applications. Each composite consists of a number of widgets, usually laid out in one or more panels. You have to answer the same type of questions you do when building an application—which widgets and panels will you use, how will they be put together, and what GWT interfaces should the widget implement?

When you're building composites, it's useful to follow a logical path of development so that you don't trip yourself up. However, unlike building an application, you don't need to use the creation tools we covered back in chapter 2; you create a new class that extends the `Composite` class.

The approach for building composite widgets is shown in table 7.1. You'll use it as we go through this section.

Table 7.1 Development steps for creating composite widgets

Step	Name	Description
1	Identify widgets	A composite widget is made out of a number of other widgets, which may be standard GWT widgets or other composites. Before you build a composite, it's useful to know what widgets you'll be including.
2	Choose layout	Determine how the widgets will be laid out in your composite. You can think of composite widgets as being mini-GWT applications.
3	Identify interfaces	As with the other widgets and panels you've built over the last three chapters, composites should behave in a manner that the user would expect, and using the provided GWT interfaces helps. If the widget has a text element, then it should implement the `HasText` interface, for example.
4	Build	This step covers the building of the composite widget. You need to build a number of code parts: ▪ Implementing the interfaces identified ▪ Implementing any outward-facing methods you wish to expose in addition to those requested by the interfaces ▪ Creating the widget structure and setting up the event handling ▪ Implementing the code that handles events that are expected
5	Set styles	Just as you relied on the standard components having well-defined style names, any composite you build should also provide that courtesy. In this step you build a naming convention for the styles and apply them to the component widgets and panels.
6	Test	You should always test composites like other software components, although in the interest of reducing the size of this book, we don't write about this step in this chapter.

As you build the `EditableLabel` widget, mark off the development steps that you've completed using the process checklist shown in figure 7.2.

Let's get developing again. We present the `EditableLabel`!

1. Identify the composite widgets to be used ☐
2. Choose the panel layout and structure ☐
3. Identify the interfaces the composite should implement ☐
4. Build the widget ☐
5. Set the styles ☐
6. Test ☐

Figure 7.2 Composite widget development process check-off list

7.3 Building the editable label

In this section, you'll build a composite widget using the process defined in table 7.1. The purpose of the composite widget is to present a text label that can be edited by clicking it. The popular Flickr photo site uses this type of functionality to allow its users to edit a photo's title and description. As you can see in figure 7.3, you can give photographs a title and a description.

Figure 7.3 Photograph from Flickr showing how a title and a description can be displayed

How do you enter/alter these details? Pre-Ajax days, this was probably implemented as a web page including a form for entering/altering the details, which for one photograph isn't an issue. But consider if several photographs appear on the page at the same time; it will seem messy to have to navigate to a new page to change each piece of text. This is where the `EditableLabel` (see figure 7.4) comes into its own.

If you want to edit a title or a description, it's a less than optimal solution to have to open each photograph, make the change, save it, and then go back to the main screen. Ajax techniques, such as those in evident use on Flickr, allow this editing to be performed directly on the screen.

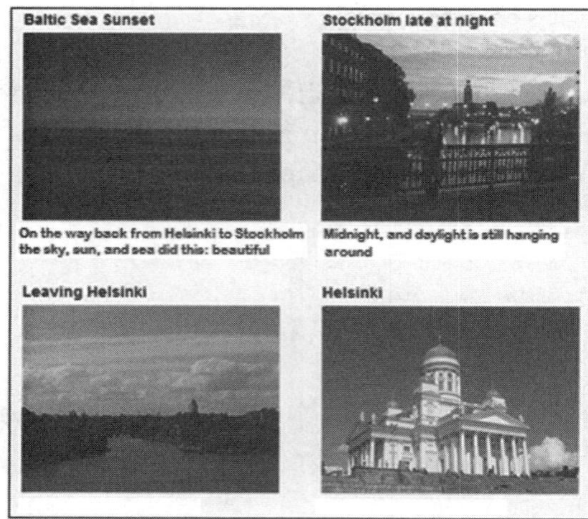

Figure 7.4
Set of photographs with titles and descriptions. Pre-Ajax user interfaces didn't allow multiple edits on a single page.

The `EditableLabel` widget provides such functionality, and it's implemented as a composite widget. It was originally built in the early days of GWT by the authors for functionality we needed at that point, and then it migrated into the GWT Widget Library for everyone to use. The functionality of the `EditableLabel` widget is defined in table 7.2.

Table 7.2 Functional description of the `EditableLabel` composite widget you'll create in this section

Step	Action
Add the widget to the panel	Only the user-defined text associated with the widget (if any is provided to the constructor) is shown.
Click text	An editable area is shown, containing the user-defined text. If the initial text is set to be word-wrapped, then the editable area presented is scrollable; otherwise a single-line editable area is used. Cancel and OK buttons are displayed.
Click the OK button	The editable area is replaced with an element of non-editable text, the value of which is set to the value last shown in the editable area. After the alteration in the user interface, a user-provided follow up action occurs. This action may, for example, save the new value of text displayed to a database.
Click the Cancel button	The editable area is replaced with an element of non-editable text, the value of which is set to exactly the same value it had prior to the last attempt to edit.
Press the Esc key	If the Esc key is pressed while focus is on the widget, then the functionality invoked is the same as clicking the Cancel button.
Press the Return/Enter key	If the Return/Enter key is pressed while focus is on the widget, then one of two functionalities is invoked. If the `EditableLabel` is identified as being word-wrapped, then a new-line is inserted in the area where the editable text is shown. If the `EditableLabel` isn't set as word-wrapped, then pressing Return/Enter invokes the same functionality as clicking OK.

Now that we've defined the functionality of the composite widget, we'll look at how to implement it. That discussion begins with identifying which existing widgets you'll employ.

7.3.1 Step 1: Identifying the components

The components you'll choose need to support the stated functionality, and often the choice is determinable from what you write down as the functionality. A quick look at the widgets provided with the GWT distribution should satisfy you that the

GWT `Label` widget is sufficient to represent the initial text—it displays text, can be word-wrapped, and is un-editable.

Another option could have been to use an `HTML` element, because you want the label to be clickable, which might imply a hyperlink. However, choosing an `HTML` element would lead users to expect that clicking the text would invoke behavior onscreen, such as the loading of a new page. It's important to keep user interfaces within the bounds of that which users normally expect.

You can easily add a click listener to a label (the API tells you that the `Label` widget implements the `SourcesClickEvents` interface) that enables you to listen and react to mouse click events. You're still left in a situation of trying to indicate to a user that they can click and edit the label, but that can be solved by, for example, changing the mouse or background color when the mouse hovers over the editable label. This can be achieved using CSS, a GWT wrapper to the script.aculo.us effects library (http://script.aculo.us—see the GWT Widget Library for a GWT wrapper) or even implementing this effect natively in GWT.

Providing the editing interface requires you to look for one or more widgets that can provide single-line and multiline editing. You'll use two simple GWT widgets for editing. A `TextBox` widget is a single-line text box that you'll be familiar with from all the forms on web sites. A `TextArea` widget is a text box that allows for multiline editing. A quick check again of the API reveals that both `TextBox` and `TextArea` extend the `TextBoxBase` class, which itself implements the `SourceKeyboardEvents` interface. By implementing the `SourceKeyboardEvents` interface, both `TextArea` and `TextBox` allow you to register the fact that you wish to listen for and react to specific keyboard presses—in this case, the Esc and Return/Enter keys.

The composite widget also needs two buttons: one to confirm the change, and the other to cancel the change, as defined in the functional description. Looking at the list of standard widgets reveals the GWT `Button` class, and the first version of the `EditableLabel` composite widget used that class. Now we've identified all the composite widgets that are used (see figure 7.5).

However, we discussed how flexible the finished version should be. It's clear that the functionality requires two objects that can be clicked, with one canceling

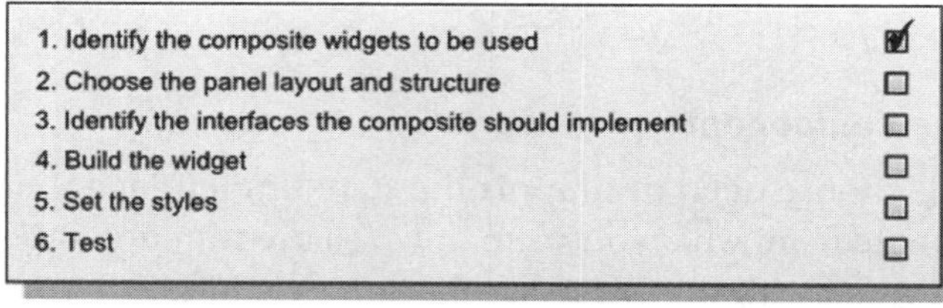
1. Identify the composite widgets to be used
2. Choose the panel layout and structure
3. Identify the interfaces the composite should implement
4. Build the widget
5. Set the styles
6. Test

Figure 7.5 Checking off step 1 of the composite widget development process

and the other affirming the edit. GWT buttons are fine, but what if someone wanted to use images or any other widget instead? Fortunately, Java provides mechanisms for interrogating objects at runtime, and we'll show in this section how to employ this to build a flexible widget with runtime checks to ensure that the functionality can be fulfilled. Before we get to that point, though, we need to look at the physical screen real-estate layout of the chosen widgets.

7.3.2 Step 2: Choosing the panel layout and structure

The components in the `EditableLabel` composite widget are shown in figure 7.6. It comprises a `Label`, a `TextBox`, a `TextArea`, and two widgets that represent the buttons.

The first decision you have to make is how these component widgets will be laid out—which panels will you use? You need at least one panel; otherwise, the widgets have nowhere to sit. But do you place all the widgets in one panel or use subpanels, perhaps with the buttons in one and the other widgets in another? Some potential groupings are shown in figure 7.7, where groups are loosely based on different views of the functionality.

When you think about layouts, consider how flexible you want the layout to be to any other user of your widget. At one end of the scale is the `FlowPanel`, which gives the greatest flexibility for another user to use CSS to reposition elements of your composite widget. Using `HorizontalPanels` or `VerticalPanels` forces a stricter positioning philosophy.

The design for `EditableLabel` went through a number of iterations as we thought about future reuse. Finally, we settled on putting the buttons in one `FlowPanel` and putting this panel and the other component widgets into another `FlowPanel`.

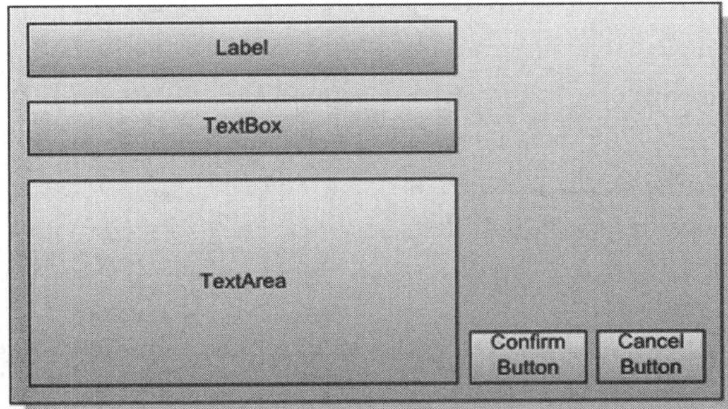

Figure 7.6 `EditableLabel` first form layout showing the components in this composite widget

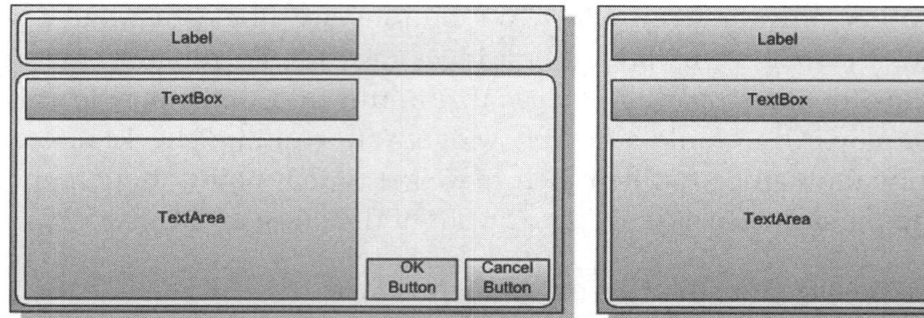

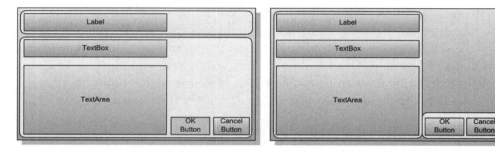

Figure 7.7 `EditableLabel` potential panel layouts showing different ways the components could be grouped

Our rationale was that the buttons and other components are clearly separable, visible components. You don't want to force another user of the widget into always having the buttons to the right of the label; perhaps they will prefer them underneath. So, you use a `FlowPanel` for the widget's main panel. Placing the buttons in their own panel allows other users to put a command such as `display: block` into their CSS to quickly move the buttons beneath the label without making any code changes.

Because only one component from the `Label`, `TextArea`, and `TextBox` is visible at any given time, there is no issue using a `FlowPanel` for the main panel. The choice of panel for the buttons could be a `HorizontalPanel`, but we wanted to cut down, if possible, the size of any compiled JavaScript code, so we again choose a `FlowPanel`.

This discussion runs the risk that you'll think we're suggesting using `FlowPanels` all the time. This isn't so; it must be considered on a case-by-case basis. For example, the composite that makes up a potential `PhotoDisplay` widget would be created using a `VerticalPanel` because this is the most appropriate panel for that widget (you don't want a user to alter the layout). See figure 7.8 as an example of what we mean.

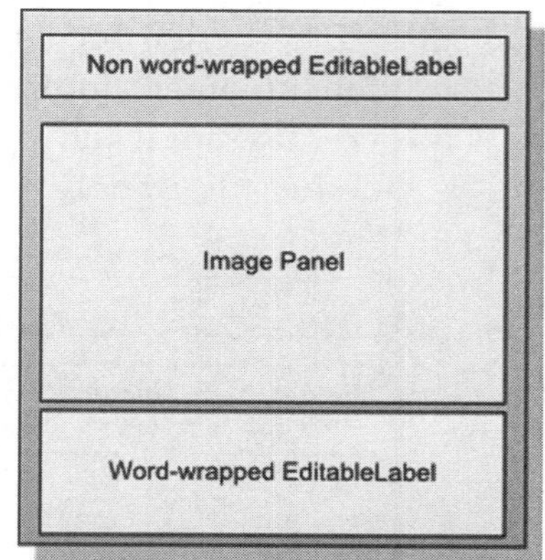

Figure 7.8 A possible `PhotoDisplay` widget panel layout demonstrating the potential use of a `VerticalPanel` and two `EditableLabel` composite widgets

Now that you've identified the components and panel layouts, you can check them off in the development process (see figure 7.9) and

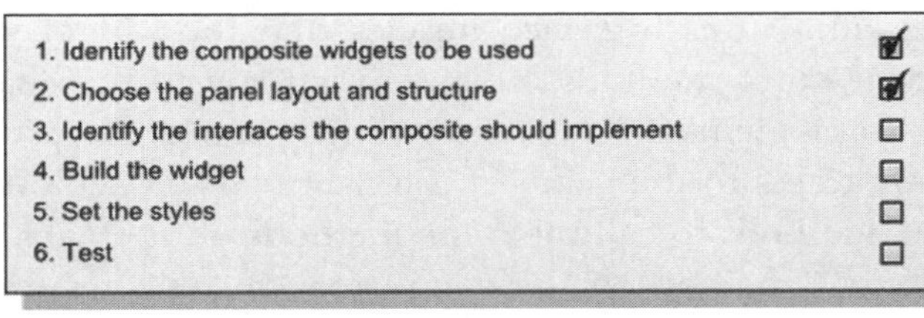

1. Identify the composite widgets to be used
2. Choose the panel layout and structure
3. Identify the interfaces the composite should implement
4. Build the widget
5. Set the styles
6. Test

Figure 7.9 Checking off step 2 of the composite widget development process

move on to considering what existing GWT interfaces the new composite widget might implement.

7.3.3 Step 3: Implementing the right GWT Java interfaces

GWT provides a number of interfaces that widgets can claim to implement. A GWT `Label`, for instance, implements the `HasText` interface, which means it provides `setText()` and `getText()` methods. When you use widgets in a composite widget, these interfaces become buried. It's possible to make the widgets your composite uses public; then, a user can call the interface methods on those widgets, but the user needs to know the structure of your composite. To improve on that and maintain consistency across widgets, you need to consider which of those interfaces the component widgets implement that the composite would be expected to implement, and also which other interfaces it would be useful to implement. In many cases, the implementation of interfaces in your composite requires a call on the appropriate method of the relevant composite part, as you'll see in just a second.

The first category of interfaces your composite implements are those it would be expected to implement. We don't mean just copying all the interfaces your component parts implement; we mean those that make sense. Consider the widgets you'll use:

- `Label`
- `TextArea`
- `TextBox`
- `Buttons`

Let's take each of these in turn and look at the interfaces that are applicable, starting with the `Label`. Because the composite widget wishes to masquerade as a `Label`, it's reasonable to expect that as far as other users of the widget are concerned, this is a `Label` and should implement the same interfaces. Let's consider these interfaces in more detail:

- HasText—Implementing this interface implies that the widget will have getText() and setText() methods, which is what you wish to have. The composite widget implements the HasText interface in order to provide the outside world with access to the value of the Label. You'll achieve this by implementing the methods to call the same methods on the Label object: Calling the getText() method on the composite will return the result of calling the getText() method on the implementation's Label, transparently to the user.
- HasWordWrap—Implementing this interface means the widget must provide setWordWrap() and getWordWrap() methods. This is perfect for implementing the required functionality switching that is based on whether the Label is word-wrapped. Again, you'll implement these methods as pass-through methods to the Label object, but also to understand whether the editable component is a TextBox or TextArea widget.
- HasHorizontalAlignment—This interface has no bearing on your functionality; you don't care if the widget is left, center, or right aligned. However, because the widget is masquerading as a Label, you should implement this interface for consistency. Calls to it will pass directly to the Label component.
- SourcesClickEvents, SourcesMouseEvents—These two interfaces allow ClickListeners and MouseListeners to be registered and unregistered against a widget implementing them. Because click and mouse events are applicable only to the Label, you'll again implement these interfaces by passing through method calls to the underlying Label widget.

The Label widget is the main component visible to most users initially. When it's clicked, the widget presents its editable area. The following list discusses the interfaces that could be implemented due to these widgets; both widgets extend the TextBoxBase class, which in turn implements a several event interfaces:

- SourcesClickEvents, SourcesMouseEvents—You don't wish to expose functionality for these events when you're in editing mode. You must still indicate that you're implementing the interfaces, because you use them for passing through to the Label when in non-editing mode.
- SourcesChangeEvents—This interface lets you register change listeners to a widget. In this instance, you don't want to allow the addition of change listeners to the TextBox or TextArea—it makes limited sense in the overall functionality of the widget to listen to changes in editing mode. However, you'll see shortly that this interface is implanted, but for other reasons.

- HasName—In forms and other techniques, this interface makes a lot of sense, allowing a TextBox or TextArea to be given a name for future manipulation. In the EditableLabel widget it makes no sense at all, because you want users to be forced to go through the Label element to set or retrieve text and the editable functionality to change values.
- HasText—You saw earlier that this interface requires the getText() and setText() methods to be implemented. These methods will already be implemented for the composite; we decided that earlier, too, but it doesn't make sense to allow access for TextArea and TextBox, because all access to the text should be through the Label.

The final component is the Button. If you were to use GWT Buttons to implement the OK and Cancel buttons, then examining the underlying ButtonBase class doesn't indicate any interfaces that it's worthwhile passing on to the user of this widget. We've mentioned that you'll allow the user of this widget flexibility in what widget is used for a button (perhaps an Image), but because we don't know, we can't guess at useful interfaces those widgets may have.

The second class of interfaces that must be considered is those you wish the new composite widget to implement in addition to those it would be expected to. A list of all interfaces is provided in the API, and you need to start considering the list and deciding which are useful.

In the case of the EditableLabel, the only interface that felt natural was SourcesChangeListener. We discarded this interface in the previous discussion because we don't want users to register change listeners against someone typing text into the TextArea or TextBox. However, it's highly useful to allow users of the widget to register change listeners that you fire when the label has been edited (changed). You'll implement this interface and manage the firing of change events yourself.

Now you know what widgets and interfaces you'll implement. Listing 7.1 shows the first outline of the composite widget code.

Listing 7.1 First version of the EditableLabel composite widget

```
public class EditableLabel extends Composite implements
                                   HasWordWrap,
                                   HasText,
                                   HasHorizontalAlignment,
                                   SourcesClickEvents,
                                   SourcesChangeEvents,
                                   SourcesMouseEvents
```

```
{
   private TextBox changeText;
   private TextArea changeTextArea;
   private Widget OK, Cancel;
   private Label text;
}
```

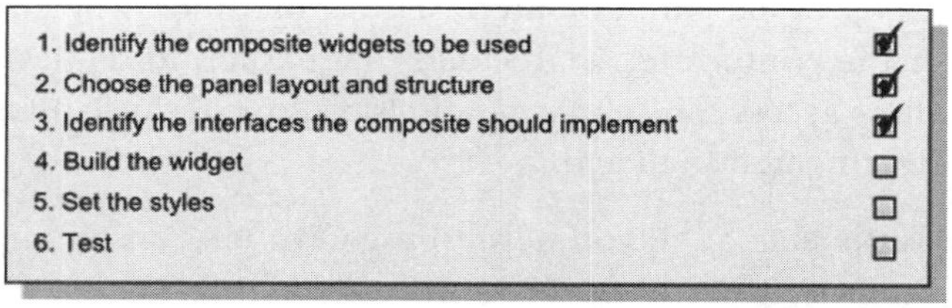

1. Identify the composite widgets to be used ☑
2. Choose the panel layout and structure ☑
3. Identify the interfaces the composite should implement ☑
4. Build the widget ☐
5. Set the styles ☐
6. Test ☐

Figure 7.10 Checking off step 3 of the composite widget development process

You can update the progress chart (see figure 7.10) and move on to the next step, where we'll begin to look at implementing the functionality.

7.3.4 Step 4: Building the composite widget

Now, we come to building the functionality for the composite widget. The code is some six pages long; rather than present the code and then talk about the various aspects afterward, as we've done with the example to this point, we'll walk through the code step by step.

The code starts as it did in listing 7.1, indicating that you're extending the `Composite` class and will handle a number of different interfaces:

```
public class EditableLabel
       extends Composite
       implements HasWordWrap,
                  HasText,
                  HasHorizontalAlignment,
                  SourcesClickEvents,
                  SourcesChangeEvents,
                  SourcesMouseEvents
{
   private TextBox changeText;
   private TextArea changeTextArea;
   private Label text;
   private String originalText;
   private Widget confirmChange;
   private Widget cancelChange;
   private ChangeListenerCollection changeListeners;
```

The methods required for the property interfaces `HasWordWrap`, `HasText`, and `HasHorizontalAlignment` are immediately passed down to the `Label` named text as shown in this sample:

```
public HorizontalAlignmentConstant getHorizontalAlignment() {
   return text.getHorizontalAlignment();
}
```

Similarly, the methods required by the `SourcesClickEvents` and `SourcesMouseEvents` interfaces are handed straight to the Label `text`, as well; for example:

```
public void addClickListener(ClickListener listener) {
   this.text.addClickListener(listener);
}
```

You want to register `ChangeListeners` against the whole widget, so the `addChangeListener` (and similarly `removeChangeListener`) is defined as follows:

```
public void addChangeListener(ChangeListener listener) {
   if (changeListeners == null){
      changeListeners = new ChangeListenerCollection();
   }
   changeListeners.add(listener);
}
```

You use of the `ChangeListenerCollection` object here and store `ChangeListeners` that are added into it (in the remove method, you take them away).

The next part generates the code for those aspects you wish to make public in addition to the identified interfaces. For `EditableLabel`, you want to do this for a few attributes, including whether the field is set to be editable, whether it's in editing mode, and whether external parties can cancel the editing state. These are simple portions of code, as shown in listing 7.2.

Listing 7.2 Methods that give external access to `EditableLabel` attributes

```
public boolean isFieldEditable (){ return isEditable; }
public boolean isInEditingMode (){ return isEditing; }
public void setEditable (boolean flag){ isEditable = flag; }
public void cancelLabelChange (){
   text.setText(originalText);
   restoreVisibility();
}
```

The next step in building the code is creating the widget and its layout. The preferred approach to creating a composite widget is to perform the following steps:

1 Create an instance of a `Panel` into which all the composite widgets and other panels that make up the composite widget will be placed.
2 Create instances of component widgets, and add required event-handling code and style names.
3 Put widgets into the defined panels (and those panels into their defined panels, if required).
4 Place all panels and widgets into the panel created in step 1.
5 Implement any programmatic styling, such as hiding of components.
6 Call the inherited `initWidget()` method with the panel created in step 1 as the parameter to initialize the new composite.

These steps are shown in listing 7.3.

Listing 7.3 Creating the `EditableLabel`

```
private void createEditableLabel(String labelText,
                                  ChangeListener onUpdate,
                                  String okButtonText,
                                  String cancelButtonText){
   FlowPanel instance = new FlowPanel();
   text = new Label(labelText);
   text.setStyleName("editableLabel-label");
   text.addClickListener(new ClickListener(){
      public void onClick (Widget sender){
         changeTextLabel();
      }
   });
   changeText = new TextBox();
   changeText.setStyleName("editableLabel-textBox");
   changeText.addKeyboardListener(new KeyboardListenerAdapter(){
      public void onKeyPress (Widget sender,
                              char keyCode, int modifiers){
          switch (keyCode) {
                    case 13:
                        setTextLabel();
                        break;
                    case 27:
                        cancelLabelChange();
                        break;
          }
      }
   });
   changeTextArea = new TextArea();
   changeTextArea.setStyleName("editableLabel-textArea");
   changeTextArea.addKeyboardListener(new KeyboardListenerAdapter(){
      public void onKeyPress (Widget sender,
```

1 Create container
2 Create Label
3 Create TextBox and listener
4 Create TextArea and listener

```
                                    char keyCode, int modifiers){
            switch (keyCode) {
                    case 27:
                        cancelLabelChange();
                        break;
            }
        }
    });
    confirmChange = createConfirmButton(okButtonText);
    if (!(confirmChange instanceof SourcesClickEvents)) {
        throw new RuntimeException("OK Must allow click events");
    }
    ((SourcesClickEvents) confirmChange).addClickListener(
     new ClickListener(){
        public void onClick (Widget sender){
            setTextLabel();
        }
    });

    cancelChange = createCancelButton(cancelButtonText);
    if (!(cancelChange instanceof SourcesClickEvents)) {
        throw new RuntimeException("Cancel must allow click events");
    }

    ((SourcesClickEvents)cancelChange).addClickListener(
     new ClickListener(){
        public void onClick (Widget sender){
            cancelLabelChange();
        }
    });

    FlowPanel buttonPanel = new FlowPanel();
    buttonPanel.setStyleName("editableLabel-buttonPanel");
    buttonPanel.add(confirmChange);
    buttonPanel.add(cancelChange);

    instance.add(text);
    instance.add(changeText);
    instance.add(changeTextArea);
    instance.add(buttonPanel);

    text.setVisible(true);
    changeText.setVisible(false);
    changeTextArea.setVisible(false);
    confirmChange.setVisible(false);
    cancelChange.setVisible(false);

    text.setWordWrap(false);

    initWidget(instance);
}
```

4 Create TextArea and listener

5 Create OK button and listener

6 Create Cancel button and listener

7 Fill button panel

8 Fill container

9 Set visibilities

10 Set default configuration

11 Start widget

You start generating the composite widget ❶ by creating the main panel in which the whole composite widget will sit. You called it `instance`. Next, you build the main visible component of the composite widget—this is the text label that will be displayed on screen. Then, you add a click listener to the `Label` and indicate that if the `Label` is clicked, you should execute the `changeTextlabel()` method ❷.

The `TextBox` called `changeText` is the first editable element you define—if you recall, this will be used if the label is edited and it isn't word-wrapped. Again, you add the style name to it according to the convention.

To the `TextBox` you add a keyboard listener, which listens for two different keypresses ❸. The first is a press of the Return/Enter key (ASCII code 13), in which case you call the `setTextLabel()` method, which changes the old label to the text now displayed in the `TextBox`. This keyboard listener also listens for presses of the Esc key (ASCII code 27); if it finds that, you call the `cancelLabelChange()` method, which restores the label to the text it had before you started to edit it.

Similar to the `TextBox`, at ❹ you set up the `TextArea`, which is used for editing the `Label` if it's word-wrapped. The difference between this code and ❸ is the setting up of the keyboard listener, which in this case only listens for the Esc key being pressed (a Return/Escape keypress in this widget means to start a new line).

Next, you begin to generate the button that is used to confirm that the changes are OK. You call a protected helper method to create the OK button (`createConfirmButton()`), which returns a widget. Doing this allows other users to subclass this class and use widgets that aren't `Buttons` for confirming and canceling edits.

However, this type of flexibility comes at a cost. In the code ❺, you add a click listener to the result of `createConfirmButton()`, and if someone subclasses and uses a widget where click listeners can't be added, you're in trouble. Luckily, you can use some Java magic to determine that the widget returned by `createConfirmButton()` is an instance of `SourcesClickEvents` (that in widget's definition, it says it implements the `SourcesClickEvents` interface). You do this with the following code segment:

```
if (!(confirmChange instanceof SourcesClickEvents))
```

If the widget isn't an instance of `SourcesClickEvents`, then you immediately raise a `RuntimeException` and stop execution of the application. Assuming that you have a valid widget, then you continue to add a click listener that calls the `setTextLabel()` method we discussed in ❸ when the widget is clicked.

You perform the same tasks at ❻ for the Cancel button, except you call the `cancelLabelChange()` method if the button is clicked.

At ❼, you start building the structure of the composite widget. You create a `FlowPanel`, set its style name, and then add to it the two buttons you just created. Then, in ❽, you begin adding objects to the base panel of this composite that you defined in step 1. You're using a flow panel for this, and, in certain circumstances, it would matter which order you started adding things because they flow in order. In this case, you have more freedom, because the next step involves hiding most of the objects and leaving only the label text visible.

You're on the home stretch! At ❾, you start performing the magic that is the `EditableLabel`. You set the visibility of all the objects in the composite to false, except for the `Label` text. Then ❿, you set the default configuration for the widget to be non–word-wrapped (remember, this parameter affects whether the editable version uses the `TextBox` or the `TextArea`).

Finally, you take the mandatory step of calling the `Composite`'s `initWidget()` method ⓫. This is the step we referred to in section 7.1, and as you can see, you create a panel called `instance` into which you place all the objects; this `instance` panel is now used as the parameter to the `initWidget()` method. As we mentioned at that time, failing to call the `initWidget()` method will result in errors at runtime. (Note that in early versions of GWT, this method was called `setWidget()`. Although it's deprecated, you may come across third-party widgets or examples that use that method—it should be replaced with `initWidget()`.)

WARNING Failure to call the `initWidget()` method when creating a composite widget will result in exceptions being raised in your code when you try and create an instance of your composite. The error, in hosted mode, states *java.lang.RuntimeException: Null widget handle. If you are creating a composite, ensure that initWidget() has been called.*

The next segment of code you should implement according to the steps in table 7.1 handles the events. We won't put all the code in this chapter, but we'll look at the methods called when you click the label and when you click the OK button. Clicking the label invokes the label's click listener, which in turn calls the `changeTextLabel()` method shown in listing 7.4.

Listing 7.4 Changing the `Label` to a `TextBox` or a `TextArea`, depending on whether it's word-wrapped

```
private void changeTextLabel (){
   if (isEditable) {
      originalText = text.getText();
      text.setVisible(false);
      confirmChange.setVisible(true);
      cancelChange.setVisible(true);
```

❶ EditableLabel editable?
❷ Save label text
❸ Change visibilities

```
    if (text.getWordWrap()){                        ❹ EditableLabel word-wrapped?
       changeTextArea.setText(originalText);
       changeTextArea.setVisible(true);             ❺ Show TextArea
       changeTextArea.setFocus(true);
    } else {
       changeText.setText(originalText);
       changeText.setVisible(true);                 ❻ Show TextBox
       changeText.setFocus(true);
    }
    isEditing = true;                               ❼ Set state of EditableLabel to editing
  }
}
```

The first check you need to make ensures that the widget is editable ❶; if it isn't, then there is no point continuing with this method. If it's editable, then you save a copy of the current label text for use in restoring the label if the cancel functionality is invoked ❷. Then, you need to hide the original label from view and display the OK and Cancel buttons ❸.

Next, you check to see whether the label is word-wrapped ❹. If it's word-wrapped, then you make the text area visible and set its contents to be the same as the label text ❺. If the label isn't word-wrapped then you make the text box visible and set its contents to the label text ❻. Finally you set a flag to indicate the widget is now in an editing state ❼.

Once the user has edited the label, they can click the OK button, which invokes the `setTextLabel()` method shown in listing 7.5.

Listing 7.5 Clicking OK invokes the `setTextLabel()` method to restore the label view with the new text

```
private void setTextLabel ()
{
   if(text.getWordWrap()){
      text.setText(changeTextArea.getText());       ❶ Set new value of text
   } else {
      text.setText(changeText.getText());
   }
   restoreVisibility();                             ❷ Hide editing components; show text
   if(changeListeners != null) changeListeners.fireChange(this);   ❸ Fire registered change listeners
}
```

First, you check to see whether the Label is word-wrapped ❶. If it is, then you need to take the new text for the label from the text area; otherwise, you retrieve it from the text box. After setting the new text, you restore the visibility of the label and hide the text box/text area and the buttons so that everything is back to normal ❷. Finally, you check to see whether anyone has registered a change listener against you. Remember that at the start of the discussion, we showed that using the addChangeListener() method adds the listener to the ChangeListenerCollection you called changeListeners. Now, you call the fireChange() method on that collection, which ensures that all change listeners registered receive the onChange event ❸.

The EditableLabel can now be used like any standard widget in GWT; for example, the creation of an arbitrary PhotoDisplay widget as in figure 7.3 would include code similar to this:

```
EditableLabel title = new EditableLabel ("");
title.addChangeListener(new ChangeListener(){
   public onChange(Widget sender){
      saveTitleChange(title.getText());
   }
});
EditableLabel description = new EditableLabel ("");
description.setWordWrap(true);
title.addChangeListener(new ChangeListener(){
   public onChange(Widget sender){
      saveDescrChange(title.getText());
   }
});
PhotoImagePanel photo = new PhotoImage();
VerticalPanel photoPanel = new VerticalPanel();
photoPanel.add(title);
photoPanel.add(photo);
photoPanel.add(description);
```

Add change listener to EditableLabel"

You also add a ChangeListener to each EditableLabel such that when a user finishes editing a label, this code is informed, and an appropriate piece of functionality can be called. In this case, the new text of the edited label is retrieved and then could be saved to a database. Table 7.3 reviews where in the code you can find the defined functionality for the EditableLabel, and which event listeners are used to drive this functionality.

We've finished our look at creating the functional aspects of the composite widget from the panel layout to identifying the necessary components and building the functional code (see figure 7.11). Next, we'll examine how styling should be applied.

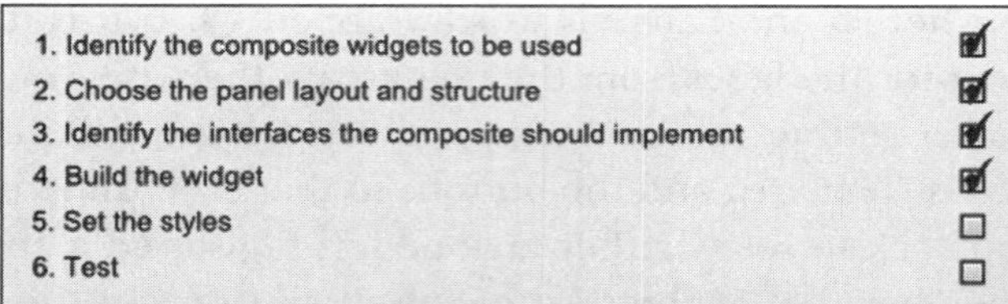
1. Identify the composite widgets to be used
2. Choose the panel layout and structure
3. Identify the interfaces the composite should implement
4. Build the widget
5. Set the styles
6. Test

Figure 7.11 Checking off step 4 of the Composite widget development process

Table 7.3 `EditableLabel` functionality with reference to how it's implemented in the composite widget code

Step	Action	How implemented in the code
Add the widget to the panel	Only the user-defined text associated with the widget (if any is provided to the constructor) is shown.	Defined in the constructor: `new EditableLabel ("Initial Text");`
Click the label	An editable area is shown, containing the user-defined text. If the initial text is set to be word-wrapped, then the editable area presented is scrollable; otherwise, a single-line editable area is used. Cancel and OK buttons are displayed.	A click listener is added to the label that executes the `changeTextLabel()` method.
Click the OK button	The editable area is replaced with an element of non-editable text, the value of which is set to the value last shown in the editable area. After the alteration in the user interface, a user-provided follow-up action occurs. This action may, for example, save the new value of text displayed to a database.	A click listener is added to the widget that represents the OK button and executes the `setTextLabel()` method.
Click the Cancel button	The editable area is replaced with an element of non-editable text, the value of which is set to exactly the same value it had prior to the last attempt to edit.	A click listener is added to the widget that represents the Cancel button and executes the `cancelLabelChange()` method.
Press the Esc key	If the Esc key is pressed while focus is on the widget, the functionality invoked is the same as clicking the Cancel button.	Keyboard listeners are added to the `TextBox` and `TextArea` widgets. If the Esc key is pressed in either the `TextBox` or `TextArea` widget, the `cancelLabelChange()` method is called. If the Return/Enter key is pressed in the `TextBox` widget, the `setTextLabel()` method is called.
Press the Return/Enter key	If the Return/Enter key is pressed while focus is on the widget, then one of two functionalities is invoked. If the `EditableLabel` is identified as being word-wrapped, then a new-line is inserted in the area where the editable text is shown. If the `EditableLabel` isn't set as word-wrapped, then pressing Return/Enter invokes the same functionality as clicking OK.	

7.3.5 *Step 5: Styling the composite widget*

Earlier in this book, we covered how styling can be applied both programmatically and through style sheets. We stated that our preference is for CSS styling wherever possible to allow the greatest flexibility, and in this final step you'll set up the CSS references for your objects.

The penultimate development stage we propose for building composite widgets is to blend in style names. We'll leave this to the later stages, because now the widget should be fairly stable and it will be easy to identify where styles are needed. In the `EditableLabel`, styling could be applied at the following places:

- The background panel for the widget, called `instance`
- The button panel
- The cancel-change button
- The confirm-change button
- The `Label`
- The `TextBox`
- The `TextArea`

We recommend, if you don't have one already, that you develop a standard way of naming styles in your widgets so you can minimize cross-widget incompatibilities. The convention suggested by Google is to use `projectname-component`. Following that convention, you end up with these style names:

- `editableLabel-buttonPanel`
- `editableLabel-buttons`
- `editableLabel-confirm`
- `editableLabel-cancel`
- `editableLabel-label`
- `editableLabel-textBox`
- `editableLabel-textArea`

In the `EditableLabel` code, you set these styles using the `setStyleName()` method for each component when it's created. You can then make appropriate entries in the CSS style sheet; for example:

```
.editableLabel-buttons {
   color: #fff;
   text-transform: uppercase;
}

.editableLabel-confirm {
   background: #0c0;
}

.editableLabel-cancel {
   background: #c00;
}
```

This style sheet would produce buttons whose labels are white and in uppercase, with the confirm button having a green background and the cancel button a red background. Some time ago, when you defined the panel layout, we suggested that using a `FlowPanel` gives maximum flexibility when using CSS to reposition the buttons. If you write the following in the CSS file

```
.editableLabel-textBox {
   display: block;
}
.editableLabel-textArea {
   display: block;
}
```

this tells the browser to put whatever flows after the `TextBox` and `TextArea` on the next line—thus you can move the buttons below the editable area, as shown in figure 7.12.

Up in the Artic Circle in
Tromso Norway ready to
enter the world's most
northern brewery.
OK
CANCEL

Figure 7.12 Buttons moved underneath the text area purely by defining this in the associated CSS

In this example, the underlying label must be word-wrapped, because the editable view is a `TextArea`.

With the styling completed (see figure 7.13), the final step is the testing of the widget; we'll cover testing in much more detail in chapter 16. As far as you're concerned, you've created your first composite widget, which is a long way from the simple example you fired up way back in chapter 1.

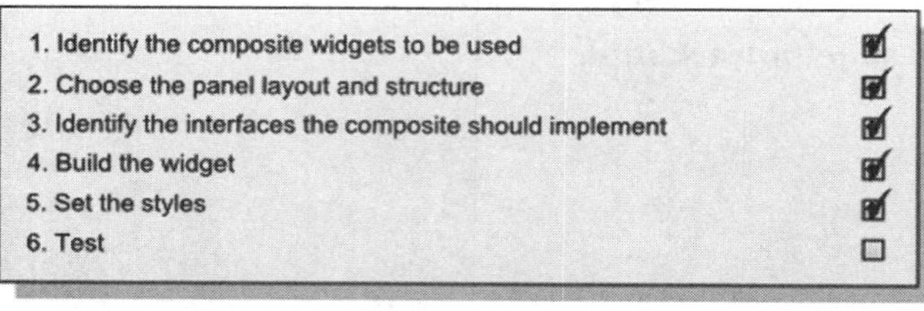
1. Identify the composite widgets to be used
2. Choose the panel layout and structure
3. Identify the interfaces the composite should implement
4. Build the widget
5. Set the styles
6. Test

Figure 7.13 Checking off step 5 of the Composite widget development process

In the next section, you'll build another Composite, but this time you'll build it from other Composites. Then, in section 7.5, you'll build the Composite class that will benefit the components you'll build for the Dashboard in the following chapters.

7.4 Creating a composite widget from other composite widgets

Let's get a little more complicated and show that you can treat composite widgets just like normal widgets. This means you can build even more complicated widgets by plugging together other composite widgets as new composite widgets.

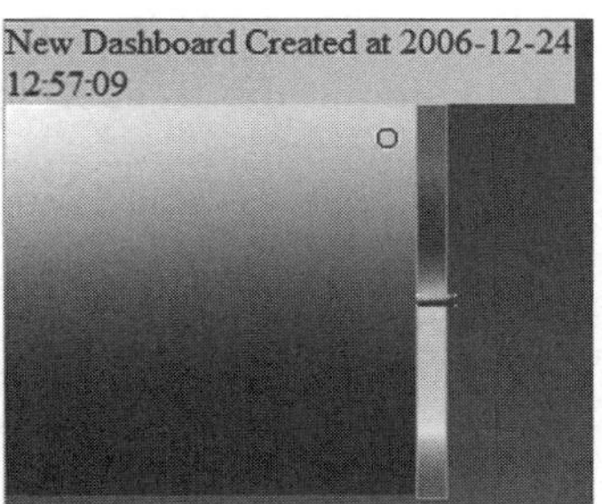

Figure 7.14 Dashboard Colour Picker application composed of other composite widgets

In this section, we'll look at the Dashboard's Colour Picker application, which is shown in figure 7.14; it can be accessed through the Create menu, allowing the user to change the color of the Dashboard name's background. The code for the sliders is included in the electronic downloads; rather than give a large code example in this section, we'll discuss some of the key aspects of the composite widget to give you an idea of how quickly you can put together fully functional components using composites.

This Colour Picker composite widget is made up from two other composite widgets—two different forms of the slider—and some other normal widgets put together in a few different panels. We show this breakdown in figure 7.15, which indicates that the whole composite is constructed in a HorizontalPanel. This

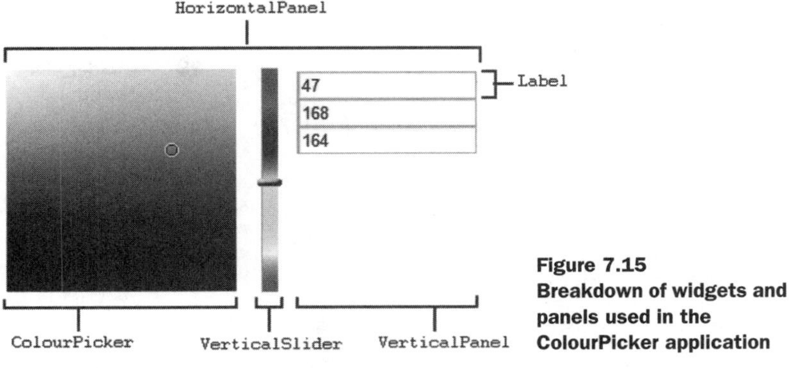

Figure 7.15 Breakdown of widgets and panels used in the ColourPicker application

horizontal panel has, from left to right, a `ColourPicker` (this component is taken from a live system one of the authors built and so retains its English spelling of the word *Colour*), `VerticalSlider`, and a `VerticalPanel` inserted into it.

The `VerticalPanel` is filled with a number of `Label` widgets that represent the RGB values of the selected color.

The `ColourPicker` and `VerticalSlider` are themselves composite widgets and are created from two `Image` widgets (`ColourPicker` is an instance of `GridSlider`). We'll first look at how these sliders are created—which begins with looking at the basic `Slider` class.

7.4.1 *Creating a slider*

The `Slider` class takes an image as a background. Another image is placed on a `PopupPanel`.

You could use the background image and thumbnail shown in figure 7.16 to create the slider shown in figure 7.17.

You take the drag functionality you saw in chapter 6 and amend it slightly to constrain dragging in the x or y plane, if needed, and to make sure that you can't drag the thumbnail off the ends of the background image. This updated `onMouseDrag()` method is shown in listing 7.6.

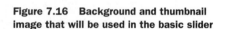

Figure 7.16 Background and thumbnail image that will be used in the basic slider

Figure 7.17 First view of a basic slider

Listing 7.6 Mouse dragging functionality for the `Slider` class

```
public void onMouseMove(Widget sender, int x, int y) {
   if (dragging) {
      absX = 0; absY = 0;
      absX = x + getAbsoluteLeft() - dragStartX;
      if (horizontalControl){
         if (absX<startX){ absX = startX; }
         if (absX>endX){ absX = endX; }
      } else {
         absX = startX;
      }
      if (verticalControl){
         absY = y + getAbsoluteTop() - dragStartY;
```

❶ Can slider slide horizontally?
❷ Make slide stay in bounds
❸ Fix horizontal position
❹ Can slider slide vertically?

```
            if (absY<startY){ absY = startY; }
            if (absY>endY){ absY = endY; }
         } else {
            absY = startY;
         }
         theSliderThumbnail.setPopupPosition(absX, absY);    ❺ Set new position of thumbnail
      }
   }
```

In the onMouseMove() method, you first check to see if this slider is a horizontal slider ❶. If it is, then ❷ you make sure that the x-index never goes outside of the left and right of the control. If the control isn't horizontal, then you make sure the x-index never changes ❸. Similar code for the y-index starts at ❹.

Once you've recalculated the new position within the constraints, you move the thumbnail pop-up ❺.

The rest of the Slider class is responsible for trying to set up the mathematics for dealing with translating screen positions to slider values (and vice versa) as well as handling one of the problems with using the pop-up panel for this functionality: If you resize the browser window, the background image moves as it flows in the new spacing of the browser page—but unfortunately, the thumbnail doesn't.

Luckily, you can get GWT to tell the code whenever the browser window is resized, by using a WindowResizeListener. This is similar to all the EventListeners we discussed in chapter 6 and lets you fire code when the particular event occurs; see listing 7.7.

Listing 7.7 The WindowResizeListener used in the Slider composite widget

```
Window.addWindowResizeListener(new WindowResizeListener(){
   public void onWindowResized(int width, int height) {      ❶ Hide thumbnail
      theSliderThumbnail.setVisible(false);
      DeferredCommand.addCommand(new Command(){       ❷ Create DeferredCommand
         public void execute(){
            redimensionalise();       ❸ Calculate new dimensions
         }
      });
   }
});
```

Now, when the browser window gets resized, the listener's methods are fired. This means you hide the thumbnail ❶ and then call the method that moves the thumbnail to the needed position ❸. You put this functionality inside a

DeferredCommand ❷ so that it gets called once the browser has completed doing all of its tasks (in this exact case, once the browser has completely resized). If we were to try and call redimensionalise() directly then there is a risk that the browser has not stabilized yet so repositioning may fail.

The final point we want to discuss in relation to the code is how you manage events. When the user drags the slider, it updates certain values, including the x and y values of the slider index. As those values are updated, you fire an onChange event to any ChangeListeners that are registered with the widget. To accomplish that, you implement the techniques shown in chapter 6. You start by making the widget implement the SourcesChangeEvents interface, which allows you to register ChangeListeners into the ChangeListenerCollection's changeListener variable. Then, whenever a change is made to the slider's x and y values, you call the changeListener.fireChange() method. You create sliders using constructors, and register ChangeListeners in the normal way:

```
Slider slider = new Slider()
Slider.addChangeListener(new ChangeListener(){
   Public void onChange(Widget sender){
      Window.alert("Slider has changed");
   }
});
```

With the basics of the slider in place, you generate three subclasses that constrain the thumbnail in its directions of movement, as shown in table 7.4.

Table 7.4 How constraints are applied to the x and y plane to create subclasses of the slider

Name	Constrain x?	Constrain y?
HorizontalSlider	N	Y
VerticalSlider	Y	N
GridSlider	N	N

The VerticalSlider used in the ColourPicker widget is created from a stripy colored background representing all the hues that could be selected and an image appropriate for the thumbnail.

The ColourPicker widget is a special form of the GridSlider. A GridSlider allows the thumbnail to move in the x and y planes, and the ColourPicker widget uses this to present the user with the swatch of colors.

7.4.2 Constructing the ColourPicker composite

To create the `ColourPicker` composite that the user uses to select the color, you use a `GridSlider` with a twist. First, you create a `GridSlider` whose background is set to the graduated transparent PNG image shown in figure 7.18. In the book, it looks black and white due to the white background color of the page; in the application, you'll apply different background colors to it, and it will show all of the available hues due to its transparency.

Figure 7.18 Background image used in the ColourPicker widget

The clever part comes when you start playing with the slider thumbnails. As you move the slider on the `VerticalPanel`, you select a different hue for the color. As this hue changes, you fire a change listener that sets the background color of the `ColourPicker` widget using the following code:

```
private void setSwatchBackground(double newHue){
   theModel.setHSV(swatch, newHue,theModel.S, theModel.V);
   String backgroundColour = "#"+theModel.RGBSwatchHexString;
   DOM.setStyleAttribute(swatchImg.getElement(),
                         "background",
                         backgroundColour);
}
```

To determine the exact color selected by the user, you take the hue value from the vertical slider; the saturation and brightness are given by the x and y positions of the thumbnail on the `GridSlider` that sits behind the `ColourPicker` widget. Values that are displayed in the text boxes are also calculated from these three values.

Putting the whole composite widget together is a simple case of creating new instances of each composite and widgets and then placing them in a `HorizontalPanel`.

You can see that composite widgets are powerful although easy to use if you plan and set them out in advance. For the Dashboard project, you'll be using composites to develop the component applications; however, you want to also provide consistent functionality across all component applications, so you'll extend the standard composite class to ensure this. Dashboard component applications will then extend this new `DashboardComposite` class.

7.5 Creating the Dashboard composite

The components created as Dashboard applications (those components that are dragged around such as a Calculator, a server monitor, and so on) will be created using composites. They also need a way of registering option menu components into the Dashboard and of setting their names (because that will be displayed in the header of the `DashboardPanel` you created in chapter 5).

You can again harness the power of writing the applications in Java by extending the standard `Composite` class to provide functions and fields that help the components sit in the Dashboard happily. Listing 7.8 shows such a class, called the `DashboardComposite`.

Listing 7.8 `DashboardComposite`: Framework code for Dashboard components

```
public class DashboardComposite
       extends Composite
       implements FocusListener{

   private String name = "Default Name";
   private MenuBar parentMenu;
   protected MenuBar optionsMenuBar = new MenuBar(true);
   private MenuItem optionsMenu ;

   public DashboardComposite(MenuBar parentMenu){
      this.parentMenu = parentMenu;
    }

   protected MenuBar getOptionsMenuBar(){ return optionsMenuBar; }
   public void setName(String newName){ this.name = newName; }
   public String getName(){return name; }

   public void onFocus(Widget sender){ addMenu(); }
   public void addMenu(){
      if (parentMenu!=null){
         optionsMenu = new MenuItem(name, optionsMenuBar);
         parentMenu.addItem(optionsMenu);
      }
   }

   public void onLostFocus(Widget sender){ removeMenu();}
   public void removeMenu(){
      if (parentMenu!=null){
         parentMenu.removeItem(optionsMenu);
      }
   }
}
```

1. Extend Composite class
2. FocusListener interface
3. Provide default name
4. Identify parent menu bar
5. Create option menu
6. Functionality when composite gains focus
7. Functionality when composite loses focus

You extend the normal Composite class ❶ as well as implementing the FocusListener interface ❷. This new interface requires you to provide onFocus() and onLostFocus() methods. These methods are called when the Composite is given and loses focus on the screen (usually by the user clicking them).

You give the DashboardComposite a default name ❸. This field is picked up by the DashboardPanel you created in chapter 5 and displayed at the top of that panel. A link is also provided back to the parent's menu bar ❹.

Next ❺, you create the basis for the Dashboard component's option menu. Each Dashboard component has the ability to create an option menu, which is embedded into the Dashboard when that component gains focus and removed when it loses focus. When focus is gained, the onFocus() method, required because you implement the FocusListener interface, is invoked ❻. It calls the addMenu() method to add the option menu to the Dashboard.

The converse of the onFocus() method is the onLostFocus() method ❼, which is called when the composite loses focus. It in turn calls the removeMenu() method to remove the options menu from the Dashboard.

With all this code in place you're almost ready to start developing the functional components of the Dashboard. These components are created by extending this DashboardComposite class and will adhere to the following template:

```
public myDashboardComponent(MenuBar menu){

    super(menu);
    setName("MyName");
    MenuBar optionsMenu = getOptionsMenuBar();
    optionsMenu.addItem(…);
    MyWidget theWidget = new MyWidget();
    initWidget(theWidget);
}
```

We have one last trick with the DashboardComposite class where you automatically create a new option menu that extends the one provided by the writer of the DashboardComposite to provide About and This Application Demonstrates menu items, but we'll cover those in chapter 14 when we discuss generators. You can see all this in action in the code by downloading it from www.manning.com/hanson. The download includes the JSNI code for the examples you'll see in the next chapters.

7.6 Summary

The last four chapters have provided quite a tour through the key aspects of GWT—believe us, it took a long time to write, and we can imagine that for you as a reader it has been a journey. We hope that, by tying everything back to the Dashboard, you're still with us! In your hands you should have code for the following:

- `PNGImage`
- `ToggleMenuItem`
- `DashboardPanel`
- `EditableLabel`
- Range of sliders
- `ColourPicker`
- `DashboardComposite`

All of these will be used in the Dashboard as we go forward.

In this chapter, you saw how composite widgets can be created and that the development of them should be treated in a similar manner to how you develop a GWT application (although without the overheads of the application-creation process). A composite is created as a single class extending the `Composite` object.

These four chapters have also been the closest that this book will come to being a reference to the components in GWT. We discussed all the standard widgets, panels, and event-handling objects and indicated where in this book you'll be using them in action. With that in mind, it's time to introduce the final user interface aspect of GWT by looking at how you can interact directly with JavaScript when you need to.

8 Building JSNI components

This chapter covers

- Overview of JSNI
- Passing Java objects to JavaScript
- Calling Java code from JavaScript
- Loading external JavaScript libraries
- Wrapping JavaScript code as Java classes

GWT's key benefit is the ability to abstract away from JavaScript, which frees the developer (you!) from concerns over browser differences and developing in an untyped programming language. But just as normal application code occasionally uses assembly-language segments for special needs, so client-side GWT applications can interact directly with JavaScript. In a normal application, you may use assembly code to get speed advantage or access hardware in the only way it can; for GWT applications, in our experience, there are four possible situations when it may be sensible to use JSNI (you may think of more):

- To enable communication between a main application and component applications using a JavaScript variable (although only when they can't be in the same variable scope)
- To access browser functionality that hasn't been included directly with GWT
- To expose an API of your GWT application to other applications on your web page that can execute JavaScript (useful if you're replacing legacy applications in an existing site)
- To access useful JavaScript libraries that you don't have either the patience or the ability to translate into GWT (you may, for example, be restricted by a license associated with the library)

For the Dashboard application, you'll enable communication between the main application and the component applications by using a JavaScript variable, which can be set by the menu system and read by the component applications when they're being deleted. The original version of the slider we discussed in chapter 7 used the JavaScript Native Interface (JSNI) to find the scroll position of the browser window to ensure that the thumbnail was moved to the correct location, regardless of how far the window had been scrolled; this functionality wasn't available directly in GWT until version 1.4.

In this chapter, we'll look at the general syntax of JSNI and how you can use JSNI to communicate to the browser and other GWT applications. We'll round off the chapter by showing you how to load and access third-party JavaScript libraries, in particular some JavaScript search libraries from Google, which allow you to produce Dashboard applications such as those shown in figure 8.1.

There is a strong caveat with all this talk about JSNI: Ask yourself if you really need to use JSNI. A lot of the time, the capability you're after may exist in the standard GWT. One key thing to remember about JSNI is that it can only be included

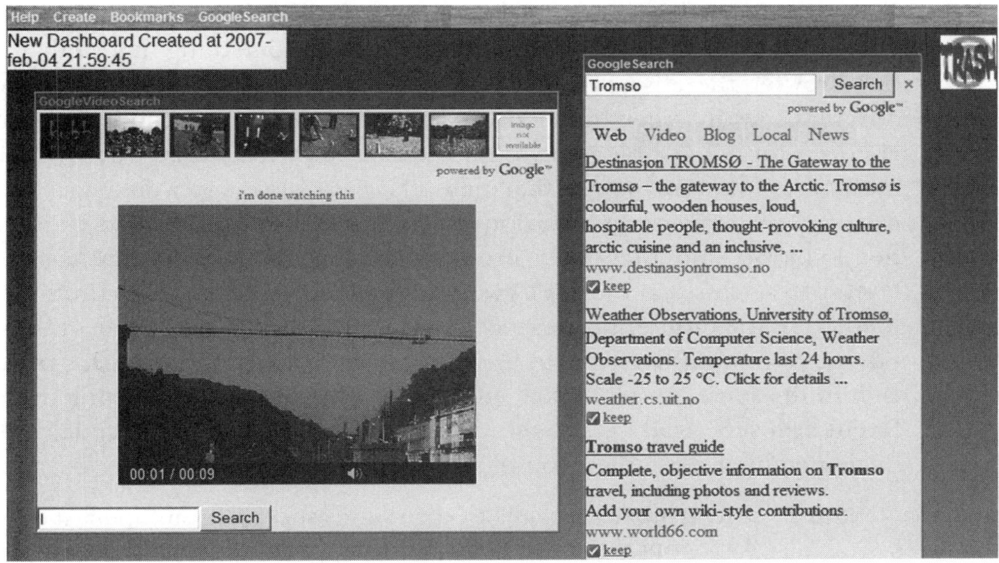

Figure 8.1 The Dashboard showing the Google Video Search application on the left and the Google Ajax Search application on the right. Both applications are JavaScript libraries wrapped as GWT widgets using JSNI.

in client-side code—so no JSNI can appear in code destined for, or on, the server. This makes sense if you step back and remember that JSNI is JavaScript code, which needs to execute in a web browser!

Before you're in the position of being able to build the two widgets for this chapter, we need to introduce and explore some of the attributes of JSNI—the basic syntax and operation.

8.1 Introducing JavaScript Native Interface (JSNI)

JSNI is GWT's mechanism to allow you as a programmer to embed JavaScript in the Java code. We can't overemphasize the point that JSNI is almost a last-resort approach. Many issues that look like they need JSNI can be solved at the GWT Java level if you spend time looking. It's possible to view the relationship between GWT Java and JSNI as you do the relationship between a high-level programming language and assembly code: Yes, you can do it, but it's sensible only if there is a clear need to do so.

It's possible to carry this analogy further, because JSNI, just like assembly language, is less portable across systems. If you write something in JSNI that works in one browser, there is a risk that it may not work at all, or perhaps may work in a different way, in other browsers. As an example, you can count the number of children for a DOM element using the simple Java GWT `DOM.countChildren()` method. If you were to write that method in JavaScript, you would have to, as GWT does for you, write several versions to cope with DOM differences between Internet Explorer and the other browsers (check out the `DOMImplStandard` and `DOMImplIE6` classes in the GWT gwt-user.jar file to see the GWT definitions for this method in the different browsers). In JSNI, you can write only one of these methods, or you would have to add the own browser detection JavaScript as well. This isn't in the spirit of GWT, which advocates writing once and running in many different browsers. There is also the risk that writing your own JSNI code could introduce memory leaks, unless you're an expert at those matters.

NOTE JSNI is applicable only to client-side aspects of your application, because JavaScript doesn't run on the server side. It's therefore not possible to use JSNI code in any server-side code or to pass an object over remote procedure calling (RPC) to the server and expect to be able to execute any included JSNI code server-side.

However, let's be a little more positive about JSNI. In the cases where you do have to use it, it can be powerful. JSNI lets you interface between Java and JavaScript in a type-safe way; you can use JavaScript objects in the Java code and rely on Java's strong typing to protect you against various programming errors. But again, the more functionality you include in a single JSNI block, the less you can rely on Java's strong typing to minimize errors.

JSNI also provides a seamless way of moving between Java and JavaScript, allowing you to pass objects and exceptions across the boundary in both directions. Through JSNI, you manage JavaScript objects from Java, and you can call back to the Java code from the JavaScript code you write. As we mentioned in the chapter introduction, one use is to wrap a third-party JavaScript library, where you create JavaScript objects from the library and pass them around the GWT Java code before perhaps sending them back to the JavaScript library.

One word of warning about JSNI: It's potentially a moving target during the early stages of GWT adoption. The existing model works well in most cases, as you'll see later in this chapter, but already several requests for reviews have been published about changing functionality of certain aspects. A guiding principle of

JSNI coding is to spend as little time as possible in "the dark side"; each JSNI method should be at an atomic level (perform one clear function) so that you isolate issues and keep as much control as possible in the strongly-types Java realm.

Let's move on and assume that you're in a situation where JSNI is the approach you need. The first thing you need to understand is how to use the syntax.

8.1.1 Understanding JSNI

If you're familiar with writing native methods in Java for other languages, then JSNI will seem relatively familiar. If you've never written native methods before, don't worry; their syntax is a little strange but not frightening. Java Native Interface (JNI) is the Java approach that allows Java code to interface with components written in other languages, for example C or C++ or assembly. JSNI is the GWT Java equivalent for interfacing with JavaScript components, and it follows a syntax similar to that of JNI.

In the next few sections, we'll look at the syntax used to cross the boundary both ways between Java and JavaScript and how the objects you pass over that boundary are treated. Here's a simple JSNI method call:

```
public static native void method_name(ObjectTyp someData)
/*-{
   someData.@org.gwtbook.client.Data::data1 == "GWT In Action"
}-*/;
```

We hope that doesn't look too scary, even with the `@` and `::` symbols sprinkled in. To start to understand why these are there, we'll first look at how you call JavaScript functionality from a GWT Java program.

Crossing the boundary from Java to JavaScript

To include JavaScript code in a GWT application, you must write it in a specific way so that both the syntax checkers of Java and the GWT Java compiler can recognize it and deal with it appropriately. For syntax checkers, that means ignoring the code because it isn't Java; and for the GWT compiler, it means merging it in a structured way into the JavaScript output of compilation.

A basic JSNI method is defined as shown here:

```
public static native void method_name()     <-- (1) Define JSNI method
/*-{      Start/end
}-*/;     (2) method definition
```

In the template, you define the method in a normal Java way, but you must include the keyword `native` as one of the modifiers ❶; this identifies the code to the Java compiler as JNI code and to the GWT compiler as JSNI code. To help any syntax checkers know that they should avoid parsing the JavaScript code, you wrap it as a comment by using a modified standard comment, which starts with the characters `/*-` (a forward slash, an asterisk, and a dash) and ends with `-*/` (a dash, an asterisk, and a forward slash) ❷. It's also important not to forget the trailing semicolon at the end of the definition; otherwise your code won't compile!

Crossing the boundary from Java to JavaScript can come in two forms: writing JavaScript code in the Java application that performs some dedicated functionality, or writing JavaScript in the Java application that calls functionality in a JavaScript library already loaded into the web browser. Both methods follow the same syntax of extending the previous template to provide parameters, a return type if necessary (otherwise the return type must be defined as `void`), and the native code. You can consider this crossing of the boundary diagrammatically as shown in figure 8.2.

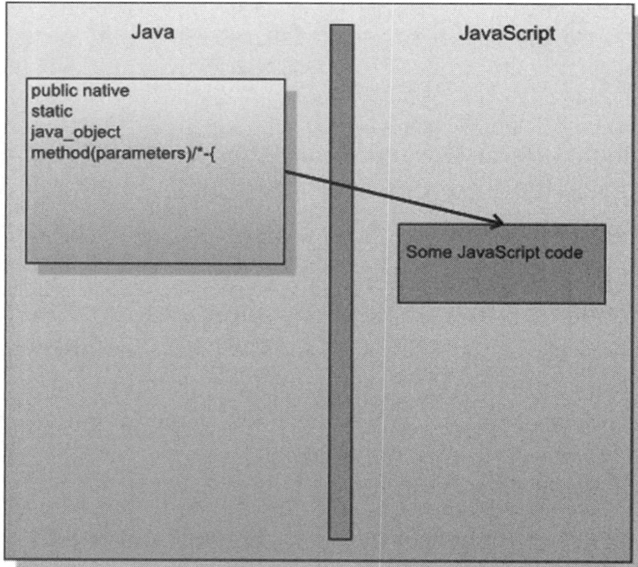

Figure 8.2 The interaction between Java and JavaScript code when crossing the Java-to-JavaScript boundary in a JSNI call from a GWT application

Here is some typical code required to cross the boundary from Java to JavaScript:

```
public static native
       return_java_type                 <-- Define function return Java type
       method(java_type parameter, …, java_type parameter)   <-- Parameter Java types
/*-{
         JavaScript code goes here and          JavaScript
         can use the passed in Java parameters  code
         return return_java_object;        <-- Return result
}-*/;
```

Overall, the definition is the same as a normal Java method; you provide a list of parameters that can be passed in and a possible return object type. If you provide a return type, rather than just a `void`, then the JavaScript must return an object of the correct type. (Be aware that JSNI code can't create new Java objects; it can manipulate ones passed in or create new JavaScript objects, but not new Java objects.)

REMEMBER It isn't possible to create new Java objects in a JSNI code block. Return types must either be primitive types, manipulated Java objects that have been passed in as input parameters, or references to newly created JavaScript objects (a `JavaScriptObject` type).

It's important to understand how the objects you provide as parameters are handled across the Java-to-JavaScript boundary, as you'll see in the next section.

Passing Java objects across the Java-to-JavaScript boundary

We have mentioned before that one of the benefits of using Java to develop the Ajax/rich Internet applications is the strong typing provided by the Java language, which isn't present in JavaScript. This missing typing model could cause problems as you start crossing the boundary from Java to JavaScript.

Unfortunately, there isn't much you can do about the typing capabilities of JavaScript. Once the objects have passed into the realm of JavaScript, they're sadly on their own. This brings us back to the point we mentioned earlier—the shorter amount of time you can spend in this potentially lawless world of JavaScript, the better. If you have to spend a long time there, it's preferable that you do so only to interact with stable third-party JavaScript libraries. What you can do, though, is ensure that a clearly defined and repeatable mapping exists between Java typed objects and JavaScript untyped objects, which is what GWT provides.

Primitive Java numeric types, such as `byte`, `short`, `char`, `int`, `long`, `float`, or `double`, become simple objects in JavaScript whose value is that of the original object. For example, if you have a Java `char`, `char keyPress = 'a'`, then it will become the JavaScript variable `var k = 'a'`. Similarly, the Java `int`, `int val = 10`, becomes the JavaScript variable `var v = 10`.

A Java `String` is translated across into JavaScript as a simple variable to which the original text is assigned. Therefore the Java object `String name = "GWT In Action"` becomes the JavaScript variable `var s = "GWT In Action"`. Finally the simple Java `boolean`, becomes another simple JavaScript variable; the Java `boolean b = true` becomes the JavaScript variable `var b = true`.

Moving on to more complicated Java objects that can be passed across the boundary, you have the Java array, a Java object, and a new object to GWT called the `JavaScriptObject`. We'll discuss the last object more in the next section; for now, you should think of it as just a reference to a JavaScript object created somewhere else that can be passed around the Java code and on to other JavaScript methods—but you can't look into its contents from the GWT Java code. This may sound strange, but we'll explain in more detail later in the section on this object.

Passing an array across the Java-to-JavaScript boundary is treated in a similar opaque way; you know you have an `array` object, but you can't look into its contents. This means that if the JavaScript code needs to use values in the array, then you should move them out of the array before you cross the boundary: either into separate parameters or into another type of user-defined Java object. You can manage Java objects in JavaScript through the JSNI interface, as we'll discuss next.

You can also pass your own defined Java objects across the Java-to-JavaScript boundary; GWT provides a special syntax allowing you to access the fields and methods of that Java object. This will take a little bit of explaining, so please, stick with us.

Let's say you have an object of type `Data`, which is defined by the class shown in listing 8.1 to contain a simple string and an integer.

Listing 8.1 Example class that will be accessed through the Java-to-JavaScript boundary

```
package org.gwtbook.client;
public class Data{
   String data1 = "GWT In Action";
   int version = 1;
}
```

You use an instance of this type in a new class defined in listing 8.2, called `DataManip`.

Listing 8.2 Example class demonstrating accessing Java objects through the Java-to-JavaScript boundary

```
public class DataManip{
   boolean correct = false;                              ❶ Define local variable

   static boolean checked = false;                       ❷ Define static variable

   public native void doSomething(Data someData)/*-{     ❸ Define JSNI method
      if(!this.@org.gwtbook.client.DataManip::correct){  ❹ Access instance's local variable

         if(!@org.gwtbook.client.DataManip::checked){    ❺ Access static variable

            if(someData.@org.gwtbook.client.Data::data1 ==
                  "GWT In Action"
               &&
               someData.@org.gwtbook.client.Data::version == 1){   ❻ Access variable in parameter object
                  //Do something else.
            }
         }
      }
   }-*/;
}
```

In the DataManip class, you have a couple of additional class variables: one called correct ❶ and then other a static variable called checked ❷ (it doesn't matter what they stand for in this example). You also define a JSNI method ❸ called doSomething(), which takes as a parameter an instance of the Data class but returns nothing (we'll cover going across the JavaScript-to-Java boundary in a short while). When doSomething() is called, you want it to look at the DataManip class' correct value ❹; if that is false, then you want to check the static field checked ❺. If that too is false, then you confirm whether the Data instance passed in as a parameter has its data1 field set to "GWT In Action" and the version value set to 1 ❻; if they are, then you do something else in the code.

To perform this functionality, you need to access an instance field, a static field, and a field in a Java object passed in as a parameter, in that order. In each case, you need to use the JSNI-specific syntax for accessing Java objects, the template for which is shown in figure 8.3.

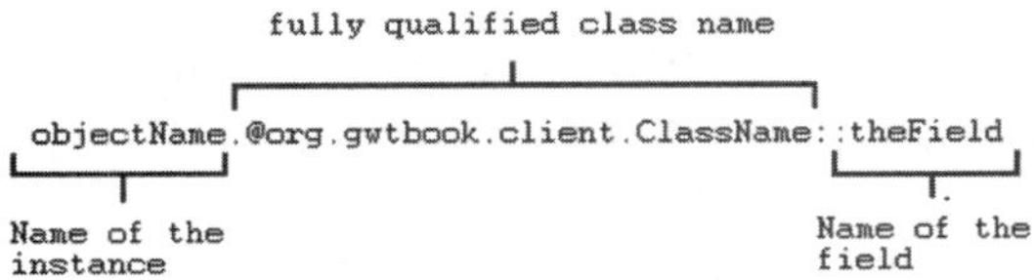

Figure 8.3 Explanation of the JSNI method to access a field in a Java object. The first part comprises the name of the instance (an object name, the keyword this, or blank for a static field). Next are the fully qualified class name and the field name.

When you access the instance field ❹, the name of the instance is `this`, the class name of this instance is `org.gwtbook.client.DataManip`, and the field you're after is called `correct`. Accessing this field is, therefore, performed by writing the following in the JSNI code:

```
this.@org.gwtbook.client.DataManip::correct
```

Accessing the static field ❺ requires you to access a field where there is no defined `objectName` (because the field is static across all instances). In JSNI, you write

```
@org.gwtbook.client.DataManip::checked
```

(Notice that the period is missing and only the `@` symbol is still required if there is no object name to reference.)

Finally, when you want to reference the `data1` field in the parameter that you've passed in, then the parameter name, `someData`, is the `objectName`, and you write

```
someData.@org.gwtbook.client.Data::data1
```

You can also access the methods from the Java object passed across the boundary in a similar way. We'll discuss how that works once you've seen how you return objects back across the boundary to the Java code.

Sending objects back across the JavaScript to Java boundary

When you've completed the functionality you need in JSNI, it's common to pass an object back in return. As with all Java methods, you need to define the return type of the JSNI method, which will either be a Java primitive, a Java object, a GWT `JavaScriptObject`, or void. Diagrammatically, you're performing the action shown in figure 8.4; once complete, program control is back in the hands of the GWT Java code.

Just as there was a defined mapping between Java and JavaScript objects for the parameters, such a mapping exists when going from JavaScript to Java for the return values.

To get a Java primitive numeric coming out of the method call, the value returned from the JavaScript must be a numeric value. You need to be careful with returning primitive numerics because GWT doesn't determine whether the type is correct. If you define the Java method to return a Java `int`, and the JavaScript returns the value `1.5`, then the result passed out of that surrounding Java method will be unpredictable.

Returning `Strings` and `booleans` is much simpler because they translate directly to their Java equivalents. Java objects can also be returned from the JavaScript; however, you can't just create Java objects in the JavaScript. If you want to return a Java object, then it must have been passed in as one of the parameters.

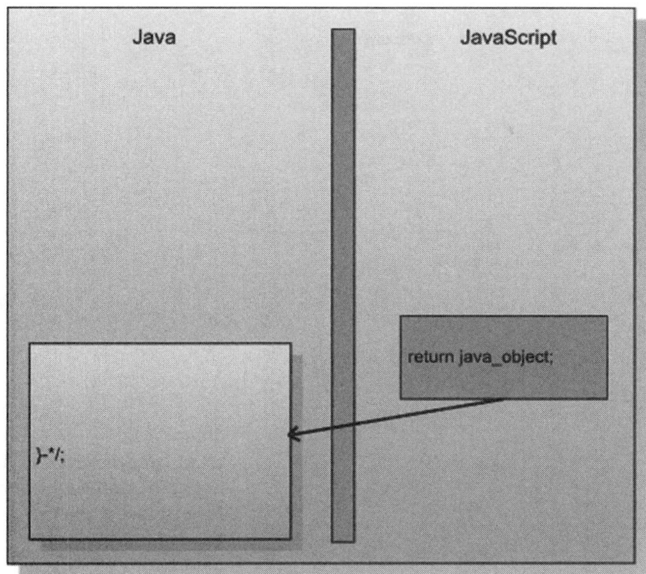

Figure 8.4
Examining the interaction between Java and JavaScript code when returning values across the JavaScript-to-Java boundary in a JSNI call from a GWT application

Take care if you're returning null objects, because the JavaScript `undefined` value isn't treated by JSNI as `null`; if it's used, unpredictable results can occur (you must always use the `null` value). You may even want to ensure that any JavaScript variable you pass back is checked to be sure it isn't the `undefined` value before it's returned.

We mentioned briefly when passing in parameters that GWT provides a special object called the `JavaScriptObject`. This type of object can be returned by the JSNI method if a new JavaScript object is created as part of the call. You'll see this in use often later in this chapter when you use JSNI methods to create new JavaScript objects from a third-party library. You need a reference to these third-party objects in the Java code because you'll later be calling methods on them, and they're therefore passed back as subclasses to the `JavaScriptObject`. This `JavaScriptObject` is opaque to the Java code—you can't use Java code to call the methods in it or even to see its fields; you need to pass them back into new JSNI methods to do that. But you'll see this in action a little later. First we need to finish our journey through the JSNI syntax by looking at how you can call Java methods from JavaScript.

Crossing the boundary from JavaScript to Java

As well as being able to access fields on Java objects from JavaScript, you can execute methods defined in those objects in a similar manner, as shown in figure 8.5.

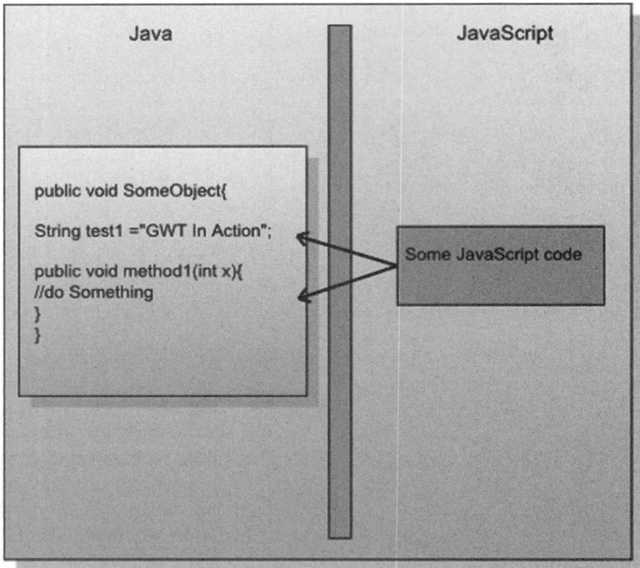

Figure 8.5 Examining the interaction between JavaScript and a Java object when crossing the JavaScript to Java boundary in JSNI

To refer to a method, you use a syntax similar to that you used to refer to fields. There are, however, some slight differences. This time, the generic template for calls to methods is shown in figure 8.6.

The first part of this should be familiar from when you were accessing fields, with the same discussion about there being no `objectName` if you're accessing a static method, using `this` if you accessing a method in the current instance, and using the parameter name if you're accessing a passed-in object to a method. The difference occurs in the second half of the template, where you see the values `param-signature` and `arguments`. The arguments part is a list of the various arguments whose types match the parameter signature. JSNI uses the internal Java

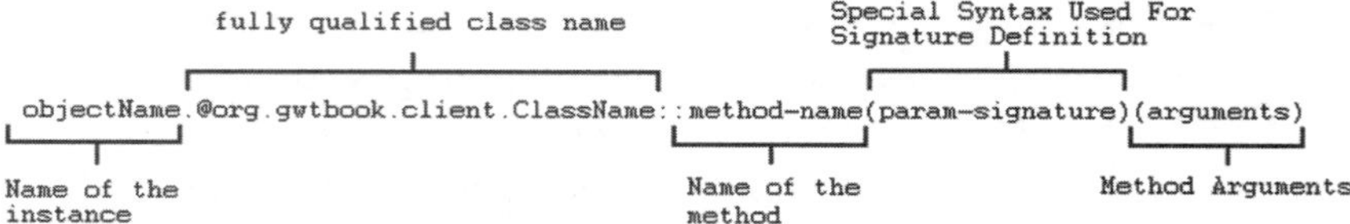

Figure 8.6 Explanation of the JSNI method to access a method in a Java object. First is the instance name, followed by the fully qualified class name. The method name is followed by the parameter signature and then the arguments.

method signature to define the parameter signature, but it doesn't require a definition of the return type to be included. Parameter type signatures are defined in table 8.1.

Table 8.1 Java type signature for various Java types

Type signature	Java type
`Z`	`boolean`
`B`	`byte`
`C`	`char`
`S`	`short`
`I`	`int`
`J`	`long`
`F`	`float`
`D`	`double`
`L` fully qualified class;	Fully qualified class
`[` type	`type[]` (an array)

Let's look at a simple example, shown in listing 8.3.

Listing 8.3 Sample attempts to call methods in a Java class from JavaScript

```
package org.gwtbook.client;
public class JSNIMethodExample{

   public void m1(String s){
      // Do something with the String s
   }

   Public void m2(int num){
      // Do something with integer num
   }

   public native void doSomething(String s, int num)/*-{
      this.@org.gwtbook.client.JSNIMethodExample::m1
              (Ljava/lang/String;)(s);                    ❶ Call method with String parameter
     this.@org.gwtbook.client.JSNIMethodExample::m2(I)(num);   ❷ Call method with integer parameter
   }-*/;

}
```

In ❶, you call the `m1()` method in this class, which takes a Java `String` as its parameter; so, you must define the parameter signature as `Ljava/lang/String;`. Then, you call the `m2()` method ❷, which expects an `integer`, so the method signature is `I`. (In your code, these definitions should all be on one line—it's sometimes difficult to get all of them on one line in the book!)

The final type of objects that can come out of the JSNI call are exceptions.

Handling exceptions

It's strongly recommended that JavaScript exceptions be handled in the JavaScript segments of the JSNI method and that Java methods be handled in Java code. The reason is that when a JavaScript exception creeps over the JavaScript boundary into the Java, it becomes, and can only become, an object of type `JavaScriptException`.

You don't necessarily lose information about the JavaScript exception, because you can use the `getName()` and `getDescription()` methods to return `String` values about the original JavaScript exception. But relying on these methods leads to messy code requiring the use of `String` comparison to handle the exceptions, whereas they can be handled more gracefully in the JavaScript code.

The only exception to this rule is where an exception is raised in Java code called by a JSNI method, which is then handed back to more Java code. In this case, the original Java exception typing is preserved through the boundaries.

With all these basics in place, let's look at the occasions when we said you may need to use JSNI, starting with how you perform different types of communication between components (browser, GWT applications, and legacy code).

8.2 *Communicating using JSNI*

You can use JSNI to allow the applications to talk to the browser, to allow GWT applications to message each other (on the client side), and to allow legacy applications to talk to the GWT application. This chapter looks at each of these types of communication in turn.

Due to the process GWT uses to load GWT applications, which we'll look at in chapter 17, you have to subtly alter the way in which you access the standard JavaScript variables `window` and `document`. The way that GWT loads the applications means you don't have direct visibility of these JavaScript variables; however, GWT fixes that in one of two ways—you can talk to the browser either using a method in the `Window` Java class or through the newly provided JavaScript variables `$wnd` and `$doc`. The `Window` class, that we'll look at next, keeps you in the realm of Java.

8.2.1 Chatting to the browser via GWT Java

If you're thinking of using functionality normally associated with the JavaScript `window` variable, you should first double-check that the GWT `Window` class (which can be found in the `com.google.gwt.user.client` package in gwt-user.jar) doesn't provide the access you're looking for. It provides access to a number of functions normally accessed through the JavaScript `window` variable (such as raising alert and confirmation windows, opening new browser windows, setting the browser title, and enabling/disabling scrolling). You'll use this class in the Dashboard to display the confirmation message when a user deletes a component, as you can see in figure 8.7.

When the user attempts to delete an application, you create a confirmation box using the code shown in listing 8.4. (If you wanted purely an alert window, then you could use the `Window.alert()` method.)

Listing 8.4 Using the `confirm()` method in the `Window` class to present a confirmation window

```
Window.confirm(
  messages.ConfirmDeleteMessage(
    this.parkComponent.getName()));
```

While we're thinking of the `Window` class, we should point out that in the Dashboard, you prevent the browser window from scrolling by using the `Window.enableScrolling()` method; passing `false` to this method lets you to stop

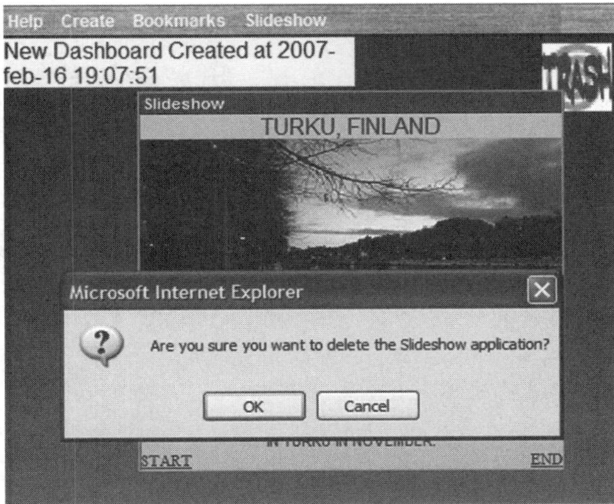

Figure 8.7 Dropping the Slideshow widget on the trash icon pops up a JavaScript confirm message. Rather than using JavaScript to get the message, you use the GWT `Window` class's `confirm()` method.

component applications from moving completely out of the browser area. The majority of the communication with the browser should be performed through the provided GWT classes. But on occasions where GWT hasn't provided a mechanism as yet, you'll have to dig down to the native JavaScript to do that.

8.2.2 Chatting to the browser via JavaScript

On rare occasions, the methods provided by the GWT Java classes for communicating with the browser won't provide the functionality you need. In these cases, you need to use JavaScript (through JSNI); but because of the way the GWT loading mechanism works, you can't use the normal JavaScript `window` and `document` variables (see chapter 17 for more on the loading mechanism). Instead, GWT provides the variables `$wnd` and `$doc`, respectively.

Prior to GWT 1.4, the `Slider` class you built in chapter 7 had an example of using these variables. When a user clicks the slider's background, you want the thumbnail to move to the appropriate location. This works fine using the standard methods, until someone scrolls the screen. Once that happens, the x and y positions the `onMouseDown` event provides you with no longer correlate with the locations on the slider's background. You need a way to obtain the scroll-off sets and then use those in the positioning calculations. The `Slider` class originally included some JSNI code that was responsible for getting those values. From GWT 1.4 on, GWT provides its own method in the `Window` class to do the same task. The code you would have used to implement that functionality is shown in listing 8.5.

Listing 8.5 JSNI code to get the y offset of scrolling in the browser window

```
private static native int getScrollYOffset () /*-{
   var scrOfY = 0;

   if(typeof($wnd.pageYOffset) == 'number' ){
      scrOfY = $wnd.pageYOffset;
   }else if($doc.body &&
              ($doc.body.scrollLeft || $doc.body.scrollTop)){
      scrOfY = $doc.body.scrollTop;
   }else{
      scrOfY = $doc.documentElement.scrollTop;
   }
   return scrOfY;
}-*/;
```

❶ Access JavaScript window variable through GWT $wnd variable

❷ Access JavaScript document variable through GWT $doc variable

You use both the `$wnd` and `$doc` variables to access y offset properties of the browser. At ❶, you retrieve the `pageYOffset` value for non-IE browsers, and at ❷ you need to use the `$doc` variable to retrieve the `body.scrollTop` variable for IE. Whichever value you eventually retrieve is the one returned to the caller of the method.

This is also a great example to point out the limitation of JSNI we spoke of earlier—managing browser differences. The code tries to identify browser differences using a number of conditional statements, checking for the existence of particular variables to understand what type of browser it's dealing with. Not exactly elegant, and it could be solved using class replacement based on the browser property technique we discuss in chapter 15, but that would make it harder to explain the point of this example!

If you're confident that there are no browser differences, then you can proceed in the manner shown in this section. Through these `$doc` and `$wnd` variables, all the usual `window` and `document` browser functions are possible. Note that the `Slider` class now uses the GWT 1.4–provided methods `Window.getScrollleft()` and `Window.getSrollTop()` instead of your JSNI method.

Another place in the Dashboard where you use these variables is to give the Dashboard user the ability to change locale through the menu system. When the user clicks a locale in the menu system, you call the function shown in listing 8.6 with the appropriate `locale` parameter. (The GWT `Command` that is called when the menu is clicked first removes the `onWindowCloseListener()`, which you added in chapter 6, so the user isn't bombarded with warning messages; then, this code is called by that `Command`.)

Listing 8.6 JSNI code to change the locale

```
private native void changeLocale(String newLocale)/*-{
    var currLocation = $wnd.location.toString();          <-- Retrieve current location
    var noHistoryCurrLocArray = currLocation.split("#");
    var noHistoryCurrLoc = noHistoryCurrLocArray[0];       Get base URL
    var locArray = noHistoryCurrLoc.split("?");
    $wnd.location.href = locArray[0]+"?locale="+newLocale;  <-- Set new location
}-*/;
```

You'll use the `$wnd` variable often when interfacing between GWT applications and any JavaScript library that may have been loaded by the application, as well as when exposing an API into the GWT application.

8.2.3 *Talking to a GWT application via a JavaScript API*

GWT applications come in many shapes and sizes. Some, like the Dashboard, take up all of the browser's space; many others fit in a small segment of a web site. As you saw in chapter 1, there will be times when the GWT application may replace an existing application. In all these cases, you may need to talk to the application from an external entity—which may be another GWT application or some legacy code. In order to do this while preserving the standard GWT loading mechanism, you need to expose the GWT application through a JavaScript API, something that GWT can easily manage with a bit of JSNI magic.

To expose an API, you need to expose JavaScript methods outside of the application that have the following features:

- Can call parts of the application's code
- Have names that don't get obfuscated by the compiler so you can reference them

You can achieve the first part of this through using JSNI to call back to static methods in the code. The second part is achieved by carefully constructing new methods in the browser by using JavaScript definitions. You can access the main browser page through the `$wnd` object. To create new JavaScript methods at that level, you create definitions along the following lines:

```
$wnd.newMethodName = function(parameters){
   // Some code
}
```

If you make the internal part of this definition a JSNI call back to static methods in the GWT application, then you've exposed an API to external applications. Let's look at how you do this for the Dashboard application.

There isn't much of an API that you can expose for the Dashboard you're building, but for the sake of an example, you'll expose two methods for setting and getting the Dashboard's name (which is usually changed by the user clicking it and typing in a new name). In the application download, we provide another HTML file than the one you've been using so far; it's called Dashboard_APITest.html. That file provides two new buttons, Get and Set (at the top of the web browser page), which aren't part of the GWT application but call the API methods. Figure 8.8 shows that clicking the Get button displays an alert window with the current name of the Dashboard as its contents.

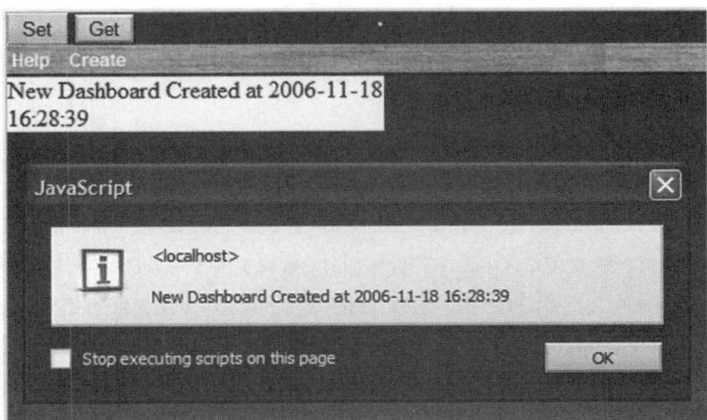

Figure 8.8 Clicking the Get button on the web page to activate the Dashboard's API `getDashboardName()` method

When you click the Set button, the JavaScript in the HTML page calls the Dashboard's `__setDashboardName()` API method, which calls back through the defined API into the Dashboard application and changes the name, as shown in figure 8.9.

In the Dashboard.java file, you'll find the segment of code that accomplishes this (see listing 8.7).

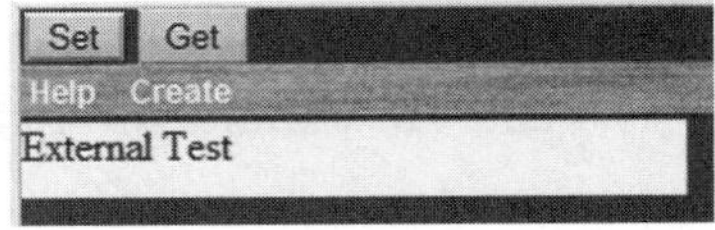

Figure 8.9 The result of clicking the Set button on the web page, which activates the Dashboard's API `setDashboardName()` method

Listing 8.7 Methods involved in providing the Dashboard's external API

```
public static void setDashboardName(String s){
   dashboardName.setText(s);
}

public static String getDashboardName(){
   return dashboardName.getText();
}

public native void setUpAPI()/*-{
   $wnd.__setDashboardName = function(s){
      @org.gwtbook.client.Dashboard::setDashboardName
            (Ljava/lang/String;)(s);
   }
   $wnd.__getDashboardName = function(){
      return @org.gwtbook.client.Dashboard::getDashboardName()();
   }
}-*/;
```

1. Internal Java method to set Dashboard name
2. Internal Java method to set Dashboard name
3. Internal JSNI method to set up API methods
4. Add set method to browser's window object
5. Add get method to browser's window object

The first two methods (❶ and ❷) provide the functionality for setting and getting the Dashboard's name in normal Java code, which is held on the `EditableLabel` widget called `dashboardName`.

The third method ❸ is the JSNI method that sets up the external methods for the API. In this method, you can see the creation of two new JavaScript methods: one for setting the Dashboard name ❹ and the other for getting the name ❺.

It works by adding two new methods to the browser's window object, which then means those methods are available to anyone else who can see the browser's `window` object. In the new method definitions, you use JSNI to refer to the static methods (❶ and ❷) in the Java class. If an external entity calls the `__getDashboardName()` JavaScript method accessible from the browser's window object, then the GWT Java `getDashboardName()` ❷ method is invoked.

To test the API, add two new buttons to the Dashboard_APITest.html file, which call the set and get methods as follows:

```
<button onClick="javascript:__setDashboardName('External Test');">
   Set
</button>
<button onClick="javascript:alert(__getDashboardName());">
   Get
</button>
```

Each button calls the appropriate JavaScript method.

You can use this API approach to provide access to whatever functions you require in the GWT applications by adding the necessary code. As we mentioned at the start of this section, this approach can be useful if you're migrating an existing web site component by component, because you can still allow legacy JavaScript code to access new GWT applications in the way they accessed the old JavaScript code the application has replaced.

Using an API is a way of calling into the GWT applications, and you could use the same approach to communicate between two separate GWT applications on a web page. Another way to do this inter-application communication is to use a variable stored in the browser page and pass values through that variable.

8.2.4 Talking between GWT applications

When you drag a Dashboard component application over the trash icon, you want it to be removed from the screen. Before it's removed, though, you need to check whether the user should be asked for confirmation about whether it should be deleted. The mechanism you'll use is for the component application to check a JavaScript boolean variable, which is set by the main Dashboard application. This

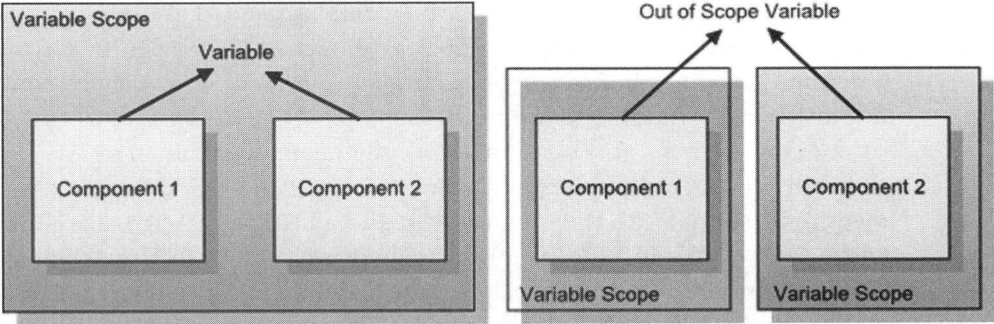

Figure 8.10 On the left, the variable is in the scope of both components and can be manipulated directly in the code. On the right, the variable is out of the scope of both components, so another mechanism is needed to alter the variable's value. For the Dashboard, you manipulate the variable using JSNI code.

is a useful approach when you need to pass data between two distinct GWT applications, but it should be limited to that situation.

The normal way of passing information between components in your application is to ensure that both components are in the same variable scope in your GWT code, as shown on the left in figure 8.10.

To understand this idea of the scope of a variable, check out the code shown in listing 8.8. The variable `confirmDelete` is visible to both objects.

Listing 8.8 How a variable can have scope over a couple of objects

```
public class Test{
   boolean confirmDelete = true;

   public class Obj1{
      public Obj1(){
         confirmDelete = false;
      }
   }

   public class Obj2{
      public Obj2(){
         confirmDelete = true;
      }
   }
}
```

Most of the time, you can make sure the variables needed are in scope of all components by having a classwide variable as shown in listing 8.8, by having setters and getters in the subclasses, or by using a static variable. Typically, components that need to share variables are in the same panel, or composite widget, or application. However, on rare occasions, you can't keep a variable in scope.

In the Dashboard application, you have a variable called `confirmDelete` that needs to be shared with the menu system and all the `DashboardPanels`. If the variable is set to `true` and the panel is dragged over the trash icon, then the panel confirms with the user whether they want to delete it. Although you can keep this in scope of the component applications by using a static variable in the `Dashboard` class, you'll break the rules slightly and implement it as a JavaScript variable outside the scope of the GWT to allow us to explain the concept shown on the right in figure 8.10.

In a model such as that shown in figure 8.10, you make a JavaScript variable in the HTML page and then use JSNI code in the Java GWT applications to access it. The code in the Dashboard.java file to "get" and "set" this JavaScript value is shown in listing 8.9.

Listing 8.9 Code used from the GWT Java code to set and get a JavaScript value set in the Dashboard.HTML file

```
private native void setConfirmDelete(boolean confirmDelete)/*-{
   $wnd.confirmDelete = confirmDelete;
}-*/;

private native boolean getConfirmDelete()/*-{
   return $wnd.confirmDelete;
}-*/;
```

At their basic level, the `getConfirmDelete()` method returns the value of the JavaScript variable `confirmDelete`, and the `setConfirmDelete()` method sets it. Similar code for getting the value can be found in the implementation of the `DashboardPanel` in chapter 5, which completes the link between the main Dashboard application and the component applications.

As well as interacting with your own GWT components using JSNI, you can also use it to interact with existing JavaScript libraries.

8.3 Loading a JavaScript library

To use an existing JavaScript library, such as the Google Video Search capability, you need to load the necessary JavaScript code into the application. In the case of the Google Video Search, this means loading in two separate JavaScript libraries, both of them downloaded from Google at runtime. The first is the Google Ajax Search library (which is common across both the Search and Video Search applications), and the second is the specific JavaScript library for the video searching. Because two different libraries are needed, we'll explore each of the two different GWT ways of loading libraries: using the HTML file, and using the module XML file. For the Google Ajax Search library, you'll use HTML.

8.3.1 Using HTML to load a JavaScript library

The first of the two ways we'll look at for loading a JavaScript library is through the HTML file the application lives in. You do so by using the normal way of linking JavaScript files to a web page, using the `<script>` tag. In the head section of the Dashboard.html file, you place the following text:

```
<script src="
      http://www.google.com/uds/api?file=uds.js&amp;v=1.0&amp;key=X"
         type="text/javascript">
</script>
```

You need to replace the `X` with a Google Ajax Search API key, which you can obtained from http://code.google.com/apis/ajaxsearch/ (when using the API in hosted mode, you should get a key that is linked to the http://localhost:8888 domain; if and when you deploy your code to your server, you'll need to change this key to one reflecting your URL at that point).

That's it for loading a JavaScript library via the HTML. As you can see, it's nothing different from the way you would normally load a JavaScript file for an HTML page. If you don't have access to the main HTML page, or you want to be more modular, add the JavaScript through the module XML file. For the video-searching JavaScript library, you'll use this module XML file method.

8.3.2 Using the module XML to load a JavaScript library

In chapter 9, we'll talk about using the ability to load JavaScript libraries for applications through the module XML file. This is a useful approach if you want to modularize the applications and ensure that everything required by the application is kept with the application. It made sense for you to load the Google Ajax search JavaScript library in the HTML page, as you just saw, because it's used by more than one application.

The Google Video Search JavaScript library, on the other hand, is only used by Google Video Search Dashboard application, so you'll load this code through that application's module XML file. In the GoogleVideoSearch.gwt.xml file, you define the following to load the gsvideobar JavaScript file:

```
<script src="
      http://www.google.com/uds/solutions/videobar/gsvideobar.js">
</script>
```

Pre–GWT 1.4, it was necessary to include some JavaScript inside a `CDATA` tag that returned `true` to indicate that the script had loaded. That isn't necessary beginning with GWT 1.4, because the bootstrapping process now guarantees that the JavaScript is loaded (assuming of course it can be found).

With the JavaScript library loaded, it's time to start using it. There are probably many different patterns of code you could use to achieve this, but we'll look next at the one we, as authors, have become comfortable with.

8.4 Wrapping a simple JavaScript library

One powerful aspect of GWT is the ability to wrap any existing JavaScript library (your own or from a third party) as a GWT widget that can then be used as normal code in the GWT applications. You'll need to do this if you can't translate the library into Java, either because it's too much effort or because you don't have the ability (perhaps due to licensing or visibility of code).

JavaScript libraries exist for Google Maps and the Google Ajax Search capabilities, all provided by Google, and all falling into the category of JavaScript code that you don't have the ability to write yourself as Java code. There already exists a useful GWT widget that wraps the Google Maps functionality (http://sourceforge.net/projects/gwt/), so we'll focus on Google's Video and Ajax search libraries.

Google's Video Search capability (http://www.google.com/uds/solutions/videobar/index.html) provides a nice video-searching application, as shown in figure 8.11.

The wrapping of this is relatively simple and a little limited, because you wrap one JavaScript object and expose only two functions: `create()` and `execute()`. But it gives us a good opportunity to examine the concepts in detail and give you an understanding of how the flow works between the objects you need to create.

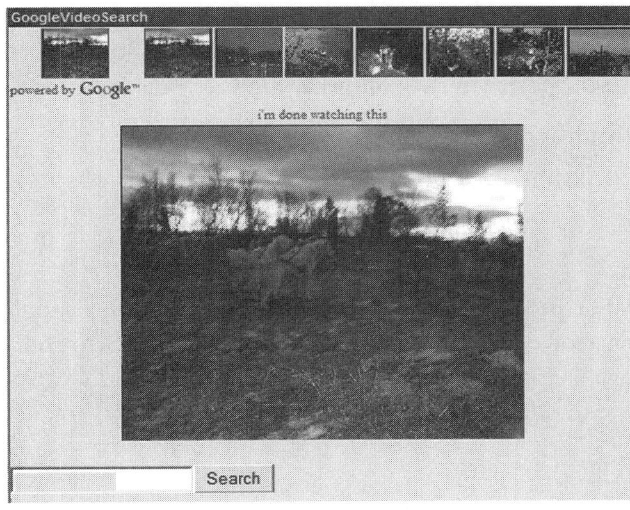

Figure 8.11 The Google Video Search application running in a browser. The whole coding for this is a JavaScript library provided by Google, which is then wrapped in JSNI for use in GWT.

To take you further into JSNI, you'll wrap the Google Ajax Search functionality (http://code.google.com/apis/ajaxsearch/); at the time of writing this book, it provides five different searchers in one search control, three of which are shown in action in figure 8.12.

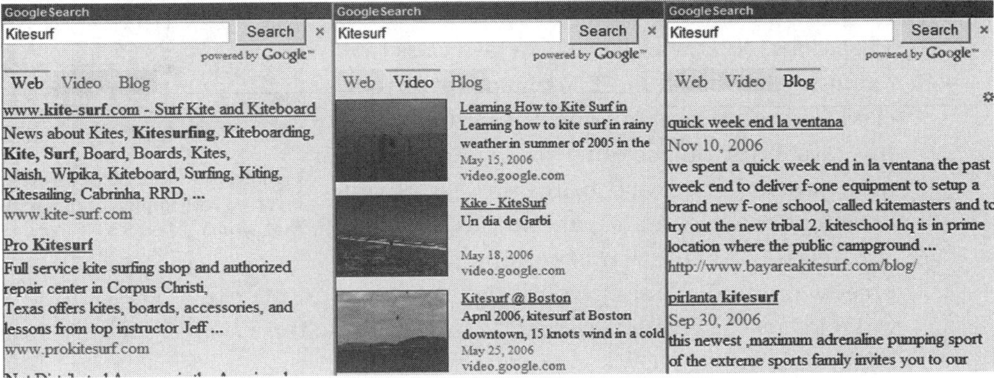

Figure 8.12 Three views of the Google Search Dashboard application, showing the Web, Video, and Blog Search capabilities on the phrase "Kitesurf"

The key to implementing both of these Dashboard component applications is, of course, JSNI and the use of all the techniques we've discussed so far in this chapter. In the general case, you perform the following steps:

1. Load the JavaScript library.
2. Access the loaded JavaScript library, and create instances of the necessary objects.
3. Use the objects.

Step 1, loading the JavaScript library, allows you to use a particular capability you need for the application (for example, to use the Google Video Search capability, you need to load two JavaScript libraries into the application). You've already seen how you can load libraries, so let's take the next step and begin to look at how you access the library.

8.4.1 Accessing the loaded JavaScript library

The journey to create and use objects in the newly loaded JavaScript library follows the hierarchy shown in figure 8.13.

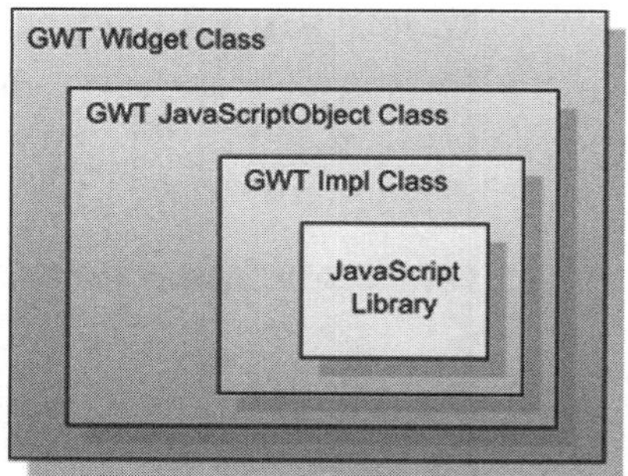

Figure 8.13 The object hierarchy involved with implementing a GWT widget that wraps a JavaScript library

First, you'll create a simple Java class that contains the JSNI code needed to interact with the JavaScript library; this is the GWT `Impl` Class. Next, you'll create a Java class that extends the basic GWT `JavaScriptObject` class. This class is an opaque object that wraps the JavaScript object obtained by creating a new JavaScript object from the JavaScript library. It also contains an instance of the `Impl` class to enable you to call the JavaScript objects methods. Finally, you'll use the `JavaScriptObject` class inside the GWT widget class to provide a widget. Let's take these three steps in a little more detail, beginning with the GWT `Impl` class.

Developing the implementation class

This is the first class you build when wrapping JavaScript libraries, and it contains all the JSNI code required for interfacing with the particular JavaScript object you'll be wrapping. It's useful to look at JavaScript examples provided by the library's documentation to see how you should create the implementation class and then identify the methods you want to expose from that. For the Google Video Search, Google provides the code repeated in listing 8.10 as an example.

Listing 8.10 JavaScript example from the Google Video Search API web site

```
<script type="text/javascript">
  function OnLoad() {
    var vbr;

    var options = {                          ← ❶ Create JavaScript options object
      largeResultSet : true
    }
    vbr = new GSvideoBar(                    ← ❷ Create JavaScript Video Search object
                document.getElementById("videoBar"),
                document.getElementById("videoPlayer"),
                options
                );
    vbr.execute("VW GTI");                   ← ❸ Execute video search
  }
</script>
```

In this Google example, an `options` object is created ❶ followed by a new `GSvideoBar` JavaScript object with two DOM elements representing where the two components will be displayed as well as the previously created `options` object as parameters ❷. Finally, the code executes a search ❸ on the newly created `GSvideoBar`.

The GWT Java implementation class will have to emulate all this, but you want to break out the functionality into different methods to make it more modular. This allows you to include the methods in the GWT approach to create new widgets, such as that in figure 8.14.

For the GWT Google Video Search functionality, you define the implementation class shown in listing 8.11, which closely follows the original GWT example.

Listing 8.11 Implementing the Java class that encapsulates JSNI calls to an underlying loaded JavaScript library

```
import org.gwtbook.client.jswrap.googleVideoSearch.GSvideoBar;

import com.google.gwt.user.client.Element;

public class GSvideoBarImpl {

   public native GSvideoBar create(Element bar,           ← ❶ Define create Java method
                                   Element player) /*-{
```

```
        var options = {
            largeResultSet : true,
            horizontal : true,
              thumbnailSize : $wnd.GSvideoBar.THUMBNAILS_SMALL
        }
        var theGSvideoBar = new $wnd.GSvideoBar(bar,player,options);
        return theGSvideoBar;
    }-*/;

    public native void execute(GSvideoBar theControl,
                                    String searchString) /*-{
        theControl.execute(searchString);
    }-*/;
}
```

❷ Create JavaScript options object
❸ Create JavaScript Video Search object
❹ Return JavaScript objects over JavaScript to Java interface
❺ Define execute Java method
❻ Execute video search

In the GWT approach, you provide a `create()` method ❶ that creates the `GSvideoBar` JavaScript object you're after. This method is written in JSNI and demonstrates nicely how you cross the Java-JavaScript boundary. The method takes two GWT `Element` objects that represent the browser elements where the search-bar and video player will be displayed. These parameters, along with some options ❷, are used directly in the JavaScript call ❸ where the GWT compiler makes sure the Java objects have become valid JavaScript objects. Notice as well that the JavaScript object is created by accessing it through the `$wnd` object.

After creating the new JavaScript `GSvideoBar` object in the JavaScript code, you return it as the result of the method call ❹. In this case, you now have a JavaScript object, so you must return an object whose type is a GWT Java `JavaScriptObject`

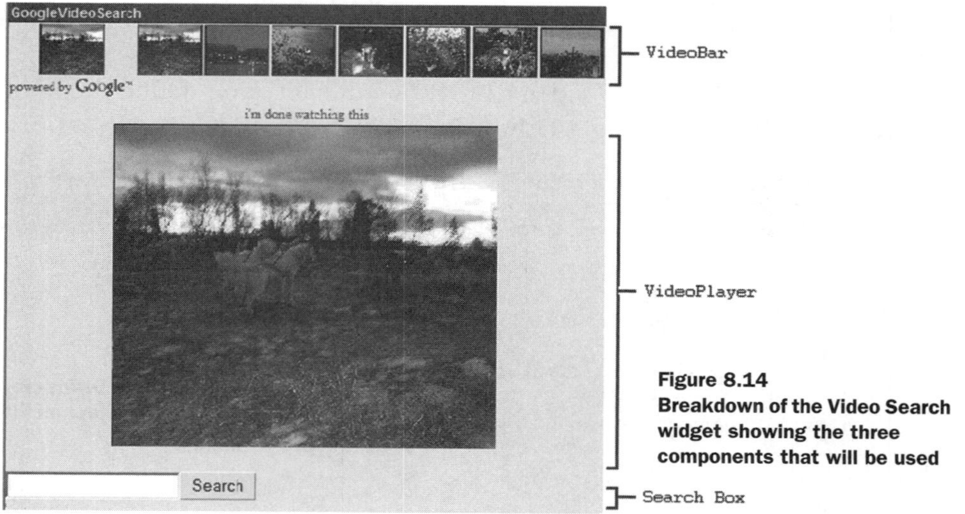

Figure 8.14 Breakdown of the Video Search widget showing the three components that will be used

object (you'll see how to handle that in the next section—the `GSvideoBar` Java object is a subclass of the `JavaScriptObject`).

The second method defined in the implementation class is the `execute()` method ❺, which performs the main work in the class by executing a search on the Google video library. You pass in as the first parameter the `GSvideoBar` object, created previously. As it crosses the boundary back into JavaScript through the JSNI interface, the opaque object turns back into a fully visible JavaScript object whose methods you can call in JavaScript—which in this case is the `execute()` method ❻.

Let's look at this mysterious `GSvideoBar` object, which in the JavaScript code is the true `GSVideoBar` JavaScript object but in the Java code becomes an instance of the `JSObject` class.

Adding the JavaScriptObject class

You will normally create JavaScript objects using the JavaScript library on which you subsequently call methods to provide the functionality you're after. In the GWT approach, you want to keep as much of the code in Java as possible and make use of the strong typing of the language and benefits of the compiler. As you saw in the last section, you try to make the GWT access to the JavaScript library as modular as possible, which results in your having to manage the initially created JavaScript object as a Java object. To do this, you use the GWT `JavaScriptObject` class.

When you pass a JavaScript object out of a JSNI segment of code and into the Java, then the GWT compiler automatically treats it as an object defined by the Java method's return type. If you define that return type to be a `JavaScriptObject` or a subclass of it, then you receive an instance of an opaque Java object. It's called *opaque* because you can't look into or execute methods on it while in the Java code. The real use of the standard `JavaScriptObject` is to act as a handle to a JavaScript object as you pass it around in the Java code.

What you do with the `JavaScriptObject` class is to extend it, hold a reference to the implementation class, and contain methods that match those you want to execute in the implementation. You can see this in action if you look at the Java `GSvideoBar` class shown in listing 8.12, which extends the GWT `JavaScriptObject` class and represents the `GSvideoBar` JavaScript object.

Listing 8.12 Implementing the Java class that embodies a JavaScript object treated as an opaque object

```
public class GSvideoBar extends JavaScriptObject{            <- Extend JavaScript-Object class

   private static GSvideoBarImpl impl = new GSvideoBarImpl();   <- Reference implementation class (1)

   public static GSvideoBar create(Element bar, Element player) {   <- Create new instance (2)
      return impl.create(bar,player);
   }

   public  void execute(String searchString){      <- (3) Execute JavaScript method
      impl.execute(this, searchString);
   }

}
```

You start the class definition by defining that you'll extend the `JavaScriptObject` class. Beginning with GWT 1.4, you shouldn't provide a constructor method for `JavaScriptObjects` or your code won't compile. (If you pick up some legacy code, it may not have been updated to reflect this change, so you may see some errors.) At ❶, you create a static instance of the implementation class that you'll use to create the new JavaScript object. There is a bit of a circular action going on here; you call the static `create()` method ❷, which in turn calls the implementation class's `create()` method, which returns a new `GSvideoBar` object.

Overriding the standard `JavaScriptObject` class offers two key benefits. First, you get to provide a name that is more meaningful (this is necessary when you start wrapping more complicated JavaScript libraries that require you to manage more than one JavaScript object). Second, you can add the JavaScript object's methods into the new class to make it act more like the opaque JavaScript object it represents.

An example of this second point is the `execute()` method ❸. In this class, you create a definition that requires the user to pass in the search string as a parameter. Inside the method, you call the implementation class's `execute()` method, passing in this `JavaScriptObject` as the first parameter followed by the search string. This means you're always addressing the correct instance of the JavaScript object.

The final step to take is to create the class that will present itself to the GWT application as the widget.

Creating the widget

Creating the widget class is an easy task; see listing 8.13.

Listing 8.13 Wrapping the JSNI and JavaScriptObject as a simple GWT widget

```
public class GVSWidget extends Composite{

   VerticalPanel theArea = new VerticalPanel();
   Label bar2 = new Label("Loading Bar");
   Label player2 = new Label("Loading Player");
   static GSvideoBar gsvideoBar = null;

   public GSvideoBar getGSvideoBar(Element bar, Element player){
      if (gsvideoBar == null){
         gsvideoBar = GSvideoBar.create(bar,player);
      }
      return gsvideoBar;
   }

   public  GVSWidget(){
      theArea.add(bar);
      theArea.add(player);
      initWidget(theArea);
      getGSvideoBar(bar.getElement(),
                    player.getElement());
   }


   public void execute(String searchText) {
      gsvideoBar.execute(searchText);
   }
}
```

❶ Create GWT label as results placeholder

❷ Create GWT label as video player placeholder

❸ Get video search component

❹ Execute video search

You need to create two GWT DOM elements where the video bar and player will reside (you use some simple labels (❶ and ❷)) and then add them to a vertical panel to provide some structure. With the visual structure in place, you call the create method in the `GSvideoBar` class using the DOM elements representing the labels ❸. You can't directly pass the labels, because the code expects DOM Elements, but a call to `Label`'s `getElement()` method resolves that.

Once completed, the create method returns a `JavaScriptObject`, which you store in the class field `gsvideoBar`. You complete the widget by defining a widget-level method for each of the methods defined in the `JavaScriptObject` class. In this case, this means creating an `execute()` method ❹. This method calls the `JavaScriptObject`'s `execute()` method, which in turn calls the implementation class using itself as a parameter to perform the video search.

That's all you need to do to perform the simple wrapping of a JavaScript library with one JavaScript object—the widget is now ready to use.

8.4.2 Using the widget in an application

All this work has created a brand-new GWT widget that you use in exactly the same manner as any other GWT widget. You can see this in the Google Video Search Dashboard application code, shown in listing 8.14.

Listing 8.14 Dashboard application that uses the new Google Video Search widget

```
public class GoogleVideoSearch extends DashboardComposite{

   VerticalPanel theArea = new VerticalPanel();
   HorizontalPanel theSearchInput = new HorizontalPanel();
   TextBox theSearch = new TextBox();
   Button startSearch = new Button("Search");
   GVSWidget theWidget;

   public GoogleVideoSearch(){
      super();
      theSearchInput.add(theSearch);
      theSearchInput.add(startSearch);
      theWidget = new GVSWidget();          <-- Create GSVideo widget instance
      theArea.add(theWidget);
      theArea.add(theSearchInput);
      startSearch.addClickListener(new ClickListener(){
         public void onClick(Widget sender) {
            performSearch(theSearch.getText());     <-- Perform search
         }
      });
      theSearch.addKeyboardListener(new KeyboardListenerAdapter(){
         public void onKeyDown(Widget sender,
                               char theKey,
                               int modifiers){
            if (theKey==13){
               startSearch.click();          <-- Perform search after user presses Return
            }
         }
      });
      initWidget(theArea);
      theWidget.execute("porjus aurora");        <-- Perform initial search
   }
}
```

In the Dashboard's video search application, you create a new `GVSWidget` and place it in a new composite that also provides the user with the ability to type in a search phrase and click a search button. When a phrase is entered and the button is clicked, you call the widget's `execute()` method, and you're presented with a number of videos to select from.

In the next section, we'll look at how you can take this wrapping strategy a little further with libraries where there are multiple objects, and we'll discuss why it isn't always efficient to wrap every single JavaScript object.

8.5 Wrapping a complex JavaScript library

The previous section wrapped a simple JavaScript library where there was only one JavaScript object. As you saw, this is a real-life example, but nowadays it's often the case that the JavaScript libraries you may want to wrap contain more than one object that you need to manage.

Let's look at the Google Ajax Search API, which you'll use to present the user with a Dashboard search component similar to that shown in figure 8.15.

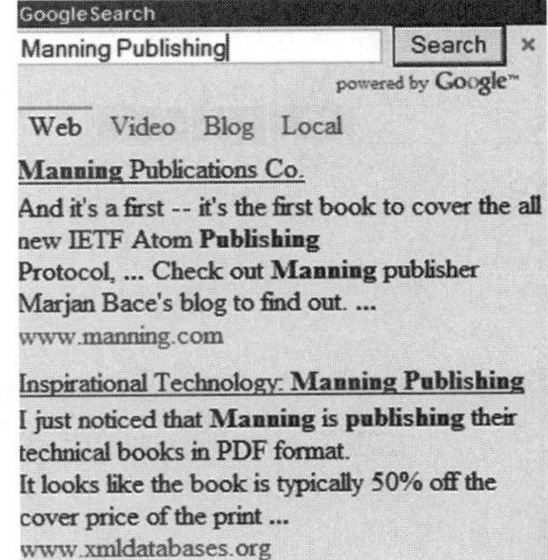

Figure 8.15 Google Ajax API Search in the Dashboard's Google Search application (showing four of the five available searchers)

We won't go into as much detail about the wrapping in this section, because we did that in the last section. What we'll look at here are the main differences between this component and the previous Video Search. First, let's consider the classes that need to be created.

8.5.1 Generating the classes

This component has a number of different JavaScript objects that could be wrapped, as shown in figure 8.16 (which is taken direct from the API documentation at http://code.google.com/apis/ajaxsearch/documentation/reference.html).

Figure 8.16 Google Ajax Search API JavaScript objects, the majority of which you need to manage in Java code, making this a complex library to wrap

For the widget, you'll wrap the GSearchControl and all the searchers, and you'll do so using the same pattern you saw in the previous section. For example, the GnewsSearch class becomes the code in listing 8.15.

Listing 8.15 The GnewsSearch class, which is part of the Google Ajax Search implementation

```
public class GnewsSearch extends GSearch{

   private static GnewsSearchImpl impl = new GnewsSearchImpl();

   public static GnewsSearch create(){
      return impl.create();
   }
}
```

The only difference between this and the previous widget is that in the GSearch-Control, you have more complicated methods such as adding new searchers to the control. Because you're working at a Java level, you have simple methods such as

```
public void addSearcher(GwebSearch theWebSearcher) {
   impl.addSearcher(this, theWebSearcher);
}
```

Here you add a JavaScriptObject to another JavaScriptObject. As we mentioned before, these are opaque objects, so you're just playing with objects; it isn't until you get to the implementation class that the real work of addition occurs. At this point, you cross the Java-to-JavaScript boundary and call the JavaScript library's addSearcher() method on the GSearchControl JavaScript object to add the GwebSearch JavaScript object:

```
public native void addSearcher(GSearchControl searchControl,
                               GwebSearch theWebSearcher) /*-{
   searchControl.addSearcher(theWebSearcher);
}-*/;
```

We made a conscious choice not to wrap the GsearcherOptions and GdrawOp-tions JavaScript objects. Next, you'll see why and what the impact is of keeping them as Java objects.

8.5.2 Keeping JavaScript objects as Java objects

When you start dealing with more than one object to wrap, you face a decision: Do you try to wrap every single object that is available, or do you take a more relaxed strategy and wrap only those for which it's necessary? Sometimes you don't want to go through the process of creating full Java classes for all JavaScript objects, due to time constraints or for other common-sense reasons. In the Google Search functionality, two objects perform no function except to hold values of options.

Although you could create all the implementation and `JavaScriptObject` classes for the `GdrawOptions` and `GsearcherOptions` JavaScript objects, you would end up writing vast amounts of code for little benefit. It's easier to keep these objects as simple Java classes and then convert them only when necessary, which, in this example case, is when you draw the control or add searchers.

When you draw the search control, you call the `draw()` method in the `SearchControlImpl`, which takes as parameters a `JavaScriptObject` (the search control), a DOM element (where the control will be drawn), and a Java object representing the options. Unfortunately, GWT won't translate the options object from Java to the required JavaScript object, so you must do that; but it's relatively simple to achieve, as shown in listing 8.16.

Listing 8.16 The Google Search `draw()` method, where options objects become JavaScript objects

```
public native void draw(GSearchControl searchControl,
                        Element div,
                        GdrawOptions options) /*-{
   var theOptions = new $wnd.GdrawOptions();
   if (options.@org.gwtbook.GdrawOptions::isInputAttached()()) {
       theOptions.setInput(
           options.@org.gwtbook.GdrawOptions::getInputElement()());
   }
   if (options.@org.gwtbook. GdrawOptions::isDrawModeSet()()) {
      if (options.@org.gwtbook.GdrawOptions::getDrawMode()() ==
          @org.gwtbook.GSearchControl::DRAW_MODE_LINEAR) {
            theOptions.
                 setDrawMode($wnd.GSearchControl.DRAW_MODE_LINEAR);
        } else {
        theOptions.
                 setDrawMode($wnd.GSearchControl.DRAW_MODE_TABBED);
      }
   }
   searchControl.draw(div,theOptions);
}-*/;
```

❶ Get GdrawOptions JavaScript object
❷ Variable set?
❸
❹ Draw search object

You create a new JavaScript object of the `GdrawOptions` by writing the code at ❶ (remember that you need to get the new object through the `$wnd` object). Once you have the JavaScript `GdrawOptions` object, you walk through the fields in the Java object, checking for values and then setting up the appropriate equivalent in the JavaScript object (for example, at ❷, you check if an alternative input area is provided; if so, you set it up in the JavaScript `theOptions` object ❸). Finally, you call the Java `SearchControl` object's `draw()` method with the new JavaScript `theOptions` object as a parameter ❹.

The Google Search control also provides the functionality for the user to save search results through a call-back mechanism. Let's check out how you can implement and support such functionality.

8.5.3 Calling user-defined code from a library

It isn't unusual for a third-party JavaScript library to provide the ability to call some user-defined JavaScript code if an event happens in the library. In the case of the Google Search Library, you can tell it to display a label after each search result, which, if clicked, performs a user-defined action (typically, the result of the search is stored). Figure 8.17 shows this in action in the Dashboard.

Because this is GWT, you'll implement this in a GWT style. The first step is to try to emulate the GWT event-handling mechanisms you saw in chapter 6. You'll create a new `KeepListener` interface, which requires a simple `onKeep()` method to

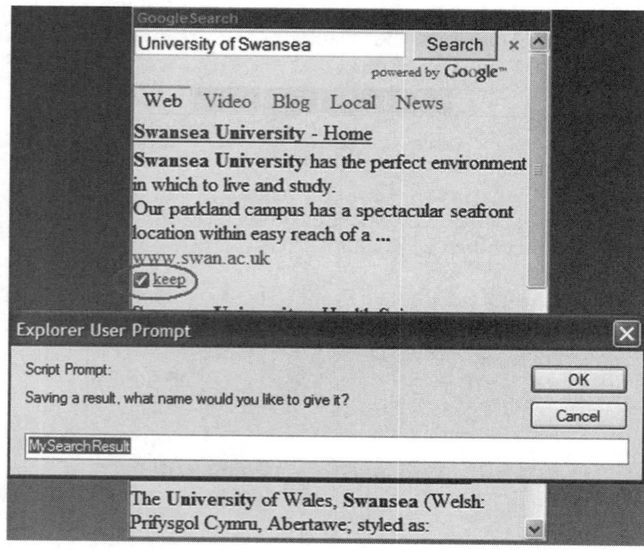

Figure 8.17 Implementing the feedback mechanism of Google Search to display an alert when the Keep label is clicked

be implemented that is executed when the user clicks the label in the widget. The listener is defined as the interface shown in listing 8.17.

Listing 8.17 The `KeepListener` class

```
public interface KeepListener {
      public void onKeep();
}
```

You use this listener as shown in listing 8.18 by adding it as an anonymous class to a search control and implementing the `onKeep()` method.

Listing 8.18 Using the `KeepListener` class

```
searchWidget = new GSearchWidget();
GSearchControl sc = searchWidget.getGSearch();
sc.addOnKeepListener(new KeepListener(){
   public void onKeep() {
      Window.prompt("Saving a result, what name would you
                     like to give it?", "MySearchResult");
   }
});
```

For our keep listener in listing 8.18 we simply pop up a prompt (using the GWT 1.4 `Window.prompt()` method) to ask for the user to provide a name to save the result as. In the implementation of `GSearchControl`, you place the code that ties the listener to the call-back functionality of the library. The way this is performed usually depends on the library; in the case of the Google Search, you need to call the `setOnKeepCallback()` method. Google define this method as follows:

"For instance, if this method is called as `.setOnKeepCallback(foo, MyObject.prototype.myKeephandler)`, when a user clicks on the keep label, a call to `foo.myKeephandler()` is called."

This isn't so easy for you to implement in GWT! However, you can use the trick that you employed when creating an API again and implement the callback as shown in listing 8.19.

Listing 8.19 Implementing the feedback

```
public native void setOnKeepCallback(GSearchControl searchControl,
                                     KeepListener theListener) /*-{
   $wnd.__callbackMethod = function(){                    <-- 1 Add callback method
      theListener.@org.gwtbook.KeepListener::onKeep()();
```

```
    }
    searchControl.setOnKeepCallback(null,                    ❷ Set up callback method
                                                               in JavaScript library
                                  $wnd.__callbackMethod,
                                  $wnd.GSearchControl.KEEP_LABEL_KEEP);
}-*/;
```

At ❶, you register a new JavaScript method that calls the `onKeep()` method of the listener passed in as the parameter. To tie this together, you then register the new method with the search control ❷ to be the method called if the user clicks the Keep label after a search result.

The final step in completing the generation of the Google Search widget is to create the widget.

8.5.4 Using a complex wrapped widget in an application

When used in the Dashboard application, you add the widget as a single component in a `DashboardComposite`, resulting in the application shown in figure 8.18 (where we searched for one of the best contributions Finland has given the world for a cold winter's night—the sauna).

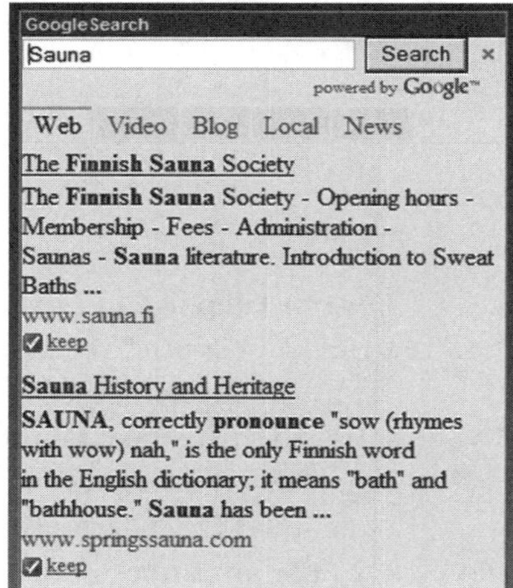

Figure 8.18 The Google Search application in full

Creating a widget from a third-party JavaScript library means that you must adhere to any rules the underlying JavaScript library may place on you. In the case of the Google Search Library, tasks must be performed in a specific order, as provided in the documentation:

1. Create the search control.
2. Add the searchers.
3. Create any options.
4. Draw the control.

Listing 8.20 shows how you achieve this to create the widget shown in figure 8.18.

Listing 8.20 Creating a complicated Google Search application using only a few lines of Java code

```
searchWidget = new GSearchWidget();                              ❶ Create Widget Instance
GSearchControl sc = searchWidget.getGSearch();                   ❷ Get search control reference
webSearch = GwebSearch.create();
webSearch.setSiteRestriction("www.manning.com");                 ❸ Create and add web searcher
sc.addSearcher(webSearch);
videoSearch = GvideoSearch.create();
sc.addSearcher(videoSearch);
newsSearch = GnewsSearch.create();                               ❹ Create and add other searchers
sc.addSearcher(newsSearch);
blogSearch = GblogSearch.create();
sc.addSearcher(blogSearch);
localSearch = GlocalSearch.create();
sc.addSearcher(localSearch);                                     ❺ Create and set drawing options
GdrawOptions options = new GdrawOptions();
options.setDrawMode(GSearchControl.DRAW_MODE_TABBED);            ❻ Draw search control
searchWidget.draw(options);
```

First, you create a new instance of the search widget ❶. Then, you use the `getGSearch()` method on the widget to create the JavaScript instance from the library ❷. Next, you add a few searchers to the widget: a web searcher ❸, along with video, news, blog, and local searchers ❹. With the searchers added according to the Google Ajax Search specification, you create a new set of drawing options to tell the widget it should draw itself in tabbed mode ❺. Finally, you draw the search control in ❻.

8.6 Summary

JSNI is an extremely powerful way of interfacing with existing JavaScript libraries and filling in the gaps where GWT may not yet have the functionality you need. It allows you to apply some of the good control and typing aspects of Java to the JavaScript interfaces; however, you should keep your use of JavaScript to a minimum. View using JSNI as you would writing assembly-language code segments in a high-level language project—it's for specialized tasks, not for everyday use. The main reason for restricting the use of JavaScript is cross-browser issues, just as assembly-language coding restricts your ability to move projects to other machines.

If you're going to use JSNI, remember that it's valid only in your client-side components, and you'll need to use the `$wnd` and `$doc` variables instead of the standard JavaScript `window` and `document` variables because of the way GWT loads your application. Also remember that when you're executing JavaScript code, you don't have the protection of GWT when it comes to browser differences (for example, the JavaScript `getElementById()` method isn't as robust as the GWT's cross-browser `DOM.getElementByID()` method). Finally, GWT and JSNI don't allow you to get around any normal restrictions of JavaScript coding; for example, you still can't subvert the security mechanisms that browsers employ.

We've reached the end of our journey through the more client-side related aspects of GWT, and it's time to consider the flexibility that GWT provides when building a real-sized application—using GWT's modularization aspects.

9 Modularizing an application

This chapter covers

- Configuring GWT modules
- Including external modules
- Injecting CSS and JavaScript
- Packaging modules as JAR files

Now that you've built all the user interface components, it's time to start looking at how you modularize the application. A principle of software design, which has now been with us since the 1960s, is the ability to develop code in a modular fashion in order to increase reuse and reliability. GWT supports modular development in two ways. First, because you're building a Java application, you have access to all the benefits of Java's package structure. Second, and this is new to GWT, is the XML module concept. There is a certain amount of synergy between GWT modules and Java packages, but they aren't the same. Just because a Java package appears on your classpath doesn't mean it's automatically visible by the GWT compiler. Don't worry; we'll explain this and the steps you need to take in this chapter, but this topic is often a source of confusion.

DEFINITION A *module* is a logical collection of classes and resource definitions that it makes sense to manage as its own entity.

So far, you've probably been thinking of the Dashboard application as a single chunk of software, which isn't incorrect; but it's also true that an application can be constructed out of a number of modules, each module defined in a module XML file where you also define a number of resource-related items. The Dashboard lends itself naturally to modularization because it has a main application and a number of component applications.

9.1 Creating a modularization structure

We mentioned previously that there is a synergy between GWT modules and Java's package structure. They're similar but different things. A *Java package* consists of a set of classes organized together for convenience into the same directory. A *GWT module* consists of a set of configuration information, relating to a particular GWT project—including entry points (if any), style sheet references, other modules this module depends on, and so on. We'll discuss all this in more detail in section 9.3 when we show how the Dashboard is modularized.

One word of caution: It isn't unusual to see a set of Java packages relating to a particular project and, therefore, a GWT module—it's possible to get confused that a GWT module equals a set of Java packages, when it doesn't. Also be aware that just because you reference a module doesn't mean the Java packages loosely associated with that module are available to your code; you still need to add them to your classpaths (and that means to both the hosted- and web-mode tools' classpaths (and with Eclipse, also the .launch configuration)). Failure to do this will result in your Java compiler (or IDE) informing you it has no idea where to find the necessary code—and this can be a frustrating error if you forget that GWT modules and Java packages aren't the same thing!

9.1.1 Modularization in GWT

Is modularization used in practice? Yes; the GWT distribution is made up of a number of modules, including the DOM, TextBox, History, JUnit, i18n, JSON, and so on. You can see these modules in their hierarchy in figure 9.1.

If you were to look at the module XML file for i18n, you would see that it defines the default `locale` property, provides the JavaScript code for determining which web browser is being used, and also identifies a special Java class called a *generator* that should be executed on all the i18n interfaces in your application to produce Java classes that bind the interface to the various property files. Modules can be powerful.

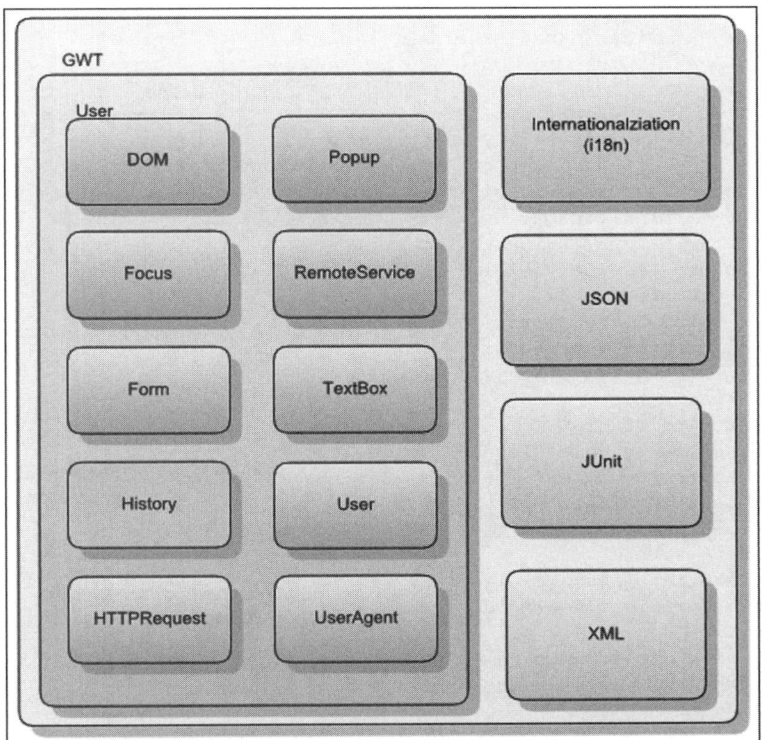

Figure 9.1 Hierarchy of GWT 1.3 modules supplied with the standard installation of GWT

In this section, we'll look at two things. First, we'll examine all the elements that can be included inside a module's XML module, which can resemble the comprehensive version shown in listing 9.1. It's a busy listing, because it includes all the aspects, but we'll go into more detail in the remainder of this section.

Listing 9.1 Comprehensive module XML file demonstrating the tags that are available

```
<module>
   <inherits name="com.google.gwt.user.User"/>
   <inherits name="org.mycompany.client.Sliders"/>
   <inherits name='org.gwtwidgets.WidgetLibrary'/>
   <public path="GenericPublic"/>
   <servlet path='/upload'
            class='org.mycompany.server.FileUploadServlet'/>
   <define-property name="externalvisible"
                    values="internet,intranet" />
   <property-provider name="externalvisible">
      <![CDATA[
         try{
            var externalvisibility;
            externalvisibility =
                parent.__gwt_getMetaProperty("externalvisibility");
            if (externalvisibility == null){
            externalvisibility = "intranet";
         }
         return externalvisibility;
         } catch(e){
            $wnd.alert("Error: "+e);
            return "intranet";
         }
      ]]>
   </property-provider>
   <extend-property name="locale" values="sv"/>
   <extend-property name="locale" values="en_UK"/>
   <generate-with class="MyStubGenerator">
      <when-type-assignable class="MyGenTagInterface"/>
   </generate-with>
   <replace-with class="NewClassName">
      <when-type-is class="OldClassName"/>
      <any>
         <when-property-is name="user.agent" value="ie6"/>
         <when-property-is name="user.agent" value="Opera"/>
      </any>
   </replace-with>
  <script src="InjectedScript.js">
      <![CDATA[
         if ($wnd.bar)
            return true;
         else
```

Annotations: Inherit core GWT functionality; Inherit module you defined; Inherit third-party module; Set path to public folder; Define interface-to-server resource; Define property values; Define property provider; Extend property; Register GWT generator; Define browser-specific replacements; Inject JavaScript library

```
            return false;
        ]]>
    </script>
    <stylesheet src="InjectedCSS.css">                    Inject JavaScript library
    <entry-point class="org.mycompany.client.MyApp"/>     Set entry point
</module>
```

The second thing we'll look at in this section involves defining how you'll break the application into modules and provide the definitive module structure for the Dashboard. Let's get started with looking at the various parts that may be included in a module XML file by examining how you include other modules in an application.

9.1.2 Including other modules in an application

In this section, we'll discuss how you indicate that a module will include other modules. All GWT modules inherit at least one other GWT module, called the `User` module. This is performed by writing the following in the module's XML module file:

```
<module>
    <inherits name="com.google.gwt.user.User"/>
</module>
```

If you look at the definition of the User module, you see that it directs the compiler to include the majority of the GWT system. How do you know that? You can look at the User.gwt.xml file included in the `com.google.gwt.user` package (see gwt.user.jar). In that module definition is the following:

```
<module>
    <inherits name="com.google.gwt.core.Core"/>
    <inherits name="com.google.gwt.user.RemoteService"/>
    <inherits name="com.google.gwt.user.DOM"/>
    <inherits name="com.google.gwt.user.HTTPRequest"/>
    <inherits name="com.google.gwt.user.History"/>
    <inherits name="com.google.gwt.user.Popup"/>
    <inherits name="com.google.gwt.user.Form"/>
    <inherits name="com.google.gwt.user.TextBox"/>
    <inherits name="com.google.gwt.user.Focus"/>
    <inherits name="com.google.gwt.user.ImageBundle"/>
    <inherits name="com.google.gwt.user.ClippedImage"/>
    <inherits name="com.google.gwt.user.SplitPanel"/>
</module>
```

The `inherits` tag indicates that the module should inherit all the contents from the specified module. As you can see, you can have multiple `inherits` tags in a module definition; in this case, you link to all the basic functionality of GWT.

(Notice that XML, JSON processing, and internationalization aren't included by default. Also, despite `HTTPRequest` appearing in the previous list, this is an internal GWT module; if you wish to use, for example, GWT's `XMLHTTPRequest` or `RequestBuilder` object, you need to add additional inherits, which we discuss later.)

Most modules inherit the User module (User.gwt.xml), because it contains the "inherits" for the majority of GWT functionality. Thus it would be expected to find as a minimum the following entry in your module file:

```
<inherits name='com.google.gwt.user.User'/>
```

If you're planning to use some of the extended functionality provided with GWT, such as the ability to handle JSON responses, internationalization, or the Ajax style interaction, then you need to include the appropriate `inherits` tags in your module XML file. Following are the four tags that represent what we just mentioned:

```
<inherits name="com.google.gwt.xml.XML"/>
<inherits name="com.google.gwt.json.JSON"/>
<inherits name="com.google.gwt.i18n.I18N"/>
<inherits name="com.google.gwt.i18n.HTTP"/>
```

Ajax calls can be slightly confusing. You saw earlier that the GWT User module inherits `HTTPRequest`. However, this module definition just helps GWT decide which class it needs to use for the GWT RPC approach. If you wish to use traditional Ajax approaches, then you need to explicitly inherit the `com.google.gwt.i18n.HTTP` module.

TIP Basic applications just need to inherit the `com.google.gwt.user.User` module. It can be easy to forget that if you use i18n, XML, JSON, or `HTTPRequest` methods, such as `RequestBuilder`, then you need to explicitly inherit the appropriate GWT modules.

Note that GWT modules shouldn't be confused with the Java classpath—the two are complementary but not dependent upon each other. The classpath is used by the Java compiler and hosted mode to find code that is required. The module XML file explains to the GWT compiler what GWT modules it needs to find and use in the application. Remember that the module file can contain many different aspects of the application, not just more includes!

As well as inheriting aspects of the standard distribution, you can inherit your own, or third-party, components in exactly the same way. If you do so, then you must take care to set the qualified name of the module correctly. For example, using the GWT Widget Library, which we discuss near the end of this chapter, requires the following `inherits` tag:

```
<inherits name='org.gwtwidgets.WidgetLibrary'/>
```

And it's at this point where confusion may begin between setting Java classpaths and inheriting modules. By inheriting a module, you're telling the compiler certain things about a module, but you aren't saying where the actual code is—you do that by setting the classpath to include the code location. (This classpath needs to be set both in the web- and hosted-mode commands. For the Dashboard, you need to set it in `Dashboard-shell` and `Dashboard-compile`. If you're using an IDE, then you may need to set the classpath in that too—for example, adding the code as an external JAR in Eclipse as well as setting the path to the code in the launch configuration. Other IDEs have similar needs.)

For the Dashboard, you'll create the module structure shown in figure 9.2. This contains one module for the main Dashboard application, which inherits the modules for each of the individual component applications.

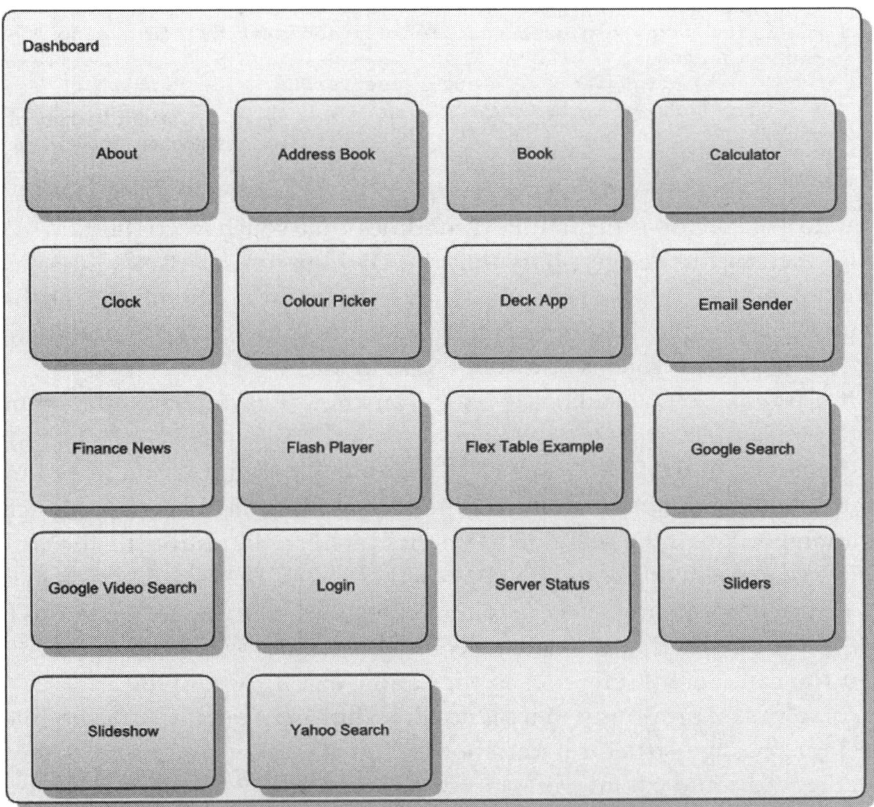

Figure 9.2 The module structure that will be used in developing the complete Dashboard application. The component application modules will all be inherited by the main Dashboard module.

The benefit of creating a structure like this is that you can treat each component application in isolation, allowing it to have, for example, its own style sheet and resources. If these applications need to change in the future, you've isolated those changes to just that component. The Dashboard application's module XML file is shown in listing 9.2.

Listing 9.2 The initial definition of the Dashboard module XML file

```
<module>
   <inherits name='com.google.gwt.user.User'/>
   <inherits name="com.google.gwt.i18n.I18N"/>
   <inherits name="com.google.gwt.i18n.HTTP"/>
   <inherits name="com.google.gwt.i18n.XML"/>

   <inherits name="org.gwtbook.client.ui.about.About"/>
   <inherits name="org.gwtbook.client.ui.calculator.Calculator"/>
   <inherits name="org.gwtbook.client.ui.addressBook.AddressBook"/>
   <inherits name=
             "org.gwtbook.client.ui.serverStatus.ServerStatus"/>
   : [Add others as necessary]
</module>
```

Inherit core GWT functionality

Inherit other GWT functionality

Inherit Dashboard component applications

Why do you include the standard modules that you have (i18n and XML)? We mentioned in the design phase that the Dashboard uses GWT's internationalization capabilities, so you need to include that module. Similarly, the Bookmark menu bar is populated by retrieving an XML file from the server and then processing its contents, so you also need the XML module.

If you've peeked ahead in the book, you know that you have other components that, for example, process JSON data. You may expect to see GWT's JSON functionality included in the Dashboard's XML module file. But you don't need to include it here, because you can include it in the XML module file that relates directly to that component. This is the reusability benefit in action—by putting the JSON reference in the component application, as opposed to at the Dashboard level, you can easily reuse the component elsewhere, safe in the knowledge that all it needs is kept with it. If you've already downloaded the code from http://www.manning.com/hanson, then you can see this reference in the YahooSearch.gwt.xml file.

As we've said previously, there is no direct link between the GWT module file and the Java package structure you choose, but it's often pragmatic to tie the two together. To some extent, you can see this in listing 9.2, where each component application's module definition is in a new Java package reference. It makes sense to place the Java code for each application in the same named package. For example, the XML module file for the Calculator component application is stored as Calculator.gwt.xml in the package/directory `org.gwtbook.client.ui.calculator` (according to the module definition shown in listing 9.2)—you'll also store the necessary Java code in the same package.

With the basic module inheritance out of the way, it's time to look at the other configuration aspects that can be stored in a module definition, starting with setting source and other resource paths.

9.1.3 Setting source and other resource paths

By default, the GWT compiler uses the client directory relative to the module file to look for the source files of your GWT application/module. For example, if your module file's fully qualified name is org.mycompany.MyApp.gwt.xml, then it will be stored in the org/mycompany directory, and the compiler will assume that the source code is in the org/mycompany/**client** directory. If you've used the GWT applicationCreator tool, then this structure is automatically set up for you.

Sometimes you may decide that this location isn't best. In that case, you can set the source path to a different location. Placing the following entry into your module XML alters the default path on which code is searched for:

```
<source path="path-to-code"/>
```

`path-to-code` must be a package name, and any classes found in that package or subpackages must follow the same rules as other classes that are to be translated by the compiler into JavaScript (typically, the source code must be available and, at present, that it must conform to Java 1.4 syntax). If this entry isn't included, the value `<source path="client"/>` is assumed.

Similarly, the compilation process assumes that any files in the public subpackage relative to the module XML file are publicly accessible resources and so will be copied into the compilation output as is (in the Dashboard, the public folder is used to store all of the trash icon images, for example). To alter this value, you can use the following tag:

```
<public path="path"/>
```

The path must again be a package name, but there are no restrictions on the content of that package or any subpackages because those contents are copied to the output folder by the compilation process.

It's possible to filter the files that will be copied from the development structure to the run structure as public resources using pattern-based filtering. This places fine-grained control over which resources get copied to the output directory; the control is based on the FileSet notion from Apache Ant implementation. Not all aspects of the Ant FileSet are supported; table 9.1 identifies those attributes and tags that are.

Table 9.1 Attributes and tags used in pattern-based filtering of GWT public resources

Attributes	Tags
includes	include
excludes	exclude
defaultexcludes	
casesensitive	

By default, the `defaultexcludes` attribute of the `public` tag is set to `true` and excludes a comprehensive set of file patterns: for example, **/*~ , **/.#*, **/CVS, and **/vssver.scc (it excludes by default, for example, any files in the CVS folder and the vssver.scc file—files that are associated with versioning control software). To enable any of these patterns, set the attribute to `false`:

```
<public path="public" defaultexcludes="false"/>
```

To explicitly include or exclude files, you can specify them using the `includes` or `excludes` element, placed in the definition of the `public` tag. As an example, to exclude a file called do_not_include_this.js, you write the following:

```
<public path="public" defaultexcludes="true">
   <exclude name="do_not_include_this.js"/>
</public>
```

As with the code path, if no entry for the `public` tag is provided, then it's assumed that it defaults to `<public path="public"/>`.

Another path-related aspect that is definable in the module XML file is the path of servlets, or server resources used in hosted mode execution.

9.1.4 Defining an application's server resources

When running in hosted mode, you need to be able to deploy any GWT remote procedure call (RPC) code you have as servlets into the hosted-mode web server. The first step toward doing this is to register the servlet path and class in the module XML file using the `servlet` tag. You'll do this for a few of the applications given in chapters 10 through 13. Let's take one of those as an example now (remember, you'll add what you see next into the appropriate component application's module file and not the Dashboard's).

For the Server Status component application, you'll require the application to talk to a servlet that will return status details for the server. In the Java code, you'll refer to this servelt as having a path of /server-status. In the Server Status application's module file, you'll bind that path to the actual Java class that provides the functionality using the `<servlet>` tag. In this examples case, the Java class that provides the functionality is called `ServerStatusImpl` and is found in the `org.gwtbook.server` package. To use this servlet in the code, you define a servlet entry in the module XML file as follows:

```
<servlet path="/server-status"
      class="org.gwtbook.server.ServerStatusImpl"/>
```

You'll see later in chapter 10 that your application will use this path in the code when it sets the entry point for the service, using the `setServiceEntryPoint(String)` method. For hosted mode, this is all you need to do to get the client-side code talking to the server code, because hosted mode deploys the server code for you into the internal web server. You'll see in chapter 16 that this isn't the final step required to set up servlets if you're deploying outside of hosted mode (in that case, you need to create a web.xml file for use on the servlet server).

TIP The `<servlet>` tag is relevant only for hosted mode. When your application transitions to web mode, you need to set up your web.xml file appropriately for the server resources you're using (we'll cover this in chapter 16).

Now, we'll move on to look at a few tags that start driving the number of permutations of JavaScript the compiler will be required to produce: the tags associated with properties.

9.1.5 Managing an application's GWT properties

We'll discuss properties in detail in chapter 15; but because they're set and manipulated in the module XML file, we need to talk about them here, too. The clearest impact of involving and managing properties for a GWT application that you've seen to this point in the book is that they drive the number of JavaScript permutations that are produced. The most obvious example where you can see properties used in GWT is in the generation of a separate piece of JavaScript code per browser that is supported. You may not have noticed this yet, because the processing happens in the background and requires no interaction by you. You don't even touch the properties involved in these decisions regarding browser choice.

You were a little more hands-on with properties when we looked at internationalization. Earlier in this book, you extended the `locale` property to include the Swedish locale. Adding locales to be managed tells the GWT compiler that it needs to include additional permutations for those new locales. Even if you've included properties files for all of the new locales, if you forget to extend the property in the XML file, then they won't be used.

Note that GWT properties aren't directly accessible to your application; they're used to drive permutations. This means you can't write code in your application to get, for example, the current locale. GWT is deliberately set up to resolve all the permutations of properties at compile time to reduce the size of delivered JavaScript code. If you desperately need to understand what locale your user interface is currently presented in, then you can hijack the i18n approach by including a specific key to describe the locale. Under this approach, you could have a key called `currlocale` and in the English local properties file you would write `currlocale = en`; the Swedish local properties file would have `currlocale = en`. GWT's i18n approach would provide a method `getCurLocale()` that returns the defined value for the current locale property.

In this section, we'll look at the following:

- Defining and extending properties
- Handling properties

On to the first item on the list: defining properties.

Defining and extending properties

Properties are defined using the simple `define-property` tag.

```
<define-property name="name" values="val1,val2,..."/>
```

For example, the user agent property that defines the browsers for which GWT can create JavaScript is given as follows:

```
<define-property name="user.agent"
                 values="ie6,gecko,gecko1_8,safari,opera"/>
```

You can see this in the UserAgent module XML in the `com.google.gwt.user` package. Similarly, the i18n module XML defines one value for locale as follows:

```
<define-property name="locale" values="default" />
```

If you want to define your own properties, you use the `define-property` tag to set the property name and optionally a set of initial values. You do so as follows:

```
<define-property name="client-property-name"
                 values="comma-separated-values"/>
```

In chapter 15, we'll introduce our own user-defined property using this approach to determine whether the user is looking at the Dashboard from the Internet or an intranet.

You also saw in chapter 3, where we introduced internationalization, that you can add new values to the already-defined `locales` property. You do so using the `extend-property` tag. For example, adding the ISO language code for Swedish was performed with the following tag:

```
<extend-property name="locale" values="sv"/>
```

You use the extension idea when you inherit a set of properties from an existing module and you want to add new values. In general, you can extend already-defined properties using the `<extend-property>` tag, as follows:

```
<extend-property name="client-property-name"
                 values="comma-separated-values"/>
```

If you're wondering where these values appear in your code after compilation, for the Dashboard application you should look at the org.gwtbook.Dashboard.nocache.js file in the compiled output. It contains automatically generated JavaScript representing values for the user agent property, similar to the following:

```
values['user.agent'] = {
   'gecko':0,
   'gecko1_8':1,
   'ie6':2,
   'opera':3,
   'safari':4
};
```

Similar JavaScript is set up for the locales. In this case, you have the default locale that comes with the i18n module you've inherited and, in addition, the Swedish locale property that the Dashboard XML module has extended:

```
values['locale'] = {
   'default':0,
   'sv':1
};
```

For the Dashboard, you'll define new properties in chapter 15 that allow you to restrict the component applications that are available based on whether the application is being accessed from an intranet or the Internet. In your applications, if you define new properties, then GWT takes care of producing the additional JavaScript to representing the values. However, you still need to define how you determine which property is the one selected—in other words, how to handle the properties.

Handling properties and managing differences

Once properties are provided, you need to provide a mechanism to select one value over another. The compilation process produces a number of permutations of JavaScript, covering all the possible property-value permutations; subsequently, the application-loading mechanism selects the appropriate one.

The simplest way to determine the appropriate property value is to define it directly in the application's HTML file (similar to how the `locale` property is set). You can alternatively provide code that allows the application's loading mechanism to determine the correct property (which is how the browser selection works). Each approach needs some JavaScript code to be provided in a `<property-provider>` tag in the module file. For the GWT standard properties, i18n and user.agent, GWT provides the code, for your own user properties, you will have to do this.

The generic pattern for providing such code is

```
<property-provider name="property-name">
<![CDATA[
   Some JavaScript code that returns values of the
   property based on some defined criteria
]]>
</property-provider>
```

Let's look at the relatively simple JavaScript code shown in listing 9.3. This is the code used by GWT to determine the user agent property (which browser the application is about to be executed in).

Listing 9.3 GWT-provided JavaScript code that determines the browser into which the application is being loaded

```
var ua = navigator.userAgent.toLowerCase();
if (ua.indexOf("opera") != -1) {
   return "opera";
}
else if (ua.indexOf("safari") != -1) {
   return "safari";
}
else if ((ua.indexOf("msie 6.0") != -1) ||
          (ua.indexOf("msie 7.0") != -1)) {
   return "ie6";
}
else if (ua.indexOf("gecko") != -1) {
```

```
    var result = /rv:([0-9]+)\.([0-9]+)/.exec(ua);
    if (result && result.length == 3) {
       var version = (parseInt(result[1]) * 10) +
                     parseInt(result[2]);
       if (version >= 18)
          return "gecko1_8";
    }
    return "gecko";
 }
 return "unknown";
```

This code is wrapped in the property-provider tag in the UserAgent module XML. After compilation of the Dashboard application, the org.gwtbook.Dashboard.nocache.js file includes this code wrapped as a function in the window array:

```
providers['user.agent'] = function(){
   var ua = navigator.userAgent.toLowerCase();
   if (ua.indexOf('opera') != -1) {
      return 'opera';
   }
   // rest of the code
}
```

If other properties are present, then a similar process occurs of creating JavaScript object for their values and copying the property-provider code into the window array.

It's left to GWT's bootstrapping process to determine which permutation of application JavaScript code needs to be selected (for the browser, `locale`, and `externalvisibility` properties in the Dashboard's case). This method uses a number of helper functions to extract the correct JavaScript permutation. Here's simple extraction from one of the helper methods:

```
unflattedKeylistIntoAnswers(["true","default","opera"],
                            "A0AB2AB8620D2637C30C022EB05A60C3");
unflattedKeylistIntoAnswers (["true","sv","opera"],
                            "AC776AB13824B447160C27D2A18B383F");
```

Ignoring the first parameter, both these entries match the user agent being "opera". The first entry matches the locale being the default locale, and the second to the locale being set to `sv` (for Sweden). The final parameter refers to the MD5 file name that the compiler has given this particular JavaScript permutation and is the one that will be loaded. (If you look in your compiled application output, you'll see a number of these types of named files—one for each permutation. The more different families of properties you want your application to manage, the more permutations there will be; by default, there are five, representing each of the browser types that GWT supports.)

In chapter 15, you'll write some JavaScript code that determines the user's visibility (intranet or Internet) of the application. That code will check the metatags of the HTML file and is used to restrict the number of component Dashboard applications the user can access.

That is how property files drive the generation of numerous permutations of JavaScript code and how the link is made for loading the correct permutation. In addition to permutations being driven by properties, their generation can also be driven by the need to replace class files, which is also property based.

9.1.6 Replacing classes based on property values

One GWT technique that we haven't explored fully yet is the replacement of Java files with others based on the value of a property. You used this functionality already, when creating the `PNGImage` widget, and GWT uses it a bit to select appropriate browser-specific behavior, such as the DOM manipulation class. But because that happens in the compiler, you've probably been unaware of it.

The technique isn't restricted to the user agent property (browser type). You'll use it again in chapter 15 to see how complete application components can be altered based on the locale property.

The most common place that class replacement occurs relates to the different ways browsers deal with the DOM. GWT copes with these differences by providing a simple DOM class you use in the Java code; this class is implemented by a number of increasingly specific classes that inherit the original class, which provide browser specific methods. You can see this hierarchy in figure 9.3.

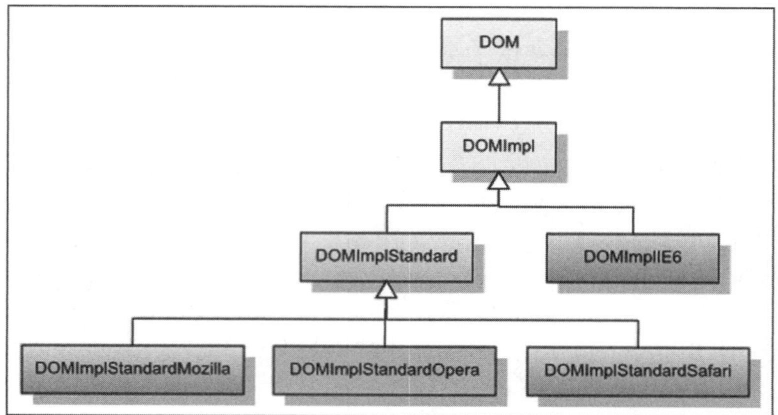

Figure 9.3 The various DOM implementation classes shown in their hierarchy. This allows GWT to cope with all the browser differences in DOM implementation.

When the code is compiled or executed in hosted mode, you need to be able to select the correct implementation for the browser. Luckily, GWT will do all this work for you in the background, as long as you tell it the rules in a module XML file. To tell GWT which class it should use for a particular property value, you use the `replace-with` tag inside the appropriate module XML file. The generic format is

```
<replace-with class="new-class-name">
   <when-type-is class="old-class-name"/>
   <when-property-is name="property-name" value="property-value"/>
</replace-with>
```

Let's look briefly at a concrete example of this from the DOM module XML. In this example, you replace the generic `DOMImpl` class with the `DOMImplOpera` class if the user agent property is set to the value "opera":

```
<replace-with class="com.google.gwt.user.client.impl.DOMImplOpera">
   <when-type-is class="com.google.gwt.user.client.impl.DOMImpl"/>
   <when-property-is name="user.agent" value="opera"/>
</replace-with>
```

Replacing classes is one mechanism that GWT uses to manipulate your basic code based on directions given in the module XML file (or one it inherits from). This functionality relies on the various classes existing in the first place. You can additionally create code on the fly using generators, the existence of which is also defined in the module XML file.

9.1.7 Registering generators in the XML module file

Generators are used to create new code based on the existence of an existing class or interface. This is used in the i18n approach, where GWT takes the interface you use in the Java code and the properties files you've defined and then at compile time produces a number of Java classes that implement the interface and bind method names to values in the properties file. They're also used in the ImageBundle approach, where a generator is used to combine a number of individual images that you specify into one image (reducing communication between client and server). Generators are powerful objects and are registered using the `generate-with` tag, whose generic format is as follows:

```
<generate-with class="generator-class-name">
   <when-type-assignable class="class-or-interface-name"/>
</generate-with>
```

Several examples of generators provided with GWT show how they're used to generate i18n Java classes from the interfaces and properties files you provide. In chapter 14, you'll build your own generator that takes the `DashboardComposite` Dashboard applications and extends them by adding a default About menu item as well as a This Application Demonstrates menu item in the option menu bar. This is done by a class you'll write called `DashboardCompositeGenerator`, which is executed for every instance of the `DashboardComposite` class the compiler finds. The compiler knows to do this because you place the following entry in the Dashboard module XML file:

```
<generate-with
    class="org.gwtbook.rebind.DashboardCompositeGenerator">
    <when-type-assignable
          class="org.gwtbook.client.DashboardComposite"/>
</generate-with>
```

In the `DashboardComposite` generator, you perform introspection on the Java class; we show this by creating an About dialog box that lists the internal methods and fields of the class under scrutiny. It's important to note that this introspection happens at compile time and is therefore no use to you if you're looking for a way to perform introspection at runtime (something that currently isn't possible in GWT).

We're nearly there; two more entries in the module XML to go. The first of these is the ability to inject resources (JavaScript library or a Cascading Style Sheet) into an application.

9.1.8 Injecting resources into an application at runtime

GWT provides the ability to inject into applications JavaScript and CSS resources at runtime (as opposed to defining them in the applications HTML file). You may want to do this, for example, if you're embedding a GWT application into an existing web page and you want to keep the application's CSS separate from the web page HTML. We'll look at both types of injection in turn: first, injecting JavaScript resources into applications; and second, injecting style-sheet resources into applications at runtime.

Both types of injection again demonstrate the power of GWT's modularization approach. In the Dashboard, you inject a CSS style file for the Dashboard in the Dashboards module file. Each component application is then made responsible for injecting any CSS or JavaScript code it requires. This way, if you reuse a component application in another application, it comes already bundled with the necessary references to make it work.

Injecting JavaScript and CSS is a useful technique in supporting reusability of the code. We'll examine this now, starting with injecting JavaScript code.

Injecting JavaScript resources into an application

To automatically inject a previously written JavaScript library or code into the web page for use by the GWT application, you use the `script` tag. This is generically written as follows:

```
<script src="js-url">script ready-function body</script>
```

The `js-url` is the URL of the JavaScript file you want to be injected.

In GWT versions prior to 1.4, you're required to insert code within the `script` tag that returns `true` when you're sure the JavaScript code has loaded and `false` otherwise. From GWT 1.4 on, this code is no longer necessary, because the new bootstrapping processes ensures that your scripts have loaded prior to starting the module. But let's do a quick review, in case you haven't upgraded to GWT 1.4 or you come across some legacy code.

It's often enough just to check whether a particular function exists in the browser's model in order to return the `true` value. However, when you're injecting the JavaScript, it's evaluated such that any JavaScript code required to be executed is. Consider this simple JavaScript segment that you may want to inject, which includes two functions and some executable script:

```
function fn1() {
  // some functionality
}

doSomething();

function fn2() {
  // something other functionality
}
```

When you inject this code, the `doSomething()` function may take some time to execute, so it's wise to check for the availability of the `fn2` function. For example:

```
<script src="InjectedScript.js">
   <![CDATA[
      if ($wnd.fn2)
         return true;
      else
         return false;
   ]]>
</script>
```

Once the injected JavaScript is loaded into the page, it's safely available for access through GWT's JavaScript Native Interface (JSNI). It's also possible to load JavaScript this way and not check whether objects exist—but if you want to do that, you still need to provide code that returns the value `true`; otherwise, GWT will wait forever. You did this in the Google Video Search Application you built in chapter 8. In this case, the injection command looks like this:

```
<script
  src="http://www.google.com/uds/solutions/videobar/gsvideobar.js">
   <![CDATA[
      return true;
   ]]>
</script>
```

As we mentioned earlier, beginning in GWT 1.4, the requirement for this code disappears. The second type of injection is the injection of style sheets.

Injecting style sheets into an application

Although you can add style sheets to your application by adding the appropriate links into the application's HTML page, there may be occasions where an application sits in existing pages that you don't want to affect. For the Dashboard application, you want to keep style sheets for the component applications together with the application. Rather than having to put a link to all the style sheets in the Dashboard.html file, you can use each application's module XML file to inject the appropriate style sheet as needed. This is performed by the `<stylesheet>` tag:

```
<stylesheet src="css-url"/>
```

`css-url` is the URL to the CSS file you want to inject. You can indicate a number of CSS files to be injected into the application. (GWT sometimes gets hung up in hosted mode when there is more than one style sheet to inject. This is nothing to worry about, because clicking the hosted browser screen gives GWT the kick it needs to continue, and this doesn't happen in web mode.) Figure 9.4 shows the Dashboard when we haven't bothered to inject any styles via the module XML files except the Slideshow application.

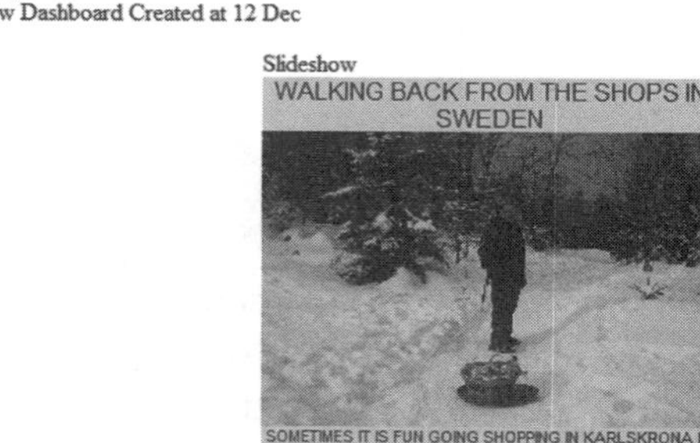

Figure 9.4
Dashboard application where styles have only been injected for the Slideshow component application. (The figure also shows the unstyled Calculator and Clock applications in an unstyled Dashboard.)

The order in which those files are injected is the order in which they're listed in the module XML. If you include the same name-style rule in several style sheets, only the last used one is used. You use this ordering in the Google Video Search Dashboard application where you load a style sheet provided by Google, and then you want to alter some of those aspects, such as the video size. The GoogleVideo-Search.gwt.xml file contains the following two entries in this exact order to achieve this:

```
<stylesheet src=
     "http://www.google.com/uds/solutions/videobar/gsvideobar.css"/>
<stylesheet src="CSS/GoogleVideoSearch.css"/>
```

We've now looked at all but one of the aspects that can be placed in a module XML file. You've seen how to inject code and style sheets, how to tell the compiler to replace code with generators or property-specific classes, and how to inherit other modules. Now, we'll look at the tag that turns a simple module into an application.

9.1.9 Setting an application's entry point

If the module XML relates to a GWT application, then you need to place an `entry-point` tag in its associated module XML file. The value of this tag is used by the compilation process to identify what code needs to be executed upon loading the application.

The generic template for the `entry-point` tag is

```
<entry-point class="org.mycompany.client.MyApp"/>
```

This section is short and sweet, because there isn't much to say about the entry point apart from the fact that the class mentioned must extend the `EntryPoint` class. Only the main application needs an entry point, so this tag is in the Dashboard's module XML:

```
<entry-point class='org.gwtbook.client.Dashboard'/>
```

But there are no corresponding entries in the component applications, because they aren't entry points to the Dashboard application.

Now we've listed all the theoretical aspects that could be included in module XML file. Let's look at this in practice by considering a version of the module XML file for the Dashboard application.

9.1.10 The Dashboard's module XML file

If you look at Dashboard's module XML file, you'll see that it uses almost all the techniques we've discussed:

```
<module>
   <inherits name='com.google.gwt.user.User'/>
   <inherits name="com.google.gwt.i18n.I18N"/>          ❶
   <inherits name='com.google.gwt.xml.XML'/>

   <inherits name='org.gwtwidgets.WidgetLibrary'/>      ❷

   <inherits name="org.gwtbook.client.ui.calculator.Calculator"/>
   <inherits name="org.gwtbook.client.ui.addressBook.AddressBook"/>
   <inherits name="org.gwtbook.client.ui.login.Login"/>
   <inherits  name=
      "org.gwtbook.client.ui.googlevideosearch.GoogleVideoSearch"/>
   <inherits name="org.gwtbook.client.ui.googlesearch.GoogleSearch"/>
   <inherits name="org.gwtbook.client.ui.slideshow.Slideshow"/>
   <inherits name="org.gwtbook.client.ui.DashboardUI"/>                ❸
   <inherits name=
      "org.gwtbook.client.ui.serverstatus.ServerStatus"/>
   <inherits name="org.gwtbook.client.ui.deckapp.DeckApp"/>
   <inherits name="org.gwtbook.client.ui.yahoosearch.YahooSearch"/>
   <inherits name=
      "org.gwtbook.client.ui.flextableexample.FlexTableExample"/>
   <stylesheet src="CSS/Dashboard.css"/>     ❹
   <entry-point class='org.gwtbook.client.Dashboard'/>     ❺
   <extend-property name="locale" values="sv"/>
   <extend-property name="locale" values="en_US"/>      ❻
   <define-property name="externalvisibility"
                    values="intranet,internet"/>        ❼
   <property-provider name="externalvisibility">
   <![CDATA[
      try{
         var externalvisibility =
                parent.__gwt_getMetaProperty("externalvisibility");
         if (externalvisibility==null){
            externalvisibility = "internet";
         }                                                              ❽
         return externalvisibility;
      } catch (e) {
         return "internet";
      }
   ]]>
   </property-provider>
   <generate-with
        class="org.gwtbook.rebind.DashboardCompositeGenerator">
      <when-type-assignable
         class="org.gwtbook.client.ui.DashboardComposite"/>      ❾
   </generate-with>
   <replace-with class="org.gwtbook.client.Dashboard_intranet">
      <when-type-is class="org.gwtbook.client.Dashboard"/>
      <when-property-is name="externalvisibility" value="intranet"/>   ❿
   </replace-with>
</module>
```

This module XML description covers that majority of the areas we have talked about so far. At ❶ you introduce the standard GWT functionality that you be using in the Dashboard—the standard user modules, as well as the XML handling and internationalization. If you've looked further forward in the book already, then you know that you'll be using GWT's JSON capability; but you don't list that here because the Dashboard doesn't use JSON; the module XML file for the appropriate component application is responsible for including that JSON functionality.

After including the necessary standard GWT functionality, you include the GWT Widget Library ❷ and all the component applications included in the Dashboard application ❸. You inject the Dashboard's style sheet ❹, but note that this style sheet includes only the main Dashboard-specific styling; styling for the component applications is delegated to the module XML files for each of those applications.

At ❺, you set the entry point for the Dashboard application. Then, you extend the locale property ❻ to include a Swedish locale and a locale for American English (see chapter 15). Not content with extending the `locale` property, you create a user-defined property (again, see chapter 15) at ❼ and provide some code in a property provider ❽ that determines the initial value of the user-defined property.

Finally, you define a generator (see chapter 14) that supports the Dashboard component applications ❾ and performs some introspection on the classes. You wrap the whole file with replacement functionality that makes the application use (see chapter 15) an intranet version instead of the default restricted Internet version ❿. (*Restricted* here is our definition and refers to the fact that the Internet version of the Dashboard offers fewer component applications than the intranet version.)

You saw in ❷ that you inherit the GWT Widget Library, which is a third-party set of modules and functionality authored by a number of people (found at http://gwt-widget.sourceforge.net/). Just including this line in the module XML file isn't enough to fully integrate a third-party library; you need to perform a couple of other steps, and we'll look at those next.

9.2 Including third-party modules

One of the real benefits of GWT's modularization approach is the ability to package together chunks of your application for reuse in other applications. By including the resource aspects in the XML module file, all the necessary information to use the components remains together, ready for reuse.

This bundling opens up the opportunity for you to reuse your code in your other projects, to offer your code for use by others, and use code provided by other people. A few examples of third-party packages are available for GWT—we, of course, are partial toward the GWT Widget Library (http://gwt-widget.sourceforge.net/), but there is also a project looking at combining the various efforts so far into a consistent gwt-commons library of third-party components (http://groups-beta.google.com/group/gwt-commons).

Using a third-party library in your code takes a few simple steps, shown in table 9.2. Forgetting any of them is likely to cause issues!

Table 9.2 Steps involved in using a third-party GWT library in an application

Step	Description
1	Download the third-party library.
2	Update the Java classpaths so the compiler (`application-compile` command) and shell (`application-shell` command) scripts can access the new Java code for the library. These classpaths must point to the source code of the library, because that is what the GWT compiler uses; just having class files won't work. If you're using an IDE, you may need to update any launch configurations that are also used. This is the case for Eclipse, where you need to right-click the project, select Run As, and then add the JAR file to the classpath as an external JAR.
3	Update the application's XML module file to inherit the new XML module definitions from the appropriate parts of the third-party library.

The first step is to download your library of choice—in the case of the GWT Widget Library that you'll use in the Dashboard, go to http://gwt-widget.sourceforge.net/ and retrieve the latest file. In the download is a gwt-widgets-*version*.jar file that you need to copy to your project—we normally place the library files in lib directory of the project; for the Dashboard, this is the DashboardDir/DashboardPrj/lib directory (you may need to create this directory before using it).

As with any library in Java, you need to add details of the third-party library to the classpath. For GWT, it's easiest to do this to the command line tools: `Dashboard-compile` and `Dashboard-shell`. After updating, for example, `Dashboard-shell` looks similar to this:

```
@java -cp "%~dp0\src;%~dp0\bin;
     C:/Program Files/gwt/gwt-user.jar;
     C:/Program Files/gwt/gwt-dev-windows.jar;
     C:/GWTApp/DashboardDir/DashboardPrj/lib/gwt-widgets-0.1.3.jar" #1
com.google.gwt.dev.GWTShell -out "%~dp0\www" %*
      org.gwtbook.Dashboard/Dashboard.html
```

1 Add third-party GWT JAR archive to classpath

where ❶ shows the additional entry for the GWT Widget Library.

In the code, you need to update the application's XML module file to indicate that you'll be using resources from another module in the code. For the Dashboard, you change the top of the Dashboard XML module file to show the following:

```
<inherits name="com.google.gwt.user.User"/>
<inherits name="com.google.gwt.i18n.I18N"/>
<inherits name="com.google.gwt.xml.XML"/>
<inherits name="org.gwtwidgets.WidgetLibrary"/>
```

Include third-party widget library XML module file in Dashboard's XML module

Now you can use components of the GWT Widget Library in the application. To add some spice to the Dashboard, you'll use the Scriptaculous (http://script.aculo.us/) wrapper included in the GWT Widget Library to hide the color picker in a flashy way. (Currently, no effects are included directly by GWT—but they're being worked on and may appear in a future version!) When the user clicks the color picker's close button, you'll hide it, but using the `switchoff` effect. This is easily achieved by using this code:

```
Effect.switchOff(colourPicker);
```

Here, you use the static `Effect` object, call the `switchOff()` method, and pass the instance of the GWT `ColourPicker` widget as a parameter. Before this works, though, you need to include the script.aculo.us JavaScript in the application; this is done in the Dashboard.html file (although as we discussed in chapter 8, it could be done by injecting the JavaScript through the module XML file).

By including the GWT Widget Library module this way, all the other functionality in the library is available to you. But sometimes you'll build your own functionality that will be useful either to other people or across various applications of yours. In that case, you'll be interested in packaging your own modules.

9.3 Packaging your own modules

When you're developing GWT applications, you're bound to come across a situation where you write some widgets or functionality that you end up thinking about using again in another application. The simple way to solve this is to copy across the necessary class files into your new application; but that isn't the best engineering practice, because you have to remember when you make changes in one copy to do so in the others (to maintain consistency).

It's far better to package your functionality as its own module and treat it the same way you would when importing a third-party module, as we just discussed. Luckily, this is easy to do and effectively just requires you to create a JAR file of the classes you require—but it does take some care, because you need to conform to the rules of GWT and ensure that your JAR file contains the source code (in a normal Java sense, your "libraries" would contain only the compiled classes).

For example, for one application we were building, we had to construct some chat functionality over the GTalk network. It initially started as functionality in another application, and then we decided it could be shared across other applications (to be honest, a little pre-thought/design would have identified this at the outset, and it could have been set up in such a way initially).

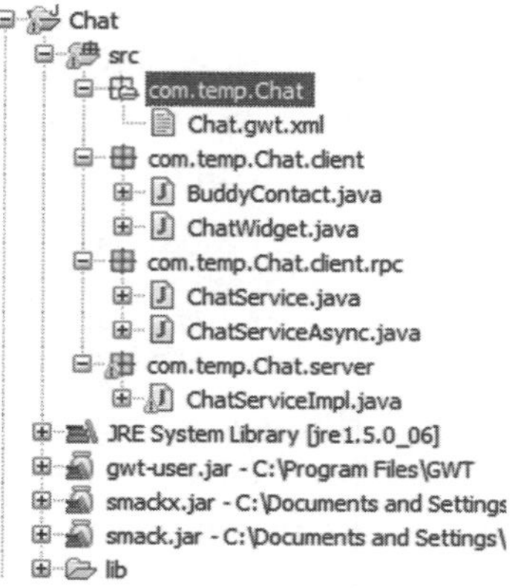

Figure 9.5 Structure for GWT code to package as your own module

To create your own package, you need to set up a mini GWT project that comprises at least a client package where your code goes (and perhaps server and RPC packages, if needed) as well as a module XML file that describes the module. The Chat module (which isn't included in the downloadable code for the book, due to size considerations) was set up with the structure shown in figure 9.5.

This looks like a standard GWT project, which it is; however, there is no need for any of the compilation or shell commands, HTML files, or entry points normally associated with a GWT application. The `smackx` and `smack` libraries in the figure are libraries used to support the Extensible Messaging and Presence Protocol (XMPP; Jabber) protocol for instant messaging. The module XML file is simple and is defined as importing the standard GWT user module. It follows the same rules defined earlier in this chapter. For example, if you wanted your code in a package other than client, then you'd need to add a `source` entry (see section 9.1.3):

```
<module>
   <inherits name="com.google.gwt.user.User" />
   <source path="path-to-code" />
</module>
```

Now that you have a standalone GWT module, the next step is to export it into a JAR file. You do this using whatever technique you're most familiar with—for us, using Eclipse, it's as simple as right-clicking the project and selecting the Export option. When you're creating the JAR file, it's vitally important that you include the Java source files as well as ensuring that you select the Add Directories option in the Options section of the export wizard. If you don't do so, then when you use the module in another application, GWT won't be able to locate the source code and will be unable to work (remember that the GWT compiler and shell mode both work on the Java source files).

With a JAR file produced that includes a module XML file, and the Java source files, using them in another application is as simple as following the steps given in the previous section.

But enough of GWT modules. We've said before that the module file structure and Java package are independent, but it's often convenient to link them together.

9.4 *Creating the Java package structure*

GWT binds your hands slightly in the choice of package names and structure. When you used the creation tools in chapter 2, you saw that the application's entry point code had to be in a package with the subpackage `client` as the last name. Thus the Dashboard.java file must be found in that package.

GWT applications are beginning to adhere to some other conventions (mainly as a result of the example code shipped with GWT). Any server-side code is generally placed in a sub-package called `server`; and if you're using GWT generators, their code is usually found in a subpackage called `rebind`. You can see all these packages in figure 9.6.

After the conventionally named packages, you're free to pick your own package names and structure. For the Dashboard, as you can see in figure 9.6, you'll create a subpackage called `ui`, under `client`, which contains a new subpackage for each component application; here, you can find each component application's module file. Additionally, the `ui` package contains all the new widgets, panels, and composite widgets you need to build for the application.

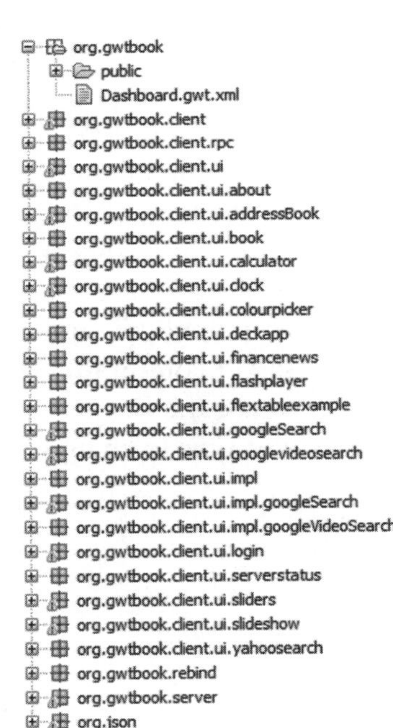

Figure 9.6 Java package structure used in the Dashboard example

9.5 Summary

This chapter concludes our demonstration of the basic client-side aspects of a real-life application—the Dashboard. We started in chapters 2 and 3 where you created the first version of the Dashboard application. It was limited in functionality but showed how you need to take the default GWT application and change a number of files to produce your own application. In chapters 4 through 6, we examined all the widgets, panels, and event handling that GWT provides by looking at how they're employed in the running Dashboard application or its components.

Chapter 9 discussed how you can lay the foundations for an application whose size is similar to one that may be found in the real world. You should now have a clear understanding of the notion of GWT XML module files and their relationship with Java package structuring. From this understanding, you've developed the module and package structure that you'll be using for the Dashboard. The code for the Dashboard, and all the component applications discussed in this book, can be downloaded from www.manning.com/hanson.

We haven't discussed the detailed construction of the component applications in this book, because we've focused on their being vehicles to understand aspects of GWT. In the following few chapters, we'll introduce more complicated component applications including the Server Status application, which introduces client-server communication; using RPC; the Yahoo Search application, which shows how to use the classic Ajax `XMLHttpRequest` approach as well as parse a JSON response; and how to change components of your application based on GWT properties.

Part 3

Advanced techniques

Part 2 explored the user-interface components of GWT, explaining how to create custom widgets and bundle them as a reusable library. Part 3 takes you to the next step by looking at GWT's advanced toolset for making remote procedure calls, code generators, application configuration, and internationalization tools.

10 Communicating with GWT-RPC

This chapter covers

- Asynchronous communication
- Overview of the GWT-RPC mechanism
- Step-by-step instructions for using GWT-RPC
- Building an example widget using GWT-RPC

When you're building a rich Internet application, it's likely you won't get too far before you need to contact the server. The reasons for doing so are numerous and can range from updating the contents of a shopping cart to sending a chat message. In this chapter, we'll explore the primary remote procedure call (RPC) mechanism that ships with the GWT toolkit. Throughout this chapter, and the chapters that follow, we'll refer to this mechanism as GWT-RPC to distinguish it from other general RPC flavors.

If you're unfamiliar with RPC, it's a term used to describe a mechanism that allows a program to execute a program on another computer and return the results of the calculation. This is a simplistic view of RPC, but this is essentially what you'll be doing in this chapter.

Throughout this chapter, as well as the next, you'll learn by building and extending an example component. This component, once completed, periodically requests performance data from the server and displays the values to the user. We call this example component the "Server Status" component.

To make the task of writing RPC code as intuitive as possible, this chapter follows a strict organization. In the first section, we'll define the component you're going to build, including a basic UI layout and defining the data that will be displayed in the component. In that context, we'll discuss asynchronous communication and some security restrictions of browser-based RPC.

In the second section, we'll examine all the nuts and bolts of GWT-RPC. We'll define the data object that will be passed on demand between the client and server, and the serialization of data objects. We'll then get down to business and write the code for the component from beginning to end.

At the end of the chapter, we'll wrap up the discussion with a detailed overview of the project and a review of the core participants of the GWT-RPC mechanism. But it doesn't end there; chapter 11 extends the example component by applying software patterns and polling techniques, providing for reusable and maintainable code.

Without further delay, let's begin the journey by defining the Server Status example project and examining the fundamental concepts behind the GWT-RPC mechanism.

10.1 Underlying RPC concepts

In this section, we'll explain how the GWT-RPC mechanism works by building a sample component. We wanted the component to be of interest to the widest audience possible, so we chose to create what we call the Server Status component. The purpose of the component is to provide up-to-date memory and thread usage for the Java Virtual Machine (JVM). As you go through the process of building the component, think about what other information you may want to add, like perhaps the number of logged-in users or maybe disk usage. Once it's completed, you'll be able to use this component in the GWT Dashboard project introduced in chapter 3 or in any of your own GWT projects.

You need to assemble three pieces of the puzzle to have a working RPC application: the service that runs on the server, the client in the browser that calls the service, and the data objects that are transported between the client and the server. Both the server and the client have the ability to serialize and deserialize data so the data objects can be passed between the two as ordinary text.

Figure 10.1 provides a visual representation of what the completed Server Status component will look like, along with an example service request and response. The connection between client and server in figure 10.1 is initiated by the client and passed through a proxy object provided by GWT. The proxy object then serializes the request as a text stream and sends it to the server. On the server, the request is received by a special Java servlet provided by GWT. The servlet then deserializes the request and delegates the request to your service. Once your service returns a value to the GWT servlet, the resulting object is serialized and sent back to the client. On the client side, the response is received by the GWT proxy, which deserializes the data back into a Java object and returns the object to the calling code.

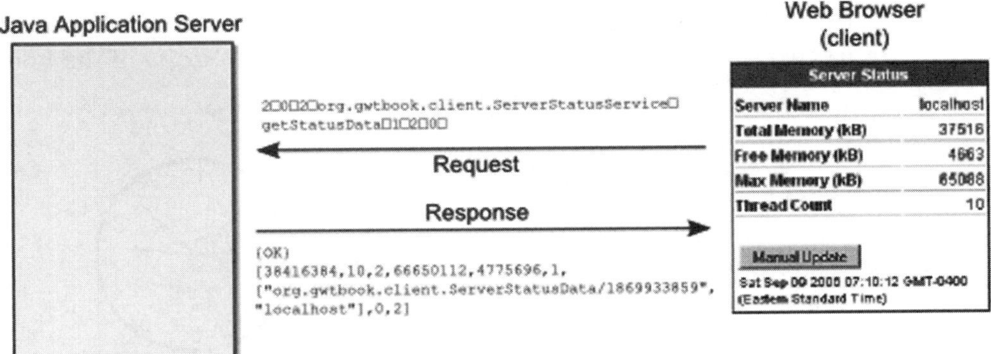

Figure 10.1 The completed GWT-RPC based Server Status component receiving serialized data from the server. The three pieces of the RPC application include the service that runs on the server, the client in the browser that calls the service, and the data objects that are transported between the client and the server.

The important part to remember about the round trip of the request is that the code deals with ordinary Java objects, and GWT handles serialization and deserialization of the data automatically. The example transaction in figure 10.1 shows the request and response data that is passed between the client and server; in practice you'll never deal with this data directly, although it may sometimes be helpful to view the data when debugging a problem. In this book, we won't explain the serialization scheme; it isn't a documented part of GWT and will likely change in later GWT versions as performance enhancements are introduced.

The idea of GWT doing most of the work for you sounds great, but the devil is in the details. You must understand a few things before you start coding, the first of which is the asynchronous nature of browser-based communication.

10.1.1 Understanding asynchronous communication

Calling a remote service with GWT-RPC is just like calling a local method with a couple additional lines of code. There is one caveat: The call is made in an asynchronous manner. This means that once you call the method on the remote service, your code continues to execute without waiting for a return value. Figure 10.2 shows this graphically; a gap of time exists between the call to the server and the response.

Asynchronous communication works much like an event handler in that you provide a callback routine that is executed when the event occurs. In this case, the event is the return of the call to the service. If you haven't dealt with this sort of behavior before, it may feel foreign at first, and it can require some additional planning when building applications. GWT uses this type of communication due to the way the underlying `XMLHttpRequest` object works. The reason why the `XMLHttpRequest` object behaves this way is beyond the scope of the book, but in

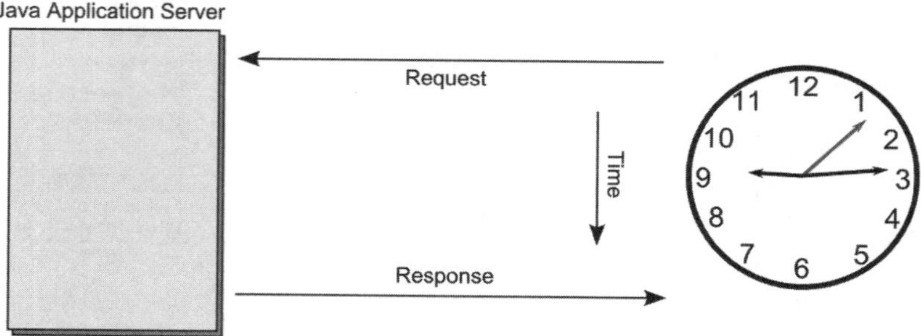

Figure 10.2 A visual representation of the time-delay of asynchronous communication used in browser-based communication

part it's due to the nature of JavaScript implementations. This asynchronous nature, though, has some advantages.

The first advantage is that network latency and long-running services can slow down communication. By allowing the call to happen asynchronously, the call won't hold up execution of the application waiting for a response; plus it feels less like a web application and more like a desktop application. The other benefit is that you can use some tricks with this to emulate a *server-push.*

DEFINITION *Server-push* is a mechanism where the server pushes data out to the client without it being requested. This is used in applications like chat, where the server needs to push messages out to its clients. We'll look at how to emulate server-push along with some polling techniques in chapter 11.

Besides asynchronous communication, another RPC issue we need to deal with is security, which affects how you use any browser-based RPC mechanism.

10.1.2 Restrictions for communicating with remote servers

Security is always a concern on the Internet, especially when a call can be made to a server that potentially returns sensitive data to the client, or perhaps provides access to secure systems. We have no intention of conducting a complete examination of security for web servers, which we leave to the experts. We do, though, want to explain one feature of making remote calls from the browser, which may seem like more of an annoyance than a feature. When you make a remote call from the browser, it *must* make the call to the same server from where the JavaScript code originated.

This means your GWT application running in the browser, which was loaded from your web server, can't call services hosted by other sites. For some people, this is more than an annoyance; it's a problem that means they may not be able to deploy their code in the manner they intend. Before we explain why this is truly a feature, understand that there are ways around it by providing a proxy on your server that calls the remote server. In chapter 13, you'll use such a proxy to communicate with a third-party search service.

Note that some browsers may let you override this behavior. For example, with Internet Explorer, you can tell the browser to allow the remote connection to proceed, even though it's attempting to contact a foreign server. Requiring your users to bypass restrictions like this is never a good idea, and it can make your users vulnerable to attacks. This is a strong statement; but as you'll see shortly with cross-site request forgery, there is a good reason for this.

To help you better understand how an attack like this might play out, let's examine a hypothetical situation. Pretend you're a high-ranking executive for company X-Ray Alpha Delta, and you're logged in to the top-secret extranet application doing some product research. Once you log in to the top-secret application, it keeps track of who you are by giving you a web cookie. The connection between the client and server is an encrypted connection provided by SSL. Using cookies as a way of handling user sessions and SSL are common tools used by most secure web applications.

While working on the top-secret extranet, you receive an email prompting you to review some competitor content on the Internet. You click the link and start reading the page, which seems to be a legitimate news site. Unknown to you, the "news" site is running JavaScript in your browser and is making requests against your top-secret extranet. This is possible because your browser automatically passes your session information contained in a cookie to the top-secret extranet server, even though the JavaScript calling the server originated from the "news" site. Figure 10.3 shows the order of events in such an attack, allowing the malicious JavaScript access to the "protected" site.

This scenario is plausible and has been proven to work when the web browser allows JavaScript to call foreign servers. At the Black Hat convention in 2006, the security firm iSEC Partners provided details about how they used this technique to remove $5,000 from a stock account. The user was logged in to a financial site and then viewed a foreign site, which contained the malicious JavaScript code. The JavaScript code in question was contained in five separate hidden iframes. Each script ran in turn, making one call to the financial service. The scripts changed the user's email notification settings, added a new checking account for transfer-

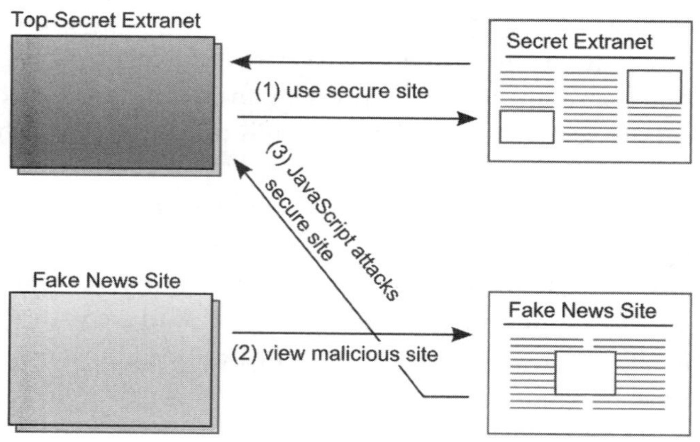

Figure 10.3 Cross-site scripting attack, using JavaScript to break in to a "secure" application

ring funds, transferred $5,000 out of the account, deleted the checking account, and restored the email notification settings. All of this occurred while the user was viewing the malicious site. This is a scary scenario, and it's why browsers don't typically allow JavaScript code to contact foreign hosts.

We've gotten far off track and need to get back to where we started: an overview of RPC architecture of GWT. So far, we've discussed its asynchronous nature and automatic data serialization, and addressed why the service must be provided by the same host that served the GWT application (for critical security reasons). To get back on track, you'll create a new GWT project that will be used to house the Server Status component.

10.1.3 Creating the Server Status project

By now, you know how to set up a new GWT project, but this one will be a little different. When you create a GWT project that will perform RPC, you need to account for the fact that it will contain both server-side and client-side code. The GWT compiler should compile only the client-side code to JavaScript without including the server-side portion of the code. You'll be including code for both the client and server in this project, so you need to do a few extra things to inform the GWT compiler which source files it needs to compile.

The first step is to use the `projectCreator` and/or `applicationCreator` command-line tool to create a new project. If you need a refresher on how to do this, consult chapter 2. For our purposes, this chapter assumes you already know how to do this. The following command and subsequent output creates the project:

```
applicationCreator -out ServerStatus org.gwtbook.client.ServerStatus

Created directory ServerStatus\src
Created directory ServerStatus\src\org\gwtbook
Created directory ServerStatus\src\org\gwtbook\client
Created directory ServerStatus\src\org\gwtbook\public
Created file ServerStatus\src\org\gwtbook\ServerStatus.gwt.xml
Created file ServerStatus\src\org\gwtbook\public\ServerStatus.html
Created file ServerStatus\src\org\gwtbook\client\ServerStatus.java
Created file ServerStatus\ServerStatus-shell.cmd
Created file ServerStatus\ServerStatus-compile.cmd
```

Next, you need to remove the sample Java code provided by the `applicationCreator` tool. The following code is ServerStatus.java after removing the sample application:

```
package org.gwtbook.client;

import com.google.gwt.core.client.EntryPoint;

public class ServerStatus implements EntryPoint
{
  public void onModuleLoad ()
  {
    // code
  }
}
```

You also want to start with a new HTML page. Listing 10.1 shows the ServerStatus.html page in the project. You can remove the various comments, provide a better page title, and add an empty style block. Once you finish the component, we'll provide some style code you can use to make the component look like figure 10.1.

Listing 10.1 The minimal HTML page you'll use to host the Server Status project

```
<html>
  <head>
    <title>Server Status</title>

    <!-- used to load module in GWT versions through 1.3 -->
    <meta name='gwt:module' content='org.gwtbook.ServerStatus'>

    <!-- used to load module in GWT versions 1.4+ -->
     <script language='javascript'
       src='org.gwtbook.ServerStatus.nocache.js'></script>

    <style type="text/css">
    </style>
  </head>
  <body>

    <!-- used to load module in GWT versions through 1.3 -->
    <script language="javascript" src="gwt.js"></script>
  </body>
</html>
```

NOTE Because GWT is thriving, it's subject to regular improvements. In listing 10.1, we've inserted HTML comments to identify the lines that are required to load the Server Status module in the current 1.3 release of GWT as well as the proposed loading method that will be used in GWT version 1.4. The older module-loading method, using `gwt.js`, will still work in GWT version 1.4, but it has been deprecated.

The CSS styles in listing 10.2 style the Server Status component to look like the example look and feel provided in figure 10.1. Feel free to adjust the styles to your liking or use your own. You can place the following CSS code into the `<style>` element in the HTML page or put the CSS code into an external file and reference it with the HTML `<link>` element.

Listing 10.2 A CSS file for styling the Server Status component

```
.server-status {            <-- Set component width and height
  width: 200px;
  height: 200px;
  border: 1px solid black;
}

.server-status td {         <-- Set font style
  font-family: Arial;
  font-size: 12px;
}

.server-status .title-bar {      <-- Set title-bar styles
  text-align: center;
  background: #666;
  padding: 2px 0;
  color: white;
  font-weight: bold;
}

.server-status .stats-grid {     <-- Set inner data-grid width
  width: 200px;
}

.server-status .stats-grid td {     <-- Add row lines to data-grid
  border-bottom: 1px solid #ccc;
}

.server-status .stat-name {      <-- Set statistic title styles
  font-weight: bold;
}

.server-status .stat-value {     <-- Right justify data values
  text-align: right;
}

.server-status .last-updated,      <-- Set styles of status label and update button
 .server-status .update-button {
  font-size: 10px;
  margin: 0 5px;
}
```

Now that you have a new project to work with, you can get down to writing some code. In the next section, you begin by creating a data object that will be passed from the server to the client and then get into creating the service and calling it from the client.

10.2 Implementing GWT-RPC

As we stated at the beginning of this chapter, there are three parts to the GWT-RPC mechanism, as you can see in figure 10.4. The first is the service that runs on the server as a servlet, the second is the web browser that acts as a client and calls the service, and last are the data objects that pass between the client and server.

We'll start with the last of these, the data objects, and explain what types of objects GWT can serialize for you. Following this, we'll look at the server side of the threesome and how you implement the service on the server. Finally, you'll call the service from your browser.

During the course of the discussion, we'll reference the Server Status project that you started in the previous section. We'll also provide code examples not related to the Server Status project when doing so helps explain details of the GWT-RPC mechanism that aren't explicitly used by the Server Status component. By the end of this section, you'll have completed the Server Status component, and you'll be able to reuse it with any of your own GWT projects. Now, let's look at the serializable data objects.

10.2.1 Understanding serializable data objects

We need to begin our discussion of GWT-RPC with data objects because the data is what gives GWT-RPC life. Describing the functionality of GWT-RPC without data would be akin to describing the function of the human heart without first understanding the purpose of life-giving blood.

At the beginning of section 10.1, we mentioned that with the GWT-RPC mechanism, you can call methods that are executed on the server, and a resulting value

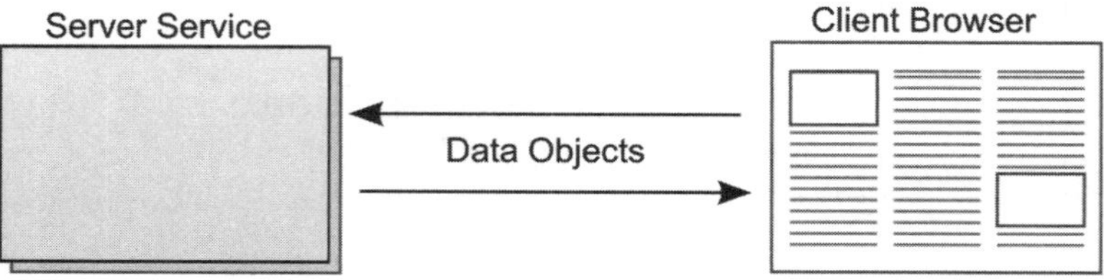

Figure 10.4 The three parts of GWT-RPC: client, server, and data objects

is passed back to the client. Just like any Java method, you may pass arguments to the method, which may be a primitive like an `int`, an object like a `String`, or an array of values. The list of value types that GWT can serialize, though, is finite:

- *Java primitive types*—`boolean`, `byte`, `char`, `double`, `float`, `int`, `long`, `short`
- *Java primitive wrapper types*—`Boolean`, `Byte`, `Character`, `Double`, `Float`, `Integer`, `Long`, `Short`
- *Subset of JRE objects*—Only `ArrayList`, `Date`, `HashMap`, `HashSet`, `String`, `Vector` (future versions of GWT may add to this)
- *User-defined classes*—Any class that implements `IsSerializable`
- *Arrays*—An array of any of the serializable types

CHANGES IN GWT 1.4 Added in GWT 1.4 is the ability to have your GWT serializable classes implement the java.io.Serializable interface instead of the GWT-specific IsSerializable interface. The change is being introduced to make it easier to share data objects with server-side persistence frameworks like Hibernate, which require data objects to implement java.io.Serializable. It's important to note that this change in GWT 1.4 is only intended to make it easier to integrate with persistence frameworks; it doesn't imply that GWT serialization follows any of the semantics of java.io.Serializable.

The first two groups of value types—primitives and their wrapper counterparts—are self explanatory, and all are supported. Only a limited number of Java data types are supported. In chapter 1, we discussed the JRE Emulation Library provided by GWT, and how GWT allows only certain Java classes to be used in client-side code. The list of supported Java classes here includes all of the value object types from the emulation library.

The first three groups consist of types that are part of standard Java, but what about user-defined types? The `IsSerializable` interface answers this question.

Implementing the IsSerializable Interface

The second from the last of the list of serializable types is any class that implements the `IsSerializable` interface. This interface is part of the GWT library, and it's used to signify that a class may be serialized. This serves a similar purpose as Java's own `java.io.Serializable` interface but is specific to GWT applications. Most of this section will be about using the `IsSerializable` interface.

The `IsSerializable` interface has no methods. It's only used to let the GWT compiler know that this object may be serialized, and it implies that you created the class with serialization rules in mind:

- The class implements com.google.gwt.user.client.rpc.IsSerializable.
- All non-transient fields in the class are serializable.
- The class has a zero-argument constructor.

By *non-transient field* we mean any field not using the transient modifier. GWT also won't serialize fields that have been marked as final; but don't rely on this, and be sure to mark all final fields as transient. That isn't to say that bad things will happen if you don't mark the final fields as transient, but you want the intention of the code to be clear if you or someone else ever needs to revisit the code for maintenance:

```
private transient String doNotCopy = "some value";
```

GWT serialization also traverses relationships between parent and child classes. You could have a superclass that implements IsSerializable and a subclass that doesn't; but, because the superclass is serializable, so are all of its subclasses:

```
public class Person implements IsSerializable {
  String name;
  Date birthday;
}

public class Programmer extends Person {
  String favoriteLanguage;
}
```

Another thing to consider when working with serializable data objects is that they will be used by both the client and server code, and, therefore, must adhere to the rules for client-side code. This includes being compliant with the Java 1.4 language syntax and may only reference classes that are part of the JRE Emulation Library or are user created classes.

In terms of optimizations for the GWT compiler, it's good to be as specific as possible when specifying the types of your fields in the data object. For example, it's common practice to specify java.util.List as a type instead of either ArrayList or Vector. The benefit of using a generalized type is that it allows you to change the underlying implementation without changing the type declaration. The problem is that when you generalize the type, it's harder for the GWT compiler to optimize the code, and you often end up with larger JavaScript files. The rule of thumb it to try to be as specific as possible in your typing.

You may have noticed the catch-22 situation we've run into. You're limited to the Java 1.4 syntax, which rules out using generics. If you're to be as specific as possible, you need a way to let the GWT compiler know what types of objects are contained in an ArrayList or Vector. This leads us to the typeArgs annotation.

Using the typeArgs annotation

Specific typing isn't possible when your data object has a member that is a collection of objects. Collections in Java 1.4 hold values of type `java.lang.Object`, and this is as generic of a type you can get. This would be an issue if, for example, your data class had a member type of `ArrayList`, `Vector`, `HashSet`, or any other type that implements `java.util.Collection`.

In the following example, the GWT compiler has no way of knowing what types of objects are held by either `listOfNames` or `listOfDates`, so it won't be able to properly optimize the client-side JavaScript:

```
private ArrayList listOfNames;
private Vector listOfDates;
```

GWT provides an annotation that allows you to let the compiler know what types of objects are in a collection. This isn't a Java 5 annotation, so it isn't part of the Java language; instead, you provide the annotation inside a Java comment. Figure 10.5 shows the syntax of the `typeArgs` annotation.

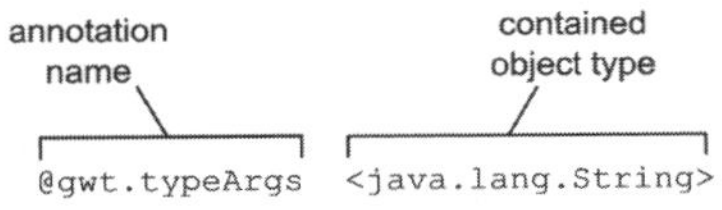

Figure 10.5 The `typeArgs` annotation is specified in a Java comment preceding a field in the class to provide a hint to the GWT compiler about the contents of a `java.util.Collection`.

There are two variations of this annotation, the second of which will be described later in this chapter when you define the service interface. In this first variation, the only parameter is the contained object type inside angled brackets. The contained type is specified using its full package and class name. When you apply this to the two fields `listOfNames` and `listOfDates`, it looks like this:

```
/**
 * @gwt.typeArgs <java.lang.String>
 */
private ArrayList listOfNames;

/**
 * @gwt.typeArgs <java.util.Date>
 */
private Vector listOfDates;
```

Now that you understand the basics, let's apply that knowledge to the example component.

Implementing the Server Status data object

To get back to the Server Status component we introduced at the beginning of this chapter, you need a data object that will be used to hold server statistics data that will be requested by and sent to the client browser. Here is the complete data object:

```
package org.gwtbook.client;

import com.google.gwt.user.client.rpc.IsSerializable;

public class ServerStatusData implements IsSerializable
{
    public String serverName;
    public long totalMemory;
    public long freeMemory;
    public long maxMemory;
    public int threadCount;
}
```

The class complies with both rules of serializable objects: It implements `IsSerializable`, and all the fields are also serializable. We built this class with only public fields, but it would be just as appropriate to provide private or protected fields with associated getter and setter methods, which is common in Java programming.

Also note that this class is in the `org.gwtbook.client` package, and it will be compiled into JavaScript to allow it to be used in the browser. On the server, you'll also use this class, but the server will use a compiled Java version of the class. As part of the data serialization handled by GWT, it will handle the mapping for the fields of the client-side JavaScript version to the server-side Java version of this same class.

Now that you have your data object, the next step is to define and implement your service. You need to define a service by using a Java interface and then implement a servlet that adheres to that interface.

10.2.2 Defining the GWT-RPC service

The next step in using the GWT-RPC mechanism is to define and implement the service that will live and be executed on the server. This consists of one Java interface which describes the service, and the service implementation. When you write a server-side service, you'll probably want to integrate it with other backend systems like databases, mail servers, and other services. In addition to the basics of using GWT-RPC, we'll touch on how you might do some of these things. First, we'll look at the GWT `RemoteService` interface.

Extending the RemoteService interface

To define your service, you need to create a Java interface and extend the GWT `RemoteService` interface. This is as easy as it sounds. If you recall, the Server Status project calls an RPC service method that returns a `ServerStatusData` object, which contains various server metrics. The interface looks like the following:

```
package org.gwtbook.client;

import com.google.gwt.user.client.rpc.RemoteService;

public interface ServerStatusService extends RemoteService
{
  ServerStatusData getStatusData ();
}
```

That is all there is to it: Provide a name for the interface, in this case `ServerStatusService`, and have it extend GWT's `RemoteService` interface. The `RemoteService` interface doesn't define any methods, so you won't need to implement anything special to get the service running. There are some additional fairly subtle requirements when defining this interface:

- The interface must extend `com.google.gwt.user.client.rpc.RemoteService`.
- All method parameters and return values must be serializable.
- The interface must live in the client package.

We have covered the first of these, but we want to explain it a little further. GWT automatically generates proxy classes for the client-side application and forwards to methods using reflection on the server. To put it another way, GWT goes out of its way to make RPC easy by minimizing the amount of code you need to write. The `RemoteService` interface is used to signal which interfaces define the remote service. This is important because this may not be the only interface the server implementation implements.

The second requirement is that all parameters and return values must be serializable. As we mentioned in the previous section, this includes all primitive Java types, certain objects that are part of the standard Java library, and classes that implement the `IsSerializable` interface. For the `ServiceStatusService` interface, the only method, `getStatusData()`, returns a `ServerStatusData` object that you created in the last section, and it implements `IsSerializable`. Here are some more examples, all of which include parameters and return values that can be serialized:

```
boolean serviceOne (String s, int i, Vector v);
String[] serviceTwo (float f, Integer o);
```

The last requirement is that the interface must be in the client package—the interface code must be in your project where it's compiled by GWT into JavaScript. Typically, this is in a package name ending in `.client` unless you have configured your project differently. This interface needs to be compiled to JavaScript because it's used by both the client and the server. On the server, the service implementation will implement this interface. We'll look at how you reference this interface from the client side when we get to the next section and call the service.

Using the typeArgs annotation

We introduced you to the `typeArgs` annotation in the previous section when you used it to define the contents of collections in a serializable object. Here, we'll introduce an alternate syntax, but with the same purpose—to provide a hint to the GWT compiler about what type of object a collection is holding. The specific collection types that GWT supports are `ArrayList`, `Vector`, `HashSet`, and their respective interfaces `List` and `Set`.

You should provide the `typeArgs` annotation for each parameter and return value that is a collection. Figure 10.6 shows the syntax, which differs in what you saw in the last section, because it also allows you to specify the parameter name. When you add an annotation for the return value, you don't specify the parameter name.

The following code defines a method that takes a `List` of `Integer` values and a `Vector` of `Date` values, and returns an `ArrayList` of `String` values:

```
/**
 * @gwt.typeArgs arg1 <java.lang.Integer>
 * @gwt.typeArgs arg2 <java.util.Date>
 * @gwt.typeArgs <java.lang.String>
 */
ArrayList operationThree (List arg1, Vector arg2);
```

In practice, you can probably leave off the `typeArgs` and everything will run fine. If you decide to leave it off, you may end up with additional JavaScript code being generated for the client because the GWT compiler won't be able to optimize the serialization code for handling `Collection` parameters and return values.

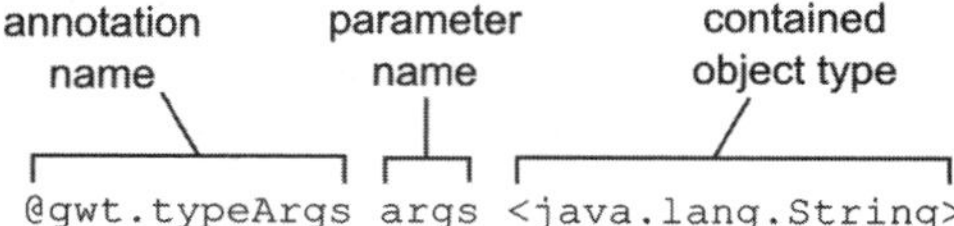

Figure 10.6 The second version of the `typeArgs` syntax, which is used to provide hints to the GWT compiler about the underlying data types contained by Collection arguments to the service

This covers serialization. But if you want remote calls to be able to pass Java objects, you also want them to have the ability to pass exceptions.

Throwing exceptions

Often, it's desirable to let a method throw an exception that will be handled by the calling code. For example, you may have a login function that returns a user-data object on success but, on failure, throws an appropriate exception:

```
UserData loginUser (String username, String password)
  throws FailedAuthenticationException;
```

When GWT calls the service method and throws an exception, it serializes the exception and returns it to the client browser. The only requirement is that the exception be serializable just like any data object. In other words, it must implement `IsSerializable`, all of its fields must be serializable, and the class must be in the client package. See the previous section, "Understanding serializable data objects," for a complete discussion of creating serializable objects.

As an alternative to writing your own serializable exception class from scratch, GWT supplies an exception class `SerializableException`, in the package `com.google.gwt.user.client.rpc`. You can use this exception class instead of writing your own, or you can use this as the base class for your exceptions.

Next, let's look at how you can implement the service interface.

Implementing the service

With the service interface defined for your service, you need to implement its methods. You do this by creating a servlet that extends GWT's `RemoteService-Servlet` and implements the service interface. Listing 10.3 shows the complete `ServerService` implementation.

Listing 10.3 Server Status server-side implementation

```
package org.gwtbook.server;

import org.gwtbook.client.ServerStatusData;
import org.gwtbook.client.ServerStatusService;
import com.google.gwt.user.server.rpc.RemoteServiceServlet;

public class ServerServiceImpl
       extends RemoteServiceServlet
       implements ServerStatusService
{
  public ServerStatusData getStatusData () {
```

```
        ThreadGroup parentThread =
          Thread.currentThread().getThreadGroup();
        while (parentThread.getParent() != null) {
          parentThread = parentThread.getParent();
        }

        ServerStatusData result = new ServerStatusData();

        result.serverName = getThreadLocalRequest().getServerName();
        result.totalMemory = Runtime.getRuntime().totalMemory();
        result.freeMemory = Runtime.getRuntime().freeMemory();
        result.maxMemory = Runtime.getRuntime().maxMemory();
        result.threadCount = parentThread.activeCount();

        return result;
    }
}
```

Find root Java server thread

Create result object

Populate result object

Return result

The benefit of using GWT-RPC, which listing 10.3 shows, is that there is nothing special you need to do to make your class a service other than extend the `RemoteServiceServlet` and implement an interface that extends `RemoteService`. When the service is called, the underlying `RemoteServiceServlet` parses the request, converting the serialized data back into Java objects, and calls the service method. When the method returns a value, it is returned to the `RemoteServiceServlet` that called the method, and it in turn serializes the result and returns it to the client browser.

Unlike what you've seen with the rest of GWT, there are no restrictions on the server-side code. You can use any Java class, you can use Java 5 syntax, and there are no special annotations you need to use. There is one restriction, however: the package name. Because the server-side code contains Java code that can't be compiled into JavaScript, and because there is no need for this to be served to the client, you need to make sure this class lives outside the client package. To refresh your memory, figure 10.7 shows what the current project directory layout looks like.

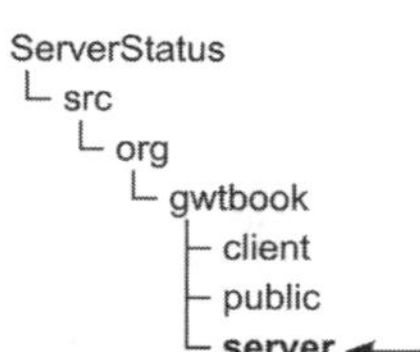

Figure 10.7 Reviewing the current project directory layout

The root of the project is the Java package `org.gwtbook`, and that package contains the `client` package and the public folder. The public folder contains any non-Java assets for the project, like the HTML file, and the `client` package contains Java classes that will be compiled to JavaScript. For the server-side code, it's the standard practice to create a `server` package just beneath the root package, which for this project is org.gwtbook.server. Don't get too hung up on this; depending on what you're building, it may be more appropriate to use a different package name, and this is fine as long as it isn't in the client package.

Next, we'll look at how to configure the development environment to use the new servlet.

Setting up your service for hosted-mode testing

There is one last step: registering your service with GWT by adding it to the project configuration file. The project configuration file is located in the root package, and it's named the same as the entry-point class with a .gwt.xml extension; in this case, it's found under org.gwtbook and named ServerStatus.gwt.xml. By default, it contains both an `<inherits>` element to provide access to the core GWT libraries and an `<entry-point>` element indicating the runnable class for this project. To this, you need to add a `<servlet>` element to register your new service. The completed ServerStatus.gwt.xml file looks like this:

```
<module>
  <inherits name='com.google.gwt.user.User'/>
  <entry-point class='org.gwtbook.client.ServerStatus'/>

  <servlet path="/server-status"
           class="org.gwtbook.server.ServerServiceImpl"/>
</module>
```

We've stripped out the comments that the GWT application creator added, to shorten the example, so it may not look exactly like yours. The `<servlet>` element has two attributes: `path` to indicate the URL of your service, and `class` to indicate the servlet that should be run when this URL is requested. Note that just like a Java application server, the path to the servlet is relative to the web project root and not the root of the server. With this project, the default project URL in hosted mode is the following:

```
http://localhost:8888/org.gwtbook.ServerStatus/ServerStatus.html
```

When you specify /server-status as the path to the servlet, it's accessible with the following URL:

```
http://localhost:8888/org.gwtbook.ServerStatus/server-status
```

If you've worked with the servlet path setting before, this will be the expected behavior; but for some, this is a common cause of frustration when configuring a servlet.

With your service defined, implemented, and configured on the server, the next step is to address the client-side issues and finally call the service from the client.

10.2.3 Preparing the client side of a GWT-RPC call

When you call the remote service from the client, GWT does most of the work for you; however, you need to create one last interface. The GWT compiler uses this interface when it generates the service proxy object. A *proxy object* is an object instance that forwards the request to another target. In this case, you'll call a local method, and the proxy object is responsible for serializing the parameters, calling the remote service, and handling the deserialization of the return value. You don't write the code for the proxy class; the GWT compiler handles this for you. In the client-side code, you create the proxy object by writing the following:

```
GWT.create (ServerStatusService.class)
```

Here you call the static method `create()` of the `com.google.gwt.core.client.GWT` class, passing it the class object of the remote service interface. This returns a proxy object that you can use to set the service URL and call the remote methods. The proxy object returned implements two interfaces: one that you need to create, and one supplied by GWT (as shown in figure 10.8).

In figure 10.8, the proxy object is an instance of `ServerStatusService_Proxy`, which implements two interfaces. The proxy class is created at compile time, so you can't reference this class directly in your code. Instead, you need to cast it to each interface separately to be able to call its methods.

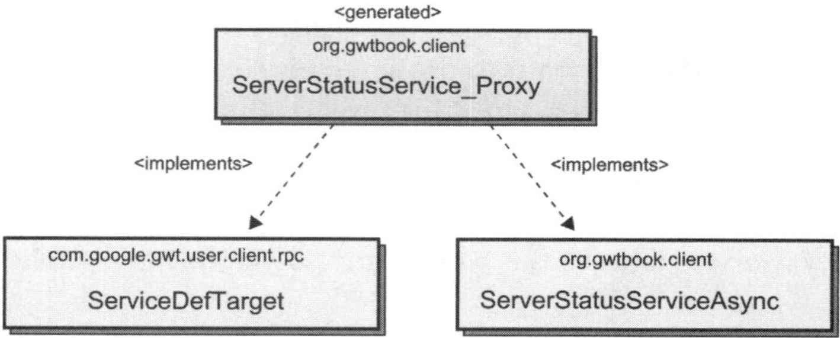

Figure 10.8 The client-side service proxy generated by the GWT compiler, and the interfaces it implements

Of the two interfaces, ServiceDefTarget is part of the GWT library and includes a method setServiceEntryPoint() for specifying the URL of the remote service. The other interface, ServerStatusServiceAsync, provides asynchronous methods for calling the remote service. You'll need to write this second asynchronous service interface yourself, as we'll discuss next.

This asynchronous service interface always has the same name as your service, with the name "Async" appended to it. The methods in the interface must match all the method names in your original service interface, but the signatures need to be changed. Specifically, for each method in the original interface, you must do the following:

- Set the return value to void.
- Add an extra com.google.gwt.user.client.rpc.AsyncCallback parameter.

Table 10.1 shows side-by-side examples of how a method in the service interface looks in the asynchronous service interface.

Table 10.1 Comparing methods in the service interface to how they look in the asynchronous interface of GWT-RPC

Service interface	Asynchronous service interface
`String methodOne (int i);`	`void methodOne (int i, AsynCallback cb);`
`List methodTwo ();`	`void methodTwo (AsynCallback cb);`
`boolean methodThree (int a, int x);`	`void methodThree (int a, int x, AsynCallback cb)`

This interface is used only by the client code and not the server. Because of this, you don't need to include this interface in any code deployed to the server, and you must place the interface in the client package. Here is what you get when you apply this to the ServerStatusService interface:

```
package org.gwtbook.client;

import com.google.gwt.user.client.rpc.AsyncCallback;
public interface ServerStatusServiceAsync {
  void getStatusData (AsyncCallback callback);
}
```

This sets you up for the last piece of the puzzle: calling the remote service from the client.

10.2.4 Calling the remote server service

Now that you have the remote service interface defined and implemented, you've created the remote asynchronous interface, and you've created a serializable object to pass between the server and client, all that remains is to call the service from the client browser. To do this, you need to do the following:

1. Instantiate a proxy object that will forward method calls to the server.
2. Specify the URL of the service.
3. Create a callback method to handle the result of the asynchronous method call.
4. Call the remote method.

The first time you do this, it doesn't feel natural, especially because you're calling the method asynchronously; but after a few tries, it becomes second nature. We'll examine each of these steps in turn and explain what needs to be done—and, perhaps more important, why it needs to be done. We'll also point out any areas of common mistakes.

Step 1: Creating the proxy object

Step 1 is to create your proxy object. You do this by calling `GWT.create()`, passing the remote service class as an argument. In return, the `create()` method returns a proxy object that you need to cast to the asynchronous interface. A common mistake is passing the wrong class as an argument to `GWT.create()`, so be sure to pass the remote service interface and not the asynchronous interface that will be implemented by the proxy object:

```
ServerStatusServiceAsync serviceProxy =
  (ServerStatusServiceAsync) GWT.create(ServerStatusService.class);
```

With the proxy object in hand, you can move on to the next step and use it to target the remote service.

Step 2: Casting the proxy object to ServiceDefTarget

The second step is to cast this same object to `ServiceDefTarget` so that you can specify the remote service URL. As you saw in the last section, the proxy object implements both the asynchronous service interface and `ServiceDefTarget`. All you need to do is cast this same object to the `ServiceDefTarget` interface. Once you do this, you can use `setServiceEntryPoint()` to set the URL for the service:

```
ServiceDefTarget target = (ServiceDefTarget) serviceProxy;
target.setServiceEntryPoint(GWT.getModuleBaseURL()
   + "server-status");
```

Or, alternatively, you can use a single-line syntax without creating a new variable:

```
((ServiceDefTarget)serviceProxy)
  .setServiceEntryPoint(GWT.getModuleBaseURL() + "server-status");
```

This sets the URL to /org.gwtbook.ServerStatus/server-status, which matches your servlet definition in the .gwt.xml file but may not match your production environment when you deploy the application. The `GWT.getModuleBaseURL()` method returns the location of the client-side code and appends a slash to the end, which works fine for hosted-mode development; but when you deploy your service, this may not be what you want.

Instead, you can detect whether the code is being executed in hosted mode, and use the appropriate service URL. You can do this by calling `GWT.isScript()`, which returns `true` when the application isn't running in hosted mode:

```
String serviceUrl = GWT.getModuleBaseURL() + "server-status";
if (GWT.isScript()) {
  serviceUrl = "/services/server-status.rpc";
}
((ServiceDefTarget)serviceProxy).setServiceEntryPoint(serviceUrl);
```

It may even be useful to take this a step further and define the web-mode service path in a `Constants` file or as a `Dictionary` object. You can get more information on how to use `Constants` and `Dictionary` in chapter 15.

You've set up the proxy object, so now you need to construct your callback object.

Step 3: Create a callback object

The third step in calling the RPC service is to create a callback object. This object implements the GWT `com.google.gwt.user.client.rpc.AsyncCallback` interface and is executed when a result is returned from the server. As you may recall, you added an `AsyncCallback` parameter to every method in the asynchronous service interface. The callback object is passed as this additional parameter. Here, you create an anonymous object instance that implements `AsyncCallback`:

```
AsyncCallback callback = new AsyncCallback() {

  public void onFailure (Throwable caught) {
    GWT.log("RPC error", caught);
  }

  public void onSuccess (Object result) {
    GWT.log("RPC success", null);
  }

};
```

The `AsyncCallback` interface has two methods that must be implemented: `onSuccess()` and `onFailure()`. If an error occurs where the service can't be reached, or if the server-side method throws an exception, the `onError()` method is called with the exception that occurred. If the call is successful, then the `onSuccess()` method is called, and it receives the return value of the remote method call. The previous sample uses the `GWT.log()` method to log information to the hosted-mode console. This would be replaced with code that does something with the resulting object and handles the error in an appropriate manner for the application.

Step 4: Make the remote service call

The fourth and final step in calling a remote service is to make the call. This is a little anticlimatic because it all comes down to one line of code:

```
serviceProxy.getStatusData(callback);
```

This method kicks off a chain of events. Any parameters other than the callback object are serialized and passed to the remote service, and the appropriate callback method is executed based on the server response.

10.3 Project summary

The GWT-RPC mechanism is simple; but with all the details, it's easy to lose site of the overall architecture. As promised earlier, we'll provide a summary of GWT-RPC, using a lot of visuals to make it easy to understand the system as a whole. We'll begin with an overview of the files in the project and then look at the server-side code, followed by the code on the client.

10.3.1 Project overview

The entire project thus far includes only seven files. Figure 10.9 provides a list of these files. It contains the usual configuration file, project HTML page, and entry point. That leaves only four files that represent the concepts covered in this chapter.

The *service interface* defines the remote service. It extends `RemoteService` and may only reference parameters and return values that can be serialized by GWT. When a method accepts arguments that implement `java.util.Collection`, or returns a `Collection`, you use the `@gwt.typeArgs` annotation to provide a hint for the GWT compiler, letting it know what types of objects it can contain. Your methods may declare that they throw exceptions, as long as any exception thrown can be serialized by GWT.

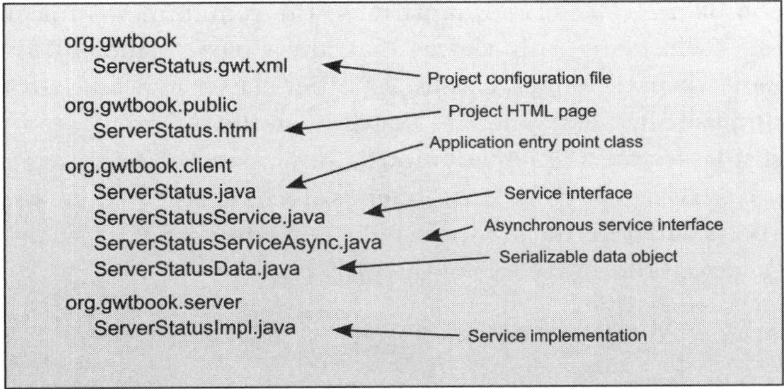

Figure 10.9 An overview of the Server Status project files you've created

The *asynchronous service interface* contains the same method names as the service interface, but with altered method signatures. Each method's return type is changed to `void`, and an `AsyncCallback` parameter is added as the last argument to each method.

The project may contain *serializable data objects*, each of which implements the `IsSerializable` interface. GWT serializes any field not marked as transient or final in the class, and every field not marked as transient must be of a GWT serializable type.

The *service implementation* is in a package outside the other client-side code because it doesn't need to be compiled to JavaScript by the GWT compiler. Typically, server-side code lives in a package at the same level as the client side code, in a package with the last part named `server`. The service implementation extends the `RemoteServiceServlet` and implements the service interface.

That is a description of each part of the project in a nutshell. In practice, the only difference between this service and other services you write will be the number of serializable data objects. You may also find that, in a large project, you wish to reorganize the package structure and place all the interfaces and data objects relating to a single service into a package by themselves.

Let's take a closer look at the server side of the project.

10.3.2 Server-side service implementation

Figure 10.10 presents a class diagram of all the classes on the server and their relationship to each other. We've used the stereotype `<<client-side>>` to mark those classes that are used on the client side as well as the server and need to be compiled by the GWT compiler. Those classes must meet the requirements for client-side code, including referencing only classes that are a part of the JRE Emulation Library, or client-side user-defined classes. All other classes may take advantage of Java 5 syntax and use any classes that are available on the server.

The server-side service implementation is just a servlet, because it extends `RemoteServiceServlet`, which in turn extends `HttpServlet`. When you deploy your service. you install it on the server just like any other servlet.

Finally, let's look at the client side of the project.

10.3.3 Calling the service from the client

You call the remote service by creating an instance of a service proxy object, specifying the URL of the service, and calling the server-side method on the object.

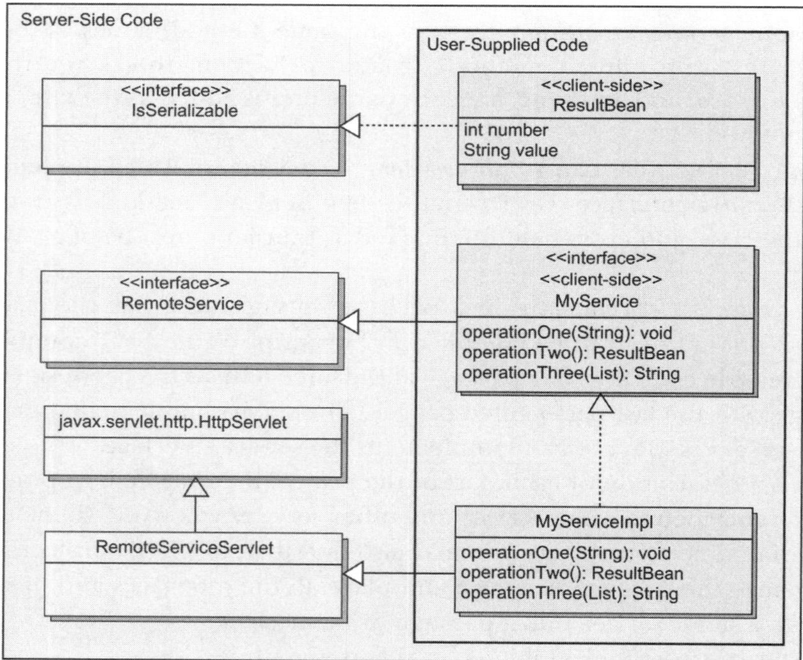

Figure 10.10 Overview of the server-side classes used for the Server Status project, but user generated and GWT supplied

The last parameter to any such method call is a callback handler, which is executed following the server returning a result. Listing 10.4 is a complete listing of the entry-point class that sets up and calls the remote service.

Listing 10.4 Client-side implementation

```
package org.gwtbook.client;

import com.google.gwt.core.client.EntryPoint;
import com.google.gwt.core.client.GWT;
import com.google.gwt.user.client.rpc.AsyncCallback;
import com.google.gwt.user.client.rpc.ServiceDefTarget;

public class ServerStatus implements EntryPoint
{
  public void onModuleLoad ()
  {
    ServerStatusServiceAsync serviceProxy =
        (ServerStatusServiceAsync)
        GWT.create(ServerStatusService.class);

    ServiceDefTarget target = (ServiceDefTarget) serviceProxy;
    target.setServiceEntryPoint(GWT.getModuleBaseURL()
        + "server-status");

    AsyncCallback callback = new AsyncCallback()
    {
      public void onFailure (Throwable caught)
      {
        GWT.log("Error", caught);
      }

      public void onSuccess (Object result)
      {
        ServerStatusData data = (ServerStatusData) result;
        GWT.log("Server Name: " + data.serverName, null);
        GWT.log("Free Memory: " + data.freeMemory, null);
        GWT.log("Max Memory: " + data.maxMemory, null);
      }
    };

    serviceProxy.getStatusData(callback);
  }
}
```

10.4 Summary

In this chapter, you created an RPC service using the GWT-RPC mechanism and called the service from the web browser, passing serialized Java objects. This chapter covers the basics of how to call a remote service, but we haven't yet discussed how to solve common real-world problems. For instance, how do you continuously poll a server for updates, and what is the best way to architect client-side RPC? In chapter 11, we'll answer both of these questions as we finish the Server Status project and take a hard look at client-side architecture.

11 Examining client-side RPC architecture

This chapter covers

- Patterns for simplifying GWT-RPC code
- Server polling techniques
- Emulating server-push data communication
- Custom GWT-RPC field serializers

In chapter 10, you began building a component called the Server Status component. The purpose of this example component is to present information about the Java Virtual Machine running on the server, including vitals such as memory and threads. During the course of that chapter, we took a deep look at how to use the GWT-RPC mechanism to solve the problem of sending data between the client and server.

When you finished that chapter, you had some code but not quite a finished component. It still needs polish. Some of the missing parts include structuring the presentation logic for your component, implementing a polling mechanism, and encapsulating the component so that it can be used over and over.

In this chapter, we'll begin by jumping back into the project and finishing it, as we take a long look at architecting a reusable and maintainable client-side component—one that takes advantage of server-side resources.

11.1 Structuring the client code

So far in the Server Status project, which you started in chapter 10, you've unceremoniously plopped the RPC code into the entry-point class with little care about application architecture. In this chapter, you continue the Server Status project and polish it, allowing it to be easily extended and maintained. You do this by applying some software patterns to the RPC code; none of them are GWT specific, but you'll apply them in a GWT-specific manner.

You'll begin by encapsulating the entire Server Status component as an extension of the GWT `Composite` class, which you've seen in prior chapters, and adding some RPC-specific code. Following that, you'll see how the Façade software pattern can be used to simplify RPC interaction. Finally, we'll look at how you can use the Command software pattern to simplify the calling of remote methods.

Let's begin with encapsulating the component.

11.1.1 Encapsulating the Server Status component

The first step in building a component is to formulate the basic visual layout of the component and then decide which widget class should be extended. For the Server Status component, figure 11.1 shows the desired structure and the resulting styled HTML.

The Server Status component is a `VerticalPanel` with four components. The first compartment inside of the component is the Server Status title bar. You'll use a `Label` for this, and with a little CSS styling you can center it and make the title appear bold and white.

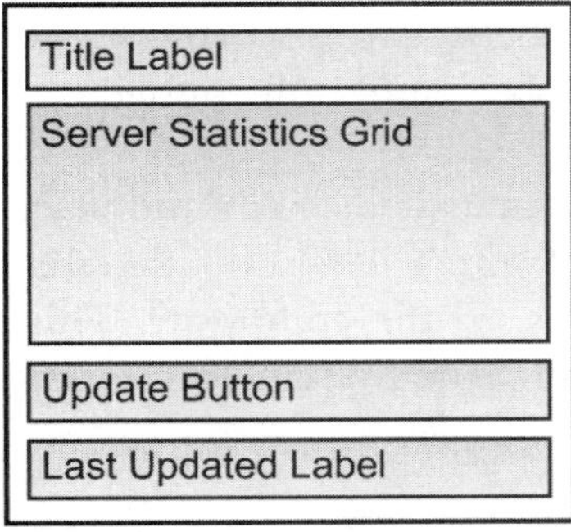

Server Status	
Server Name	localhost
Total Memory (kB)	37516
Free Memory (kB)	4663
Max Memory (kB)	65088
Thread Count	10

Manual Update

Sat Sep 09 2006 07:10:12 GMT-0400 (Eastern Standard Time)

Figure 11.1 The structure of the Server Status component, and what the finished component looks like

The second component you'll employ is a `Grid` component to display the server statistics you're retrieving via RPC. The grid is two cells wide and five cells tall to hold the five labels and five data values. These labels, like Server Name and Total Memory, are added to the grid as plain text. The values, on the other hand, are separate `Label` components so you'll be able to update their values using the `setText()` method of the `Label` component. You could set the text directly in the grid for these, but by providing a named `Label` instance for each value in the code the code is somewhat self-documenting, making it easier to understand and maintain.

At the bottom of the Server Status component is an update `Button` component, used to manually update the statistics, and a `Label` to indicate the last time the values were updated. It's our intention that this component will use some sort of polling mechanism to update itself periodically, but the manual update button can be used to force an early update. You'll hook the Server Status component up to a polling mechanism when we discus polling techniques in the next section.

Once you've designed a general structure, the next step is to code this as a component.

Writing the component shell

In writing the shell for the component, you'll deal with the layout of the component and not worry much about the inner workings yet. Once you complete the shell, you can move on to the next step and start having the component display data.

As we stated earlier, you need to decide which GWT user-interface component to extend. In figure 11.1, we showed that the outer shell of the component uses a `VerticalPanel`, but this isn't a good choice for the basis of the component. The reason is that `VerticalPanel` exposes several methods that you don't want the component to support. For example, the `add()` and `remove()` methods of `VerticalPanel` could be used to add or remove widgets from the finished component, changing the desired layout. For this reason, you want to extend `com.google.gwt.user.client.ui.Composite`. The `Composite` class provides several protected methods for use by an extending class and only publicly exposes a `getElement()` method.

In listing 11.1, you create the class `ServerStatusComponent` and place it in the `org.gwtbook.client` package with the rest of your client code. You define a private variable for each component that makes up the composite. This includes each of the components we discussed, including the five labels to hold the statistics you receive from the server.

Listing 11.1 Coding the structure of the `ServerStatusComponent`

```
package org.gwtbook.client;

import java.util.Date;
import com.google.gwt.core.client.*;
import com.google.gwt.user.client.rpc.*;
import com.google.gwt.user.client.ui.*;


public class ServerStatusComponent extends Composite
{
  private Panel composite = new VerticalPanel();     <-- Container component

  private Label titleBar = new Label("Server Status");
  private Button updateButton = new Button("Manual Update");
  private Grid serverStats = new Grid(5, 2);
  private Label labelLastUpdated = new Label();
                                          Subcomponents
  private Label labelTotalMemory = new Label();
  private Label labelFreeMemory = new Label();
  private Label labelThreadCount = new Label();
  private Label labelMaxMemory = new Label();
  private Label labelServerName = new Label();
                                          Individual statistic containers
  public ServerStatusComponent ()
  {
    initWidget(composite);

    composite.add(titleBar);
    composite.add(memStats);
    composite.add(updateButton);
    composite.add(labelLastUpdated);
  }

}
```

Thus far, the only code you've included is the constructor for the `ServerStatusComponent`. The constructor calls the `initWidget()` method of the superclass, passing it a newly created `VerticalPanel` instance. This sets the user interface component that will be used as the outer shell for the component. To this, you add the title bar label, the statistics grid, the update button, and the last-updated label.

Next, you need to update the entry-point class to reflect that you're now packaging the Server Status as a component. Notice that by encapsulating the `ServerStatusComponent` as a component, you're able to instantiate it and add it to the `RootPanel` with only two lines of code (see listing 11.2).

Listing 11.2 Instantiating the `ServerStatusComponent`

```
import com.google.gwt.core.client.*;
import com.google.gwt.user.client.rpc.*;
import com.google.gwt.user.client.ui.*;

public class ServerStatus implements EntryPoint
{
  public void onModuleLoad ()
  {
    ServerStatusComponent serverStatus =
        new ServerStatusComponent();
    RootPanel.get().add(serverStatus);
  }
}
```

You can now view the project in the hosted-mode browser; it should look like figure 11.2.

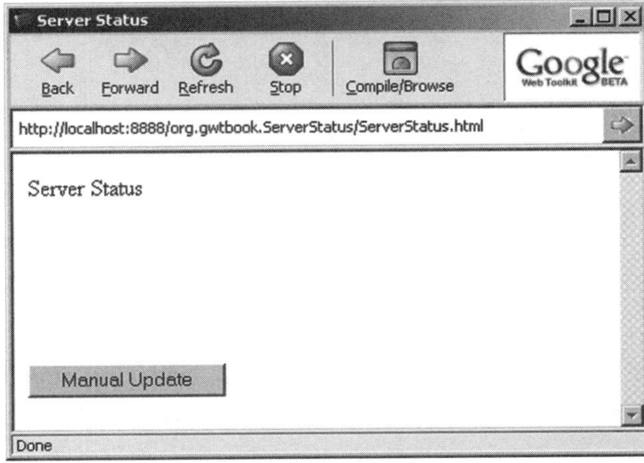

Figure 11.2 The incomplete shell of the Server Status component example running in the hosted-mode browser

The component looks a little sparse at this point, not only because you haven't supplied any data, but also because you haven't yet applied CSS styling.

Adding style and labels to the component

As you saw in chapter 4, you can attach CSS class names to the individual parts of a component. You need to specify separate style class names for the title-bar, `Grid` component, update button, last-updated label, and the `Composite` as a whole. You also need to add labels to each row in the grid, to the left of where each data value will be displayed. See listing 11.3.

Listing 11.3 Adding style classes and labels to the Server Status component

```
public ServerStatusComponent ()
{
  initWidget(composite);

  composite.setStyleName("server-status");
  titleBar.setStyleName("title-bar");
  serverStats.setStyleName("stats-grid");
  updateButton.setStyleName("update-button");
  labelLastUpdated.setStyleName("last-updated");

  updateButton.addClickListener(new ClickListener() {
      public void onClick (Widget sender) {
          getStatusDataFromServer();
      }
  });

  addRowToGrid("Server Name", labelServerName, 0);
  addRowToGrid("Total Memory (kB)", labelTotalMemory, 1);
  addRowToGrid("Free Memory (kB)", labelFreeMemory, 2);
  addRowToGrid("Max Memory (kB)", labelMaxMemory, 3);
  addRowToGrid("Thread Count", labelThreadCount, 4);

  composite.add(titleBar);
  composite.add(serverStats);
  composite.add(updateButton);
  composite.add(labelLastUpdated);

  getStatusDataFromServer();
}
```

Annotations: **Set style classes** (style name lines); **Attach update button listener** (addClickListener line); **Add components to grid** (addRowToGrid lines); **Retrieve values from server** (final getStatusDataFromServer call).

In listing 11.3, you reference two methods that you haven't yet defined. The first is `addRowToGrid()`, which helps you populate the statistics grid; and the second is `getStatusDataFromServer()`, which is the method that triggers a call to the server.

For each row, `addRowToGrid()` sets the title of the value, which appears on the left side of the grid, and inserts the `Label` component to the right of it. For each title, you set the style class name to be `stat-name`, and for each value you set the style name to be `stat-value`. Creating methods like this that group repetitious code is extremely helpful, especially because GWT code can easily become verbose.

`getStatusDataFromServer()` will be used to trigger an RPC call to the server. We'll describe this method and its purpose shortly, but for now you leave that method as an empty stub. Listing 11.4 shows the two methods you will add to the Server Status component.

Listing 11.4 Adding the `addRowToGrid()` and `getStatusDataFromServer(` method

```
private void addRowToGrid (String name, Widget widget, int row)
{
  serverStats.setText(row, 0, name);
  serverStats.setWidget(row, 1, widget);
  serverStats.getCellFormatter().setStyleName(row, 0, "stat-name");
  serverStats.getCellFormatter().setStyleName(row, 1, "stat-value");
}

private void getStatusDataFromServer ()
{
}
```

If you run the application now, you see that it's starting to come together. Figure 11.3 shows what the application should look like.

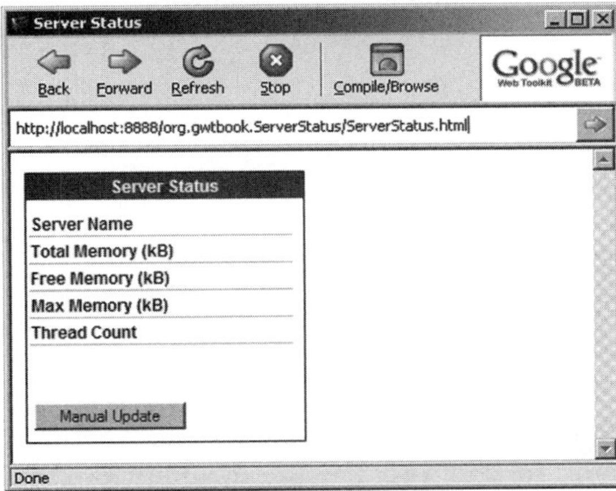

Figure 11.3
A nearly complete version of the Server Status component example

This assumes you've been following the example throughout the chapter and are using the CSS provided in section 10.1.

Now that you have the majority of the application's moving parts, you need to fill in the `getStatusDataFromServer()` method, which calls the remote method. You'll do this a little differently than you did in the prior section: This time, you'll encapsulate the interface to the server as a façade.

11.1.2 Encapsulating remote calls in a façade

The Façade pattern is one of the software patterns described in the famed book *Design Patterns: Elements of Reusable Object-Oriented Software* by Gamma, Helm, Johnson, and Vlissides. This book defines the Façade software pattern as a way of providing a higher-level interface to make a subsystem easier to use. In this case, you want to encapsulate all of the RPC logic into a class that provides a simple interface in an effort to achieve the following:

- Reduce complexity by reducing the number of classes you need to interact with.
- Promote weak coupling, allowing you to alter the underlying RPC mechanism without affecting the client.

We all like reduced complexity, because easier is almost always better, so it isn't hard to understand the motivation for wanting the first point. You'll realize this by creating a new class named `ServerService` with one method for each remote method plus a single `getInstance()` method (see listing 11.5).

Listing 11.5 `ServerService` class

```
package org.gwtbook.client;

public class ServerService
{
  public static ServerService getInstance();
  public void getStatusData (AsyncCallback callback);
}
```

This class follows the Singleton software pattern, providing a single static method to retrieve an instance of the `ServerService` class. From this instance, you provide a `getStatusData()` method to call the remote service. It may be tempting to do away with the `getInstance()` method and make the remote method call static, but this isn't a good idea. Doing so would reduce the flexibility of the class and make it more difficult to do things such as allowing multiple instances to be created. It's one of those cases where you need to make the code a little more verbose to make future maintenance easier.

With the interface for the service class defined, you now need to implement the RPC service it will provide. In this case, your needs are simple: You have only a single endpoint (service URL) to call on the server, and you have only one method. The implementation is straightforward; see listing 11.6.

Listing 11.6 The service façade

```
package org.gwtbook.client;

import com.google.gwt.core.client.GWT;
import com.google.gwt.user.client.rpc.AsyncCallback;
import com.google.gwt.user.client.rpc.ServiceDefTarget;

public class ServerService {

  private static ServerService instance;
  private ServerStatusServiceAsync proxy;

  private ServerService() {
    proxy = (ServerStatusServiceAsync)
      GWT.create(ServerStatusService.class);
    ((ServiceDefTarget) proxy).setServiceEntryPoint(
      GWT.getModuleBaseURL() + "server-status");
  }

  public static ServerService getInstance() {
    if (instance == null) {
      instance = new ServerService();
    }
    return instance;
  }

  public void getStatusData(AsyncCallback callback) {
    proxy.getStatusData(callback);
  }
}
```

In this implementation, you make the constructor private, allowing only the `ServerService` class to create an instance of itself. When `getInstance()` is called, it creates a new instance of the `ServerService` class only if one has not been created. This ensures that there will only ever be one instance of this class. When the `ServerService` class is instantiated, it creates the proxy instance that will be needed to call the server. When the `getStatusData()` method is finally called, the proxy object has already been created and can pass the callback object to the proxy.

You've effectively met your initial goals for using a façade. You've reduced the complexity of the `ServerStatusComponent` class because it no longer needs to deal with any of the underlying RPC code, including the creation of a proxy object and specifing an endpoint. You've also decoupled the calling class from the RPC implementation. You could potentially replace the GWT-RPC call with some other RPC mechanism such as XML-RPC, and you could do this without having to change any code in the Server Status component. You can do so only because you've completely delegated the RPC responsibility to the `ServerService` class.

Now that you have the façade class implemented, you can write the rest of the code for the Server Status component. You'll do so by using the Command software pattern to provide future flexibility.

11.1.3 *Callback routine using the Command pattern*

Early in our discussion of RPC, we addressed the fact that calls to the server are done in an asynchronous fashion, where the call to the server is as a separate thread of execution. We then examined how you can pass an anonymous instance of the `AsyncCallback` interface to receive the result from the server. Here's the example we provided earlier:

```
AsyncCallback callback = new AsyncCallback() {
  public void onFailure (Throwable caught) {
    GWT.log("RPC error", caught);
  }

  public void onSuccess (Object result) {
    GWT.log("RPC success", null);
  }
};
```

This is a valid way of providing a callback object, but it has a couple of drawbacks. First, it locks you into using this specific functionality; if you wanted to change the functionality, you would need to rewrite the existing routine. Second, you can't extend the functionality of the callback because it's an anonymous class.

The solution to both of these issues is to use the Command pattern. The benefits you hope to achieve are as follows:

- Create a new callback without having to rewrite or remove an existing callback.
- Extend and reuse the callback.
- Have the ability to create a callback that can execute other callbacks.

Applying the Command pattern is easy, especially given the way the existing callback mechanism works in GWT. All you need to do is create a named class for your callback; see listing 11.7.

Listing 11.7 A callback command

```
private void getStatusDataFromServer ()
{
  ServerService.getInstance().getStatusData(
    new ServerStatsUpdater());
}

class ServerStatsUpdater implements AsyncCallback
{
  public void onFailure(Throwable caught) {
  }

  public void onSuccess(Object result) {
    ServerStatusData data = (ServerStatusData) result;
    labelServerName.setText(data.serverName);
    labelTotalMemory.setText(toKB(data.totalMemory));
    labelFreeMemory.setText(toKB(data.freeMemory));
    labelMaxMemory.setText(toKB(data.maxMemory));
    labelThreadCount.setText(Integer.toString(data.threadCount));
    labelLastUpdated.setText(new Date().toString());
  }
}
```

In the `getStatusDataFromServer()` method, you pass a new instance of `ServerStatsUpdater`, an inline class, instead of passing an anonymous callback routine. The `ServerStatsUpdater` class is the *command* object. In this case, you make the command an inline class due to the fact that it needs to update various `Label` objects inside the Server Status component. This, however, doesn't take away from the fact that you've added flexibility with almost no additional coding time, and this code is easier to read than if you had used an anonymous `AsyncCallback` instance.

To provide an example of how this can add flexibility to your application, let's add an additional requirement to the callback. Let's require that you use the GWT logging mechanism on all callbacks to log the result of a callback. You could add this directly to the `onFailure()` and `onSuccess()` methods as in the following anonymous `AsyncCallback`, but there are some problems with this design:

```
AsyncCallback callback = new AsyncCallback() {
  public void onFailure(Throwable caught) {
    GWT.log("RPC Error", caught);
  }
```

```
    public void onSuccess(Object result) {
      GWT.log("RPC Success", null);
      ...
    }
  };
```

In practice, you'll likely have many different RPC commands, and you'd need to add this code to each callback. This in itself isn't the problem; the problem occurs when you change your mind about how to log this information. For example, the previous code doesn't let you know which RPC command was executed; it only lets you know whether it was successful. As developers, we aren't fortune-tellers; a good design can prevent pain later when you need to update existing code. Using chains of callbacks is one solution you can apply to this problem.

Chaining callbacks for separation of activities

If you go back to the Command pattern example, there are two ways in which you can provide shared logging functionality. The first is by chaining callbacks, and the second is to provide a superclass to the `ServerStatsUpdater` class, which includes logging capabilities. Let's examine how to solve this problem by chaining callbacks. To do this, you need to create a new class called `LoggingChainingCallback` (see listing 11.8).

Listing 11.8 `LoggingChainingCallback` class

```
package org.gwtbook.client;

import com.google.gwt.core.client.GWT;
import com.google.gwt.user.client.rpc.AsyncCallback;

public class LoggingChainingCallback implements AsyncCallback {

  private AsyncCallback callback;

  public LoggingChainingCallback(AsyncCallback callback) {
    this.callback = callback;
  }

  public void onFailure(Throwable caught) {
    GWT.log("RPC Failure ["
        + GWT.getTypeName(callback) + "]", caught);
    callback.onFailure(caught);
  }
```

```
    public void onSuccess(Object result) {
      GWT.log("RPC Success ["
          + GWT.getTypeName(callback) + "]", null);
      callback.onSuccess(result);
    }
  }
```

The `LoggingChainingCallback` class implements the `AsyncCallback` interface and, as such, includes the `onFailure()` and `onSuccess()` methods. Notice that you add a constructor to this class. It takes an `AsyncCallback` as a constructor argument and stores the object in a private instance variable. You reference this instance in both the `onFailure()` and `onSuccess()` methods, using it to pass the result to that object after logging the event.

To use this class, all you need to do is alter the calling code slightly. You now pass the new `ServerStatsUpdater` callback to the constructor of the `LoggingChainingCallback`. The `LoggingChainingCallback` instance is then passed as an argument to the `getStatusData()` method:

```
private void getStatusDataFromServer ()
{
  ServerService.getInstance().getStatusData(
    new LoggingChainingCallback(new ServerStatsUpdater())
  );
}
```

If you're confused about the chain of events, figure 11.4 will help. It shows the sequence of what happens when a successful result is returned from the server. The `ServerService` calls the `onSuccess()` method of the `LoggingChainingCallback`. This class logs the event and then passes the result on to the `ServerStatsUpdater`, which updates the fields.

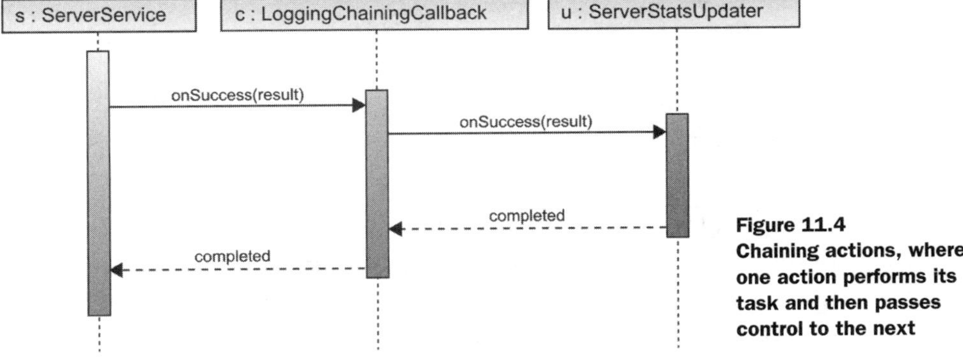

Figure 11.4 Chaining actions, where one action performs its task and then passes control to the next

You've chained two callbacks together, where each performs its own function without overlap. In this design, you separate out the logging portion of the application so that it can be shared and modified independently of the callbacks to which it passes the request. With a little architecture, you've helped to future-proof the application, making it easier to alter logging functionality at a later date.

Besides chaining callbacks, we also mentioned that the Command software pattern allows you to subclass the command to enhance or replace the existing functionality.

Using an AsyncCallback superclass

As you've seen, you've applied the Command software pattern by creating a class that implements the `AsyncCallback` interface. One of the original reasons for doing this was so you could extend the command class, which is something you can't do if you use an anonymous class for the callback. Again, the goal goes back to the need to separate out the logging for all RPC commands into a single class that can be reused and maintained in a single place.

You can achieve this two ways with a superclass. The first is by convention, and the second is to create a new type of callback interface. By *convention*, we mean that it's up to the developer to follow the rules; if the rules are followed, the system works. In general, it's a bad idea to allow a developer the ability to *not* follow the rules when functionality could break. But this approach is still useful when you can enforce the convention. For other times, there is a second approach. The goals you'll attempt to achieve include the following:

- Provide an abstract callback superclass that can be subclassed to add specific behaviors (such as logging).
- Give the superclass the ability to handle the RPC result before the subclass.

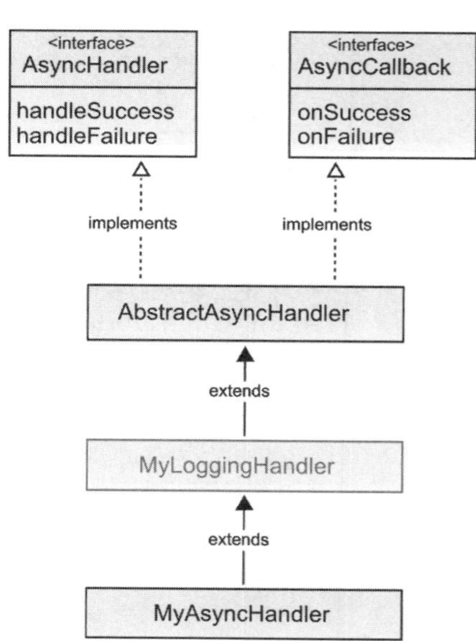

Figure 11.5 Creating your own handler interface so you can add functionality, like logging, in a reusable manner

To do this, you need to do a little design work. Figure 11.5 shows a high-level overview of what the new structure will look like.

Figure 11.5 introduces a new interface called `AsyncHandler` that contains the two methods `handleSuccess()` and `handleFailure()`. You then create the class `AbstractAsyncHandler` that implements both the new interface and GWT's `AsyncCallback` interface. You achieve the desired behavior by having this new abstract class intercept the RPC `onSuccess()` or `onFailure()` event and then forward it on to either the `handleSuccess()` or `handleFailure()` method.

The abstract handler in this sense is passing on the event to a method of a different name. You want to do this so the `MyAsyncHandler` will implement only the `handleSuccess()` and `handleFailure()` methods, and not the methods defined by the `AsyncCallback` interface. This allows you to extend the `AbstractAsyncHandler` with a handler with a specific function, like a logging handler, which only overrides the `onSuccess()` and `onFailure()` methods.

To build this, you'll start at the top and work your way down. First, you create the `AsyncHandler` interface, which defines the two new methods:

```
package org.gwtbook.client;

public interface AsyncHandler {

  void handleSuccess(Object result);

  void handleFailure(Throwable caught);
}
```

The `AsyncHandler` interface mirrors the `AsyncCallback` interface in that it has two methods with the same parameters and return values; the only difference is the method names. Next, you need to create the `AbstractAsyncHandler` class (see listing 11.9).

Listing 11.9 `AbstractAsyncHandler` class

```
package org.gwtbook.client;

import com.google.gwt.user.client.rpc.AsyncCallback;

public abstract class AbstractAsyncHandler
  implements AsyncCallback, AsyncHandler {

  public void onFailure(Throwable caught) {
    handleFailure(caught);
  }

  public void onSuccess(Object result) {
    handleSuccess(result);
  }
```

```
    public abstract void handleFailure(Throwable caught);

    public abstract void handleSuccess(Object result);
  }
```

You declare the class as abstract, as well as the `handleFailure()` and `handleSuccess()` methods. This forces subclasses to either declare themselves as abstract or implement the two abstract interfaces. The next class in figure 11.5 is `MyLoggingHandler` class, but we're going to skip this one for now because it's just a placeholder for a handler class containing any type of needed functionality. Let's skip to `MyAsyncHandler`, which is the specific handler you need to create for a specific RPC call.

In the Server Status component RPC call, you implemented `ServerStatsUpdater` as the callback handler. Let's revisit that handler and alter it to use the new `AbstractAsyncHandler` as its parent class. The following code replaces the code you used earlier for both the call to the service class and the response handler:

```
private void getStatusDataFromServer ()
{
  ServerService.getInstance().getStatusData(
    new ServerStatsUpdater());
}

class ServerStatsUpdater extends AbstractAsyncHandler {

  public void handleFailure(Throwable caught) { }

  public void handleSuccess(Object result) {
    // success code
  }
}
```

This is essentially the same thing you started with, except the `ServerStatsUpdater` now extends the new `AbstractAsyncHandler` instead of implementing GWT's `AsyncCallback` interface. With this change comes the fact that the handler method names are different, matching the abstract methods of the `AbstractAsyncHandler` class.

This new structure adds flexibility. As a reminder, these were the goals set forth for organizing the classes in this manner:

- Provide an abstract callback superclass that can be subclassed to add specific behaviors (such as logging).
- Give the superclass the ability to handle the RPC result before the subclass.

To demonstrate that you've achieved both of these goals, let's go back to the logging example and create a subclass of the `AbstractAsyncHandler` that will automatically log RPC events. Name the class `LoggingAsyncHandler` to indicate that it provides automatic logging (see listing 11.10).

Listing 11.10 `LoggingAsyncHandler` class

```
package org.gwtbook.client;

import com.google.gwt.core.client.GWT;

public abstract class LoggingAsyncHandler
    extends AbstractAsyncHandler {

  public final void onSuccess(Object result) {
    GWT.log("RPC Success [" + GWT.getTypeName(this) + "]", null);
    super.onSuccess(result);
  }

  public final void onFailure(Throwable caught) {
    GWT.log("RPC Failure [" + GWT.getTypeName(this) + "]", caught);
    super.onFailure(caught);
  }
}
```

Notice that you make the `LoggingAsyncHandler` class abstract, so it doesn't need to implement the `handleSuccess()` and `handleFailure()` methods. You also override the `onSuccess()` and `onFailure()` methods and make them final. The purpose of making them final is so subclasses can't alter the behavior of the class, which would most likely break it.

The `onSuccess()` and `onFailure()` methods are overridden to add the required logging capabilities and log the event prior to the handling of the event by its subclasses. This meets both requirements you set out to achieve.

Figure 11.6 summarizes the chain of events when a response is returned from the server. The `LoggingAsyncHandler` gets the first look at the response and passes the response up to its parent class, which then passes it down to the only class that implements the abstract `handleSuccess()` and `handleFailure()` methods.

It may seem as though you went the long way around to add a couple of simple logging statements, but as your GWT application gets larger, it becomes increasingly important to have a good design. The payback from this additional work comes from reuse of the logging handler and ease of maintenance.

Now that we've discussed a couple of patterns for maintainable client-side code, we can turn our attention back to the more general concept of polling.

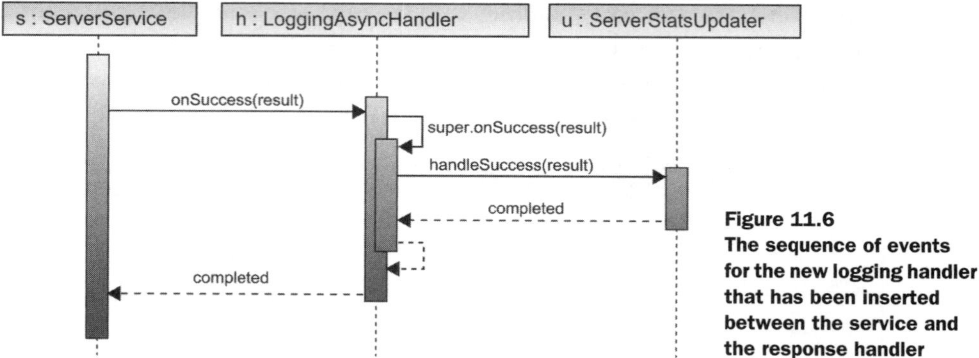

Figure 11.6 The sequence of events for the new logging handler that has been inserted between the service and the response handler

11.2 Examining different polling techniques

Often, you may need to keep in constant contact with the server via RPC calls to keep the client updated. This is usually to inform the client browser of some event like the arrival of an email, a new chat message, a server being out of disk space, and so on. The solution is to *poll* the server. This can be done by contacting the server via RPC on a regular basis, such as every five minutes. Some applications require more frequent updates and may want to be as close to real-time as possible. In this section, we'll explore GWT's functionality for scheduling tasks and examine various polling techniques.

We'll begin our examination by providing a high-level overview of polling terminology, including pull versus push. Then, we'll look at the GWT `Timer` class and explain how it works. You'll use the `Timer` class to enhance the Server Status component by making it update its contents on a regular basis. Following this, we'll look at a technique called *blocking* to emulate a server-push mechanism.

11.2.1 Understanding polling issues

Before we get into implementing polling, it's useful to understand the different ways of delivering content and the consequences of each. Delivery techniques can be broken into two categories: server push and client pull. A *push* is when the server pushes content out to a client, and *pull* is when the client requests data from the server—the primary difference between these two being who initiates the request. Let's look a little closer at these types: first push, then pull.

Examining server-push

In theory, pushing data out to your clients is useful. You use it daily when you send an email or an instant message. For example, when you send an email, you're sending it to a mail server, which in turn pushes the mail to another mail server. The same goes for instant messaging, where the message gets pushed to the intended recipient.

By pushing data out to clients, you can have any number of clients, perhaps many thousands, and no server or bandwidth resources are used until you have something to send. This scales well, and you can easily support any number of clients with this scheme with relative ease.

There is one hitch: Web browsers don't have this capability. During the 1990s, quite a bit of work went into this area, but it never caught on. Part of the problem is that if you could push data to the browser, it would likely pose security issues, opening the user to a new breed of attack.

Although you can't achieve true server-push, you're often required to emulate it—for example, if you want to build a chat client that immediately broadcasts messages it receives. There are several techniques for doing this, like Comet, Pushlet, Pjax, and others. For the most part, these are difficult to implement in GWT, so we won't discuss them here. Blocking server threads, on the other hand, is easy to implement in GWT; we'll provide a full example of implementing this a little later.

The opposite of *push* is *pull*; we'll examine pull technologies next.

Examining client-pull

Client-pull is another name for the standard request-response sequence used by the browser. When you go to a URL with your browser, you request a page from the server or, in other words, pull the page from the server. This technique is useful when a delay between the publication of an event and the receiving of an event is acceptable.

Client-pull has its own challenges. Because there can be a delay between sending and receiving the event, you often need to queue up data on the server, waiting for a client to check in. For example, if you write a chat application using client-pull, the server needs to store any unsent messages for a user until that user pulls the messages.

Between the two types of delivering data, pulling is the natural for web browsers. We'll examine a client-pull implementation first by implementing a continuously updating component.

11.2.2 Implementing a continuously updating component

In this section, we'll revisit the Server Status component and allow it to periodically update itself. To do this, you'll add the ability to set the refresh rate for the data, as well as add the ability to change or stop the automatic updates. In doing so, we'll need to look at the GWT `Timer` class, which allows you to trigger timed events.

If you've been following along with us, your Server Status component should be working and have a method that can be called to have it update its information from the server. If you haven't been following with us, here is the basic shell for the Server Status component, which includes a `getStatusDataFromServer()` method that triggers an RPC call and updates the displayed data:

```
package org.gwtbook.client;

import java.util.Date;
import com.google.gwt.core.client.*;
import com.google.gwt.user.client.rpc.*;
import com.google.gwt.user.client.ui.*;

public class ServerStatusComponent extends Composite
{
  public ServerStatusComponent () {
    ...
  }

  private void getStatusDataFromServer () {
    ...
  }
}
```

In the full version of the Server Status component, the `getStatusDataFromServer()` method is called when the component is first initialized or when an update button is clicked. Next, you'll add a timer to trigger an update as well.

Using the GWT Timer class

The `Timer` class can be found in the `com.google.gwt.user.client` package. It provides a no-argument constructor and several methods. The method signatures are as follows:

```
public abstract class Timer {
  public abstract void run();
  public void schedule(int milliseconds);
  public void scheduleRepeating(int milliseconds);
  public void cancel();
}
```

The first thing to point out is that the `Timer` class is abstract, so you must subclass it to be able to use it. You can do this by creating an anonymous class or creating your own specialized timer class. When you implement your class, you need to implement the abstract method, run(), that is called when the timer is triggered. In this example, you create a timer that alerts the user with a "hello" message when a timer event is triggered:

```
Timer example = new Timer() {
  public void run () {
    Window.alert("hello");
  }
};
```

To trigger a timer event, you need to set either a one-time event with the schedule() method or a recurring event with the scheduleRepeating() method. In the case of schedule(), you specify the number of milliseconds to wait before executing the run() method. The scheduleRepeating() method also takes the number of milliseconds as a parameter, and it repeatedly executes the run() method. The first execution of run() begins in the number of milliseconds specified and then continuously recurs at that same interval.

The cancel() method, as apparent by its name, allows you to stop the timer. Once it's stopped, you may start it again by calling either the schedule() or scheduleRepeating() method. The following example sets the timer for five seconds and then cancels it:

```
example.schedule(5000);
example.cancel(); // just kidding
```

The next step is to add additional methods to the Server Status component to provide the ability to set the update interval as well as the ability to stop the automatic updates. You'll do this via a schedulable class.

Creating a schedulable class

There are many ways to implement a timer, but you'll use an approach we think is highly reusable. The code not only can be used in the Server Status component, but also applies to any Composite component. It's also possible, with some minor changes, to adapt it to other base classes.

You'll accomplish this by creating a subclass of Composite called UpdateableComposite, shown in figure 11.7, that provides methods for setting and stopping the update timer. Before you start coding, look at the class diagram to see the relationships between the new class and the existing ServerStatusComponent class.

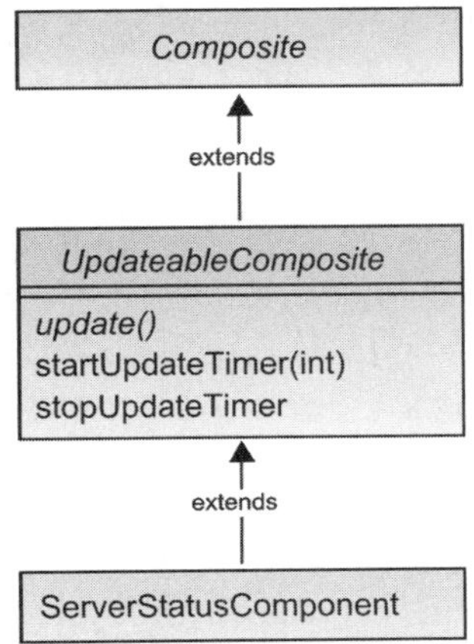

Figure 11.7 A structural overview of the reusable, updateable-composite

We'll begin by introducing the new `UpdateableComposite` as a subclass of `Composite`. `UpdateableComposite` is an abstract class, meaning that it must be subclassed to use it, and it contains three methods. The `startUpdateTimer()` method starts the update timer. It allows you to specify the number of seconds between updates; you can use this same method to change the update interval. The `update()` method is an abstract method and must be implemented by the subclass.

Once you implement `UpdateableComposite` class, you alter the Server Status component to implement the `update()` method, and then set the timer (see listing 11.11).

Listing 11.11 Abstract `UpdateableComposite` class

```
package org.gwtbook.client;

import com.google.gwt.user.client.Timer;
import com.google.gwt.user.client.ui.Composite;

public abstract class UpdateableComposite extends Composite
{
  private Timer timer = null;

  public abstract void update();

  public void startUpdateTimer(int seconds)
  {
    if (timer != null) {
      stopUpdateTimer();
    }

    timer = new Timer() {
      public void run() {
        update();
      }
    };

    timer.scheduleRepeating(seconds * 1000);
  }

  public void stopUpdateTimer()
  {
    if (timer == null)
      return;

    timer.cancel();
    timer = null;
  }
}
```

The implementation is straightforward but is worth some explanation. The class contains a single private field called `timer`, which holds the `Timer` object. You need to hold onto a reference to the `Timer` object so that you can cancel it when `stopUpdateTimer()` is called. Looking at the `stopUpdateTimer()` method, you can see that the method calls `cancel()` on the `Timer` object and then sets the timer field to null.

The `startUpdateTimer()` method first checks to see if the timer field is null. If it isn't null, this is a sign that it has already been started. The method responds by calling `stopUpdateTimer()` to cancel the existing timer. This allows you to use `startUpdateTimer()` to change the interval period without having to worry about stopping the existing timer. The method then goes on to create a `Timer` instance. You're creating the `Timer` as an anonymous class, which prevents external clients of this class from being able to control the timer directly. In the timer's `run()` method, you call the abstract method `update()`. It will be left up to the subclasses of `UpdateableComposite` to determine what the `update()` method does.

With the `UpdateableComposite` complete, the only thing left to do is alter the Server Status component to take advantage of the scheduling capabilities:

```
public class ServerStatusComponent extends UpdateableComposite
{
  ...

  public void update() {
    getStatusDataFromServer();
  }
}
```

The only change is that you now extend `UpdateableComposite` instead of `Composite` directly, and you implement the `update()` method. The `update()` method, in turn, calls the private method `getStatusDataFromServer()`, which you created before triggering an RPC call to the server. In projects other than the Server Status component, you can include whatever code is required to update the component in the `update()` method.

With this mechanism in place, you can now easily create and schedule updates for the component. The code to do this for the Server Status component is here, but it will be essentially the same for any custom component that subclasses `UpdateableComposite`:

```
ServerStatusComponent serverStatus = new ServerStatusComponent();
serverStatus.startUpdateTimer(60);
```

In summary, using the GWT `Timer` class, it's easy to schedule a piece of code to execute on a schedule. The concepts for doing this are the same no matter if you're using a timer to schedule polling of the server or updating a display. In either case, it's always a good idea to think through the design and use the tools that Java provides to create reusable code. The `UpdateableComposite` is just one example.

Now that we've explored timers and, in conjunction, the concept of polling, it's time to look at how you can emulate server-push and push events to the client browser.

11.2.3 Emulating server-push by blocking server threads

As we briefly mentioned earlier, no true server-push is available to browsers, meaning the server can't send data to the browser without the browser requesting it. The reasons are security and lack of a standard. To accommodate for this lack of functionality, there are several schemes for emulating server-push. In this section, we'll discuss and implement one such variation called *blocking server threads.*

From a high level, RPC involves a client browser requesting data from a server. The server then processes the request and returns a result. Not only is this how browser-based RPC works, but it's also how web pages are served. With blocking server threads, you add one small alteration: You hold up the processing on the server until data is available to process. It's similar to a company with poor customer service—you end up waiting on hold until there is someone to talk to you.

To help understand how this works, figure 11.8 provides a visual comparison between polling and blocking server threads.

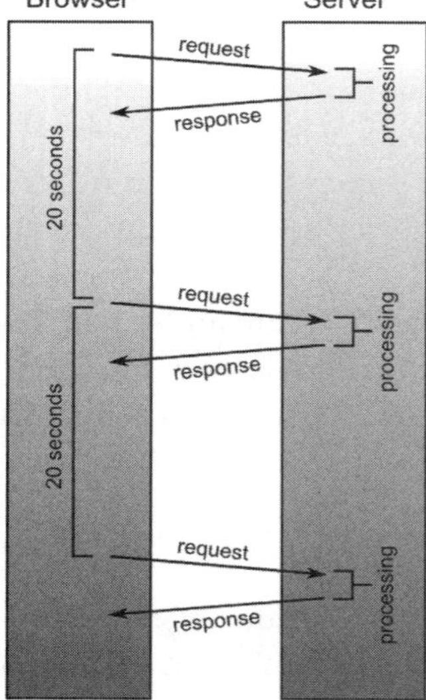

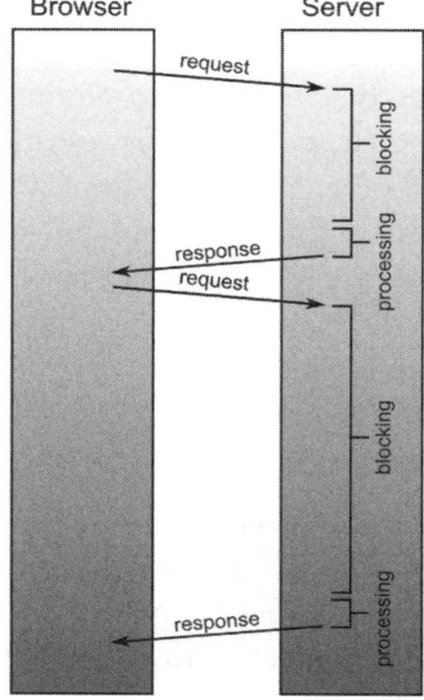

Figure 11.8 A visual comparison of server polling and the blocking-threads technique

In figure 11.8 you can see that when you use polling, the browser handles the orchestration by calling the server every 20 seconds. With blocking, the server becomes the conductor, placing the request on hold until it needs to process the request. Another important difference is that with blocking, you have an almost constant connection between the client and the server.

A web-based chat client is the classic example of the need for blocking server threads, and we'll use this type of application as our example. You won't build a complete component because doing so would require covering a lot of the same topics we've already discussed; but we'll explain the few changes required to make it work. We'll start with the code required on the client and then look at what changes are needed on the server.

Implementing blocking on the client

When you implement the client side of blocking server threads, there is little that you need to do. The only requirement is that each time you get a response from the server, you need to initiate a new request. Take the following `AsyncCallback` implementation for example. We've removed the implementation details, but notice that it calls the method `getDataFromServer()` on both success and failure:

```
class ChatPanelUpdater implements AsyncCallback
{
  public void onFailure (Throwable caught) {
    ...
    getDataFromServer();
  }

  public void onSuccess (Object result) {
    ...
    getDataFromServer();
  }
}
```

You'd need to define `getDataFromServer()`; the only requirement is that this method triggers another RPC request. In the Server Status component, the method `getStatusDataFromServer()` serves the same purpose.

With this one minor change, we can turn our attention to the more interesting aspects of blocking server threads on the server.

Implementing blocking on the server

Implementing the server portion of a blocking RPC server can be done the same way you block any Java thread: by issuing a *sleep* command. When you issue a sleep command to the JVM, it stops processing that specific thread of execution for some amount of time. Once the sleep time is finished, the thread wakes up and continues processing. Issuing a sleep command involves a single statement. The method `Thread.sleep()` takes a number of milliseconds to sleep; passing 1000 to the method causes the thread to sleep for one second:

```
Thread.sleep(1000);
```

For our purposes, you need to do more than just block the thread for some amount of time. You need to first determine whether you should process the request, which in the case of a chat application is when you have a message that you want to send the user. On the other hand, if you don't have a message to send, you should put the thread to sleep for a short period of time. Once the thread wakes up, you check again whether you should process the request. To do so, you use a loop similar to this:

```
public List getMessages ()
{
  List result = new ArrayList();

  try {
    while (true) {
      if (canProcess()) {
        result = process();
        break;
      }

      Thread.sleep(1000);
    }
  } catch (InterruptedException ignore) {
  }

  return result;
}
```

You use the `while(true)` loop to create an endless loop, and at the end of the loop, you use `Thread.sleep()` to sleep for one second. Prior to sleeping, you check to see if you can process the request by calling `canProcess()`; if you can, you call `process()` to get the result of the RPC call and then break out of the `while` loop. The `try` statement catches an `InterruptedException`, which could result from the call to `Thread.sleep()`—for example, if the application server was being shut down.

This loop is fine, but what happens if the user closes their browser or navigates to a different web page? Unfortunately, you don't have a good way to be notified of these events, so potentially a thread could loop forever even though the browser client is no longer present. To solve this problem, you need to introduce a timeout (see listing 11.12).

Listing 11.12 Blocking threads example with the introduction of a timeout

```
public List getMessages ()
{
  List result = new ArrayList();
  long timeout = System.currentTimeMillis() + (30 * 1000);

  try {
    while (true) {
      if (canProcess()) {
        result = process();
        break;
      }

      if (System.currentTimeMillis() > timeout) {
        break;
      }

      Thread.sleep(1000);
    }
  } catch (InterruptedException ignore) {
  }

  return result;
}
```

To the original example, you added a timeout value: You set the value to the current time in milliseconds and add 30 seconds to that value. You also added a check, and, if the current time exceeds the timeout value, it breaks the loop. The timeout value you use depends on your specific project, but in most cases 30 seconds is sufficient to keep the number of requests down while removing stale connections quickly.

The exact implementation of `canProcess()` and `process()` depends a lot on the purpose of the method. For example, with the chat application, you'll likely have a queue of messages for each user of the system, in which case `canProcess()` returns `true` if any messages are in the queue for that user. The `process()` method then returns the list of messages and clears out the queue, or marks the messages in the queue as being delivered.

Now that we've shown how you can easily implement polling, let's turn our attention to a completely different, although equally important, topic: how to create custom serialization routines for your objects.

11.3 Writing custom field serializers

With GWT's basic serialization system, you can create data objects that implement the `IsSerializable` interface, which can be passed between the client and server. When you implement this interface, GWT handles all the details of serialization and deserialization for you. This is usually sufficient for most work with GWT, but occasionally this mechanism isn't sufficient for a given project. Three common reasons for needing to write a custom field serializer are as follows:

- The default serialization causes performance issues for a complex object.
- The class that needs to be serialized doesn't implement `IsSerializable` (or `Serializable` as of GWT 1.4).
- The class that needs to be serialized doesn't have a zero-argument constructor.

Writing a custom field serializer is fairly easy. In this section, you'll take the `ServerStatusData` class that you used as the data object for the ServerStatus component example, and you will write a custom serializer for it. To begin, let's look at the original implementation of the `ServerStatusData` class, shown in listing 11.13.

Listing 11.13 Original implementation of the `ServerStatusData` class

```
package org.gwtbook.client;

import com.google.gwt.user.client.rpc.IsSerializable;

public class ServerStatusData implements IsSerializable
{
  public String serverName;
  public long totalMemory;
  public long freeMemory;
  public long maxMemory;
  public int threadCount;
}
```

The data object is fairly simple, including only five fields; the custom field serializer will also be fairly simple, but it will highlight the important concepts. You'll begin by creating a custom field serializer class, and we'll look at implementing both serialization and deserialization. We'll then discuss how to serialize objects that don't have a zero-argument constructor.

11.3.1 Creating a custom field serializer class

To begin, you need to create a class for each custom field serializer, which must follow some rules:

- The serializer class must reside in the same package as the class that it serializes.
- The serializer class must have the same name as the class that it serializes plus `_CustomFieldSerializer`.
- It must implement `serialize()` and `deserialize()` methods.
- It may optionally implement an `instantiate()` method if the class requires custom creation.

These rules require the convention of adding the suffix "`CustomFieldSerializer`" to a class to specify that it's a custom serialization class. Also, as you'll see shortly, the three methods have signatures that depend on the class type being serialized. To help you understand how all this works, you'll start by building the shell of the class; then, we'll discuss each of the method signatures it contains. (See listing 11.14.)

Listing 11.14 Beginnings of the `ServerStatusData_CustomFieldSerializer` class

```
package org.gwtbook.client;

import com.google.gwt.user.client.rpc.SerializationException;
import com.google.gwt.user.client.rpc.SerializationStreamReader;
import com.google.gwt.user.client.rpc.SerializationStreamWriter;

public class ServerStatusData_CustomFieldSerializer
{
  public static ServerStatusData instantiate(
    SerializationStreamReader reader)
      throws SerializationException
  {
  }

  public static void serialize(
    SerializationStreamWriter writer,
    ServerStatusData instance)
      throws SerializationException
  {
  }
```

```
    public static void deserialize(
      SerializationStreamReader reader,
      ServerStatusData instance)
        throws SerializationException
    {
    }
  }
```

The first method, `instantiate()`, is a static method that takes a `SerializationStreamReader` as an argument (which we'll discuss shortly) and returns an object of the type this class was built to serialize, namely the `ServerStatusData` class. The `instantiate()` method is optional and is required only when the target class doesn't have a zero-argument constructor. It must return the same type of object that you've built this class to serialize and deserialize—in this case, a `ServerStatusData` instance. The `instantiate()` method, like the other two methods, throws `SerializationException`.

The `serialize()` method is a static method that takes a `writer` object, used for adding data to the serialization stream, and an `instance` object, which is the object that is being serialized (in this case, a `ServerStatusData` object). This instance object is of the same type that you're serializing, so if your custom field serializer was serializing an object of type `Foo`, then the instance parameter would be of type `Foo`.

The `deserialize()` method receives a `reader` object, which can read data from the serialized stream, and an `instance` object of the type of object that you're deserializing (in this case, a `ServerStatusData` object). The `instance` object is the same object that was created by the `instantiate()` method, and the `reader` object is the same reader that was given as a parameter to `instantiate()`. The pattern for deserialization is that `instantiate()` is called first and is given an opportunity to read data from the serialized stream and use it in the creation of the object. The instance created by `instantiate()` is then passed to `deserialize()` along with the reader, allowing it to continue reading from the stream and setting any properties of the object.

Now that you have a basic shell, let's discuss the usage of the serialization reader and writer classes by implementing the methods in the class.

11.3.2 Implementing custom field serialization

Thus far, we've looked at the method signatures for the custom field serializer, but you haven't yet implemented them. Let's inspect each method individually and explain its purpose and how it should be implemented.

Implementing the instantiate() method

When GWT serializes or deserializes an object using your custom field serializer class, it calls `instantiate()`. The purpose of this method is to create a new instance of your object, including passing any values to the constructor required for its creation. This method has a default behavior, and you don't need to implement the method unless you need to override the implementation. The default behavior as shown here, calls the zero-argument constructor of the data class and returns the instance:

```
public static ServerStatusData instantiate(
  SerializationStreamReader reader)
  throws SerializationException
{
  return new ServerStatusData();
}
```

In this implementation, you implemented a field serializer for the data class `ServerStatusData`. If you were writing a field serializer for a different class, the method signature would change to return an object of that type.

A `SerializationStreamReader` object is passed to this method and can be used to read values from the serialized stream and use those values in the construction of the object. For example, in the following example, the class `FakeData`'s constructor takes a `String` argument, which you pull from the reader:

```
public static FakeData instantiate(SerializationStreamReader reader)
  throws SerializationException
{
  String val = reader.readString();
  return new FakeData(val);
}
```

We'll discuss using the `SerializationStreamReader` in more detail when we look at the `deserialize()` method (after the `serialize()` method).

Implementing the serialize() method

The `serialize()` method of the custom field serializer is passed a `writer` object, which is used to write data to the serialized stream, and an existing object instance, which is the object you'll serialize. Serialization works by reading some data from the object you're serializing and then writing that data to the writer.

The writer is an instance of `SerializationStreamWriter` from the package `com.google.gwt.user.client.rpc`; it includes methods for writing different types of data to the serialized stream. Following is a list of available writer methods, all of which may throw a `SerializationException`:

- `writeBoolean(boolean value)`
- `writeByte(byte value)`
- `writeChar(char value)`
- `writeDouble(double value)`
- `writeFloat(float value)`
- `writeInt(int value)`
- `writeLong(long value)`
- `writeShort(short value)`
- `writeString(String value)`
- `writeObject(Object value)`

The writer includes a method for each of the Java primitive types as well as the `String` and `Object` classes. Writing an object to the stream in turn calls the serializer for that type of object, which could be one of the serializers that comes with GWT or another custom field serializer.

You may write the fields to the stream in any order. The only restriction is that the `deserialize()` method reads the values from the stream in the same order you wrote them.

Implementing the deserialize() method

The `deserialize()` method is passed the object instance created by `instantiate()` and passed a reader so that it can continue reading from the serialized stream. The reader is an instance of `SerializationStreamReader` from the package `com.google.gwt.user.client.rpc`. It has a set of methods that allow you to read one value at a time from the serialized stream. The reader methods mirror the writer methods we looked at previously. It's important that you read the values in the same order as you wrote them, or you'll likely cause a `SerializationException` to be thrown—or, even worse, end up with a deserialized object with the wrong data in the wrong fields.

The reader object has the following methods, all of which throw `SerializationException`:

- `boolean readBoolean()`
- `byte readByte()`
- `char readChar()`
- `double readDouble()`

- `float readFloat()`
- `int readInt()`
- `long readLong()`
- `short readShort()`
- `String readString()`
- `Object readObject()`

Just like the writer, there is one method for each of Java's primitive types, plus `String` and `Object`. Calling `readObject()` in turn causes the deserialization of the value you're reading.

Here is the `deserialize()` method for the `ServerStatusData` object:

```
public static void deserialize(
  SerializationStreamReader streamReader,
  ServerStatusData instance) throws SerializationException
{
  instance.serverName = streamReader.readString();
  instance.totalMemory = streamReader.readLong();
  instance.freeMemory = streamReader.readLong();
  instance.maxMemory = streamReader.readLong();
  instance.threadCount = streamReader.readInt();
}
```

The `deserialize()` method, like the `serialize()` method, is simple; you read each value from the stream in the proper order and set the appropriate field of the object.

11.4 Summary

In chapter 10, we introduced an example component, Server Status, which makes calls to the server and displays statistics on memory usage and the number of server threads. As we progressed through the chapter, we followed an entire build process for the component and presented something new at each step.

In chapter 11, we polished this working example by focusing our attention on the architecture and design of the application. You started by encapsulating your code as a reusable composite component. We looked at how the Façade software pattern can be used to hide the implementation details of the RPC call, providing the flexibility for changing this later without disturbing the entire application. We then focused our attention on the callback routine that receives the data from the server. You encapsulated this object as a Command object, and we discussed how this pattern allows you to easily add functionality like logging or chaining multiple commands together.

Once you had a stable and reusable component, we looked at polling techniques, starting with a comparison of server-push and client-pull. You created an abstract `Composite` class, which can be reused and will allow any component that subclasses it to pull data from the server on a scheduled basis. We followed this up with a discussion of how you can emulate server-push by blocking server threads.

Last, but not least, we discussed cases where the built-in serialization routines aren't enough. You can write your own custom field serializer class to handle a data object that can't follow the requirements of the `IsSerializable` interface.

We've covered quite a bit, but GWT offers even more with respect to RPC. In this chapter, we looked at GWT's proprietary RPC mechanism, which is tailored to deliver Java objects between the client and server. But what if your server isn't Java? In the next chapter, we'll look at the rest of GWT's RPC offering, including the ability to communicate with non-Java servers.

12 Classic Ajax and HTML forms

This chapter covers

- Classic Ajax support
- Loading and parsing external XML data
- Using FormPanel
- Widgets for use with FormPanel

In chapter 10, we showed you how you can use the GWT-RPC mechanism to communicate between the Java application server and the browser to pass Java objects. But what if you don't have a Java application server? What if you use PHP, .NET, or even plain vanilla CGI scripts? Or, what if you want to load static configuration files from the server? These are just some of the situations where the GWT-RPC mechanism doesn't quite do the job.

In this chapter, classic Ajax and good old HTML forms come to our rescue. These tools are generic and flexible, and GWT provides a set of objects that allows you to take advantage of them. In the first half of the chapter, we'll examine the `RequestBuilder` class, which provides support for classic Ajax communication.

In the second half of this chapter we explore GWT's `FormPanel` component, which allows the building of traditional HTML forms in a smart and powerful way. We'll show you some different ways of using this component, including using it for handling file uploads.

With the path set, let's begin this journey by looking at the `RequestBuilder` class.

12.1 Classic Ajax with RequestBuilder

In chapter 10, we discussed asynchronous communication and the role of the underlying `XMLHttpRequest` object. To recap, the `XMLHttpRequest` object is a tool that is a part of modern browsers, which can be scripted with JavaScript. This `XMLHttpRequest` object allows you to fetch content from a remote URL and handle the response programmatically. The benefit of loading content this way is that you can use code to communicate with the server without needing to refresh the web page, making your web application feel more like a desktop application and more user friendly. The GWT-RPC mechanism that you saw in chapters 10 and 11 is a higher-level tool built on top of this lower-level JavaScript object.

In this section, you'll get a lot closer to the `XMLHttpRequest` object than you did when you used GWT-RPC. There are many reasons why you might need to do this. One such situation is where you need to communicate with legacy systems, which often aren't written in Java, and it's too costly to rewrite the server components. Another motivation for not using GWT-RPC arises when you aren't running a Java application server (which is a requirement of GWT-RPC). Whatever the reason, we'll explore how you can access this basic functionality.

We'll begin the discussion with a brief overview of HTTP and the difference between a `GET` and a `POST`. This will provide the groundwork for exploring `RequestBuilder`, which requires you to specify which of these two methods you want to use. If you're already well versed in HTTP, you may still want to quickly browse through the material; we promise to keep it focused and short.

After going over the basics of the communication protocol, we'll examine the `RequestBuilder` class. `RequestBuilder` provides a simple interface with sensible defaults for making remote calls to the server without sacrificing the ability to alter the low-level details of the request when you need it. This includes the ability to alter and add HTTP headers to the request and specifying a timeout.

Let's get some background on the HTTP protocol and the request-response cycle.

12.1.1 Examining HTTP methods

When you load a web page into your browser, the Hypertext Transport Protocol (HTTP) is used to communicate the transaction. HTTP involves a request and a response. The browser sends the request to the server, and the response is sent from the server back to the browser. The exact details of HTTP can get complex, but for the purpose of using GWT we only need to discuss how the basic HTTP messages work.

Each request in HTTP involves issuing a command to the server that includes a method name, a URL, header name-value pairs, and potentially a message body. There are numerous methods; but with GWT, we only need to focus on `GET` and `POST`, because these are the only methods supported by GWT. Both `GET` and `POST` can be used to send data to the server, but the way they accomplish this differs.

Let's look at the `GET` method first.

Dissecting the HTTP GET method

The `GET` command sends all its data as part of the URL. Before we get into the specifics, let's look at an example URL, which is the URL used to perform a Google search for "GWT":

```
http://www.google.com/search?hl=en&q=GWT&btnG=Google%2Bsearch
```

When your browser sends this URL request to google.com, it sends the following `GET` message using HTTP:

```
GET /search?hl=en&q=GWT&btnG=Google%2BSearch HTTP/1.1
Host: www.google.com
```

The URL is still intact, except that the host name has been added as a header. For clarity, we have only included the Host header, but you could use any number of additional name-value pairs to identify information about your browser.

The server at google.com parses this HTTP request and handles it accordingly. In Java and most other server-side platforms, you can get complete information about the request, including the method used, the URL requested, and any of the header name-value pairs. This can be useful if you need to know what specific types of content the client-browser can handle.

The Uniform Resource Locator (URL) may reference an HTML page, an image, or just about anything. The URL is made up of various parts (see figure 12.1).

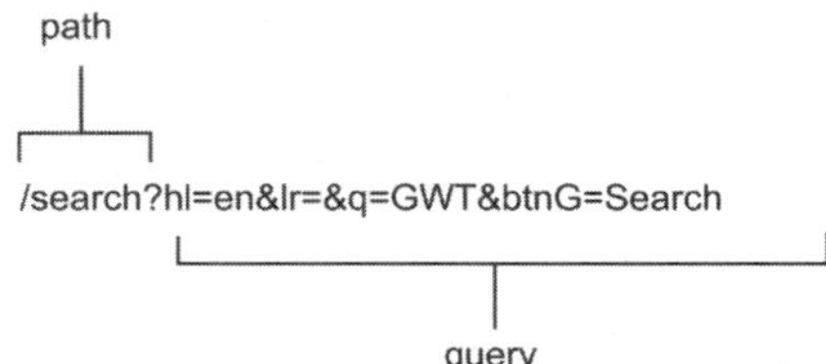

Figure 12.1 The anatomy of a URL, used to reference some piece of content on a server

The important part for us is the query portion of the URL. A single question mark separates the query from the path, and it contains name/value pairs. The name/value pairs are separated by ampersands (&), and the individual pairs use an equal sign (=) to separate the name from the value. The example URL contains the following names: "hl", "lr", "q", and "btnG".

This query is how a `GET` can be used to pass data to the server. Because the query uses both equal signs and ampersands to delimit data, you may not use either of these characters in a name or value. There are several reserved and unsafe characters, including percent (%), star (*), slash (/), space, period (.), plus (+), and hash (#); it's important to escape these characters before you pass them to the server. GWT provides a tool to perform this function for you:

```
String safe = URL.encodeComponent("=unsafe value=");
```

To decode an escaped value, you use the `decodeComponent()` method. The following example decodes the escaped value `"=unsafe value="`:

```
String val = URL.decodeComponent("%3Dunsafe+value%3D");
```

The `URL` class belongs to the `com.google.gwt.http.client` package, and you must specifically import the HTTP module to your module configuration file. You can do this by adding the following line to your module configuration:

```
<inherits name='com.google.gwt.http.HTTP'/>
```

URL escaping involves converting unsafe characters to hexadecimal values and prefixing them with a percent sign. For example, a slash (/) becomes %2F. The only exception is that a space is encoded as a plus (+) symbol. You typically don't need to worry about these details, though, because the encode methods do all the work for you.

With the encodeComponent() method, you can use the following code to build a query whose values were variables that could potentially contain unsafe characters:

```
StringBuffer query = new StringBuffer();
query.append("param1=" + URL.encodeComponent(value1));
query.append("&");
query.append("param2=" + URL.encodeComponent(value2));
query.append("&");
query.append("param3=" + URL.encodeComponent(value3));

String url = "/search?" + query.toString();
```

Notice that you need to escape each potentially unsafe value individually. You also need to make sure that each parameter name is separated from the value by an equal sign (=) and that each name/value pair is separated by an ampersand (&). Once you have a completed query string, you can then attach the script or servlet URL to the beginning and separate it from the query string with a question mark (?).

One limitation of the GET method is that the entire URL has a maximum length that is allowed. Unfortunately, this isn't documented, and each browser and server may impose different length restrictions. Generally, the maximum length is 1,024 characters—but again, it can vary depending on the browser and server. If you expect your URL to be more than a few hundred characters, you shouldn't use the GET method; instead, you'll want to use POST, which brings us to our next topic.

Comparing GET to the POST method

The POST method is typically used for HTML forms, where there can be a lot of data that needs to be transmitted. The POST method differs from the GET method in how it sends data to the server. Instead of including the data as part of the URL query, it uses the *body* of the HTTP message. In HTTP, the command and headers are separated from the body with a single blank line. When we looked at GET, we issued a simple query to a web server. This time, we'll look at the same query, but sent as a POST:

```
POST /search HTTP/1.1
Host: www.google.com
Content-type: application/x-www-form-urlencoded
Content-length: 32

hl=en&q=GWT&btnG=Google%2BSearch
```

We've left out some of the common HTTP header values, but we've added new ones that apply to a POST. The header now includes the content type of the message body as well as the length of the body. The message body isn't limited to a certain size, so any amount of data can be passed to the server in this fashion.

The body content in this example is URL-encoded data, as noted by the `Content-type` header. The content-type value is important because the server needs to know how to read the data so that your server-side application can use it. For example, if you don't specify that the data is URL-encoded, like the previous example, a Java application server won't make this data available to the request object. This is important to know because the default content-type for the `RequestBuilder` class, which we'll look at next, is "text/plain", which isn't always appropriate.

12.1.2 Simple RPC with RequestBuilder

The `RequestBuilder` class allows you to call a URL and register a handler to receive the result. The handler works in a similar fashion as to how it worked with GWT-RPC in chapter 11, except that you can only send and receive text-only data. Any data that isn't in a text form, like a `Date` value, must be converted to text when the data is sent. The data can be sent by either `GET` or `POST`, which implies URL-encoded data when using a `GET`; but for a `POST`, you can pass any sort of text-based data. For both `GET` and `POST`, you can also specify a username and password to gain access to the server resource you're requesting. In most cases, you won't need to do this, but it's offered if the need arises.

`RequestBuilder` resides in the `com.google.gwt.http.client` package, which is part of the HTTP module. To be able to use this class and its helper classes, you need to add the following `inherits` line to your module configuration file:

```
<inherits name='com.google.gwt.http.HTTP'/>
```

The `RequestBuilder` must be instantiated in order to use it. Its only constructor takes two parameters: a method and a URL. The method can be one of two static constants, `RequestBuilder.GET` or `RequestBuilder.POST`. Here is an example of setting up the `RequestBuilder` to use a `POST`:

```
RequestBuilder builder = new RequestBuilder(
  RequestBuilder.POST, "/rpc/storedata");
```

Creating the builder is just the first step. You now have the opportunity to set the properties of the request. This includes adding header pairs, setting the credentials to use, and specifying a timeout:

```
builder.addHeader("Content-type",
    "application/x-www-form-urlencoded");
builder.setUser("mikem");
builder.setPassword("100ta$1nai");
builder.setTimeoutMillis(500);
```

By default, the content-type is set to "text/plain", which isn't always appropriate. If you'll be passing a query string payload to the server, you should specify a content-type of "application/x-www-form-urlencoded". On many server platforms, this content-type value is used to signify that the URL-encoded data should be automatically parsed and decoded by the server. An example of such a server-side framework is a Java application server, which makes the data available via calls to `request.getParameter()` only if this specific content type is used.

Once the additional parameters are set, you need to make the call. To do this, you call the `sendRequest()` method of the `RequestBuilder` object, passing it any data to add to the body of the HTTP message and a callback handler to handle the server response (see listing 12.1). The `sendRequest()` method throws a checked exception `RequestException` if an error occurs when sending the message.

Listing 12.1 Initiating the `RequestBuilder` request

```
Request req = null
try {
  req = builder.sendRequest(
     "storeItem=5893&action=fetch",
     storeCallbackHandler
  );
}
catch (RequestException e) {
  GWT.log("Error", e);
}
```

When you make the call to the server, the `RequestBuilder` returns a handle to the `Request` object. This is often useful if you want to ensure that only one request hits the server at a time, or if you need the ability to check the status of a long-running request.

For example, to ensure that you have only one server request executing at any given time, you can set up a property in your class called `currentRequest`, which holds the last executed request. You can then check the status of the request by calling `isPending()`, and if it's still active, call `cancel()` to cancel the request:

```
Request currentRequest = null;
...

if (currentRequest != null && currentRequest.isPending()) {
  currentRequest.cancel();
}
...
```

```
currentRequest = builder.sendRequest(
  "storeItem=5893&action=fetch", storeCallbackHandler
);
```

The callback handler implements the `RequestCallback` interface and must implement two methods, one for handling a completed request and one for handling an error:

```
RequestCallback storeCallbackHandler = new RequestCallback() {

  public void onError(Request request, Throwable exception) {
    GWT.log("Error", exception);
  }

  public void onResponseReceived(
      Request request, Response response) {
    ...
  }
};
```

When an error occurs, the handler's `onError()` method is called. This can happen for any number of reasons, including communication errors or the request's timeout being exceeded.

If the result returns successfully from the server, the `onResponseReceived()` method is called, and the `Request` and `Response` objects are passed to it. It's important to understand that a "successful" response means the server returned a valid result; it doesn't mean the server-side application behaved properly.

In order to verify that the response isn't just from a server error, it's a good practice to check the status code of the response by calling the method `getStatusCode()`. The status codes are part of the HTTP protocol, where a code of 200 indicates a successful response:

```
public void onResponseReceived(Request request, Response response) {
  if (response.getStatusCode() == 200) {
    Window.alert(response.getText());
  }
  else {
    GWT.log("Error status code", null);
  }
}
```

Other codes are grouped by type. Codes in the 300 range indicate that the object has been moved, the 400 range indicates that the resource is either missing or otherwise inaccessible, and the 500 range indicates some sort of server-side error or exception.

Other methods of the Response object include getStatusText(), which provides a description of the status code. For a 200 code, this method returns the text "OK", and for a 500 error, it returns "Internal Server Error".

The Response object also provides several methods to investigate the headers returned with the HTTP message from the server. You can use getHeader(name) to retrieve the value of a specific header, getHeaders() to get an array of Header objects, or getHeadersAsString() to get a String value with all the headers. In most cases, the header data is relatively useless, unless your server-side service specifically returns data in the header pairs. For example, you could use custom header values to augment the data sent in the result.

We've spent a lot of time discussing the API and the differences between POST and GET. What we haven't yet done is put all this together into a good example. In the next section, we'll provide an example of using the RequestBuilder to read configuration information from a static XML file.

12.1.3 Using RequestBuilder to load XML data

Describing the API as we've done is useful, but a real-life example can help put everything into context. In this section, you'll put RequestBuilder to work by using it to load and parse an XML configuration file. There are real-world reasons why you might need to do this; even the Dashboard offers lots of places where this technique could be used. Because we need to pick a reason, we've decided to use an external XML file to add bookmarks to the menu bar.

The idea is simple: You'll create an XML file of bookmarks, load the bookmarks via RequestBuilder, and add them to a menu bar. Because using an XML configuration file to set the values of a menu bar isn't specific to the Dashboard project found throughout this book, it's our hope that you'll find other uses for this example in your own projects. Toward that end, we provide the example as an encapsulated piece that can be easily added to any project.

We'll begin with a visual of the project and then discuss the overall architecture of the Bookmarks menu.

Designing the Bookmarks menu

Because you aren't building a new component type, the design is relatively simple. It consists of a main MenuBar, to which you'll add the menu item Bookmarks. When the Bookmarks menu item is clicked, it opens a submenu populated by your XML data file. (See figure 12.2.)

Because the intention is to add this to the existing Dashboard project, we'll assume the main MenuBar object already exists. You need to write a method that

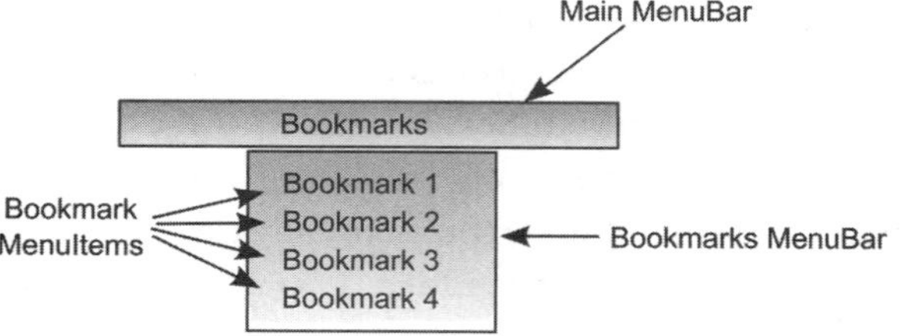

Figure 12.2 A wireframe representation of the example project, which loads an external data file and populates a menu bar

takes this menu as input, as well as the URL of the XML file. In turn, the method you'll create loads the XML data file and populates the submenu. The steps it will perform are listed in table 12.1.

Table 12.1 The flow of the main method of the example, which adds a list of bookmarks to a `MenuBar` based on the contents of an external XML file

Step	Description
1	Load the external XML file based on the URL passed to the method.
2	Parse the XML data file using GWT's `XMLParser` class.
3	Create a Bookmarks `MenuBar` for the drop-down menu listing the bookmarks.
4	Create a `MenuItem` for each bookmark in the data file. Clicking the `MenuItem` will trigger the bookmarked page to load into the existing window. Each `MenuItem` is added to the `MenuBar`.
5	Attach the Bookmarks `MenuBar` to the main `MenuBar`. This main `MenuBar` will be passed to your method as a parameter.

If you've been skipping around in this book, we covered the `MenuBar` and `MenuItem` controls in chapter 4. Fortunately, they're simple to use; if this is your first time seeing these controls, you probably won't require any explanation as to what is going on. If you do have a question, you can go back and review the details of these controls.

Because this book is about GWT, not XML, we'll keep the message format simple and (we hope) self-explanatory.

Creating the Bookmark XML data file

For the purposes of the example, the data file is static, short, and extremely simple. It uses `<bookmarks>` as the root element and contains a list of `<bookmark>` elements. Each `<bookmark>` element uses attributes to specify the name and URL for each link. As you read through this example, think of other extensions that could be added. A possible extension would be the ability to group bookmarks by submenu, or attach icons to each bookmark. The possibilities are endless, but because this chapter can't be, we'll stick to the basics:

```
<bookmarks>
  <bookmark title="Official GWT Site"
        url="http://code.google.com/webtoolkit/"/>
  <bookmark title="GWT Dev Forum"
        url="http://groups.google.com/group/Google-Web-Toolkit"/>
  <bookmark title="GWT Widget Library"
        url="http://gwt-widget.sourceforge.net/"/>
  <bookmark title="Gpokr Online Poker"
        url="http://gpokr.com/"/>
</bookmarks>
```

The list of bookmarks was handpicked to provide invaluable resources to the GWT developer. The first two are for the official GWT site and for developer's forum; both are great places to go when you're trying to find a solution to a problem. The third is our favorite third-party GWT library, which we briefly discussed in section 9.2 in our discussion of installing third-party libraries. The last bookmark is one of the best examples of what GWT is capable of, not to mention a good way to spend a little down time.

With the plan spelled out, and now with the data format defined, you should be starting to understand how you'll implement your method.

Implementing the submenu reader method

The implementation of the Bookmarks reader is broken into several parts to make it easier to understand and to add value for code reuse. The main method that triggers the building of the submenu is named `loadSubMenu()`. Because you'll request an external resource, you need a response handler, which is provided as a private class named `MenuLoaderHandler`. Last, you need a Command object that loads a given bookmark when the menu item is clicked. You'll create a private class to encapsulate this command, called `LinkCommand`.

This one method and two private classes provide the desired functionality. You can drop this method and two classes into the entry-point for the Dashboard, or any other project, to add the functionality. The method signatures are summarized by this code snippet:

```
private void loadSubMenu(
    MenuBar menu,
    String menuTitle,
    String bookmarksUrl) {
}
```

```
private class MenuLoaderHandler
  implements RequestCallback {
}

private class LinkCommand
  implements Command {
}
```

In addition to dropping this code into the entry-point class, you also need to ensure that you've imported both the XML and HTTP modules. You can do this by adding these two lines into your configuration file, if they aren't already listed:

```
<inherits name='com.google.gwt.http.HTTP'/>
<inherits name='com.google.gwt.xml.XML'/>
```

We'll approach the solution to this problem in reverse, starting with the `LinkCommand` class, then the `MenuLoaderHandler`, and finally the `loadSubMenu` method. Typically, you'll code this in the reverse order; but because the two private classes require variables to be passed to them, it's easier to explain and understand by starting at the bottom and working our way up.

Implementing the LinkCommand class

The purpose of the `LinkCommand` is to load a web page when it's triggered. The `LinkCommand` implements the `Command` interface, which is part of the `com.google.gwt.user.client` package. Implementing the `Command` interface requires you to implement a single method `execute()`. Look at the implementation in listing 12.2, and then we'll explain.

Listing 12.2 The `LinkCommand` implementation

```
private class LinkCommand implements Command {

    private String url;

    public LinkCommand(String url) {        // Object constructor
        this.url = url;
    }

    public void execute() {                 // Open new page
        Window.open(url, "_self", "");
    }
}
```

The `execute()` method uses the `Window.open()` method to open the provided URL. The special window name `_self` indicates that the page should open in the same browser window that the GWT application is running in. If you decide that you always want the URL to open into a new window, you should replace this with the special window name `_blank`. Both `_self` and `_blank` aren't specific to GWT; they're part of the HTML specification.

To open the URL, you need a URL to open. To do this, you must provide a constructor for the command, which takes a URL as a parameter. The constructor stores this value into an instance variable so it can be referenced later by the `execute()` method. By creating your command this way, you achieve encapsulation while still allowing the command to take parameters.

Moving up the call stack, the `LinkCommand` class is used by the `MenuLoaderHandler`.

Implementing the MenuLoaderHandler

The `MenuLoaderHandler` class for the example implements the `RequestCallback` interface so that it can receive events from remote call that originate from the `RequestBuilder` class. At this point, you haven't made the remote call (we'll get to that next); for now, you need to define the handler. In the example of populating a menu from remote data, the handler is where all the real work is done. (See listing 12.3.)

Listing 12.3 The `MenuLoaderHandler` implementation

```
private class MenuLoaderHandler implements RequestCallback
{

  private MenuBar parentMenu;
  private String menuTitle;

  public MenuLoaderHandler(MenuBar menu, String menuTitle) {     ❶
    this.parentMenu = menu;
    this.menuTitle = menuTitle;
  }

  public void onError(Request request, Throwable exception) {     ❷
    Window.alert("Some problem has occurred, we are"
      + " unable to load your bookmarks");
  }

  public void onResponseReceived(Request request, Response response)
  {
    if (response.getStatusCode() != 200) {     ❸
      Window.alert("Some problem has occurred, the serve"
        + " returned a status code "
        + response.getStatusCode());
      return;
```

```
      }

      MenuBar subMenu = new MenuBar(true);      ❹

      Document doc = XMLParser.parse(response.getText());                   ❺
      NodeList elements = doc.getElementsByTagName("bookmark");

      for (int i = 0; i < elements.getLength(); i++) {      ❻
        Node element = elements.item(i);
        NamedNodeMap attrs = element.getAttributes();

        String title = attrs.getNamedItem("title").getNodeValue();        ❼
        String url = attrs.getNamedItem("url").getNodeValue();

        MenuItem bookmark =
          new MenuItem(title, new LinkCommand(url));       ❽
        subMenu.addItem(bookmark);
      }

      parentMenu.addItem(menuTitle, subMenu);      ❾
    }
  }
```

There is quite a bit going on in listing 12.3, so we'll take it one step at a time. Rest assured that you've already seen most of this, so there isn't much new.

You begin with a constructor ❶ that serves the same purpose as the one you saw with the `LinkCommand` class in listing 12.3, which is to allow you to pass parameters to your handler. In this case, you need a reference to the main menu bar to which you're attaching the submenu. You also receive a title for the submenu that provides you with some additional flexibility—for example, if you wanted your submenu to be named something other than Bookmarks.

As part of the interface, you need to implement the `onError()` method ❷, which may be called for various network-related reasons or if a timeout occurs. You provide a generic error message using the `Window.alert()` method to inform the user of the problem.

As you implement the `onResponseReceived()` handler, you first check ❸ that the status code returned by the server indicates success. If any code other than the successful 200 code is received, you display it to the user as an error message.

At this point in the code, you have your response from the server, so you first create ❹ a `MenuBar` to hold your submenu items, passing `true` to the constructor to indicate that it should appear vertically. Next, the response text is parsed ❺ and the `<bookmark>` elements are extracted from the external configuration file.

The next step ❻ loops over each of these elements and ❼ extracts the `title` and `URL` attributes from the XML element. These values are then turned into a new `MenuItem` ❽ and added to the submenu `MenuBar`.

The handler ends ❾ by utilizing the `parentMenu` and `menuTitle` variables that were initially passed to the constructor. The code attaches the submenu to the `parentMenu` using the title that is stored in `menuTitle`.

All this could be done by employing anonymous classes, eliminating the need for the constructor. The drawback of that approach is that it can make the code difficult to read, and it makes the code impossible to reuse without copying and pasting each time it's needed. Unless the handler is small, it's always a good idea to shy away from anonymous classes.

To get back to our example, only one piece is left: implementing the `loadSubMenu()` method.

Implementing the loadSubMenu() method

When we examined the code for the `MenuLoaderHandler`, we mentioned that the handler did most of the heavy lifting. It may not come as a surprise that the implementation of the `loadSubMenu()` method in listing 12.4 is simple.

Listing 12.4 Implementing the `loadSubMenu()` method

```
private void loadSubMenu(
    MenuBar menu, String menuTitle, String bookmarksUrl) {

  RequestBuilder builder = new RequestBuilder(RequestBuilder.GET,
      bookmarksUrl);                                    // Create RequestBuilder

  try {
    String requestData = "";
    RequestCallback callback =
        new MenuLoaderHandler(menu, menuTitle);

    builder.sendRequest(requestData, callback);        // Trigger request to be made
  }
  catch (RequestException e) {
    Window.alert(e.getMessage());
  }
}
```

You create a new `RequestBuilder` instance, specifying that it should use the `GET` command for interacting with the server, and the URL of the configuration file. This URL, as well as the parent `MenuBar` and the submenu title, are passed into the method as parameters.

Listing 12.4 breaks out the two arguments to the `sendRequest()` method to make it clear what you're sending. The first argument is a list of data to be passed in the body portion of the HTTP message, which for this example is blank. The second argument, shown as the variable `callback`, is a new instance of the `MenuLoaderHandler()` method.

To have this code add a submenu to the Dashboard project or any other project, you add a call to this method in the entry-point class, after instantiating the main `MenuBar` object. For example, if you have an external configuration file bookmarks.xml, and the main menu is defined by the `mainMenu` variable, a call like the following adds the Bookmarks submenu.

```
loadSubMenu(mainMenu, "Bookmarks", "bookmarks.xml");
```

This example has been lengthy, but we hope you find a few gems in it. The example doesn't need to end here. If you find that this functionality, or similar functionality, is useful, you may wish to extend it. One possible enhancement would be to replace the static XML file on the server with a Java servlet or CGI script capable of generating XML configuration data from a database or other source. Another idea would be to extend it to allow for submenus on the submenu, so you could group your bookmarks by category. This example should give you ideas for many possibilities.

Next, we'll look at another form of client-sever communication, falling back to the ever-useful HTML form.

12.2 Examining FormPanel basics

GWT provides an interesting twist on the HTML form. It mixes the standard form support of HTML and adds to it some old-school RPC techniques. In the old days, some time after the dinosaurs but before being able to use the `XMLHttpRequest` object, you had to use other techniques for communicating with the server. One popular technique was to create a hidden iframe for sending and receiving data. You sent data by loading content into the iframe via JavaScript, passing parameters via the query string to the server. Once the iframe loaded, you could then inspect the contents of the hidden page to see what was returned. The `FormPanel` uses this technique to allow a standard form submission to return a response to your application without refreshing the page.

You've already seen a few RPC tools provided by GWT: Why is the `FormPanel` better than the others? The `FormPanel` isn't better, it's just different. The `FormPanel` is best used when you want to present a set of input controls to the user and where that form data is destined to be sent to the server for processing. You could use GWT-RPC or `RequestBuilder` for this as well, but doing so would require more code to get the same effect.

There is one area where `FormPanel` functionality can't be matched by any other RPC mechanism: when you want the browser to upload files to the server. In HTML, a file-input tag allows a user to select a file on their local system via a browse dialog box, which can then be uploaded to the server by submitting an HTML form. Currently modern browsers have no mechanism other than an HTML form for uploading files.

In this section, we'll present the functionality of the `FormPanel` in several parts. We'll begin with an overview of how the `FormPanel` works and explore its functionality. We'll then look at the controls you can use with the `FormPanel` including `CheckBox`, `RadioButton`, `TextBox`, and others. We'll round out our exploration with perhaps the most interesting use of the `FormPanel`: processing file uploads. Let's begin with a detailed look at how the `FormPanel` works.

12.2.1 Introducing the FormPanel

It's likely that you've seen dozens of forms on the Internet. They're used for everything from webmail to shopping, registrations to subscriptions. If you've done web development before it's likely that you're well aware as to how they work, but in case you haven't run into them before we'll provide a quick overview.

HTML forms consists of a `<form>` element, inside of which are *form controls*. Each control is given a name to identify it. For example, a registration form might use the names `fullName`, `streetAddress`, `cityState`, and `phoneNumber`. Most forms also include a submit button that triggers the form and sends the data to the server. The example form we just described would look like the following code example in an HTML page:

```
<form method="POST" action="process.jsp">
  <input type="text" name="fullName" />
  <input type="text" name="streetAddress" />
  <input type="text" name="cityState" />
  <input type="text" name="phoneNumber" />
  <input type="submit" name="submitButton" value="Submit" />
</form>
```

You may have noticed the `method` and `action` attributes of the `form` element. The `method` attribute identifies the HTTP message type that should be used to send the data to the server; it may be either `POST` or `GET`. We discussed the difference between these two methods earlier in this chapter, in section 12.1.1. The `action` attribute specifies the URL to which the form data should be sent. The action URL may reference any server-side application that can normally handle processing form data. The example points to a JSP page, but it could be a .NET application, CGI, PHP, or just about anything. As you'll see shortly, the `method` and `action` concepts carry over to the `FormPanel` component.

Inside of the `form` element are several *form controls*. In the example, the first four are text-box controls and the last is a submit button. Each of these controls, including the submit button, has a name associated with it. These names are passed to the server, along with the values, when the form is submitted. It's possible to use the same name for multiple fields, but this isn't usually done because it complicates the processing of the data on the server. There is one exception to this rule: the handling of radio buttons, where only one in a group of buttons can be selected. We'll take a closer look at the controls a little later; for now, all you need to know is that each control has to have a name.

Here's the way a form works. When the user clicks the submit button, it triggers the data to be sent to the server. The rule is that any control inside the `form` element is sent to the URL specified by `action`. Because only the controls inside the `form` element are sent, you may have multiple forms on the same page. You might, for instance, have a search form and a registration form on the same page with two different actions. The `FormPanel` works the same way: When you submit the `FormPanel`, it sends the data for all the controls contained in the component. Figure 12.3 shows the relationship between the controls and the `FormPanel` container.

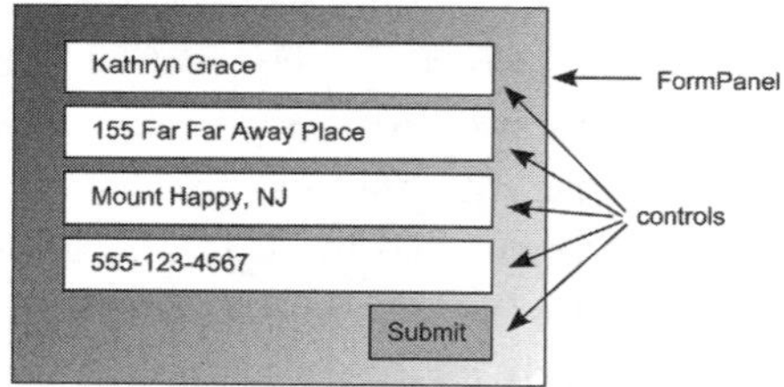

Figure 12.3 A visual representation of the relations between the controls and the `FormPanel` in which they're contained

Setting up a new `FormPanel` is a little different than other panels because you want to set some of the properties we mentioned, like `action` and `method`. Let's start by constructing the `FormPanel` and setting some of these values:

```
final FormPanel form = new FormPanel();
form.setAction("/process.jsp");
form.setMethod(FormPanel.METHOD_POST);
```

The `setAction()` method, as you probably guessed, sets the `action` we already mentioned; its value is set to a the URL of your application. The `setMethod()` method sets the HTTP method to use for sending the data. You can use one of two constants for this: `FormPanel.METHOD_POST` or `FormPanel.METHOD_GET`. Unless there is a reason to do otherwise, you should use the `POST` method, because the `GET` method is usually limited in the amount of data that can be sent.

The `FormPanel` is a subclass of `SimplePanel`, which means it can only contain a single widget or panel. Unless your form has only one control, you need to place your controls into a panel and then add that panel to the `FormPanel`. For a simple registration, you'll use a `VerticalPanel` to hold the form controls, displaying them one above the next:

```
VerticalPanel layout = new VerticalPanel();
form.setWidget(layout);
```

Next, you need to add some controls to the `VerticalPanel`. Figure 12.3 shows a form with four text fields. To keep things simple, for now you'll do the same.

```
final TextBox fullName = new TextBox();
final TextBox streetAddress = new TextBox();
final TextBox stateZip = new TextBox();
final TextBox phoneNumber = new TextBox();

layout.add(fullName);
layout.add(streetAddress);
layout.add(stateZip);
layout.add(phoneNumber);
```

When we examined HTML forms earlier, we mentioned that each control contained in the form needs a name associated with it. This is required so you can access the data by name when you process the form on the server. To allow for this, the `TextBox` control and all other controls that can be used in a `FormPanel` to send data to the server implement the `HasName` interface. All such implementations include `getName()` and `setName()` methods:

```
fullName.setName("fullName");
streetAddress.setName("streetAddress");
stateZip.setName("stateZip");
phoneNumber.setName("phoneNumber");
```

The only thing you're missing is a way to submit the `FormPanel`. Submitting a `FormPanel` is done by executing the `submit()` method of the `FormPanel` instance. In a standard HTML form, you'd use the special submit button control; but in GWT, you need to create a `Button` instance and attach a listener to trigger the form submission:

```
Button submit = new Button("Submit");
layout.add(submit);

submit.addClickListener(new ClickListener() {
    public void onClick(Widget sender) {
        form.submit();
    }
});
```

Up to this point, the FormPanel doesn't differ much from an ordinary HTML form. You created a FormPanel, the equivalent of the <form> element, and added TextBox controls that are rendered as <input> elements in the form. So far so good, but FormPanel has an added trick up its sleeve: event handling.

12.2.2 Listening to FormPanel events

The FormPanel allows you to register an event listener, allowing you to write handler code for exposed events. The two events are the submission of the form and the completion of the submission:

```
form.addFormHandler(new FormHandler() {

  public void onSubmit(FormSubmitEvent event) {
    // ...
  }

  public void onSubmitComplete(FormSubmitCompleteEvent event) {
    // ...
  }
});
```

The onSubmit() handler is triggered just before the form submission, allowing you to validate the form and even cancel the submission. To cancel the submission, you call setCancelled(true) on the event object passed to the method. Here you added validation code to the onSubmit() method from the previous example and verify that the user supplied their name:

```
public void onSubmit(FormSubmitEvent event)
{
  if (fullName.getText().length() == 0) {
    Window.alert("You must enter your name");
    event.setCancelled(true);
    return;
  }
}
```

If the onSubmit() method returns without setting the cancelled flag, the form is submitted to the server. The FormPanel by default specifies the *target* of the form to be a hidden frame. By doing this, it instructs the browser to load the server response into this hidden frame instead of the main browser window. We'll discuss the options for setting the target frame shortly; for now, we'll stick with the default.

When the response is returned from the server, the handler's onSubmitComplete() method is called, and it's passed a FormSubmitCompleteEvent object. This object has a getResult() method that returns the content returned by the server. For the example, the server returns the text "success" if everything went well.

```
public void onSubmitComplete(FormSubmitCompleteEvent event)
{
  String result = event.getResults();

  if (result.equals("success")) {
    Window.alert("Registration accepted");
  }
  else {
    Window.alert("Sorry, we cannot accept your registration");
  }
}
```

The beauty of this system is that the server result isn't limited to plain text. For instance, the server can return HTML code that can then be inserted into the page by your handler. Or, the server may return a complex data structure like XML data. Because the result isn't limited to text, the `FormPanel` is usable in a wide variety of operations.

To take a short step backward, we mentioned that you can alter the default target of the `FormPanel` submission.

12.2.3 Altering the FormPanel target

There is a good reason why you may want to change the target of the form submission, and it goes back to how traditional HTML forms work. Typically, when you submit a form on the Web, the browser loads a completely new page. Although the idea behind Ajax techniques is that the page doesn't need to reload, you still may need to do this.

With the `FormPanel`, you can set the target of the form with the constructor only, and you can't change it once it has been set. There are three constructor options: use the default hidden frame, use a named frame, or use a `NamedFrame` object.

We already discussed the default behavior, so let's start with the named frame. In HTML, each frame may be given a name, and there are also a couple of special frame names. The following special frame names can be used to identify the target of the form:

- `_self`—Specifies the target frame as being the frame in which the `FormPanel` resides. For most GWT applications, this is the same as `_top`.
- `_top`—Specifies that the target frame is the entire browser window. The results sent back from the server completely replace what is currently displayed in the browser.

- `_blank`—Specifies that the results from the server should be placed into a new pop-up window. This is a useful target, but you should only use it when there is a good reason to do so, because users tend to dislike new windows. Note that you can't set the *features* of the target window—you can't specify the height/width, remove toolbars, or similarly affect the new window.
- `_parent`—Frames may be placed into other frames, creating a hierarchy. The parent frame is the frame above the current frame in that hierarchy. We've included this target for completeness, but you'll almost never need to use it.

Besides these special frames, you may want to specify a specific named frame. The description of `_blank` provides a hint as to one reason for doing this: When you want the results of the form submission to appear in a pop-up window, you often want to set some of the features of the pop-up, such as setting the window dimensions or hide toolbars. To do this, you need to create the pop-up window first and then submit the form into that window.

You must first alter the `FormPanel` creation by passing in a named frame. You set the named target frame to `resultPopUp` (we made up this name):

```
final FormPanel form = new FormPanel("resultPopUp");
```

You now have the `FormPanel` targeting a named frame that doesn't yet exist. By default, if you don't create a frame for this name and submit the results, the browser creates a new window for you with the specified name, similar to what happens if you specify `_blank`.

To get the desired behavior, you need to alter the `onSubmit()` method in your `FormHandler` code. Use `Window.open()` to open an empty pop-up with the name `resultPopUp`, with a height of 300 pixels and a width 400 pixels:

```
public void onSubmit(FormSubmitEvent event)
{
  if (fullName.getText().length() == 0) {
    Window.alert("You must enter your name");
    event.setCancelled(true);
    return;
  }

  Window.open("", "resultPopUp", "width=300,height=400");
}
```

As you can see in the example, the window features are passed as a comma-delimited `String`. In addition to setting the height and width, you can also turn on and off various features of the window. For example, the following code turns off the menu bar and turns off the ability to resize the window:

```
String features = "width=300,height=400,menubar=no,resizable=no";
Window.open("", "resultPopUp", features);
```

These features aren't specific to GWT—and there are a large number of them, some of which are available only in certain browsers. In general, only a few are used frequently. The most-used features are as follows:

- `height`—The height of the window in pixels
- `left`—The number of pixels from the left edge of the screen
- `location`—Specifies whether the address bar is displayed (yes/no)
- `menubar`—Specifies whether the menu bar is displayed (yes/no)
- `resizable`—Specifies if the new window is resizable (yes/no)
- `scrollbars`—Specifies whether scroll bars will be available (yes/no)
- `status`—Specifies whether the status bar should be displayed (yes/no)
- `toolbar`—Specifies if the toolbar will be displayed (yes/no)
- `top`—The number of pixels from the top edge of the screen
- `width`—The width of the new window in pixels

We've spent a lot of time talking about the named frame constructor of the `FormPanel`. Most of this information also relates to the last constructor of the `FormPanel`, which takes a `NamedFrame` object as an argument:

```
NamedFrame frame = new NamedFrame("resultFrame");
final FormPanel form = new FormPanel(frame);
```

`NamedFrame` is a subclass of the `Frame` widget, with the only real difference between the two being that the `NamedFrame` can be identified by its name. The `NamedFrame` instance renders as an iframe when it's added to the page. You'll use the `NamedFrame` as the submission target of `FormPanel` when you want the form submission results to appear inside of an iframe on the page.

With `FormPanel`, you have several options for the constructor, based on what you're trying to accomplish. Table 12.2 summarizes them.

We've spent most of our time looking at the `FormPanel` and how the overall mechanism works. Next, we'll take a tour of the GWT widgets that can be used in the `FormPanel`.

Table 12.2 `FormPanel`**-related issues and the appropriate** `FormPanel` **constructor to solve the problem**

Problem	Solution
You need to send form data to the server and optionally be notified of the server response.	Use the default constructor.
You need to send the form results to a specific frame, and the frame has a name.	Use the `String` constructor, passing in the name of the frame.
You need to send the form results into a pop-up window.	Use the `String` constructor, specifying a name for the pop-up window, and then use `Window.open()` to create the pop-up.
You need to send the form result into a GWT `Frame` control.	Modify your code to use `NamedFrame` control instead of the `Frame` control. Pass the `NamedFrame` control to the `FormPanel` constructor.

12.2.4 Using the various form controls

The underlying functionality of the `FormPanel` lies in the standard functionality of the HTML form. The `FormPanel` is a wrapper around this existing functionality that is supplied by the browser. Any controls you use to pass form data to the server must be rendered in the page as a control type supported by standard HTML forms. The GWT components we'll list here mirror existing HTML control types.

For each component, we'll offer a brief explanation, a short code example, and a visual example of what the control looks like in an application. You'll find that you've already used many of these controls in earlier chapters. We'll start with what is likely to be the most often used component: the `TextBox`.

Using TextBox to capture text

You see the standard `TextBox` control everywhere. The `TextBox` renders a text input box that consists of a single line but may be any width. The following snippet creates a new `TextBox` with the name `name` and a character limit of 100 characters (see figure 12.4):

Your name
David Oliver

Figure 12.4
A `TextBox` **control**

```
TextBox text = new TextBox();
text.setName("name");
text.setMaxLength(100);
```

Don't confuse the width of the `TextBox`, which can be set with CSS, and the `maxLength` property. The `maxLength` property is the maximum number of characters the field can hold. This is useful when your data will be inserted into a fixed-width database column.

The `TextBox` has a sister component, the `PasswordTextBox`.

Using PasswordTextBox to hide text

The `PasswordTextBox` is the same as `TextBox`, with one small difference: Any characters typed in the box appear as stars or a round circles to obscure the contents of the field. As the name implies, this input component is typically used only for password fields; someone looking over your shoulder won't be able to read what you've typed. Here's an example (see figure 12.5):

Figure 12.5 A `PasswordTextBox` control

```
PasswordTextBox pass = new PasswordTextBox();
pass.setName("password");
```

As with the `TextBox`, you must explicitly set the `name` property of the component if you plan to send the data to a server as form data. This name is then used on the server to fetch the data by field name.

If `PasswordTextBox` is the sister to `TextBox`, then both of them have a big brother that is used to capture long text: the `TextArea`.

Using TextArea to capture long text

The `TextArea` is like the `TextBox` except that it can span multiple lines and include a scrollbar when the text exceeds the bounds of the display area. The following example creates a `TextArea` that is 30 characters wide and 5 lines tall (see figure 12.6):

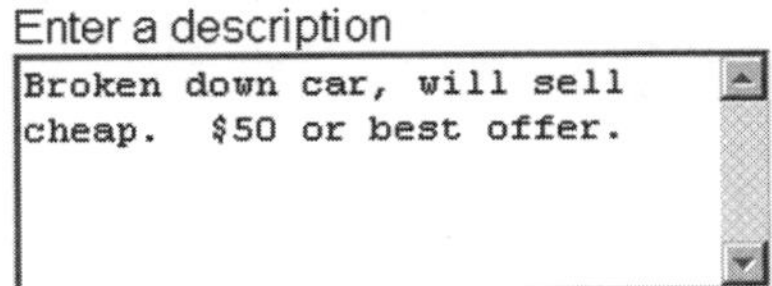

Figure 12.6 A `TextArea` control

```
TextArea textArea = new TextArea();
textArea.setName("description");
textArea.setCharacterWidth(30);
textArea.setVisibleLines(5);
```

The width of a character and height of a line will differ between browsers, so it may be preferable to set the height and width using CSS.

In addition to text controls, several other input types are probably familiar. These input types include check boxes, radio buttons, and list boxes.

Using CheckBox for boolean values

The `CheckBox` component is rendered as a square that can be checked by the user. The `CheckBox` constructor takes an optional label as an argument. The label, if specified, appears to the right of the check box. The following snippet asks the user to subscribe to a newsletter (see figure 12.7):

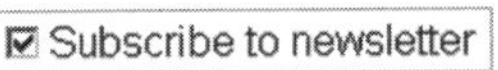

Figure 12.7 A `CheckBox` control

```
CheckBox subscribe = new CheckBox("Subscribe to newsletter");
subscribe.setName("subscribe");
```

On the server, the `CheckBox` data is handled a little differently than the data of other form controls. Instead of the value being a specific `String` value, it's either `on` or `null`. If the user doesn't check the box, the browser doesn't send any information about that control to the server, resulting in the `null` value.

The `RadioButton` control is similar to the `CheckBox`.

Using RadioButton to offer options

Like the `CheckBox`, the `RadioButton` presents a control that can be selected, but it looks to the user like a circle instead of a box. The user is provided a list of options, and selecting a single option deselects the others. In a *group* of radio buttons, only a single radio button can be selected. Here is a code snippet that provides four age options (see figure 12.8):

How old are you?
18-25
26-30
31-40
> 40

Figure 12.8 A `RadioButton` control

```
RadioButton age18 = new RadioButton("age", "18-25");
RadioButton age26 = new RadioButton("age", "26-30");
RadioButton age31 = new RadioButton("age", "31-40");
RadioButton other = new RadioButton("age", "> 40");
```

The `RadioButton` constructor includes the group name for the radio buttons. In the example, all four buttons use the name `age` as the group name, which is what links them together. The browser allows you to select only one option from this group. When your selection is sent to the server, the name of the group can be used to retrieve the value.

`RadioButton` widgets are useful when you're presenting a short list to the user, but they aren't appropriate when the list is lengthy, like a list of countries. In this case, the `ListBox` is more appropriate.

Using ListBox to display an option list

The `ListBox` is rendered as a single line, similar to the `TextBox`, except that at the right of the `ListBox` is a small arrow. Clicking the arrow opens the list and reveals all the possible values that can be selected. The following example creates a list with three country names that appear in the same order in which they're added (see figure 12.9):

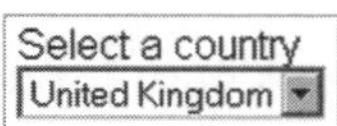

Figure 12.9 `ListBox` control

```
ListBox list = new ListBox();
list.setName("country");
list.addItem("Canada", "CA");
list.addItem("United Kingdom", "UK");
list.addItem("United States", "US");
```

On the server, the value in this example can be referenced by the `country` parameter of the form data. Each of the items on the list includes a name and a value. The name appears on the list to the application user, and the value is sent to the server. If the user selects Canada from the list, the value CA is passed to the server.

The `ListBox` has an alternate style that displays a scrolling list of options instead of a drop-down list. To use this alternate style, you specify the number of items that should be visible. If the list includes more items than can be visible, a scrollbar appears to the right of the list, allowing the user to scroll through the options (see figure 12.10):

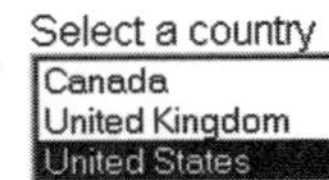

Figure 12.10 A `ListBox` control that displays multiple items

```
list.setVisibleItemCount(3);
```

The `ListBox` by default allows the user to select only a single item. When an item is selected, any previously selected item is deselected. On occasion, it may make sense to allow a user to select multiple options. To do so, you need to set the `multipleSelect` property to `true`, as follows:

```
list.setMultipleSelect(true);
```

This lets the user select multiple items by holding down the Ctrl key as they select additional items. In practice, this typically isn't used because it has a tendency to confuse users.

So far, we've only talked about the user entering content in some fashion; but HTML and GWT also support hidden data.

Using Hidden to hide data

Hidden data passes a value to the server with the form data when you don't want the user to see or interact with the data. For example, if the user is logged in to your application and has obtained a security key, you need to pass that key to the server, but it doesn't make sense for the user to be able to edit it. The following example creates a hidden form field with the security key data:

```
Hidden hidden = new Hidden("securityKey", "KLHiuky$45eEW98h%YS");
```

When you use the `Hidden` control, make sure you don't abuse it. Just because the data is hidden from the web page doesn't mean it can't be detected. It's always a good idea to ask yourself whether it would be a potential security risk to allow a user to see and modify this data. If the answer is yes, then you're probably building flaws into your application that could be exploited by malicious attackers.

Along the same lines, there is another form control that should be used cautiously: the `FileUpload` component.

Using FileUpload to upload files

The `FileUpload` control presents a text box along with a Browse button. Clicking the Browse button allows the user to select a file on their system; once selected, the file's path appears in the text box. When the form is submitted, the browser sends the contents of the selected file along with the form data (see figure 12.11):

Upload a file
C:\shopping-list.txt Browse...

Figure 12.11 A `FileUpload` control

```
FileUpload upload = new FileUpload();
upload.setName("file");
```

To be able to use the `FileUpload` control, you must set the method type of the `FormPanel` to `POST` and set the encoding-type to `multipart`. `Multipart` is a special content-type that allows different types of data to be mixed in a single message. If you ever sent an email with an attachment, then you've sent a multipart message. The form passes the data to the server using the same technique your mail client uses to send attachments:

```
FormPanel form = new FormPanel();
form.setMethod(FormPanel.METHOD_POST);
form.setEncoding(FormPanel.ENCODING_MULTIPART);
```

On the server, handling a file upload can be a messy task. The tools you use depend on the language you're using on the server, but most languages have tools available to make the task more manageable. In Java, our tool of choice for handling uploaded files is the `commons-fileupload` library, which is one of the Apache Jakarta projects. You can download the library from http://jakarta.apache.org/commons/fileupload/.

Listing 12.5 provides an example of using `commons-fileupload` in a servlet. The servlet iterates over the data passed to the servlet, processing only uploaded files and ignoring all other data.

Listing 12.5 A servlet using the Jakarta commons-fileupload library to capture uploaded files

```
import java.io.*;
import java.util.*;
import javax.servlet.ServletException;
import javax.servlet.http.*;
import org.apache.commons.fileupload.*;
import org.apache.commons.fileupload.disk.DiskFileItemFactory;
import org.apache.commons.fileupload.servlet.ServletFileUpload;

public class UploadServlet2 extends HttpServlet
{
  public void service(
    HttpServletRequest request, HttpServletResponse response)
    throws ServletException, IOException
  {
    if (!ServletFileUpload.isMultipartContent(request))        ❶
      return;

    FileItemFactory factory = new DiskFileItemFactory();           ❷
    ServletFileUpload upload = new ServletFileUpload(factory);

    List items = null;
    try {
      items = upload.parseRequest(request);        ❸
    }
    catch (FileUploadException e) {
      e.printStackTrace();
      return;
    }

    for (Iterator i = items.iterator(); i.hasNext();) {       ❹
      FileItem item = (FileItem) i.next();

      if (item.isFormField())      ❺
        continue;

      String fileName = item.getName();      ❻

      int slash = fileName.lastIndexOf("/");
      if (slash == -1) {
        slash = fileName.lastIndexOf("\\");
      }                                                       ❼
      if (slash != -1) {
        fileName = fileName.substring(slash + 1);
      }

      try {
        File uploadedFile = new File("/uploads/" + fileName);       ❽
        item.write(uploadedFile);
```

```
      }
      catch (Exception e) {
        e.printStackTrace();
      }
    } // end for

  } // end service()

}
```

The handling of uploaded files may look intimidating at first, but it isn't that complex thanks to the `commons-fileupload` library. When the servlet's `service()` method is called, the first thing you do ❶ is make sure the form was submitted as multipart content. As we mentioned previously, this is required in order to use a form to submit files to the server. To accomplish this, you use the static routine `ServletFileUpload.isMultipartContent()` from `commons-fileupload` to perform the check for you. If the form data isn't multipart, you return from the method, doing no additional work.

The `commons-fileupload` library requires a little setup before it will parse the form data for you. You create a new instance of `ServletFileUpload` ❷ and pass it a reference to a `FileItemFactory`. The `FileItemFactory` generates a `FileItem` instance for each file that was uploaded to the server. In this example, you use a `DiskFileItemFactory` instance. The `DiskFileItemFactory` stores the uploaded file in memory if it's less than 10 KB or save it in a temp directory otherwise. This is currently the only `FileItemFactory` that ships with `commons-fileupload`, so you don't have a lot of choices; but it lets you create your own factory for cases where special data handling is required.

You then parse the request data ❸, which builds a list of `FileItem` objects. If an error occurs during the parse, a `FileUploadException` is thrown, providing information about the problem. In the example, if an error occurs, you return, although this may not be appropriate for all applications.

Next, you loop through each of the `FileItem` instances ❹. If the `FileItem` is a simple form field ❺ or, rather, *not* a file, you ignore it and continue with the next `FileItem` instance.

If the `FileItem` is a file, you get the filename ❻. The filename isn't what you may expect, because it isn't just the filename but instead is the full path to the file on the client's computer. For instance, the name might be C:\Document and Settings\rhanson\Desktop\shopping_list.txt, which has limited value for you on the server. You need to strip the path information from the name ❼ so that you have only the filename. In listing 12.5, you look for the last forward-slash (Unix style) or backslash (Windows style), stripping anything up to that point.

What you do next depends on the application. In the example servlet, you store the file in the /uploads/ directory ❽. You accomplish this by creating an instance of `java.io.File` and passing it to the helper method `write()` of the `FileItem` instance. This writes the file to disk at the location you specified.

We don't expect that you'll use this servlet as is, because it probably won't fit general application usage. For example, it's bad practice to place all the files in the same directory. If your application uses user accounts, perhaps it's better to store each user's files in their own directory. Or, if your system is an issue-tracking system like Bugzilla or Jira, it may be better to store the file in a directory that has the same name as the ticket number. How you store the files depends on what you're building.

NOTE Many web servers and servlet containers place a restriction on the maximum file size that can be uploaded to the server. If the files your users are uploading are more then a few megabytes, you should consult your server documentation for the default maximum file-upload size and associated configuration settings.

With the end of our discussion on the `FileUpload` control, so ends our discussion of the `FormPanel` component.

12.3 Summary

In this chapter, we looked at two different tools: `RequestBuilder` and `FormPanel`. Both of them pass data to the server, so it's a question of the best tool for the job.

If you need to send or request data from the server behind the scenes without presenting a form to the user, the `RequestBuilder` should be your tool of choice. `RequestBuilder` is easy to use and offers good error handling, allowing access to the server-status code so you can handle errors appropriately. The `RequestBuilder` also lets you set a timeout for the request, cancel the request, and set and modify the headers that are sent to the server. Modifying the headers is useful if you want to set the content type to URL-encoded so server-side systems like JSPs and servlets know that they should parse the message data.

The `FormPanel` class takes a completely different approach to sending data to the server by wrapping existing HTML form functionality found in web browsers. This makes it useful when you want to send user-supplied data to the server, where the data is submitted via a form. In the same way that the `RequestBuilder` response handlers work, event handlers can be registered with the `FormPanel` to listen for form-submission and submission-complete events. On completion, the results returned by the server are sent to a hidden frame, which can be read by your code, allowing you to provide feedback to the user on the server's response.

Arguably, you could use `RequestBuilder` along with some additional coding to provide the same functionality as the `FormPanel`, but one specific function sets the `FormPanel` apart. Web browsers let you use an HTML form to upload files to the server. In modern web applications, this approach is being used more and more, especially as traditional desktop applications are ported to the Web as run-anywhere applications. With the `FormPanel`, along with the `FileUpload` control, you can provide this functionality in your GWT application. Handling file uploads on the server isn't a simple task, but tools are available for most languages to make this easier. Java has the `commons-fileupload` library, available from www.apache.org, which makes it easy to write a servlet that can read uploaded files. Table 12.3 summarizes these tools and compares them to GWT-RPC from chapters 10 and 11.

Table 12.3 Benefits of the three main tools for sending data to the server, to help you pick the right tool for the job

RPC tool	Underlying request mechanism	Benefits	Disadvantages
GWT-RPC	`XMLHttpRequest`	Automatic serialization and deserialization of Java classes.	Can only communicate with a server that is running a Java servlet-container. Complex setup; requires several interfaces to be built in addition to your servlet.
RequestBuilder	`XMLHttpRequest`	Easy to use. Good error handling. Allows control over the HTTP headers and request timeout.	Can only send text data. If you need to send complex data structures like XML or data objects, you must write custom serialization and deserialization code.
FormPanel	HTML form	Uses a standard HTML form. Allows for simple integration with server-side frameworks like Struts, and allows for uploading files.	Requires form fields to be displayed on the page for use, which makes it inappropriate for some tasks.

In the next chapter, you'll build on the functionality of `RequestBuilder` by using it to pass structured data to the server. The format you'll use is called JavaScript

Object Notation (JSON). As you'll see, JSON makes it easy to send structured data to server-side applications written in not just Java, but in any popular programming language.

13

Achieving interoperability with JSON

This chapter covers

- Overview of the JSON data format
- Using GWT's JSON support
- Yahoo's JSON search service
- Examples of JSON server-side in Java, Perl, and Ruby

JavaScript Object Notation (JSON) is a message format designed to be lightweight and easy to learn. The format it provides is meant to be JavaScript friendly and, at the same time, easy to read and write in any language. You can find the JSON specification at json.org; it has met with quite a bit of success, assuming that you equate success with adoption. On the home page of the JSON site are nearly 40 implementations in no fewer than 20 different languages. Because JSON is easy to learn and is widely available, it's an ideal choice for communication between your GWT application and any type of server.

In this chapter, we'll discuss the basic structure of a JSON message and provide an overview of the different objects the JSON format supports. We'll then map the JSON format to the JSON support found in GWT and present details of how to use JSON in your applications.

Finally, we'll round out our discussion by implementing a search component that takes advantage of Yahoo's JSON API. Because developers using JSON are most likely doing so because they don't run Java on the server, you'll implement the server portion of your component in not only Java, but in Perl and Ruby as well. Let's begin with an introduction to JSON.

13.1 Introducing JavaScript Object Notation (JSON)

In this section, we'll begin with a brief overview of the JSON message format and how you can use the GWT `JSONParser` class to read JSON messages. This lays the groundwork for the rest of the chapter where we get into the details of JSON value objects and provide an example application. To help you understand what the `JSONParser` is doing under the hood, we need to first understand what a JSON message looks like.

13.1.1 Understanding the JSON data format

JSON is a message format that was designed specifically to take advantage of JavaScript's ability to evaluate strings as code. The JSON format is valid JavaScript code; when evaluated, it can rebuild the object. The benefit is that the code required to deserialize a JSON message is only a single line of JavaScript. To understand how this works, consider the following snippet of JavaScript code:

```
var code = '["this","that","other",1,2,3]';
var x = eval(code);
```

In this example, the variable `code` is a string value that contains valid JavaScript code. The brackets denote an array value, which contains six values—both strings and numbers. The second line evaluates the string and assigns the result to the variable x. The result is that x is now an array of values.

JSON works by evaluating whatever is in the string. You could use `eval()` to execute any JavaScript code, but the JSON specification puts some limits on this. The reason for limiting the syntax is that JSON endeavors to be easy to implement in any language, not just JavaScript. Toward this end, JSON is limited to only a few basic values: `null`, `true`, `false`, `string`, `number`, `array`, and `object`. Let's look at another example that uses all these different types:

```
var code = '{
 "name" : "John Doe",
 "age" : 25.0,
 "married" : true,
 "children" : null,
 "pets" : ["Maxie", "Minnie"]
}';
var x = eval(code);
```

We've spaced out the `code` variable for readability; it would usually be a single long value. In the value, the curly braces create a JavaScript object containing name/value pairs. This object is roughly equivalent to a `Map` in Java. Each name/value pair consists of a string name and a value that can be any of the allowable types we mentioned. JSON arrays, like objects, can contain any of the value types, including different value types mixed in the same array. This allows you to create complex data structures any number of levels deep.

One type we want to focus on is the JSON `number` value. This is a generic type used to hold integers and floating-point values of any size. Numbers may be negative or positive and may use scientific notation:

```
var code = ' [-90823, 987345, 24345.23445, 1.234e8]';
var x = eval(code);
```

For further information on the JSON format, visit the json.org web site. It spells out in minute detail the allowed JSON values. It also lists quite a few JSON implementations in various languages that can be used on the server to parse and build JSON messages.

None of these implementations is especially useful with GWT on the client side, so GWT provides its own JSON support. The first (and arguably most important) GWT class for using JSON is `JSONParser`.

13.1.2 Using JSONParser to parse JSON messages

The `JSONParser` is responsible for deserializing JSON data into Java objects, and it's extremely easy to use. You parse a JSON message by calling the static `parse()` method of `JSONParser`, passing in the raw JSON message. If the JSON message is malformed, the parser throws a `JSONException`:

```
JSONValue valueObject;
try {
  valueObject = JSONParser.parse(jsonData);
} catch (JSONException e) {
  GWT.log("JSON parse exception", e);
}
```

The `JSONValue` object that is returned by the parse is a generalized JSON type that can be any one of a number of `JSONValue` subclasses. We'll examine the `JSONValue` class as well as its subclasses next.

NOTE `JSONParser` doesn't "parse" the JSON message. Instead, it evaluates the JSON message as JavaScript, essentially executing it, much as you would do if you were writing your JSON client code in JavaScript.

13.2 Examining GWT's JSON data objects

As we mentioned in the last section, JSON consists of only a few basic data types: `string`, `number`, `boolean`, and `null`. JSON also has the concept of objects and arrays, which hold collections of JSON values. GWT provides a set of classes that correspond to each of these JSON values types. In this section, we'll provide class diagrams of each of these data types as well as examples of how to use them.

In addition to having these JSON data objects constructed as the output of the `JSONParser`, we'll also show you how to construct JSON objects, tie them together as an array or object, and generate a JSON message that can be sent to the server.

Before we get to these specific JSON types, we need to start at the beginning and examine the parent of all JSON types in GWT: the `JSONValue` object.

13.2.1 Introducing the JSONValue object

At the top of the JSON stack is the `JSONValue` object. This is the abstract superclass of all JSON value objects. It contains a test method for each JSON type and a `toString()` method that returns a JSON message string. Each of the test methods returns either an object of the specific type or `null` if the object isn't of that type. For example, the `isArray()` method returns the `JSONArray` object if the value is an array or `null` if it isn't. Figure 13.1 shows the methods of the `JSONValue` class.

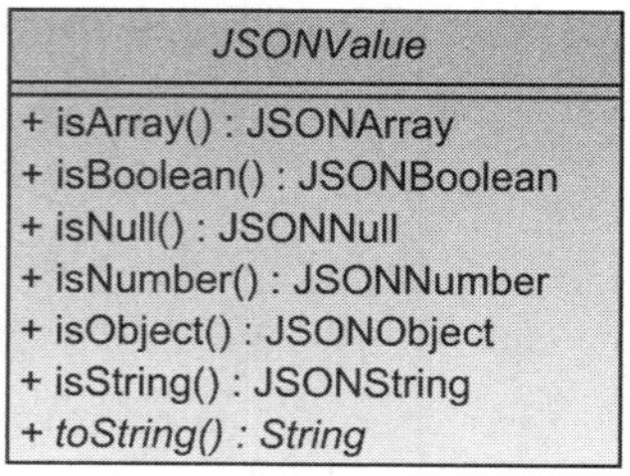

The test methods allow for some creative coding. In this example, a JSON value is stored in the variable `jsonValue`, and you want to log an error if it isn't a `JSONString` value:

```
JSONString data;
if ((data = jsonValue.isString()) == null) {
  GWT.log("bad data", null);
}
```

JSONValue

+ isArray() : JSONArray
+ isBoolean() : JSONBoolean
+ isNull() : JSONNull
+ isNumber() : JSONNumber
+ isObject() : JSONObject
+ isString() : JSONString
+ *toString() : String*

Figure 13.1 A class diagram of the `JSONValue` class, which is the superclass of all JSON data objects in GWT

Inside the `if` statement condition, you call `jsonValue.isString()`, which returns a `JSONString` object into the variable `data` if it's a string, or `null` if it isn't. You then test the contents of the variable `data` to determine whether it's `null`. If it's `null`, you log the error. This format may take a little getting used to if you haven't used it before, but it's concise and compact. Another way to code the same thing is the following:

```
JSONString data = jsonValue.isString();
if (data == null) {
    GWT.log("bad data", null);
}
```

The style you use depends a lot on your coding style and how much error-checking you want to include. If you don't require any error-checking, you can simply cast the value object to the appropriate type:

```
JSONString data = (JSONString) jsonValue;
```

Next, we'll look at the specific JSON data.

13.2.2 Examining basic JSON types

In addition to the `array` and `object` types, JSON includes four basic value types: `string`, `number`, `boolean`, and `null`. Figure 13.2 provides a visual of these classes and shows their relationship to the `JSONValue` parent class.

To construct a `JSONString`, you pass the `String` value as a argument to the constructor. The value can then be retrieved using the `stringValue()` method:

```
JSONString name = new JSONString("John Doe");
String value = name.stringValue();
```

The `JSONNumber` class is similar in that you pass the value, which is a Java `double`, to the constructor. JSON doesn't include support for granular number types like

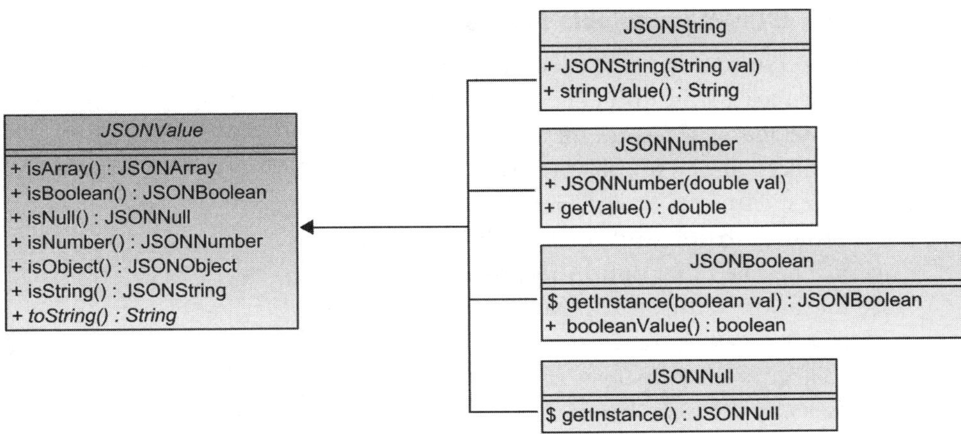

Figure 13.2 A class diagram of the basic JSON data types that are part of the GWT library

Java; in JSON, all numbers are equal. For example, Java provides several primitive number types like `short`, `integer`, `long`, `float`, `double`, `char`, and `byte`. To retrieve the encapsulated value from a `JSONNumber` instance, you call the `getValue()` method:

```
JSONNumber age = new JSONNumber(25);
double value = age.getValue();
```

To create a `JSONBoolean` instance, you call the static method `getInstance()`, passing a Java `boolean` to indicate the JSON value type to return. To test the value of the object once it's created, you call the `booleanValue()` method:

```
JSONBoolean married = JSONBoolean.getInstance(true);
boolean value = married.booleanValue();
```

A `JSONNull` object is the equivalent to a Java `null` value. To get an instance, you call the static method `getInstance()`:

```
JSONValue children = JSONNull.getInstance();
```

All of these objects are subclasses of the `JSONValue` class and, therefore, inherit all of its methods, including `toString()`, which returns a JSON message that represents the object's value. Several of these values can also be tied together as an array or map.

13.2.3 Storing JSONValue objects in a JSONArray

The two container type objects supported by JSON are arrays and objects. A JSON array is, as you probably guessed, an array of JSONValue objects. It's a simple ordered collection of values, with get() and set() methods to read values from and write values to the array. The class diagram in figure 13.3 shows the methods of the JSONArray class.

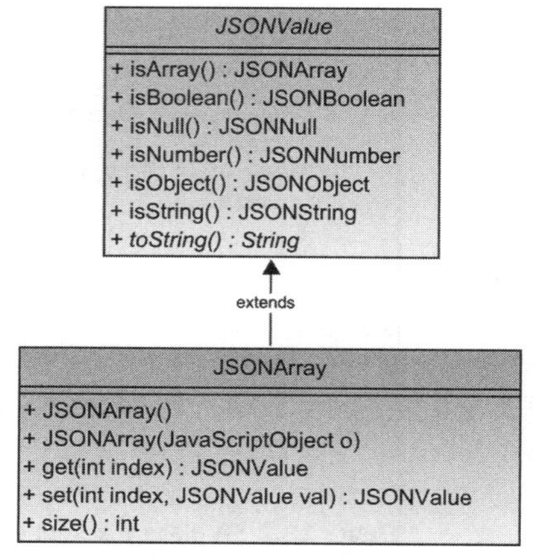

Figure 13.3 The `JSONArray` class, which can be used to store collections of `JSONValue` objects

The JSONArray has two constructors: one a zero-argument constructor, and the second taking a JavaScriptObject. The second constructor is typically used only from within the JSON parser, but you could use it to read values returned from native JSNI methods that return a JavaScript value type.

To fill a JSONArray, you first create a new instance and add values using the set() method, providing the index of the value being added to the array. The JSONArray doesn't include an add() method like you find with Java's Vector or ArrayList, so if you want to append a value to the end of the array of an unknown size, you need to call the size() method to get the current size:

```
JSONArray pets = new JSONArray();
pets.set(0, new JSONString("Maxie"));
pets.set(pets.size(), new JSONString("Minnie"));
```

When you're putting values into an array, you must ensure that you don't skip any indices. When you call toString() on the JSONArray, it throws an exception if any of the array indices don't contain an object:

```
JSONArray pets = new JSONArray();
pets.set(0, new JSONString("Maxie"));
pets.set(5, new JSONString("Minnie"));
String jsonValue = pets.toString(); // throws exception!
```

If your code could potentially skip indices, you can use the following method to fix the array by inserting JSONNull values where no values exist. Any value in the array that returns a Java null value won't be able to be converted to a JSON message and needs to be set with an instance of JSONNull:

```
private void fixJsonArray(JSONArray array)
{
  for (int i = 0; i < array.size(); i++) {
    JSONValue val = array.get(i);
    if (val == null) {
      array.set(i, JSONNull.getInstance());
    }
  }
}
```

To read data from a `JSONArray`, you can use the `size()` method to determine the number of values and use the `get()` method to retrieve each value:

```
for (int i = 0; i < pets.size(); i++) {
  JSONValue val = pets.get(i);
  // ... processing ...
}
```

`JSONArray`s are useful for ordered data, but we still have yet to look at a way to store mapped data. The `JSONObject` fills that need.

13.2.4 Collecting JSONValue objects in a JSONObject

The JSON `object` type, shown in figure 13.4, is roughly equivalent to the Java class `java.util.Map`: It's a collection of name/value pairs. In languages other than Java, this type of data structure may be known as a *hash*, an *associative array*, or, as in JavaScript, an *object*.

The `JSONObject`, like the `JSONArray`, may be constructed with the zero-argument constructor or by passing a JavaScript object. The ability to pass a `JavaScriptObject` is handy if you want to convert a JavaScript object that was returned from a native JSNI function to a `JSONObject`.

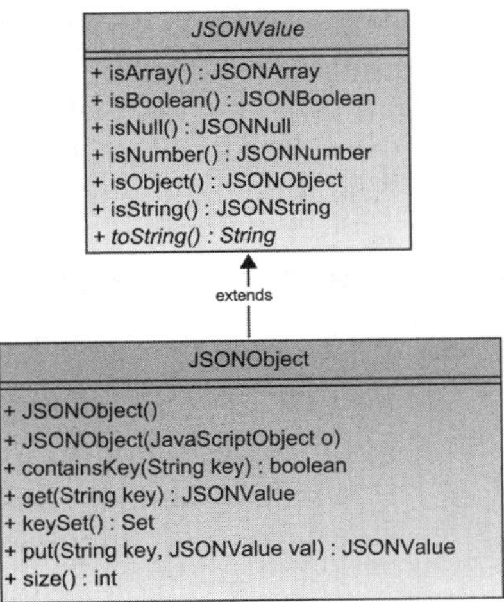

Figure 13.4 A class diagram of the `JSONObject` class, used to hold a collection of named `JSONValue` objects

Adding values to a `JSONObject` is the same as a Java `Map`. It provides a `put()` method that takes a `String` as the key and a `JSONValue` object as the value:

```
JSONObject person = new JSONObject();
person.put("name", name);
person.put("age", age);
```

```
person.put("married", married);
person.put("children", children);
person.put("pets", pets);
```

To iterate over the values in the JSONObject, you can use the keySet() method to return a java.util.Set of keys. You can then pass each key to the get() method to retrieve the stored JSONValue:

```
Set keys = person.keySet();
for (Iterator i = keys.iterator(); i.hasNext();) {
  String key = (String) i.next();
  JSONValue value = person.get(key);
  // ... processing ...
}
```

The JSONObject class also includes a size() method to get the number of name/value pairs and a containsKey() method to test for the existence of a key.

```
int pairs = person.size();
boolean hasName = person.containsKey("name");
```

No remove method is available; once you place something in the JSONObject, you can't remove the name/value pair without rebuilding the entire object. In most cases, this isn't an issue because JSON objects are typically used only for transport and not modified after creation.

This concludes our examination of JSONObject and all the JSON value objects. Now, let's put JSON to work as you build a search component that uses the Yahoo Search API.

13.3 Creating a search component using JSON

Yahoo is one of those companies that has provided a lot of open APIs that developers can use. One of the APIs provided by Yahoo is for its search engine; Yahoo's API provides support for several data formats including JSON. Over the course of this section and the next, you'll implement a search component that displays search results from the Yahoo search engine (see figure 13.5).

You'll break the component into two parts: the client side and the server side. On the client, you'll send a JSON request to the server and then display the results of the search by parsing the JSON response. On the server side, you'll utilize a third-party Java API to read the JSON request from the client, and then you'll call the remote Yahoo server API. The server portion will then return the raw JSON response from Yahoo to the client browser. Once you finish that, you'll reimplement the server-side code in Ruby and Perl.

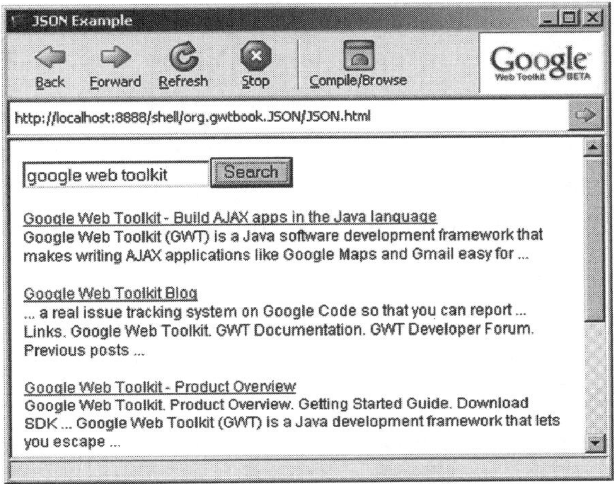

Figure 13.5
The completed Yahoo-service search component running in the GWT hosted browser

To begin, we'll explain the Yahoo Search API and provide details on the returned JSON data.

13.3.1 Examining the Yahoo Search API

Yahoo provides a rich set of Search APIs, allowing you to write applications that can search for audio, images, web sites, and videos, and also provides a ton of options. For the purposes of your search component, you'll be using the web-search service, and you'll request that the returned data be in the JSON message format. Due to space constraints, we can cover only a small portion of the Search API and its options; if you decide to explore more of what Yahoo has to offer, you can find the full details at http://developer.yahoo.com/search.

You can access the Yahoo API by passing the search arguments in a URL. This is the base URL for the Yahoo Search API:

```
http://search.yahooapis.com/WebSearchService/V1/webSearch
```

To this, you can add various query parameters. Following are some of the available parameters, which you'll use in your component:

- `appid`—The application ID: a required parameter. The Yahoo developer network provides information for registering your `appid` and the terms of use. Visit http://developer.yahoo.com/faq/index.html#token for additional information.
- `output`—The output format. These include `json`, `xml`, `php`, and `string`. For this application, you'll use `json` as the value for this parameter.

- `results`—The number of results to return. The default is 10.
- `query`—Used to pass the search terms to the Yahoo service. This is a required parameter.

When you pass the value `json` as the `output` parameter, the results are returned as JSON data. You can test this by appending the following search parameters. When you use this, replace the `appid` value "GWT-Book" with your own:

```
?appid=GWT-Book&output=json&results=1&query=Manning
```

The results returned from this search look like those shown in listing 13.1. Note that we've reformatted the data to make it more readable; when you use this in your browser or application, the data is on a single line.

Listing 13.1 JSON formatted message received from Yahoo's Search API after a search on the term "Manning"

```
{
  "ResultSet" : {

    "type" : "web",
    "totalResultsAvailable" : 22800000,
    "totalResultsReturned" : 1,
    "firstResultPosition" : 1,
    "moreSearch" : "\/WebSearchService\/V1\/webSearch...",

    "Result" : [
      {
        "Title" : "Manning Publications Co.",
        "Summary" : "Publisher of computer books...",
        "Url" : "http:\/\/www.manning.com\/",
        "ClickUrl" : "http:\/\/uk.wrs.yahoo.com\/_ylt=A9ib...",
        "DisplayUrl" : "www.manning.com\/",
        "ModificationDate" : 1160722800,
        "MimeType" : "text\/html",
        "Cache" : {
          "Url":"http:\/\/uk.wrs.yahoo.com\/_ylt=A9ib...",
          "Size":"62363"
        }
      }
    ]
  }
}
```

The root object returned is a JSON object, as denoted by the curly braces. Inside the object is a single property named `ResultSet`. `ResultSet` is an object that contains various properties like type, total available results, total results returned, a link to additional results, and a `Result` property. The `Result` property is an array of results, each of which is a JSON object. Each result object contains the title of the result, a summary, a display URL, a click URL, and other details about the result.

Now that you have an idea what the Yahoo data looks like, you need to create the client application and implement the code to read this JSON data.

13.3.2 Implementing the Yahoo search component

You've built several components at this point, so we won't repeat the steps for creating a new project here. Instead, you'll get right into the project. Your project name may vary, but for the purposes of the code examples found here, the entry point class is `org.gwtbook.client.JSON`.

Setting up your JSON project is the same as any other, with one addition: By default, the JSON classes aren't in the build path for the GWT compiler, so you need to add them to your project configuration file. To do so, you inherit the `com.google.gwt.json.JSON` module, which lets the GWT compiler find the JSON classes. With this addition, the project configuration looks like the following:

```
<module>
  <inherits name='com.google.gwt.user.User'/>
  <inherits name='com.google.gwt.json.JSON'/>
  <entry-point class='org.gwtbook.client.JSON'/>
</module>
```

For this component, you'll create a class called `YahooSearchComponent` that extends the GWT `Composite` class and resides in the `org.gwtbook.client.ui` package. Listing 13.2 provides the component's basic structure. Again, we've covered how to do this several times, so we'll only briefly describe the general structure of the component.

Listing 13.2 The `YahooSearchComponent`

```
package org.gwtbook.client.ui;

import com.google.gwt.core.client.*;
import com.google.gwt.json.client.*;
import com.google.gwt.user.client.*;
import com.google.gwt.user.client.ui.*;

public class YahooSearchComponent extends Composite
{
  FlowPanel component = new FlowPanel();
  TextBox searchBox = new TextBox();            Construct
  Button searchButton = new Button();           components
  FlowPanel resultsArea = new FlowPanel();
```

```
    public YahooSearchComponent()
    {
      initWidget(component);
      setStyleName("yahoo-search");

      searchButton.setText("Search");
      searchButton.addClickListener(
        new ClickListener() {
          public void onClick(Widget sender) {
            search();
          }
        }
      );

      component.add(searchBox);
      component.add(searchButton);
      component.add(resultsArea);
    }
  }
```

Add listener for button

The widget you're using for the top level of this component is a `FlowPanel`. Inside it, you include a text box, where the user enters their search text; a button to trigger the search, and a flow panel to hold the search results. In the constructor for the component, you add a `ClickListener` that triggers the `search()` method, which you'll define shortly.

If you comment out the `search()` call, you should be able to create an instance of the component from your entry point and test it in the hosted browser. The following is the code for the entry point (nothing special here; you instantiate the `YahooSearchComponent` and add it to the `RootPanel`):

```
public class JSON implements EntryPoint
{
  public void onModuleLoad()
  {
    YahooSearchComponent search = new YahooSearchComponent();
    RootPanel.get().add(search);
  }
}
```

Figure 13.6 shows what you should have so far: a simple page with a search box and a button. We haven't provided any special CSS styling for this component—we leave that up to you.

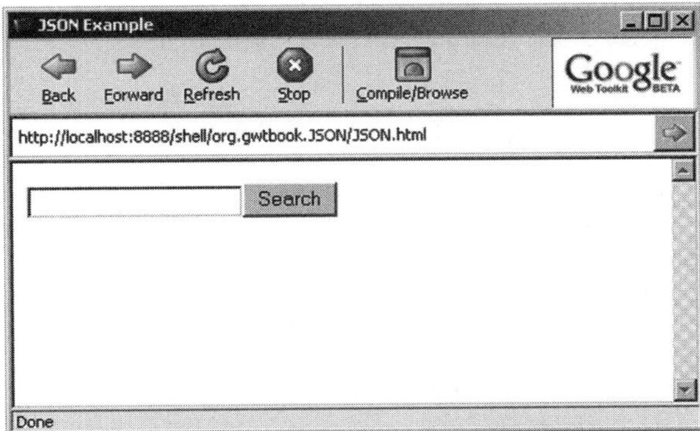

Figure 13.6
The beginnings of the Yahoo search component

Now that you have the basic structure of the component set, it's time to use some of your JSON knowledge and make the component work. Part of this process involves having the search component send data to the server.

13.3.3 Sending JSON data to the server

When you use JSON to communicate with the server, you do so with the `RequestBuilder` class that we looked at in chapter 12. JSON by itself isn't a transport mechanism; it's a message format, so you need to use `RequestBuilder` to transmit the message. In the discussion that follows, we'll no doubt repeat some of what we stated in the section on `RequestBuilder`, but this isn't a substitute for our earlier explanation. If you don't understand something about the transport of the JSON message, you should refer to the appropriate topic in chapter 12.

First, in order to use `RequestBuilder`, you need to import the `com.google.gwt.http.HTTP` module by adding the following line to the module configuration for this project:

```
<inherits name='com.google.gwt.http.HTTP'/>
```

This lets the `RequestBuilder` class and associated classes be included into your project path, making them available to the GWT compiler.

When we ended our coverage of implementing the search panel in the last section, you'd created a click listener to trigger a `search()` method. This method, as we explained, triggers the search. Listing 13.3 defines the `search()` method that provides an example of sending a JSON message.

Listing 13.3 The search() method

```
private void search()
{
  String searchString = searchBox.getText());          ← ❶ Get search keywords

  JSONObject o = new JSONObject();
  o.put("searchString", new JSONString(searchString);  ← ❷ Construct JSON message
  o.put("maxResults", new JSONNumber(5));
                                                       ❸ Clear results area
  resultsArea.clear();

  RequestBuilder rb = new RequestBuilder(RequestBuilder.POST,   ← ❹ Create request
    GWT.getModuleBaseURL() + "search");

  try {
    rb.sendRequest(o.toString(), new SearchResultsHandler());   ← ❺ Send request
  }
  catch (RequestException e) {
    GWT.log("Could not send search request", e);
  }
}
```

First, if you haven't been following along, you get the search terms for the `YahooSearchComponent` from the text box ❶. Following this, you ❷ build the JSON message. You construct a new `JSONObject` and add two properties to it: `searchString` and `maxResults`. You do this by creating the appropriate JSON object type and adding it to the `JSONObject`. Again, this should all be review; if you missed that part, go back and read section 13.2, where we define the JSON class types.

Next, you clear the search results panel and send your request to the server, removing any previously return results ❸. After that, you're ready to make the actual RPC request. You construct a new `RequestBuilder` instance using the `POST` method ❹. You need to use this HTTP method instead of an HTTP `GET` because you want the JSON message to be passed in the body of the HTTP message. We favor this over passing the data in the HTTP query string because an HTTP `POST` doesn't limit you as to the length of the JSON message.

The `sendRequest()` method ❺ takes two parameters: the `POST` message and a reference to a `RequestCallback` object. For the `RequestCallback` parameter, you pass a new instance of `SearchResultsHandler`, which we'll define shortly, whose job it is to parse and display the resulting JSON message and display the search results to the user. For the `POST` message, you call the `toString()` method on your JSON object. This builds a JSON message from the object, which looks like the following:

```
{"searchString":"google web toolkit", "maxResults":5.0}
```

With the JSON format, the curly braces denote the boundary of a JSON object; within are two properties. The `searchString` property in this example contains the string "google web toolkit", and the `maxResults` property contains the value 5.0. As we mentioned earlier in this chapter, JSON doesn't distinguish between integer and floating-point numbers, which is why the value 5, which you set in the code, is passed as 5.0. (We discussed the JSON format in section 13.1.1.)

The only thing left on the client side of the component is to implement the `SearchResultsHandler` class that parses and validates the results from the server and displays them to the user.

13.3.4 Parsing and validating a JSON server response

When you receive the JSON message results from the server, you should add comprehensive validation to the message. Because this requires a bit of code, you'll break up the functionality into several bite-sized pieces. Listing 13.4 is the shell for the response handler; it contains four methods, three of which aren't currently defined.

Listing 13.4 Response handler shell

```
class SearchResultsHandler implements RequestCallback
{

  public void onError(Request request, Throwable exception)     <- Handle errors
  {
    GWT.log("Search request failed", exception);
    Window.alert("Sorry, the search request could not be sent.");
  }

  public void onResponseReceived(Request request, Response response)     <- Handle results
  {
    if (response.getStatusCode() != 200) {
      Window.alert("Sorry, there was an error...");
      return;
    }

    JSONArray results;
    results = extractYahooResults(response.getText());     <- Extract result data
    updateResultsArea(results);     <- Update display
  }

  private JSONArray extractYahooResults(String responseText) {}

  private void updateResultsArea(JSONArray results) {}

  private String getString(JSONValue value) {}
}
```

The flow of the handler is fairly simple. It first examines the JSON response and extracts just the `JSONArray` that contains the search results. This is done in the method `extractYahooResults()`, where you'll provide a lot of error handling. The results are passed to `updateResultsArea()`, which updates the results panel of your component. The last method is a simple utility method that takes a `JSONValue` and returns the `String` representation. Remember that calling `toString()` on a JSON object returns a JSON message string. This isn't always what you want, and it's the reason for this method, because it would automatically add quotes to a `String` value.

Next, let's define the `extractYahooResults()` method (see listing 13.5).

Listing 13.5 Handling the Yahoo API response

```
private JSONArray extractYahooResults(String responseText)
{
  JSONArray results;
  JSONValue resVal;
  JSONObject resObject;
  JSONObject resultSet;

  if (responseText == null || responseText.equals("")) {
    GWT.log("no response content", null);
    return null;
  }

  try {
    resVal = JSONParser.parse(responseText);
  } catch (JSONException e) {
    GWT.log("JSON parse exception: " + responseText, e);
    return null;
  }

  if ((resObject = resVal.isObject()) == null) {
    GWT.log("resObject is unexpected type", null);
    return null;
  }

  if ((resultSet = resObject.get("ResultSet").isObject()) == null) {
    GWT.log("ResultSet object not found", null);
    return null;
  }
  if ((results = resultSet.get("Result").isArray()) == null) {
    GWT.log("Result array not found", null);
    return null;
  }

  return results;
}
```

1 Test for blank response

2 Parse response

3 Validate response format

You need to write the validation of a JSON message yourself, and it can become verbose. Because of this, you may have a strong desire to skip it and assume that everything will work. This approach may work out most of the time, but when something isn't working right, it can be difficult to debug. In the validation routine, you want to make it easy to find problems; in the long run, it's usually worth the time involved in writing a detailed validation routine.

You begin the validation by verifying that the message you're going to parse isn't `null` and that it isn't empty ❶. If either of these is true, the parse automatically fails and throws either a `NullPointerException` or an `IllegalArgumentException`. By making this check, you can log the root cause of the problem without causing an exception.

Next, you attempt to parse the JSON message ❷. If something goes wrong, the `JSONParser` throws a `JSONException`. This is *not* a checked exception, so you don't need to surround it in a `try` block; but again, you're attempting to make it easy to debug any issues with the message you receive from the server.

Following this are three separate checks ❸ as you dig deeper in the JSON message to find the search results you need. You first verify that the object you get back from the `JSONParser.parse()` call is a `JSONObject`. You then verify that this object has a `ResultSet` property that is also a `JSONObject`, and that the object has a `Result` property that is a `JSONArray`. This follows the result format for the Yahoo JSON message, as we discussed in section 13.3.1. In each check, you call the appropriate `isXYZ()` method, which returns `null` if the underlying object isn't of that type. If everything checks out, you return a `JSONArray` of search results.

The next method you need to define is `updateResultsArea()`, which displays the results to the user (see listing 13.6).

Listing 13.6 Updating the component's display

```
private void updateResultsArea(JSONArray results)
{
  for (int i = 0; i < results.size(); i++) {
    JSONObject result;
    if ((result = results.get(i).isObject()) == null) {      ❶ Validate result object
      GWT.log("Result[" + i + "] not an object", null);
      continue;
    }

    String title = getString(result.get("Title"));             ❷ Extract field data from result
    String summary = getString(result.get("Summary"));
    final String clickUrl = getString(result.get("ClickUrl"));
```

```
      Hyperlink link = new Hyperlink(title, "result");
      link.addClickListener(new ClickListener() {
        public void onClick(Widget sender) {
          Window.open(clickUrl, "_blank", "");
        }
      });

      resultsArea.add(link);
      resultsArea.add(new Label(summary));
      resultsArea.add(new HTML(" "));
    }
  }
```

❸ **Create result link**

In this method, you loop over the results in the `JSONArray` and add each to the `resultsArea` `FlowPanel`. Again, you're cautious with the JSON data and verify that each result is a `JSONObject` ❶. You then get the string value of the title, summary, and link ❷. For each of these, you use the `getString()` method, which we'll define shortly. You then create a `Hyperlink` for each result ❸ and add a `ClickListener`, which sends the user to the URL for the result when clicked.

The only method left to define is `getString()`, which returns the `String` representation of a `JSONValue` object. Again, be careful not to make any assumptions about the JSON data:

```
private String getString(JSONValue value)
{
  if (value == null)
    return "";
  if (value.isString() != null)
    return value.isString().stringValue();
  return value.toString();
}
```

Here you plan for three cases. If the value is `null`, you return an empty `String`. This makes the method null-safe and prevents `NullPointerExceptions`. You then test to see whether the value is a `JSONString`, in which case you call the `stringValue()` method to return the value. In the third case, you don't know what the value is, so you call `toString()` and return a JSON-formatted message for the object.

You've come a long way, but you don't quite have a working search. You have a client, but you still need to write the code for the server. For the server, you'll create a server-side application that will proxy requests between the browser client and the Yahoo search service.

13.4 Implementing a Yahoo Search proxy service

When you began this project, we stated that you'd build the server-side portion of the application using Java, Perl, and Ruby. In the sections that follow, you'll do that. We expect that only one or two of these may be of interest to you, so feel free to look at only those languages you're interested in. In each of the implementations, we'll explain everything you need to know with regard to that language, and we don't reference any text across those sections (you won't miss anything if you skip a section).

We're calling this a *proxy* service, meaning that your server code is merely the man in the middle, passing data between the client browser and the Yahoo service. The reason for doing this is that due to security restrictions in the browser, your client application won't be able to hit the Yahoo service directly. If you missed the section on RPC security concerns, you can look at section 10.1.2, where we explain the reasoning behind this.

In each of the following sections, the purpose of the code is to first read the request from the client browser and pass it along to the Yahoo service. The request from the client browser comes to the server as a JSON message; in each implementation, we'll include notes on the JSON implementation that we used and where you can get it.

When you call the Yahoo service, you do so by hitting a URL that has been provided by Yahoo. Again, in each language, you need to use a language-specific library to do this, and we'll provide some information about the library we used. The content returned by the Yahoo service isn't processed by your server-side code; instead, the server passes the content to the browser to be processed on the client. The server code completes its work by "printing" the contents to your client.

With that brief explanation of what we're trying to accomplish, let's look at how this works, first with Java.

13.4.1 Using JSON with Java on the server

As we stated, you need to implement a proxy service for your Yahoo-based search component. For this project, you'll implement this as a Java servlet and use third-party libraries to allow you to parse JSON data and hit an external web address. There is no requirement that this be implemented as a servlet, but we've done so because we feel that, as a standalone application, this it the best fit.

To begin, you need to first address the source of external libraries that will be required to deploy this project. To let your servlet hit a remote web site, you'll use the Jakarta Commons HttpClient library. If you aren't familiar with the Jakarta project, it's a highly respected project in the Java world and is the Java arm of the

Apache Foundation. You can download the latest version of HttpClient library from the following URL: http://jakarta.apache.org/commons/httpclient/.

The other external library you need is a library for parsing JSON objects. When we visited the JSON.org web site, several Java implementations were available, as well as a reference implementation provided by JSON.org. Each of the libraries has its own set of features and tools, some easier than others. In the end, we decided to use the reference implementation because it doesn't depend on third-party libraries. The reference implementation can be found at this URL: http://www.json.org/java/. Unfortunately, there is one downside: The JSON.org folks don't currently have their code packaged as a JAR file, so you have to download the source and add it to your project.

Our decision to use this implementation was based on the need to make this example easy to implement, and we didn't want our readers downloading dozens of external libraries to get the application working. On the other hand, if you don't mind tracking down dependencies, you may find one of the other implementations more appropriate for your project needs. Look on the JSON.org home page for a list of alternate Java distributions.

Once you have the prerequisites downloaded and added to your classpath, you can proceed with the implementation. Compared to the other languages we'll look at, the Java implementation is by far the longest. It isn't more difficult, though; it's just that Java, by its nature, tends to be more verbose than dynamic languages. We want you to know this because the code in listing 13.7 looks daunting—but it isn't complex.

Listing 13.7 A JSON server proxy in Java

```
package org.gwtbook.server;

import java.io.*;
import java.net.URLEncoder;
import javax.servlet.ServletException;
import javax.servlet.http.*;
import org.apache.commons.httpclient.HttpClient;
import org.apache.commons.httpclient.methods.GetMethod;
import org.json.*;

public class YahooSearchService extends HttpServlet
{

  protected void service(
      HttpServletRequest request,
      HttpServletResponse response)
         throws ServletException, IOException
```

❶ Servlet method signature

```
{
  BufferedReader input = new BufferedReader(
    new InputStreamReader(request.getInputStream()));

  StringBuffer data = new StringBuffer();
  String buf = input.readLine();
  while (buf != null) {
    data.append(buf);
    buf = input.readLine();
  }

  String searchString = null;
  int maxResults = 0;

  JSONObject json;
  try {
    JSONTokener tokenizer = new JSONTokener(data.toString());
    json = new JSONObject(tokenizer);
    searchString = json.getString("searchString");
    maxResults = json.getInt("maxResults");
  } catch (JSONException e) {
    e.printStackTrace();
  }

  GetMethod get = new GetMethod(
    "http://search.yahooapis.com/WebSearchService/V1"
       + "/webSearch?appid=GWT-Book&output=json"
       + "&results="
       + maxResults
       + "&query="
       + URLEncoder.encode(searchString, "UTF-8"));

  HttpClient client = new HttpClient();
  client.executeMethod(get);
  String result = get.getResponseBodyAsString();
  get.releaseConnection();

  response.getWriter().print(result);
 }
}
```

❷ **Read input data**

❸ **Parse and extract request data**

❹ **Prepare call to Yahoo service**

❺ **Call Yahoo service**

❻ **Return result to client browser**

As we mentioned, you implement this service as a Java servlet ❶. The entry-point method for a servlet is the `service()` method, which takes a `request` object and a `response` object as parameters. These objects can be used as handles to read input from and write output to the browser.

Because the content being sent by the browser isn't a standard query, you need to do a little work to extract the JSON data ❷. Here, you use the request object to get a handle on the input stream, and then you read it into the `StringBuffer` variable `data`. This code should be fairly standard if you plan to use servlets to handle JSON requests, so it may be worthwhile to package this code as a method so that you can easily reuse it.

Once you read in the JSON message request from the browser, you need to parse the message and extract the parameters ❸. The exact code here depends on the JSON library you use. In this case, you're using the reference Java implementation from JSON.org. To parse the message, you create an instance of the `JSONTokenizer` and pass it to the constructor of the `JSONObject`. The `JSONObject` constructor uses the tokenizer to parse the message, and, if something is wrong with the message, it throws an exception. Once the message has been parsed, you call the appropriate methods on the `JSONObject` to get the data—in this case, `getInt()` and `getString()`. The names `searchString` and `maxResults` are the parameter names you defined when you built the search client in the last section.

Next, you utilize the Commons `HttpClient` library and build a `GET` request ❹. The URL you're building is the one defined for the Yahoo search service; note that you URL-encode any `String` values. You must encode values that are sent in the URL because the search text may include characters that are considered reserved in the URL query format.

Once you have your request, you need to send it to the Yahoo service ❺. This involves creating a HTTP client, executing the request, grabbing the result, and closing the HTTP client. This is analogous to opening your web browser, going to a URL, reading the page, then closing your browser.

With the result in hand, all that is left to do is print the JSON message that came from the Yahoo service ❻. You print this value using a special writer that ultimately delivers the data to the client browser. This last part ends the request-response cycle between the browser and the servlet.

There is one issue to be aware of, depending on the remote service you're trying to proxy to. Some services attempt to detect the type of client hitting their service and may deny access to the service in some cases. The service can do this because your web browser, as well as the `HttpClient` class, sends information about what type of client (also known as the *user agent*) it is. This is what allows web-site log analyzers, for example, to determine the types of browsers being used by the users of a web site.

One example of a service that does this is Google Groups, which denied access to a servlet that we wrote from being able to access an RSS feed. To access the service, we had to provide a user agent name other than the default used by the Commons `HttpClient` library:

```
HttpClient client = new HttpClient();
HttpClientParams clientParams = new HttpClientParams();
clientParams.setParameter(HttpMethodParams.USER_AGENT,
   "SecretAgent");
client.setParams(clientParams);
```

When we made a request with this `HttpClient`, it reported our agent type as being `SecretAgent`. There are many other reasons to set this value to something other than the default, including masquerading as a specific browser type or including your contact information as part of the agent name (which is a common practice).

We hope we've covered everything you need to know to start writing JSON services in Java. With that, we'll move on to the second implementation, in Perl.

13.4.2 Using JSON with Perl on the server

Perl is one of the old workhorses of the Web, and it's still popular today. In this section, we'll provide the code required to get the server portion of your Yahoo-based search service project up and running in Perl. In the course of doing so, you'll see how Perl can work with JSON messages, as well as its ability to act as a proxy between the client and a remote service.

As with the Java version, you need to get a few external libraries, the first of which provides support for JSON. As with all things Perl, there is more than one way to do it; with a quick search of CPAN.org, we found many. We settled on the module `JSON`, by Makamaka Hannyaharamitu, which you can download from the following URL: http://search.cpan.org/~makamaka/JSON/.

The second library you need calls the Yahoo web service from your Perl script. The obvious choice is `libwww-perl` (LWP) by Gisle Aas. This is probably one of Perl's most popular libraries, so you may already have it installed; if you don't, you can download it from the following address: http://search.cpan.org/~gaas/libwww-perl/.

If you aren't sure whether LWP is installed on your system, you can run the following command, which prints the version number of LWP if it's installed. If you're running this command on Windows, replace the single quotes in the command with double quotes:

```
perl -MLWP -e 'print $LWP::VERSION'
```

For the Perl example, you need a third library as well: the `URI::Escape` module, again by Gisle Aas. This library is used to URL encode strings and can be found here: http://search.cpan.org/~gaas/URI/URI/Escape.pm.

Once you have the prerequisites installed, it's time to write some code. Due to Perl's concise nature, this example is rather short; see listing 13.8.

Listing 13.8 A JSON server proxy in Perl

```
#!/usr/bin/perl

use strict;
use JSON;
use CGI;
use LWP::Simple;
use URI::Escape;

my $cgi = new CGI();                                    ❶ Print
print $cgi->header('text/plain');                         headers
                                                                  ❷ Read and parse
my $req = jsonToObj($cgi->param('POSTDATA'));                       JSON message

my $query =
  sprintf("appid=GWT-Book&output=json&results=%d&query=%s",     ❸ Build
    int($req->{maxResults}),                                        query
    uri_escape($req->{searchString}));

getprint("http://search.yahooapis.com:80/WebSearchService/V1"
  . "/webSearch?$query");
                                               Call Yahoo service ❹
```

The first thing you need to do is create a new `CGI` instance and print the content headers ❶. CGI is the de facto standard module when it comes to CGI support in Perl. Here, you use it to print the standard `Content-type` header. This header tells your web server what type of content you're printing out, which in this case is plain text.

Next, you read in the JSON message that was passed to the client and parse the message so that it can be read ❷. The CGI module makes the first task easy by allowing you to retrieve the `POSTDATA` parameter, which returns the entire message that was posted by the client browser. The parsing of the JSON message is done by calling `jsonToObj()`, which is one of the methods automatically imported when you used the JSON module. The `jsonToObj()` method converts the JSON message to a regular Perl object.

With the JSON request in hand, you now build the query that will ultimately be sent to the Yahoo service ❸. You use `sprintf()` to help you format the string, and you call `uri_escape()` to URL-encode the search string. The `uri_escape()` method is automatically imported when you use the `URI::Escape` module.

The last two steps needed to finish up your proxy—calling the Yahoo service and printing the result—are performed by the last statement in the script ❹. The `getprint()` method is automatically imported when you use `LWP::Simple`, and it handles both of these tasks.

With fewer than 20 lines of code, you should be up and running in Perl. We expect that the `JSON` module, along with `LWP::Simple`, will cover most of your JSON needs; if not, your first stop should be CPAN: http://search.cpan.org/. CPAN has thousands of modules available; if you require some bit of functionality, it's likely that someone else needed the same functionality and shared their code. For example, one interesting module we found in our search is `DBIx::JSON`, which generates JSON messages from database queries.

With that, we conclude the Perl version of the implementation. Next, we'll look at how you can implement it in a language that has been gaining a lot of popularity lately: Ruby.

13.4.3 Using JSON with Ruby on the server

The third and final implementation of the Yahoo search service proxy is in Ruby, a popular language that has been gaining a lot of momentum the last few years. If you've read either the Java or Perl sections that preceded this one, this one follows a similar pattern and starts by discussing the third-party libraries required for the example. Then, we'll look at the implementation and explain in detail what it's doing.

With Ruby, you require only one external library, which parses the JSON data. We chose to use the `json` library, by Frank Florian. You can download the `json` library from RubyForge at the following address: http://rubyforge.org/projects/json. Alternatively, you can use RubyGems to install the package by executing the following command at the command line:

```
gem install json
```

With the `json` library installed, it's time to look at the Ruby implementation; see listing 13.9.

Listing 13.9 A JSON server proxy in Ruby

```
#!/usr/bin/ruby

require 'rubygems'
require 'json'
require 'net/http'

if $stdin.eof
  raise "no data defined"
end

input = $stdin.read
data = JSON.parse(input)

if data.has_key? 'Error'
  raise "data parse error"
end

searchString = data['searchString']
maxResults = data['maxResults'].to_i

base_url = "http://search.yahooapis.com:80/WebSearchService/V1"
base_url << "/webSearch?appid=GWT-Book&output=json"

url = "#{base_url}&query=#{URI.encode(searchString)}"
url << "&results=#{maxResults}"

resp = Net::HTTP.get_response(URI.parse(url))
result = resp.body

puts "Content-type: text/plain\n\n"
puts result
```

❶ Verify data available
❷ Read and parse JSON message
❸ Extract search request
❹ Build Yahoo service query
❺ Call Yahoo service
❻ Print results to client browser

Out of the gate, the first thing you want to do is verify that you received a request from the client browser. You do this by checking the `stdin` file handle ❶ and verifying that the end-of-file flag isn't set to `true`.

Next, you read the contents of the `stdin` handle and call `JSON.parse()` to convert the JSON message to a data object that you can use ❷. Again, you add some error-checking by looking for the key `Error` in the data object. If this key is found, it signals that there was a parse error, in which case you raise an error.

With the contents of the JSON message parsed, you extract the two parameters from the object ❸. The `searchString` and `maxResults` parameters are the ones you defined in your client for this service in the previous section.

You now use these parameters to build the URL, which will be used to call the Yahoo service ❹. Note that you use the `URI.encode()` method to escape any reserved characters that appear in the search string.

Next, you call the Yahoo service with the `Net::Http::get_response()` method ❺. This method calls the service and returns a `response` object. You can then read the `body` property of the `response` object to get the JSON message returned by the Yahoo service.

The only thing left to do is print the `Content-Type` header and the JSON message ❻. The web server then sends this output back to the browser that called your service.

That concludes the third implementation of a JSON server proxy service. You aren't limited to one of the languages we've presented here, because JSON implementations are available in many other languages: Python, PHP, Haskell, Delphi, C#, Lisp, OCaml, and others. Visit json.org for a long list of implementations.

13.5 Summary

In this chapter we covered the nuts and bolts of GWT's support of the JavaScript Object Notation format (JSON). We began by showing that the JSON format is simple to read and understand and that it's executable as JavaScript code. This simplicity has brought wide-spread adoption of JSON as a language-agnostic format that can be consumed and produced by a variety of languages.

We discussed each of the JSON value types: `string`, `number`, `boolean`, and `null`. We also examined the structure and format of the composite types `array` and `object`. The simplicity and small number of types makes the format lightweight. On the other hand, the lack of complexity means your data may need to be massaged to fit the message format. For example, because JSON doesn't include an explicit `date` object, you need to handle serialization of a Java `Date` object yourself.

With the JSON tour out of the way, you finally got to put JSON to work by building a Yahoo search component. To show off JSON's ability to work with a variety of languages, we explained how to implement the server side of the component in Java, Perl, and Ruby.

During the course of implementing the Yahoo search component, we provided a short tour of the Yahoo search API. We used only a subset of the API, but we tried to provide with enough information so that you can customize the component to meet your specific needs.

This ends our discussion of JSON and also our discussion of GWT's RPC tools: We began with GWT's proprietary RPC mechanism in chapter 10, moved on to client-side architecture in chapter 11, and then explored the `RequestBuilder` object and `FormPanel` in chapter 12. But it doesn't end here, because there is more of GWT to explore. In chapter 14, we'll focus on using code generators to write code for you. If you want to squeeze every last ounce of goodness from GWT, then you'll likely find it an interesting topic.

14 Automatically generating new code

This chapter covers

- Overview of GWT generators
- Writing custom generators
- Accessing input and context
- Using introspection

Everything we've done so far has involved you, as a developer, writing GWT Java code for your application. But you can do more with GWT. Is your ideal development project one that includes sitting back with your feet up and letting a tool write the code for you? With GWT, your dreams are about to come true—almost. Using GWT generators, it's possible, at compile time, to take an existing interface or class (a type) and automatically generate a brand-new type. This new type could implement the input interface or extend the input class, giving new functionality to your applications. The output type of a generator generally contains more implementation details than the input type.

Your task in this chapter is to create a generator that takes all of your Dashboard applications and automatically creates an About menu option in the application's standard option menu bar. When the user clicks the About menu option, you'll show them an alert box containing a list of all the fields and methods in the application's class (if the application is in Internet mode, you'll display only the public fields and methods). In practice, this means you must build and register a generator that takes all of the `DashboardComposite` classes in your application and creates a subclass that provides the About menu item and uses GWT introspection of the class to access the fields and registers.

Additionally, you'll create a This App. Demonstrates menu item that displays the comment defined for the class to the user of the application. This task is also performed using the generator you'll develop.

14.1 Generating new types

You've already used generators, albeit in the background, while developing the Dashboard application (although it's understandable if you haven't been aware of it). Remember when we talked about internationalization and how you provide an interface and a number of properties files? A generator takes that interface and generates a set of classes that bind methods defined in the interface to the values in the various language-specific properties files you also provided. These classes are then used in the deferred binding approach, where the appropriate locale class is selected in the compilation process.

GWT uses generators for more than internationalization. You also used them when you implemented the RPC technique (to talk to the server) in chapter 10. They took the proxies and interfaces and implemented all the code to plumb everything together. When you use JUnit to perform some testing in chapter 16, you'll again use generators to take your test classes and produce the necessary classes in the format needed by JUnit. Table 14.1 indicates the class and packages where you can find the source code for these generators if you're interested in seeing how GWT performs these tasks in detail.

Table 14.1 Package and class names of existing generators in GWT

Generator	Package	Class name
JUnit	`com.google.gwt.junit.rebind`	`JunitTestCaseStubGenerator`
	Description Creates a JUnit-readable class from a user-provided GWT JUnit class.	
I18n	`com.google.gwt.i18n.rebind`	`LocalizableGenerator`
	Description Takes an interface that extends the `Localizable` interface and then generates classes that bind keys in a number of properties files to methods in the interface. One class is produced for each property-specific locale added to the module's XML file.	
RPC	`com.google.gwt.user.rebind.rpc`	`ServiceInterfaceProxyGenerator`
	Description Creates all the plumbing code necessary to implement GWT RPC based on the interfaces you provide.	
Image Bundling	`com.google.gwt.user.rebind`	`ImageBundleGenerator`
	Description Bundles together a number of user-provided images into a single image.	

Unfortunately, not much documentation is available for generators at present, but at least some people are at work decoding how these beasts work and looking at putting them to use (ourselves included!). This chapter represents our knowledge of how generators function, based on our investigation, and also shows you how to produce a practical implementation for the Dashboard.

14.2 Investigating GWT generators

The first point to note about generators is that most of the classes they use don't reside in the JAR archives you've been comfortably using so far. Up to now, you've included the gwt-user.jar file into your projects, which includes all the standard GWT functionality required. For generators, you must venture into the gwt-dev-*platform*.jar archive (substitute your development environment for *platform*, such as gwt-dev-windows.jar). As always, to use these classes, you must add that archive to the classpath (for the commands that launch hosted mode and the compiler for web mode). Our classpath on our Windows development machine is included in the Dashboard-shell command script and looks like this:

```
@java -cp
        "%~dp0\src;%~dp0\bin;C:/Program Files/gwt-win/gwt-user.jar;
         C:/Program Files/gwt-win/gwt-dev-windows.jar"
        com.google.gwt.dev.GWTShell
        -out "%~dp0\www" %* org.gwtbook.Dashboard/Dashboard.html
```

With the classpath amended, there are three key steps to producing your own generator. First, you need to write the code that makes up your generator (we did say that automatic code generation was *almost* a case of the code writing itself). Next, you need to register the fact that you wish the generator to be used with the GWT system. Finally, you must use the deferred binding approach to create the objects that will be generated by a generator.

Writing a generator involves extending the com.google.gwt.core.ext.Generator class with the functionality you require. Registering the generator is performed through your application's module XML file, where you indicate which type the generator should be executed on and what generator's class name is—package_name.TypeToGenerateFor and package_name.GeneratorClassName in the following example:

```
<generate-with class="package_name.GeneratorClassName ">
   <when-type-assignable class="package_name.TypeToGenerateFor"/>
</generate-with>
```

By using the GWT.create(classLiteral) method to create your objects, you're signaling to the compiler that it should use a deferred binding approach—meaning that at compile time (for web mode) or invocation time (for hosted mode), there is a little more work to do to get the appropriate class. In the case of deferred binding to a class created by a generator, you're telling the GWT system that the appropriate class needs to be generated.

Be careful, though, because the classLiteral that you pass into the GWT.create() method should be the name of the type you've written, such as Clock.class, not the name of the type you expect the generator to produce. (The generator works by either implementing your interface or subclassing the class you provide as an input. The result can't have the same name as the input, which is a standard Java rule.)

NOTE You must use the deferred binding approach for creating instances of classes that will be generated. Otherwise, the compiler doesn't know that it needs to invoke a generator.

The process of a generator's action is shown in figure 14.1.

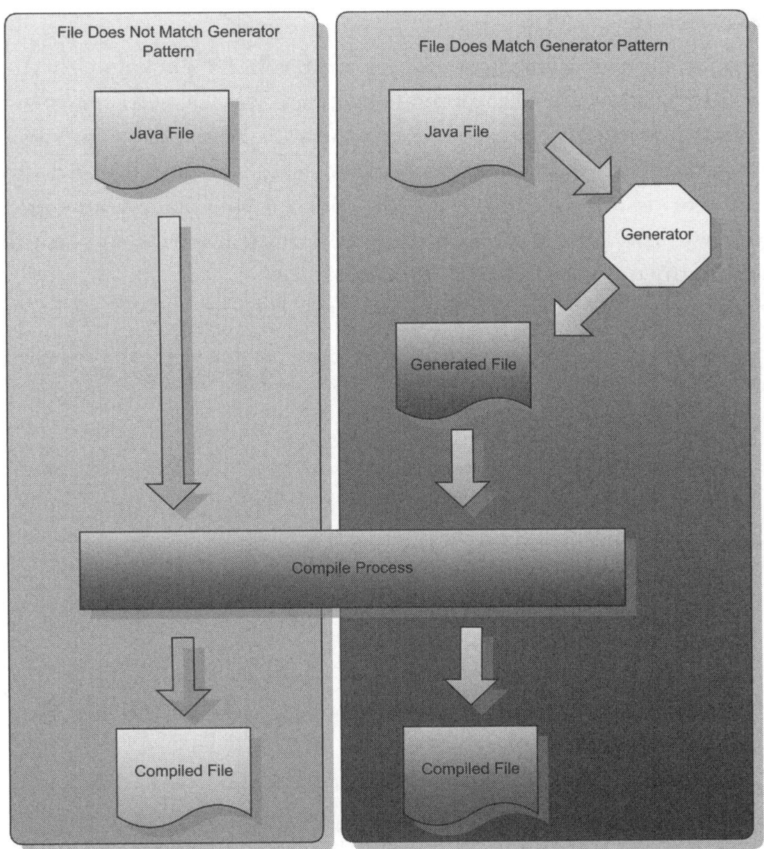

Figure 14.1 How generators change the code before the compilation process starts

When the compiler comes across a deferred-binding instantiation for a class/type, it checks the module XML file (together with any included module XML files) to see if any direction is given to it. If the *assignable type* of the class/type under consideration matches the definition given in the module XML definition, then the generator is applied to it, creating a new type that is used in place of the existing type in the program. If no match is found, then the original class is used.

You know how to register a generator, and what happens at compile time. But what does a generator look like?

14.2.1 Basic generator code

By convention, you place generator classes in a `rebind` package; for the Dashboard, this resides under the `org.gwtbook` package. Just as with server-side code, you should avoid placing a generator under the `client` package for two reasons: It doesn't naturally fit in that package; and you can use Java 1.5 and other constructs that aren't possible in the client-side code (if you place your generator in the client package, then the GWT compiler automatically tries to compile it and complains about any non-GWT compliant code).

Let's look at the basic structure of any generator, shown in listing 14.1.

Listing 14.1 The template of a generator

```
import com.google.gwt.core.ext.Generator;
import com.google.gwt.core.ext.GeneratorContext;
import com.google.gwt.core.ext.TreeLogger;
import com.google.gwt.core.ext.UnableToCompleteException;

public class MyGenerator extends Generator{          ❶ Extend Generator class

   public String generate(TreeLogger logger,
                          GeneratorContext context,
                          String typeName)
                          throws UnableToCompleteException {   ❷ generate() method
      return null;
   }
}
```

This generator doesn't do much, but it does show that all generators need to extend the basic `Generator` class ❶ and implement the `generate()` method ❷. The inputs to the `generate()` method are all supplied by the compiler during the compilation process. These inputs include the context in which the generator executes; you can use that context to access classes, files, and properties. A `TreeLogger` is also supplied, which allows you to output your own logging information in the compilation logger. The final parameter is the name of the type that is being presented to the generator by the compiler.

At present, the result of the `generate()` method in listing 14.1 is the value `null`—which tells the compiler that the generator hasn't created a new type and that it should use the original type passed in as the parameter. If you want to create a new type, then you need to provide the code to create that new type as well as return the name of this new type. You'll do that now for the Dashboard example.

14.3 Creating a generator for the Dashboard

When you built the components for the Dashboard, you put in place a mechanism to let component applications display an option menu when they gain focus; but there is no requirement that a component application must have such a menu. By using a generator, you'll now extend the Dashboard functionality by doing the following:

- Setting the name of the `DashboardPanel` that the `DashboardComposite` sits in to be the name of the `DashboardComposite` class (this is then displayed on the application's title bar and as the option menu name)
- Adding an About menu item to the option menu
- Creating an About alert box, which describes the fields and methods of the `DashboardComposite` (if the Dashboard is in Internet mode, then only the public fields and methods are listed)

Once an application has gone through the generator, it will appear in the Dashboard. Clicking the About menu gives a result similar to that in figure 14.2, which shows the About dialog for the GoogleSearch component application in intranet mode.

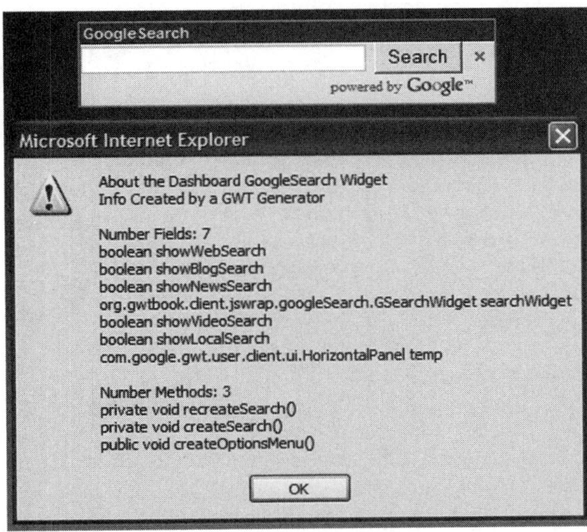

Figure 14.2
The About dialog for the GoogleSearch Dashboard application, showing the methods and fields in the class. (The information was gathered by introspecting the class at compile time using a GWT generator.)

The generator that performs this follows this template:

- Gets information about the input type and property values from the current context
- Creates a new object that is used to create the new type (a `SourceWriter` object)
- Builds the new type, including introspecting the input type, extending that input type, and adding some new methods
- Returns the new type's name to the compiler

In the next few sections, we'll look at each of these steps.

14.3.1 Accessing the input class

The `generate()` method takes as a `String` parameter the name of the input type. For the generator to be of any use, you need to access the type itself and not a reference to its name. Listing 14.2 shows how you do this.

Listing 14.2 Accessing the `TypeOracle` and various type aspects within a GWT generator

```
public String generate(TreeLogger logger,
                       GeneratorContext context,
                       String typeName)
      throws UnableToCompleteException {
   try{
      TypeOracle typeOracle = context.getTypeOracle();
      JClassType requestedClass = typeOracle.getType(typeName);
      String packageName = requestedClass.getPackage().getName();
      String simpleClassName = requestedClass.getSimpleSourceName();
      String proxyClassName = simpleClassName + "Proxy";
      String qualifiedProxyClassName =
                   packageName + "." + proxyClassName;
   } catch (NotFoundException e) {
      logger.log(TreeLogger.ERROR, "Class '" + typeName +
                                  "' Not Found", e);
      throw new UnableToCompleteException();
   }
}
```

❶ Access TypeOracle for current context
❷ Retrieve class
❸ Get details of class
❹ Create type name
❺ Catch exceptions

GWT provides a `TypeOracle` class, an instance of which you can retrieve ❶ from the also-passed `generatorContext` object, which allows you to access information about the type. Once you have the `TypeOracle`, you can get a reference to the class through the `getType()` method ❷. In the example, you have no nested classes to find; but if you do, you need to use the source name (with periods) rather than the binary name (with `$`).

This use of `TypeOracle` is fairly simple: to get access to one named type. It can also be used to examine the whole set of types and packages in the context that is being compiled through various methods with the words `package` and `type` in their names.

The returned type from the `getType()` method is a `JType`, which is one of a number of GWT classes that represent Java constructs. There are also GWT Java classes for packages, classes, methods, parameters, fields, and so on; you can use these objects to perform introspection on classes, as you'll see later in this chapter. For now, you use a couple of methods in the `JType` class to retrieve the package name of the input class as well as its simple source name ❸. Both of these pieces of data are then used in creating the fully qualified name of the class you'll generate ❹, which is the input class with the text `Proxy` appended to the class name. Any exceptions that are raised by your generator are handled at ❺, where you output an error message to the current `TreeLogger` object.

In certain circumstances, such as with internationalization, you'd like to know the values of the properties in this context so that the correct binding to constants/messages can be performed. Access to these values is through the `PropertyOracle` object.

14.3.2 Accessing properties of the context

When the GWT system creates the bindings required for internationalization, the generator needs to know which locale the current context is all about in order to select the appropriate properties file (this is why the files must be named in the particular manner they have been). Similarly, for the Dashboard, you wish to know if you're generating for the Internet or intranet version. In chapter 15, we'll introduce a user-defined property called `externalvisibility` that you can set as either `intranet` or `internet`. If the context you're compiling for has the `externalvisibility` property set as `internet`, then you only show public fields and methods in the About dialog; you determine that by looking in the `PropertyOracle` (see listing 14.3).

Listing 14.3 Accessing the PropertyOracle and a property from within a GWT generator

```
public String generate(TreeLogger logger,
                       GeneratorContext context,
                       String typeName)
     throws UnableToCompleteException {
   try{
      PropertyOracle properties = context.getPropertyOracle();
      String version = properties.getPropertyValue
                        (logger, "externalvisibility");
      } catch (BadPropertyValueException e) {
         logger.log(TreeLogger.ERROR,
                    "Could not find property value", e);
         throw new UnableToCompleteException();
      }
}
```

❶ Access PropertyOracle for current context

❷ Retrieve property value

❸ Handle failure

You accessed information about types through the TypeOracle object, which you retrieved from the GeneratorContext object. Similarly, you access information about GWT properties through a PropertyOracle retrieved from the GeneratorContext object ❶. Retrieving properties is slightly easier than class details because there is only one thing to look for. You use the getPropertyValue() method ❷ to get access to the value of the externalvisibility property.

Unlike other points in GWT where we discuss properties, in the generator case you're only concerned with the value of a property in the particular context being compiled at that point. For example, when you set up the locale property in chapter 3, you gave two values—an English one and a Swedish one. When the generator executes the locale, the property has only one value: that of the locale currently in context. In hosted mode, that means the locale currently being used; when compiling for web mode, the generator is called multiple times, once for each locale being managed.

If you can't find the property you're looking for, this is handled by the catch statement ❸. You can also keep track of what's going on in your generators by implementing logging.

14.3.3 Adding logging to a generator

Logging in a generator is performed by writing log statements to the TreeLogger class that is passed to the generate() method. You can log either a message or an exception using the following template:

```
Logger.log(TreeLogger.LEVEL, message, exception)
```

Figure 14.3 Output from the generator when running in hosted mode

Only one of the `message` or `exception` can be provided; the other should be left as the `null` object. Values of the `LEVEL` all come from the `TreeLogger` class and include the `INFO` and `ERROR` levels you've used in the Dashboard example as well as `ALL`, `DEBUG`, `INFO`, `SPAM`, `NULL`, `TRACE`, and `WARN`.

When you run the application in hosted mode, the generator is invoked whenever you create an instance of a `DashboardComposite`. The output in the hosted-mode window is shown in figure 14.3.

In web mode, all of the compilation is performed at once to generate the numerous permutations of JavaScript code (see chapter 17 for details). Figure 14.4 shows the output produced when we compiled the code.

```
                   Computing all possible rebind results for 'org.gwtbook.client.
dashboard.clock.MyClock'
                      Rebinding org.gwtbook.client.dashboard.clock.MyClock
                         Invoking <generate-with class='org.gwtbook.rebind.Dashbo
ardCompositeGenerator'/>
                            Starting rewriting using: DashboardCompositeGenerator
 for internet version
                            Completed rewriting
```

Figure 14.4 Output from the generator when preparing for web mode

Or, you can ask the compiler to use the `TreeLogger` by including the `-treeLogger` flag in the `compile` command (see chapter 2). Adding this flag means the output appears in hosted-mode style window, as shown in figure 14.5.

```
Output will be written into C:\Documents and Settings\tacyad\Desktop\Dashboard\DashboardPrj\www\org.gwtbook.Dashboard
  Analyzing permutation #1
    Rebinding org.gwtbook.client.ui.calculator.Calculator
      Invoking <generate-with class='org.gwtbook.rebind.DashboardCompositeGenerator'/>
        Starting rewriting using: DashboardCompositeGenerator for internet version
```

Figure 14.5 Output from the generator when preparing for web mode with the compile provided with the `-treeLogger` flag set

The log statements are added to your generator code, as shown in listing 14.4.

Listing 14.4 Logging progress within a GWT generator

```
public String generate(TreeLogger logger,
                       GeneratorContext context,
                       String typeName)
        throws UnableToCompleteException {
   try{
      logger.log(TreeLogger.INFO, "Starting rewriting using:"+
                                  this.getClass().getSimpleName()+
                                  " for "+version+" version",
                                  null);
      // Other code
      logger.log(TreeLogger.INFO, "Completed rewriting", null);
      } catch ...
      }
}
```

You're almost in a position to start writing your new functionality, but first you must get an object that represents the new type—the `SourceWriter` object.

14.3.4 Generating the new type structure

You write your new type by printing lines of text to a `SourceWriter` object (which, unlike the other classes used in generators, can be found in the gwt-user.jar archive under the `com.google.gwt.user.rebind` package). The route to it is slightly convoluted and is shown in listing 14.5 as a separate method in the Dashboard `Generator` class.

Listing 14.5 Creating the `SourceWriter` object

```
protected SourceWriter getSourceWriter(TreeLogger logger,
                                       GeneratorContext context,
                                       String packageName,
                                       String className,
                                       String superclassName){
   PrintWriter printWriter = context.tryCreate(logger,
                                               packageName,
                                               className);       ❶ Create PrintWriter

   if (printWriter == null) return null;                         ❷ Handle when new type already exists

   ClassSourceFileComposerFactory composerFactory =
       new ClassSourceFileComposerFactory(packageName, className);   ❸ Get new ClassSourceFileComposerFactory
```

```
    composerFactory.addImport("com.google.gwt.user.client.Command");
    composerFactory.addImport("com.google.gwt.user.client.Window");
    composerFactory.addImport("com.google.gwt.user.client.MenuItem");
                                                          Add imports ❹
    composerFactory.setSuperclass(superclassName);
                                                          ❺ Set superclass
    return composerFactory.createSourceWriter(context, printWriter);
}                                                         Create SourceWriter ❻
```

First, you try to create a standard Java `PrintWriter` object from the current `GeneratorContext` through the `tryCreate()` method ❶ using the new fully qualified class name as a parameter. If you fail to get a `PrintWriter`, it's because the class you're trying to create already exists ❷. This isn't unusual, particularly because at compilation time the generator is called many times; you may have created the necessary new type in a previous permutation.

Note that if the generated type is to be an interface rather than the default of a class, then you additionally call the `makeInterface()` method on the composer factory.

Let's assume you're applying the generator to the Clock component application. If the `PrintWriter` has been successfully created, then ❸ creates your new type, which resembles the following:

```
package org.gwtbook.client.ui.clock

public class ClockProxy{
}
```

At ❹, you tell the new class to have some imports. Because you're going to add a `MenuItem` and an associated `Command`, these are prime candidates to be included, as is the `Window` class, because you're going to show an alert box with the `Window.alert()` method. Next, you tie the new type to the old type by setting its superclass ❺. The class is now as follows:

```
import com.google.gwt.user.client.Command;
import com.google.gwt.user.client.Window;
import com.google.gwt.user.client.ui.MenuItem;
package org.gwtbook.client.ui.clock

public class ClockProxy extends Clock{
}
```

Finally, you create the `SourceWriter` from this `ComposerFactory` ❻, which is subsequently used to create the methods in the new class.

14.3.5 Creating the new class

Assuming the result of getting the `SourceWriter` isn't `null`, you need to take the last result and provide your new functionality. You do this by adding new methods, overriding methods in the superclass, or manipulating the input class. New methods and fields are written out to the `SourceWriter` object. We'll look at creating two methods: one that overrides the `DashboardComponent`'s `getName()` method, and another that creates the About menu item.

Overriding an existing method

To override an existing method, you write out the details to the `SourceWriter`, as shown in listing 14.6.

Listing 14.6 Using a generator to override an existing method

```
public void writeClassNameMethod(TreeLogger logger,
                                 String className,
                                 SourceWriter writer){
   writer.beginJavaDocComment();
   writer.println("Overides DashboardComposite getName() method");
   writer.endJavaDocComment();
   writer.println("public String getName()");
   writer.println("{");
   writer.indent();
   writer.println("return \"" + className + "\";");
   writer.outdent();
   writer.println("}");
}
```

Add JavaDoc comment

Define method

Indent text

Implement functionality ❶

Outdent text

Complete method definition

You first write out a JavaDoc comment for the new method. Then, you write the method definition you want using calls to the `println()` method. Although you generally won't see the new method definition written down, here you use the `indent()` and `outdent()` methods to structure your code—it's useful to structure the code in a sensible way for those occasions where you make errors. In these circumstances, the compiler will direct you to the error, and in our experience it's often due to forgetting to put the semicolon in at the end of the command you're constructing. Look at this line of code, which could be written instead of ❶ in listing 14.6:

```
writer.println("return \"" + className + "\"");
```

The syntax checker in Java won't complain about this, because it's valid Java. But when you try to use your new class, you get the error message shown in figure 14.6.

The error happens because you forgot to put a semicolon at the end of the code you're generating, not because a semicolon is missing from the `println()`

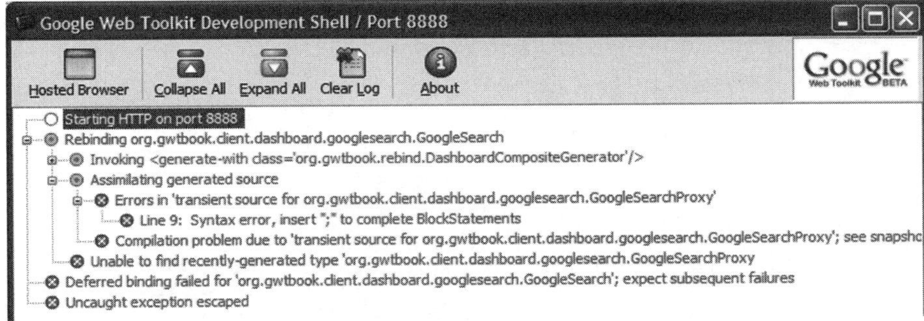

Figure 14.6 A common error when developing generators is to make a mistake in the code.

command. In this case, hosted mode tells you the error is in Line 9, and the next line in the error points you to the location of the temporary file containing Java code that has been generated, a segment of which is shown here:

```
package org.gwtbook.client.dashboard.clock;

import com.google.gwt.user.client.Window;
import com.google.gwt.user.client.Command;

public class ClockProxy extends
             org.gwtbook.client.dashboard.clock.Clock {
   public String getName()
   {
      return "Clock"
   }
}
```

❶ **Missing semicolon in the generated code**

The offending error line is marked ❶, and you can see that a semicolon is indeed missing.

You can see in figure 14.6 that the compiler tells you where to find the generated class, but remember from chapter 3 that you can direct the compiler where to place these generated classes by using the `-gen directory` flag.

This method was easy to write. More complicated ones are possible, including those that include an element of introspection on the input class, as you can see in the method that creates the About menu dialog.

Creating a method that uses introspection

When it comes to manipulating the input class, we briefly mentioned earlier that GWT provides a set of classes that allow you to introspect an existing Java class. These are depicted in figure 14.7.

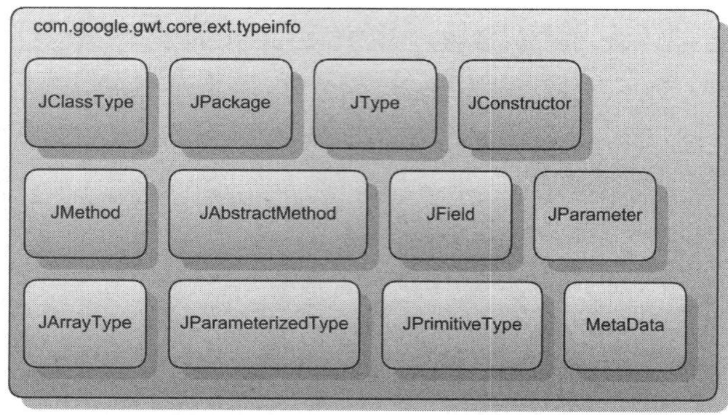

Figure 14.7 Classes that can be used in the generator to manipulate GWT Java classes

NOTE It's only possible to introspect a Java class at compile time—and that introspection has to use the GWT classes in figure 14.7 rather than the normal Java way.

You use these classes when it comes to manipulating the input class. The starting point for introspection is the `JClassType` object, which you obtain from the `OracleType` at the start of the generator's `generate()` method. Once you have this object, you can start asking for the class's methods using the `JClassType.getMethods()` method or its field using `JClassType.getFields()` method. You can find out the modifiers of the type, such as whether it's public or private, what type it subclasses or implements, its metadata, and various other aspects.

Return objects from methods in the `JClassType` class generally come from those classes shown in figure 14.7. For example, if you wanted to list all the methods of the `requestedClass` object you retrieved from the `TypeOracle`, you would write the following:

```
JMethod[] methods = requestedClass.getMethods();
for(int loop=0;loop<methods.length;loop++){
   writer.println(methods[loop].toString()+"\n);
}
```

You use these introspection approaches in the generator to create the About menu option we've previously discussed. Listing 14.7 shows the code.

Listing 14.7 Creating a new option menu using source code introspection

```
protected void writeCreateOptionsMenu(TreeLogger logger,
                                      SourceWriter writer,
                                      String name,
                                      JClassType requestedClass,
                                      String version){
   JMethod[] methods = requestedClass.getMethods();
   JField[] fields = requestedClass.getFields();
   writer.println();
   writer.println("public void createOptionsMenu(){");
   writer.indent();
   writer.println("super.createOptionsMenu();");
   writer.println("optionsMenuBar.addStyleName(\"submenu\");");
   writer.println("optionsMenuBar.addItem(
                      \"About\", new Command() {");
   writer.indent();
   writer.println("public void execute(){");
   writer.indent();
   writer.println("String aboutMessage =
                      \"About the Dashboard "+name+
                 " Widget ("+version+" version)\\n\";");
   writer.println("aboutMessage +=
                      \"Info Created by a Generator\\n\\n\";");
   writer.println("aboutMessage +=
                     \"Number Fields: "+fields.length+"\\n\";");
   for(int loop=0;loop<fields.length;loop++){
      if ((fields[loop].isPublic())||(version.equals("intranet")))
         writer.println("aboutMessage+=
                     \""+fields[loop].toString()+"\\n\";");
   }
      writer.println("aboutMessage +=
                     \"\\nNumber Methods: "+
                     methods.length+"\\n\";");
   for(int loop=0;loop<methods.length;loop++){
      if ((methods[loop].isPublic())||(version.equals("intranet")))
         writer.println("aboutMessage+=\""+methods[loop].toString()+
                     "\\n\";");
   }
   writer.println("Window.alert(aboutMessage);");
   writer.outdent();
   writer.println("}");
   writer.outdent();
   writer.println("});");
   writer.outdent();
   writer.println("}");
}
```

1. Introspect class for methods and fields
2. Call parent create() method
3. Start alert message
4. Loop through fields
5. Intranet mode or public field?

At ❶, you use GWT's version of introspection to get the fields and methods of the class. Next, you make the method call the overridden parent's `createOptionsMenu()` method ❷ so you ensure that the `MenuItem` you're adding always gets added as the last item in the list. You create a `String` object to hold the alert message ❸, and at ❹ you start looping around the fields in the input class. You check at ❺ that you're generating for the intranet version—or, if it's the Internet version, whether the field is public. If either of those cases is true, then you add the details to the alert string.

You can see the complete generator in the downloadable code, which includes all this code plus more logging. The result of the generator, so far, on the Clock Dashboard component application for the intranet version is shown in listing 14.8.

Listing 14.8 The generated version of the `Clock` class (`ClockProxy`)

```
package org.gwtbook.client.ui.clock;

import com.google.gwt.user.client.Window;
import com.google.gwt.user.client.Command;
import com.google.gwt.user.client.ui.MenuItem;

public class ClockProxy extends org.gwtbook.client.ui.clock.Clock {

  /**
   * Overides DashboardComposite getName() method
   */
  public String getName(){
    return "Clock";
  }

  public void createOptionsMenu(){
    super.createOptionsMenu();
    optionsMenuBar.addStyleName("submenu");
    optionsMenuBar.addItem("About", new Command() {
      public void execute(){
        String aboutMessage = "About the Dashboard Clock Widget
                               (intranet version)\n";
        aboutMessage +="Info Created by a GWT Generator\n\n";
        aboutMessage +="Number Fields: 4\n";
        aboutMessage+="org.gwtbook.client.ui.clock.Clock.AlarmTimer
                       alarm\n";
        aboutMessage+="private com.google.gwt.user.client.ui.Label
                       clockLabel\n";
        aboutMessage+="private boolean local\n";
        aboutMessage+="org.gwtbook.client.ui.clock.Clock.ClockTimer
                       clock\n";
```

```
            aboutMessage +="\nNumber Methods: 2\n";
            aboutMessage+="public java.util.Date getTime()\n";
            aboutMessage+="public void createOptionsMenu()\n";
            Window.alert(aboutMessage);
         }
      });
   }
}
```

It's not only methods that you can extend; you can also read and react to tags in the class's comments or methods. You did this when you created an ImageBundle in chapter 4, where the path to the image was stored as a tag in the method's comment. Let's look at how you can use this mechanism to create the Dashboard components' This App. Demonstrates menu item.

Getting information from tags in comments

When you created an ImageBundle in chapter 4, you created an interface that included definitions such as this:

```
/**
* @gwt.resource org/gwtbook/public/ToolbarImages/ChangeEvents.png
*/
AbstractImagePrototype ChangeEvents();
```

The tag @gwt.resource defines the location of the image that should be included in the ImageBundle. GWT's image bundle generator will ensure that this identified image is included in the bundle.

In the Dashboard, you use a similar approach to extract information in the class's comment to display to the user when they click the This App. Demonstrates menu item. Listing 14.9 provides an overview of the Clock class.

Listing 14.9 Clock class definition showing comment displayed as the This App. Demonstrates menu item

```
/**
 * @dashboard.description Generally shows off how to use various
 *  GWT Timer objects to:                                 Tagged comment ❶
 *   <ul>
 *      <li>Display and update a clock</li>
 *      <li>To set an alarm through the options menu (set time for
 *          10 seconds in the future)</li>
 *      <li>Cancel a set alarm</li>
 *      <li>Clean up all Timers when component is removed</li>
 *   </ul>
 */
```

```
public class Clock extends DashboardComposite
{
   //Clock code.
}
```

❷ **Class definition**

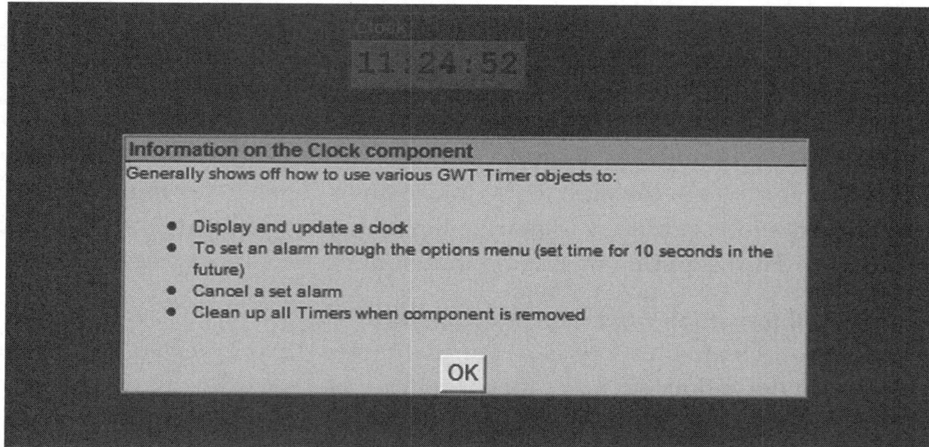

Figure 14.8 Comment displayed when the user clicks the This App. Demonstrates menu item

In the Dashboard generator, you extract the comment ❶ for the class ❷ and wrap it up to be displayed when the user clicks the This App. Demonstrates menu item, as shown in figure 14.8.

You ensure that the text you want displayed from the comment starts with a specific tag—in this case, `@dashboard.description`. Then, in the generator, you write some code that extracts this text from the class's metadata. For the Dashboard, this code is shown in listing 14.10.

Listing 14.10 Generator code that extracts the metadata value from the class

```
String[][] metaData =
            requestedClass.getMetaData("dashboard.description");
String newAppDescription = "";
if (metaData.length >= 1){
   int lastTagIndex = metaData.length -1;
   for(int loop=0; loop < metaData[lastTagIndex].length;loop++){
      newAppDescription += metaData[lastTagIndex][loop]+ " ";
   }
```

❶ **Get metadata reference**

❷ **Examine metadata**

```
} else {
   newAppDescription =  "No Class Meta Data set for "
   newAppDescription += "this Dashboard application";
}
```

❸ **Default text if no metadata**

First, you get a reference to the class's metadata, which is tagged with the tag `@dashboard.description` ❶. With the reference established, you either extract all the text related to the tag ❷ or create default text ❸. The next step is to wrap the `newAppDescription` variable into some code that creates a display similar to figure 14.8.

There is one final step to take before you use your newly generated class: You have to return its name to the compiler.

14.3.6 Using the classes that have been generated

The final task that the generator needs to perform is to return the name of the class the compiler should use. In listing 14.1, you saw that the compiler uses the input class if you return the `null` value. For the `DashboardGenerator`, you always return a class name, which is the name of the proxy class that either the generator just generated or was generated in the past.

To use the generated class in your code, you must use GWT's deferred-binding approach to allow the compiler to generate the code for you. Fortunately, there isn't much difference between normal Java object creation and GWT's deferred-binding approach, except that you can't pass parameters into the deferred approach. To create an object this way, write the following code:

```
DashboardComposite newObject =
    (DashboardComposite)GWT.create(Calculator.class);
```

Here you use the `GWT.create()` method, which is in the `com.google.gwt.core.client` package, to create a new object of the `Calculator.class` type. The parameter must be a class literal; and, frustratingly, you can't use a variable in its place. This last fact explains why in the `Dashboard.java` code you'll find the same code shown in listing 14.11 repeated for each Dashboard application.

Listing 14.11 Creating an instance of the Server Status Dashboard application through deferred binding

```
class CreateServerStatusCommand implements Command{
   public void execute(){
      DashboardPanel thePanel;
      String panelName = "serverstatus";
      if (!panels.containsKey(panelName)){
```

❶ **Created panel before?**

```
            DashboardComposite newObject =                    Create component app ❷
               (DashboardComposite)GWT.create(ServerStatus.class);

            newObject.addParentMenu(menu);                    Create DashboardPanel ❸
            thePanel = new DashboardPanel(newObject,true, trash);

            panels.put(panelName, thePanel);                  Add new panel
                                                          ❹ to panel store
         } else {
            thePanel = (DashboardPanel)panels.get(panelName);
            thePanel.show();
         }                                                    Get panel
      }                                                   from panel store ❺
   }
```

If the panel hasn't already been created ❶, then you use the deferred binding approach to create a new instance of the appropriate `DashboardComposite` ❷; place it in its own panel ❸, which is set to automatically display when created; and add it to your list of panels ❹. In the case where the panel already exists, you make the old panel visible ❺. (This means only one instance of a Dashboard application is ever in the Dashboard at a time.)

With this generator in place and the Dashboard.gwt.xml file updated, you register the generator as follows:

```
<generate-with
      class="org.gwtbook.rebind.DashboardCompositeGenerator">
   <when-type-assignable
          class="org.gwtbook.client.ui.DashboardComposite"/>
</generate-with>
```

Then, every class you have that extends the `DashboardComposite` class will be passed to this generator and have a new About menu item stamped on it, as well as have its class name added as the title bar of the window it sits in. In our discussion, we briefly touched on some properties the generator can access—in this case, the `externalvisibility` property. GWT properties such as this are another way to alter what is displayed to the user.

14.4 Summary

We've covered client-side and client-server techniques and looked at how you can change an application by using generators or harnessing the power of GWT properties.

As you've seen, you can do a lot with these advanced techniques in GWT. The best way to get used to them is to use them and play with the `Dashboard` demo, adding a few more locales, including other domains on top of `internet` and `intranet`, or enhancing the `DashboardCompositeGenerator`.

For generators, the key things to remember is to make sure you return the correct name from the `generate()` method—if you don't, then the results of the compiler won't be correct! If you want the compiler to use the original class, return a `null` value to use the newly generated class return its new name. And don't forget, if the result of the `SourceWriter` creation is `null`, the class already exists; return its new name and not `null`.

When you're dealing with property-based coding, remember that the general pattern is to create a default class and then the variations, all of which extend the default class. Then, you can use `replace-with` tags in the module XML file to replace the default file when properties match values; or, if you're using the i18n approach, the default class must implement `Localizable`, and all class names should follow the i18n naming structure.

In the next chapter, we'll look at another advanced technique, which allows you to change your application based on the values given for a set of properties.

15 Changing applications based on GWT properties

This chapter covers

- Managing browser-specific code
- Internationalization (dynamic and static)
- Altering application functionality based on locale
- Implementing and using user defined properties

So far in your journey, you've used GWT properties without making too much out of them. GWT properties are defined in various module XML files and are used at compile time to change your application based on their values. The most obvious case of this in action is GWT's ability to work with many browsers. GWT provides a `user.agent` property that defines, in the `com.google.gwt.user.UserAgent` module XML file, a number of values for different browsers. At compile-time, the compiler produces a JavaScript permutation for each value of the `user.agent` property value, replacing a number of core class files with browser specific versions. These replacements are defined in various other module XML files—for example, `com.google.gwt.user.DOM` defines which browser-specific DOM class is used.

NOTE GWT properties are designed to be used at compile-time to help produce various permutations of your application as well as at load-time to help select the appropriate permutation. They aren't intended to be accessed via your code at runtime (if you're trying to do the latter, then you should think of redesigning your application).

You can also use GWT properties in your programming. Internationalization is one area where you've seen this already: You extended the property values of the `locale` property to include the Swedish locale for the Dashboard application. In this chapter, we'll look at how you can use GWT properties to your advantage, including creating a compact Flash widget (which sends only the necessary code to the browser). We'll explain fully how you can change parts of the application based on the locale and look at the full range of internationalization. Finally, we'll introduce our own GWT property to indicate whether the Dashboard application is executing in an intranet or Internet mode (the mode indicated alters the functionality of the application).

Before we zoom into the chapter, let's recap the information about properties from chapter 9 to save you having to flip back through the book.

15.1 Quick summary of properties

Properties are defined in the module XML file. You can set up an initial set of values initially using the `define-property` tag, such as this one:

```
<define-property name="property-name" values="val1,val2,..."/>
```

It's possible to extend this set in later modules that inherit the module where the properties are defined, using the `extend-property` tag:

```
<extend-property name="property-name" values="additional-values,..."/>
```

Once the property values are defined, you need to identify which of those values you should use; you can do that either declaratively or programmatically. Declaratively, you set property values in the application's HTML file through an HTML `meta` tag:

```
<meta name='gwt:property' content='property-name=value'>
```

You can also provide some simple JavaScript code in the module XML file that returns valid values from the set of property values based on a calculation. For example, you can define a `property-provider` tag as follows that returns a `property-value` based on the success of a particular condition statement:

```
<property-provider name="property-name">
<![CDATA[
   if (condition1 == true) return value1
   if (condition2 == true) return value2
   // other code
   else return valuen
]]>
</property-provider>
```

The programmatic approach is used to decide which browser is in use and then set the appropriate value for `user.agent`.

Now that we've recapped properties, it's time to see how you can put them to use as opposed to letting GWT have all the fun. We start our discussion by looking at how you can plug into the way GWT manages browser differences by building a Flash widget.

15.2 Managing browser differences

Throughout this book, we've referred to the benefit of GWT as a write-once, run-across-many-browsers type of affair. This is true, and don't be misled by the title of this section—we aren't saying you should go out of your way to write applications that behave differently in different browsers. But on some occasions, you need to manage the fact that differences exist between the way browsers perform actions (most often at the DOM or JavaScript level).

We don't think you'll need to deal with browser differences often, unless you're implementing specific functionality that requires it. You'll do it in this section, for example, to build a widget that displays a Flash movie. In normal web pages, you need to send code for both Internet Explorer and other browsers to ensure that the movie is displayed; using GWT, you can send only the code needed. Before we move on to the widget, let's look at how GWT manages browser differences to see what you can reuse.

15.2.1 How GWT manages browser differences

We'll look at the DOM implementation and see how GWT deals with browser differences, and we'll examine the patterns you can use if you need to. The hierarchy of classes provided for the GWT DOM implementation is shown in figure 15.1.

You can see a number of classes in this hierarchy, some marked with specific browser names—Safari, Opera, and so on, as well as Standard and plain Impl. All these different classes provide browser-specific implementations of DOM manipulation methods. GWT uses our old friend deferred binding in order to create an instance of the DOM classes it uses:

```
DOMImpl impl = (DOMImpl) GWT.create(DOMImpl.class);
```

This allows the compiler to select the appropriate class for the browser as directed by the DOM module XML definition. The module XML file contains a number of replace tags (see chapter 9 for a complete definition) like the following:

```
<replace-with class="com.google.gwt.user.client.impl.DOMImplIE6">
   <when-type-is class="com.google.gwt.user.client.impl.DOMImpl"/>
   <when-property-is name="user.agent" value="ie6"/>
</replace-with>
```

The `replace` statement tells the compiler to replace the `DOMImpl` class with the `DOMImplIE6` class if the `user.agent` property is set to a value of `ie6`.

In this section, you'll build a widget that performs in a similar manner, sending the necessary code to display a Flash movie in Internet Explorer or all the other browsers.

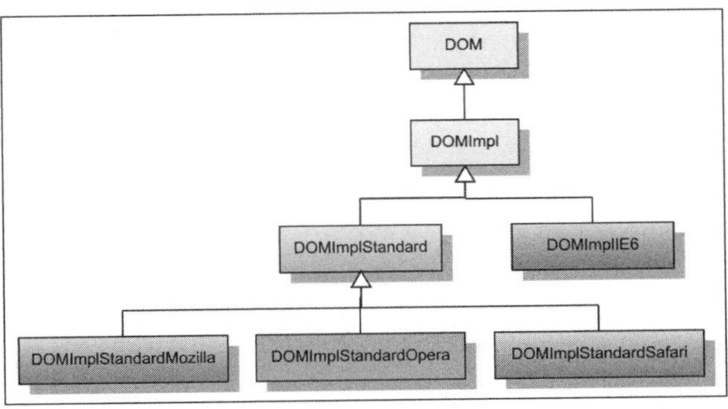

Figure 15.1 Class hierarchy of DOM classes in the GWT distribution

15.2.2 Building the Flash widget

When displaying Flash movies in a web browser, you must use two different tags to ensure that cross-browser functionality is achieved. Internet Explorer needs to use the `OBJECT` tag, and the other browsers use the `EMBED` tag. Figure 15.2 shows the simple Flash movie used in the Dashboard—we specifically set the text to distinguish the browser (*IE6* for Internet Explorer and *Other* for Firefox, Opera, and Safari).

Normally, you write both tags in the HTML page, and the browser ignores the irrelevant one, as shown in listing 15.1.

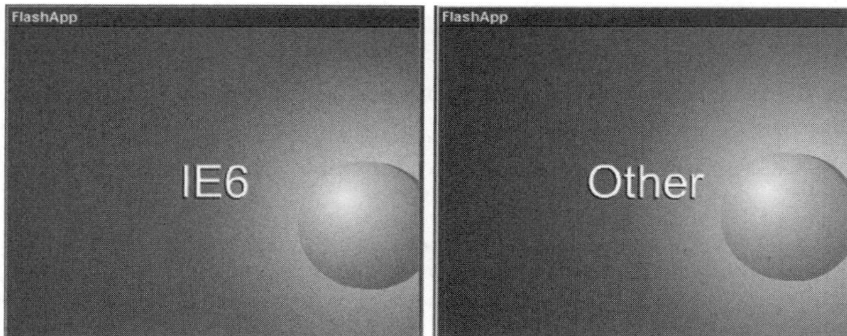

Figure 15.2 Two versions of our test Flash movie, one showing the word *IE6* and the other the word *Other*. You'll use GWT's browser-specific code capabilities to show the right movie in the right browser.

Listing 15.1 Standard way of dealing with browser differences when loading a Flash movie

```
<OBJECT classid="clsid:D27CDB6E-AE6D-11cf-96B8-444553540000"
codebase="http://download.macromedia.com/pub/shockwave/cabs/flash/
          swflash.cab
        #version=6,0,40,0"
        WIDTH="550" HEIGHT="400" id="myMovieName">
   <PARAM NAME=movie VALUE="myFlashMovie.swf">
   <PARAM NAME=quality VALUE=high>
   <PARAM NAME=bgcolor VALUE=#FFFFFF>
   <EMBED src="/support/flash/ts/documents/myFlashMovie.swf"
          quality=high bgcolor=#FFFFFF
          WIDTH="550" HEIGHT="400"
          NAME="myMovieName" ALIGN=""
          TYPE="application/x-shockwave-flash"
          PLUGINSPAGE="http://www.macromedia.com/go/getflashplayer">
   </EMBED>
</OBJECT>
```

But you can do better than that by using GWT browser-specific code: You can create a widget whose implementation is set up for either Internet Explorer or for all the other browsers. First, you'll create a simple Flash movie using one of the free online Flash generators (we chose this approach because we're not exactly the world's best artists!). The benefit of the movie is that it allows you to change the text as a parameter to the movie's URL, and thus you can change the movie text as shown in the two images in figure 15.2 so you can easily see what browser you're running in.

You'll follow the pattern used in the majority of GWT browser-specific code, in that you create a main class that instantiates one of the specific implementation classes to provide the functionality. The appropriate implementation is chosen by the compiler based on `replace` tags you'll place in the component application's module XML file.

Creating the Flash widget

The Flash widget is a simple extension of the `Composite` class that uses deferred binding to get a reference to a `FlashMovieImpl` class, the implementation class, as shown in listing 15.2. You set up the code so it can be made flexible in the future with the ability to pass in a set of parameters in the `FlashMovieParameters` class, but for now this isn't used.

Listing 15.2 Creating a simple Flash widget

```
public class FlashMovie extends Composite{

   FlashMovieImpl impl =
      (FlashMovieImpl) GWT.create(FlashMovieImpl.class);

   public static class FlashMovieParameters{
      public String movieName;
   }

   public FlashMovie(FlashMovieParameters params){
      SimplePanel panel = new SimplePanel();
      String tag = impl.createMovie(params);
      DOM.setInnerHTML(panel.getElement(), tag);
      initWidget(panel);
   }

   public FlashMovie(){
      new RuntimeException("Need Flash Movie Parameters!");
   }
}
```

Annotations: ❶ Access implementation class; ❷ Implement constructor; Prevent constructor with no parameters

In the widget, you create an instance of the implementation class ❶, which is then used in the constructor to create the appropriate tag for the browser ❷. In the constructor, you create a simple panel in which the Flash movie will reside, and then you obtain the appropriate tag from the implementation. Once you have that, you use DOM manipulation to place the tag in the HTML or the panel and then initialize the panel as the widget.

Next, we'll look at the two implementation classes: one for the majority of browsers and the other specifically for IE.

Implementing the standard Flash widget

The standard implementation for the Flash widget creates the `EMBED` tag, as shown in listing 15.3, by stringing together a number of `Strings`. In a real implementation, you would use the parameters passed in to set dimensions, and so on, but, in this example, you hard-code all the parameters. Note that in the URL, you set the title value to be the word *Other*, which is what you expect to be displayed on screen.

Listing 15.3 Defining the Flash widget's implementation class for the majority of browsers supported by GWT

```
public class FlashMovieImpl {
   public String createMovie(FlashMovieParameters params) {
      String theMovie = "";
      theMovie += "<EMBED src=\"flash_movie.swf?slogan=&
                        slogan_white=&title=Other&
                        title_white=Other&url=\" ";
      theMovie += "width=\"318\" height=\"252\" play=\"true\"
                  loop=\"false\"";
      theMovie += " quality=\"high\" ";
      theMovie +=
    "pluginspage=\"http://www.macromedia.com/go/getflashplayer\">";
      theMovie += "</EMBED>";
      return theMovie;
   }
}
```

Now that you've defined the standard implementation, you need to provide the IE-specific implementation.

Implementing the Internet Explorer–specific Flash widget

The IE implementation returns the `OBJECT` tag equivalent of the standard implementation. The two key things to note with the code shown in listing 15.4 is that it must extend the standard implementation and that its URL sets it up to display the text *IE6*.

Listing 15.4 Defining the Flash widget's implementation class for Internet Explorer

```
public class FlashMovieImplIE6 extends FlashMovieImpl{
   public String createMovie(FlashMovieParameters params) {
      String movie =
            "<OBJECT classid=
                     \"clsid:D27CDB6E-AE6D-11cf-96B8-444553540000\"
                     codebase=\"http://download.macromedia.com/pub/
                     shockwave/cabs/flash/swflash.cab#\\
                     version=6,0,40,0\" name=\"demoMovie\"
                     id=\"demoMovie\" width=\"318\" height=\"252\">";
      movie += "<param name=\"movie\" value=flash_movie.swf?slogan=&
                       slogan_white=&title=IE6&title_white=IE6&
                       url= />";
      movie += "<PARAM name=\"play\" value=\"true\" />";
      movie += "<PARAM name=\"loop\" value=\"false\" />";
      movie += "<PARAM name=\"quality\" value=\"high\" />";
      movie += "</OBJECT>";
      return movie;
   }
}
```

With the implementation files in place, it's time to set up the module XML file so you can replace the standard version with this one if you need to.

15.2.3 Setting up the property replacement

The `FlashMovie`'s module file contains only one entry: the directive to replace the standard implementation with the IE-specific one if the `user-agent` property is `ie6`. It's written as shown in listing 15.5.

Listing 15.5 Replacing `FlashMovieImpl` with `FlashMovieImplIE6` if the user agent is set to `ie6`

```
<module>
   <replace-with
         class="org.gwtbook.client.ui.impl.FlashMovieImplIE6">
      <when-type-is
         class="org.gwtbook.client.ui.impl.FlashMovieImpl"/>
      <when-property-is name="user.agent" value="ie6"/>
   </replace-with>
</module>
```

Now, when you create an instance of `FlashMovie`, you get an object that contains only the relevant tag necessary to display the movie in the browser you're using.

In addition to changing the application components based on the `user-agent` property, you can also manipulate the way GWT uses the standard internationalization functionality to change components based on the locale. But before you change components based on the locale, you need to fully understand how GWT manages internationalization.

15.3 Supporting internationalization in full

You've seen GWT's static i18n approach twice already in this book. In this section, we'll explain it in full, as well as looking at the dynamic approach you can use, which is particularly useful if you already have an existing i18n approach. In the static approach, you define a default properties file, say `Filename.properties`, and then define a number of locale-specific properties files whose filenames follow a predetermined structure, as shown in figure 15.3.

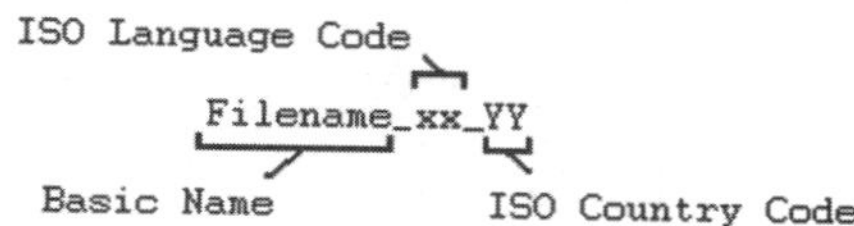

Figure 15.3 How locale-specific filenames are constructed

It isn't necessary to have an ISO country code, but if one is present, then the ISO language code must be, too. Locales also exist in a hierarchy, as shown in table 15.1.

Table 15.1 Permutation selected when using types that implement the `Localizable` interface

If the locale is set to	Then use this type
Unspecified value	The default type, `Type`
xx	The type called `Type_xx`, if it exists; or the default type `Type`, if `Type_xx` doesn't exist
xx_YY	The type called `Type_xx_YY`, if it exists; or the type called `Type_xx`, if that exists; or the default type `Type`, if neither `Type_xx_YY` nor `Type_xx` exists

In the Dashboard, you've already used the ISO language codes en for English and sv for Swedish; in the full Dashboard version, you'll also add a properties file for `en_US` (American English) where you provide the distinction in spelling of color from the en version: *colour*. This hierarchy has been chosen deliberately because GWT 1.4 introduces localization of times, dates, and currencies, and your choices of hierarchy could cause issues, as you'll see later.

First, we'll look at the static approaches you've already used in the Dashboard application.

15.3.1 Using static-string internationalization

The concept of string internationalization stems from the same principles used in standard code development. In normal code, it's common practice to avoid writing constants directly and instead to define the `String` literal as a constant in the code and then refer to that. You can also take it a step further by moving the constants out of the code and into a resource file. Table 15.2 shows each of these three ways, writing the constant directly, and defining and referring to the constant as a string literal, and defining the constant in a separate resource file.

Table 15.2 Different approaches to using strings in code

Approach	Code
Writing a constant directly in code	`Label newLabel = new Label("Some Label Text");`
Referring to a string literal in code	`final String labelText = "Some Label Text";` `Label newLabel = new Label(labelText);`

Referencing constants in a resource file	`MyConstants constants =`
	`    (MyConstants)GWT.create(MyConstants.class);`
	`Label newLabel = new Label(constants.labelText());`

The approach shown in the second row (defining a string literal constant first and then referring to it in the code) makes it easy to change the value of `labelText`, especially if it's used in numerous places in the code. You can take this a step further by moving the constants out of the code and into a resource file, referencing them from that file; this way, they're available across different classes. At this point, GWT static-string i18n can step in.

In the static approach, the compile uses generators that you saw in the last chapter to tie together an interface file and the variety of programmer provided properties files (one for each locale defined as in use). Because the GWT compiler creates permutations for each locale you identify by extending the `locale` property in the application's module XML file, it can employ the power of static analysis to include only those constants and messages that are used in the code. It also only includes code related to the specific locale for which the permutation is being created, further reducing the size of code per permutation, which translates to faster loading times for applications.

To implement static-string internationalization, you first provide a series of one or more properties files and a single Java interface that extends one of the following three GWT-provided Java interfaces:

- `Constants`—Simple user-interface constants. The compiler removes unused constants to improve efficiency.
- `ConstantsWithLookup`—Simple user-interface constants. The compiler keeps all provided key/value pairs. You can look up constants by name.
- `Message`—Simple user-interface messages that can take parameters, which are placed in predetermined locations of the message. The compiler removes unused constants to improve efficiency.

These three interfaces extend the `Localizable` interface, which is the link into the i18n generator, as we discussed in the last chapter. In this section, we'll look at these three interfaces and see how they're used. First is the `Constants` interface.

Defining static string internationalization constants

GWT i18n constants are simple strings that, as the name suggests, are constant—as opposed to messages that allow parameters to be displayed in the string. You need two types of files to implement i18n constants functionality in GWT, and we'll look at them in turn:

- A set of one or more properties files
- A Java interface that extends the `Constants` interface

The properties files are where the key-value pairs are defined. They're simple files that follow the naming convention shown for localized classes: There is a default file, say `myAppConstants.properties`, and you can define locale-specific files such as `myAppConstants_en.properties` and `myAppConstants_en_US.properties`. These files live in a hierarchy, and constants are searched for in that hierarchy in the same manner as indicated in table 15.1. For example, if the locale is set to `en_US` then a constant is searched for in the following order of properties files:

1. myAppConstants_en_US.properties
2. myAppConstants_en.properties
3. myAppConstants.properties

In the Dashboard application, you use this hierarchy (although the standard English text is kept in the default file) to cope with the different spelling of *colour/color* between English and the version of English used in USA. Try it: When the application loads, the Help menu contains an entry for the Colour Picker; if you change the locale to American, then that entry is spelled Color Picker.

This hierarchy also means you don't have to define all constants in all files. Look at the properties files shown in table 15.3. You can see the contents of a non-locale-specific properties file—`myAppConstants`—which provides no values for any constants apart from the `ok` key. There are also three location-specific properties files' contents—an English (`en`) locale `myAppConstants_en`, an American one, and a Swedish (`sv`) locale `myAppConstants_sv`. In these locale-specific files, language-specific values are defined for all keys except `ok`.

Table 15.3 The contents of three i18n properties files that exist in a hierarchy

myAppConstants	myAppConstants_en	myAppConstants_en_US	myAppConstants_sv

`Colour: colour`
`hello:`
`hi:`
`yes:`
`no:`
`ok:OK`
	`hello: Hello there`
	`hi:Hi`
	`yes:Yes`
	`no:No`
		`Colour:color`	`Colour: färg`
			`hello:Hejsan`
			`hi:Tjena`
			`yes:Ja`
			`no:Nej`

You could now use the i18n tool provided in the GWT download to create the appropriate interface file (see chapter 3), or you could create it by hand. Either way, you would end up with an interface that looks as follows:

```
public interface MyAppConstants extends Constants{
   String hello();
   String hi();
   String yes();
   String no();
   String ok();
}
```

Note that this interface contains a method name for each of the constant keys in the properties file that you may wish to access—including the OK key. Regarding your part in coding the i18n setup, this is all you need to do; the GWT generator performs the task of creating necessary Java class files at runtime/compile time.

To use the Swedish, English and American locales in the application, you must extend the `locale` property using the module XML file by adding the appropriate `extend-property` tags:

```
<extend-property name="locale" values="en"/>
<extend-property name="locale" values="en_US"/>
<extend-property name="locale" values="sv"/>
```

You let the application know which locale to start with by setting a new `meta` tag in the head section with the name `gwt:property`; its content sets the locale of choice. Alternatively you can also change the locale by setting it as a parameter in the URL. For example, to use the Swedish version, the URL is

```
http://www.example.org/myapp.html?locale=sv
```

Look in the i18n module file (in the `com.google.gwt.i18n` package) to see how the system copes with changing the locale through URL parameters. In that file, a `property-provider` tag is defined to extract the URL and find the locale. This provides a good base code to use if you ever implement properties that are also changeable through URL parameters.

Finally, to use the different constants in the Java application code, you first need to obtain an independent version of the `MyAppConstants` class. Because this is an interface to your code, you use the `GWT.create()` method to indicate that you'll use the deferred binding approach to allow the compiler to decide the exact implementation at compile time. You do that by using the following code:

```
MyAppConstants constants =
     (MyAppConstants)GWT.create(MyAppConstants.class);
```

You use constants by calling the appropriate method defined in the interface:

```
Label newLabel = new Label(constants.hello());
```

The aim is to produce a menu that appears similar to figure 15.4.

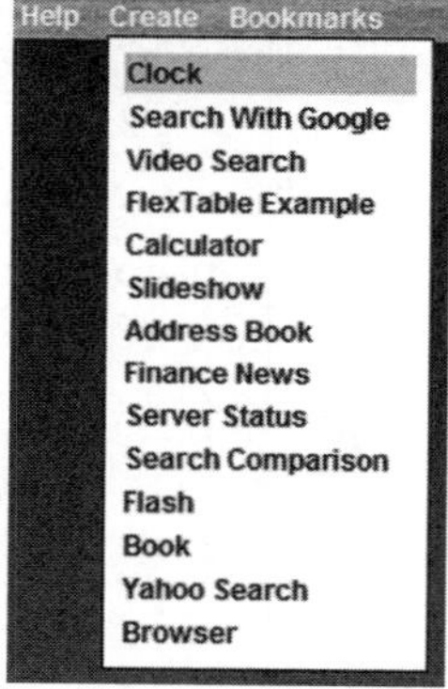

Figure 15.4 Menu system when the locale is set to the default

To create the text for the menu items in the default locale, you take the DashboardConstants.properties file previously created in chapter 3 and replace its contents with those shown in listing 15.6.

Listing 15.6 Defining the constants used in the default locale

```
HelpMenuName: Help                          <-- Menu bar constants
CreateMenuName: Create
AboutMenuItemName: About                        Construct components
LoginMenuItemName: Login
ConfirmDeleteMenuItemName: Confirm Delete   <-- Menu item constants for Create menu
LocaleMenuItemName: Locale                  <-- Menu item constants for Locale menu
CalculatorMenuItemName: Calculator
ClockMenuItemName: Clock
AddressBookMenuItemName: Address Book
```

```
SlideshowMenuItemName: Slideshow
GoogleSearchMenuItemName: Search With Google
GoogleVideoSearchMenuItemName: Video Search
FinanceNewsMenuItem: Finance News
ServerStatusMenuItem: Server Status
FlashMovieMenuItem: Flash
FlexTableMenuItem: FlexTable Example
SearchComparisonMenuItem: Search Comparison
BookMenuItem: Book
YahooSearchMenuItem: Yahoo Search
SendEmailMenuItem: Send Email
ColourPickerMenuItem: Colour Picker          <-- Color constants
NameChangeOK: Change
NameChangeCANCEL: Don't Change               <-- Text constants for EditableLabel buttons
EnglishLocale: English
SwedishLocale: Svenska
AmericanLocale: English (US)
CurrentLocale: en                  <-- See the following tip
```

TIP At runtime, it isn't directly possible to determine the locale currently used by the application (because the compilation process removes this information). However, if you really need to do this, you can write the locale string value as a constant in the properties files: for example, a `CurrentLocale` entry. Then, you can retrieve the value using the `constants.CurrentLocale()` method.

With the default locale established, you should add constants for the other locales you expect the Dashboard to manage.

You also need to replace the Swedish locale that you created in chapter 3 to match the entries in the default locale, but with Swedish text. (Don't forget that the encoding of the text file you're using should be set to UTF-8 if you're using a language's special characters.) Replace the `DashboardConstants_sv.properties` file's contents with those shown in listing 15.7, which produces a menu similar to that shown in figure 15.5.

Listing 15.7 Defining the constants used in the Swedish locale

```
HelpMenuName: Hjälp          <-- Menu bar constants
CreateMenuName: Ny
AboutMenuItemName: Om Dashboard                      <-- Menu item constants for Create menu
ConfirmDeleteMenuItemName: Godkännar Delete
LocaleMenuItemName: Välj Språk          <-- Menu item constants for Locale menu
CalculatorMenuItemName: Kalkylator
ClockMenuItemName: Klocka
AddressBookMenuItemName: Adressbok
```

```
SlideshowMenuItemName: Galleri
GoogleSearchMenuItemName: Sök med Google
GoogleVideoSearchMenuItemName: Sök Video
FinanceNewsMenuItem: Finans Nyheter
SearchComparisonMenuItem: Search Comparison
BookMenuItem: Boken
YahooSearchMenuItem: Sök med Yahoo
SendEmailMenuItem: Skicka en Email
ColourPickerMenuItem: Välj Färg          <-- Color constants
NameChangeOK: Byta
NameChangeCANCEL: Ej Byta                <-- Text constants for EditableLabel buttons
CurrentLocale: sv
```

We made a subtle "error" in the properties file for the Swedish locale in order to discuss a specific attribute of GWT i18n. If you compare the default and Swedish locales, you'll see that the Swedish properties file misses a number of constants. When GWT comes across this situation, it simply goes to the next level in the hierarchy to find the constant value (in this case the default locale—which explains the English words visible in figure 15.5.)

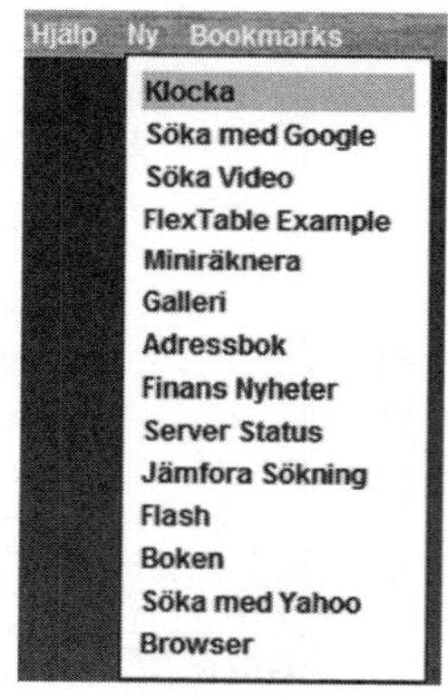

Figure 15.5 Menu system when the locale is set to Swedish by changing the `DashboardConstants_sv.properties` file's contents

Finally, you create the American English properties file (`DashboardConstant_en_US.properties`) which makes heavy use of the hierarchy to only define the following two lines:

```
ColourPickerMenuItem: Color Picker
CurrentLocale: en_US
```

If you want to add additional locales, now is a good time to do so. Remember that the filename must follow the format specified in chapter 15 and that you also need to add an `<extend-property>` tag to the Dashboard.gwt.xml file defining each locale you're adding (if you've not already done so, then you need to add the `en_US` locale to the Dashboard.gwt.xml file).

Once you're happy that your default properties file contains all the constants you need in the application, then you need to execute the `DashboardConstants-i18n` tool again (remember that this tool was created in chapter 2). It regenerates the necessary `DashboardConstants` interface file, taking into account any changes you've made since the last time it was executed. The result of executing the tool for the default file is shown in listing 15.8.

Listing 15.8 Result of the DashboardConstants-i18n tool

```
public interface DashboardConstants extends
                 com.google.gwt.i18n.client.Constants {

  String AboutMenuItemName();
  String CreateMenuName();
  String HelpMenuName();
  String CalculatorMenuItemName();
  String SlideshowMenuItemName();
  String AddressBookMenuItemName();
  // other signatures
  String NameChangeOK();
  String NameChangeCancel();
  String SwedishLocale();
  String EnglishLocale();
  String CurrentLocale();
}
```

In addition to a `Constants` interface, GWT provides a `ConstantsWithLookup` interface, which we'll look at next. The main difference is that `ConstantsWithLookup` doesn't perform any static code reduction.

Defining static string internationlization constants with lookup

The `ConstantsWithLookup` interface works exactly the same way as the `Constants` interface, and values in the properties file can be accessed in exactly the same way. What sets these two apart is that `ConstantsWithLookup` sends all constants into the JavaScript file (so there's no reduction in file size), and it additionally provides a number of specific retrieval methods that return the constant as a variety of Java objects. These retrieval methods are as follows:

- `getBoolean(String)`—Looks up a particular method name, and returns a `boolean` value
- `getDouble(String)`—Looks up a particular method name, and returns a `double` value
- `getFloat(String)`—Looks up a particular method name, and returns a `float` value
- `getInt(String)`—Looks up a particular method name, and returns a `int` value
- `getMap(String)`—Looks up a particular method name, and returns a `map` value

- `getString(String)`—Looks up a particular method name, and returns a `String` value
- `getStringArray(String)`—Looks up a particular method name, and returns a `String[]` value

An exception is raised if the method name doesn't exist in your interface or if it isn't possible to cast the constant type to the object expected (for example, a `String` to a `boolean`). If you define the interface as follows

```
public interface MyAppConstants extends ConstantsWithLookup{
   String hello();
   String hi();
   String yes();
   String no();
   String ok();
}
```

then you can look up values from your properties files using one of the following two approaches:

```
constants.hello();
```

or

```
constants.getString("hello");
```

If you tried to look up `constants.getString("farewell")`, it would throw a runtime exception because the method name `farewell()` doesn't exist (if you had used the static approach, this error would have been picked up at compile time). Similarly, looking up `constants.getInt("ok")` would throw a runtime exception because the `ok()` method returns a `String` and not an `int`.

Let's get even racier with our examples and start defining i18n messages—something you didn't do earlier—that you'll use in the Dashboard application. In addition to constants, you can use messages in the same style by extending the `Messages` interface. Messages allow parameters to be passed in the interface; the values of those parameters appear in predetermined sections of the messages. If you're using the GWT creation tools to create the files, don't forget to include the `-createMessages` flag when you're running the `i18nCreator` tool. In the next section, we'll look at how these messages are created.

Defining static-string internationalization messages

Messages differ from constants in that they're parameterized. As with constants, you need two types of files:

- A set of one or more properties files
- A Java interface that extends the `Messages` interface

The properties files are again where the key-value pairs are defined, and they follow the same naming convention and hierarchical properties as those discussed for constants. As an example, you can define `myAppMessages.properties` file as the following:

```
hello:Hello {0},
```

Defining a message is like creating a template where values will be slotted in. The example Hello message has one slot, denoted by the text `{0}`. Other messages may contain more slots: for example, `goodbye:Goodbye {0} at {1}`. This message has two slots; in the interface, you define what goes into them. You can, of course, define messages with zero slots, in which case they act like constants in the way we described earlier.

The interface you need to define for messages is almost the same as for constants, except that you should extend the `Messages` interface, and you define the parameters the methods should take—one parameter for each slot in the message. For the properties file example, you define the interface method as follows:

```
public interface MyAppMessages extends Messages{
   String hello(String name);
}
```

You're saying that the `hello()` method takes one parameter, which is a `String`.

Using the code in the application and setting the locale is performed the same way as for the other two techniques we've just discussed, except that you need to pass the appropriate number of parameters to the chosen method. For example, to display the message "Hello Tiina Harkonen", you write the following code:

```
MyAppMessage messages = (MyAppMessage)GWT.create(MyAppMessage.class);
Label newLabel = new Label(messages.hello("Tiina Harkonen"));
```

Other specific locale properties files are created the same way as for the other interfaces we've looked at. For example, a properties file for the Finnish locale, `fi`, is called `myAppMessages_fi.properties` and may have the contents

```
hello: Tervetuloa {0},
```

If the application was set to the Finnish locale, then the hello message would become "Tervetuloa Tiina Harkonen".

In chapter 2, we discussed that the `i18nCreator` tool can be used to create messages as well as constants (messages allow you to add a parameterized value into the text at runtime, whereas constants don't). You'll now bring in a message that you'll use to set the default name on the Dashboard (which is stored in the `EditableLabel`). The first thing to do is to create the necessary structure and files using the `i18nCreator` tool.

Establishing the messages file and directory structure

To create the messages structure, you should execute the appropriate command line shown in table 15.4, depending on whether you're using the Eclipse IDE (this will work, assuming you've followed the same structure you created in chapter 2).

Table 15.4 Different versions of the `i18nCreator` tool used to create the message framework for the Dashboard internationalization

Version	Command Line
Non Eclipse	`i18nCreator -createMessages -out DashboardDir org.gwtbook.client.DashboardMessages`
Eclipse	`i18nCreator -eclipse DashboardPrj -createMessages -out DashboardDir org.gwtbook.client.DashboardMessages`

Successful execution of the command results in a new DashboardMessages.properties file in the code directory and a new application called `DashboardMessages-i18n`. (If you use the Eclipse version, you also get a new Eclipse launch configuration. In Eclipse, you should now refresh your project by right-clicking it and selecting the Refresh option; doing so shows these new files in your Package Explorer view.)

Now that you've created the message structure, let's create the default locale implementation.

Creating messages for the default locale

Just like creating constants for the default locale, creating messages for the default locale means you must update the `DashboardMessages.properties` file created by the `i18nCreator` tool. Find it now, and replace it with the contents shown in listing 15.9.

Listing 15.9 Part of the default DashboardMessages.properties file

```
DashboardDefaultNameMessage = New Dashboard Created at {0}        ❶
ConfirmDeleteMessage = Are you sure you want to delete the
                       {0} application?                           ❷
BookmarkOnErrorMessage = Some problem has occurred, we are unable to
                         load your bookmarks.
```

```
BookmarkOnResponseErrorMessage = Some problem has occurred, the
                                 server returned a status code {0}
                                 (perhaps you are running this with
                                 no server?)
WindowResizedMessage = New window size: ({0},{1}) \n Turn Off Resize
                       Notifications?                                  ❸
SaveDashboardNameMessage = We would normally save the \n Dashboard
                           Name now it is changed.
WindowClosingText: You are attempting to close the Window - are you
                   sure?
WindowClosedText: Window is now closing, typically at this point       ❹
                  we would now save the state of the application.
```

Notice that in the messages, you use the equals sign (=) as well as the colon (:) to separate the keys from the message; this is just to show the flexibility we mentioned earlier. At ❶ is a message that takes two parameters: in this case, the x and y dimensions of the resized window.

This code creates a set of GWT i18n messages, each with a differing style. The first line ❶ places the variable text at the end of the message (you'll use this in the Dashboard as the initial text for the `EditableLabel` that represents the Dashboard's name). It's simple to place the variable text in the middle of the message, as shown on the second line ❷, or it can go at the start. Placing two or more variables in the message? Not a problem; you do that at ❸. Finally, you hit a slightly philosophical point where there are no variables to add to a message—should it be a message or a constant? Technically, it should be a constant, but in the last line, ❹, it's a message. Where should it be placed? In professional development, you can always refer back to your coding standards for guidance (or, if it isn't there, create it). For the Dashboard, we decided that where the text is presented to the user as a message, it should sit in the messages area regardless of whether it has variables.

If you execute the new `DashboardMessages-i18n` command (created by the `i18nCreator` tool), it creates a new interface file called `DashboardMessages.java`. The interface's contents resemble listing 15.10 (you will explicitly set the parameter type for the `WindowResizedMessage` to `int`).

Listing 15.10 Results of the `DashboardMessages-i18n` tool

```
public interface DashboardMessages extends
  com.google.gwt.i18n.client.Messages {
   public String DashboardDefaultNameMessage(String time);    | Message with one
   public String ConfirmDeleteMessage(String appName);        | String variable
```

```
    public String WindowResizedMessage(int x, int y);    <-- Message with two int variables
    public String WindowClosingText();    <-- Message with no variables
    // Other signatures
}
```

The resulting Java interface is similar to the constants interface, except the method takes a parameter, the value of which is inserted in the place-marker {0} defined in the message.

You must add similar messages for the different locales the application will manage.

Adding messages for other locales

GWT's i18n approach is standard. To create different locale messages, you create different properties files named according to the same naming convention used for constants. In this case, you create a DashboardMessages_sv.properties file for the Swedish locale and place the following in it:

```
DashboardDefaultNameMessage = Ny Dashboard, frambringade @ {0}
```

But you needn't stop with localizing constants and messages; you can do the same thing with components in the application. For example, the trash icon changes based on the locale. We'll explain how you can alter components based on the locale in more detail in section 15.4.

One of the restrictions of using a static approach is that changing locale requires you to reload your GWT application. For small applications, this may not be a major problem; but if your application becomes substantial in size, then a simple locale change may begin frustrating your user. However, the static nature which finds errors at compile time and reduces code size should usually outweigh the reloading problem.

GWT (version 1.4) also provides a number of classes that deal with localization of dates, times, and currencies.

Localization of dates, times, and currencies

When you create the message that is the default value for the `EditableLabel` (in the Dashboard's `onModuleLoad()` method), you use the `DashboardDefaultName-Message` from your messages files to display the date and time the Dashboard was created.

To do so, you use the `DateTimeFormat` i18n classes provided from GWT 1.4. You create two new objects, one that creates a full date format

```
String fullDateFormat =
      DateTimeFormat.getFullDateFormat().format(new Date());
```

and one that creates a short time format:

```
String shortTimeFormat =
       DateTimeFormat.getShortTimeFormat().format(new Date());
```

In the com.google.gwt.i18n.client.constants package, you can find hundreds of classes covering dates and number formats for all the potential language and country codes. The date format object, for example, provides details about the short and full date/time formats. Listing 15.11 gives the details of the default English locale properties file for the DateTimeFormat.

Listing 15.11 DateTimeConstants_en properties file

```
eras = BC, AD
eraNames = Before Christ, Anno Domini
narrowMonths = J, F, M, A, M, J, J, A, S, O, N, D
months = January, February, March, April, May, June, July, August,
         September, October, November, December
shortMonths = Jan, Feb, Mar, Apr, May, Jun, Jul, Aug, Sep, Oct,
              Nov, Dec
// More month data
weekdays = Sunday, Monday, Tuesday, Wednesday, Thursday, Friday,
           Saturday
shortWeekdays = Sun, Mon, Tue, Wed, Thu, Fri, Sat
narrowWeekdays = S, M, T, W, T, F, S
// More weekday data
ampms = AM, PM
dateFormats = EEEE\\, MMMM d\\, yyyy, MMMM d\\, yyyy, MMM d\\,
              yyyy, M/d/yy
timeFormats = h:mm:ss a v, h:mm:ss a z, h:mm:ss a, h:mm a
```

These definitions in the locale-specific files are used by the DateTimeFormat class the same way you've been using i18n properties files to ensure the appropriate set of definitions is used for your locale. You use the DateTimeFormat class to get text representing dates and times in the format you desire. In the Dashboard, you use the following code to create the EditableLabel:

```
dashboardName = new EditableLabel(
                    messages.DashboardDefaultNameMessage(
                          medTimeFormat +" "+ fullDateFormat),
                    constants.NameChangeOK(),
                    constants.NameChangeCANCEL());
```

You tie together the GWT DateTimeFormat classes to get the presentation of dates and times for your locale (for example, the U.S. uses a 12-hour clock as opposed to the 24-hour clock used in Europe). In the U.S. locale, the variable `medTimeFormat` might hold

```
03:02 PM
```

whereas in the English and Swedish locales, it would hold

```
15:02
```

However, here is the subtle problem in the i18n approach applied so far. The default English locale in the Dashboard is English, and we specifically included an American English locale (`en_US`) to resolve the spelling of *colour/color*. When you include GWT's date and time formats, then they define the default English locale as American English—and you have a mismatch. In the Dashboard's default English locale, the spelling of *color* is English (*colour*), but the time format uses the 12-hour clock rather than the expected 24-hour clock.

Correct or incorrect is a debate that could go on for a long time, but you should be wary of this in your applications, especially if you're developing from a non-American viewpoint (it isn't just a debate over English primacy—the default Spanish locale, as another example, is Argentinian). Be particularly careful if you're using currencies, because, for example, the default English currency is U.S. dollars, and the default Spanish currency is Argentinian Pesos (unless GWT changes this in the future). To be 100 percent safe, if you're using currency/date/time formats, you may want to avoid default locales and specifically use both language and country codes.

We've exhausted the static approaches; they're the ones you should use unless you have an existing i18n approach. Whether you use constants, constants with lookup, or messages will depend on your application.

Dynamic-string i18n is the other approach that GWT provides; it's a more flexible approach to i18n with regard to changing locales, although this flexibility comes at the expense of static analysis. The dynamic approach also lets you use existing approaches to i18n that you may already have in the rest of your site/organization. We'll now look at this dynamic approach.

15.3.2 Using dynamic string internationalization

The dynamic approach was originally designed to allow existing i18n approaches to be quickly incorporated into GWT applications. If your existing approach used JavaScript associative array objects containing sets of key-value pairs, like those shown in table 15.5, then dynamic-string i18n would potentially work for you.

Table 15.5 Two JavaScript associative array objects containing English and Swedish user interface constants

`var  userInterfaceEN = {`
`   hello:Hello,`
`   hi:Hello,`
`   yes:Yes,`
`   no:No,`
`   ok:OK`
`};`
	`var  userInterfaceSV = {`
	`   hello:Hejsan,`
	`   hi:Tjena,`
	`   yes:Ja,`
	`   no:Nej,`
	`   ok:OK`
	`};`

In this approach, the two JavaScript objects list key-value pairs for a simple user interface, the first in English and the second in Swedish. In JavaScript, it's easy to select an element in an associative array by referencing it via the key. To select the correct text to display for the index `hello` in a Swedish locale, you write

```
userInterfaceSV[hello];
```

which results in the text "Hejsan" being selected.

If this is the approach you currently use for i18n, then implementing it in GWT is swift and easy. You need to insert the JavaScript objects into the HTML file as you normally would; they're accessed using the GWT `Dictionary` class.

Assuming the HTML file into which the GWT application is to be loaded has the `userInterfaceSV` associative array included, then you create an object that accesses it using the `getDictionary()` method, as follows:

```
Dictionary uiText = Dictionary.getDictionary("userInterfaceSV");
```

The `Dictionary.get(key)` method retrieves values based on the supplied key. In this case, to retrieve the value to display for the index `hello` in a Swedish locale, you can write

```
uiText.get("hello")
```

Dynamic-string i18n offers a few benefits:

- You can quickly use existing i18n approaches you currently have.
- No code recompilation is required to make any changes or additions to the constants.
- Changing locale doesn't necessarily require a complete reload of the application.

However, the disadvantage of the dynamic approach is that GWT provides no help to determine whether constants you're referring to exist. With the dynamic approach, it's possible to refer to keys that don't exist, creating unexpected results in your UI. In addition, the compiler can't perform any optimization by removing unused keys. This means all key-value pairs, used or not, are sent by the web server, increasing the application's size and, therefore, slowing down the delivery of applications.

GWT's i18n approach is great for dealing with the display of different messages and constants based on locales, but you can go one better and start changing complete components of the application based on the locale.

15.4 Altering the application for the locale

Let's imagine that one of the Dashboard applications will access restricted information. That information could be anything, but for the sake of the example, we'll say that it's financial information for a company that is restricted by financial market regulations. Although GWT's i18n approach is set up for dealing with messages and constants, you can subvert it to change application components based on locale by borrowing the code structure.

You need to implement two basic types to get the differing functionality by locale (this pattern should be becoming familiar to you now!):

- A default class
- A set of zero or more localized classes

Let's look at both cases in more detail through examining the Dashboard Finance News component application.

15.4.1 Implementing the default component

When companies make certain announcements, it's common for this information to be restricted to certain financial markets due to regulations. For example, the details of one company intending to purchase a controlling stake in another company listed on the UK market isn't usually for release in the USA or Australia. You can use localization to restrict this access.

For the financial system application's functionality, you want to display a button allowing access to the announcement if a user is in a locale that can see the announcement and a label expressing regret if not. As a starting point, you'll define the default type, in this case a class, and provide a single method that returns a GWT widget. Because you wish to be safe and not attract the wrath of regulatory bodies, you want users coming in from any locale to be treated to a display of the default screen shown in figure 15.6.

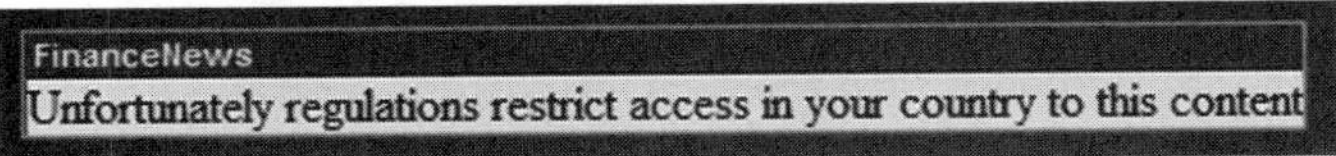

Figure 15.6 Finance application running in a locale that isn't allowed to view financial information

To do this, you set the default class to return a `Label` containing denial message. Call the class `Proceed`, and write the following:

```
public class Proceed implements Localizable{
   public Widget getProceed(){
      return new Label("Unfortunately regulations restrict
                        access in your country to this content");
   }
}
```

The default class is simple and has the basic rule that it must implement the `Localizable` interface. Let's move on to the locale-specific classes.

15.4.2 Locale-specific classes

Let's say that a financial announcement is made on the Swedish stock market. Users in the Swedish locale can read the text, and instead of the previous message, you want to present a button allowing the user to click through to the announcement.

In theory, a user in the Swedish locale will see the full release after they click on the proceed button, but for this example, you will just show them an alert box as shown in figure 15.7.

You distinguish users from the Swedish locale by defining that the locale they're in has the ISO language code `sv`. You want to write a class that is used for this locale instead of the default class, and you want this new class to return a button rather than a label. To do so, you write a class that extends the original `Proceed` class and is named following a simple naming convention. Here it is:

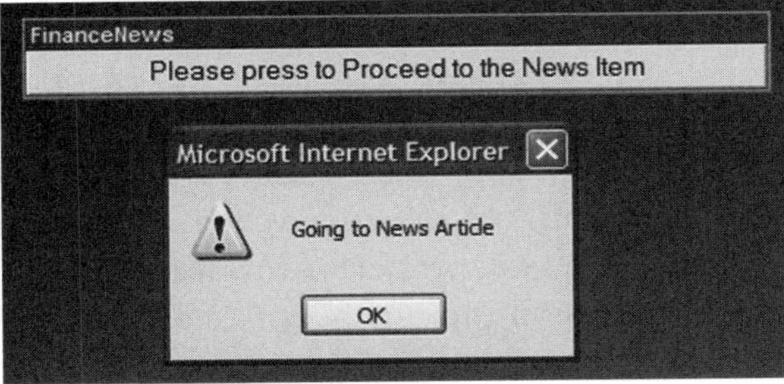

Figure 15.7
Finance application in `sv` locale (even though the text is written in English so the majority of users can see the functionality)

```
public class Proceed_sv extends Proceed{
   public Widget getProceed(){
      Button theButton = new Button
                     ("Please press to Proceed to the News Item");
      theButton.addClickListener(new ClickListener(){
         public void onClick(Widget sender) {
            Window.alert("Going to News Article");
         }
      });
      return theButton;
   }
}
```

That is all you need to do from a code perspective to implement localization classes in a GWT application. Unfortunately, it doesn't mean your localized code is available to your application—that takes a couple more steps. The first step is to tell the application which locales it needs to be concerned about, and the second is to tell it which locale to use (you already did this for the Swedish locale in the Dashboard application some chapters back).

Unlike with browser-specific code, when you replace components due to locale, there is no need to enter anything beyond the locales in the module XML file. The existing setup provided by GWT in i18n's module XML file is sufficient.

Now that you've seen how to use the existing approaches for properties with your code, it's time to take the next step and begin defining and managing new properties.

15.5 Implementing user-defined properties

You've seen that GWT provides a nice way to manage different browsers through properties; it also gives you a way to manage different locales for messages and constants, which you can subvert to manage the changing of application components based on locales. It's possible to take this property-based approach further and define your own properties and handling code.

In this section, you'll do that for the Dashboard application to present an intranet view and a more restricted Internet view. In your applications, you may need to do something similar so that external users get a restricted set of functionality compared to users on your intranet. There are many ways to provide this type of division outside of GWT; this is just an approach that you may want to investigate. (You set the property in the HTML file, which isn't that secure because the user can override it; but you can expand the property-provider approach and generate JavaScript that selects which version the user sees based on IP addresses or something similar.)

15.5.1 Defining user-specified properties

The property definition is simple. You'll define a user-defined property that has two values—intranet and internet—and you'll call it externalvisibility. You set this up using the standard approach that we described a few sections back, by making the following entry in the Dashboard.gwt.xml file:

```
<define-property name="externalvisibility" values="intranet,internet"/>
```

Before it can be used in any meaningful way, you need to be able to get the value of this property.

15.5.2 Defining a user-specified property provider

In the Dashboard example, you look at the meta tag defined in the HTML file to determine the start value for the external visibility flag. More realistically, you might implement IP-checking code to set the value, but we'll stick with getting it from the HTML file. You do that in the property provider shown in listing 15.12, which is placed in the Dashboard's module XML file.

Listing 15.12 Defining the property-provider that handles your externalvisibility property

```
<property-provider name="externalvisibility">
<![CDATA[
   try{
      var externalvisibility =
              __gwt_getMetaProperty("externalvisibility");    ❶ Access HTML meta definition
      if (externalvisibility==null){                        ❷ Set default property value
         externalvisibility = "internet";
      }
      return externalvisibility;                            ❸ Return value
   } catch (e) {
      return "internet";                                    ❹ Return default value in case of error
   }
]]>
</property-provider>
```

In the property provider, you first try to get the externalvisibilty value from the meta tag in the Dashboard.html file using the getMetaProperty() method ❶. If that isn't available, then an exception is raised, which you catch at ❹; you then set the value to the most restrictive value, internet. If you successfully get a value at ❶, then you check to make sure it isn't null ❷; if it is, you set it to be the value internet; otherwise, you return the value that you found ❸. How do you know the value is OK? We'll look at that next.

15.5.3 Checking the provided property value

Just retrieving a value from the metatag doesn't necessarily mean it's a valid value that you can work with. Fortunately, you can harness GWT again to ensure the value is in the list of defined properties—or, if it isn't, to handle that error.

In the Dashboard.html file, you define a `gwt:onPropertyErrorFn meta` tag as follows:

```
<meta name='gwt:onPropertyErrorFn' content='handleWrongVisibility'>     ❶
   <script>
      function handleWrongVisibility(propName,
                                      allowedValues,                   ❷
                                      badValue){
         if (propName == "externalvisibility"){      ❸
            window.alert("You are looking at the application from
                           an unknown area\nCheck the
                           externalvisibility property.");              ❹
            window.location.href = ("http://www.google.se");
         }
      }
   </script>
```

Here you define the `meta` tag ❶ followed by some JavaScript that is executed when GWT determines that the property value given to the application is invalid. You indicate in the `meta` tag that the function `handleWrongVisibility` should be called if there is a property error. At ❷, you begin to provide the definition of the `handleWrongVisibility` method. At ❸, you check whether the error is with the `externalvisibility` property, and if so, display an error and navigate the user to the Google home page ❹. You can extend this approach to all the properties you have, if you wish.

With the basics in place, you can now build the code.

15.5.4 Building the code

Finally, you can build the complete final version of the Dashboard, which comes in two flavors: one for the Internet and one for the intranet. The Internet version provides access a small number of component applications; the intranet version provides those same component applications plus many more.

You implement this by following the same pattern you have for all the property-based functions. First, you build the `Internet` class as a default class for the property, which you'll call `Dashboard`. In this `Dashboard` class, you create the menus containing the limited number of menu items corresponding to component applications. Next, you build a `Dashboard_intranet` class that extends that `Dashboard` class and overrides the methods in `Dashboard` that are responsible for building the menus (and therefore giving access to the additional component applications).

To complete the functionality, add a `replace-with` tag in the Dashboard's module XML file:

```
<replace-with class="org.gwtbook.client.Dashboard_intranet">
   <when-type-is class="org.gwtbook.client.Dashboard"/>
   <when-property-is name="externalvisibility" value="intranet"/>
</replace-with>
```

This entry says that the `Dashboard` class must be replaced by the `Dashboard_intranet` class if the `externalvisibility` property is set to `intranet`.

15.6 Summary

This concludes our walk through using properties to change the application—a powerful tool, particularly if you need to alter aspects of your application to suit differing locales. Just remember that the general pattern is to create a default class and then the variations, all which extend the default class. Then, you can use `replace-with` tags in the module XML file to replace the default file when properties match values; or, if you're using the i18n approach, the default class must implement `Localizable`, and all class names should follow the i18n naming structure.

In the next part of this book, we'll look at the final practical aspects of GWT, including testing and deploying applications.

Part 4

Completing the understanding

Part 3 examined the more advanced tools of the GWT toolset for communication and internationalization. Part 4 of this book completes your understanding of GWT by examining how to write tests for your application and how to deploy to a web server. This is followed by a detailed look under the hood, showing you the magic behind the tools.

16 Testing and deploying GWT applications

This chapter covers

- JUnit testing of GWT applications
- Testing asynchronous code
- Deploying GWT applications
- Installing GWT-RPC servlets

At some point, you'll make the leap from evaluating GWT to deploying it on production systems. This chapter shows you how to write tests for your application, making long-term maintenance easier, and also shows you how to migrate applications from hosted-mode development to a server.

In this chapter, we won't assume that you're a JUnit wizard or that you know your Java application server backward and forward. Although we provide useful information for experts, we also give you step-by-step information if this is your first time working with these tools.

We'll get to setting up your production environment shortly. First, let's examine testing, starting with an overview of JUnit.

16.1 Testing GWT code using JUnit

Many developers (and entire organizations) have taken up the notion of test-driven development, or at least recognize the importance of writing tests. The return on investment when creating tests comes in the form of time saved as the application gets larger and also during the maintenance phase of the software lifecycle. Almost in contradiction to the notion of writing automated tests as being a good thing, we find that writing those tests for JavaScript applications can be difficult and time consuming.

In Java-land, we've had powerful testing tools available for many years. At the top of the testing framework heap is JUnit, which is so popular that it has been ported to many other languages. It has remained popular because it's easy to use and has been integrated with IDEs and build tools like Eclipse and Ant.

In the land of JavaScript, we haven't seen the success of any single testing framework, and none can match the usability and ease of use of JUnit. The lack of a good testing framework for JavaScript may be because writing complex JavaScript applications is a relatively new idea, or perhaps it's because it isn't easy to test code that is meant to be run by the browser. Whatever the reason, testing JavaScript is hard, but GWT provides a solution.

When it came time to add testing capabilities to GWT, the GWT development team turned their attention to the de facto standard: JUnit. But instead of creating something similar to JUnit, they harnessed the power of JUnit itself. What this means for you as a developer is that you get to use a time-tested framework for testing, and all the tools that go along with it.

In this section, we'll look at how to use JUnit to test your GWT code, and we'll point out areas where the support isn't perfect. Before we get started, we need to have a quick review of JUnit.

16.1.1 Overview of JUnit for GWT developers

If you haven't seen or heard of JUnit, the best place to start is the JUnit project site at www.junit.org. The site contains links to dozens of articles about the framework, dating back to 1999. Our overview in no way replaces the thousands of pages written on the subject, but it provides enough detail to allow you to write some simple tests even if this is your first experience with JUnit.

Unless you already have JUnit ready to go, you need to visit the JUnit site to download the latest release of the 3.8.x branch. When you visit the JUnit site, you may notice that a 4.x version available, but this version isn't compatible with GWT. JUnit 4.x takes advantage of new functionality that was added in Java 5; but as we explained in chapter 1, GWT doesn't yet support the Java 5 syntax.

Let's begin by opening an IDE or a text editor and writing a simple test case.

Writing a simple test case

In JUnit, a *test case* is a class that may contain one or more tests. The purpose of the test case is to group a set of tests together, typically based on their function. For example, you may want to place all tests for a calendar widget in the same class, potentially allowing you to write private methods that can be shared among the tests.

In the example, you'll write a test case that tests basic math functionality, giving you a feel for how to use JUnit. You begin by creating a new class named `MathTestCase` and having it extend JUnit's `TestCase` class, as shown in listing 16.1.

The next step is to add some tests to the class. For each test you add, you need to create a method. The method name must begin with the name `test`. JUnit works by interrogating the methods in the class; any method that begins with the word `test` is taken to be a unit test. In listing 16.1, you create four methods, each of which tests a different mathematical function.

Listing 16.1 JUnit test-case that provides several examples of testing mathematical functions

```
package org.gwtbook.test;

import junit.framework.TestCase;

public class MathTestCase extends TestCase
{
  private int x = 100;
  private int y = 10;

  public void testAdd() {
    assertEquals(110, x + y);          ❶
  }
```

```
    public void testSubtract() {
      assertTrue(x - y == 90);        ❷
    }

    public void testMultiply() {
      assertEquals("test #1 failed", 1000, x * y);    ❸
      assertEquals("test #2 failed", 1000, y * x);
    }

    public void testDivide() {
      if (x / y != 10) fail();        ❹
    }
}
```

The JUnit `TestCase` class includes dozens of methods that can be used to test for a valid value; listing 16.1 provides several examples. In the test `testAdd()` ❶, you use the method `assertEquals()` from the parent `TestCase` class to test the equality of two `int` values. You pass two values to the assertion method: the expected result (110) and your tested value. In this case, you're testing that the variables `x` plus `y` are equal to 110. The `TestCase` class includes similar variations of the `assertEquals()` method for testing each of the primitive types, as well as `String` and `Object` values.

In `testSubtract()` ❷, you use another of the `TestCase` methods to test the truth of the statement `x - y == 90`. If this statement returns a `false` value, the test fails. Other similar methods in the `TestCase` class include `assertNull()`, `assertNotNull()`, and `assertFalse()`, each of which behave as the name implies.

In `testMultiply()` ❸, you see a variation on the `assertEquals()` method that includes an error message as the first argument. You may have as many assertions in a single test as you like, which can cause confusion if you can't tell which assertion in the test failed. If you add a message to the assertion and the test fails, the message is displayed in the test results, making it easy to determine what part of the test failed.

The last variation in the example is used in `testDivide()` ❹. Here you test the value, and if the result isn't correct, you call the `fail()` method. The `fail()` method does as you may expect: It fails the test. The `fail()` method takes an optional message parameter that can be used to provide additional information about the failure.

These are the `TestCase` assertions that you'll use most often, but there are a few more. You can use the `assertSame()` method to test that two object references point to the same object. `failSame()` does the opposite, failing if the two references point to the same object. There is also a variation of the `assertEquals()` method for `float` and `double` values that allows the addition of a delta argument. The delta is used to specify a maximum difference between the values being tested. For example, the following assertion is true because 99.5 is within 0.6 of 100.0:

```
assertEquals(100.0, 99.5, 0.6);
```

When you add up all the variations of assertions with and without messages and deltas, you have three dozen different assertion methods to choose from.

Now that you have your test-case written, you need to have JUnit run your tests.

Running tests

JUnit provides two tools for executing unit tests, called *test runners*. One runs your tests at the command line, and the second presents you with a GUI tool for point-and-click testing. Unfortunately, the GUI version of the testing tool doesn't behave as expected when running your tests against a GWT application, so we'll only explain how to use the command-line version.

To run your tests at the command line, you need to execute the class `junit.textui.TestRunner` that is bundled in with the JUnit JAR file. It takes a single parameter: the class name of your test case class. You also need to include the path to the JUnit JAR file and the path to your compiled test-case class file. If you don't typically run Java applications at the command line, you would execute something like the following command:

```
java -cp junit.jar;./classes" \
  junit.textui.TestRunner \
  org.gwtbook.test.SampleTestCase
....
Time: 0

OK (4 tests)
```

Note that in this example you use a backslash at the end of the line to denote that the command continues onto the next line. This is supported only in UNIX and UNIX-like shells; in Windows, don't include the backslash in the command.

As the tests execute, JUnit prints dots to indicate the progress of the testing. Once completed, it displays the total time it took to run the tests along with the results of the testing. In this case, JUnit displays that all four tests ran successfully.

It's nice to see that all the tests passed—but if this was always the case, you wouldn't need to write tests to begin with. Let's introduce some failures into the code. You can do this by altering the value of the y variable in the test-case class, changing it from 10 to 11:

```
private int y = 11;
```

After making this change, you need to recompile the test-case code. Then, run the tests again, and you'll see the following output:

```
.F.F.F.F
Time: 0.016
There were 4 failures:
...
FAILURES!!!
Tests run: 4,  Failures: 4,  Errors: 0
```

In the output, we used ellipses (...) to denote the additional messages that appear in the output. When you run this yourself, you'll see a message and a partial stack trace indicating the reason for the failure. For example, the following message is displayed at the command line for the failure report on the testAdd() method:

```
1) testAdd(org.gwtbook.test.SampleTestCase)
 junit.framework.AssertionFailedError:
 expected:<110> but was:<111>
```

Notice that JUnit tries to provide a helpful message by displaying not only the expected value but also the result. This may help you in debugging the problem without the need to add logging to your test case.

At the bottom of the output, JUnit tells you that failures occurred and provides a count of the tests run, the number of failures, and the number of errors. The difference between these last two may seem confusing at first, but a *failure* isn't an *error*.

Writing a test to properly handle errors

When JUnit reports an *error*, it means that a runtime exception was thrown and the test didn't properly account for it. This is different from a *failure*, which indicates that an assertion failed. To illustrate this point, let's use the following test example:

```
public void testDataProvider()
{
  List data = DataProvider.getData();
  String value = (String)data.get(0);
  assertEquals("Testing", value);
}
```

This test may seem correct, but a lot of runtime errors could potentially occur, which means that JUnit wouldn't be able to properly report on them. First, you don't test that getData() returns a value, which could cause a null pointer exception. You also don't check that there is a value in the List, so grabbing the first element could result in an index out of bounds exception. Last, you cast the value to a `String`, but if it isn't a `String` value, a class cast exception will be thrown. If any of these runtime exceptions occurred, they would be reported by JUnit as *errors*, not *failures*.

A better way to write the test is as follows:

```
public void testDataProvider()
{
  List data = DataProvider.getData();
  assertNotNull("data is null", data);
  assertTrue("data is empty", data.size() > 0);

  Object value = data.get(0);
  assertTrue("value is not a String", value instanceof String);
  assertEquals("value is incorrect", "Testing", (String)value);
}
```

You now test for each of the possible error conditions using assertion methods and provide a message for each assertion that adds value to your test report if the test fails. Also notice that you don't need to use conditional blocks in your test to prevent any of the runtime errors from occurring. Specifically, after you call `assertNotNull()` to test for a valid return value from the `DataProvider` class, you don't need to provide code to prevent the next line from executing if it fails, which would result in a null pointer exception. This isn't necessary because JUnit ends the execution of a test as soon as any assertion fails.

This means that any cleanup in the test that follows a failed assertion won't be executed, so it's important to not use tests for cleanup. This can be problematic, because on some occasions you may need to free up some resources used by the test to properly handle errors.

Setting up and cleaning up the test

Because you'll often need to perform some setup prior to a test and cleanup after, JUnit provides two methods for this purpose. The `setUp()` method is called before executing each test in the `TestCase` class, and `tearDown()` is called after each test.

Listing 16.2 is an example of using the `setUp()` method to create a connection pool using the Jakarta `commons-dbcp` library before each test and shutting it down after the test has completed.

Listing 16.2 An example of overriding the `TestCase setUp()` method

```
BasicDataSource dataSource;

protected void setUp() throws Exception
{
  dataSource = new BasicDataSource();
  dataSource.setDriverClassName("oracle.jdbc.driver.OracleDriver");
  dataSource.setUsername("scott");
  dataSource.setPassword("tiger");
  dataSource.setUrl(connectURI);
}

protected void tearDown() throws Exception
{
  dataSource.close();
}
```

Although managing a connection pool is more relevant to testing server-side code than it is to GWT code, it's a concept that most developers can understand. You initialize or reset the services needed by the test in the `setUp()` method, and you shut down or release the services in `tearDown()`. Although you may not use these methods often, it's good to know that JUnit makes it easy to do.

At this point, you know everything you need to get started writing tests. In the next section, we'll discuss the specifics of using JUnit to test your GWT projects.

16.1.2 Creating a new test case

Back in chapter 2, we briefly discussed the `junitCreator` tool that ships with GWT. In this section, we'll provide additional details and point out some important points that can help you avoid pitfalls.

The first question is, what does the `junitCreator` tool do? The short answer is that it creates a single `TestCase` class, two shell scripts you can use to execute that single test, and optionally two launch files for Eclipse. The first shell script or launch file is for executing your test case in hosted mode, and the second executes the test case in web mode. Let's take a closer look at the options for `junitCreator` and the files it creates.

Running junitCreator

The command-line options for the `junitCreator` tool are similar to those for other tools. Following is the command-line syntax:

```
junitCreator -junit pathToJUnitJar -module moduleName
 [-eclipse projectName] [-out dir] [-overwrite] [-ignore] className
```

Here's a description of the available options:

- `-junit`—Path to the JUnit libraries. This option is required, and it must point to the location of the JUnit JAR file. Again, note that it must point to JUnit version 3.8.x, because 4.x isn't yet supported. This path is used in generating the scripts, where the path to JUnit is added to the classpath.
- `-eclipse`—Name of the Eclipse project (optional). If included, this option generates the Eclipse launch files that can be used to execute the test case.
- `-module`—GWT module of the application you wish to test. This option is also required and is the name of the module that contains the code that you want to test. The module name is added to the generated Java source code. We'll look at what the generated code looks like shortly.
- `-out`—Directory to write output files into (defaults to current).
- `-overwrite`—Overwrites any existing files (optional).
- `-ignore`—Ignores any existing files; doesn't overwrite (optional).

When you're running `junitCreator`, you'll want the output to be directed to the same directory as your project. The scripts and launch files are placed in the root of the directory, and the test-case source is placed under a new source directory called `test`. For example, if you had an existing project called ExampleProject, the structure would look something like the left side of figure 16.1.

When you add a test case using `junitCreator`, you might use the following command from inside the ExampleProject directory:

```
junitCreator.cmd -eclipse ExampleProject -junit <pathToJunit>
  -module org.gwtbook.ExampleProject org.gwtbook.client.ExampleTest
```

After running this command, the project would look like the right side of figure 16.1. It creates the two scripts for executing the tests and two Eclipse launch files, and it creates the test case class `ExampleTest` under a new test source tree.

When you're running `junitCreator`, the test case you're creating must reside in the same client package used by the project. In the case of figure 16.1, the project has a client package `org.gwtbook.client`. The test case must reside in this package or a subpackage under it.

Now, let's take a closer look at the generated code for the test case and explain the slight differences between a GWT test case and a standard JUnit test case.

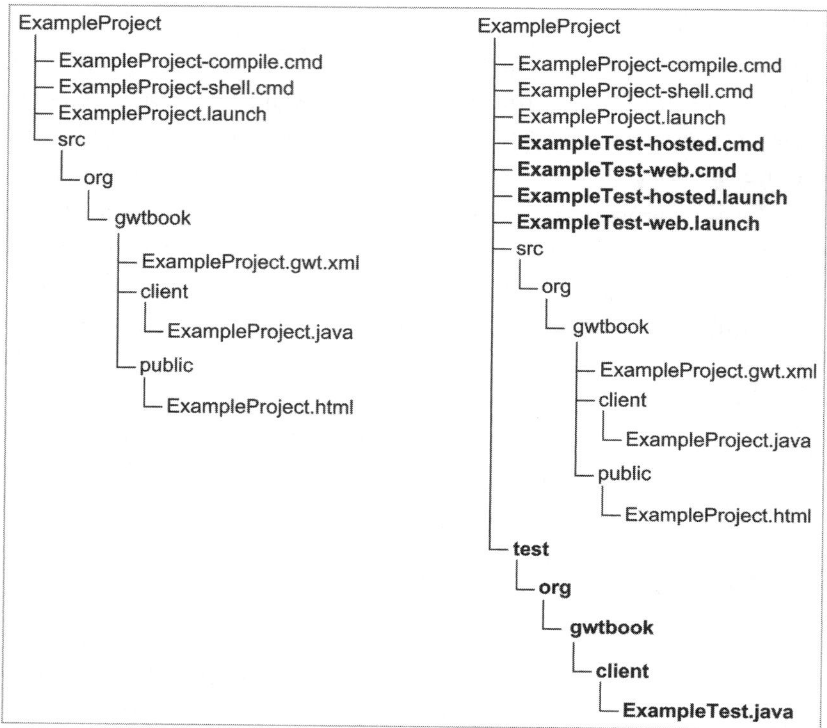

Figure 16.1 A sample project directory structure before and after adding a test case with `junitCreator`

Examining the generated test case

The full source for the generated test case, minus comments, is shown in listing 16.3.

Listing 16.3 Source code for the basic test case generated by the `junitCreator` tool

```
package org.gwtbook.client;

import com.google.gwt.junit.client.GWTTestCase;

public class ExampleTest extends GWTTestCase {

  public String getModuleName() {
    return "org.gwtbook.ExampleProject";
  }
```

Extend GWTTestCase

New GWT-specific method

```
    public void testSimple() {
      assertTrue(true);
    }

  }
```

The code shows a basic JUnit test case with a single sample test named `testSimple()`, which will succeed. What is different is that the test case extends the class `GWTTestCase` instead of the normal `TestCase` class from the JUnit library.

The second difference is the addition of the `setModuleName()` method. This method tells the testing system the name of the GWT module that contains this test case. Because this test case is essentially a GWT entry point, the module needs to point to the source of this test case. When you create the test case, you specify the module name as the same as the main project, which means you don't need to create a separate one just for the test case.

From here, you can create tests just as you did at the beginning of this chapter when we examined the basics of JUnit. The rules for writing individual tests are the same as when you're writing a GWT application. You may only reference core Java classes when they exist in the JRE Emulation library, and you may include JavaScript Native Interface (JSNI) methods in the test case.

This covers the basics, but GWT also provides an additional feature that makes testing RPC-driven GWT applications a little easier.

16.1.3 Testing asynchronous code

When we looked at the various flavors of RPC in chapters 10 through 13, one thing in common was that they're all asynchronous. That makes it difficult to test because your tests may potentially end before the server returns a response. To allow for this, the `GWTTestCase` provides a mechanism you can use to tell the test to delay ending for some period of time, allowing your server code to return a response to the client. In this section, we'll look at how you can use this mechanism to test your server-side functions.

For the purpose of discussion, you'll use the `RequestBuilder` class for performing your RPC. We chose this method because it's the simplest of the available mechanisms, but you could use any of the available RPC mechanisms.

To delay the ending of a test, `GWTTestCase` provides the method `delayTestFinish()`, which takes a number of milliseconds to delay before ending the test. Calling this method puts the test into *asynchronous mode*, and with that come some important semantics. In asynchronous mode, you must call `finishTest()` before the delay expires, or the test will fail—the idea being that if `finishTest()` was never called, it's likely that your RPC call never returned. Listing 16.4 shows a sample test so you can see how this might work.

Listing 16.4 Using `delayTestFinish()` to test asynchronous application logic

```
public void testLoginService()
{
  delayTestFinish(5000);                          ❶ Delay test finish

  RequestBuilder rb = new RequestBuilder(RequestBuilder.GET,
    GWT.getModuleBaseURL() + "login?user=david&pass=m0mmy");

  try {
    rb.sendRequest("", new RequestCallback() {

      public void onError(Request req, Throwable ex) {
        fail();                                   ❷ Fail on receive error
      }

      public void onResponseReceived(Request req, Response res) {
        assertEquals(200, res.getStatusCode());
        assertEquals("OK", res.getText());        ❸ Verify result

        finishTest();                             ❹ Complete test
      }

    });
  }
  catch (RequestException e) {
    fail();                                       ❺ Fail on send error
  }
}
```

In this example, you're testing your login service. You first set a five-second delay so the server code has time to complete execution and return a result ❶. This delay starts only after the test has ended normally, so it can be set anywhere in the test and doesn't need to be set before the RPC call.

Next, you make an asynchronous call to your login service, which could be a servlet or any other server-side service that is accessed via login.rpc. In order to handle the response, you pass in a `RequestCallback` that has an `onResponseReceived()` method to receive the server response. The `onResponseReceived()` method contains an `assertEquals()` method to test the server response: both the HTTP status code and the text result passed back from the server ❸. You then call `finishTest()` to signal a successful test completion ❹. If the remote call throws an exception or fails, you call the JUnit `fail()` method to indicate failure ❷, ❺. The end result is a clean, simple test case for testing remote calls.

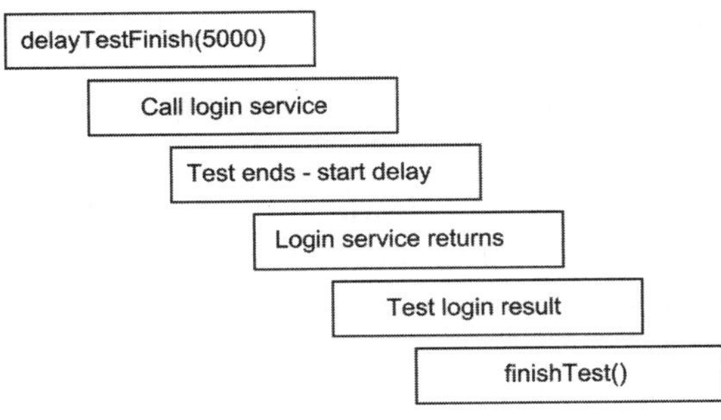

Figure 16.2
A diagram showing the flow of execution of your sample unit test, where the test performs an asynchronous call

Due to the asynchronous nature of the RPC call, the order in which the code is executed differs from its order in the method. Figure 16.2 shows the real order, with the `onCompletion()` handler being called after the normal execution of the test has ended.

During the delay period, three events will end the delay and complete the test:

- If `finishTest()` is called, the delay ends, and the test completes successfully.
- If an exception is thrown, including one caused by one of the assert methods, the delay ends, and the test shows an error.
- If the delay ends normally, without `finishTest()` being called, the test shows a failure due to a timeout.

As you can see, the `GWTTestCase` extension to JUnit allows you to test client-side code the same way you test server-side code. This allows Java developers already familiar with JUnit to leverage their existing knowledge without needing to learn yet another testing framework.

Once you've tested your application and feel confident that everything is working properly, you need to deploy the application.

16.2 Deploying GWT applications

It's fairly typical to spend most if not all of your development time using just your IDE and the hosted-mode browser. The hosted-mode browser—and web mode as well—make it easy to write and test your application without ever deploying it to the server. When it comes time to deploy your application to a server, it would be nice if you could just toss it up on the server, and it would start working. Unfortunately, this isn't the common case; deployment is often a source of pain. This section means to help alleviate that pain by providing tips to making the move to your server an easy one.

Throughout this section, we'll discuss general deployment issues as well as those relating to RPC. When we discuss RPC, we do so with an eye toward the Apache Tomcat application server, which is freely available and widely used. You may be using a different server, such as Resin or JBoss, but the discussion still generally applies. We also assume that you know a little about your application server—at the least how to stop and start it.

At the time of this writing, we find ourselves between releases of GWT. GWT 1.4, which is still in development at the time of this writing, alters the way applications are loaded by the browser. Throughout this section, we'll point out differences that exist between 1.4 and prior versions.

We'll begin by looking at a simple GWT application that uses no RPC and examining how you can better organize the files in the project.

16.2.1 Organizing your project

The files generated by GWT aren't organized. If this is the first application you're deploying, this may not seem like a big deal; but as you add modules, images, CSS, and other supporting files to the server, it can quickly become a mess. In this section, we'll examine the compiled output of a project and the options available for organization.

As an example project, you'll write an application that prints "Hello World" to the browser window. The entire application contains two lines of code along with the usual imports and class declaration. The application is shown in listing 16.5. It's far from earth-shattering, but it suits our need for a simple application.

Listing 16.5 Sample application that displays "Hello World" in the browser

```
package org.sample.client;

import com.google.gwt.core.client.EntryPoint;
import com.google.gwt.user.client.ui.Label;
import com.google.gwt.user.client.ui.RootPanel;

public class HelloWorld implements EntryPoint
{
  public void onModuleLoad() {
    Label output = new Label("Hello World");
    RootPanel.get().add(output);
  }
}
```

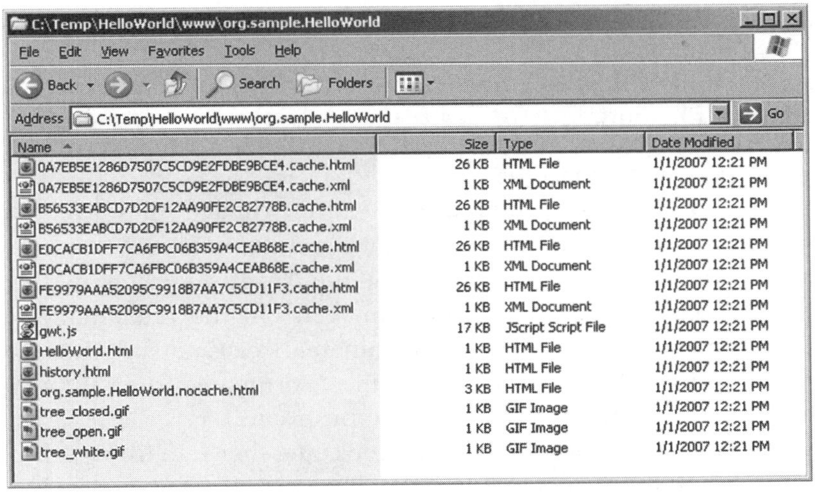

Figure 16.3 A plethora of files is created when you compile the GWT project to JavaScript.

This application generates quite a few files when it's compiled. It may come as no surprise that you don't need most of them, especially given the simple nature of the project. Figure 16.3 shows the list of compiled files when you use GWT 1.3 to compile the project. If you're using GWT 1.4, the list of files includes all of these plus additional ones.

Before we go any further, let's remove the files you don't need, starting with the rebind decision files.

Removing unneeded rebind decision files

The *rebind decision* files are all of those files that end with cache.xml, found in both GWT versions 1.3 and 1.4. These files provide information about the choices the compiler made when generating the JavaScript for the project. As we discussed in chapter 9, the GWT compiler generates a different JavaScript file for each target browser based on the `<replace-with>` tags found in the module configuration files used by the project. These files specify the choices the compiler made for each version of the JavaScript file. For example, if the compiler was compiling the IE version of the JavaScript code, you would see this line in this file, indicating that it used the IE6 implementation of the DOM class:

```
<rebind-decision
  in="com.google.gwt.user.client.impl.DOMImpl"
  out="com.google.gwt.user.client.impl.DOMImplIE6"/>
```

Although this information may be useful for debugging, it isn't used by the deployed application.

Next, we'll look at the three tree images in the directory and explain what you can do to clean them up.

Cleaning up the TreeItem images

The next set of files to prune are the three image files: tree_closed,gif, tree_open.gif, and tree_white.gif. These images are used by the `TreeItem` widget that comes with GWT. If you aren't using the `Tree` widget, as in this sample project, you should remove these three images. On the other hand, if you're using a tree in your application, it's unfortunate, because it isn't the best idea to have images intermingled with your HTML files. Fortunately, the GWT `Tree` widget allows you to move them someplace more appropriate.

Let's begin by looking at some sample tree code, shown in listing 16.6. This is a simple tree of fictitious beasts that have been reportedly seen in the wild, but for which no proof exists.

Listing 16.6 Example code that produces a small tree listing several fictitious beasts

```
Tree tree = new Tree();

TreeItem myths = new TreeItem("Mythical Beasts");
myths.addItem("Loch Ness Monster");
myths.addItem("Big Foot");
myths.addItem("An under-budget software project");
tree.addItem(myths);

RootPanel.get().add(tree);
```

This code produces the small tree shown in figure 16.4. The figure shows both the open and closed state of the tree, including the small plus (+) and minus (-) images used to indicate the open or closed state of the tree branch. This accounts for the tree_open.gif and tree_closed.gif images. The third image, tree_white.gif, is used as a spacer for leaf items that don't have children.

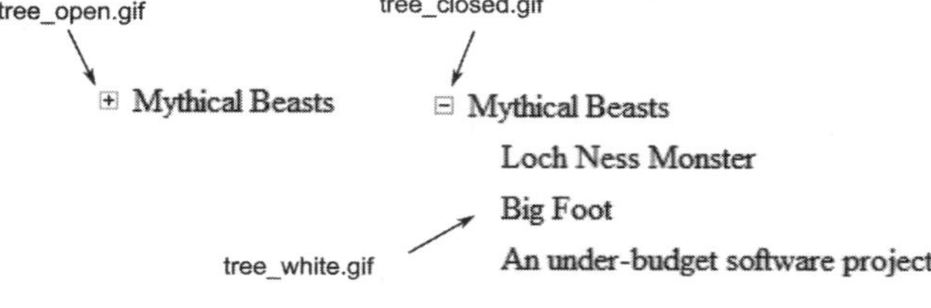

Figure 16.4 A Tree widget with sample data, showing the images used by the widget for the different tree states

To change the location of these images, the `Tree` widget provides a method `setImageBase()` that can be used to set a path that is added to the beginning of image name. If you wanted the images to be pulled from the images directory, you could use the following code when constructing your tree:

```
Tree tree = new Tree();
tree.setImageBase("images/");
```

The trailing slash is important because the code for `Tree` won't automatically add it. With it, the code uses the paths images/tree_open.gif, images/tree_closed.gif, and images/tree_white.gif. After adding this to your code, you need to manually create the images directory and move those three images into it. Until you move the images, they appear as broken images.

Going back to the original code sample, you still need to do some more cleaning. We'll continue by looking at the history.html file.

ADDITIONAL IMAGES IN GWT 1.4 GWT 1.4 introduces two new images: disclosure.png and clear.cache.gif. The disclosure.png image (which may be renamed disclosure.gif prior to release) is used by the new `DisclosurePanel`. The second image, clear.cache.gif, is a clear spacer image used by the new `ClippedImage` and perhaps other widgets. If you aren't using either of these widgets, you can remove the files; otherwise, you should keep them in the same directory as the nocache.js file for the project.

Removing an unneeded history file

In the generated project files, you'll find a history.html file. This is used by the history subsystem that we discussed in chapter 4. If you aren't using the `History` class, as in the example, then you should remove this file along with the reference to it in the HTML page.

In the HTML page that is generated by the `applicationCreator`, you'll see these lines in the body:

```
<!-- OPTIONAL: include this if you want history support -->
<iframe id="__gwt_historyFrame" style="width:0;height:0;border:0">
</iframe>
```

As the comment states, this is optional and is used only for the history system. If you aren't going to use the history system, remove these two lines from the HTML file along with the history.html file.

With this file removed, your project space is looking quite a bit cleaner—but it isn't organized, because all the files are still lumped into a single directory. In the next section, you'll organize your JavaScript files by placing them in subdirectories.

Relocating the JavaScript code in GWT 1.3

Because there are some significant differences between the generated files in GWT 1.3 and 1.4, we'll discuss each version in its own section. We'll begin by examining GWT 1.3 and then immediately follow with version 1.4.

If you've been following along and removing the unused files from the sample project, you'll see that there aren't many files left. Figure 16.5 shows the current file list for the project. Remaining are the project HTML file (HelloWorld.html), the gwt.js file, the one loader script ending in .nocache.html, and the four browser-specific script files ending in .cache.html.

You could deploy this lump of files as is without any further organization; but if you're deploying a GWT project with other pages on your web site, you may want to keep the GWT project files separated from other site pages. In this section, we'll assume that your Hello World application files need to be segregated from the rest of the pages on the site. This will involve creating a script directory and moving all the supporting files into that directory. You'll also separate the files that are specific to the `org.sample.HelloWorld` module from other GWT projects while still sharing the common gwt.js file for all GWT applications on your site.

The first step is to create a new directory to hold the JavaScript code; name it scripts. Next, create a directory under scripts for the files specific to the module; name this directory the same as the module (org.sample.HelloWorld). Now, move the gwt.js file into the scripts directory and all the other script files into scripts/org.sample.HelloWorld. When you get done, your project should look like figure 16.6.

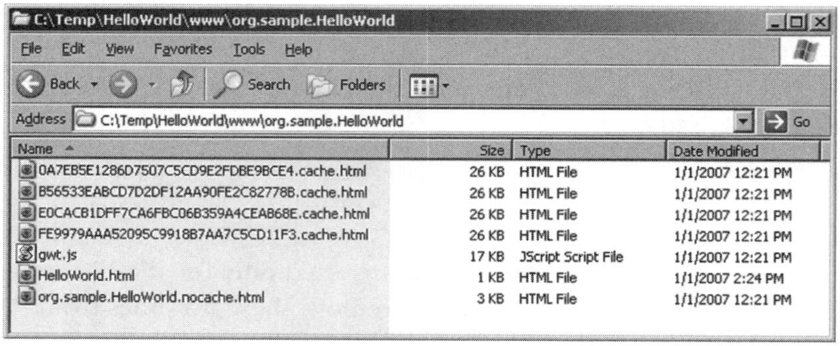

Figure 16.5 The current list of files in your GWT 1.3 project after pruning unused files like the rebind decision files, tree images, and the history file

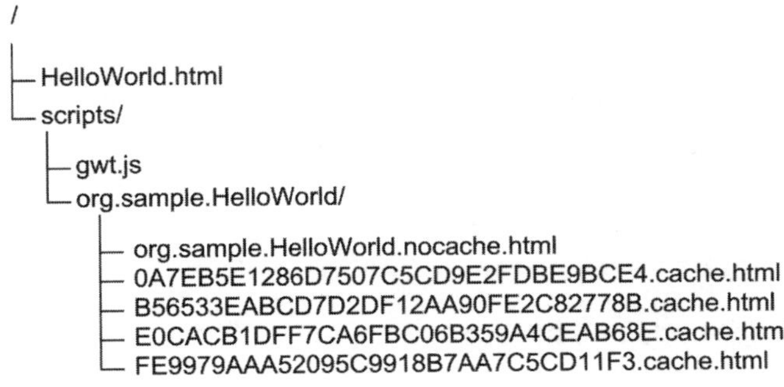

Figure 16.6 An example of a reorganized GWT application that uses a directory to hold scripts and modules

This structure makes it easy to deploy additional modules to the same server: You can add a new directory under scripts for the new module and place the files for the new module there. As for the gwt.js file, all the modules may share this file.

NOTE If you're using the GWT resource-injection mechanism to include external JavaScript files or CSS files from your module configuration, you'll need to move the injected files into the same directory as the nocache.html file. This requirement also applies to any images referenced from injected CSS files that are using a relative path.

Now that your files are reorganized, you need to make some minor changes to the HelloWorld.html file to point to these new locations. In the HelloWorld.html file, you need to change two lines. The first is the script tag that points to the gwt.js file. Here, you need to update the `src` attribute to point to the gwt.js file in the scripts directory. When you get done, it should look like this:

```
<script language="javascript" src="scripts/gwt.js"></script>
```

The second change is to the metatag that specifies the name of the module to load. The following snippet shows the tag before you make your change:

```
<meta name='gwt:module' content='org.sample.HelloWorld'>
```

Without any additional path information, this tag will cause the GWT loader to look for the module JavaScript files in the same directory as this HTML file. Because you've moved these files into the scripts/org.sample.HelloWorld directory, you need to add this path information to the metatag. You do so by adding the path to the `content` attribute, followed by an equal sign (=) and then the module name. With this change in place, the updated metatag looks like this

```
<meta name='gwt:module'
  content='scripts/org.sample.HelloWorld=org.sample.HelloWorld'>
```

The equal sign separates the path from the module name. The GWT loader looks for the module at this alternate path instead of in the current directory.

With this last organizational change in place, you now have a tidy little application ready to be deployed to the server. Deploying the application from here is as simple as copying the files to any place on the server and optionally renaming HelloWorld.html to some other name, like index.html.

Now let's take a look at how to clean up the JavaScript files when using GWT 1.4.

Relocating the JavaScript code in GWT 1.4

Although GWT 1.4 still hasn't finalized, we want to examine what we see so far and explain how you'll change the way you deploy your applications. The first noticeable difference is that the GWT compiler generates a lot of additional files. Figure 16.7 shows the files from the Hello World application; compare it to figure 16.5, the files generated by GWT 1.3, and you'll see the difference.

The reason for all these files is to not only let you load a GWT application from your own server, but also allow others to load your GWT application from pages hosted on their server. Looking at 16.7, notice that for each *.cache.html, file there is a *.cache.js file. The HTML versions of these files are for use on pages originating from the same site that hosts your GWT code, and the JavaScript versions are for use on externally hosted sites. The difference between the two is that the HTML versions can be compressed by your server, whereas the JavaScript versions can't be.

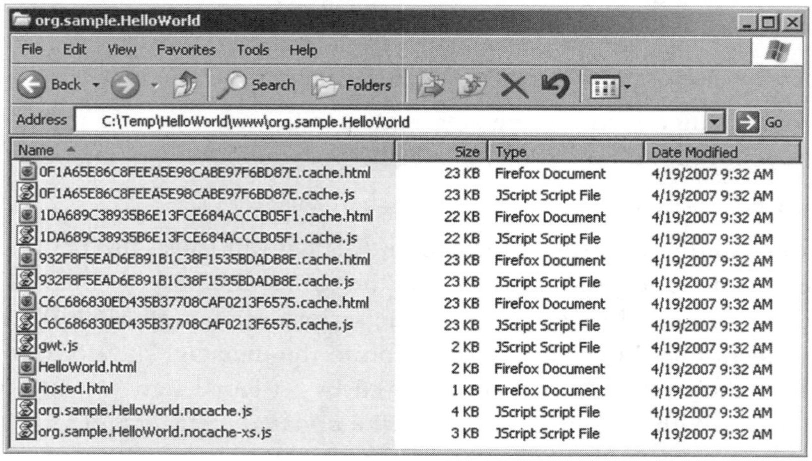

org.sample.HelloWorld

File Edit View Favorites Tools Help

Back Search Folders

Address C:\Temp\HelloWorld\www\org.sample.HelloWorld Go

Name	Size	Type	Date Modified
0F1A65E86C8FEEA5E98CABE97F6BD87E.cache.html	23 KB	Firefox Document	4/19/2007 9:32 AM
0F1A65E86C8FEEA5E98CABE97F6BD87E.cache.js	23 KB	JScript Script File	4/19/2007 9:32 AM
1DA689C38935B6E13FCE684ACCCB05F1.cache.html	22 KB	Firefox Document	4/19/2007 9:32 AM
1DA689C38935B6E13FCE684ACCCB05F1.cache.js	22 KB	JScript Script File	4/19/2007 9:32 AM
932F8F5EAD6E891B1C38F1535BDADB8E.cache.html	23 KB	Firefox Document	4/19/2007 9:32 AM
932F8F5EAD6E891B1C38F1535BDADB8E.cache.js	23 KB	JScript Script File	4/19/2007 9:32 AM
C6C686830ED435B37708CAF0213F6575.cache.html	23 KB	Firefox Document	4/19/2007 9:32 AM
C6C686830ED435B37708CAF0213F6575.cache.js	23 KB	JScript Script File	4/19/2007 9:32 AM
gwt.js	2 KB	JScript Script File	4/19/2007 9:32 AM
HelloWorld.html	2 KB	Firefox Document	4/19/2007 9:32 AM
hosted.html	1 KB	Firefox Document	4/19/2007 9:32 AM
org.sample.HelloWorld.nocache.js	4 KB	JScript Script File	4/19/2007 9:32 AM
org.sample.HelloWorld.nocache-xs.js	3 KB	JScript Script File	4/19/2007 9:32 AM

Figure 16.7 The current list of files in your GWT 1.4 project after pruning unused files like the rebind decision files, tree images, and the history file

Along with the two sets of *.cache.* files are two bootstrap files: <*module-name*>.nocache.js and <*module-name*>.nocache-xs.js. The second version is the cross-site loader (ending with xs.js), and is for use on external sites. The first version is for use on the local server, the same server hosting your HTML pages. In most cases, you won't need both sets of files, so you should remove either the local or cross-site versions. In figure 16.8, we make the assumption that you'll be using the local loader for your application; the figure shows the cross-site files removed.

That leaves you with a lot fewer files than you started with, but you can still remove two more: hosted.html and gwt.js. The gwt.js file is used for compatibility with the GWT 1.3 loading style, so if you aren't using the GWT 1.3 style of application loading with the `meta` tag, you can remove this file. The hosted.html file makes its debut in GWT 1.4 and is only needed for hosted-mode support. Removing these two files leaves you with only the necessary files to deploy your application.

From here, you could easily deploy the files you have left, but it's common practice to relocate your JavaScript files into a scripts directory, making your file system more organized. When you relocated these files for GWT 1.3, you had to do some extra work to accomplish this; but with GWT 1.4 compiled files, all you need to do is relocate the *.nocache.js file along with the *.cache.html files into your scripts directory. Our recommended practice is to place these files in a directory named for the project; with the Hello World application, you place the JavaScript files under /scripts/org.sample.HelloWorld/. By placing the files in a directory named for the project, you can deploy additional GWT projects in the same manner, keeping the files for each application separate. The only change you need to make in the HTML page is to alter the `script` tag to point to the new location.

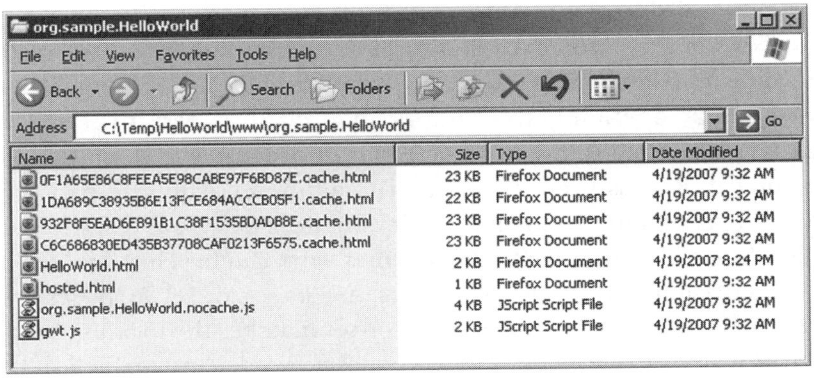

Figure 16.8 The current list of files in the GWT 1.4 project after pruning unused cross-site compatibility files

For more information about the GWT bootstrapping mechanism and all the files mentioned here, visit chapter 17, where we cover both topics in detail. Now that you've cleaned up the file system, let's turn our attention to installing the servlets for the GWT-RPC services. In the next section, we'll begin by providing a brief tutorial of setting up a servlet, in case you've never done so before.

16.2.2 Installing RPC servlets

If you need to install an RPC servlet, we need to assume that you already know how to write one and that you probably already have it running in hosted mode. In this section, we'll show you how to deploy your servlet to a server that supports Java servlets, also known as a *servlet container*. For the purposes of exploration, we'll keep it fairly light and generic when we talk about the server, which is all you need to deploy a servlet. This section won't discuss connection pooling, caching, or other functions that are typically specific to the server software you're running. We'll cover the basics of the web.xml configuration file and how the organization choices from the previous section affect your application settings.

To begin, we'll provide a high-level look at how a Java servlet container works and how it processes incoming servlet requests.

How servlet containers work

A *servlet container* is the part of a web server or application server that handles a network request and manages servlets throughout their lifecycle. Some servlet containers are also application servers, meaning they meet the requirements of the Java Enterprise Edition in addition to the servlet specification. JBoss is a freely available application server. Other servlet containers are only servlet containers, like the freely available and popular Apache Tomcat server.

If this is your first attempt at setting up a servlet container, we recommend Apache Tomcat, which can be found at http://tomcat.apache.org. It's available for most popular operating systems, and it's relatively easy to install and use. Throughout this section, any server-specific information that we provide is for Apache Tomcat. Rest assured that if you run a different software package, nearly all of the information in this section is relevant; we'll keep it as generic as possible.

For developers new to servlets, the way they work can be a little confusing, especially if you're familiar with how CGI scripts, ASP pages, or HTML pages are served. With these technologies, the URL in the browser matches the location of the file on the file system. For example, if a user requests /works/gwt_in_action.html, you expect that there is a file on the system named gwt_in_action.html in the directory works. Servlets don't work like this. Instead, you use a configuration file to map a

URL to a servlet class. This allows you to map any arbitrary URL or set of URLs to any servlet by using wildcards. The configuration file that is used to map URLs to servlets is named web.xml, and it always resides under the WEB-INF directory on your site.

When you're developing a GWT application using the hosted-mode browser, you're using Tomcat. Because this provides a good example of servlet configuration, it's a good place to start the discussion about the web.xml file.

Understanding servlet configuration in the development environment

When you tested your RPC servlet in hosted mode, you may have noticed that a directory named tomcat was created. In that directory, under tomcat/webapps/ROOT/WEB-INF/, is a file named web.xml, which is known as a *deployment descriptor.* Unless you manually modified this file to integrate other services into your development environment, it looks like listing 16.7.

Listing 16.7 Default deployment descriptor used by the GWT development environment in hosted-mode

```
<?xml version="1.0" encoding="UTF-8"?>
<web-app>

  <servlet>
    <servlet-name>shell</servlet-name>
    <servlet-class>
      com.google.gwt.dev.shell.GWTShellServlet
    </servlet-class>
  </servlet>

  <servlet-mapping>
    <servlet-name>shell</servlet-name>
    <url-pattern>/*</url-pattern>
  </servlet-mapping>

</web-app>
```

Define servlet

Map URL to servlet

If you take a good look at listing 16.7, you'll see that it isn't complicated. It first defines a servlet by giving it an arbitrary name and specifying the full package and class name of the servlet. In this case, the servlet is `GWTShellServlet`. It's important to note that you shouldn't use this servlet on your server; it's only meant for use only in the GWT development environment.

The second part of the configuration maps a URL to the servlet. It does so by specifying a URL pattern and the name of the servlet that handles requests to that URL—in this case, the URL is /*. The URL may include the wildcard * to match anything, so the pattern /* matches any request to the server. This isn't typically what you want; but in this case, the `GWTShellServlet` servlet was written to read your project's module file and dispatch the request to the right place. If you recall, the module configuration uses the `<servlet>` tag to define your GWT-RPC servlets. This information is used by the `GWTShellServlet`, but it isn't used when you move your code to a production server.

Let's apply these basics to how you configure your production environment.

Configuring the production environment

The first step is to find the directory your server uses to deploy web applications. If you're using Apache Tomcat, figure 16.9 shows this directory structure for the Tomcat installation. Figure 16.9 shows the directory structure on Windows, but it's the same regardless of the platform.

In figure 16.9, you see a bin directory to hold executables, conf for the overall server configuration, logs to store log files, and a few others. The directory that you need to be concerned with is webapps. This directory holds individual web

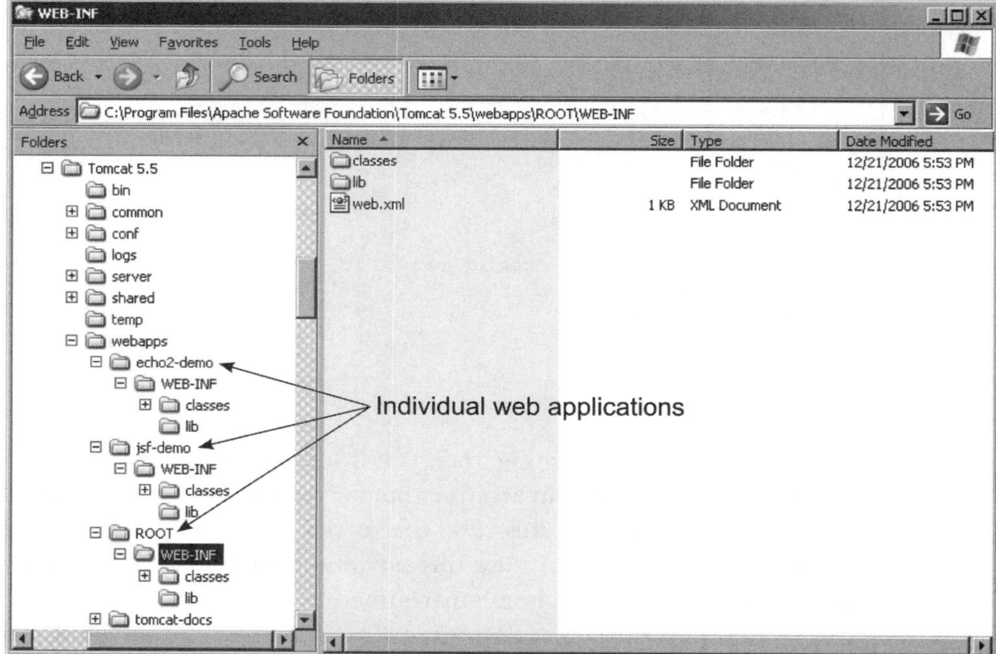

Figure 16.9 The directory structure of an Apache Tomcat installation on Windows

applications running in Tomcat. Figure 16.9 shows a few applications we've placed there, like echo2-demo and jsf-demo. To access these applications in a browser, you use the URLs http://*your-host-name/*echo2-demo and http://*your-host-name/* jsf-demo. Each application directory in the webapps folder is accessible in your browser by using the same name as the application directory.

We're pointing this out because the ROOT directory under webapps works a little differently. You can access the ROOT directory in the browser via http://*your-host-name* without specifying the application directory. This is important because you need to decide if you want your application to be accessed using just the host name in the URL or in an application directory. For example, if you want the Dashboard application to be accessible as http://*your-host-name*, then you place it under ROOT; otherwise, you create a new directory under webapps, perhaps called Dashboard, and the application is then accessible as http://*your-host-name/* Dashboard. For the purposes of the discussion that follows, it doesn't matter what you choose because all applications, including the root application, have the same directory structure.

Inside, each application directory follows a specific structure. Figure 16.10 shows this structure, including the location of the web.xml file that is used to configure the application.

You place the HTML and JavaScript files generated by your project in the root of the application. In the WEB-INF/lib directory, you place any JAR files your project relies on. If you're using GWT-RPC, this includes at least the gwt-servlet.jar file that is part of the GWT distribution. This JAR includes all the GWT classes required for the GWT-RPC mechanism. You should never deploy the gwt-user.jar and gwt-dev.jar files to your server, because they will probably interfere with your server; these JAR files contain their own Tomcat server code, which is used when you're testing in hosted mode.

The WEB-INF/classes directory can be used for loose classes. You need to place any necessary compiled class files for your project under the WEB-INF/classes directory or package them as a JAR and place it in the WEB-INF/lib directory. The

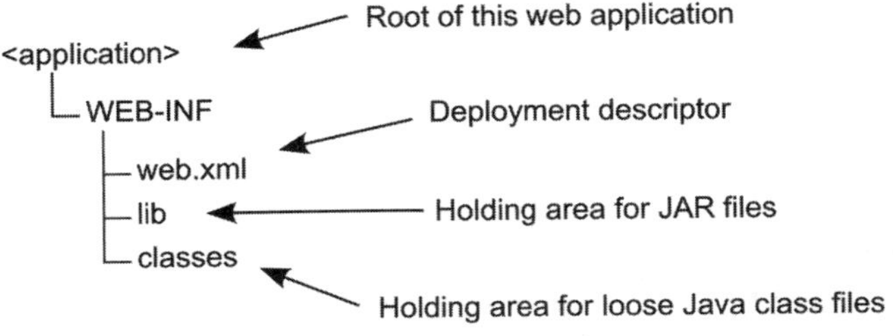

Figure 16.10 The directory structure inside a web application, including the location of the deployment descriptor

servlet container automatically includes all the classes and JAR files in these directories in the classpath for the application. Note that this only applies to code that needs to be run on the server. For example, if you're using GWT-RPC, you must include the class files for your servlet and any Java interfaces it references. However, you don't need to include any classes that are used only on the client side, such as widgets, because these aren't executed on the server. Also note that it won't hurt anything if you do deploy class files that are used only on the client, because they will never be called.

Once that is complete, the only step left is to create the web.xml file, known as the deployment descriptor, and reference your servlets.

Writing the application deployment descriptor

When you're creating the deployment descriptor, you need to map each individual GWT-RPC servlet to a URL. You can do this in the same manner as you saw previously when we looked at the deployment descriptor used by the GWT development environment.

The easiest way to explain this is to provide an example. Listing 16.8 provides the deployment descriptor file that could be used to deploy the Server Status project from chapter 10. In most cases, you can copy the example and alter it to match your servlet classes.

Listing 16.8 Deployment descriptor for the Server Status project from chapter 10

```
<?xml version="1.0" encoding="UTF-8"?>
<web-app>

  <servlet>
    <servlet-name>server-status</servlet-name>
    <servlet-class>
      org.gwtbook.server.ServerStatusImpl
    </servlet-class>
  </servlet>

  <servlet-mapping>
    <servlet-name>server-status</servlet-name>
    <url-pattern>/server-status</url-pattern>
  </servlet-mapping>

</web-app>
```

Define servlet (annotates the <servlet> block)

Map URL to servlet (annotates the <servlet-mapping> block)

Just as you saw with the deployment descriptor used in hosted mode, you first define the servlet using the <servlet> tag, providing a name and class. You then provide a `<servlet-mapping>` tag that maps the servlet to a specific URL. The servlet you list in the deployment descriptor is your GWT-RPC class that extends the `RemoteServiceServlet` class. If you have multiple servlets, you'll have multiple `<servlet>` blocks, one for each servlet you need to define.

The servlet-mapping is usually where it's easy to run into problems. First, understand that the forward slash (/) at the beginning of the pattern refers to the root of this specific web application, not necessarily the root of the web site. This may seem confusing at first; but if you look back at figure 16.7, we showed you that each subdirectory in the Tomcat webapps directory is its own "application." If you place the Server Status application in the webapps/status directory so that it's accessible via the URL http://*your-host-name/*status, then the servlet-mapping / server-status refers to the URL http://*your-host-name/*status/server-status.

You also need to be concerned about the use of the method `GWT.getModuleBaseURL()` in your code, which typically references GWT-RPC and other server-side resources. Understand that this method returns the path to your project's JavaScript file that ends with nocache.html. At the beginning of this chapter, we showed how you can relocate this file, as well as the other JavaScript files, to better organize your site. If you used `getModuleBaseURL()` to reference an RPC servlet, you need to account for this in the servlet-mapping.

As an example, if you look back at figure 16.6, you'll see that we moved the generated JavaScript files for the module into the directory /scripts/org.sample.HelloWorld/. Let's imagine that some code in this module referenced the following URL in an RPC call:

```
GWT.getModuleBaseURL() + "/hello-world-service"
```

In this case, you would use a servlet-mapping that looks like the following code. Notice how it takes into account the path to the generated JavaScript:

```
<servlet-mapping>
  <servlet-name>service</servlet-name>
  <url-pattern>
    /scripts/org.sample.HelloWorld/hello-world-service
  </url-pattern>
</servlet-mapping>
```

When you get done setting up your deployment descriptor, you should restart the servlet container to make sure the changes take effect. After you carefully write the deployment descriptor, if the RPC doesn't seem to be working, then check the server logs. They will show you what URL the client browser is calling; you can compare this to web.xml and make any necessary changes.

16.3 Summary

In this chapter, we showed you how to use JUnit and how it can be used to test your GWT code. We showed you how you can use the included `junitCreator` tool to painlessly create new JUnit test cases for testing your client-side and RPC interactions, which isn't typically available when building a non-GWT Ajax application.

We then turned our attention to deploying the GWT application to the server. We showed how you can better organize your project and what unused files can be safely deleted. In the end, we showed how you can keep your deployments organized, allowing you to deploy multiple GWT applications to the same server without having a mess of files.

After a good cleanup, we examined how a servlet container works and how it's used to host GWT-RPC servlets. We looked at the deployment descriptor file in some detail, and we compared the hosted-mode deployment descriptor against what you would use in your production environment.

Now that the application is tested and deployed, the next chapter looks under the hood. There is a lot to GWT, and the more you know about how the magic works underneath, the better you'll be able to maintain and debug your GWT application.

17 Peeking into how GWT works

This chapter covers

- GWT compilation process
- GWT compiler outputs
- GWT loading mechanism

We've arrived at the final chapter in our discussion on GWT, where we'll round off by looking at how GWT performs the magic that it does. When we started using GWT, we were first interested in building applications; then, as our curiosity got the better of us, we started wondering how GWT works behind the scenes.

We asked ourselves questions like, how does the compilation work? Why are so many HTML and XML files produced, and what do they do? How is an application loaded into the web browser? What does the produced JavaScript look like? How does GWT manipulate the DOM? There were, and still are, many more questions, and we suspect you may have the same questions now that you've gotten this far in the book. After showing you the practical uses of GWT and how to develop a web application using this toolkit, we'll finish by setting out to answer a number of those questions that hounded us once we got past the initial learning curve with GWT.

To answer the questions, we felt the best place to start was by looking at the compilation process. We hope we'll begin to answer your questions, as well.

17.1 Examining the compilation process and output

The GWT compilation stage, Stage 4 in the lifecycle defined in chapter 2, involves taking the source files you've written in Java and producing output that can be executed in a number of web browsers. We've spent the majority of this book discussing the Java source files. In this section, our goal is to look at the output from the compiler; but to get there, we need to look at how files get from the source to the compiled side.

17.1.1 Investigating compilation

If you look at the compilation process, it isn't a one-for-one translation of Java to JavaScript files. In figure 17.1, you can see that many more files are produced as the result of the compilation process than are supplied to it.

The files that are produced fall into three types: those that are passed straight through, such as the style sheets and the resources in the public folder; those that are "magically" created by the compiler almost from thin air; and those that are created by the true compilation of source Java files to produce object JavaScript files. The files that fall into these categories are as follows:

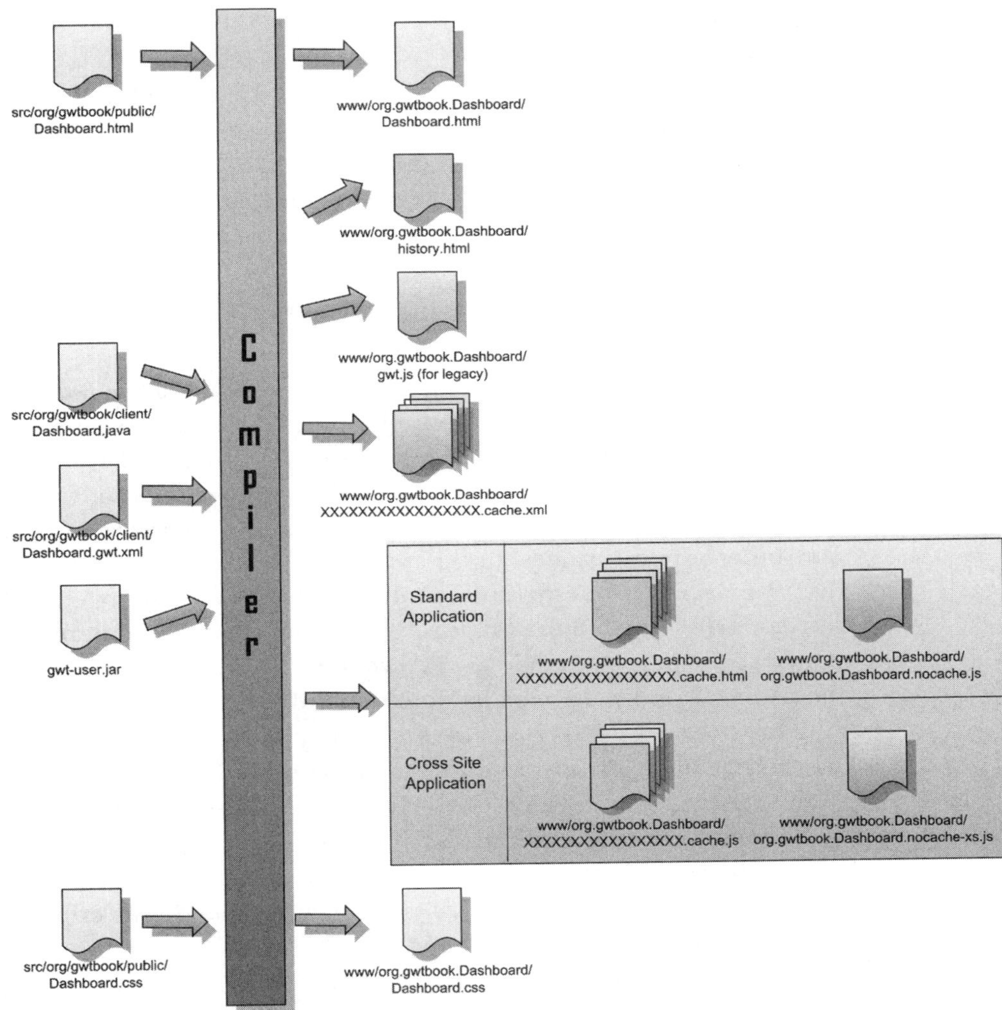

Figure 17.1 Source-to-object file mapping in the compilation process of GWT Java files to files that can be used in a web browser

- *Dasboard.html*—The HTML file you created in which the GWT modules will be placed.
- *gwt.js*—Produced to support legacy GWT applications. Pre-1.4, it was the basic GWT JavaScript code used to bootstrap your GWT modules into the browser and get them up and running. From GWT 1.4 on, it's provided only to support legacy code—you should include either `org.gwtbook.Dashboard.nocache.js` or `org.gwtbook.Dashboard.nocache-xs.js` to bootstrap the Dashboard instead.
- *history.html*—A simple HTML file that is used to manage the history of a GWT application.
- *org.mycompany.Dashboard.nocache.js or org.mycompany.Dashboard.nocache-xs.js*—The first file loaded by the bootstrapping mechanism (unless you're using legacy applications, in which case gwt.js is loaded first, and then that loads org.mycompany.Dashboard.nocache.js). It contains all the code necessary to derive the set of properties this application has: the browser, which locale, and any other property values. In the case of the Dashboard, this is the `externalvisibility` property (it determines all of these values by directly using the code described in the `property-provider` tag of the XML module file). Once all the property values are determined, the necessary permutation can be deduced, and is then loaded into the browser.

  The two versions relate to how the GWT application could be loaded. The nocache.js file loads the appropriate cache.html file, enabling the application to use any compression the server provides. Use the nocache-xs.js file if you want to load the application's pure JavaScript directly into the browser. Using the second approach, it isn't possible to take advantage of any web server functionality, but your browser gets unwrapped JavaScript code that can be used in mashups and so on.
- MD5_coded_name.*cache.xml*—A set of files, all prefixed by an MD5-coded name, that lists in XML format the various choices made by the compiler in producing this particular permutation of JavaScript code.
- MD5_coded_name.*cache.html*—A set of files, all prefixed by an MD5-coded name, that corresponds to a matching cache.xml file. Unlike the XML file, the HTML file contains the actual JavaScript code for this permutation of

the application. Marking the files as HTML allows the web server to send them as compressed files to the browser.

- MD5_coded_name.*cache.js*—A set of JavaScript files, all prefixed by an MD5-coded name, that corresponds to a matching .cache.xml file. Like the HTML files, these contain the actual JavaScript code for this permutation of the application, but they can't be compressed by the web server (however, they can be used by other JavaScript applications).

We'll now look at each of these files in more detail.

17.1.2 Examining the output

In this section, we'll look at the contents of the various compiler outputs, starting with the file that was the first one loaded by GWT applications prior to the arrival of version 1.4.

The gwt.js file

Until GWT 1.4 came along, the first file a GWT application had to load into the browser was gwt.js. It set up a few variables and then tried to load an application.nocache.html file (for the Dashboard, that would have been the Dashboard.nocache.html file). The arrival of GWT 1.4 turned this bootstrapping process around, and gwt.js became obsolete.

It's still produced to support legacy HTML pages that haven't changed to the new process, but it's reduced to checking for the `gwt:module` tag, extracting the *module* name, and then loading the appropriate *module*.nocache.js file (note that beginning with GWT 1.4, the loading mechanism ignores the `gwt:module` tag). We'll next look at the *module*.nocache.js file.

The module.nocache.js and module.nocache-xs.js files

Whereas GWT previously loaded a *module*.nocache.html file from the gwt.js script, you now put a link in your HTML directly to the module's JavaScript file. The benefit of this approach is that you link directly to your application and can in theory load several applications into your HTML page. There are two different ways to refer to the module's JavaScript file, depending upon the strategy you wish to follow to load your GWT application. You load one of the following two files:

- *module*.nocache.js
- *module*.nocache-xs.js

The first strategy, which we'll call the *standard approach*, lets the server compress your files as much as possible. In this case, you load the *module*.nocache.js file, which in turn loads the appropriate cache.html file. The second strategy, which we'll call the *cross-site approach*, trades off the potential compression and speed of the HTML files for getting pure JavaScript files in order to mash up your application. In this case, you load the *module*.nocache-xs.js file.

In both cases, the files perform similar tasks: They set up a number of variables, process metadata tags, and identify which permutation of the module is required to be loaded. Permutations are generated under the direction of the compiler, considering the various options and paths that can be taken. The most obvious permutations are driven by the different browsers supported by GWT—one permutation for each. Other permutations can be driven by using more advanced GWT techniques. Internationalization, for example, drives a number of permutations based on the number of locales that the application is told to manage, as does the user-defined property `externalvisibility` for the Dashboard.

If you're interested in seeing the type of code GWT uses to determine browser type, it's reproduced in listing 17.1. At present, GWT recognizes the following types of browser: Opera, Safari, IE6, Gecko, and Gecko 1.8 (for example Firefox and Mozilla).

Listing 17.1 Looking at the code GWT provides to perform browser detection

```
window["provider$user.agent"] = function() {
  var ua = navigator.userAgent.toLowerCase();
  if (ua.indexOf('opera') != -1) {
    return 'opera';
  }
   else if (ua.indexOf('safari') != -1) {
    return 'safari';
  }
   else if (ua.indexOf('msie 6.0') != -1 ||
            ua.indexOf('msie 7.0') != -1) {
    return 'ie6';
  }
   else if (ua.indexOf('gecko') != -1) {
    var result = /rv:([0-9]+)\.([0-9]+)/.exec(ua);
    if (result && result.length == 3) {
      var version = parseInt(result[1]) * 10 + parseInt(result[2]);
      if (version >= 18)
        return 'gecko1_8';
    }
    return 'gecko';
  }
  return 'unknown';
};
```

Similar code is used to determine other properties that may be used to select permutations—such as the code we introduced in chapter 15 to look for your user-defined `externalvisibility` property.

Each *module*.nocache file is also responsible for loading the CSS and JavaScript libraries that you've indicated must be loaded in the module XML file. With all the resources loaded, the loading attempts to set up its own `onLoad` and `onUnload` handlers. Finally, the *module*.nocache.js file tries to start the module (this doesn't happen for the *module*.nocache-xs.js file because you're expected to either start or use parts of the code yourself).

Next, we'll look more at the JavaScript application permutations. Two types of files are produced: an XML file that details the options chosen by compiler, and associated HTML and JavaScript files that contain the JavaScript permutations corresponding to the options chosen.

The cache.xml files

The compilation process relies heavily on the module XML file and knowledge of the types of browsers that are supported in order to produce numerous permutations of JavaScript files. In the simplest case, the only property dealt with is `user.agent`; subsequently, there are four permutations—one JavaScript file for each browser that GWT supports.

Using GWT more extensively—for example, by using its internationalization aspects—drives up the number of permutations required. Using two locales means that two sets of browser-specific permutations are required: a set of four for the first locale and another set of four for the second locale. This scales linearly, so if you have 10 locales for your application, you'll have some 40 different permutations.

What is the benefit of this madness? It considerably reduces the amount of code that needs to be sent to the browser, decreasing download size and times. The downside is the amount of time necessary to perform the compilation. If you've already tried to compile the Dashboard application, you'll have noticed how long it takes (we hope compiler optimizations will appear in the near future, especially because GWT is now open source). One way to reduce this compilation time during the testing phase is to restrict the number of permutations that are created by adding an entry such as

```
<set-property name="user.agent" value="ie6"/>
```

in the module XML file, which restricts the number of `user.agent` permutations to one (you could easily replace `ie6` with whatever browser you prefer). In the case of the example we mentioned, with 10 different locales to manage and 40 permutations, placing this line in the module XML file reduces the number of permutations to 10.

> **TIP** To reduce the number of permutations created during web-mode testing, and therefore speed up compilation, add a `set-property` tag to your application's module XML file. Set the name to `user-agent` and the value to the browser you'll test with (`ie6`, `safari`, `opera`, and so on).

The purpose of the cache XML files is to allow the compiler to keep track of the permutations it has already created and to know what more it needs to do. Once compilation has finished, the files are of limited use; they serve only as a record of what the compiler did. This is why we suggested in chapter 16 that you can get rid of them when you package the application to deploy.

Sometimes, it's useful to examine these cache XML files, particularly if your compiled application isn't performing nicely and you wish to look at what the compiler did. When we compiled the Dashboard application on our system, the compiler produced a number of .cache.xml files, including one called E36B89235-ACF98A4C55874ACEBBDF6E8.cache.xml (see listing 17.2).

Listing 17.2 Example cache XML file from the Dashboard application

```
<cache-entry>
<generated-type-hash
   class="org.gwtbook.client.ui.slideshow.SlideshowProxyintranet"
   hash="56AB4931F5D118966FAB4EC5937F0C51"
/>
:
<generated-type-hash class="org.gwtbook.client.DashboardMessages_"
   hash="1FB08CF8556128D1B892F2AAEB7D38FA"
/>
:
<rebind-decision
in="com.google.gwt.xml.client.impl.XMLParserImpl"
out="com.google.gwt.xml.client.impl.XMLParserImplOpera"
/>
:
<rebind-decision
in="org.gwtbook.client.DashboardMessages"
out="org.gwtbook.client.DashboardMessages_"
/>
:
<rebind-decision
in="org.gwtbook.client.ui.slideshow.Slideshow"
out="org.gwtbook.client.ui.slideshow.SlideshowProxyintranet"
/>
:
</cache-entry>
```

1 Result of GWT generator working

2 GWT generated default locale class

3 Compiler picked Opera version of GWT class

4 Compiler decided to use default locale class

5 Compiler chose intranet version of Slideshow generated

OK, so the cache.xml file doesn't readily say that the compiler chose the default locale and compiled for the Opera browser using the `intranet` property as the value for the `externalvisibility` property (and listing 17.2 is an edited highlight of the file). You can, though, conclude this by looking at the rebinding decisions listed in the xml file. At ❸, the compiler decided to use `XMLParserImplOpera` in place of the `XMLParserImpl` class. (If you were to look into the bowels of GWT, you would see this rebinding direction defined in a module XML file where the property of `user.agent` was set to Opera.)

The choice of the default locale occurs at ❹, where the `DashboardMessages` interface used in the code is to be replaced by the `DashboardMessages_` class. You know this is the default locale because GWT uses a generator to produce a set of classes that bind the user provided interface to the user provided properties files, which must conform to a particular naming convention. The generated classes also conform to the same naming convention, where `DashboardMessages_` represents the default locale class (`DashboardMessages_sv` would be the Swedish locale class). But you didn't write these classes: The compiler did that for you using a GWT-provided generator, and at ❷ you can see a reference to that generated class. ❶ shows a class that was created by the user-defined generator; in this case, the `Slideshow` class has been generated into the `SlideshowProxyintranet` class as the generator provided in chapter 14 requires. Finally, ❺ indicates where the generated class for the slideshow is chosen for use in this permutation.

Closely associated with cache XML file is the JavaScript file implementation relating to the permutation described. As we've previously mentioned, GWT produces both a JavaScript and an HTML version for each compiler permutation.

Specific HTML and JavaScript files

For each permutation identified in specific XML files, there is an associated cache.html file that the browser can load under the first loading strategy and a cache.js file that can be loaded under the second strategy. For the XML file mentioned earlier, there is an E36B89235ACF98A4C55874ACEBBDF6E8.cache.html file and an E36B89235ACF98A4C55874ACEBBDF6E8.cache-xs.js file. These files contain the JavaScript specific to the Opera browser, where the `externalvisibility` property is set as `intranet` and `locale` is the default locale (the JavaScript in the first file being wrapped in HTML).

The final file produced by the compilation process is History.html, which is used for managing history.

The History.html file

History.html is an HTML file that contains JavaScript for managing history in the application. Listing 17.3 shows the definition of the `hst()` history function that is used to decode any URL that has a history token and subsequently move the application to the necessary state.

Listing 17.3 GWT code used in the history management subsystem;

```
<html>
   <head>
      <script>
         function hst() {
            var search = location.search;
            var historyToken = '';
            if (search.length > 0)
               historyToken = search.substring(1));
            document.getElementById('__historyToken').value =
                                                   historyToken;
            if (parent.__onHistoryChanged)
               parent.__onHistoryChanged(historyToken);
         }
      </script>
   </head>
   <body onload='hst()'>
      <input type='text' id='__historyToken'>
   </body>
</html>
```

Decode history token in URL

Set start history token value

Move history state to the token value

History is stored in the input element with id_`historyToken` and is accessed and managed via your application when it uses the history management operations.

Now that you've seen the various outputs from the compilation process, the next logical step is to look at how the application is loaded into the web browser in web mode (hosted mode is out of scope for this book, although the recent open sourcing of GWT means the mechanics behind hosted mode are more readily accessible).

17.2 The GWT application-loading mechanism

As a final step in examining the Dashboard example, we'll look at what happens when a GWT application is loaded. You've seen all the files that you need to create a GWT application and the result of the compilation process. When you load the Dashboard.html file, from either the file system or a web server, what is going on? It's one of the three processes shown in figure 17.2.

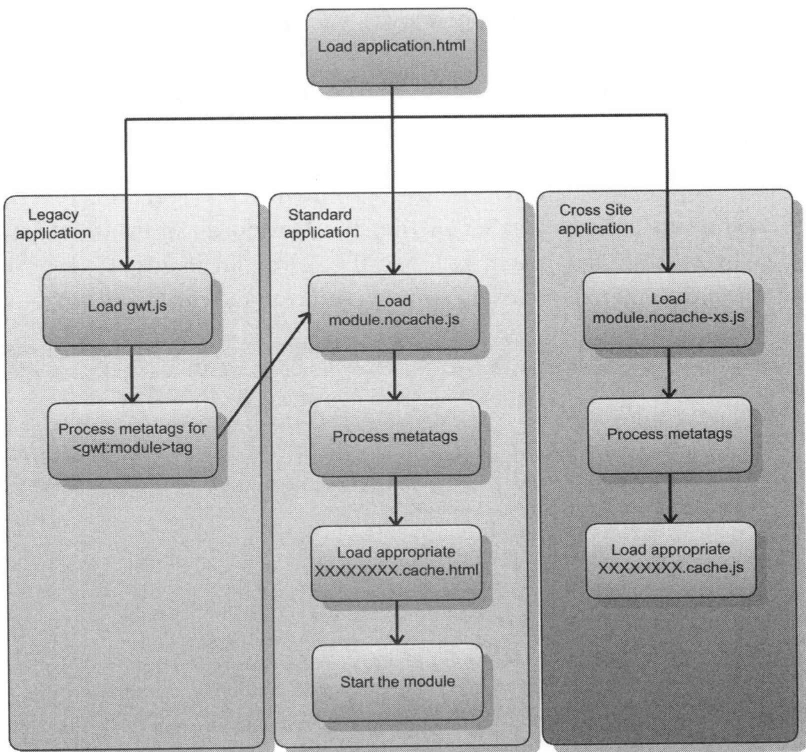

Figure 17.2 Steps performed behind the scenes in the loading process of a GWT application

There are three processes because GWT supports the pre-1.4 version loading approach of including a gwt.js file that then bootstraps the application, as well as the new two versions (standard and cross-site). Let's look at each of these approaches in more detail, starting with the legacy approach.

17.2.1 Legacy applications

The legacy approach is provided for applications that haven't upgraded to the new approach. Its purpose is to allow the application's HTML file to include a `gwt:module` tag and load a gwt.js JavaScript file as it would have done under the initial bootstrapping approach for GWT. From GWT 1.4 on, `gwt:module` and the gwt.js file are no longer used.

Once the gwt.js file is loaded, it processes the HTML file's metatags looking for the `gwt:module` tag. When this is found, the script sets up the HTML page to load the *module*.nocache.js file used in the standard approach, which we'll look at next.

17.2.2 Standard applications

In a standard application approach, the application's HTML file directly references the *module*.nocache.js JavaScript file. It's loaded as soon as the HTML file loads. Let's review the Dashboard's HTML file, given in listing 17.4; you haven't seen it for some time, and we can use it as a concrete example.

Listing 17.4 Dashboard.html file from a perspective of the loading mechanism

```
<html>
   <head>
         <meta name='gwt:property'
               content='externalvisibility=intranet'>
         <meta name='gwt:onPropertyErrorFn'
               content='handleWrongVisibility'>
         <script>
            function handleWrongVisibility(propName,
                                           allowedValues,
                                           badValue){
              if (propName == "externalvisibility"){
            window.location.href=("http://www.manning.com/hanson");
              }
           }
         </script>
         <script type="text/javascript" language="javascript">
            confirmDelete = true;
         </script>
         <script src="http://www.google.com/uds/api?file=uds.js&
                       amp;v=1.0&amp;key=X" type="text/javascript">
         </script>
         <script src="Scriptaculous/prototype.js"
                    language="javascript"/>
         <script src="Scriptaculous/effects.js"
                    language="javascript"/>
   </head>
   <body>
      <iframe id="__gwt_historyFrame"
              style="width:0;height:0;border:0"></iframe>
      <script language="javascript"
              src="org.gwtbook.Dashboard.nocache.js"></script>
   </body>
</html>
```

❶ Set GWT property value

❷ Define function to execute if visibility set wrong

❸ Load JavaScript file

You set the value of the user-defined GWT `property` variable ❶ as well as provide functionality to deal with someone setting the property variable incorrectly ❷. At ❸, you load the nocache.js file.

With this HTML in mind, we'll go through each of the steps identified in figure 17.2. We'll assume that you've loaded the HTML into a browser, so the first step is bootstrapping the application by loading in the nocache.js file.

17.2.3 Bootstrapping the standard application

When the HTML loads, it automatically loads in the nocache.js. This file is responsible for bootstrapping your complete application through the following well-oiled process:

1. Establish property-providers for this module.
2. Compute the script's base location.
3. Process all the metatags.
4. Determine the MD5 name that matches the permutation for the property values.
5. Insert the appropriate cache.html file into an iframe in the current document.
6. Load all resources.
7. Try to start the module.

We'll look at some of these steps in more detail now.

Establishing property-providers

In chapter 15, you set up your own property, `externalvisibility`, as well a property provider for it. We also discussed the fact that GWT has standard properties, such as `user.agent`, which is used to identify the browser the application is loaded into. Your own property provider and those GWT uses are found in the nocache.js file after compilation.

Establishing the property providers means the script creates a new JavaScript function for each property. Listing 17.5 shows this for the `externalvisibility` property.

Listing 17.5 `externalvisibility` property-provider from the perspective of the loading mechanism

```
providers['externalvisibility'] = function(){
   try {
      var externalvisibility = __
                    gwt_getMetaProperty('externalvisibility');
      if (externalvisibility == null) {
         externalvisibility = 'internet';
      }
      return externalvisibility;
   } catch (e) {
      return 'internet';
   }
};
```

In addition, this file defines values that are allowed for the properties (allowed values are specified in module XML files, if you recall). For the `externalvisibility` property, this file defines

```
values['externalvisibility'] = {'internet':0, 'intranet':1};
```

Now, we'll look at how the metatags are processed.

Processing the metatags

GWT also lets you define metatags covering the situations shown in table 17.1.

Table 17.1 Metatags that can be entered into an application's HTML file

Metatag	Description
`gwt:module`	Defines any modules and entry points that you'll be using in the web page. (This is now deprecated under the new bootstrapping process.) `<meta name="gwt:module" content="qualified_class_name">`
`gwt:property`	Defines a deferred-binding client property. It can cover many aspects, such as the locale of the application (which would drive the loading of other locale-specific constant files if you had defined them). `<meta name="gwt:property" content="_name_=_value_">`

Table 17.1 Metatags that can be entered into an application's HTML file *(continued)*

Metatag	Description
`gwt:onPropertyErrorFn`	Specifies the name of a function to call if a client property is set to an invalid value (meaning no matching compilation will be found). `<meta name="gwt:onPropertyErrorFn" content="_fnName_">`
`gwt:onLoadErrorFn`	Specifies the name of a function to call if an exception happens during bootstrapping or if a module throws an exception out of `onModuleLoad()`. The function takes a `message` parameter. `<meta name="gwt:onLoadErrorFn" content="_fnName_">`

Managing property metatags

In the Dashboard application, you define one property tag, which indicates whether the application is in an intranet or the Internet. This property is used in the user-defined property approach shown in chapter 15. Under the bootstrapping process, each property is stored in an associative JavaScript array called metaProps; for example, in the Dashboard, the intranet value is stored as follows:

```
metaProps['externalvisibility'] = intranet;
```

Although this example defines one gwt:property tag, it's feasible for you to define the initial locale as a property tag (if not, then the default locale is used).

Registering a property error function

GWT lets you register JavaScript functions that execute under two error conditions during the loading process. First is the gwt:onPropertyErrorFn metatag, which allows you to register a function to be executed if a defined property value doesn't appear in the list of valid properties. (We'll discuss the second condition in the next section.)

The Dashboard example includes the externalvisibility property, which can have values of internet and intranet. You'll set up an error handler that redirects the user to the book's web page if an invalid property value is used (to test this in action, you can change the property's value in the Dashboard.html file and run the application). If the property is wrong, then you receive the alert shown in figure 17.3.

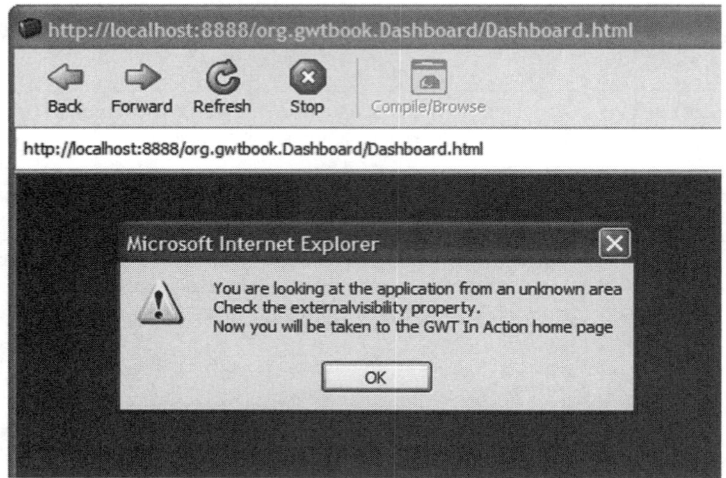

Figure 17.3 The result of running the Dashboard example when there is an error in the user-defined `externalvisibility` property

Listing 17.6 shows the code in the Dashboard.html file that achieves this redirection when an error occurs.

Listing 17.6 JavaScript function called if an incorrect value is set for the `externalvisibility` property

```
<meta name='gwt:onPropertyErrorFn' content='handleWrongVisibility'>   ❶ Define function to call in case of a property error
<script>
function handleWrongVisibility(propName,
                               allowedValues, badValue){   ❷

   if (propName == "externalvisibility"){   ❸ Confirm failed property

      window.location.href = ("http://www.manning.com/hanson");   ❹ Redirect user on error
   }
}
</script>
```

You first need to set the name of the JavaScript function to execute if there is a property error; you do that by setting the content property of the metatag ❶. With the name set up, you need to provide the JavaScript function, which you can do within normal script tags—usually following our definition, but this isn't mandated because the error-handling calls the JavaScript function given to it.

The error function, in this case `handleWrongVisibility()`, can take up to the three parameters ❷, allowing you to present a complex error message if you wish. For the Dashboard, you redirect the user to the book's web page using simple JavaScript code ❹. Before you can handle the error, though, you first must check that the property that erred is `externalvisibilty`; you do so with an equality check on the `propName` variable ❸.

Registering a loading error function

You can also register a function that is executed if the loading process errors, in a similar manner to the property error just shown, using the `gwt:onLoadErrorFn` metatag—although you don't do that for the Dashboard application.

Determining the MD5 name of the file to load

Next, the GWT application determines the name of the cache.html file it will try to load. It does this by trying to flatten out the lists of property values against the property value set for this run (see listing 17.7).

Listing 17.7 Determining the filename of the nocache.html file to load

```
try {                                                    Set properties to name ❶
   unflattenKeylistIntoAnswers(['intranet', 'default', 'ie6'],
                               '0154B171C285D65E6187DF0D30FD12C6');
   unflattenKeylistIntoAnswers(['intranet', 'sv', 'gecko1_8'],
                               '05B292B62BD4D184310C95932CF27787');
   unflattenKeylistIntoAnswers(['intranet', 'en_US', 'opera'],
                               '0ACD8C827FA60AC018F0846D4687F633');
   strongName = answers[computePropValue('externalvisibility')]
                       [computePropValue('locale')]
                       [computePropValue('user.agent')];
} catch (e) {                                            Calculate ❷
   return;                                               name to use
}                                             ❸ Create
strongName += '.cache.html';                    filename
```

The script establishes a set of patterns against filenames ❶. At ❷, it determines which MD5 name should be used for the set of properties of the current application. Then, it tags on the text *.cache.html* to create the full filename for the bootstrapping mechanism to load ❸.

With this name, the script can now load the appropriate JavaScript permutation and attempt to start it.

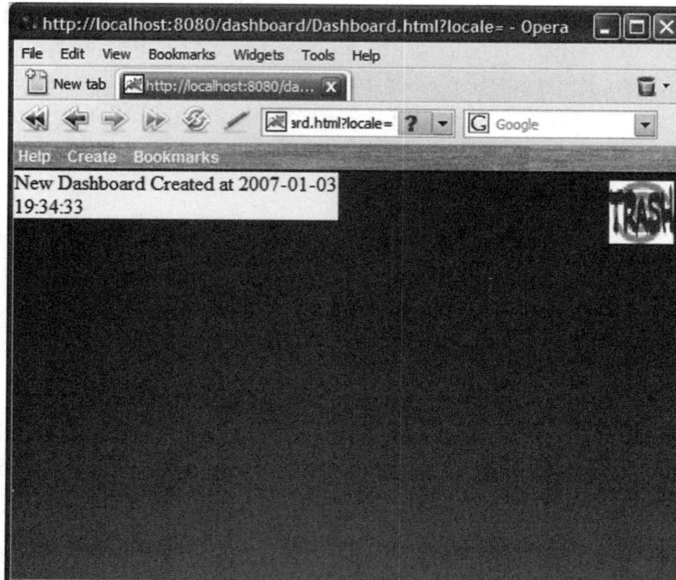

Figure 17.4
The result of loading the Dashboard GWT application

Executing the application

Throughout the loading process, the code makes calls to the `maybeStartModule()` method in the *module*.nocache.js file. This method tries to execute the `gwtOnLoad()` method in the JavaScript permutation code; when it can do so, the GWT application is officially up and running, as shown in figure 17.4.

17.2.4 Cross-script applications

The cross-script application performs mainly the same task as the standard application approach, but with two subtle differences. First, it doesn't load a *nocache.html* file; rather, it loads the *nocache.js* version. Second, it makes no attempt to start the application; that is left for you to do, which is just how you want it if you're going to mash up your GWT application with some other code.

Now that we've looked into the loading process, it seems only natural to turn our attention to how the content that is to be loaded is created.

17.3 Compiling Java to JavaScript

Although you'll write your code in Java, the output of the GWT compiler is pure JavaScript to enable it to execute on a user's web browser. The code written for the client side uses a subset of the Java 1.4 definition; the main reasons for this restriction are the applicability of packages to web applications and the ability to represent the OO Java concepts in JavaScript. Those parts of Java that are available for the client side were discussed in detail in section 1.1.2, although you should again note that there are no restrictions on the Java used for server-side components, as you saw earlier.

In this section, we'll look at the output of the compiler to give you a bit of confidence that the Java code you write is nice, if not that simple, JavaScript.

17.3.1 Exploring the produced JavaScript

When you have GWT Java code that you wish to execute, you need to decide if you're going to execute it in hosted or web mode. In hosted mode, the Java code remains Java code and is executed in a special hosted environment. For web mode, which this section deals with, the GWT compiler is invoked to compile the Java code to JavaScript files. The result of compilation is then viewed through a normal web browser as a user would.

The compilation process is complicated and produces a number of output files, which vary depending on the number of browsers supported and various options you may use (for example, internationalization). Code produced from the compilation can be broken down into the three segments shown in figure 17.5.

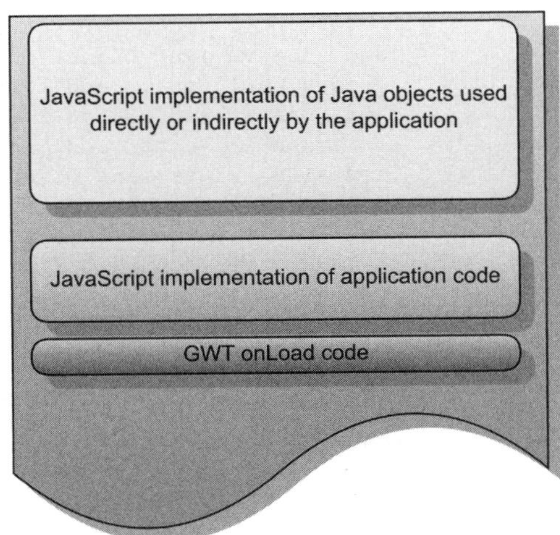

Figure 17.5 Structure of compiled code

This visual breakdown isn't immediately obvious if you go to a GWT application and open one of the JavaScript files, because by default the compiler obfuscates its output. You can turn off the obfuscation by sending the `-style PRETTY` (or `-style DETAILED`) flag to the compiler.

In the first part of the JavaScript file is the JavaScript definition of the standard Java objects supported by the compilation process. To reduce the file size, the compiler outputs only those Java objects that have been used either directly or indirectly in your program code. Further file-size reductions are made by including only the object's methods used rather than all the object's possible methods. We'll now look at the following:

- An example of a standard object that has been compiled (we show the vector object in the example)
- Some of our compiled code
- An application's initialization code

We'll start with an example of how a standard Java object is compiled behind the scenes of the GWT code.

17.3.2 Reviewing standard Java objects: the vector object

Let's look briefly at the implementation of the Java `Vector` class—this commonly appears even if you don't explicitly used `Vector`. As soon as you use events in your code, `Vector` is included because it's used in the internal process of GWT event handling. The prototype JavaScript definition for the `java.util.Vector` class appears in listing 17.8 (you used `-style DETAILED` for this view).

Listing 17.8 Prototype JavaScript definition for the `java.util.Vector` class

```
function java_util_Vector(){
}

_ = java_util_Vector.prototype = new java_util_AbstractList();
_.add__ILjava_lang_Object_2 =
    java_util_Vector_add__ILjava_lang_Object_2;
_.add__Ljava_lang_Object_2 =
    java_util_Vector_add__Ljava_lang_Object_2;
_.contains__Ljava_lang_Object_2 =
    java_util_Vector_contains__Ljava_lang_Object_2;
_.equals__Ljava_lang_Object_2 =
    java_util_Vector_equals__Ljava_lang_Object_2;
_.get__I = java_util_Vector_get__I;
_.hashCode__ = java_util_Vector_hashCode__;
_.indexOf__Ljava_lang_Object_2I =
    java_util_Vector_indexOf__Ljava_lang_Object_2I;
_.size__ = java_util_Vector_size__;
_.toString__ = java_util_Vector_toString__;
_._1get__I = java_util_Vector__1get__I;
_.initArray__ = java_util_Vector_initArray__;
_.java_lang_Object_typeName = 'java.util.Vector';
_.java_lang_Object_typeId = 16;
```

Annotations: **Object definition** (the function declaration); **Object inheritance of java.util.AbstractList** (the prototype line); **Signature definition** (the method assignments); **Internal definitions** (the typeName and typeId lines).

Notice that everything in the JavaScript keeps its fully qualified class name, with the periods (.) replaced by underscores (_). The Java class `java.util.Vector`, for example, becomes the JavaScript class `java_util_Vector`. Classname and method are separated by one underscore, and the types of any inputs are separated from the method name by two underscores. This notation is shown in figure 17.6, which represents the `Vector.add(Object)` method.

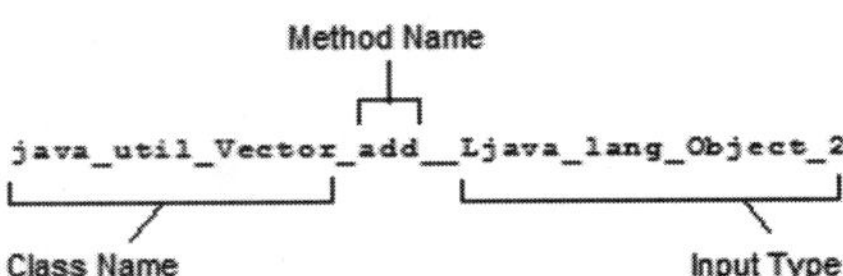

Figure 17.6 Explanation of JavaScript call format

The definition in the JavaScript code for adding an object to a vector is as follows:

```
_.add__Ljava_lang_Object_2 =
          java_util_Vector_add__Ljava_lang_Object_2;
```

Or, executing the `.add` method on a vector is the same as executing the `java_util_Vector_add` method; the parameter is of type `java.lang.Object` (which is the same as the Java definition). Further, in the file you find the definition of this function to be the addition of the new object to the end of the array representing the current vector:

```
function java_util_Vector_add__Ljava_lang_Object_2(o){
  var a = this.array;
  a[a.length] = o;
  return true;
}
```

Similarly, the method to retrieve an indexed element from the vector, the `Vector.get(int)` method, is referenced as follows:

```
_.get__I = java_util_Vector_get__I;
```

(`int` is a primitive type in Java and isn't treated as an object; thus the input to the `get` method has type `I` rather than the incorrect `Ljava.lang.int`. If you were using the Java `Integer` object, then the argument would indeed be `Ljava.lang.Integer`.) The `get` method is implemented in the JavaScript function

```
function java_util_Vector_get__I(index){
  return java_util_Vector_$get__Ljava_util_Vector_2I(this, index);
}
```

which calls the second form of the `get` operation with arguments `(this,index)`:

```
function java_util_Vector_$get__Ljava_util_Vector_2I(this$static,
                                                     index){
  if (index < 0 || index >= this$static.size__())
    throw java_util_NoSuchElementException_$NoSuchElementException__
```

```
            Ljava_util_NoSuchElementException_2
                          (new java_util_NoSuchElementException());
    return this$static._1get__I(index);
  }
```

Here it's easy to see some bound-checking taking place. An exception is thrown if the index is less than 0 or greater than the size of the vector (or, in reality, the underlying JavaScript array implementation). If all is OK, then a value is retrieved from the call to the `1get_I(index)` method, which returns the value at the correct index in the underlying array implementation:

```
function java_util_Vector__1get__I(index){
  return this.array[index];
}
```

You've seen that standard Java objects are compiled into JavaScript in a systematic way that is relatively easy to read if you tell the compiler to produce human-readable code. What happens to the JavaScript you write? How does it relate to the Java code?

17.3.3 Exploring program code as JavaScript

In the next segment of code, you find the JavaScript relating to your Java code. Consider the Dashboard again; listing 17.9 shows the compiled version of the `onModuleLoad()` method (this time using the flag `-style PRETTY` to cut down on the verbose output).

Listing 17.9 `onModuleLoad()` method in JavaScript using the `-style PRETTY` flag

```
function _$onModuleLoad(_this$static){
  var _menuCreate, _menuHelp;
  _dashboardName = _$EditableLabel(new _EditableLabel(),
       _$DashboardDefaultNameMessage(_this$static._messages,
                                    _$Date0(new
  _Date())._toLocaleString0()),
                                    'Byta', 'Ej Byta');
  _$setWordWrap0(_dashboardName, true);
  _$addChangeListener0(_dashboardName, _$Dashboard$3
                                          (new _Dashboard$3(),
                                           _this$static));
  _$setStyleName(_dashboardName, 'dashboard-Name');
  _menuCreate = _$buildCreateMenu0(_this$static);
  _menuHelp = _$buildHelpMenu0(_this$static);
  _$loadSubMenu(_this$static, _this$static._menu, 'Bookmarks',
              'bookmarks.xml');
  _$addItem2(_this$static._menu, 'Hj\xE4lp', _menuHelp);
  _$addItem2(_this$static._menu, 'Nya', _menuCreate);
  _$setAutoOpen(_this$static._menu, true);
```

```
    _$setIcon(_this$static._trash);
    _$addStyleName(_this$static._trash, 'trash');
    _$setUpWindowEventHandling(_this$static);
    _$add2(_get3(), _this$static._menu);
    _$add2(_get3(), _this$static._trash);
    _$add2(_get3(), _dashboardName);
    _this$static._setUpAPI0();
}
```

If you recall the original Java code for the `onModuleLoad()` function, this will look familiar. As you can see, the JavaScript for the Java code is written in the same style as the rest of the code. The rest of the functions are also included in JavaScript permutation—feel free to browse, although if you've forgotten to put `-style PRETTY` or `-style DETAILED` as a flag to the compiler, it will be extremely difficult to follow the output, which will resemble listing 17.10.

Listing 17.10 Sample compiled code using the default style flag (`-style OBFUSCATED`)

```
function a(){return window;}
function b(){return this.c + '@' + this.d();}
function e(f){return this === f;}
function g(){return h(this);}
function i(){}
_ = i.prototype = {};
_.j = b;_.k = e;
_.d = g;_.toString = function(){return this.j();};
_.c = 'java.lang.Object';_.l = 0;
function m(n){return n == null?null:n.c;}
o = null;function p(){return ++q;}
function r(s){return s == null?0:s.$H?s.$H:(s.$H = p());}
function t(u){return u == null?0:u.$H?u.$H:(u.$H = p());}
q = 0;function v(){v = a;w = y('[N',[0],[24],[0],null);return window;}
function z(){var A,B;A = m(this);
B = this.C;
if(B !== null){return A + ': ' + B;}else{return A;}}
function D(E,F){if(E.ab !== null)throw bb(new cb(),
                                     "Can't overwrite cause");
if(F === E)throw db(new eb(),'Self-causation not permitted');
E.ab = F;
return E;}
function fb(gb){v();return gb;}
function hb(ib,jb){v();ib.C = jb;return ib;}
```

In the final segment of the JavaScript, from figure 17.5, you can find the code that is called when a module is initialized.

17.3.4 Understanding the initialization code segment

Finally, the JavaScript is completed with the initialization code segment. This segment includes a method called `gwtOnLoad()`, which is called by the GWT application-loading process. In this example, the following JavaScript code was produced:

```
function gwtOnLoad(errFn, modName){
  if (errFn)
    try {
      init();
    }
     catch (e) {
      errFn(modName);
    }
   else {
    init();
  }
}
```

The `init` function is defined as firing up your application; it looks something like the following:

```
function init(){
      HelloWorld_$onModuleLoad__LHelloWorld_2(
            new HelloWorld()
      );
}
```

At first glance, this example may appear to have a lot of overhead associated with it, and you could easily start thinking that a hand-coded version would be smaller and more efficient. This is probably true for such a trivial example; but when you turn your mind to industrial-strength applications, the true benefits of coding in Java and letting a compiler produce all this code become clearer. Remember as well these two quotes from Google that list important things you should keep in mind:

- “A typical, full-featured GWT application will require the user to download about 100K of cacheable JavaScript, which is in line with most hand-written AJAX applications.”
- “GWT applications are almost always as fast as hand-written JavaScript. The GWT compiler avoids adding any wrappers around any functionality that is implemented natively in the browser.”

Of course, we'll have to wait and see as the facts and figures emerge to confirm the validity of these statements, once industrial applications start becoming a reality; but each permutation of the Dashboard application, ignoring any third-party JavaScript libraries, comes in at around 228KB in obfuscated mode. On the size side, we're doubling Google's estimate, but considering all the functionality on the Dashboard, that's not unreasonable.

Speedwise, we didn't find any problems on the development machines or any machines we tested on, but we haven't built an equivalent directly in JavaScript to compare.

> **TIP** If your compilation is slow, you can alter the parameters for the Java Virtual Machine, which may increase the compilation speed. Try the `Xms` and `Xmx` parameters to the Java command; we use `-Xms256m` and `-Xmx512m`.

To be frank, and this is probably *the* key point of GWT, we don't even want to think about the amount of effort that would be required to program, let alone debug, any issues or perform maintenance across six different browsers for an application such as the Dashboard directly in JavaScript.

17.4 Summary

As you've seen, GWT is a powerful tool firmly based in delivering standards-compliant web technologies compiled from Java code and using CSS for styling. It doesn't bring any magic proprietary technologies that need to be downloaded by your application users, which is good news in these days of Internet security and trojans. The use of these technologies makes GWT easily expandable and flexible in the ways you need. Coupled with the ability to bring the power of the existing Java toolsets to bear on development, it's a great proposition.

It's simple to access and manipulate the DOM through GWT at a low level via the JavaScript Native Interface, through low-level method calls in the GWT DOM implementation classes, and through the more natural Java approach of creating objects and using widget and panel API methods such as `add()`. These widgets and panels are simple HTML elements, and you've seen them all in use.

On the client side, functionality is provided by writing code in GWT Java and subsequently compiling it to JavaScript code using the provided compiler code. You saw that the resulting JavaScript code contains the code you've produced, or which has been generated; and implementations of the standard Java objects used by your code.

Server-side integration is possible with your choice of language. If you want to use Java, then GWT provides the RPC approach to make the boundary between client and server almost disappear.

Is GWT the answer to every Ajax development problem? Probably not, but it goes a great way toward making Ajax applications easier to develop. GWT enables you to use the mature tooling of Java in the development of Ajax applications, as well as access JavaScript directly if you need to do that. To sum up, we'll go back to the last sentence of the previous section, which sums up our thoughts on GWT at present:

"To be frank, and this is probably *the* key point of GWT, we don't even want to think about the amount of effort that would be required to program, let alone debug, any issues or perform maintenance across six different browsers for an application such as the Dashboard directly in JavaScript."

index

Symbols

A

B

C

E

H

M

N

R

S

X

Y

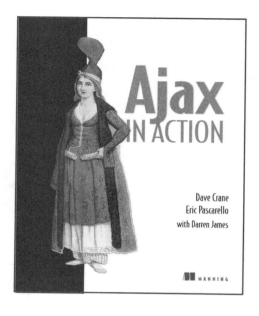

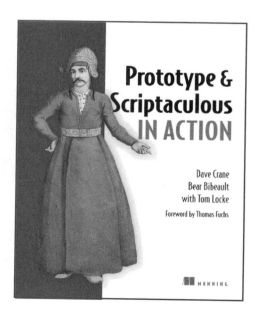

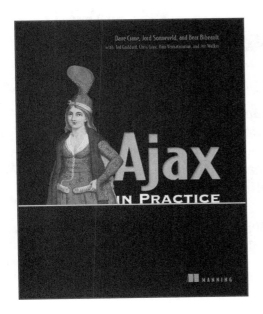